The Great Ascent

A World Bank Publication

The Great Ascent
The Rural Poor
in South Asia

Inderjit Singh

Published for the World Bank
The Johns Hopkins University Press
Baltimore and London

The Johns Hopkins University Press
Baltimore, Maryland 21211, U.S.A.

The textile pictured on the cover shows rice growers in an Indian
village. It is one of more than 250 appliqué and embroidered pieces
produced by Les Ateliers au Fils d'Indra in Pondicherry, India. Founded in
1968, the workshop provides employment for women and preserves embroidery
techniques and styles that are centuries old. The artwork is distributed
in Western Europe through nonprofit associations.

Library of Congress Cataloging-in-Publication Data

Singh, Inderjit, 1941–
    The great ascent : the rural poor in South Asia / Inderjit Singh.
      p. cm.
    Includes bibliographical references and index.
    ISBN 0–8018–3954–8
    1. Rural poor—South Asia. 2. Agricultural productivity—South
Asia—Regional disparities. 3. South Asia—Economic conditions—
Regional disparities. I. Title.
    HC430.6.S59 1990
    338.05419054'73'4—dc20

                                     90–5122
                                     CIP

Contents

Foreword

The rural performance since independence in India, Pakistan, and Bangladesh has inspired thousands of papers, books, and surveys. The flow has increased since high-yielding cereals were introduced in the mid-1960s. For scholars and administrators, the task now is to evaluate this work. Three things are needed for such a task, and Inderjit Singh's book brilliantly provides them.

The first is a comprehensive, ordered guide to the literature. Singh thoroughly searches official series and research studies, neoclassical and Marxist approaches. Furthermore, he organizes them into a coherent story with four central themes: the trends in rural poverty as they are affected by agrarian structure, landlessness, and unemployment; the sources of growth for small farms, especially the role of technical progress; the impact of nonfarm employment and rural public works; and the scope and limits of land reform.

The second requirement is a critical examination of the literature. It is necessary to weigh the worth, not merely measure the mass, of the research materials. This book does more than count the pieces of evidence on each side of an issue; it assesses their quality and considers the number of rural people to whom they apply.

Third, a guidebook needs a clearly stated point of view. Only thus can it organize evidence or challenge readers to disagree intelligently. This book's viewpoint is that, although massive poverty persists in South Asia, economic growth has helped to ease it. "Where agricultural output per capita has been stagnant or declining," says Singh, "the living conditions of the rural poor have deteriorated," and where it has been growing at over 2 percent a year, all rural classes, even the poorest agricultural labor households, have gained (p. 41).

Singh's optimistic view of what rapid farm growth *can* do must be set against his recognition that many rural South Asians, "unable to support themselves by farming because their landholdings are very small or nonexistent, . . . seem increasingly to suffer from underemployment and the erosion of the real value of their earnings" (p. 93). Indeed, rural unemployment—while low overall—is highest among the poorest, is rising over time, and is concentrated in places and times of low wage rates and low work force participation (see my World Bank working paper, *Labor and Poverty*). Many underemployed people are poor not only because their landholdings are inadequate, but also because the "dramatic expansion of [nonfarm incomes] has been confined . . . to areas in which agricultural growth has been high" (p. 93).

Thus Singh's main recipe for reducing rural poverty in South Asia is to promote fast growth of output on small farms. Because such growth is usually needed for farm *and* nonfarm employment, both poor farmers and even poorer rural employees benefit. Singh, however, is worried that concentrating on small-farm growth, so desirable on equity grounds, may sometimes damage efficiency. He argues that the "inverse relationship"—the tendency of small farms to show higher yields per acre than large farms—may be reversed by the Green Revolution (p. 101). Fortunately, growing recent evidence suggests that once cultivation with improved seeds settles down, small farmers once again do better (as R. Longhurst and I argue in *New Seeds and Poor People*, pp. 142–44).

Using data from Bangladesh and Pakistan, Singh also shows that small farmers are dramatically more likely to double-crop than large farmers. Moreover, the gap has been widening (p. 117 and tables 4.9–4.10). "Multiple cropping promises to be more effective in creating [rural] employment and income . . . than either rural industries or rural work programs" (p. 128). It depends critically on improved water control (including drainage) and further research into appropriate short-duration, and hence drought-avoiding, crops and varieties.

What of the problems small farmers have with rural credit and marketing? Singh does not fully review the evidence of bias against small farmers in markets. He does note that India's commercial banks have served farmers better since nationalization, but other institutional agencies still neglect smallholders (p. 137). Yet farmers operating less than two hectares are much likelier to get credit from a bank or a coop, instead of a moneylender, if they use high-yielding seeds than if they do not (p. 142). This finding lends support to the view that small-farm growth in South Asia need not face a credit constraint, provided that in areas where such a constraint might indeed bite, there is no dogmatic objection to modest, carefully managed credit subsidies.

South Asia's small farms are at least as efficient as big ones—largely because they employ more labor per acre—and, if growth prospects are attractive, small farms can often overcome credit and marketing biases against them. How, then, have small farmers been affected by the new cereal varieties? In a few areas these varieties have brought a veritable revolution in output (for example, by doubling wheat yields and almost tripling rice yields in the Indian Punjab between the mid-1960s and the early 1980s). Small farmers' adoption of these varieties "did lag, but . . . lags diminished rapidly" (p. 159), although sometimes the lagging, poorer adopters then faced a cost-price squeeze, in contrast to the economic rents enjoyed by earlier and better-off innovators. In regard to the use of fertilizer, however, small farmers may fare even better than is suggested here (p. 168); in Southeast Asia they use at least as much inorganic fertilizer per hectare as big farmers do (Herdt and Capule 1983).

Mechanization and eviction sometimes erode the small farmer's gains from new seed technology and may even reverse the employee's. Singh argues that the gains "arise more from the agrarian structure . . . and from the economic policies" than from the new varieties themselves (p. 177). But a more socially conscious approach to farm research would steer it toward varieties—and also crops, seasons, techniques, and environments—where the interaction with such structure and policies was relatively likely to favor the poor.

Singh argues that the Green Revolution has pushed up wage rates, kept down food prices, and hence favored the poor as workers and consumers (pp. 176, 185, 195). The poor would certainly be worse off without the new seeds, but these particular benefits are precarious. A poor and landless work force, especially one that is growing fast because the population as a whole is rising, readily moves toward areas with a higher demand for labor. As a result, employment may increase, but even with a Green Revolution wages may not rise significantly over the long term. If food prices are restrained, the ready availability of labor means that employers can restrain wage increases. Partly to boost the demand for labor against such eventualities, Singh argues for the Chinese approach to rural industrialization—"upgrading village crafts by transforming their technologies [rather than preserving] outmoded and stagnant production methods"—together with "medium-term relief to the unemployed" through rural works, along the lines of Maharashtra's Employment Guarantee Scheme (pp. 256, 259).

Yet, if both farm and nonfarm employment—and hence poor people's incomes—depend on agricultural growth through transformed technology, and if small farms are at least as good at attaining such growth as large, then is there not an overwhelming case for land reform? Singh rightly rejects reform based on restrictions on tenancy.

There is little tenancy anyway, and it is declining. Some of it entails rentals by the poor to the rich; the rest often helps the poor and land-less by allowing them to "sell" their managerial skills for usufruct claims (pp. 291–92). Anyway, can such reforms be imposed on pow-erful landlords, who enjoy increasing competition among tenants to rent land? Given the rural "balance of economic and political power . . . further tenancy reform is useless," Singh concludes (p. 299). "It is poverty that leads to sharecropping, and not sharecropping that causes poverty" (p. 287).

Yet Singh accepts the strong case for redistributing owned hold-ings, though he does so more for reasons of equity than in confident anticipation of productivity gains. "The 'structuralist' viewpoint . . . that the only long-run remedy to the problems of rural poverty is . . . radical land reform . . . is correct [because] the numerous [other] remedies . . . may not be enough. . . . The case for redistributive land reforms is further strengthened by the evidence . . . that smaller hold-ings could enhance employment and [cropping] intensities" (pp. 288–90).

Land redistribution has in fact achieved little, though more than Singh suggests here (see my World Bank working paper, *Land Assets and Rural Poverty*, p. 28). Singh contends that "a relatively modest re-distribution program could usefully give the landless plots for simple homesteads and space for small-scale vegetable or livestock farming" (p. 307). The experience of Kerala supports this approach, but also reveals the political obstacles (described by Ronald Herring in *Land to the Tiller*).

Singh makes a convincing and thoroughly documented case that "the great ascent" of South Asia's rural poor, though patchy and slow, has indeed begun. It is most noticeable where agricultural growth is really rapid (such growth does indeed "trickle down," at least to the moderately poor) and where, despite unsatisfactory growth, the poor are both literate and organized, as in Kerala. The book argues force-fully for labor-intensive, agriculture-based technical progress to bene-fit the poor. Rural employment programs also have a role. History strongly suggests two further requirements. One is much more politi-cal organization among the rural poor. The other is a shift in the pat-tern of research and technical change.

High-yielding cereals were in some ways ideal innovations for the rural poor: divisible to the level of the smallest farm, generally reduc-ing risks of moisture stress and (at least in the short run) pest attack, permitting the buildup of cereal reserves, moderating the price of food, and boosting farm employment. But this last effect—in-creasingly important because a growing proportion of poor rural people's incomes is earned from hired labor—has been subverted by tractors, threshers, weedicides, mechanical rice transplanters, even combines. New technology can be progressive, but subsidies should not selectively encourage labor-replacing inputs, such as fuel or credit.

Agricultural research should concentrate on achieving advances that productively demand rural labor in neglected areas (those without reliable irrigation) and for neglected crops (those eaten principally by the poor). The Indian national crop research programs and the Hyderabad-based International Crops Research Institute for the Semi-Arid Tropics (ICRISAT) have shown what is possible, by making progress on two crops that very poor people eat and grow labor-intensively: ragi in Karnataka and hybrid sorghum (in the main monsoon season only) in Maharashtra. Progress is much slower for millets, winter sorghum, and root crops and for the densely populated, ill-drained rice areas of eastern India and parts of Bangladesh and Kerala.

Two other issues face agricultural researchers. First, how can the emphasis on poverty be reconciled with the need to sustain long-run agricultural productivity, especially to reduce soil erosion on marginal lands and to avoid groundwater depletion almost everywhere? Poor people, more of them all the time, need income and food now. The short-run response is to find methods and incentives to *substitute employment for environment*: using fertilizers in root-zone placement (mudballs) and other ways of reducing the agrochemicals required to achieve a given output; cross-bunding and micromanagement of water; contour plowing associated with vetiver grass; appropriate improvements to terracing; and establishing research priorities, by crop and region and varietal selection, to improve the private returns to such methods.

The long-run response has to involve slower population growth. In Kerala—with its disappointing agricultural performance—the improved health of children and the dramatic drop in mortality have been accompanied by such a rapid decline in fertility that the net reproduction rate has fallen almost to the replacement level. Elsewhere in India, including the Punjab, total fertility has fallen more slowly, especially among the poor. It is very important to focus research—and subsequent action—on the long-run effect on fertility of *alternative* paths of agricultural progress and health provision.

The thesis of this book—that fast small-farm growth is the best cure for rural poverty—raises a second issue for agricultural researchers. Simply stated, it is that the potential yield of major tropical and subtropical food crops must increase significantly. Rice has not done so since the IR-8 variety was released in 1963; for wheat, the rate of increase is only about 1 percent a year. The green revolution has therefore increasingly required farmers to narrow the gap between field performance and nearly stagnant yield potential. But such narrowing eventually becomes uneconomic or too risky, unless researchers are driving that potential upward. Field performance is itself eroded by new pest biotypes and by the depletion of micronutrients and groundwater.

By exploring the effectiveness of rapid small-farm growth in reducing poverty—and the scope of social action to improve that effectiveness—this splendid book should capture the attention of policymakers and researchers. Researchers, however, tend to do what they have previously done well. Policymakers tend to overstress fashionable issues of aggregate economic management. It will take a major effort to focus both groups, once again, on labor-intensive technical progress for the main staple crops of the rural poor.

Michael Lipton

Preface

After World War II the economies of the developing world were predominantly agrarian. To improve living standards and eliminate rural poverty, rural productivity had to increase. This was a goal of all developing countries, and in South Asia—India in particular—it became the central one. (Throughout this book "South Asia" includes Bangladesh, India, and Pakistan.)

In the early 1950s and 1960s, agriculture was seen as tradition-bound and stagnant, contributing little to national development. Development plans therefore placed heavy emphasis on industry. The Mahalonobis plan, for example—which was based on the Soviet development experience and on the blueprint for India's second plan (1956–61)—stressed capital-intensive investment in basic industries to reap the productivity gains from technology. Farming was neglected: it received few resources, and its output was seen mainly as feeding industrial growth. Such thinking continued to underpin development theory through the early 1960s.

A fundamental change came with the breakthrough of high-yielding varieties of cereal (HYVs) in the mid-1960s. Norman Borlaug was awarded the Nobel Prize for developing high-yielding varieties of maize in Mexico, and new adaptive wheat and rice varieties soon followed. Pioneering research organizations, such as the International Rice Research Institute (IRRI) and the International Center for Corn and Wheat Improvement (CIMMYT), were set up under the Consultative Group on International Agricultural Research. Their technical innovations soon found intellectual support from economists. Theodore Schultz won the Nobel Prize for his theory that the economic potential of agricultural development had been largely unexploited and that peasant agriculture could be highly responsive and productive. The bulk of poor farmers then came to be seen not as inefficient but as constrained by distortions introduced by the government; that is, by interventions to keep food prices low for politically important urban dwellers and industrial workers. The ability of the agricultural sector to become an engine of growth then became development orthodoxy. Without major productivity growth in agriculture, economists began to argue, efficient industrialization would be unlikely.

The initial neglect of agriculture meant that by the mid-1960s population growth was outpacing growth in agricultural productivity, and South Asia was growing more dependent on massive imports of food aid. During the late 1960s one ship a week carried grain from the Mississippi Delta ports of the United States to India, which required more than a million metric tons a month. Projections of the combined future import demands of Bangladesh, India, and Pakistan became enormous, and their agrarian takeoff seemed increasingly distant. At the same time, the Indian government realized that it would have to halt the growing dependence on foreign food aid and imports if it were to maintain political sovereignty. Given the combination of HYV technology and political imperatives, India embarked on the massive task of creating the research, extension, irrigation, and marketing infrastructure necessary to deliver the new HYV seeds, water, and fertilizers to farmers.

By the late 1960s a rapid agrarian transformation had started in South Asia. But bureaucratic and intellectual perceptions of the situation continued to lag. As late as the mid-1970s international institutions were forecasting that India would need 15 million to 18 million—even 20 million—tons of food imports a year in the 1980s to feed its burgeoning population. Far from draining the supplies in international markets, however, India was already starting to become self-sufficient, and by the early 1980s it had 20 million tons of food-grain surpluses. Instead of being a food deficit country, India was able to build a growing volume of food stocks. Pakistan had in the meantime also become self-sufficient and started to export food. And Bangladesh, despite its late start and the horror stories that suggested the need for triage, had started on its way to self-sufficiency.

At the heart of these dramatic changes is the transformation of the lives of 800 million people in the rural areas of South Asian countries—the "great ascent" from poverty and despair to a more materially rewarding existence.

If increases in agricultural productivity and output are a prerequisite for industrial development and the great ascent, these countries have taken the first steps. But this very success has led to other problems. Most of the new productivity was concentrated in a few parts of the subcontinent, which gave rise to distinct regional disparities. Three broad belts of differentiated development have emerged:

- *Northwest India and Pakistan*, including the states of Gujarat, Haryana, Kashmir, Punjab, western Uttar Pradesh, parts of Rajasthan, and Pakistan. In this region productivity and output have grown faster than the population.
- *The central "Hindu heartland" of India and Bangladesh*, including Andhra Pradesh, Bihar, Madhya Pradesh, Maharashtra, eastern Uttar Pradesh, West Bengal, parts of Gujarat, and the eastern states of India. In this region population has grown at a higher rate than productivity.
- *South India*, including Karnataka, Kerala, and Tamil Nadu. This region has increased its agricultural productivity but barely enough to meet the growing population demands.

A core of progressive states in the Northwest has thus been generating the surpluses in the subcontinent. By the mid-1970s, 65 to 75 percent of the total food-grain stocks of the central government of India was coming from two states, Punjab and Haryana, which have only about 5 percent of the agricultural area. At harvesttime India has to divert all its freight trains to these states to transport the millions of tons of food to central depots and then redistribute them to the deficit states. It has set up a central mechanism for state purchasing, storage, and distribution, with fair-price food shops to sell food grains at subsidized prices. The political implications of these changes have been dramatic. A political minority is producing food surpluses for the political majority. The large deficit states in the central heartland of India generate 60 percent of the the votes and 70 percent of the members of parliament, and yet they depend on states at the periphery (Punjab and Haryana) that are often in the hands of opposition parties.

Interstate disparities have also widened because of differences in endowments and commitment to the agricultural sector. Provinces with water, progressive agricultural policies, and programs for extension services and irrigation did well. (Agriculture in India is organized and funded by the states, not the central government.) In short, the states that paid attention to their rural constituencies and to agriculture got ahead, while others lagged. Bengal, eastern Bihar, and eastern Uttar Pradesh have been left behind because their state legislatures failed to provide the funds for irrigation, research, extension, roads, and agricultural support services.

A similar dualism sprang up in the villages. The new HYV technologies favored the landed over the landless, who were unable to raise credit and buy the new seeds and fertilizers. A new fragmentation of the rural economy replaced the traditional *jajmani* system of shared tasks and shared rewards. Landowners with large or medium-size holdings produced the surplus, those with smaller holdings were relatively self-sufficient, and the rural landless and tenants became the deficit group, dependent on the surpluses of the others.

Because the unequal distribution of incomes is an initial condition, unequal rewards prevail in the markets. The real tradeoff, according to A. K. Sen, is between the value of food and the value of labor. A poor landless laborer's "entitlement" depends on his ability to market his labor (in excess supply) and his ability to buy food (in short supply). With the changes in South Asia's rural economy, the entitlement a laborer received for one hour of labor dropped, so that some of the rural poor became even poorer. As a result, the idea developed that government intervention was needed to change the market tradeoffs between labor and food.

Governments could correct the market imbalances by setting up special services for the poor—cheaper credit, food shops, rural works programs, and so on. But governments are no more neutral than markets. Governments in South Asia responded to the vested interests of the landed classes, and they were not about to transform the terms of trade to favor the rural poor. Pakistan, for example, started few direct programs to reduce poverty because its policy formulation was dominated by elites—from the army, the bureaucracy, or the landed aristocracy.

In India the poor had no money but at least they still had the vote. The middle-class farmer began to form a significant political bloc of votes by the late 1970s and early 1980s, and the government set up special programs for the rural areas. But those who benefited from these antipoverty programs were usually those who had the grassroots power. Deciding who was "poor" and therefore eligible for aid depended on the administrators of these programs, generally the rural elite. So, rather than being a neutral agent for the distribution of gains, government became a trough where different social groups fed in relation to their economic power. Many antipoverty programs in India—such as the Drought Areas Program, the Rural Works Program, and special credit programs—delivered the greater share of their benefits to the richer, not the poorer, segments of society.

As a result, the Green Revolution decades were marked by the pessimistic view that growth was making the poor poorer and the rich richer. The failure of both markets and governments to deliver gains equitably fueled a whole series of articles in the 1970s.

In response to the debate about the effectiveness of the new technologies, this book follows two lines of inquiry. It first questions whether the changes from the Green Revolution have really failed to help the rural poor. Is it true that growth has been impoverishing? Have the rich benefited at the expense of the poor? Or is it more correct to say that the rich have become richer, but the poor are also better off? Second, this book looks at the other side of the coin. The efforts may not have succeeded as well as planned or as hoped, but what would South Asia look like without these changes? Imagine India still dependent on U.S. food aid and imports with twice the population it had twenty years ago. What would Indian politics be if the government had not set up programs to try to overcome some of the faults of the markets and had failed to tackle some of the faults in those programs? The answer is obvious. The poor would have been far worse off today, and there would have been political and economic chaos.

The results of these two lines of inquiry support a series of generalizations:

- Growth has not been impoverishing but has been essential in redressing poverty.
- Inequality has increased, but the increase has been exaggerated, as have the problems.
- The Green Revolution has had major benefits, especially in view of the alternative.
- Tenancy is not as important a barrier to developmental change as has been assumed.
- The real problem is not unemployment, but productive employment; that is, how much a laborer can get in return for one hour of work, whether employed or not.
- Nonfarm and noncrop income are just as important as land for transforming the rural economy.
- The growth of the nonfarm economy depends on the vitality of the farm economy; without agricultural growth in the rural areas, redresssing poverty is an impossible task.
- Rural work programs can succeed, especially when tied to a well-managed grain distribution system (the Maharashtra Employment Guarantee Scheme is an excellent example).
- Ancillary industries that tie rural industrialization to the development of rural areas are important but too often neglected.
- Land reform, though critical, is no panacea, and even without land reform, progress is still possible in other areas.
- Institutional reforms and policy changes are needed, but much has already been done to develop the appropriate institutions, such as research universities and extension agencies.
- South Asian countries cannot tackle the problems of poverty without considering the future of the industrial sector. Because

agriculture cannot continue to absorb the continuing population increases, there must be rapid industrial growth, which undoubtedly will in turn become a source of problems.

The two lines of inquiry in this book converge on a larger question: has South Asia started on its great ascent? The first few steps have clearly been taken. And just as clearly, more problems will arise. In development the solution of one set of problems, seemingly simple, leads to a set of more complex problems. In addition to the foregoing problems in agriculture, four problems outside agriculture require further attention.

First, there must be a policy of population control. India's population growth has slowed to 2.2 percent a year, but Pakistan and Bangladesh are still growing at 2.6 and 3.1 percent a year respectively. Industrial and technical progress cannot keep pace. Even in India, agricultural productivity barely keeps up with population growth, which remains a driving mechanism for perpetuating poverty.

Second, without education the poor will neither demand new programs and new technologies nor have the ability to respond to those opportunities. China, Japan, and the Republic of Korea owe their success to an educated and informed population. Without an educated peasantry, long-term development in South Asia will continue to lag.

Third, an industrial revolution is needed to absorb the labor from the transformation of the agrarian sector. If employment in the industrial and service sectors is not forthcoming, the gains from agricultural growth will collapse dramatically. As 200 million to 300 million people in South Asia move into urban and urban-related activities, ways must be found to organize the industrial sector to provide productive employment, income, and higher living standards—the major challenge for the decades ahead in South Asia.

Fourth, researchers and administrators need to change their perspective. Their pursuit of the best solutions may make it difficult to carry out good solutions. There may be ten good programs that will help farmers, five that will help small farmers, and only two to help the landless. Finding one that helps only the poor and not the rich is rarely feasible, and we should not throw out the good because of a feckless search for the best. Patience is also needed. The transformation from agrarian to modern industrial state takes generations. What Europe did in twenty generations and Japan did in ten the developing world is trying to do in five. So far, this experiment in South Asia has had only forty years. Now the third generation is laying the foundation for another two generations beyond us. South Asia may not see the last steps of the great ascent until the middle of the 2000s. But that would be a tremendous accomplishment—in a hundred years to go from a traditional, feudal, agrarian economy to a modern welfare state.

In addition to eschewing perfection and haste, researchers must avoid oversimplification. As the book points out, there are nuances within nuances. For example, the division between the landless and farmers is complex: some farmers spend time as wage earners, and some of the landless have access to land. Simple breakdowns and simple notions do not help much. To say that poverty has either increased or decreased is an oversimplification—especially when considering economies the size of India's, with hundreds of millions of people and some 600,000 villages.

Another change in perspective is that government administrators and nongovernmental organizations should not try to do everything for the poor. More is accomplished when people take command of their lives and find their own solutions. Administrators should understand that and allow more room for it to happen. Their job should be to enable people to help themselves—to find out what people want to do with their lives and give them the means to do it.

Three additional areas of inquiry that have some bearing on the lives of the rural poor are not adequately addressed in this book. First is the importance of arid agriculture and its prospects, since many of the rural poor live in arid and semiarid areas of South Asia. Although experimental research has reported some initial progress in raising productivity in arid areas, big breakthroughs in application are yet to come. When they do, a further assessment of their impact on the rural poor will be needed. Second, how to provide the rural poor with greater access to credit, water, knowledge, and other services remains a question for further research. Significant work is being done, however, both to make markets operate more effectively and to develop new institutions to overcome market biases. A full treatment of this topic would require a separate undertaking. Third, there has been considerable growth in the number of programs designed to assist the rural poor directly, especially in India. Their coverage, effectiveness, and shortcomings constitute another important area of inquiry, and the considerable amount of work that is being done needs to be assessed carefully.

Policymakers and administrators should know that sharecropping is not bad, that risk is not an ultimate barrier to adoption, that credit systems can be made to work, that markets generally operate better without interventions, that crop insurance is costly and generally not feasible, that price support systems have given tremendous stability, that extension has worked, and that rural works programs and dairying can succeed. International agencies, which formulated many of the schemes discussed in the book, will find a wealth of project-related solutions, drawn not only from the recent academic literature but also from the World Bank's operational experience. Researchers will find that the theories and development notions prevalent in the 1950s need to be reformulated. This book argues for a new theoretical paradigm, perhaps a more complex paradigm to replace our earlier and more naive concepts about rural poverty.

This book stems from a paper written for the 1978 edition of the World Bank's *World Development Report*. After subsequent research in 1979 and the first half of 1981, I compiled a 1,200-page draft, which for a variety of reasons had its publication repeatedly delayed. This manuscript has now been updated with new empirical evidence for the intervening years and has been cut in half. The original chapters on tenancy, agrarian structure, and the productivity of small farms have been published separately (Singh 1988a, b, and c) and are merely summarized here.

Shankra Acharya, Montek Ahluwalia, D. C. Rao, and Martin Wolf initiated some of the early ideas for this work and reread my drafts; without their support the book would not have been written. My thanks also go to Robert McNamara and Ernest Stern, who supported my efforts to produce a book from the original research. I would also like to thank Bevin Wade, chief economist for India at the time, who insisted that I incorporate a wider research literature and stressed the importance of the book. Mark Leiserson, my former division chief in the Agriculture and Rural Employment Division of the Development and Economics Department, has been an unfailing source of moral support throughout all the vicissitudes. Even after the abolition of that department, he constantly asked how the book was coming and urged its publication. My thanks also go to my three directors—Benjamin King, Gregory Ingram, and Ardy Stoutjesdijk—who provided invaluable support and research assistance even when I was transferred to other departments in the World Bank.

I am indebted to my editor, Peter Bocock. He produced the first organized draft and the revised drafts under great personal pressure and strain. A special word of thanks goes to Tribhuwan Narain, who worked with me on the first paper for *World Development Report 1978*, traveled with me to South Asia for three months, visited hundreds of universities and researchers, helped ship and compile the data, and sorted through some 6,000 articles. He undertook the work on all the tables, and even though subsequently employed elsewhere in the Bank, he has never failed to come back and help update the final copy. I would also like to thank the hundreds of researchers throughout South Asia for giving so generously of their time and their latest research work. In addition, I am grateful to Bruce Ross-Larson and Miranda Elgin for helping me produce the final version under extreme pressure, and to Jane Carroll for copyediting voluminous material with a fine-tooth comb.

Finally, I want to thank my family for their support and humor through eight long years of my bringing this manuscript home to finish—"one more time."

Acronyms and Abbreviations

ADB	Asian Development Bank
ADBP	Agriculture Development Bank of Pakistan
AERC	Agro-Economic Research Center
BARC	Bangladesh Agricultural Research Council
BIDS	Bangladesh Institute of Development Studies
CAD	command area development
CIMMYT	International Center for Corn and Wheat Improvement
CSRE	Crash Scheme for Rural Employment
DDP	Desert Development Program
DPAP	Drought Prone Areas Program
EGS	Employment Guarantee Scheme
FMS	Farm Management Surveys
FWP	Food for Work Program
GDP	gross domestic product
HYV	high-yielding varieties
IDA	International Development Association
IFDC	International Fertilizer Development Center
IFPRI	International Food Policy Research Institute
ILO	International Labour Organisation
IRDP	Integrated Rural Development Program
IRRI	International Rice Research Institute
MFLA	Marginal Farmers and Landless Labor Agencies
MNP	Minimum Needs Program
NCAER	National Council of Applied Economic Research
NDDB	National Dairy Development Board
NDP	net domestic product
NREP	National Rural Employment Program
NSS	National Sample Survey
NWFP	Northwest Frontier Province
PIREP	Pilot Intensive Rural Employment Program

PRS	personal responsibility system
RIP	Rural Industries Projects
SFDA	Small Farmers Development Agencies
T&V	training and visit
TIP	Thana Irrigation Program
TVE	township and village enterprise
USAID	U.S. Agency for International Development
WAPDA	Water and Power Development Authority

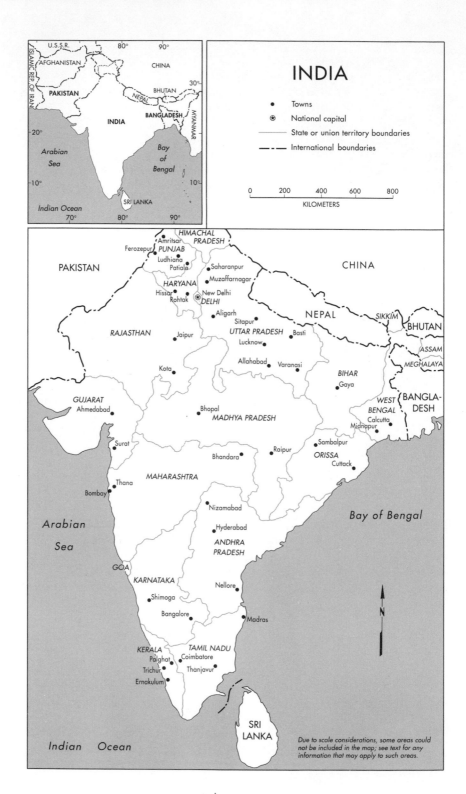

INDIA

- Towns
- ⊛ National capital
- State or union territory boundaries
- ·—·— International boundaries

0   200   400   600   800
KILOMETERS

U.S.S.R.
AFGHANISTAN
PAKISTAN
INDIA
CHINA
BHUTAN
NEPAL
BANGLADESH
MYANMAR
Arabian Sea
Bay of Bengal
Indian Ocean
SRI LANKA
80°   90°   30°   20°   -10°   10°   70°   80°   90°

PAKISTAN

CHINA

NEPAL

HIMACHAL PRADESH
Amritsar
Ferozepur
PUNJAB
Ludhiana
Patiala
Saharanpur
Muzaffarnagar
HARYANA
Hissar
Rohtak
New Delhi
DELHI
Aligarh
Sitapur
UTTAR PRADESH
Basti
Lucknow
SIKKIM
BHUTAN
ASSAM
MEGHALAYA

RAJASTHAN
Jaipur
Kota
Allahabad
Varanasi
BIHAR
Gaya
WEST BENGAL
BANGLA-DESH
Calcutta
Midnapur

GUJARAT
Ahmedabad
Bhopal
MADHYA PRADESH
Sambalpur
ORISSA
Cuttack

Surat
Bhandara
Raipur

MAHARASHTRA
Thana
Bombay

Arabian Sea

Nizamabad
Hyderabad
ANDHRA PRADESH

Bay of Bengal

GOA
KARNATAKA
Shimoga
Bangalore
Nellore
Madras

N

KERALA
Palghat
Trichur
Ernakulum
TAMIL NADU
Coimbatore
Thanjavur

SRI LANKA

Indian Ocean

Due to scale considerations, some areas could not be included in the map; see text for any information that may apply to such areas.

xxvi

PAKISTAN

- Towns and cities
- ⊛ National capital
- Province boundaries
- International boundaries

0   200   400
KILOMETERS

U.S.S.R.

CHINA

AFGHANISTAN

NORTHWEST
FRONTIER
PROVINCE

Peshawar

Kohat
Islamabad ⊛

Approx. Line
of Control

Jhelum
Gujranwala

D.I. Khan

Fort Sandeman

Faisalabad
(Lyallpur)

Quetta   Loralai

Sahiwal

PUNJAB

Kalat   Sibi

BALUCHISTAN
Kharan

Rahimyar
Khan

Khuzdar

Jacobabad

ISLAMIC REP.
OF IRAN

Larkana

SIND

Bela

N

Turbat

Nawabshah

Hyderabad

INDIA

Arabian   Sea

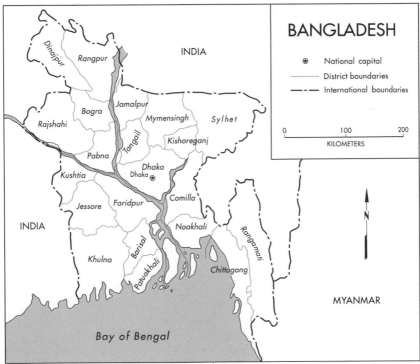

BANGLADESH

- ⊛ National capital
- District boundaries
- International boundaries

0   100   200
KILOMETERS

Dinajpur

Rangpur

INDIA

Bogra   Jamalpur

Rajshahi

Mymensingh   Sylhet

Tangail

Kishoreganj

Pabna

Kushtia

Dhaka
Dhaka ⊛

Comilla

Jessore   Faridpur

INDIA

Noakhali

Ranganati

Barisal

Khulna

Chittagong

Patuakhali

MYANMAR

N

Bay of Bengal

1

Introduction

No society can surely be flourishing and happy of which
the greater part of the members are poor and miserable.
                                        —ADAM SMITH

Since the countries of South Asia—Bangladesh, India, and Pakistan—
gained independence, the reduction of mass poverty has been a fundamental goal of their social and economic policies. Yet in spite of
nearly four decades of effort, the number of people living below the
poverty line (however arbitrarily defined) has continued to increase,
especially in rural areas.

Rural poverty is deeply rooted in the economic and social structure
of South Asia, and many observers have contended that poverty cannot be alleviated without radical changes—particularly in the unequal
distribution of rural assets and the power and privilege that go with
them. True, rural poverty would have been easier to eradicate, and
the gains from technological and institutional improvements would
have been more widely distributed, if structural reforms had been undertaken soon after independence. But at a minimum such reforms
would have included the redistribution of landed assets—and they
would have been revolutionary. The nature of the polity in South
Asia was such that fundamental changes of this kind were not undertaken, and the subsequent difficulties in tackling the problems of
rural poverty are the historical legacy of that missed opportunity.

The chances of such redistributive reforms being undertaken today
are even slimmer; but they would not be a panacea even if they could
be undertaken. In areas where redistribution is most desirable there
is little land available to distribute. Demographic pressures have further subdivided holdings, increased landlessness and the number of
small and marginal farmers, and made the problems of poverty more
intractable than ever.

It has been wrong to insist that little has been or can be done to reduce poverty without structural reforms—that since the "best" was not done no "second-best" alternatives will suffice. One of the main themes of this book is that, notwithstanding the pessimism expressed in various quarters, significant progress has actually been made in reducing the proportion of those living in poverty in South Asia. The changes have been slow and in many cases the trends have been hardly discernible; but they do exist, and they are in the right direction.

The trends have been most visible where per capita growth in the agricultural sector has been high. Annual rates of per capita growth in excess of 2 to 2.5 percent, when sustained for a decade or more, have had a significant impact on rural poverty. Such growth has occurred in relatively few areas of South Asia, however. The relative neglect of growth as an explicit strategy for attacking rural poverty has been one of the consistent threads in the evidence reviewed throughout this book. The central message is that growth *does* matter, and that it is the lack of growth—or rather the overwhelming stagnation in large parts of South Asia until recently—that is responsible for the continuing poverty observed in the subcontinent.

The lesson is clear: without vigorous and continued agricultural growth, poverty cannot be alleviated. Where growth has been vigorous and sustained, even the poorest have benefited—directly through increased income and employment opportunities in the agricultural sector and indirectly through second-round employment opportunities generated in the rural sector and greater supplies of wage goods. Without growth in per capita terms, it is the poorest who will remain the longest in poverty and continue to suffer most from the degradation associated with it.

Experience with various projects and programs during the past four decades clearly indicates the types of investments that have spurred agricultural growth:

- Investments in irrigation, especially in semidry and arid areas where the returns are enormous and the potential impact on growth very large, or in flood control and bunding in areas with heavy rainfall where multiple cropping is possible
- Investments in new technologies associated with the Green Revolution, together with associated investments in essential inputs (including the timely and adequate provision of improved seeds, fertilizers, information, water, markets, and credit)
- Investments in physical infrastructure—roads, transport, electrification, communications, and marketing—especially with the spread of technologies for high-yielding varieties (HYV) of seed,

which increase the marketed surpluses of small farmers and require greater labor mobility and specialization on farms

- Investments in rural education that enhance the productivity of
farmers and laborers by enabling them to take advantage of new
opportunities
- Investments in research and extension that allow the dissemination and adoption of existing technologies and a continuing flow
of new ones to small farmers
- Investments that encourage crop intensification, multiple cropping, and shifts to higher-value crops, including fruits and vegetables.

The positive implications of the Green Revolution have been
swamped in much of the relevant literature by the criticism that it has
not provided the rural poor with assets and opportunities equal to
those of their richer and more powerful neighbors (who are said to
have garnered all the gains from the new cereal technologies). I show
that much of this criticism is misplaced. The best bet for the poor
throughout South Asia, and especially in the chronically poor regions
in the subcontinent, is to acquire, adapt, and adopt these technologies
as rapidly as possible. It is futile to labor the point that the gains from
these technologies would have been even more widespread and more
beneficial had rural assets been more evenly distributed. The hard
fact is that they are not. But this is a political failure, not a consequence of any shortcomings in the new technologies. To continue to
argue against the rapid extension of these technologies and of the institutions and investments needed to disseminate them as widely as
possible—or to make structural reforms a precondition of their
extension—is to argue against good solutions because the "best" solutions are not available. Thus in much of the public policy debate on
this issue, the best has become the enemy of the good.

None of the above should be taken as an argument against the in-
trinsic desirability of reforming South Asia's agrarian structures. This
book unsparingly outlines the inequities and inefficiencies in the existing situation. Where reforms are possible—and I show that they are
in many areas of South Asia—they must remain on the urgent agenda
of policymakers. The policy debate needs to shift its focus, however,
from their desirability to their political feasibility. Where appropriate reforms are feasible, they should certainly be carried out. In
order of priority and their likely impact on the rural poor, these
include:

- Redistribution of land—still the most effective way to change the
prospects of those without land

- Consolidation of holdings—shown to be both feasible and highly desirable
- Increasing the security of land tenancy—where there is the political will needed to implement and monitor such programs effectively.

In addition to programs for accelerating per capita growth and land reform in the farm sector, complementary programs in the nonfarm sector are needed if overall prospects for the rural poor are to be improved. Those with the greatest potential benefits for the rural poor include:

- Dairy programs, especially the cooperative arrangements first tried out at Anand and later extended through Operation Flood and the National Dairy Development Board in India, but yet to be tried in Pakistan and Bangladesh
- Small stock programs, which have yet to be fully developed and extended on a national scale anywhere in the subcontinent
- Small fisheries, whether private or cooperative undertakings in freshwater or seawater, which have yet to be fully exploited but offer considerable potential benefits for the rural poor
- Poultry programs, which also have yet to be tried on a cooperative basis—the only way to make them accessible to the rural poor
- Agroprocessing programs, again along cooperative lines, to bring together small producers of oilseeds, fruits, and vegetables; now being tried for oilseeds on the Anand model
- Development of rural manufacturing and service industries, which would offer a host of opportunities for small-scale entrepreneurship and nonfarm employment for the rural poor—notably by providing goods and services to meet the expansion of rural demand once per capita agricultural incomes begin to rise.

Of the initiatives listed above, only the dairy programs have been seriously tried on a national basis. Although there has been some development of rural industry, it has been mainly the result of individual efforts prompted by and dependent on the rate of agricultural growth rather than a government plan based on conscious policy choices. But these are programs that can work—and when they have been tried they have had a significant impact on the rural poor. They need to be given a more explicit role in an overall strategy for alleviating rural poverty.

Opportunities like these are a necessary but not a sufficient condition for the alleviation of poverty, however. All the evidence suggests that although growth is absolutely essential for reducing rural poverty in the long run, it cannot be accelerated immediately in most of South Asia. Moreover, even if it were accelerated, it would take time to have a significant impact on poverty. Even if all the programs listed above were to be pursued vigorously, therefore, another decade or two would be needed for their impact to become substantial in many parts of South Asia. What is to be done in the interim? Public policy, especially in a democracy, cannot afford to wait for the long run to address this issue.

By the early 1970s it became obvious, at least in India, that direct antipoverty programs were needed to address the problem. Four categories of programs were developed for different purposes. The first group was designed to provide direct benefits to individuals. It includes the Small Farmers Development Agencies (SFDA) and the Marginal Farmers and Landless Labor Agencies (MFLA), which were later supplemented by the Integrated Rural Development Program (IRDP). They enabled poor households to acquire assets (mainly through subsidized credit) that could generate both income and self-employment. A second group included the Crash Scheme for Rural Employment (CSRE), the Pilot Intensive Rural Employment Program (PIREP), and the Food for Work Program (FWP)—later restructured and called the National Rural Employment Program (NREP)—which provided wage employment in rural areas through public works. A third group was designed for the development of ecologically disadvantaged areas and included the Drought Prone Areas Program (DPAP) and the Desert Development Program (DDP). Fourth were those designed to raise standards of living through the direct provision of social services; an example is the Minimum Needs Program (MNP), which provided clean water, health care, and family planning.

The most extensive of these programs are the IRDP and the NREP. The IRDP was started in 1978–79 to cover the areas in which the SFDA and MFLA had been operating and was extended to the entire country in 1980. It mainly provides subsidies and credit for purchasing livestock and milk animals. Its outlays have grown very rapidly from about Rs4 billion in 1980–81 to about Rs10 billion in 1982–83, and it covers about 3 million families a year. In fact, the IRDP has grown too rapidly and has failed to reach the poorest rural groups. Because of political pressures it caters to many who are not poor and has therefore suffered extensive leakages. Since more than 260 million rural people were estimated to be in poverty in 1979–80 and the program reaches only about 9 million of them, it is generally considered inadequate in its scale and coverage.

The Food for Work Program started in 1977 and was extended in 1980 to all of India under the NREP. From 1980–81 to 1984–85 the program created about 350 million additional days of employment a year and executed a wide variety of useful public works projects, including afforestation, village water tanks, drinking water wells, minor irrigation works, rural roads, soil and water conservation, and land reclamation throughout India (Dantwala 1986). The program cost about Rs5 billion in 1984–85.

Dantwala (1986) estimated that the outlays for all the direct antipoverty programs together amounted to no more than about 1.5 percent of the net national product of the sectors in which they are supposed to eliminate poverty. In view of the size of the poverty problem, he rightly concluded that these programs are too small to tackle it adequately. He believes, again rightly, that most of the resources going to a variety of programs should be concentrated in the NREP because food for work programs provide employment directly to the poor, avoid leakages to the bogus poor, and provide directly productive works that are badly needed in rural areas. Such programs are also less subject to political pressure to benefit the rural rich, because the latter are mainly attracted to the credits and subsidies provided under other programs, such as the IRDP. The weight of evidence from Maharashtra's Employment Guarantee Scheme (EGS), reviewed in chapter 7, confirms this view. Indeed, the experience of the EGS spurred the Indian government to expand rural public works via the NREP. Although India has taken the first steps toward experimenting and gaining experience with direct antipoverty programs (such as the NREP) on a national scale, nationwide programs have yet to be taken up in Pakistan and Bangladesh.

Most of the direct antipoverty programs are less than a decade old even in India, and it is too early for a full-scale assessment of their failures and successes. Excellent reviews of individual programs are provided in Desai (1979) and India, Planning Commission (1982, 1985a). The point stressed here is that programs of this kind are an essential complement to strategies to accelerate growth, and in the final analysis they depend on rapid agricultural growth to sustain them over time.

One reason why India could experiment with the NREP is that it had a surplus of foodstocks—an estimated 25 million metric tons in 1985. It has always been recognized that the poor are in dire hunger because they lack the necessary purchasing power, a view formalized by Amartya Sen in his seminal work (1981), which cited the lack of "entitlements" on the part of the poor as the main cause of famines in South Asia. Food for work programs such as the NREP bring together poor people who need work, and the surplus food grains to provide wages in kind, with essential public works that need to be put in place. These programs create direct entitlements for the poor, enabling them to exchange their work for food—the main item in their budget.

It is essential to underscore the point, however, that it is only because of rapid agricultural growth in states such as Punjab and Haryana that the government has the surplus stocks of food that make a scheme such as the NREP feasible on a national scale. (It would be possible for Pakistan to undertake a similar effort, again thanks to rapid agricultural growth.) Without surpluses generated in fast-growing regions, direct national antipoverty programs—whether NREP or IRDP—would have to rely on food imports or food aid. Dependence on food imports would rapidly run into balance of payments problems and stimulate inflation, which is just what happened when large food for work programs were tried in the 1960s. And Bangladesh would face these constraints now if it were to extend nationwide its small food for work program, which depends heavily on food aid.

To summarize, a workable antipoverty strategy involves a three-pronged approach consisting of: (a) policy reforms and action programs to accelerate growth in both farm and nonfarm rural activities; (b) a well-funded and effectively implemented rural work program aimed at the poor, with payments in food or, better still, money; and (c) supplemental but well-targeted programs in health, education, sanitation, family planning, and potable water supply to improve the quality of life in rural areas. These three elements—growth in the longer run, guaranteed employment in the short run, and improvements in the quality of rural life—should remain the central focus of policies for reducing rural poverty and its degrading impact in the coming decades.

Meanwhile, the number of the landless and near landless will continue to grow, as will the number of the rural poor—at least in absolute terms. Underlying demographic trends make it certain that poverty will continue to increase in areas where agricultural stagnation persists. But in areas where per capita agricultural growth accelerates, poverty can certainly be expected to continue to decline. In the long run, however, the inexorable pressure of rising population on rural land can be relieved only by reducing the rate of population growth and increasing employment opportunities in the industrial sector. The former is inextricably tied to the growth of employment opportunities and the incomes and access to education (especially for women) that come with them. The heart of the problem is therefore the failure to transform the economies of South Asia by adequately expanding industrial employment opportunities. The reasons for this failure require a separate and detailed analysis, but it is certain that in the long run mass poverty—rural as well as urban—can be eradicated only by the industrial transformation of South Asia. On this path the economies of the region are now embarked.

2
Rural Poverty: Incidence and Trends

In 1986 India, Pakistan, and Bangladesh together had 983 million people (see table 2-1). About 76 percent of them—some 741 million people—lived in rural areas, as do most of the poor; about 67 percent of the combined labor force of the three countries work in agriculture. Overall growth rates of gross domestic product (GDP) per capita have been small except in Pakistan, and the distribution of income suggests that even the modest increases may not have been shared equally. Agricultural output has barely exceeded population growth in Pakistan and India and has fallen behind in Bangladesh. It is consequently inferred that rural living standards have declined and that the incidence of rural poverty in South Asia has increased (see ILO 1977a).

This inference has been reflected in a growing and disquieting literature on trends in rural poverty in South Asia. Starting with the pioneering work of Dandekar and Rath (1971), the literature is fairly extensive for India, and some recent work has also been done for Pakistan and Bangladesh.[1] Many of the relevant studies, though not all, suggest that where agricultural growth has stagnated, the incidence of poverty in the rural population has definitely increased and that the absolute number of the rural poor has increased everywhere (see table 2-2 for selected aggregate estimates). More serious, some analysts have argued that even vigorous and sustained agricultural growth has been accompanied by a steady deterioration in the distribution of incomes—not only a relative decline in the incomes of the rural poor but also an absolute decline in real terms.[2]

This powerful myth, accepted by a growing number of policymakers, has serious implications for the poor. If the incidence of poverty increases with growth, the poor are bound to become the direct and innocent victims of policies designed to increase growth, and the con-

Table 2-1. *South Asia: Basic Economic Characteristics*

Item	Bangladesh	India	Pakistan
Population			
Total population, mid-1986 (millions)	103.0	781.0	99.0
Rural population, 1986			
Number (millions)	84.5	585.5	70.9
Percent	82	75	71
Annual rate of growth, 1980–86			
(percent)	2.6	2.2	3.1
GDP (current prices)			
Total GDP, 1986 (billions of U.S. dollars)	15.5	203.8	30.1
Per capita GDP (1986 U.S. dollars)	140	261	303
Agriculture, 1986			
Agricultural GDP as a percentage			
of total GDP	47	32	24
Rural population per square kilometer			
of agricultural area	990	345	280
Labor force, 1985 (percent)			
1985 estimated population of			
working age (15–64 years)	53	56	53
Percentage of labor force			
in agriculture	75	70	55
Average annual growth rates (percent)			
GDP, 1980–86	3.7	4.9	6.7
Agriculture, 1980–86	2.7	1.9	3.3
Labor force, 1980–85	2.8	2.0	2.0

Sources: World Bank (1988a and b).

flict between equity and growth objectives consequently becomes acute. For this argument to hold, however, it must be shown both that GDP per capita has grown and that it has increased the incidence of rural poverty.[3] As I shall show in this chapter, the factual basis for these suppositions is by no means sound.

Patterns of Poverty

Has absolute and relative rural poverty increased substantially in South Asia in spite of (or because of) agricultural growth? A careful examination of the evidence shows that much of it is based on poor data and the slippery concept of the poverty line. Where the data are reliable, no clear trends emerge.

Table 2-2. South Asia: Estimates of Rural Poverty, Selected Years and Studies

Definition of poverty (per capita income or expenditure)	Year	Percentage of rural population in poverty	Implied size of rural population in poverty (millions)
Bangladesh			
Based on a food bundle of 2,100 calories and 45 grams of protein[a]	1963–64	88	49.9
	1966–67	62	37.9
	1968–69	79	50.7
	1973–74	94	64.0
Absolute poverty: Tk23.6 (monthly per capita income at constant 1963–64 prices), equivalent to 95 percent recommended calorie intake[b]	1963–64	40	22.2
	1968–69	76	47.0
	1973–74	78	53.5
	1975 (1st quarter)	62	43.6
Based on food bundle of 2,122 calories[c]	1981–82	74	60.9
India			
Rs480 annually[d]	1968–69	75	307.7
	1969–70	72	305.3
	1970–71	68	295.7

Consumer expenditure level of Rs15 per 30 days at 1960–61 rural prices[e]	1959–60	49	172.8
	1960–61	42	152.4
	1963–64	49	189.1
	1965–66	51	204.7
	1967–68	58	241.1
	1970–71	49	216.6
	1973–74	48	221.3
Pakistan			
Rs300 annually (at constant 1959–60 prices)[f]	1963–64	61	23.5
	1966–67	60	24.8
	1968–69	62	26.7
	1969–70	60	26.5
	1970–71	55	25.3
	1971–72	58	27.5
Rs27.5 per capita per month (at constant 1959–60 prices)[g] equivalent to 95 percent recommended calorie intake	1963–64	72	27.7
	1966–67	64	26.5
	1968–69	62	27.6
	1969–70	68	30.0
	1970–71	71	32.7
	1971–72	74	35.1

a. Alamgir (1975).
b. Khan in ILO (1977a), pp. 144–47.
c. World Bank (1987b), p. 137.
d. NCAER (1975), p. xv.
e. Montek S. Ahluwalia (1978).
f. Alauddin (1975).
g. Naseem in ILO (1977a), pp. 41–60.

India

One of the most reliable estimates of the trends in rural poverty in India (where comparative data permit careful analysis) was first made by Montek Ahluwalia (1978). He used consumer expenditure data drawn from the National Sample Survey (NSS) for 1956–57 to 1973–74 to calculate the percentage of the rural population below a given poverty line for India as a whole as well as for individual states.[4] Table A1 reproduces results from his study. (Tables with numbers preceded by "A" are found in the statistical appendix at the back of the book.) The most important findings of his study through the early 1970s were as follows:

- For India as a whole, the extent and incidence of rural poverty varied markedly over time, with no overall trend to increase or decrease, at least before the Green Revolution.

- Since the population grew steadily and the incidence of poverty did not fall markedly, the absolute number of rural poor grew significantly over time. Ahluwalia calculated the increase to average about 5 million people every year during that period.

- The incidence of poverty in the states followed a pattern similar to that for India as a whole. Poverty fell in almost all states until the early 1960s, peaked in 1967–68 or 1968–69, and declined again thereafter. Only two states (Assam and West Bengal) showed a significant increase in poverty, while two others (Andhra Pradesh and Tamil Nadu) showed a decline.

Ahluwalia also looked at an alternative and more reliable measure of poverty—Sen's poverty index, which takes into account the percentage of the population in poverty, the gap between the poverty line and the mean consumption of the poor, and the extent of inequality among the poor.[5] The Sen index showed a pattern of fluctuation similar to that described above with "no evidence for asserting a trend increase or decrease in rural poverty over [the] period as a whole" (Ahluwalia 1978, p. 304). But that was before more recent data were available for the decade after the Green Revolution, from the late 1970s to the early 1980s. Ahluwalia included the most recent NSS data available (1956–57 to 1977–78) in his 1985 analysis and wrote:

The NSS data permit the firm conclusion that there is no basis for the view that the incidence of rural poverty has increased over time, especially in the period after the green revolution. The data for 1956/57 to 1977/78 show no significant trend, and the data for the period after the green revolution show a *more or less steady decline.*

The second issue considered . . . is the relationship between rural poverty and agricultural income levels per head. Three conclusions have emerged: (1) There is fairly strong evidence of an inverse relationship between agricultural income per head and the incidence of rural poverty, especially if account is taken of lagged effects; (2) there is no evidence that this relationship has weakened since the green revolution; and (3) reliance on growth alone will not bring about a large reduction in the incidence of poverty in the near future. These conclusions underscore the need for rural development programs aimed especially at the rural poor. (Ahluwalia in Mellor and Desai 1985, p. 72)

Robin M. Mukherjee (1986) arrived at similar conclusions when examining all-India data and further evidence from selected states. Using evidence from the NSS 38th Round (India, Ministry of Planning, 1983), he found significant declines in the incidence of poverty in Haryana, Kerala, Punjab, Tamil Nadu, and even West Bengal starting around 1970 and continuing into the 1980s. C. H. H. Rao (1986) confirms further declines in the incidence of poverty in all states except Rajasthan between 1977–78 and 1982–83. The incidence of rural poverty in India as a whole fell from 40 percent to 32 percent between 1978 and 1983 (tables A2 and A3). The combined evidence on long-term trends suggests that the incidence of poverty fell from around 55 percent in the late 1950s to around 35 percent by the early 1980s (see table 2-3 and figure 2-1).

Although the debate about the reliability and usefulness of the NSS data for measuring poverty continues, they are the only data that allow consistent comparative analysis over more than three decades. Data from earlier studies have been consistently used to argue that growth has little or no impact on poverty. That conclusion predated the later advances in agricultural growth, however. More recent evidence should lay to rest the view that growth has in general made rural poverty worse or has failed to alleviate it. The fact is that growth as an explicit strategy for relieving poverty has never been high on the agenda of policymakers, especially in India. The new evidence should convince policymakers of the absolute importance of accelerating rates of growth, especially in regions where poverty is widespread, and of introducing special programs to alleviate poverty among those who have benefited less from this growth.

Pakistan

The evidence on rural poverty in Pakistan is less extensive than that for India and is based on less reliable and noncomparable data. Khan

Table 2-3. *Trends in Rural Poverty in India*

| Year | Percentage of population in poverty | | Sen's poverty index | |
	Ahluwalia	Mukherjee	Ahluwalia	Mukherjee
1956–57	54.1	n.a.	0.23	n.a.
1958	50.2	n.a.	0.22	n.a.
1959	46.5	n.a.	0.19	n.a.
1960	44.4	n.a.	0.17	n.a.
1961	38.9	n.a.	0.14	n.a.
1962	39.4	n.a.	0.14	n.a.
1963	n.a.	n.a.	n.a.	n.a.
1964	44.5	n.a.	0.16	n.a.
1965	46.8	45.7	0.17	0.17
1966	53.9	48.7	0.21	0.19
1967	56.6	56.0	0.24	0.24
1968	56.5	55.5	0.20	0.23
1969	51.0	49.0	0.18	0.20
1970	n.a.	45.2	n.a.	0.19
1971	47.5	n.a.	n.a.	0.17
1972	41.2	46.4	n.a.	n.a.
1973	43.1	46.1	0.17	0.18
1974	46.1	n.a.	0.14	0.16
1975	39.1	n.a.	n.a.	n.a.
1978	39.1	40.2	0.14	0.14
1983	n.a.	32.8	n.a.	0.11

n.a. Not available.

Sources: Ahluwalia (in Mellor and Desai 1985), and personal communication from Robin M. Mukherjee, Economic Research Unit, Indian Statistical Institute, Calcutta.

and Bose (1968) showed that per capita incomes in the agricultural sector in East Pakistan (now Bangladesh) fell between 1949–50 and 1963–64. In West Pakistan (now Pakistan) incomes increased (though very gradually) during the same period; even in the West, however, the study found that the majority of the farming population had less than the average income, which was itself barely above the subsistence level.

In a more extensive study, Naseem (1973) showed that findings based on national income data revealed substantially higher increases in rural per capita income than expenditure data drawn from household surveys, especially after 1963–64. Using this latter data base, he estimated that the percentage of those in West Pakistan below a given poverty line had fallen substantially between 1963–64 and 1969–70. In a subsequent study, however, Naseem (in ILO 1977a) qualified his earlier findings. He defined three separate poverty lines by consump-

Figure 2-1. *Rural Poverty in India and Selected States, 1956–83*

Percentage of rural population in poverty

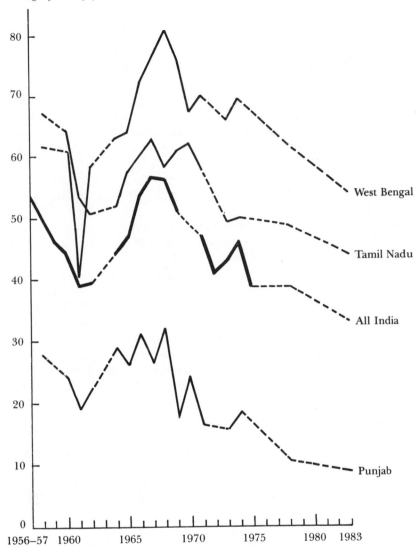

Note: Broken line indicates extrapolated data.
Sources: Tables 2-3 and A3.

15

tion levels of 95, 92, and 90 percent of the "minimum calories required per capita." He concluded that the proportion of the population in poverty varies considerably according to the poverty line
chosen[6] and that there was no definite trend in the incidence of poverty even when an arbitrary index was used to define it. When he defined poverty in "the most extreme intolerable terms" (that is, a level
of expenditure that permitted the consumption of no more than 90
percent of the minimum number of required calories), he found that
in 1971–72, 54 percent of rural households and 43 percent of the
rural population were below these extreme levels of poverty and that
the percentage of people in poverty had remained roughly the same
over the years. In view of the growth in population, the implication
is that the absolute number of Pakistanis living in poverty had increased substantially—a finding similar to that for India for the same
period, but more disquieting because Pakistan had had higher rates
of agricultural growth.

Naseem's findings have not been universally accepted, however.
Alauddin (1975) studied the same period and used the same data but
reached the opposite conclusion (see table 2-2). Alauddin's calculations suggested that the percentage (though not the absolute number)
of persons below the poverty line had fallen in West Pakistan since
1963–64. But Alauddin's poverty line was not the same as Naseem's,
and he used a different price index to make data for several years
comparable. It is not possible to establish which of these studies is
more credible, although Naseem's finding that "extreme poverty" had
risen in West Pakistan is difficult to reconcile with World Bank data
on rural wages presented in a 1977 internal report. The latter showed
that real wages of casual agricultural workers remained stable between 1959 and 1966, but began to rise after 1966 at a rate of about
2–5 percent a year. The real wages of permanent agricultural workers
showed a similar trend between 1966 and 1973, with a fairly uniform
pattern of increase in all districts.[7]

Reviews of more recent studies on the incidence of poverty in Pakistan suggest that it has declined substantially, from around 20–30
percent in the mid-1970s to around 10–15 percent in the mid-1980s
depending on the poverty line used (Allison 1989; Ahmad and Ludlow 1989). Because of sustained high rates of agricultural growth
and substantial out-migration from rural areas (especially to the
Middle East), poverty certainly appears to be far less evident in Pakistan than in India. A conjecture about the present incidence of rural poverty in Pakistan would place it close to that found in Punjab
and Haryana in India—that is, about 10–12 percent of the rural
population.

Bangladesh

Work on the incidence of rural poverty in Bangladesh is also limited and has problems similar to those of the Pakistani studies, but the findings are perhaps less equivocal, at least through the 1970s.[8] As noted above, Khan and Bose (1968) found that agricultural incomes in East Pakistan had actually fallen between 1949–50 and 1963–74. From more detailed data Bose (1968) concluded that per capita agricultural incomes fell during the entire decade of the 1950s except for a slight reversal observed in 1963–64. He observed that rural wage earnings in Bangladesh were lower in every year between 1951 and 1960 than they had been in 1949. After falling in 1962, earnings peaked in 1964 but then fell again, so that "by 1966 rural wages were at a level lower than in 1959." Alamgir (1975) seems to confirm these broad results for 1963–64 to 1973–74 (see table 2-2). No clear trend can be attributed to Alamgir's findings, however, and his study relies on two surveys which are probably not comparable.

A. R. Khan (in ILO 1977a) noted that most analyses, including those for Bangladesh, make no allowance for differences in calorie requirements for different types of workers.[9] To deal with this problem, he split the poor into two groups—the absolutely poor (whose calorie intake is only 90 percent of the "recommended requirements for their occupation") and the extremely poor (whose calorie intake is only 80 percent of the recommended requirements). Using these categories, Khan showed that there was a sharp increase in the incidence of poverty in Bangladesh after the early 1960s. His calculations suggested that only 5 percent of the rural population could be categorized as "extremely poor" in 1963–64, but that the proportion rose to over 40 percent in the 1970s. He further estimated that the "absolutely poor" made up about 40 percent of the population during 1963–67 and nearly 62 percent of the total in 1975. Khan also examined the evidence on real agricultural wages; although he found no trend for the entire period from the early 1950s to the 1970s, he stated categorically that real wages started to fall after 1964 and that this decline accelerated sharply in the early 1970s.

In view of this evidence, Khan concluded that the living standards of the vast majority of the rural population in Bangladesh fell in absolute terms through the 1970s; real wages of agricultural laborers fell; and per capita rural incomes and output fell, especially during the first five years of the 1970s. All groups may not have shared in this fall, however; many households at the top of the scale had increases in real incomes during that period.

Studies of rural poverty also showed an increase in the incidence of rural poverty through the 1970s. According to Muqtada (1974) this incidence increased significantly from 44 percent in 1963–64 to over 68 percent by 1976–77 and was accompanied by continuing population growth in spite of war and natural disasters. As a result, the absolute number of the poor in Bangladesh grew dramatically—more than doubling according to Muqtada—in this period.

No recent reliable data are available on the incidence of rural poverty in Bangladesh. Per capita agricultural production, however, declined or stagnated throughout the first half of the 1970s, and this trend was reversed in the latter half of the 1970s and the first half of the 1980s. If the relationship between the incidence of poverty and agricultural growth is similar to that confirmed elsewhere in South Asia, rural poverty must also have declined in Bangladesh in recent years. There is some recent evidence of this. A careful study carried out by the World Bank using household expenditure survey data concluded that the overall incidence of poverty declined between 1974 and 1982 from 82 percent to 73 percent; the incidence of extreme poverty (daily consumption of only 1,850 calories per person) increased from 43 to 50 percent; and there were 4 million more poor and 1.3 million more "hard core" poor in 1982 than in 1974. The study adds that as a result of continuing increases in per capita income and substantial increases in food for work programs, the poverty situation does not seem to have deteriorated further (World Bank 1987b).

These findings are disturbing, for even where the incidence of poverty has declined and when the data are interpreted conservatively, they suggest the enormity of the problem.[10] It would, however, be wrong to take them (and the numbers they imply) at face value. There are serious problems with both the quality of the data and the methods used. (A few of the problems associated with deriving and interpreting data on the incidence of poverty are discussed in appendix A.) One should therefore accept the *numbers* on rural poverty as merely indicative, and one should be extremely cautious in accepting the evidence on *trends*.

Trends in Agricultural Output and Incomes

Another problem with the notion that growth was impoverishing rural people in South Asia is that there was little real growth in per capita terms in most parts of South Asia during the 1970s. Increases in food-grain output per capita were confined to a few regions and slowed considerably in the latter half of the 1970s. Furthermore, agricultural net domestic product (NDP) per capita, a more appropriate measure, stagnated or actually declined in most parts of the subcontinent in the 1960s and 1970s.

Table 2-4 gives the relevant data on food-grain production in the 1970s. Per capita food output—generally used in arguments about the impoverishing consequences of growth—did show positive trends in the 1970s for most of the Indian states (although only a few had high growth rates) and for Pakistan; the trends for Bangladesh were negative (figure 2-2). Growth rates were generally much lower in the 1960s except in East Punjab and Haryana, states which experienced an early breakthrough in the adoption of HYV wheat. But it is highly misleading to concentrate on food-grain production alone as an indicator of growth in the rural sector. The sector includes other products and income opportunities—and it is well known that food-grain production was increased by diverting land and resources from these other crops.[11]

A more complete picture emerges from the data on net domestic product in the agricultural sector shown in table 2-5. The figures for India show that between 1960 and 1970 agricultural NDP per head of the rural population rose on average by about 3 percent a year in six states—Gujarat, Haryana, Himachal Pradesh, Karnataka, Punjab, and Rajasthan—that accounted for 19 percent of the rural population; it rose by less than 1 percent in four other states accounting for another 31 percent of the rural population, but actually fell in the remaining seven states that made up 50 percent of the rural population.[12] This last group included Bihar and Madhya Pradesh, each of which had had a per capita NDP below the all-India average in 1960–61. By 1970–71 per capita NDP had fallen below the Indian average in three more states—Assam, Maharashtra, and West Bengal.

Data for the entire decade of the 1970s are not available to allow a comparable analysis, but a state-by-state breakdown of national accounts data for agriculture between 1970 and 1975 illustrates what happened in the first half of the decade.[13] Agricultural output continued to fall, and the per capita agricultural NDP of the rural population fell by 1 percent a year for the country as a whole. The states that had shown vigorous growth in the 1960s (agricultural NDP per capita growth of over 2 percent a year) actually experienced a decline; the second group, which had recorded only moderate growth, also registered an overall decline (though of a smaller magnitude). Only four states, which accounted for 18 percent of the rural population, experienced positive growth rates in agricultural NDP per capita, and only two of them—Himachal Pradesh and Maharashtra—had rates above 2 percent a year. The rest of the country, accounting for 91 percent of the rural population in 1976, experienced a relative de-

Table 2-4. South Asia: Annual Growth Rates of Population and of Food-Grain Output

Country and state	1960–70			1970–79		
	Rural population	Food-grain output		Rural population	Food-grain output	
		Total	Per capita[a]		Total	Per capita[a]
Bangladesh	2.8	2.0[b]	–0.8[b]	2.40	1.13	–1.27
India	2.00	1.85	–0.15	1.88	2.74	0.86
Andhra Pradesh	1.68	0.39	–1.29	1.50	3.46	1.96
Assam	1.34	2.47	1.13	3.02	2.11	–0.91
Bihar	1.78	0.21	–1.57	1.83	2.51	0.68
Gujarat	2.29	3.16	0.87	2.00	2.07	0.07
Haryana	2.78	5.20	2.42	2.01	3.09	1.08
Karnataka	1.93	2.85	0.92	1.70	2.24	0.54
Kerala	2.22	2.01	–0.21	1.94	–0.14	–2.08
Madhya Pradesh	2.31	–0.42	–2.73	2.44	0.92	–1.52

Maharashtra	2.03	−0.52	−2.55	1.52	9.15	7.63
Orissa	2.03	2.16	0.13	2.00	0.95	−1.05
Punjab	1.89	9.54	7.65	1.36	5.15	3.79
Rajasthan	2.32	−0.40	−2.72	2.65	2.93	0.28
Tamil Nadu	1.53	0.69	−0.84	0.97	1.44	0.47
Uttar Pradesh	1.68	2.27	0.59	1.72	2.34	0.62
West Bengal	2.37	2.80	0.43	2.22	1.34	0.88
Pakistan	2.7	5.0	9.3	3.0	3.3	0.32

Notes: These are trend growth rates for comparable periods (1959–60 to 1968–69, and 1976–77 for Pakistan; 1960–61 to 1969–70, and 1978–79 for India; and 1960–65 to 1965–70, and 1978–79 for Bangladesh).

a. Per capita growth rates are simply the difference between the growth rates for rural population and food-grain output.

b. For rice production only.

Sources: M. H. Khan (1981), p. 29 for Pakistan (log linear trend); Alagh and Sharma (1980), pp. 100–01 for India (linear and log linear estimates corrected by output regression coefficients and standard errors); and World Bank data for Bangladesh (annual growth rates). Rural population growth rates for India and its states are from Census of India, 1971, series J, paper I of 1979 "Report of the Expert Committee on Population Projections," pp. 158–59.

Figure 2-2. *Growth of Rural Population and Per Capita Food-Grain Output in South Asia, 1960–70 and 1970–79*

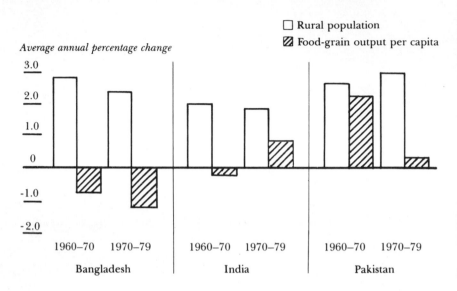

Source: Table 2-4.

cline in per capita agricultural NDP in the first half of the 1970s. Except in the record harvest years from 1975–76 to 1977–78, agricultural output per head of rural population in India as a whole stood below its 1960–61 levels.[14]

Even state-level data are too highly aggregated to show the diverse patterns of output. The localized nature of growth in agricultural output is confirmed by Bhalla and Alagh (1979). In a careful study of agricultural performance based on *district* data between 1962–65 and 1970–73, they showed that of the 282 districts studied in India, nearly a quarter (70 districts) had negative rates of growth; another 62 districts (22 percent) had rates of growth ranging between 0 and 1.5 percent a year, while 102 districts (36 percent) had growth rates varying between 1.5 and 4.5 percent. Once population growth is accounted for, only the remaining 48 districts with growth rates in excess of 4.5 percent can be said to have experienced positive per capita growth. All of these districts—except four in Karnataka and two in Tamil Nadu—were concentrated in six states in the north and west—Rajasthan (twelve), Punjab (eleven), Western Uttar Pradesh (eight), Haryana (five), Gujarat (two), and Jammu and Kashmir (two). These districts are in the arid zones in northwestern India where the productivity base was very low to begin with or where irrigation, particularly tubewell irrigation, has had a major impact.

This spatial distribution of growth suggests that, since growth has been confined to particular regions, it is in those regions that one should test the hypothesis that growth further impoverishes the poor. It also suggests a need to look carefully at district data. Even statewide figures can be misleading since they aggregate districts that have done poorly with ones that have done well. District-level data on poverty are very difficult to obtain, however, and few studies are based on them. (Bardhan in Mellor and Desai 1985 is an exception.)

Although differences in the land and in irrigation facilities are important determinants of these regional inequalities, there is growing evidence that public policy contributed significantly to them. Subbarao (1985b) analyzed state incentive policies in India as factors explaining the long-term prospects for growth in various states. He calculated that in India total subsidies for agriculture and rural development programs rose from Rs10,000 million in 1974–75 to about Rs25,000 million by 1980–81 at constant prices. Of the easily identifiable state incentives, benefits from price supports accrued mainly to four states—Haryana, Punjab, Tamil Nadu, and Uttar Pradesh. Benefits from fertilizer subsidies (estimated at Rs9,000 million in 1983–84) also accrued to four states—Andhra Pradesh, Punjab, Tamil Nadu, and Uttar Pradesh—which accounted for half of the nation's gross irrigated area and claimed 55 percent of the subsidies. Subsidies to institutionalized credit also went disproportionately to a few states. He concludes correctly that public incentive policies—mainly agricultural price supports, input subsidies, and subsidized credit—accrued disproportionately to the prosperous states that already had access to water and fertilizers. Public policies have reinforced rather than compensated for existing regional inequalities and have thus accentuated regional disparities. These "state-induced market price distortions," as Subbarao calls them, have aided growth in advanced states and retarded it in others. As a result, fewer public resources have been left for investments in poorer areas.

Available data for Bangladesh show that agricultural output barely kept pace with population growth in the 1960s and that agricultural NDP per capita of the rural population declined slightly between 1969–70 and 1977–78—for all practical purposes a record of stagnation over two decades.

Overall performance in Pakistan was similar to that in the Indian Northwest, at least in the 1950s and early 1960s, with a growth rate of 1.6 percent a year. More recent data reveal, however, that per capita agricultural output of the rural population stagnated between 1969–70 and 1977–78, a period corresponding to most of the poverty studies in Pakistan. The better than average performance in the Punjab and Sind provinces dominated the overall Pakistan figures, how-

Table 2-5. *South Asia: Agricultural Growth per Capita of Rural Population*
(percent)

Country and state	1960–70 growth rates			1970–75 growth rates			Rural population, 1976
	Rural population	Agricultural NDP[a]		Rural population	Agricultural NDP[a]		
		Total	Per capita		Total	Per capita	
Bangladesh	2.50	2.56	0.06	2.40	2.10	−0.30	72.8[b]
India	2.00	2.24	0.24	1.88	0.88	−1.00	481.5[b]
Gujarat	2.29	4.00	1.71	2.00	−10.10	−12.10	4.4
Haryana	2.78	5.09	2.31	2.01	−0.97	−2.98	1.9
Himachal Pradesh	2.02	6.66	4.64	2.01	5.13	3.12	0.7
Karnataka	1.93	3.42	1.49	1.70	2.40	0.70	5.0
Punjab	1.89	4.60	2.71	1.36	0.53	−0.83	2.3
Rajasthan	2.32	5.18	2.86	2.65	−5.00	−7.65	5.0
Regional aggregate	2.19	4.89	2.70	2.03	−2.24	−4.27	19.3
Andhra Pradesh	1.68	2.35	0.67	1.50	0.13	−1.37	7.9
Jammu and Kashmir	2.39	3.37	0.98	2.47	0.42	−2.05	0.9

Kerala	2.22	2.74	0.52	1.94	−1.76	−3.70	4.1
Uttar Pradesh	1.68	2.58	0.90	1.72	−3.10	−4.82	17.2
Others	2.52	3.02	0.50	n.a.	n.a.	n.a.	n.a.
Regional aggregate	1.79	2.56	0.77	1.73	1.78	−3.51	15.5
Assam	1.34	0.99	−0.35	3.02	1.70	−1.32	3.3
Bihar	1.78	1.38	−0.40	1.83	−0.34	−2.17	11.5
Madhya Pradesh	2.31	−0.03	−2.34	2.44	−2.77	−5.21	8.2
Maharashtra	2.03	−2.07	−4.10	1.52	7.10	5.58	7.8
Orissa	2.03	1.12	−0.91	2.00	2.14	0.14	4.6
Tamil Nadu	1.53	1.42	−0.10	0.97	−3.87	−4.84	6.3
West Bengal	2.37	1.67	−0.70	2.22	−0.43	−2.65	7.7
Regional aggregate	1.95	0.56	−1.39	−1.87	0.40	−1.47	49.4
Pakistan	3.34	4.90	1.56	2.28	2.36	0.08	52.6[b]

n.a. Not available.
Notes: Ordinary least square regressions are used to calculate all growth rates.
a. Net domestic product.
b. Millions.
Sources: Data from the World Bank, Reserve Bank of India, and National Accounts Statistics of India.

ever, and there is evidence to suggest that the Northwest Frontier Province (NWFP) and Baluchistan may have fallen considerably behind.

Agricultural Growth and Poverty

For India, where relatively reliable production data are available, Ahluwalia (1978 and in Mellor and Desai 1985) shows that there is clear evidence of an overall inverse relationship between the incidence of poverty and indices of food production, agricultural production, and net domestic product per capita of the rural population. He found that this relationship held in at least seven of the fourteen states that he examined. These states—Andhra Pradesh, Bihar, Karnataka, Madhya Pradesh, Maharashtra, Tamil Nadu, and Uttar Pradesh—accounted for 56 percent of the rural population and about three-quarters of the rural population in poverty.[15]

Ahluwalia's first results for Punjab and Haryana, based on data from the 1960s and early 1970s, are of special interest because other studies have purported to show an *increase* in rural poverty in these states despite the success of the Green Revolution in raising agricultural output.[16] His results showed that despite a dramatic growth in agricultural output per rural person, there was no evidence of any significant increase in the incidence of poverty and no discernible negative relationship between the incidence of poverty and the index of agricultural production per capita. So although there was no case for an increasing incidence of poverty as other studies have maintained, there was also no sign that real consumption had increased among the poorest 25 percent of the population.

There are three possible explanations. One frequently used is that the real consumption levels of the poorest 25 percent dropped because the labor-displacing technologies that accompanied growth in the region had reduced employment opportunities (and perhaps real wages) for agricultural laborers and the landless. This explanation fails, however, to square with the evidence of heavy migration into Punjab and Haryana from Bihar and eastern Uttar Pradesh in response to rapidly rising labor demand. Ahluwalia puts forward a different hypothesis. He suggests that the poorest quarter of the rural population in the high-growth states contains a rising proportion of immigrants. Although real consumption levels have indeed remained stagnant, this group "consists increasingly of individuals whose consumption is higher than it would have been if they had not migrated."[17] The implication is that the benefits of agricultural growth have in fact "trickled down," not only to poorer Punjabis (who have presumably moved into higher expenditure groups) but also to the poor from other states who have migrated to areas of relatively rapid growth in search of employment. The ample evidence of the dramatic expansion of demand for rural labor in high-growth states, of increasing in-migration (seasonal and permanent) from other states, and of increases in average real wages in rural areas makes this second explanation at least as plausible as the first.[18]

A third explanation is that most studies do not cover a long enough period and in fact fail to cover the evidence from more recent years. Ahluwalia (in Mellor and Desai 1985) re-examined his results on the incidence of poverty and its relationship to agricultural growth using data from 1956–57 to 1977–78. The evidence is now clearer. There is a significant and consistent negative relationship between agricultural growth and the percentage of rural population below poverty (table 2-3). This relationship is also borne out by C. H. H. Rao (1986), who compares the incidence of poverty across regions using data for 1977–78 and 1983–84. Almost everywhere in India—in the lagging eastern and central regions as well as in the south—the rural population below poverty has declined significantly.

As mentioned earlier, similar evidence is provided by Robin M. Mukherjee (1986), who extends Ahluwalia's results to include data from the 32nd and 38th Rounds of the NSS for 1978 and 1983 (tables A2 and A3). They all show a clear trend of decline in the incidence of poverty for all the states studied and for India as a whole.

A continuing problem with most poverty studies in South Asia is that they cover very short time spans. Some are based on data from the 1960s only, a period of low growth rates; others focus on even shorter periods. Few cover periods exceeding two to three decades. A few studies, carried out mainly by anthropologists or historians, have used longer time frames of five decades or more. Their findings are in sharp contrast to the more shortsighted views of economists and report significant amelioration in the conditions of the poor. Attwood (1979), for example, analyzed economic change over fifty years (1920–70) in a village in western India. He concluded that there was considerable upward as well as downward mobility; landholding had become less concentrated; some of the poor had gotten richer, while the rich had not gotten richer, at least in terms of their share of land—indeed some had gotten poorer; and "no less than 25% of the landless in 1920 had moved upward into the landed category" while "44% of those who were landed in 1920 had lost their lands by 1970" (p. 500).

Bruce (1982) covered an even longer period, 1800–1979, in his study of villages in Bellary district in Karnataka. He concluded that agrarian change had led to a more equitable distribution of resources and more widely dispersed economic opportunities. In particular, technological change between 1945 and 1980 had greatly benefited agricultural laborers, and real wages for agricultural labor reached historic highs while employment opportunities nearly doubled. Extensive evidence is available on the progress of the Green Revolution in the Punjab at the state level (see Gill 1976 and Blyn 1983). At the local level, Leaf (1983, p. 268), reports that in one village between 1965 and 1978 "the gains have gone at least as much to the poorer villagers as to the wealthier."

Thus, the evidence for "impoverishing growth" in South Asia seems shaky, at least on the basis of direct evidence on poverty and its relationship to growth. Before the issue can be resolved, however, more time series data at the district and household levels will need detailed analysis. As Bardhan (1981) has pointed out, to trace the specific impacts of growth we need a much larger number of micro studies, even down to the district level. Without them, it is impossible to settle the controversy.

More generally, growth in agricultural output per capita can be reconciled with a rising incidence of poverty only if the distribution of the benefits of growth is uneven or growth has ceased. The available evidence on income inequalities, at least at the aggregate level, does not support the view that growth has increased poverty.

Ahluwalia (1978) has tested for trends in inequality over time by calculating Gini coefficients of the distribution of rural consumption expenditures (in nominal terms) for India as a whole and for individual states between 1957–58 and 1973–74 (see table A4).[19] He found that far from increasing, relative inequality appeared to be diminishing for India as a whole and for seven of the fourteen states that he examined. None of the states that showed a significant trend toward increasing output per capita of rural population had experienced an increase in relative inequality (which would have occurred if growth had been accompanied by absolute impoverishment, as some analysts contend). In particular, Ahluwalia found that the Gini coefficients for Punjab and Haryana showed a significant decline in inequality over two decades. The same general conclusions can be drawn from data on trends in income distribution in India from other sources (table 2-6).

Some authors have asserted that inequalities have also increased in Pakistan and Bangladesh. On the basis of the available evidence (table 2-6) this assertion cannot be supported, at least for Pakistan. A study by Guisinger and Hicks (1978) clearly shows that rural income inequality did not increase in Pakistan between 1963 and 1971 and that the income shares of the poorest 20–40 percent of households showed no tendency to shrink over this period. De Kruijk (1986b) shows that inequality in Pakistan is due to inequality *within* provinces

Table 2-6. *South Asia: Income Distribution in Rural Households*
(share of income in selected years)

Country and year	Lowest 20%	Lowest 40%	Middle 40–60%	Highest 20%	Highest 5%	Gini coefficient
Bangladesh						
1963–64	7.8	19.2	15.5	43.1	17.2	0.35
1966–67	8.1	19.9	16.0	41.7	16.1	0.33
1968–69	10.4	23.6	16.6	37.0	13.1	0.27
1973–74	6.8	18.3	11.2	41.7	n.a.	0.35
India						
1960	3.9	13.8	14.9	49.6	23.8	0.45
1962	5.9	16.2	14.5	48.1	n.a.	0.41
1964–65	7.5	19.3	15.4	44.6	21.9	0.37
1966–67	4.9	13.2	12.7	53.3	n.a.	0.46
1967–68	4.7	13.0	13.0	53.1	24.6	0.48
1968–69	5.3	14.8	14.0	50.6	n.a.	0.43
1969–70	6.3	16.6	14.7	47.1	n.a.	0.39
1970–71	6.4	17.1	15.1	46.6	n.a.	0.38
1975–76	7.3	17.1	15.1	46.4	n.a.	0.39
Pakistan						
1963–64	6.8	18.0	16.5	43.0	17.0	0.36
1966–67	8.5	20.5	16.0	41.4	16.5	0.33
1968–69	8.8	21.6	16.8	30.0	14.6	0.30
1969–70	8.6	21.5	16.9	39.0	14.8	0.30
1970–71	9.2	21.9	16.9	38.6	15.0	0.29

n.a. Not available.
Source: Calculated from data in Jain (1975).

rather than *between* provinces, as is widely believed. Although no direct evidence on trends in inequality is available for Bangladesh, supplementary evidence makes it at least possible that the picture there was not dissimilar from that in Pakistan.

Agricultural Wage Rates

Since a majority of the poor belong either to rural labor households or to small cultivating households that depend on wage employment for a large share of their income, trends in real wage rates in rural areas and their relationship to agricultural growth yield additional evidence relevant to this controversy (table 2-7).

The evidence from Bangladesh is clear. A. R. Khan's study (in ILO 1977a), based on earlier data reported by S. R. Bose (1974b), shows a general decline in real average rural wages.[20] Although no clear trends exist, these studies have used a long time series from 1949 to 1975 and have concluded that real wages fell sharply up to the early

Table 2-7. Indexes of Money and Real Wage Rates for Male Agricultural Laborers, 1956–57 to 1971–72

| | North India | | West India | | | South India | | | | East India | | | | | |
| | Punjab and Haryana | Uttar Pradesh | Gujarat | Madhya Pradesh | Maharashtra | Andhra Pradesh | Karnataka | Kerala | Tamil Nadu | Assam | Bihar | Orissa | West Bengal | Pakistan | Bangladesh |
Year															
						Index of money wage rates (1956–57 = 100)									
1957–58	n.a.	n.a.	n.a.	n.a.	n.a.	n.a.	n.a.	n.a.	n.a.	n.a.	n.a.	n.a.	n.a.	n.a.	n.a.
1958–59	112	129	110	11	101	122	114	107	98	97	111	97	101	n.a.	n.a.
1959–60	110	249	131	125	92	121	126	114	102	101	100	95	106	n.a.	n.a.
1960–61	n.a.	n.a.	n.a.	n.a.	n.a.	n.a.	n.a.	n.a.	n.a.	n.a.	n.a.	n.a.	n.a.	n.a.	n.a.
1961–62	126	141	122	121	115	138	128	133	108	102	104	127	114	n.a.	n.a.
1962–63	127	140	124	121	117	136	128	155	112	100	102	146	110	n.a.	n.a.
1963–64	n.a.	n.a.	n.a.	n.a.	n.a.	n.a.	n.a.	n.a.	n.a.	n.a.	n.a.	n.a.	n.a.	n.a.	n.a.
1964–65	144	178	139	129	144	159	160	170	140	105	135	192	129	n.a.	n.a.
1965–66	182	221	144	142	146	168	142	195	142	123	160	187	155	n.a.	n.a.
1966–67	180	250	158	163	175	189	145	230	159	138	n.a.	211	177	n.a.	n.a.
1967–68	229	284	178	n.a.	189	213	156	282	170	n.a.	n.a.	176	191	n.a.	n.a.
1968–69	276	290	181	179	195	217	156	301	183	162	196	n.a.	175	n.a.	n.a.
1969–70	303	303	185	190	217	233	n.a.	308	187	167	n.a.	n.a.	185	n.a.	n.a.
1970–71	304	315	213	194	212	261	188	337	194	178	n.a.	212	183	n.a.	n.a.
1971–72	305	326	233	210	211	239	198	338	217	180	n.a.	226	202	n.a.	n.a.

Index of real wage rates (1956–57=100)

Year															
1957–58	n.a.	n.a.	n.a.	n.a.	n.a.	n.a.	n.a.	n.a.	n.a.	n.a.	n.a.	n.a.	n.a.	n.a.	90
1958–59	101	114	110	104	99	119	112	103	97	89	98	98	92	n.a.	87
1959–60	106	122	137	126	87	111	114	107	96	96	98	91	96	n.a.	87
1960–61	n.a.	n.a.	n.a.	n.a.	n.a.	n.a.	n.a.	n.a.	n.a.	n.a.	n.a.	n.a.	n.a.	n.a.	102
1961–62	121	143	117	119	114	124	114	118	94	95	100	119	109	n.a.	99
1962–63	121	144	116	113	107	122	111	136	105	87	94	115	90	n.a.	106
1963–64	n.a.	n.a.	n.a.	n.a.	n.a.	n.a.	n.a.	n.a.	n.a.	n.a.	n.a.	n.a.	n.a.	110	120
1964–65	103	110	102	93	93	116	98	121	99	74	89	128	95	100	100
1965–66	131	135	103	92	90	112	74	123	97	78	89	110	91	105	86
1966–67	102	120	101	81	98	110	73	134	90	67	n.a.	105	90	113	86
1967–68	118	122	109	n.a.	101	122	74	155	97	n.a.	n.a.	80	79	113	92
1968–69	142	165	111	93	108	118	76	146	101	72	104	n.a.	88	116	100
1969–70	153	156	107	93	116	121	n.a.	144	96	83	n.a.	n.a.	93	125	101
1971–72	140	172	125	102	99	119	92	151	113	78	n.a.	96	96	130	72

n.a. Not available.

Sources: India: Jose (1974); Lal (1976); Yelamanchili (1981). Bangladesh: A. R. Khan (in ILO 1977a), reporting data from Swadesh R. Bose (1974b) deflated by the cost of living index; the series of data is very close to that in Clay (1976). p. 424. Pakistan: FAO *Production Yearbook 1974*, deflated by cost of living index of agricultural laborers.

Table 2-8. Bangladesh: Trends in Real Wages by Sector, 1969–70 to 1985–86
(index of real wage rates; 1973–74 = 100)

Sector	1969–70	1973–74	1981–82	1984–85	1985–86	1985–86 (taka per day)
Rural						
Agriculture (unskilled without food)	113	100	88	104	120	29.5
Fishery (unskilled)	166	100	157	122	132	25.4
Urban[a]						
Cotton textile	186	100	107	106	116	28.7
Jute textile	113	100	77	67	83	28.3
Engineering	194	100	97	102	130	36.4
Vegetable oil	179	100	92	81	84	20.9
Small-scale industry	131	100	103	141	139	31.5
Construction	123	100	101	91	104	33.3

Notes: Nominal wages deflated by rural and urban cost of living indexes.
a. Average wage rates for Chittagong, Dhaka, Khulna, and Rajshahi.
Source: Bangladesh Bureau of Statistics in World Bank (1987b), table 6.4, p. 141.

1950s, rose steadily for about a decade thereafter, but began to fall again after 1964. Despite some fluctuations, the recent direction of change has been generally downward, reaching a nadir between 1973 and 1975—years of near famine in Bangladesh.

The real wage rates in Bangladesh seem to have shown a persistent decline over most of the last three decades. A. R. Khan and others (1981) estimate that real wage rates for agricultural laborers declined nearly 17 percent between 1949 and 1970 and fell by almost 40 percent between 1949 and 1980. The most recent data, however, show that between 1981–82 and 1985–86 wages of unskilled agricultural laborers may have increased by some 36 percent. The steady decline in real wages for agricultural workers between 1970 and 1982 seems to have been halted—even reversed—in Bangladesh (table 2-8.)

These wage indices are consistent with Khan's earlier finding (in ILO 1977a) of a growing incidence of poverty in Bangladesh in the 1970s. Although agricultural output and the associated demand for labor were virtually flat, demographic conditions were worsening. Consequently, the living standards of a substantial part of the rural population (especially those who depended primarily on wage labor) must have fallen sharply during the 1970s. Notwithstanding the caveats noted earlier about the data and methodologies used to measure the incidence of poverty, this particular conclusion is clear—and every recent observer of rural Bangladesh seemed to concur with it.

By contrast, real agricultural wages in Pakistan appear to have risen. Guisinger and Hicks (1978) found a pronounced trend for real wages to increase, particularly in the period 1966–73. Even the wages of casual laborers (mostly the landless or very small farmers) rose in real terms at a rate of 2–5 percent a year after 1966; by 1973 they were about 60 percent higher than their 1952 level. The real wages of permanent workers showed a similar trend, and the broad pattern of increase was fairly uniform across districts.[21] This is consistent with other evidence of increasing rural productivity and incomes in Pakistan in the 1970s and 1980s. These developments were brought about by the Green Revolution and rising demand for labor, together with labor shortages during harvest periods in spite of increased mechanization. Extensive out-migration from rural areas in Pakistan to the Middle East and elsewhere has produced trends toward new labor shortages and higher rural wage rates, together with higher levels of remittances to rural areas.

The evidence from India is extensive and mixed, as would be expected given the diversity of agrarian conditions and agricultural performance. The findings of some early studies on trends in money and real wages in agriculture have been very thoroughly reviewed by Bardhan (1977a and b) and are summarized below.[22]

Although some studies showed a declining trend in real wages between the mid-1950s and the mid-1960s (before high-yielding varieties had been adopted even in the Punjab, the heartland of the Green Revolution), analysis over a longer period does not reveal any underlying trends in most states. In the fifteen years from 1956–57 to 1971–72, real wages rose in the first five years, declined by varying amounts between 1961–62 and 1967–68 in most states except Kerala,[23] and then rose again except in the states where both agricultural output and wages generally stagnated—Assam, Bihar, Madhya Pradesh, Orissa, and West Bengal.

Lal (1976) analyzed relatively recent and reliable NSS evidence on wage levels and found that real agricultural wages rose in most Indian states (other than those in the east) between 1956–57 and 1970–71 (except for West Bengal, for which there were no data for 1970–71). From 1956–57 to 1964–65, before the Green Revolution, real wages rose in only seven states and were constant or fell in six others; they subsequently rose generally, however, most notably where the impact of the Green Revolution was beginning to be felt—in Gujarat, Haryana, Punjab, and western Uttar Pradesh. This is confirmed by the rising disparity in real wage rates between agriculturally growing and agriculturally stagnant states and regions in India (Jose 1974; Krishnaji 1971). Lal thus surmises that earlier studies were wrong to conclude that agricultural growth was unlikely to raise the real wages of agricultural laborers and that it was accompanied by their further impoverishment. He shows that the percentage of total income accruing to the poorest three deciles of the population *increased* in all states where real wages rose between 1956–57 and 1970–71, years for which comparable NSS data were available for analysis.[24]

The most careful review of wage data for India is by Yelamanchili (1981), who analyzed state-level data. His results, in the form of indices of money and real wages of agricultural workers, are given in table 2-8. These data support later conclusions that real wages have risen in states where agricultural growth has been rapid.

A recent study by Parthasarathy (1987) also supports the view that real wages for agricultural laborers have increased in several states—Madhya Pradesh, Kerala, and even Bihar—especially where the percentage of wage laborers in the rural population has declined (table 2-9). His evidence on declining real wages in Punjab and Haryana is, however, refuted by other evidence. He does show that because of large-scale in-migration the share of wage labor in the rural population has increased in these states—a finding evident to any visitor.

Available evidence suggests that indices of real agricultural wages have generally increased in periods and areas in which agricultural growth has been rapid enough to outstrip population pressures. The data do not support the view that agricultural growth has failed to raise the standard of living of the rural poor and may even have been accompanied by their further impoverishment.[25] But where agricultural output has lagged behind or barely kept pace with population growth, it is not surprising that rural poverty has increased, in some instances dramatically, in the predominantly agrarian economies of South Asia.

To summarize, agricultural growth does benefit even the poorest, and some (albeit small) benefits have trickled down to them, directly or indirectly, through rising real wage rates.[26] But not enough! For the poor continue to grow in number, and the areas in which significant benefits have accrued to the rural poor account for only a small share of the total rural population of the subcontinent. This is a direct consequence of the general stagnation in the agricultural sector. *The proper conclusion to draw, therefore, is that it is stagnation, not growth, that has brought impoverishment.* Without general and rapid increases in agricultural output per capita there is no chance of further redressing rural poverty in the subcontinent, irrespective of whether or not radical institutional changes are brought about.

Who Are the Rural Poor?

Census data in South Asia do not make it easy to break down income or expenditure data by rural occupational classes and thus classify the poor by some easily recognizable features. One characteristic of the rural poor in South Asia—the smallness of their landholdings, if any—does, however, command general agreement among those who have studied the subject. Most of the rural poor, as Minhas (1974) points out, are made up of agricultural laborers without land, agricultural laborers with very little land, other rural laborers without land, and small landholders who usually have less than 5 acres.

Landholding Characteristics

The earliest study to confirm that most of the rural poor in India have little or no land and rely mainly on wage labor was done by Dandekar and Rath (1971). Using NSS survey data for 1956–57, they found that nearly 60 percent of all agricultural labor households had no land and 57 percent had less than the minimum level of per capita consumption. Agricultural labor households constituted 40 percent of all households in the category they called "rock bottom physical existence." Three-quarters of the households that were cultivating between 1 acre and 1.5 acres of land lived below poverty levels.[27] The incidence of poverty remained high even among those with larger

Table 2-9. India: Exponential Growth Rates of Money and Real Wages of Male Agricultural Laborers for Selected Villages, 1974–75 to 1984–85
(percent)

State	District	Village	Sowing		Harvesting		Field labor	
			Money wage	Real wage	Money wage	Real wage	Money wage	Real wage
Bihar	Patna	Mahadevpur	6.4[a]	0.3	0.5[b]	−6.2[a]	n.a.	n.a.
Bihar	Muzaffarpur	Narasingpur	11.7[a]	5.2[b]	15.7[b]	9.6	n.a.	n.a.
Bihar	Ranchi	Gaitalsood	7.0[a]	0.9	6.5[b]	0.4	n.a.	n.a.
Haryana	Karnal	Uggarkheri	8.3[a]	1.7	5.1[a]	−1.3	n.a.	n.a.
Madhya Pradesh	Hoshangabad	Sangkherakatan	10.1[a]	5.1[b]	10.0[a]	5.0[a]	n.a.	n.a.
Madhya Pradesh	Surguja	Basdei	11.5[a]	6.4[b]	9.5[a]	4.5[b]	n.a.	n.a.
Madhya Pradesh	Morena	Bijaipur	10.3[a]	4.3[b]	8.1[a]	3.2	n.a.	n.a.
Madhya Pradesh	Satna	Kotar	9.7[a]	4.7[b]	9.1[a]	4.1[b]	n.a.	n.a.
Kerala	Kozhikode	Koduvally	12.4[a]	6.5[a]	n.a.	n.a.	n.a.	n.a.

State	District	Village					
Kerala	Palghat	Elapully	6.7[a]	3.7[a]	n.a.	n.a.	n.a.	n.a.
Punjab	Ludhiana	Pakhowal	6.1[a]	−0.4	3.6	−2.7	n.a.	n.a.
Rajasthan	Kota	Dhoti	6.6[a]	0.9	8.4[a]	2.5	n.a.	n.a.
Tamil Nadu	Thanjavur	Alangudi	n.a.	n.a.	1.0	−4.0	n.a.	n.a.
Tamil Nadu	Tirunelveli	Malayankulan	n.a.	n.a.	4.3[a]	−1.9	n.a.	n.a.
Uttar Pradesh	Varanasi	Awajapur	10.4[a]	3.8	8.1[a]	1.6	n.a.	n.a.
Uttar Pradesh	Varanasi	Keshavpur	10.0[a]	3.4	6.9[a]	0.5	n.a.	n.a.
Andhra Pradesh	Krishna	Ghantasala	n.a.	n.a.	n.a.	n.a.	10.1[a]	4.8[a]
Andhra Pradesh	Guntur	Tadikonda	n.a.	n.a.	n.a.	n.a.	12.7[a]	7.3[a]
Andhra Pradesh	Rangareddy	Arutla	n.a.	n.a.	n.a.	n.a.	13.2[a]	7.8[a]
Karnataka	Bangalore	Harisandra	n.a.	n.a.	n.a.	n.a.	9.7[b]	8.0
Karnataka	Tumkur	Gaddahalli	n.a.	n.a.	n.a.	n.a.	6.5[a]	0.4

n.a. Not available.
a. Significant at the 1 percent level.
b. Significant at the 5 percent level.
Source: Parthasarathy (1987), table V, p. 12.

amounts of land; nearly 60 percent of households that cultivated landholdings of between 3.5 and 5 acres lived in poverty in 1963–64.

Minhas (1974) reached similar conclusions. He stated, for example, that between 75 and 85 percent of all households that were operating holdings of fewer than 5 acres lay below a poverty line that he calculated for 1960–61.

There is little evidence that conditions have changed substantially in the 1980s. Other studies also state that the rural poor consist almost exclusively of landless laborers and small operators. In a study of the per capita income distribution of different rural groups, Bhatty (in Srinivasan and Bardhan 1974) found that for any given poverty line the incidence of poverty was far higher for agricultural laborers than for cultivators, with nonagricultural workers falling in between. The more accurate Sen poverty index revealed, however, that cultivators at the lower end of the poverty scale were far worse off than agricultural laborers.[28] Thus the small cultivator (owner and tenant) and the landless are not readily distinguishable by their standards of living.

The poorest groups in Bangladesh belong to the same categories. A. R. Khan (in ILO 1977a) noted that agricultural households that were entirely dependent on wage income fell in the category of "extremely poor"; even if they had significant nonwage income, they generally fell in the category of "absolutely poor." He also noted that nearly a sixth of the agriculturally active population and about a quarter of the rural population as a whole depended on wages as the major source of their income.[29] It is clear from his study and that of Alamgir (1978) that the rural poor are agricultural laborers and those with small owned or tenanted holdings of fewer than 5 acres.

The situation in Pakistan is no different, but, as Naseem (1971, 1979) points out, the real dichotomy may be not between large and small farms (the differences in size are getting smaller) but between those who own land and those who do not. He states that a large number of small and marginal farmers were forced to sell and leave their land in the last decade and to eke out their existence by grazing livestock on communal land. These, along with small tenant farmers and agricultural laborers, constitute the core of the rural poor. He estimates that whereas 60 percent of owner-cultivators and nearly 67 percent of tenants fell below the subsistence level, only 38 percent of owners who are also tenants belonged in this category. It is the medium-size owners (those with holdings of 5–25 acres) who have gained the most and have further enlarged their holdings by leasing-in land from smallholders or evicting their own smaller tenants. Agricultural labor households and small tenants were the worst off, with per capita incomes about half that of small farming households (those with holdings of less than 7.5 acres) and about one-tenth that of large farming households (those with holdings of over 12.5 acres).[30] A study by Albrecht (1976) gives figures of a similar order of magnitude.

Other Socioeconomic Characteristics

The poor lack not only food and land, but also access to many other basic necessities—health, education, shelter, and security, for example. Most of the rural poor share economic, demographic, and social characteristics that can help us to identify them (at least in a broadly qualitative sense) and to understand their economic plight.

The assets and employment of the rural poor are examined in chapter 3. Other socioeconomic factors that set apart the poorest in the rural population of South Asia are outlined briefly below.[31] In comparison with better-off groups, the poor (and especially the poorest) have:

- Higher birth rates, but not necessarily larger families because they also have higher infant and child mortality (mainly because of malnutrition)[32]
- Poorer health (as indicated by higher morbidity rates, lower weight to height ratios, higher incidence of protein-calorie malnutrition, and lower access to health care)[33] and lower life expectancy
- Larger households (but landless households are smaller than those with land, other things being equal)[34]
- A higher proportion of infants and small children (an especially vulnerable group) in their households[35]
- A larger proportion of young people (below 14 years)[36]
- A larger proportion of women of childbearing age and a higher number of pregnancies per adult woman.

As a consequence of these demographic and health characteristics, the very poor:

- Tend to have few earners and much higher dependency ratios, so that the ratio of workers to consumers, or of earners to nonearners or part-time earners, is low[37]
- Have lower average labor force participation rates but higher age-specific participation rates among those (especially women) of working age[38]

- Have lower literacy rates, less education, fewer skills, and hence lower overall endowments of human capital (again, especially true of women)[39]
- Are more likely to be members of nuclear families—rather than joint or extended households, which are common among the not-so-poor—and so lack the support of extended families in times of adversity
- Are less able to migrate in search of better opportunities in rural or urban areas, and if they do migrate, are more likely to do so temporarily[40]
- Are especially vulnerable to adverse contingencies—chronic illness, bad harvest, crop failure, death in the family, seasonal loss of employment— which often strike simultaneously and cause extreme deprivation[41]
- Are particularly vulnerable during certain seasons of the year, especially the wet, slack seasons (May through August in South Asia) when labor demand and wages are low, food prices are high, the harvest has come and gone, income flows are few, and illness and malnutrition often reach their peaks[42]
- Are more likely to belong to lower castes and as social outcasts are more likely to suffer both economic deprivation and social prejudice. Members of higher castes are more likely to be landowners, moneylenders, merchants, and traders while lower castes are more often sharecroppers, agricultural laborers, and landless peasants.

These characteristics and their implications for policy will barely be alluded to in the rest of this book. A full examination of their incidence and consequences would require another set of studies. Nonetheless they should be borne in mind as background for the more narrowly economic characteristics discussed here. Poverty in South Asia has many dimensions, and no single policy approach can be expected to solve all the problems that beset the rural poor.

Conclusions

Despite disagreement among the experts about the conclusions to be drawn from some of the available evidence, the following general points about rural poverty in South Asia seem reasonably clear:

- However poverty is measured, a large percentage of rural households are poor and their absolute number has been increasing in the subcontinent.

- Where agricultural output per capita has been stagnant or declining, the living conditions of the rural poor have deteriorated (particularly those of the small landholders and agricultural laborers who make up the lowest two to three income deciles of the rural population). These conditions have prevailed in Bangladesh and in the majority of the Indian states, especially those in eastern India—Assam, Bihar, Madhya Pradesh, Orissa, eastern Uttar Pradesh, and West Bengal—since the early 1960s. Together, these areas account for most of the rural population of South Asia.

- Where agricultural output per capita has been growing relatively rapidly (over 2 percent a year), this growth has benefited all classes of the rural population. Even the poorest agricultural labor households have gained, directly or indirectly, although the extent of the benefit accruing especially to the poorest group is uncertain. These conditions have prevailed in only a few regions of the subcontinent, including the Indian and Pakistani Punjabs and the Indian states of Gujarat, Haryana, Himachal Pradesh, and Rajasthan, which account for a small minority of those living in rural South Asia.

- The rural poor consist predominantly of agricultural labor households (mainly the landless and some who cultivate very small plots of land) and small landholders with cultivated holdings of less than 5 acres. This group is largely made up of tenants, but includes some who own their land.

- The very poor also exhibit socioeconomic characteristics that set them apart from other groups and increase both the severity of their problems and the intensity of their need for greater earnings.

Notes

1. For India see Bardhan (1970), Raj (1976), Minhas (1974), Lal (1976), Rao (1977a and b), and articles in Srinivasan and Bardhan (1974) and ILO (1977a). For a comprehensive treatment of the available evidence on India, see Ahluwalia (1978). For Pakistan, see S. M. Naseem (1973, 1979, and in ILO 1977a), T. M. Khan and Bose (1968), and Khandker (1973). For Bangladesh see Bose (1968, 1974b), ILO (1977a), Alamgir (1975, 1978), Alauddin (1975), and Chaudhry and Chaudhry (1974).

2. The most persistent advocates of this view have been Griffin and Khan (in ILO 1977a), Griffin and Ghose (1979), Naseem (in ILO 1977a), and Alamgir (1978). Data purporting to support this argument are given in ILO (1977a).

3. If output growth has been outstripped by population growth, then, other things being equal, one would expect poverty to increase.

4. The poverty line was estimated at Rs15 per person for thirty days at 1960–61 rural prices. Any line is necessarily arbitrary in all work of this kind, but Ahluwalia (1978, pp. 6–7) states that this particular figure has an "established pedigree" in Indian literature. It is supposed to correspond to an expenditure level at which food consumption on the average provided a "norm of 2,250 calories per day," and represents "an extremely low level of living."

5. The Sen index is defined as $I = x [c^* - \bar{c}(1 - g)]$ where x = percentage of population below poverty line, c^* = the poverty line, $\bar{c}$ = mean consumption of the poor, and g = the Gini coefficient of consumption of the poor. See A. K. Sen (1973) for an explanation of the superiority of this measure both to the usual head count of those below an arbitrary poverty line and to standard measures of relative inequality (such as the Gini coefficient by itself).

6. This is true of all studies that specify more than one poverty line. Because each poverty line is somewhat arbitrary, calculations of the number of poor from such studies are also arbitrary. See appendix A for the implications of this arbitrary choice and of the use of calorie intake to define a poverty line.

7. Naseem also examined the evidence on real wages and found that the evidence for Punjab did not provide a firm basis for the conclusion that real wages had increased significantly during the period under consideration (1960–73). This is contrary to his own data (based on three observations over thirteen years), which show increases in real wages of 2.1 percent a year between 1960 and 1966 and 2.8 percent between 1966 and 1973. He finally compromised by saying "the evidence does not rule out the possibility of some increase in the real wages" (in ILO 1977a, p. 58).

8. See Khan and Bose (1968), Bose (1974b), Salimullah and Islam (1976), and A. R. Khan (1972).

9. Khan (in ILO 1977a) argues that most agricultural workers work as hard during the peak season as some rickshaw pullers whose calorie requirements are as high as 5,000 calories per day. Men engaged in exceptionally heavy work, such as harvesting without mechanical help, have reached levels of 5,000 calories per day over a few days. These include smallholders and landless laborers, who are among the poorest classes in Bangladesh. But having made this seemingly telling point, he proceeds to define the "extremely poor" as those consuming only 1,720 calories. Presumably using the higher calorie figures would make everyone in Bangladesh either poor or undernourished or both.

10. If Ahluwalia's estimate of the percentage of the 1973–74 rural population in poverty were applied to the rural population in 1981, an estimated 252 million people in rural areas of India would be living below the poverty line he defines. A similar exercise using Khan's conservative percentage for 1973–74 gives a 1981 figure of 71 million in poverty for Bangladesh; using Alauddin's (1975) equally conservative Pakistani percentage for 1971–72 gives 46 million in poverty in that country in 1981. These figures cannot be added because they are not based on comparable poverty lines.

11. There has been a significant decline in area and output of minor cere-

als (such as jowar, ragi, barley, and gram), pulses, oilseeds, and jute in India. See Bhalla and Alagh (1979).

12. There are serious problems in using these data, and alternative methods give different rates. Growth rates have been calculated by first deflating the agricultural NDP, with the use of state-specific agricultural price deflators, and then estimating an exponential trend with the use of ordinary least squares.

13. These results for 1960–70 are consistent with the findings of Katyal and Sood (1976). They have done no comparable analysis for later periods.

14. In 1978–79 the worst drought in recent history caused output to decline by 15–50 percent for the kharif season in some states.

15. Ahluwalia's state-level results, based on data for 1953–54 to 1973–74, have been questioned by Griffin and Ghose (1979), who argue that if the reference period for the analysis is restricted to 1960–61 to 1973–74, there is no significant inverse relationship between the incidence of poverty and the rate of agricultural growth. The dropping of the first two observations to arrive at this conclusion seems arbitrary.

16. Bardhan (1971) reported an increase in the incidence of poverty for these two states between 1960–61 and 1967–78, while Rajaraman (1975) reported a similar result for Punjab between 1960–61 and 1970–71 on the basis of small samples. Ahluwalia (1978) points out that although the conclusions of these studies stand as long as their particular starting and finishing points are used, they are misleading about underlying trends. One of the general problems in evaluating this type of evidence is that the choice of different starting and end points leads different studies to different conclusions based on the same data, when the data in fact show only fluctuations rather than broad trends.

17. For this argument to hold, the in-migration would have to be permanent to allow migrants to be included in the NSS sample over time.

18. See especially Lal (1976), Johl (1975), Kahlon and Singh (1973), and Sidhu and Grewal (1981).

19. Distributions of real consumption were not used because they required fractile-specific price indices that were unavailable. It is therefore possible that the data are somewhat biased. Further, the distribution of consumption tends to be less unequal than the distribution of income, so that disparities in welfare are underestimated by the coefficients used. The data do, however, provide a basis for gauging broad trends.

20. Since wages vary by season, region, and type of task performed, an unweighted index of average wages is misleading. The data needed to assign appropriate weights to different wage series would be very difficult to obtain, however.

21. Naseem (in ILO 1977a), using rural-labor-specific price indices provided by Chaudhry and Chaudhry (1974) to deflate money wages, calculates annual increases in real wages of 2.6 and 2.8 percent for permanent and casual laborers respectively in the Punjab between 1966 and 1973. He nonetheless erroneously concludes that "the evidence for Punjab, the most prosper-

ous province, does not provide a firm basis from which to conclude that real wages have increased significantly during the period under consideration. It should, however, be noted that the evidence does not rule out the *possibility* of *some* increase in real wages in the Punjab" (p. 58; italics added).

22. The major studies reviewed by him include his own work (1970, 1973a) based on the NSS data; Jose (1974) and Krishnaji (1971) based on the agricultural wage data collected by the Ministry of Food and Agriculture and published in *Agricultural Wages in India Bulletin*; and Bardhan (1976) based on wage data available in various farm management surveys.

23. According to Bardhan (1970) real wage rates rose in Kerala but declined in the Punjab between 1956–57 and 1964–65, in spite of higher growth in agricultural output in the Punjab. In a subsequent study covering a longer period (1956–57 to 1970–71), Bardhan (in Srinivasan and Bardhan 1974) found the initial decline in real wage rates in Punjab and Haryana to be temporary, with real wages rising after the mid-1960s. But he found that real wages rose faster in Kerala in spite of its higher proportion of landless labor and slower rates of growth. He attributed this to the bargaining power of Kerala's agrarian trade unions.

24. A similar conclusion was stated earlier by Herdt and Baker (1972). The 1970–71 25th NSS Round was geared toward the "weaker sections" so that it included both small cultivators and noncultivating wage earners, and the 1956–57 12th NSS Round dealt with agricultural labor households. These surveys are thus especially useful for assessing changes in the incomes of the poorest groups.

25. See Griffin (1974), Byres (1972), Farmer (1977), and Frankel (1971) among others for relevant bibliographies of what might be termed "the new orthodoxy of rural poverty."

26. I. G. Patel is perhaps too sanguine, but he has put the matter succinctly: "While those glib of tongue may repeat the cliche of the rich getting richer and the poor getting poorer, and while the first part of this statement is almost universally true, I doubt if there are many countries where the second part of the charge is even remotely valid. The poor may seem poorer to eyes accustomed to plenty and this is perhaps as it should be. But impatience with what could be should not lead to the denigration of the good that has already taken place." (*Eastern Economist*, March 26, 1982.)

27. Cultivating households with less than half an acre were classed as agricultural labor households, both because they derived their main income from labor and because their level and pattern of expenditure were similar to those of labor households.

28. The lower end of the poverty scale refers to the lowest two income deciles of the population; for these two decile groups, annual per capita incomes were Rs180 and Rs240 for cultivators, compared with Rs360 or Rs420 for agricultural laborers in 1968–69.

29. In 1964–65 they included landless wage earners (10.5 percent), landless wage earners who were also sharecroppers (1.3 percent), domestic servants who were also cultivators (3.6 percent), wage earners owning some land

(6.2 percent), and wage earners-cum-sharecroppers owning some land (3.8 percent) (A. R. Khan in ILO 1977a, p. 150).

30. Naseem (in ILO 1977a) cites Eckert's (1972) study in the Punjab, which shows 1970–71 per capita incomes as follows: large farmers, Rs1,102; small farmers, Rs318; tenants, Rs200; agricultural laborers, Rs192 and Rs173 for permanent and casual labor respectively. The surveys of the Punjab Board of Economic Inquiry give the following: large farmers, Rs933; small farmers, Rs633; tenants, Rs343; and agricultural laborers, Rs180.

31. It is beyond the scope of the present study to present detailed evidence on these other characteristics. For more detailed data, see Visaria (1979, 1980) and World Bank (1980). Lipton (1983a) has paid special attention to the question of whether there are any discontinuities that separate the "poor" from the "poorest" in terms of the socioeconomic characteristics cited here.

32. In Karnataka, for example, laborers and tenants had 67 percent higher levels of infant and child mortality rates than owner-cultivators farming more than three acres (see Lipton 1983a). Also see Visaria (1980) for evidence from West India and Chen (1973) for Bangladesh.

33. Morbidity rates among the lowest income groups were 12.8 percent higher than the average, even in Sri Lanka where the poor have access to extensive health care systems. In India as many as 75 percent of all hospitals and 89 percent of all hospital beds were in urban areas having only 20 percent of the population (Grawe, Krishnamurti, and Baah-Dwomoh 1979).

34. The poorest have slightly larger households than the poor, and the poor have larger households than the nonpoor, because household size and per capita income are positively correlated. But household size and assets (mainly land) are negatively correlated in general. Thus land available per household exaggerates per capita poverty, while income per household understates it. See Lipton (1983b) for a thorough statement.

35. For all of India in 1972–73, the ratio of children per rural household drops from 0.5–0.54 for the four lowest classes of monthly expenditure per person to 0.29–0.33 for the three highest classes in the NSS samples. The percentage of children in the rural population drops from around 50 percent for the class with monthly outlays of Rs0–34 per person to 31 percent for the Rs150+ class in Maharashtra (see Lipton 1983a).

36. In India over a third of all household members are between the ages of 5 and 14 in the poorest decile, compared with a quarter or less in the richest decile (Lipton 1983a).

37. Dependency ratios fall dramatically as per capita income increases but rise as size of landholding increases.

38. This is so despite the fact that women from poorer households have very limited opportunities for work outside their homes owing to social sanctions (especially in Muslim households and areas) and are heavily burdened with child care, family health care, and pregnancy. Their poverty drives them into higher participation rates than those of better-off women and reduces the amount of time spent caring for the health and informal education of their children. In the poorest households, greater labor force participation

results from attempts to overcome the high burden of dependency (Lipton 1983b).

39. Literacy rates and education are generally positively associated with mean family per capita expenditures. In Gujarat, for example, only 22 percent of males and 8 percent of females in the lowest income decile participated in primary education compared with 54 percent and 51 percent respectively for the highest income decile (Visaria 1977a).

40. See Lipton (1983a and c), Visaria (1980), and Connell and others (1976). Long-term rural-urban migration tends to be highly selective by age and sex, with a high proportion of men between the ages of 15 and 30. The proportion of women in migration streams has been rising rapidly, but they are not the poorest.

41. The illness of adult workers results in losses, and crop failures lead to the loss of on-farm wage employment. The impact of multiple contingencies on the poor is especially severe because their incomes are already low (and hence vulnerable) and they have few or no assets. These interlocking contingencies can destroy the whole economic status and well-being of poor families. The descent into poverty often starts with a "bad year" on top of illness and debt. (See Lipton 1983c, Alamgir 1980, R. H. Chaudhry 1978, and Chen 1973.)

42. Physical weakness, malnutrition, sickness, and death all peak in the wet season, months before the kharif harvest. Women and children are especially vulnerable to hardship in this period when public services are least likely to be effective. (See Chambers 1979, Longhurst and Payne 1979, R. H. Chaudhry 1978, and especially Pacey, Longhurst, and Chambers 1981.)

3

The Agrarian Structure

To evaluate the prospects and problems of small farmers and the landless in South Asia, one has to understand the agrarian structure within which they seek their livelihood and the ways this structure influences the distribution of the benefits of economic progress:[1]

- The agrarian structure determines the ownership of rural assets and, in turn, the way rural people derive their livelihood, whether from land, from other assets, or from labor.
- It shapes the nature and pace of technological change and the ways in which the benefits (and costs) of these changes are distributed.
- It determines the hierarchy of rural social and political relationships, which closely follow control over land.

In general, the term "agrarian structure" encompasses all the institutions relating to land, labor, and the productive assets by which rural people earn a living, together with the network of economic, social, and political relationships linking different rural groups. This chapter focuses on two of the central features of South Asia's agrarian structure: the access to land, as owner or operator, and the access to employment in agricultural and nonagricultural rural sectors.

In rural South Asia, as in other developing areas, disparities in landholdings produce disparities in incomes, and control of land usually coincides with control of local institutions. Access to other rural factors of production is largely determined by the size of landholdings. Variables such as the quality of land, the nature of tenurial arrangements, and the intensity with which land and technology are used in different areas or by different groups may offset (or strengthen) the effects of the size of holdings. Nonetheless, the size distribution of landholdings remains the single most important determinant of agrarian relationships.

This chapter begins with a brief discussion of alternative explanations (more accurately, theories) that purport to explain the trends in the patterns of landholding and the changing agrarian structure in South Asia.

Two Theories of Agrarian Change

In recent years the rural economy of South Asia has been characterized by high population growth rates in all areas and rapid changes in production technology in many regions. These factors form the starting points for two alternative but not mutually exclusive explanations of the patterns of landholding and landlessness in the subcontinent: the Malthusian or *population pressure theory* and the Marxian or *class-polarization theory*.

The population pressure theory is based on the observation that the combination of rising rural population and a limited land base reduces the average size of owned holdings as they are apportioned among heirs, and thus adds to the problem of rural poverty. If the average rate of population increase is the same among large and small landholders, families with initially large holdings will be better off than others, but the size of all holdings will fall in absolute terms; there will be no change in the pattern of concentration. If wealthier families with larger holdings have more surviving sons whose off-farm incomes can be invested in additional land, or if they divide their land less often than other families, they may be able to compensate for the process of partitioning or actually to enlarge their holdings. If the rich wish to buy land, the poorest may be obliged to sell: partitioning by the smallest holders tends to produce holdings too small to withstand crises such as crop failures or the death of draft animals. Lack of new land prevents expansion of the cultivable area as the labor force grows and forces more people to rely on wage employment.

The class-polarization theory observes that technological changes lead to the commercialization of agriculture and to increases in the use of purchased inputs, in the proportion of total output sold for cash, and in the use of hired labor. As commercialization proceeds, the control of essential resources, including land, becomes more concentrated. Small farmers (especially tenants) facing competition from commercialized agriculture run increasingly into debt. In an economic system based on private property and with a high incidence of tenancy, the demand for credit leads to mortgages, foreclosures, and the alienation of land from small cultivators to big landlords and moneylenders. Disparities in incomes and in the ownership of land and other assets increase as small cultivators are driven into the classes of sharecroppers and landless laborers, while the land they formerly owned becomes concentrated in fewer hands.

Much of the literature on agrarian change in South Asia subscribes to one or the other of these theories.[2] Attwood (1979, pp. 496–97) demonstrates that their relative merits cannot easily be tested on the basis of available data, since most of the testable hypotheses are common to both theories. Thus both predict that

- The proportion of landless villagers will increase.
- This increase will be due mainly to downward mobility among cultivators, especially smallholders.[3]
- Most families will move downward, very few upward.
- Big landholders will make a disproportionately large share of the land purchases while smallholders will make a disproportionately large share of the sales.
- The mean or median size of holdings will decline.

But there are three predictions on which they differ:

- The Marxian theory predicts that ownership holdings are bound to become more concentrated, while the Malthusian theory suggests that although holdings of all sizes are likely to shrink, there may be little or no change in the overall degree of concentration.
- The Marxian theory suggests that the main cause of downward mobility is land sales by smaller to larger owners, while the Malthusian theory suggests that the main cause is the partitioning of holdings among multiple heirs (sales may, but need not necessarily, take place).
- The Marxian theory suggests that big holdings will get bigger and small ones smaller, so that their heterogeneity (standard deviation from the mean) will increase, while the Malthusian theory suggests that, as partitioning will reduce most holdings to a fraction of their original size, heterogeneity will decrease.

These last two hypotheses cannot be tested with aggregate data; it is necessary to trace what happened to particular landowning households over time. One useful analysis of this type is Attwood's (1979) study of the landholdings of the *same* households and their heirs over fifty years (1920–70) in a village in Maharashtra. He found both upward and downward mobility: in terms of size of landholdings, some of the poor had become richer and some of the rich had become poorer. Land had not become concentrated in only a few hands. Nearly 25 percent of the landless in 1920 had land in 1970 (a change predicted by neither theory), while 44 percent of the originally landed had lost their land. Those with the smallest holdings in 1920 had enlarged them, while the largest landowners of 1920 had lost most of their holdings. Contrary to the Marxian theory, most land purchases were by smallholders and most sales were by large owners. Consistent with the population pressure theory, repeated partitioning was an important cause of downward mobility.

This leaves the hypothesis that the distribution of owned holdings will (or will not) become more concentrated. The available evidence on trends in ownership in India and Pakistan suggests that the distribution has become *less* concentrated over time, a trend that is *not* consistent with the Marxian perspective.

Vyas (1976) showed that, over a forty-year period in Gujarat, market transactions in land were few and most changes in holdings were made in response to land reform legislation. Landless households acquired land much more frequently than small households lost their land. Evidence of the landless acquiring small plots of land is also given for Gujarat by Dantwala and Shah (1971) and for Haryana by Sheila Bhalla (1977).[4] Most of the additions to the ranks of agricultural laborers came from small-farm and artisan households. Vyas noted the strong possibility that many workers reported themselves as agricultural laborers not so much because they were landless as because they lacked *enough* land to provide a living. He found no evidence of large-scale displacement of small farmers by larger farmers.[5]

As Vyas points out in other studies (1979, 1987), a decline in the concentration of owned holdings can be caused by *market* processes, whereby marginal and small farmers may have purchased land from larger holders; *institutional* processes, whereby larger holdings may have been broken up by land reform and allocated to smaller holders; and *demographic* processes, whereby holdings have been subdivided in response to increases in population and the size of rural households. The evidence suggests that all three processes have been at work in India, and that by and large land markets have worked in favor of small and marginal farmers rather than against them. Although there was some evidence in the 1950s of larger holders purchasing land from smaller owners, this process came to a halt during the 1960s. Fear of the imposition of ceilings on landholdings, opportunities for profitable intensification of land use, and tenancy legislation that made it easier for tenants to acquire land in a number of states all made it less desirable and more difficult for larger owners to enlarge their holdings.

Even where technological change has been rapid, the "proletarianization" thesis cannot be accepted, although the superficial evidence—an increase in the "agricultural laborer" category of the rural work force and a downward shift in the structure of farm holdings—seems to support it. Sheila Bhalla's studies (1976, 1977) of changing agrarian structure and relations in Haryana during the 1960s, when the Green Revolution was in full spate, found that "the more-than-doubling of the number of male agricultural laborers from 1961 to 1971 . . . cannot be attributed to the loss of land previously owned or leased in by households which are now landless labor households," and that "no household cultivating under 15 acres today, and no landless labor household, lost any land by sale to pay off debt, or sale for any other reason. None lost land through foreclosure of mortgages and none leased out land previously self-cultivated."[6] The same analyst also found that the decline in the average size of small holdings in Haryana was caused by the subdivision of plots among families as farming became more profitable.[7]

Other microeconomic evidence, however, suggests that big farmers in Punjab and Haryana may have been acquiring more land for cultivation, though it is not certain from whom.[8] Where technologies have changed rapidly—East and West Punjab, Haryana, and Tamil Nadu—the processes predicted under both theories have accelerated, while *operational* landholdings have definitely become more concentrated. Further displacement of tenants, a sharp increase in the use of hired labor, and, among larger holders, diversification of assets away from land have all been observed, especially in irrigated areas. These trends lend some credibility to the Marxian perspective. Similar changes may be expected to accompany agricultural innovations in other areas. Government policies, however, notably in India, where they have been of special help to somewhat better-off peasants, may have limited the process of polarization.

It thus appears that both population pressures and technological change have helped to alter the agrarian structure, but that each of these determinants explains only certain aspects of the transformation of the pattern of South Asian landholdings. But what changes have there been among the landless? The relevant evidence and data sources have been examined in Singh (1988a). The main findings from that study are summarized here.

The Structure of Ownership Holdings

Land accounts for two-thirds of the value of all assets in rural areas. Those who control land, control the major source of income as well as other rural institutions. Initial disparities in landownership beget disparities in rural incomes, and access to land in the sense of who operates it and under what conditions is often the main determinant of the distribution of rural incomes.

Data on landownership are notoriously unreliable, are seldom comparable over time or across countries, and reveal an enormous diversity in the subcontinent. Nonetheless they permit some valid comparisons.

India

The data from India (tables 3-1 and 3-2) are the most reliable. They reveal that inequality in the distribution of landownership was fairly high at independence but actually declined in the 1960s. In spite of this, ownership remained extremely uneven—about 78 percent of all rural households owned no land or fewer than 2 hectares and only 25 percent of the area, while 3 percent of all households owned more than 8 hectares and nearly 30 percent of the area. The number and proportion of marginal owned holdings (those less than an acre) increased significantly and their average size declined, whereas the number of small owned holdings (1.1 to 4.9 acres) increased, their proportion declined, and their average size remained almost constant. The importance of larger owned holdings decreased both in number and in total area held with few exceptions, and the absolute number as well as proportion of households not owning any land (about 10 percent of all rural households) declined significantly. Figure 3-1 gives the percentage share of various size groups in the total number and area of owned holdings. The medium-to-large owned holdings (those more than 4 hectares) accounted for 10 percent of the total number and 54 percent of the total area of owned holdings in 1971, while the shares of this size group in 1982 declined to 7 and 48 percent respectively. The proportion of marginal holdings increased from 63 percent of the total number in 1971 to 67 percent in 1982, and from 10 percent of the total area owned in 1971 to 12 percent in 1982. This evidence contradicts the general impression that landownership is becoming more unequal and the broader generalization that landlessness has been increasing via the "proletarianization of the rural masses" through loss of landownership. There is no evidence of a direct or simple relationship between the inequality of landownership and agricultural performance in the past two decades.

Bangladesh

For Bangladesh there are few reliable data on landownership. The most recent data are from the Land Occupancy Survey (1979) and the 1983–84 Agricultural Census. They reveal that ownership is highly skewed, more so than in India, with 90 percent of all rural households owning zero or fewer than 5 acres of land and only 51 percent of the area, while 2.5 percent own more than 10 acres and

Table 3-1. India: Cumulative Distribution of Rural Households and Landownership, 1961–62 and 1971–72
(percent)

Size of holding (hectares)	North India 1961–62 N	A	North India 1971–72 N	A	West India 1961–62 N	A	West India 1971–72 N	A	South India 1961–62 N	A	South India 1971–72 N	A	East India 1961–62 N	A	East India 1971–72 N	A	All India 1961–62 N	A	All India 1971–72 N	A
0	4	0	4	0	13	0	11	0	18	0	14	0	12	0	8	0	12	0	9	0
0–1	58	11	64	16	44	7	44	9	70	10	70	12	67	14	71	22	60	9	63	13
0–2	78	30	81	49	57	19	60	38	81	21	82	28	84	37	88	54	75	24	78	26
0–4	94	65	93	73	80	46	78	59	91	43	92	49	95	64	96	77	90	52	90	62
0–10	99	85	99	92	93	70	94	83	98	73	98	76	100	89	100	95	97	79	98	85
All holdings	100	100	100	100	100	100	100	100	100	100	100	100	100	100	100	100	100	100	100	100
Number of owned holdings (millions)	16.6		17.4		17.0		18.8		19.6		20.8		19.3		20.8		72.5		77.8	
Total area owned (million hectares)	24.2		23.2		56.2		58.8		26.8		27.1		21.0		19.0		128.2		128.1	

N: Cumulative percentage of total number of owned holdings.
A: Cumulative percentage of total area owned.
Sources: National Sample Survey (NSS) 17th (1961–62) and 26th (1971–72) Rounds. The percentages have been rounded to the nearest whole number.

Table 3-2. India: Percentage Change in Number of Owned Holdings and Area Owned by Size of Holdings

Size of holding (acres)	Average area (acres), 1953–54	Percentage change, 1961–62 over 1953–54		Average area (acres), 1961–62	Percentage change, 1971–72 over 1961–62		Average area (acres), 1971–72
		Number	Area		Number	Area	
Marginal (<1)	0.27	53.5	21.5	0.21	51.2	−3.0	0.14
Small (1–4.9)	2.62	28.8	28.0	2.60	22.0	21.7	2.60
Medium (5–14.9)	8.45	16.7	15.2	8.44	4.3	2.5	8.29
Big (15–49.9)	24.80	4.8	2.3	24.20	−10.2	−11.5	23.87
Large (50+)	88.71	−37.7	−34.0	80.96	−20.0	−27.0	73.87
Total	6.25	31.0	4.1	4.97	26.6	−2.1	3.84

Sources: NSS Report 36, 8th Round (1953–54); NSS Report 144, 17th Round (1961–62); and NSS Report 215, 26th Round (1971–72).

Figure 3-1. *India: Percentage Distribution of Owned Holdings and Area Owned by Size of Holding, 1961–62, 1971–72, and 1982*

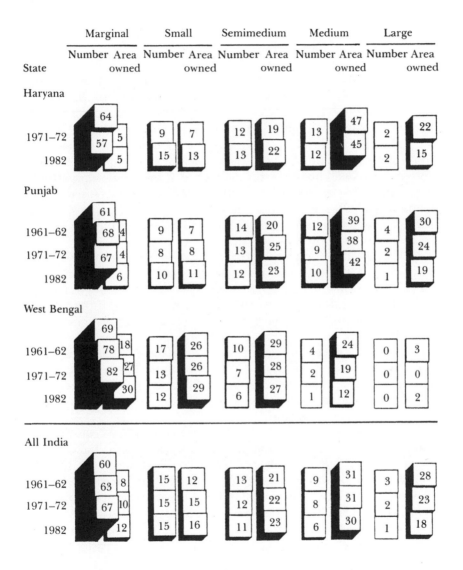

Note: Marginal holdings are less than 1.01 hectares; small, 1.01–2.02 hectares; semimedium, 2.03–4.04 hectares; medium, 4.05–10.12 hectares; and large, 10.13+ hectares.
Sources: National Sample Surveys and *Sarvekshana* 5 (3 and 4).

25 percent of the area. Nearly a third of all rural households owned no land other than their house lots (table 3-3). Supplementary evidence suggests that ownership may be becoming more concentrated through a slow process of land alienation, with smaller owners being forced to sell their land to larger owners in recent years.

West Bengal and Bangladesh

Because agrarian conditions in Bangladesh and West Bengal (India) are similar, it is worth comparing the structure of landownership in the two areas (table A5 presents the data). If anything, landownership was marginally less egalitarian in Bangladesh in 1977 than in West Bengal in 1971. This difference may have become more pronounced in recent years. Although both have a heavy concentration of ownership in very small holdings, the number and area under larger holdings is declining in West Bengal, while it has actually increased in Bangladesh. In both regions, over 50 percent of all holdings are smaller than 1 acre, although the percentage of households owning no land at all seems larger in Bangladesh.

Given the similarity between the two areas and the relatively greater reliability of the data for West Bengal (especially with regard to changes over time), it might be reasonable to use the latter as a rough guide to the kinds of changes that may have occurred in Bangladesh in the past decade. In West Bengal the average size of holdings fell for all size groups; the number of marginal (less than 1 acre) and small (1–5 acres) holdings rose, as did their share of the total owned area; the number of medium (5–10 acres) and large (10 acres and more) holdings fell, as did their share of total area; and the concentration of landholdings consequently fell, as did the percentage of rural households owning no land.

Similar trends would, in principle, be likely to have continued in Bangladesh in the past decade, with certain exceptions. Land reform in West Bengal had relatively greater success, and the devastating civil war, floods, and famine in Bangladesh are likely to have increased the proportion of those owning no land and the concentration of ownership, as the Land Occupancy Survey data seem to suggest. Recent data reported by Hossain (1988) show that both the number and share of households owning more than 5 acres increased between 1979 and 1983–84.

Pakistan

Data on landownership in Pakistan are also less reliable than in India. The information that is available shows that ownership was heavily concentrated (especially in Sind) at independence and remained so for more than two decades: over two-thirds of the owners owned fewer than 5 acres and accounted for over 18 percent of the area, while less than 1 percent owned 25 acres or more and accounted for over 12 percent of the area. This concentration was considerably reduced by the 1976 land reforms, but the concentration of land in the hands of large (25–50 acres) and very large (more than 50 acres) owners remains a salient feature that sets Pakistan apart from the rest of the subcontinent (tables 3-4 and 3-5). Yet this inequality has not been a barrier to high rates of growth.

East and West Punjab

Contrary to accepted notions, there are many basic similarities in the ownership patterns in West Punjab (Pakistan) and East Punjab (India).[9] As Singh (1988a) shows, nearly two-thirds of all owners or landowning households in both areas owned fewer than 5 acres; the number and total area of these holdings has been increasing while their average size has declined or remained constant; the number of larger owned holdings has declined, but their total area has decreased less or increased. Thus the average size of medium (5–25 acres), large (25–50 acres), and very large (more than 50 acres) holdings owned by households (East Punjab) or individuals (West Punjab) has increased, with the largest increase occurring in the medium-size groups.

The main difference between the two regions lies in the average size of farms. Very large farms still exist in Pakistan, where in West Punjab in 1976 more than 10,000 individuals owned more than 150 acres each; in the Indian Punjab fewer than 8,000 households owned holdings of more than 50 acres each.[10] Ownership holdings of fewer than 5.0–6.6 acres make up about two-thirds of all holdings in both Punjabs, but in West Punjab their average size is 2.5 times larger. Differences in the importance of large owners and the average size of small owned holdings have major consequences for agrarian structure and for the policies followed in the two areas, as will be shown later.

Conclusions

According to Singh (1988a), the broad evidence on landownership in rural India shows that the basic patterns of ownership after independence persisted for four decades, despite movements in the direction of a more even distribution because of population pressure. Nevertheless, the number of marginal and small owners as well as the total

Table 3-3. Bangladesh: Percentage Distribution of Total Owned Land in Rural Areas by Size of Holding, 1977 and 1978

Size of holding (acres)	Number of households		Total area owned[a]		Percentage of absolute change for group	
	1977	1978	1977	1978	Number	Area
0	11.07	14.69	—	—	34.8	—
0–1	47.44	44.68	9.30	8.33	-4.4	33.3
1–2	16.43	15.21	14.43	12.78	-6.0	-4.8
2–3	8.91	8.69	13.18	12.28	-1.0	0.2
3–4	5.27	5.16	11.13	10.29	-0.5	-0.5
4–5	3.29	3.08	9.00	7.93	-4.6	-5.2
5–6	2.09	2.11	6.90	6.61	2.4	3.1
6–7	1.43	1.44	5.69	5.40	2.4	2.0
7–8	1.02	0.92	4.65	3.98	-7.5	-7.9
8–9	0.69	0.79	3.60	3.86	15.9	15.3
9–10	0.42	0.56	2.46	3.06	34.0	33.7
10–11	0.34	0.51	2.15	3.05	52.5	52.7
11–12	0.29	0.32	2.03	2.14	14.7	13.1

12–13	0.16	0.30	1.18	2.17	100.0	97.6
13–14	0.22	0.22	1.82	1.69	0.0	0.2
14–15	0.13	0.16	1.19	1.37	25.0	23.6
15+	0.80	1.16	11.29	15.07	0.0	43.7
All	100.00	100.00	100.00	100.00	1.5	7.6
Total (millions)						
Number	11.85	12.03	—	—	1.5	—
Acres	—	—	19.35	20.81	—	7.6
0–5 acres						
Including landless	10.95	11.01	10.54	10.74	0.6	1.9
Excluding landless	9.64	9.24	10.54	10.74	-4.2	1.9
5+ acres	0.90	1.02	8.81	10.07	13.3	14.3
Overall Gini coefficient of concentration	0.6577	0.6842				

— Not applicable.

a. Including the house lot.

Source: Jannuzi and Peach (1980), appendix tables D.1 and E.1.

Table 3-4. Pakistan: Landownership by Size of Owned Holding, 1950s and 1970s

	1950s			1972			1976	
Size of holding (acres)	N	A	Size of holding (acres)	N	A	Size of holding (acres)	N	A
0–5	64.4	15.3	0–5	66.5	17.6	0.0–6.25	70.8	24.9
5–25	93.1	47.0	5–25	94.5	56.7	6.25–12.5	88.3	46.2
25–100	98.8	68.8	25–100	99.0	82.8	12.5–25.0	95.9	64.3
100–500	99.9	84.6	100–150	99.4	89.1	25.0–50.0	98.5	77.5
500+	100.0	100.0	150+	100.0	100.0	50.0+	100.0	100.0
Number of owners (millions)	5.07			10.06			10.3	
Total area owned (million acres)	48.64			67.64			60.13	

N: Cumulative percentage of total number of owners.
A: Cumulative percentage of total area owned.
Sources: Pakistan Land Reform Commission data in M. H. Khan (1981), landownership tables 3.1–3.5; 1972 Agricultural Census, annex.

Table 3-5. Pakistan: Distribution of Owners, Area Owned, and Average Size of Owned Holdings in Punjab and Sind, 1971 and 1976

Size of owned holding (acres)	Punjab 1971			Punjab 1976			Sind 1971			Sind 1976		
	N	A	Average size (acres)	N	A	Average size (acres)	N	A	Average size (acres)	N	A	Average size (acres)
0–6.25	60.4	20.6	1.98	69.1	26.1	1.98	36.7	5.6	2.94	40.3	8.2	3.58
6.25–12.5	25.7	25.0	5.65	19.6	24.3	6.32	23.2	10.5	8.74	23.9	12.5	9.16
12.5–25.0	9.9	20.7	12.16	7.8	18.7	12.93	19.7	19.4	18.93	17.6	18.0	17.96
25.0–50.0	2.8	12.9	27.12	2.3	12.7	28.76	11.6	20.3	33.64	10.1	19.3	33.61
50+	1.2	20.8	98.12	1.2	18.2	80.89	8.6	44.0	98.84	8.0	42.0	93.69
All	100.0	100.0	5.8[a]	100.0	100.0	5.25[a]	100.0	100.0	19.28[a]	100.0	100.0	17.62[a]
Number of owned holdings (millions)			6.27			7.45			0.59			0.66
Total area owned (million acres)			36.36			39.12			11.45			11.68

— Not applicable.
N: Percentage of total number of owned holdings.
A: Percentage of total area owned.
a. Average number of acres for all size groups.
Source: Pakistan Land Reform Commission data in M. H. Khan (1981), tables 3.3 and 3.4.

area they owned and the average size of their holdings appeared to increase, while the importance of large farms decreased. Meanwhile, the number and proportion of rural households owning no land declined significantly in many parts of India. It is generally agreed that the subdivision of landholdings and the sale and purchase of land have been more important in bringing about structural redistribution than the redistribution of land through tenancy reforms and legal ceilings on landholdings (C. H. H. Rao 1976). This statement is quite contrary to the uninformed rhetoric that suggests a growing concentration of landownership and a slow proletarianization of the small peasantry by large owners who have bought them off.

The Structure of Operational Holdings

The distribution of landownership provides a useful guide to the ownership of assets in rural areas, but it does not tell how these assets are used. Since land rental markets are a prominent feature of rural life in the subcontinent, one must look beyond the distribution of *owned* land to the distribution of *operational* holdings (those cultivated by either owners or tenants) to determine who has access to land and consequently who can benefit from strategies to make land more productive.

India

Table 3-6 shows the cumulative size distributions of operational holdings by region in India for 1961–62 and 1971–72 (including households that operate no land). For the latter year several features stand out.

- Between one-quarter and one-third of all rural households in the four regions operate no land. (Not all of these households depend wholly on wage employment, but many do.)
- Another quarter to one-third of all rural households operate marginal holdings of less than 1 hectare, and a further 15–20 percent of all rural households (20–25 percent of cultivating households) operate small holdings of between 1 and 2 hectares. Holdings are especially small in the east and south.
- There are very few medium to large holdings: only 4–8 percent of all rural households (5–12 percent of cultivating households) operate holdings larger than 4 hectares, except in western India where 22 percent (30 percent of cultivating households) operate holdings larger than this.

- Marginal and small farmers account for 80 percent of all the rural households but only a third of the cultivated land. By contrast, the 10 percent of rural households with cultivated holdings larger than 4 hectares account for nearly 47 percent of the operated area.

One might think that the size distribution of operational holdings would be less skewed than that of owned holdings, on the assumption that larger owners generally rent out land to smaller ones. The need to use land intensively, together with the diseconomies of scale associated with the management of labor, would seem to favor relatively small holdings and promote transfers of land in this direction. Thus it is commonly believed that the agrarian structure consists of large landlords at one end and small tenants at the other, with owner-cultivators lying in between.

The reality is far more complex, however. The percentage of rural households that operate no land is much larger (24–35 percent, depending on the region; see table 3-6) than the percentage owning no land (4–18 percent; see table 3-1). Further, although quite a large proportion of rural households (12–30 percent) *own* very small holdings (less than 0.5 acre), a much smaller proportion (only 3–11 percent) *operate* holdings of this size. It seems likely that because owners of very small holdings find them uneconomic to run, they rent them out to larger operators and earn their livelihood in some way other than farming.[11]

Thus, landlords and tenants cannot be divided into mutually exclusive social classes—a point that is often missed. Many of those with relatively large operational holdings are tenants of small owners. The analysis by Vyas (1979) of changes in the distribution of operational holdings tends to support this interpretation. His study reveals that the distribution of operational holdings in the 1960s was less skewed than that of owned holdings in only five states—Assam, Bihar, Orissa, Uttar Pradesh, and West Bengal—all in eastern India. It was *more* skewed in four states—Haryana, Karnataka, Punjab, and Tamil Nadu—all of which except Tamil Nadu experienced high rates of agricultural growth during the same period. No clear conclusion emerges for the remaining states.

What have been the changes in the distribution of operational holdings over time? Three trends are evident from the all-India data:

- Although operational land is still very unequally distributed, inequality has been reduced somewhat over time.
- The number of small and very small holdings increased during the 1950s, 1960s, and 1970s as a result of subdivision and the

Table 3-6. India: Cumulative Distribution of Rural Households and Operated Areas, 1961–62 and 1971–72

Size of holding (hectares)	North India 1961–62 N	North India 1961–62 A	North India 1971–72 N	North India 1971–72 A	West India 1961–62 N	West India 1961–62 A	West India 1971–72 N	West India 1971–72 A	South India 1961–62 N	South India 1961–62 A	South India 1971–72 N	South India 1971–72 A	East India 1961–62 N	East India 1961–62 A	East India 1971–72 N	East India 1971–72 A	All India 1961–62 N	All India 1961–62 A	All India 1971–72 N	All India 1971–72 A
0	23	0	26	0	21	0	25	0	33	0	35	0	29	0	24	0	27	0	28	0
0–1	56	10	61	13	42	3	43	3	67	9	67	11	63	13	68	20	56	7	61	9
0–2	76	29	80	42	56	10	59	18	79	21	82	30	82	38	87	55	74	21	83	30
0–4	90	56	93	68	74	25	78	37	91	42	92	59	94	66	96	80	86	41	90	53
0–12	99	91	100	94	94	66	96	75	98	76	99	84	100	93	100	97	98	77	99	84
All	100	100	100	100	100	100	100	100	100	100	100	100	100	100	100	100	100	100	100	100
Number of operational holdings (millions)	11.6		12.7		11.9		14.1		13.7		14.9		13.5		15.3		50.8		57.1	
Total area operated (million hectares)	25.4		22.7		57.9		58.1		28.0		26.4		22.1		18.5		133.4		125.7	

N: Cumulative percentage of total number of operational holdings.

A: Cumulative percentage of total area operated.

Sources: NSS 17th (1961–62) and 26th (1971–72) Rounds; Sirohi, Ram, and Singh (1976); Dandekar and Rath (1971); and Reserve Bank of India (1976). Since 1971–72 statewide distributions have been unavailable. These data were compiled by applying the changes in the distribution of operational holdings of various rates given in Sirohi, Ram, and Singh to the 1961–62 distributions from the NSS and Dandekar and Rath. The numbers of households were grouped by various regions using the Reserve Bank of India data. These data were then consolidated to get the all-India distribution.

growth of population, but the average size of marginal holdings (fewer than 2.5 acres) also increased.

• Larger holdings (more than 15 acres) fell proportionately (in both number and area), but their average size did not decline.[12]

Figure 3-2 gives more recent data and shows that the area operated under marginal holdings rose from 9 percent in 1971 to 12 percent by 1982. The area under large holdings dropped significantly from 29 to 18 percent from 1961 to 1982.

The view that small operators are losing their land because large ones buy them out is widely held among proponents of the class-polarization theory of changing agrarian structure and may be difficult to dislodge. It provides a convenient explanation for the rise in the number and proportion of agricultural laborers in the rural work force—an increase too large to be accounted for solely by the growing number of people in agricultural labor households. Nevertheless, the evidence presented so far on the changes in the size distribution of holdings in India is not consistent with this perception.

Changes in Punjab and Haryana have run contrary to the general findings noted above that marginal and small holdings have increased, large holdings have decreased, and inequality has declined somewhat over time (see Singh 1988a, table A.14). In this region, both the numbers and area of small owned *and* operational holdings declined in the 1960s, and inequalities as measured by Gini coefficients increased (see Sanyal 1977b; Sirohi, Ram, and Singh 1976). The number of very small holdings of fewer than 2.5 acres rose (while their combined area declined), and the number of holdings in all other size classes decreased as did their average area, the decline being greatest in the large size groups, according to the National Sample Survey (NSS) data. A tendency toward an increase in both the number and the share of area accounted for by medium-size holdings (5–15 acres) in Punjab is supported by the NSS data as analyzed by Sanyal (1977b).

Bangladesh

Data on the size distribution of operational holdings in Bangladesh do not permit systematic comparisons between the size distributions of owned and operational holdings for the same year, nor do they show what proportion of rural households operated no land.

The size distributions of operational holdings in Bangladesh in 1960–61 and 1967–68 are shown in table 3-7. By 1967–68 nearly 57 percent of these holdings were smaller than 2.5 acres, accounting for 21 percent of the cultivated area. Farms of less than 1 acre accounted for 25 percent of all holdings and less than 5 percent of the total culti-

Figure 3-2. *India: Percentage Distribution of Operated Holdings and Area Operated by Size of Holding, 1961–62, 1971–72, and 1981–82*

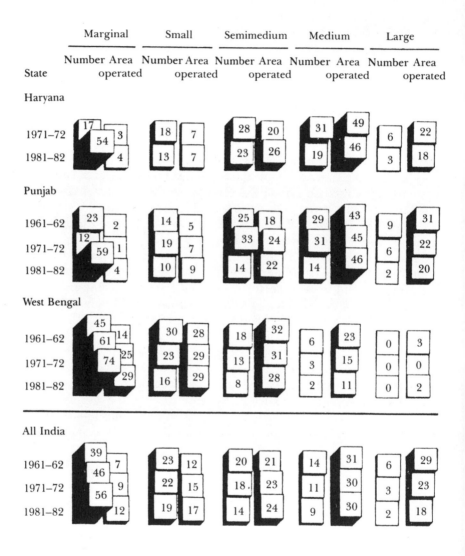

Note: Marginal holdings are less than 1.01 hectares; small, 1.01–2.02 hectares; semimedium, 2.03–4.04 hectares; medium, 4.05–10.12 hectares; and large, 10.13+ hectares.

Sources: National Sample Surveys and *Sarvekshana* 5 (3 and 4).

vated area. By comparison with 1960–61, the distribution of operational holdings had become a little less unequal.

Evidence for later years suggests a dramatic reversal. Early tabulations of the 1977 Agricultural Census show that the size distribution of operational holdings shifted quite dramatically against farms of fewer than 2.5 acres and in favor of medium-size farms (table 3-7)—reversing earlier trends during the 1960s, when both the number and total area of small farms had actually increased while that of larger farms had decreased. Combined with an increase in the average size of larger farms and a growth in their number, this evidence suggests that many small farmers either sold out their farms and became landless or stopped operating. Nearly 0.82 million holdings have dropped out of this category—their operators probably joining the class of the landless in Bangladesh. This trend in the increase in the number of small holdings has continued into the 1980s; as a result the average size of small holdings (less than 1 acre) has declined in spite of an increase in the total operated area in such holdings.

The data on operational holdings from the 1977 Agricultural Census together with the 1977 Land Occupancy Survey data on ownership holdings indicate that the distribution of operational holdings is more skewed than that of owned holdings. The implication is that, in Bangladesh as in India, very small owners are probably net lessors of land.[13]

The gaps in the data are so wide and the available information so generally unreliable that any number of conjectures is possible. It seems likely, however, that the share of land operated in small holdings has declined dramatically and that land markets have worked against smallholders, pushing them into the rural proletariat. This is supported by fragmentary evidence on rural land sales and purchases in the early 1970s (see Singh 1988a, table A.17).

West Bengal and Bangladesh

Although the eastern parts of India, particularly West Bengal in the 1960s, experienced changes similar to those occurring in Bangladesh, later changes in Bangladesh were quite dramatic. As Singh (1988a, table A.18) shows, although both West Bengal and Bangladesh in the beginning of the 1960s had fairly similar distributions of operational holdings, by 1977 the number of very small holdings in Bangladesh had decreased while those in West Bengal continued to increase. Furthermore, the area and number of medium-size holdings in West Bengal continued to decrease, whereas those in Bangladesh increased. These trends seem to have been reversed in the early 1980s in Bangladesh.

Table 3-7. Bangladesh: Size Distribution of Operational Holdings, 1960–61, 1967–68, and 1977

Farm size (acres)	1960–61		1967–68		1977		Percentage change, 1960–67		Percentage change, 1967–77		Average size (acres)		
	N	A	N	A	N	A	Number	Area	Number	Area	1960	1967	1977
<0.5	13.1	0.9	12.3	1.2	5.5	0.5	5	22	−60	−60	0.2	0.3	0.3
0.5–1.0	11.2	2.3	12.7	3.1	10.4	2.1	26	33	−25	−31	0.7	0.8	0.7
1.0–2.5	27.3	13.0	31.6	17.1	33.9	16.1	30	30	−3	−4	1.7	1.7	1.7
2.5–5.0	26.3	26.4	26.3	30.0	29.2	29.2	12	13	0	−1	3.6	3.6	3.5
5.0–7.5	11.4	19.3	9.2	17.8	11.6	19.7	−9	−9	15	13	6.0	6.1	6.0
7.5–12.5	7.2	19.1	5.2	15.5	6.6	17.4	−18	−19	15	15	9.4	9.3	9.3
12.5–25.0	3.1	14.1	2.2	11.0	2.5	11.6	−21	−23	3	7	16.0	15.6	16.3
25.0+	0.4	4.8	0.5	4.5	0.4	3.4	40	−7	1	1	33.9	28.2	32.1
All	100.0	100.0	100.0	100.0	100.0	100.0	12	−1	−10	2	3.5	3.1	3.5
Number of operational holdings (millions)	6.14		6.87		6.25								
Total area owned (million acres)	21.7		21.5		21.96								

N: Percentage of total number of operational holdings.

A: Percentage of total area operated.

Notes: Data are for farms and not households. Columns may not add to total because of rounding.

Sources: Pakistan Ministry of Agriculture and Works (1960a), table 3; Bangladesh, Bureau of Statistics (1972), table 1, and (1977).

Notwithstanding changes in the 1970s, the average size of operational holdings continued to be much larger in Bangladesh than in West Bengal: by 37 percent (in 1960–61) and 84 percent (Bangladesh in 1977 compared with West Bengal in 1970–71). This runs contrary to the general view that Bangladesh has the smallest holdings in the subcontinent; although it experienced severe demographic pressures, the concentration of landholdings did not become more pronounced. West Bengal, however, had a much greater long-term decline in the average size of holding. It is one of the most densely populated and longest settled regions in the subcontinent, but it did not experience the social and economic dislocations that in the 1970s made Bangladesh's agrarian structure more inequitable.

Pakistan

The only data on the size distribution of operational holdings in Pakistan come from the 1960 and 1972 agricultural censuses. These have been carefully examined by M. H. Khan (1981), some of whose main findings are reproduced in table 3-8 (see also Singh 1988a, tables A2.19 and A2.20). The data show that in 1972:

- In sharp contrast to Bangladesh and most of India, only a third of all operational holdings were smaller than 5 acres. Together they accounted for 5 percent of the area in 1972, and their number and area had declined rapidly nationwide since 1960. The decline was especially noticeable in the Punjab, where all other size groups increased both in number of holdings and in percentage of total cultivated area.
- The number and combined area of farms larger than 50 acres increased in Pakistan as a whole, but not in Sind, where they fell slightly. Medium-size farms—12.5 to 50 acres—increased in number and combined area, most noticeably in the Punjab: this category also declined in Sind.
- The average size of holdings fell in all size groups except the 5–12.5 acre group. Holdings of this size, small by Pakistan's standards, dramatically increased in number and area covered, especially in Sind.[14]

The conclusion is clear: especially in the Punjab, the size distribution of operational holdings in Pakistan has become more skewed, favoring medium (12.5–50 acres) and large (more than 50 acres) farms at the expense of small ones.

A comparison of the distribution of ownership (table 3-5) with that of operational holdings (table 3-8) shows that though the Punjab has

Table 3-8. Pakistan: Distribution of Operational Holdings and Area by Farm Size, 1960 and 1972

Farm size (acres)	Year	Pakistan		Punjab		Sind	
		N	A	N	A	N	A
<5.0	1960	49.5	9.4	51.6	10.9	25.6	5.5
	1972	28.2	5.2	26.1	4.8	19.0	4.5
5.1–12.5	1960	27.6	22.3	26.9	24.9	38.9	22.5
	1972	39.9	25.2	39.0	24.6	51.7	34.5
12.5–25.0	1960	15.0	25.6	14.7	28.5	23.3	28.6
	1972	21.1	26.6	23.1	28.8	21.9	29.2
25.1–50.0	1960	5.9	19.4	5.4	20.2	9.0	21.1
	1972	7.6	18.8	8.8	21.3	5.2	13.2
50.1–150.0	1960	1.8	13.4	1.3	10.6	2.1	14.2
	1972	2.7	15.1	2.7	14.7	1.7	10.7
150.1+	1960	0.3	10.0	0.2	4.9	0.3	8.2
	1972	0.4	9.1	0.3	5.8	0.4	7.0
Number of operational holdings (millions)	1960	4.86		3.33		0.68	
	1972	3.76		2.38		0.75	
Total area operated (million acres)	1960	48.93		29.21		9.71	
	1972	49.06		31.03		9.46	

N: Percentage of total number of operational holdings.
A: Percentage of total area operated.
Source: Agricultural Census data in M. H. Khan (1981), table 3.17.

the large farms, it is Sind that has the large landlords. In the Punjab, a large proportion of marginal and small owners (fewer than 12.5 acres) rent their land to owners of medium and large holdings. In Sind, by contrast, the owners of large and very large holdings rent land to small and sometimes medium-size sharecroppers. Medium and larger operational holdings predominate in the Punjab, and their operators are more likely to be owners who have rented more land to enlarge their holdings. In Sind, small operational holdings are mostly farmed by sharecroppers (haris), who rent from larger owners.

East and West Punjab

The Indian and Pakistani Punjabs share one basic similarity (see Singh 1988a, table A.21): a fall in the percentage of operational holdings of fewer than 5 acres, combined with an increase in their average size. In contrast, whereas West Punjab shows a rise in the share of medium-size holdings (12.5–50 acres) in the total number and area, East Punjab shows a decrease. As with ownership holdings, however, operational holdings are typically much larger in Pakistan than in India. In West Punjab nearly 21 percent of the operated area is in holdings between 25 and 50 acres, with another 15 percent in even larger holdings; in East Punjab, by contrast, nearly 80 percent of the operated area is in holdings of fewer than 25 acres. Thus the total area of operated holdings of fewer than 5 acres increased in Punjab-Haryana (India) but declined in West Punjab (Pakistan), and the number and combined area of holdings larger than 25 acres rose substantially in the latter but fell quite dramatically in the former. Although both regions saw a dramatic shift toward medium-size holdings, this group consisted of farms of 20–50 acres in West Punjab, but of 5–15 acres in East Punjab. In addition, West Punjab had nearly 65,000 farms larger than 50 acres compared with 11,000 in East Punjab and Haryana. These differences in the size of holdings are an important factor in the patterns of technological change that have characterized the rapid growth in these two regions. These trends have been accentuated in the 1980s and have important implications for both the type of mechanization and rural employment in the two regions.

Overstatement of Land Inequality

The data on the concentration of landholdings in South Asia do not present a true picture of the extent of inequality in the ownership and use of land assets in rural areas. The unequal distributions of both owned and operational holdings are ameliorated by two facts. First, the distribution of holdings per household (or per farm) overstates the inequality because households with smaller holdings also tend to have fewer members. In Bangladesh, for example, households owning less than 1 acre of land had only 4.7 members on the average compared with 11.2 members per family for those owning more than 15 acres. This negative relationship between size of holding and number of household members who are dependent on that holding pertains throughout the subcontinent. As a consequence, the distribution of per capita holdings is much more equitable than the data on holdings per household suggest.

Second, the size of holding is not even a close proxy for the income potential of the land held, because land quality and productivity vary significantly. Smaller holdings are generally farmed more intensely and have higher percentages of area under irrigation almost everywhere in South Asia. The inequality in income potential between small and large holdings is therefore reduced *within* a given region. Furthermore, given the enormous diversity in land quality, irrigation, and cropping intensities in different regions, comparisons by size of holding across regions are inevitably misleading. More arid areas and those with poor land and low productivity (such as Sind and Rajasthan) have larger holdings on the average than areas with assured irrigation (the Punjabs, Tamil Nadu) or adequate rainfall (West Bengal).

Thus the raw data on the size distribution of holdings both within and across regions greatly overstate the real inequality in income potential between small and large holdings. A proper comparison would require adjustments by household size and land quality. Available data are inadequate to allow such adjustments to be made, however, at national or state levels. If adjustments were made to bring out the real differences in the net returns per hectare on farms of different sizes in different regions, the resulting distribution of the per capita income streams from different size holdings would be much more evenly distributed. Although these facts are widely recognized, uncritical use of the data on landholdings continues unabated.

Landlessness

Concern for the landless has been growing in recent years, as evidenced by a rash of publications (ILO 1977a; Esman 1978). In fact, so much concern has been expressed that a certain cynicism has set in.[15] The main problem is that when the rural poor are identified with small farmers, many policies and programs currently being undertaken by both national governments and international agencies may be irrelevant or even counterproductive. In particular, it is widely believed that the landless constitute a majority of the poor; that their numbers and proportions are increasing dramatically; that they are being bypassed by programs that benefit mainly the landed; that the benefits of growth do not trickle down to them; that few if any programs have proved successful in increasing their incomes; and that apart from a radical program of land redistribution, little can be done to improve their prospects. Some observers go so far as to argue that growth has actually increased the poverty of the landless.

At least three definitions for the landless in rural areas are tenable: those who *own* no land, those who *operate* no land, and those whose *major* source of income is wage employment. Each definition includes different but not mutually exclusive subsets of the rural population (typically these subsets overlap) and has different implications for the control over rural and other assets and for how incomes are derived. The three are often hopelessly confused. Data on landlessness per se are meaningless without adequate differentiation of these categories. But the data are not up to the task.

Evidence from Indian data, which are the most complete, shows that landlessness in terms of those who own no land is large (about

29 percent) and has declined over time; landlessness in terms of those who operate no land has increased in both relative and absolute terms; but landlessness in terms of those who neither own nor operate any land is very small (around 7 percent) and has declined in both relative and absolute terms (tables 3-9 and 3-10).

Landlessness in terms of those not operating any land has increased significantly in many agriculturally dynamic states (Gujarat, Haryana, Punjab). There is no cause for alarm, however, because this increase is the result of a larger proportion of the rural population moving away from agricultural occupations and into a growing and dynamic nonfarm sector. In some agriculturally stagnant states (West Bengal and Bihar) this type of landlessness has actually declined! These data on landlessness suggest the ambiguity of the concept because they fail to distinguish between dynamic and stagnant processes that have the same outcome—fewer people owning or operating land!

Much that has been written on landlessness in Bangladesh is replete with confusion on definitions and data sources. No consistent set of data exists to verify trends in landlessness, although some have been inferred from a large set of disparate and noncomparable sources. What little is firmly known suggests that (a) in terms of nonownership of land a third of all rural households are landless, (b) about 30 percent of all rural households fall in the category of "landless labor," and (c) this category has been growing in both relative and absolute terms at a pace that may have accelerated in recent years (table 3-11).

Table 3-9. *Rural India: Agrarian Profile and Landlessness*
(household number in millions)

Year	Owning land		Not owning land		Raw total	
	Number	*Percent*	*Number*	*Percent*	*Number*	*Percent*
Operating land						
1960–61	51.8	71.5	1.6	2.2	53.4	73.7
1970–71	54.7	69.8	2.2	2.8	56.9	72.6
1980–81[a]	64.4	67.0	3.3	3.5	67.7	70.5
Not operating land						
1960–61	12.2	16.8	6.8	9.4	19.0	26.3
1970–71	16.1	20.5	5.4	6.9	21.5	27.4
1980–81[a]	23.6	24.6	4.8	4.9	28.4	29.5
Total						
1960–61	64.0	88.3	8.5	11.7	72.5	100.0
1970–71	70.8	90.3	7.6	9.7	78.4	100.0
1980–81[a]	88.0	91.6	8.1	8.4	96.1	100.0

a. Estimated by extrapolating past trends.
Sources: NSS 16th Round (1960–61); NSS 25th Round (1970–71).

Table 3-10. India: Percentage of Rural Households Not Owning and Not Operating Land, Selected States, 1954–55, 1961–62, and 1971–72

State	Not owning land			Not operating land			Owning but not operating[a]		Neither owning nor operating[a]		Leasing in land
	8th Round, 1954–55	17th Round, 1961–62	26th Round, 1971–72	8th Round,[b] 1954–55	17th Round, 1961–62	26th Round, 1971–72	17th Round, 1961–62	26th Round, 1971–72	17th Round, 1961–62	26th Round, 1971–72	26th Round, 1971–72
Andhra Pradesh	30.12	6.84	6.95	42.80	37.95	36.05	32.03	29.68	5.92	6.37	83.58
Bihar	16.56	8.63	4.34	23.84	21.71	20.65	15.28	17.52	6.43	3.13	83.56
Gujarat	n.a.	14.74	13.44	n.a.	25.41	33.75	11.78	25.47	13.63	8.28	55.98
Haryana	—	—	11.89	—	—	48.00	—	41.05	—	6.94	
Punjab	36.86	12.33	7.14	38.92	39.09	58.61	30.51	52.90	8.58	5.71	66.83
West Bengal	20.54	12.56	9.78	24.30	33.88	30.94	24.21	23.09	9.67	7.85	86.65

— Not applicable.

n.a. Not available.

a. Estimates are not available for NSS 8th Round.

b. Percentage of nonagricultural holdings deemed comparable by S. K. Sanyal (1977b) to NSS 17th and 26th Rounds.

Source: Sanyal (1977b).

Table 3-11. Bangladesh: Landlessness

Source	Year	Landless laborers as percentage of total cultivators	Landless laborers (millions)	Households with no land other than house lot
Cited in A. R. Khan (1972)				
Agricultural Census	1951	14.3	1.51	
Agricultural Census	1961	17.5	2.47	
Master Survey of Agriculture	1963–64	17.8	2.71	
Master Survey of Agriculture	1964–65	17.5	2.75	
Master Survey of Agriculture	1967–68	19.8	3.4	
		Agricultural laborers plus sharecroppers as percentage of rural households	*Agricultural laborers as percentage of total cultivators*	
Cited in Adnan and others (1978)				
Agricultural Census	1951	n.a.	15.3	n.a.
Agricultural Census	1961	n.a.	17.5	n.a.
IRDP[a] (14 villages)	1973–74	n.a.	n.a.	38
BIDS[b] (8 villages)	1974	26	n.a.	38
Land Occupancy Survey (400 villages)	1977	n.a.	n.a.	32

n.a. Not available.
a. Integrated Rural Development Program.
b. Bangladesh Institute of Development Studies.

Table 3-12. *Pakistan: Rural Households, Landownership, Tenancy, and Estimates of Landlessness, 1961 and 1972*

	Indicator	1961	1972
(1)	Rural population (millions)	35.8	47.4
(2)	Rural household size (persons)	5.5	5.8
(3)	Rural households (millions)	6.5	8.2
(4)	Number of landowners (million persons)	5.1	10.1
(5)	Total area owned (million acres)	48.6	67.6
(6)	Number of farm households (millions)	4.9	4.0
	Percentage operating as		
	Owner cultivators	41.1	41.7
	Owner-tenant cultivators	17.2	23.8
	Tenant cultivators	41.7	34.4
(7)	Area operated by farm households (million acres)	48.9	49.1
	Percentage operated by		
	Owner cultivators	38.3	39.5
	Owner-tenant cultivators	22.5	30.9
	Tenant cultivators	39.2	29.6
(8)	Percentage of farm households cultivating area other than that owned	58.9	58.2
(9)	Percentage of area operated by farm households that is not owned by the operating household	50.5	46.2
(10)	Estimated number of rural households not operating land (millions)	1.6	4.2
(11)	Estimated landless agricultural labor households (millions)	0.6	1.6[a]

a. Estimated using 1961 proportion: (11) / [(11) + (10)].

Sources: (1) World Bank data; (2) Afzal (1974), p. 47; (3) computed from (1) and (2); (4) through (9) M. H. Khan (1981); (10) by mere subtraction, (3) − (6); (11) M. H. Khan (1981) citing figure in 1961 census of approximately 2.0 million tenant "farmer-workers," confirmed by (6), which justified estimating 565,435 landless laborers belonging to separate households.

Nothing can be inferred directly about landlessness—its magnitude or trends—in Pakistan because data are practically nonexistent. Despite this serious lacuna in the agrarian data base, data can be "constructed" from a number of sources. They show that the proportion of rural households not operating any land nearly doubled in the 1960s, as did landless agricultural labor households as a percentage of all rural households. More recent data from Pakistan are very difficult to obtain and are not easily comparable with data from the 1970s. De Kruijk (1986b) used a variety of sources to construct a distribution of rural households by activity and status in 1979–80. He found that about two-thirds of all households were engaged in agricultural work;

of these only 18 percent were landless, while the rest (45 percent) were either owners, owner-tenants, or pure tenants. The proportion of landless households (18 percent) is slightly lower than that estimated indirectly in table 3-12 for 1972.

Trends in landlessness in and of themselves do not signify much. They need to be examined along with other evidence on the changing agrarian structure. One should concentrate directly on the conditions of cultivation for those who *operate* land—the size, productivity, and tenurial status of holdings—and on the conditions of wage employment for those who depend primarily on wage labor in rural areas for their incomes. For this purpose, a closer look at the occupational distribution of rural labor households is more helpful.

Rural Wage Labor

The households that depend *primarily* on wage employment in rural areas—more specifically, in agriculture (agricultural labor households)—include not only the so-called landless but also many marginal and small farmers who operate owned land as well as small tenants who lease-in land and supplement their farm incomes with wage employment.

Data on rural labor are sparse, except for India, but they all show that the proportion as well as the absolute number of rural households that have to depend primarily on wage employment are increasing (tables 3-13 to 3-16). In 1985 a third of the rural population in Pakistan and Bangladesh and more than two-fifths in India were estimated to belong in the category of rural labor. A quarter of this rural labor force in India, a third in Pakistan, and nearly half in Bangladesh were also working on their own farms—that is, they were operating land as farmers or tenants. In India nearly two-fifths of the rural labor force are casual or agricultural laborers; in Bangladesh 25 percent and in Pakistan only 6 percent (figure 3-3). But not all are dependent on agriculture. A quarter of the rural labor force in Pakistan and about 13 percent in India work in nonagricultural occupations (table 3-13 and Singh 1988a).

In India in 1974–75 more than half of all rural *labor* households (about 16 percent of all rural households) were landless—in the sense of not cultivating any land, whether owned or leased—and were dependent entirely on manual wage labor. Although the proportion remained fairly constant, the absolute number of such households increased (table 3-14). In Bangladesh nearly a third of all rural households are in this category, and to the extent that the available data allow temporal comparisons, proportions and absolute numbers seem to have declined (table 3-15).

Figure 3-3. *Composition of Rural Labor Force in South Asia*

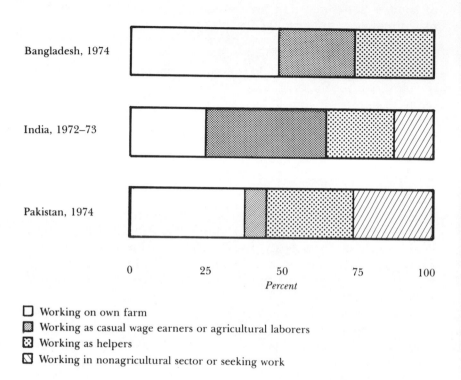

☐ Working on own farm
▨ Working as casual wage earners or agricultural laborers
▧ Working as helpers
◨ Working in nonagricultural sector or seeking work

Source: Table 3-13.

Although the proportion of rural households not operating any land seems to be high and increasing in Pakistan, many of these households engage in nonfarm occupations, and the share of those mainly dependent on agricultural labor is much smaller (table 3-16).

Several additional characteristics of the rural labor force in South Asia stand out clearly. Both small and marginal farmers depend heavily on wage labor and participate in rural labor markets, but agriculture is not the only source of their income since a large variety of nonfarm productive activities also hire wage labor. Much of the employment, however, is casual rather than permanent (Parthasarathy 1987). Rural laborers face declining wage opportunities in many parts of India and Bangladesh, but not in Pakistan or areas of rapid growth in India. They are heavily indebted and their indebtedness may be increasing. Rural labor is not at all organized in the subcontinent, with the possible exception of Kerala (Singh 1988a).

Table 3-13. **South Asia: Composition of Rural Labor Force by Usual Activity**

Item	Bangladesh 1974 Millions	Bangladesh 1974 Percent of rural labor	Bangladesh 1985 estimate (millions)	India 1972–73 Millions	India 1972–73 Percent of rural labor	India 1985 estimate (millions)	Pakistan 1974 Millions	Pakistan 1974 Percent of rural labor	Pakistan 1985 estimate (millions)	South Asia, 1985 estimate Millions	South Asia, 1985 estimate Percent of rural labor
Rural population	65.0		86.0	455.0		573.0	50.0		69.0	728.0	
Rural labor force	16.0	25[a]	26.5	200.0	44[a]	252.0	15.0	30[a]	20.7	299.0	42[a]
Working on own farm	7.5	48	12.7	50.6	25	63.0	5.7	36	7.5	83.3	28
Working as casual wage earners or agricultural laborers	4.0	25	6.6	78.0	39	98.3	0.9	6	1.2	106.1	35
Working as helpers	4.3	27	7.2	45.6	23	58.0	4.6	30	6.2	71.4	24
Working in nonagricultural sector and/or seeking work	—[b]		—[b]	25.1	13	32.8	4.3	28	5.6	38.4	13

Notes: In Bangladesh only the agricultural labor force was considered. Those working on their own farms include part-owners, and pure sharecroppers are also included here. In India the available breakdown was for farm and nonfarm work combined. It was assumed that 74 percent of the labor was for agricultural activities; the reduced numbers are shown and the last category increased accordingly. For Pakistan the 1972 Agricultural Census gives higher estimates for the labor force than the Labor Force Survey used here. Estimates for 1985 assume there is no change in the labor structure from that in the 1970s.

a. Percentage of total rural population.

b. Included in other categories.

Sources: Bangladesh, Ministry of Agriculture and Forests (1978), p. 64; World Bank data; India, Planning Commission, "Draft Five-Year Plans, 1978–83" (New Delhi, 1978), vol. 2, table 1; Pakistan, Ministry of Finance, Planning and Economic Affairs, "Labor Force Survey, 1974–75," pp. xix, 67, and 81.

Table 3-14. India: Changes in Rural Labor, 1964–65 and 1974–75

Region	Rural households (millions)	Rural labor households				Agricultural labor households			
		As percentage of rural households	All (millions)	With land (millions)	Without land (millions)	As percentage of rural households	All (millions)	With land (millions)	Without land (millions)
1964–65									
North	16.4	15.2	2.5	1.1	1.4	13.4	2.2	1.0	1.2
West	17.5	22.3	3.9	1.4	2.5	18.9	3.3	1.3	2.0
South	18.3	33.3	6.1	2.4	3.7	30.0	5.3	2.0	3.3
East	18.2	29.7	5.4	2.8	2.5	24.2	4.4	2.4	2.0
All India	70.4	25.4	17.9	7.7	10.1	26.6	15.2	6.7	8.5
1974–75									
North	19.6	18.9	3.7	1.7	2.0	14.8	2.9	1.4	1.5
West	19.7	25.4	5.0	2.3	2.7	21.3	4.2	2.0	2.2
South	21.1	40.8	8.6	3.9	4.7	34.6	7.3	3.3	4.0
East	21.7	35.0	7.6	4.2	3.4	29.5	6.4	3.6	2.8
All India	82.1	30.3	24.9	12.1	12.8	25.3	20.8	10.3	10.5
Percentage increase									
North	20		48	55	43		32	40	25
West	13		28	64	8		27	54	10
South	15		41	63	27		38	65	21
East	19		41	50	36		45	50	40
All India	17		39	57	27		37	54	24

Note: Agricultural labor households draw over half their incomes as wages for agricultural work; they constitute 85 percent of the rural labor households (which draw wages for labor in rural areas) and 22 percent of all rural households.

Source: India, Ministry of Labour (1978).

Table 3-15. *Bangladesh: Rural Labor Households*

Item	1973–74	1977	1978	Percentage change, 1973–74 to 1978
Rural population (millions)	67.6	76.0	78.0	15.4
Rural households (millions)	11.1	11.8	12.0	19.8
Households not owning[a] and not operating any land (millions)	3.7	3.3	3.1	−17.2
As a percentage of all rural households	33.3	27.9	23.3	
Estimated rural labor households (millions)	4.4	4.7	5.3	20.4
As a percentage of all rural households	39.6	39.8	40.0	
Estimated agricultural labor households (millions)	2.8	3.4	4.0	70.0
As a percentage of all rural households	25.2	28.8	29.2	
Average household size (persons)	6.1[b]	6.4[b]	6.5[b]	1.5

a. Those who owned no land other than house lots.

b. Estimated simply by dividing the rural population by number of rural households.

Sources: Government of Bangladesh and World Bank population estimates; Jannuzi and Peach (1977a); Bangladesh, Agricultural Census, 1960; Robinson (1969); Jabbar in Bangladesh, Ministry of Agriculture and Forests (1978), and World Bank data.

Because these households often constitute a majority of the "poorest of the poor," special concern must be given to increasing employment opportunities for them in rural areas in the short run and in the economy as a whole in the long run. Most of the changes in the agrarian structure can be attributed to population pressures on land—the Malthusian imperative. But changing technologies and their interaction with rural institutions have also contributed to and in some cases accelerated these changes in the agrarian structure.

Rural Unemployment

Despite the serious limitations of the available data, it seems reasonable to conclude from the previous section that more and more people in rural South Asia are earning wages rather than cultivating land they hold as owners or tenants. During recent years, however, the growth of rural employment opportunities has failed to keep pace with the number seeking jobs. Estimates of the imbalance between

Table 3-16. Pakistan: Rural Laborers

Item	1961	1972	Percentage change, 1961–72
(1) Rural population (millions)	42.9	65.3	52.2
Punjab	25.6	37.8	47.7
Sind	8.5	14.2	67.1
(2) Rural household size (persons)	5.5	5.8	5.5
(3) Rural households (millions)[a]	7.8	11.3	44.9
(4) Farm households (millions)	4.9	4.0	−18.4
(5) Rural households not operating land (millions)[b]	2.9	7.3	150.7
As a percentage of all rural households	37.2	64.6	
(6) Agricultural laborers (millions)	7.6	9.7	27.6
Punjab	4.8	5.8	20.8
Sind	1.6	2.4	50.0
As a percentage of all rural households	17.7	14.8	
(7) Agricultural labor households (millions)[c]	1.4	1.7	19.5

a. Derived by dividing population by household size.
b. Residually derived, (3)−(4).
c. (6) / (2).
Sources: M. H. Khan (1979b); Afzal (1974).

work and workers in rural areas vary, depending on how employment and unemployment are defined and how the available quantitative estimates are interpreted.[16] This section is concerned with the broad magnitude of the unemployment problem (and hence the scale of the efforts that might be needed to tackle it), the forms unemployment takes, and the characteristics of the unemployed. This information is needed to determine which measures might be appropriate to raise employment levels.

As A. K. Sen (1975) has pointed out, more has been written on unemployment in India than in any other country. Nevertheless, the estimates of rural unemployment in India vary widely, as do the figures for Pakistan and Bangladesh—largely because of differences in concepts and in measurement and estimation procedures.[17] A great deal of the confusion surrounding the figures can be avoided if some of these conceptual issues are clarified at the start. (Singh 1988a, annex 3, attempts to clarify some of the common concepts and definitions used in measuring rural unemployment. It should be referred to in interpreting the data that follow.) Given the extent of self-employment in rural areas (in farm or nonfarm enterprises), and the fact that much of the work consists of household tasks shared among members, what it means to be "employed" or "unemployed" or "seeking employment" must be interpreted with care. Most poor people—and those who rely mainly on rural wage employment fall in this category—try to engage in whatever gainful work they can find, often on a temporary or casual basis. The amount of work they do, the time they work, and the income they earn are all difficult to define and measure.

India

The available evidence from India shows that open, or chronic, unemployment is very low—about 1 percent if measured on the basis of the "usual activity" of the respondents in the rural labor force—which suggests that nearly everyone finds *some* work during the year. When measured on the basis of whether or not respondents were unemployed during the week or on the day of the survey, unemployment is not exceptionally high (about 4–8 percent), but the numbers are large—about 13 million on any given day are without jobs. There are enormous regional differences, with most of the high unemployment rates (measured in person days) concentrated in six states in India—Bihar and West Bengal in the east, Andhra Pradesh, Kerala, and Tamil Nadu in the south, and Maharashtra in the west (tables 3-17, 3-18, and 3-19).

Unemployment is a highly seasonal phenomenon, as might be expected, and the extent of unemployment in the slack period also varies by state. In general, states that have experienced high growth have both low unemployment rates and less variation between peak and slack seasons.

Much of the unemployment is heavily concentrated in landless households, and casual laborers account for between half to three-quarters of the total person days of unemployment in rural areas in some states. Women are a particularly vulnerable group with unemployment rates two to three times higher than among men. There is general agreement that of the three types of employment—self-employment, regular wage or salaried work, and casual work—it is casual work that offers the most uncertainty. There is considerable evidence that unemployment is highest among casual workers in the rural labor force (Vaidyanathan 1986b; Visaria 1980). In India the proportion of casual laborers in the rural labor force has recently been increasing (Dantwala 1987b). Moreover, casual labor is becoming the norm for wage employment in rural areas. In practically all

Table 3-17. India: Percentage Distribution of Rural Labor Force by Usual Activity, Current Activity, and Sex

Status	Usual activity, 1972–73			Activity in current week, 1977–78			Activity on current day, 1977–78		
	Male	Female	Total	Male	Female	Total	Male	Female	Total
Self-employed + helpers in agriculture	35.0	19.4	54.4	34.5	14.7	49.2	35.5	13.4	48.9
Self-employed + helpers in nonagriculture	7.0	3.4	10.4	7.7	2.7	10.4	7.8	2.4	10.2
Regular salaried farm employee	4.2	0.7	4.9	2.9	0.4	3.3	3.0	0.4	3.4
Regular salaried nonfarm employee	3.5	0.7	4.2	4.6	0.7	5.3	4.9	0.7	5.6
All casual wage earners	14.1	11.1	25.2	17.2	10.3	27.5	15.3	8.5	23.8
Unemployed	0.7	0.1	0.8	2.7	1.3	4.0	5.4	2.7	8.1
Total percentage	64.8	35.2	100.0	69.9	30.1	100.0	71.9	28.1	100.0
Millions	128.7	71.0	199.7	116.3	50.2	166.5	113.4	44.2	157.6

Note: The 1972–73 data are based on a rural labor force that was defined to include those 5 years old or older, whereas the 1977–78 sample included only those 15–19 years old.

Source: NSS data in *Sarvekshana* (1977, 1979), the journal of the NSS.

Table 3-18. *India: States by Level and Variability of Unemployment Rates, 1972–73*

Group and states	Unemployment rate (percent of labor force)	Index of variation[a]
High unemployment, high variation		
Andhra Pradesh	11.23	87
Jammu and Kashmir	8.58	595
Orissa	10.18	105
Tamil Nadu	10.45	134
West Bengal	10.66	109
High unemployment, low variation		
Bihar	10.02	31
Karnataka	8.55	24
Kerala	23.49	18
Maharashtra	9.43	46
Low unemployment, high variation		
Assam	1.89	352
Madhya Pradesh	3.41	128
Rajasthan	3.25	426
Low unemployment, low variation		
Gujarat	5.43	30
Haryana	2.93	52
Punjab	3.94	48
Uttar Pradesh	3.38	30

a. The index of variation = [(maximum − minimum) / minimum] × 100.
Source: NSS 27th Round.

states in India two-thirds to three-fourths of all wage laborers were in casual employment in 1982–83—a substantial increase over the preceding decade (Parthasarathy 1987).

Bangladesh

Data from Bangladesh are inadequate, too, but indications are that although open unemployment is low—about 10 percent—a large proportion of the population works long hours for small returns in uncertain, seasonal, and casual jobs. More than half of those who were self-employed or wage earners worked less than 250 days, with 10–15 percent working less than 150 days a year (see I. Ahmed 1978; M. H. Khan 1975; R. I. Rahman 1978; Singh 1988a; and World Bank 1987b).

Pakistan

As with Bangladesh, available data are less reliable than for India, but they show very low rates of rural unemployment—about 2 percent

Table 3-19. *India: Unemployed as Percentage of Total Males 5 Years Old and Older, According to Activity on Current Day in Rural Areas*

State	1972–73	1983
Andhra Pradesh	6.90	5.59
Assam	1.46	1.88
Bihar	5.67	4.24
Gujarat	3.48	3.02
Haryana	2.25	3.41
Jammu and Kashmir	5.24	8.36
Karnataka	4.65	4.69
Kerala	12.84	13.39
Madhya Pradesh	2.19	1.56
Maharashtra	5.60	3.99
Orissa	6.31	5.09
Punjab	2.89	4.08
Rajasthan	3.25	3.09
Tamil Nadu	7.19	12.00
Uttar Pradesh	1.95	2.16
West Bengal	7.23	8.80
All India	4.75	4.79

Source: NSS data in Parthasarathy (1987), table IV.

of the labor force—mostly among landless casual laborers. This is consistent with rising real wage rates and actual shortages of labor in recent years produced by migration to the Middle East from rural areas. (See Robinson and Abbasi 1979; Eckert 1972; Anderson and Leiserson 1978; and Singh 1988a.)

Conclusions

In aggregate terms, rates of unemployment in South Asia are low by traditional standards, but a large proportion of the population works in marginal activities with low productivity. Whether or not this is called "disguised unemployment" is less important than the fact that a high proportion of those gainfully employed are available for additional work and meanwhile work long hours with little remuneration. The problem is one of inadequate growth in labor demand; its solution lies in increasing the opportunities for productive employment of the wage labor force, a group that includes many cultivators who own or lease small holdings. The final section of this chapter briefly outlines past and current trends in the occupational distribution of these opportunities.

The Occupational Distribution of Rural Wage Employment

There are three possibilities for raising the incomes of poor rural households that depend primarily on wage earnings. First, on-farm employment in crop production may increase as a result of multiple cropping, increased output, and shifts to labor-intensive and higher-value crops such as vegetables and fruits. Second, noncrop agricultural activities (such as dairying, poultry farming, fisheries, and forestry) may offer new income-producing opportunities. Third, nonagricultural rural activities (for example, small-scale manufacturing, processing, transport, repair, marketing and other services, or rural public works programs) may provide additional jobs and wage earnings.

The extent to which increased crop production raises the demand for wage labor depends on the size distribution of holdings, the cropping patterns adopted, and, most critically, farm technologies. In some areas of rapid agricultural growth (the Indian and Pakistani Punjabs, for example), much of the potential stimulus to employment has been offset by farm mechanization (see chapter 5). Greater use of irrigation and higher cropping intensities should on balance increase the demand for farm labor (although changing from persian wheel to tubewell irrigation may not), but how much of this demand will be met by family labor rather than hired workers is not clear. In general, crop production in the 1990s is unlikely to generate enough new demand for rural labor to absorb the two main components of potential supply—the currently unemployed and underemployed in the rural labor force, together with the anticipated increments to that labor force over the years. Consequently, the rapid expansion of noncrop agricultural and nonagricultural rural activities is crucial for the prospects of the poorest in rural areas.[18] This section briefly outlines the extent to which these activities are already contributing to the incomes of rural labor households; subsequent chapters examine the prospects for growth in these activities.

Noncrop and Nonfarm Employment

Noncrop and nonfarm sources of employment and incomes are usually found in small-scale, highly dispersed, informal enterprises that are often overlooked in surveys and censuses. Data on the extent and nature of these enterprises can therefore be hard to come by. Anderson and Leiserson (1980) evaluated the available evidence from some fifteen developing countries and found that nonfarm activities in rural areas are a primary source of employment and earnings for approximately one-quarter of the rural labor force in most developing countries (one-third if the labor force in rural towns is included).[19] They are a significant source of secondary earnings for small farmers and the landless in the slack season when farm and nonfarm employment move in opposite directions. The total contribution of nonfarm activities to employment in rural areas is growing (see also Chuta and Liedholm 1979, p. 18); they include a wide variety of activities in manufacturing (20–30 percent), services (20–35 percent), commerce (15–30 percent), construction (5–15 percent), and transport and processing (5–15 percent).[20] They are generally carried out on a very small scale, rely on simple labor-intensive methods, require little capital and skills (other than those provided indigenously via apprenticeship), and are widely dispersed spatially (at least until they become concentrated in rural towns as infrastructure improves and markets grow). Most of the demand for these products and services is generated locally in rural areas and is linked closely to the growth of agricultural and rural incomes.

India

In India 39 percent of nonfarm employment is estimated to be in manufacturing, 14 percent in construction, 14 percent in trade and commerce, 24 percent in services, and 9 percent in transport and "other" categories (Anderson and Leiserson 1980, p. 245). The limited available evidence shows that noncrop incomes account for nearly half of the incomes of all rural households. The proportions are smaller but still substantial for cultivating households and depend on whether high-yielding varieties are planted. As table 3-20 shows, the nonagricultural sector accounts for about 15 percent of the rural labor force in India and Bangladesh and about 30 percent in Pakistan.[21]

Table 3-21 presents data on rural per capita incomes in India, compiled from an extensive series of surveys of 4,100 rural households by the National Council of Applied Economic Research (NCAER) between 1969 and 1971. The figures show that the proportion of income derived from crops rises with the size of holding, and that nonagricultural wages and nonfarm earnings provide nearly half of the incomes of landless and marginal farmers (those with holdings of less than 1 hectare) and between a fifth and a quarter of the incomes of small farmers (those with holdings of up to 5 hectares).[22] All these groups have very low per capita incomes; only their noncrop and nonfarm earnings permit the very poorest to match the near-destitution incomes of the small farmers.

Table 3-20. *South Asia: Rural Labor Force in the Agricultural and Nonagricultural Sectors*

| Country | Year | Rural labor force (millions) | | | Nonagricultural sector as percentage of total |
		Total	In agricultural sector	In nonagricultural sector	
Bangladesh	1951	96.8	82.8	14.0	14
	1961	96.6	84.7	11.9	14
India	1961	86.0	70.5	15.5	18
	1971	82.5	70.3	12.2	15
Pakistan	1951	86.8	63.1	23.7	27
	1961	84.5	58.3	26.2	31

Source: Country census data.

The sources of income for the landless are of special interest. It is often thought that they depend heavily on agricultural wage employment for their livelihood. For this reason, much work has gone into estimating on-farm employment elasticities (see Singh 1988a and chapter 7) and into efforts to analyze how these elasticities are translated into jobs and income for the landless. But the NCAER data reveal that only a quarter of the incomes of the landless came from agricultural wages. The rest came from noncrop and nonfarm activities, the largest proportion being in construction, manufacturing, rural services, and trades.

Vyas and Mathai (1978) have noted that comparisons of India's rural occupational structure over time show hardly any change in the proportion of the labor force working in agriculture; the figures for 1957, 1961, and 1971 were 72.1, 71.2, and 72.1 percent respectively. There has thus been little occupational diversification in the rural economy. In fact, the proportion of the rural work force employed in industrial activities actually fell (from 18 to 16 percent between 1961 and 1971). Vyas and Mathai attribute these findings to the weakness of the linkages between agricultural and nonagricultural activities in the rural economy (see chapter 7 for a discussion of these linkages and nonfarm activities generally).

Nevertheless, nonagricultural activities are important sources of rural employment in India, accounting for 15–20 percent of the labor force in nearly all states (see Singh 1988a, table A.44). If noncrop agriculture (livestock and dairying, poultry, forestry, and fishing) is included, this proportion rises to 20–25 percent. (Singh 1988a, table A.45, provides data from selected Indian states on the sources of rural per capita income by size of holding.) Even if noncrop income represents a small proportion of the income of the total rural labor

Table 3-21. India: Rural Per Capita Incomes by Farm Size and Source of Income, 1970–71

Size of cultivated land (acres)	Estimated percentage of households	Annual per capita income (rupees)	Percentage of income derived from				
			Crops (A)	Ancillary activities (B)	Agricultural wages (C)	Nonagricultural wages (D)	Nonfarm and other sources (E)
Landless[a]	28	540	—	26	26	5	43
0–1.0	9	544	33	7	16	3	41
1.0–2.5	10	457	50	10	14	2	24
2.5–5.0	15	566	67	7	7	1	18
5.0–7.5	9	672	78	5	3	1	13
7.5–10.0	8	822	82	4	2	1	11
10.0–15.0	8	905	86	4	1	...	9
15.0–25.0	8	1,040	92	2	1	...	5
25.0+	4	1,409	98	...	...	0	1
All size groups	100	677	59	9	9	2	21

(Number of households in sample survey = 4,100)

— Not applicable.
... Negligible.

Notes: Columns (A) and (B) are gross values of output from crops and other farm activities *less* operating expenses. Column (C) includes cash and wages in kind, as does column (D), where workers are laborers and not salaried. Column (E) includes salaries, remittances, property rental income, and incomes from employment and enterprises in rural areas. Ancillary activities include livestock, poultry, dairying, forestry, and on-farm processing, while nonfarm sources include incomes from rural manufacture, handicrafts, repair and construction, transport, trade, and commerce.

a. All noncultivating households.

Source: NCAER, Assets and Rural Indebtedness Survey.

force, it is a significant source of earnings for small farmers and the landless throughout India—in rice and wheat zones, arid and irrigated areas, and high and low growth states.[23]

Data from the National Sample Survey (NSS) 25th Round, 1970–71, showed that a significant proportion of poor households (35 percent of small cultivators and 43 percent of noncultivating wage earners) supplemented their incomes in noncrop agricultural activities (India, Ministry of Planning 1976a; Visaria and Visaria 1973). Evidence from farm management surveys in India indicates that off-farm employment accounted for 50 percent of small farmers' labor and somewhat less of their incomes in the 1950s (Bharadwaj 1974b). By the early 1970s, noncrop activities had assumed a greater significance; many small farmers earned much more from occupations such as dairying than they did from work associated with food crop cultivation. In Tamil Nadu, for instance, male agricultural laborers' average annual earnings from nonagricultural occupations increased from 10 percent to 38 percent of their total incomes in the 1960s and 1970s (ILO 1977b).

Microeconomic studies of small farmers and agricultural laborers carried out by Agro-Economic Research Centers confirm this trend; they also suggest that members of agricultural labor households who engage in noncrop activities have marginally higher incomes than those who cultivate very small holdings (less than half a hectare), whether owned or tenanted.[24]

Pakistan and Bangladesh

The data for Pakistan and Bangladesh are sparse and two decades old, but they confirm the importance of nonfarm sources of income in rural areas, especially for those with small holdings (tables 3-22 and 3-23). More recent evidence suggests that a rising share of the rural labor force is engaged in nonfarm work and that an increasing share of rural income comes from nonfarm sources. In 1970–71, 19 percent of rural employment in the Pakistani Punjab was in nonfarm activities; 48 percent of farm families in Pakistan relied on income from nonfarm activities, which contributed 23 percent of their total income. Nearly 70 percent of small farmers and the landless undertook nonfarm work, which accounted for nearly 39 percent of their income (Anderson and Leiserson 1980).

In the Pakistani Punjab, Haider (1977b) has documented the rapid shift into nonfarm employment produced by the Green Revolution. New jobs have emerged in distribution, repair and maintenance services (especially for farm machinery), rice milling, small engineering

Table 3-22. *Bangladesh: Farm and Other Income by Size of Holding, 1965–66*

Size of holding (acres)	Average size of holding in size group (acres)	Percentage of households in the sample	Farm	Other sources	Nonfarm as a percentage of total
			Annual household incomes (rupees)		
0–3	1.82	46	584	362	38
4–10	4.80	48	858	163	16
10+	13.51	6	2,307	1,220	34

Note: The main source of other income of small cultivators is wage labor on and off the farm, while for the medium cultivators it is petty trade and in some cases remittances from family members working elsewhere. The bulk of the nonfarm income of large cultivators is from trade, nonfarm work, and additional remittances.
Source: Rajshahi University survey data in T. M. Khan and Bose (1968).

Table 3-23. *Pakistan: Contribution of Nonfarm Income to Total Income of Farm Families by Size of Holding, 1968*

Size of holding (acres)	Nonfarm as a percentage of income
0–6.25	39
6.25–12.49	22
12.5–18.74	22
18.75–24.99	8
25+	6
All size groups	23

Source: Steele (1975).

workshops, transport, construction, marketing agencies, and financial institutions. Meanwhile, however, some of the traditional activities of village artisans—blacksmiths, carpenters, weavers, potters, cobblers, traders, millers—have declined in importance or have taken different forms on farms. Many artisans stay in villages but commute to work elsewhere.

Another feature of the rural economy in Pakistan has been extensive migration to cities and the Middle East. Most of the migrants are from landowning groups, but artisans represent a significant percentage of the total.[25] Small towns have grown rapidly as new nonagricultural occupations have flourished and attracted rural migrants. These migrants have become a major source of remittances to the rural economy, thus raising both rural incomes and the demand for nonfarm work. Farm labor is becoming scarce as higher returns in nonagricultural occupations raise rural wage rates.[26] With the extensive development of rural infrastructure, new roads and electrification have made it easier to set up small engineering shops and manufacturing facilities. D. A. Khan (1978) estimates that between 1960 and 1972 incremental employment in nonfarm occupations exceeded that in on-farm employment (which had been considerable owing to the Green Revolution).[27]

In Bangladesh, both the 1974 census and the 1973–74 Household Survey showed that nearly 30 percent of all rural households could be classified in nonagricultural occupations. Most of this activity consisted of rural trade and services, organized around small rural towns that serve as marketing centers. Small-scale and cottage industries in rural areas accounted for less than 4 percent of the total labor force in Bangladesh.

A survey by Ali (1980) documented the extent to which farmers in Bangladesh were taking up nonfarm employment to obtain additional income. Interviews with more than 2,140 farm families in 1980 showed that 84 percent of all farm operators reported off-farm employment of more than 100 days a year, but that those with holdings of more than 5 acres did not work off the farm. The percentage reporting off-farm work of 100 days or more had risen steadily, from 8.4 percent in 1951 to 30 percent in 1960 to 51 percent in 1970 to 84 percent in 1980—a tenfold increase in three decades! Only 10 percent of those engaged in part-time farming produced enough on their land to meet their yearly food needs. More than 53 percent worked on their holdings for more than nine months (270 days), another 23 percent did so for six to nine months.

Conclusions

This chapter has dealt with agrarian structures in South Asia. On the basis of the limited evidence available, I have shown that large numbers of those living in rural areas in South Asia are unable to support themselves by farming because their landholdings are very small or nonexistent. The employment opportunities for these people who make up the rural wage labor force fall short of the demand for jobs, and those who do find work as farm laborers seem increasingly to suffer from underemployment and the erosion of the real value of their earnings. Earnings from nonfarm agricultural activities and from nonagricultural rural jobs are of special importance for marginal farmers and the landless. Any dramatic expansion of these income sources in recent years has been confined, however, to areas in which agricultural growth has been high. This link between agricultural growth and the growth of nonfarm employment opportunities is criti-

Table 3-24. South Asia: Estimates of Small-Farm and Landless Households and Population, 1980
(households and population in millions)

Item	Bangladesh			India			Pakistan			South Asia	
	House-holds	Family size	Popu-lation	House-holds	Family size	Popu-lation	House-holds	Family size	Popu-lation	House-holds	Popu-lation
Landless rural labor											
Noncultivators with wage income more than half of total	3.0	4.6	13.8	15.0	4.4	66.0	2.0	4.5	9.0	20.0	88.8
Percentage of all rural	21.0	—	16.7	16.0	—	12.6	19.8	—	15.4	17.0	13.3
Near landless											
Cultivating fewer than 0.4 hectares	1.1	5.1	5.6	14.0	5.0	70.0	0.2	4.9	1.0	15.3	76.6
Percentage of all rural	7.7	—	6.8	15.0	—	13.3	1.9	—	1.7	13.0	11.5
Marginal farmers											
Cultivating 0.4–1.0 hectares	2.3	6.2	14.3	16.9	5.3	89.6	0.5	5.0	2.6	19.7	106.5
Percentage of all rural	16.1	—	17.2	18.1	—	17.1	5.0	—	4.4	17.0	16.0
Small farmers											
Cultivating 1.0–2.0 hectares	2.0	7.1	14.2	15.9	6.1	97.0	0.7	5.3	3.8	18.6	119.0
Percentage of all rural	14.0	—	17.1	17.0	—	18.5	6.9	—	6.5	15.8	17.3
Subtotal	8.4	—	47.9	61.8	—	122.6	3.4	—	16.4	73.6	386.9
Percentage of all rural	58.8	—	57.8	66.1	—	61.5	33.6	—	28.0	62.8	58.1
All rural households	14.3	5.8	82.9	93.6	5.6	524.2	10.1	5.8	58.6	118.0	665.7

— Not applicable.
Source: Based on 1970–80 changes in the population and on 1970 percentages.

cal to any evaluation of employment prospects for the rural poor in the future. (For some final numbers on the agrarian structures in South Asia see table 3-24 and figure 3-4).

Although it is widely known that unequal access to land—owned or operated—is a major source of income inequalities in rural areas of South Asia, what is less well understood is the role of wage employment, nonfarm enterprises, and ancillary activities in mitigating these inequalities. In a recent study of income inequalities in rural Pakistan, Ercelawn (1984) has shown this role to be significant. Poverty is borne primarily by those with little or no access to land; one solution is to redistribute land. But as I shall show later this is not the *only* solution to alleviating poverty. Another is to increase sources of nonfarm employment through agricultural growth.

In chapters 2 and 3, I have tried to sketch the economic environment in which small farmers and the landless in South Asia seek their livelihood. I have discussed the dimensions of rural poverty in general terms and have outlined some of the characteristics of the rural poor. In particular, I have examined two factors which both define these people and determine their economic status—their access to

Figure 3-4. *Small-Farm and Landless Households as a Percentage of Rural Households in South Asia, 1980*

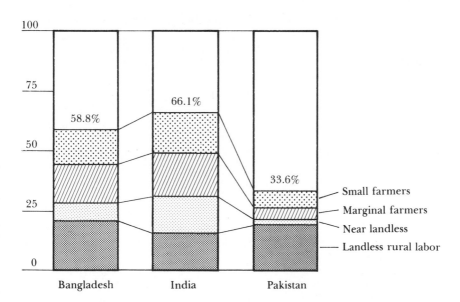

Note: The household categories are defined in Table 3-24.
Source: Table 3-24.

land and to jobs. Clearly, any coherent policy to alleviate the conditions outlined in chapter 2 must base itself on new approaches to the problems summarized here—the small landholdings that characterize most rural South Asian households and the lack of adequate income-earning opportunities for those who lack even the minimal security of an economically viable plot of land.

Chapters 4 and 5 focus on the prospects and problems of raising the productivity of small farmers in the crucially important food-grain sector and look at small farmers' access to credit and markets. Chapters 6 and 7 turn to the earnings potential of non-food-grain agriculture (especially livestock and dairying) and of nonagricultural rural activities. These possibilities for loosening the stranglehold of rural poverty will be of interest to academic researchers and practical policymakers alike. Despite the difficulties, the prospects of the rural poor need not be wholly bleak, as I hope to show in what follows.

Notes

1. See Singh (1988a) for a more detailed analysis of the issues outlined in this chapter.
2. The Marxian perspective seems to dominate the literature on rural South Asia. Among others see Alamgir (1978); A. R. Khan (in ILO 1977a); Rudra (1978a and b); Alavi in Stevens, Alavi, and Bertocci (1976); Frankel (1971); Patnaik (1987); and Sau (1973). For the Malthusian perspective, see Vyas (1979); and Stokes (1978).
3. Attwood (1979) defines a family's upward mobility as an expansion in its landholding and downward mobility as a contraction of that holding.
4. Between 1961 and 1971 some 38,000 formerly landless households in two relatively poor regions in Haryana purchased land.
5. The fact that an overwhelming number of small farmers have been able to retain their holdings does not mean that they may not have become poorer. As Vyas (1979) has pointed out, further impoverishment can occur with or without proletarianization. As family size increases, previous levels of production may become more and more inadequate, forcing households to rely more and more on agricultural labor and other supplementary occupations. Under these circumstances, and in the absence of productivity increases or easy access to off-farm employment, per capita incomes will fall.
6. Sheila Bhalla (1977), p. A–4. "Only 5.3 percent of today's landless agricultural labor households cultivated any land at all in 1962. All of them were pure tenants" (p. A–12).
7. Nearly 75 percent of those who "lost" land had in fact transferred it to other family members (Sheila Bhalla 1977).
8. See Rudra, Majid, and Talib's (1969) study of 261 farms of more than 20 acres in 1968–69. It is hard to reconcile this with the National Sample Survey (NSS) data, but since Rudra, Majid, and Talib collected their data from

block development officers at the local level, one tends to give their findings greater credence. The official NSS data reveal the de jure structure; it is doubtful whether the de facto nature of landownership will ever be known.

9. The Indian data are for both East Punjab and Haryana and have been adjusted to exclude the category of households owning no land (a category not given in the Pakistan data). The figures are still not strictly comparable because the Pakistan data are for individual owners while the Indian data are for owning households.

10. Although there must be large holdings hidden under bogus transfers in both regions, the extent of this concealment is unlikely to differ between them.

11. Small owners who rent out their land do not necessarily join the ranks of the landless or agricultural wage earners. The category "nonoperating owners" covers people engaged in occupations other than agriculture, including workers in cities.

12. These broad conclusions are supported by the analyses by Raj (1976) and H. Singh (1976) and by the analysis of state data by Sirohi, Ram, and Singh (1976), except that the latter find a dramatic decline in the average size of marginal holdings between 1960–61 and 1970–71, even in Punjab.

13. According to the Land Occupancy Survey, 72 percent of all households that owned land were in the 0.1–2 acre category and accounted for 24 percent of the owned land in 1977; according to the 1976 Pilot Census, 48 percent of all cultivators were in the 0.1–2.5 acre category and accounted for only 18 percent of the area cultivated.

14. The five-acre cutoff may represent a subsistence holding below which farmers in Pakistan cannot make an adequate living. Those with holdings smaller than this may rent them out or sell them to take up other occupations.

15. "The very recent fad about and display of interest in the landless is less due to a charitable concern on the part of the established officialdom and academia than due to a very real bout of enlightened self-interest arising out of the threat of disintegration to the established order in the face of the growing trend of landlessness and agricultural stagnation" (Adnan, Khan, and others 1978, p. 19).

16. The conceptual and measurement problems in estimating unemployment are discussed in some detail in Krishna (1976); A. Sen (1975); and Raj (1976).

17. The Indian debate on these issues can be found in Krishna (1973a and b, 1976); Dantwala (1973); Visaria (1972); and Raj (1976). There are only a few studies available for the other two countries: for Bangladesh, see Ahmed (1978); Clay and Khan (1977); and Clay in Bangladesh, Ministry of Agriculture and Forests (1978); and for Pakistan, see Eckert and others (1973).

18. Migration represents another option for the rural poor, but its potential as a solution to the oversupply of labor in rural areas is strictly limited—notably by constraints on the mobility of potential migrants and on the absorptive capacity of receiving areas and employers.

Rural-urban migration is a major subject of study in its own right and is not discussed comprehensively in this book for reasons of space. There have been a number of useful studies on the dynamics of migration in South Asia; the interested reader might begin by examining Connell and others (1976).

19. It is estimated that 20–24 percent of the rural labor force in India is employed in nonfarm activities, around 50 percent in Taiwan, 30–40 percent in the Philippines, 20–25 percent in the Republic of Korea, 30–40 percent in West Malaysia, and around 30 percent in Indonesia. Nonagricultural rural activities include manufacturing, repair, processing, construction, handicrafts and artisanal work, transport, trade and commerce—many of which are, of course, ancillary to agricultural activities and needs.

20. Manufacturing includes a wide variety of activities in food processing (including oil pressing, milling, and husking), handicrafts, leather work, textiles, wood products (including sawmilling, furniture, and carpentry), and metalworking (including blacksmithing, welding, fabrication and assembly work for machine tools and equipment); in Pakistan, East Punjab, and Tamil Nadu it includes small-scale manufacture and repairs of diesel and electric tubewells. Construction includes that of dwellings, farm buildings, roads, and civil works. In commerce, retail trade accounts for three-quarters of total employment, the remainder being made up of marketing and financial services; other services include petty trading, small business, and repair and artisanal work.

21. This proportion has declined by 3 percentage points in India and increased by 4 points in Pakistan in the intercensal decade, but this could be due to differences in what is included in the nonagricultural category.

22. These data partly overstate the importance of nonfarm incomes since they include pensions, remittances, and rental incomes. Rent is, of course, an unlikely source of income for the landless or those with small holdings if they are also cultivating land, but it could be a significant part of nonfarm income for those with larger holdings. Remittances, however, could be a significant source of income for the poorest groups; the data needed to establish their importance are unfortunately not available.

23. Biases resulting from the inclusion of remittances, pensions, and other transfer incomes in nonfarm incomes should be kept in mind, however.

24. See AERC (1974; 1975b and c; 1976a, b, c, and d), for example. But agricultural laborers are also worse off in some states; see Chauhan and others (1973) and Kaul and Kahlon (1971).

25. Over half the annual migrants from rural Punjab are derived from land-owning households of small or large farmers. An additional 10 percent come from farm tenant households. Fifteen percent are classified as unskilled laborers, while 17.5 percent bear with them the diverse skills of their respective trades (Eckert and Khan 1977).

26. Even village artisans have incomes that exceed those of permanent hired laborers by 20 percent to as much as 115 percent for such well-paid tradesmen as blacksmiths, barbers, and weavers (see Eckert 1972; D. A. Khan 1978). Between 1964–65 and 1976–77, in-kind and wage payments for farm work by permanent laborers rose by 149 percent in nominal terms; nonfarm occupations matched these increases.

27. D. A. Khan (1978, pp. 935–36) estimates that on-farm employment on small farms increased by some 0.2 million work years and on medium and large farms by 0.99 million work years. He reports that nonfarm employment increased by 1.5 million work years. These estimates are, however, based on the use of simple fixed input-output ratios of labor coefficients to crop averages; indirect employment is assumed to increase by 1.23 work years for every work year of farm employment—an estimate based on an Indian study.

4

Prerequisites for Sustained Gains in Output on Small Farms

Despite the unequal distribution of rural land in the subcontinent, large numbers of households obtain their livelihood from farming on small but viable holdings. Raising the productivity of these small-farm households must represent a central element in any strategy to reduce rural poverty in South Asia. In the subsequent chapters I will identify some of the opportunities that exist for implementing such a strategy. This chapter examines the characteristics of the small-farm sector, summarizes the available evidence on farm size as a factor in farm productivity and efficiency, and reviews the prospects for raising the output of traditional food grains through improved cultivation practices on small farms.[1]

The Small-Farm Sector

Misconceptions about small farmers abound. It is sometimes suggested, for example, that they are inefficient and relatively unproductive, grow only food crops for subsistence and do not produce for the market, do not use capital or credit extensively or effectively, and are inherently less willing to take risks than other farmers. These generalizations are often untrue and misleading.

The evidence from South Asia shows that small farmers are by no means pure subsistence farmers—if subsistence farmers are defined as those who grow only food, mainly for home consumption; rely very little on markets for the sale of their output; and use only owned factors of production, of which family labor is the most important (Wharton 1963; Nakajima 1970). In fact, although small farmers do indeed devote much of their cultivated land to food crops, they also plant a significant proportion of it with cash and other crops; and although they consume much of their food output on the farm, they also market a significant share of it locally (even though they may later have to buy some of it back).

Small farm operations are further characterized by higher irrigation and cropping intensities than on large farms, and as a result they use more inputs, especially (family) labor, per hectare and have higher total productivity per hectare. The last—the inverse relationship between farm size and productivity per hectare—is well established in traditional agriculture. There is some evidence, however, that in wheat-producing areas where the Green Revolution has had a significant impact, this relationship is being reversed (see Singh 1988b). The increased intensity in the use of cash inputs on larger farms seems to have neutralized the advantage previously held by small farms in terms of productivity. This is due not to lower efficiency on small farms, but to the better access of large farmers to these yield-increasing inputs.

Imperfections in factor markets are the main sources of productivity differences among farms, and there is nothing inherently superior or inferior about small family farms. Because these imperfections along with the economies of scale introduced by mechanization have favored larger farms, they appear to be more productive in this era of high-yielding varieties (HYV). With proper access to the relevant inputs, some differences in productivity and efficiency may disappear, but real economies of scale will persist because of the indivisibilities of capital. Tables 4-1, 4-2, and 4-3 summarize the evidence surrounding the productivity-efficiency debate reviewed in Singh (1988b).

The presumed higher productivity of small farms was one of the arguments in favor of redistribution of landholdings. The evidence suggests that redistributive land reform cannot be predicated solely on the assumed "productive superiority" of small farms. Other considerations of equity, employment, and social issues provide a much firmer basis for such a policy.

Two other characteristics set small farmers apart. They are not more risk averse but are more vulnerable to the consequences of risk than are larger, better endowed farmers, and they represent farm-household units in which interdependent decisions are made that affect both the farm and the household. Both these characteristics reduce the number of choices available to small farmers and subdue their response to economic incentives.

In evaluating prospects for increasing output and productivity, one must bear in mind that small farmers are not inefficient, tradition-bound, unresponsive to economic opportunities, or unwilling to adopt new ideas and technologies. But they do have limited means

(Text continues on page 108.)

Table 4-1. South Asia: Relationship between Farm Size and Productivity, the Pre-HYV Period

Years	Study	Region	Data	Data source	Inverse relationship	Remarks
1954–59	A. K. Sen (1962)	All India	Various districts	FMS	Holds	By and large, productivity per acre decreases with the size of holding.
1955–56	D. Mazumdar (1965)	North India	Two villages in Uttar Pradesh	FMS	Holds	Small farms may not be viable.
1955–56	C. H. H. Rao (1966)	West India	Three districts, Maharashtra	FMS/Author	Holds	Size, not wage differentials, is important in explaining relationship.
1954–57	A. P. Rao (1967)	North India	Disaggregated data from 3 villages in Punjab and Uttar Pradesh (249 observations)	FMS	May not hold	Productivity, input use, irrigation per acre do not vary by size.
	A. Rudra (1968)	North India	Disaggregated data: 17 districts, 20 villages in Punjab, Haryana, and Uttar Pradesh	AERC	Does not hold	In correlating gross area with output, does not hold; in correlating net area with output, holds for all crops, not individual crops.
1959–60	S. K. Sanyal (1969)	All India	State-level data, all states	NSS	Probably holds	Large farms have lower land use, fewer attached workers, less investable surplus, and lower use of inputs per acre.

Years	Author	Region	Data	Source	Inverse relationship	Comments
1957–64	U. Rani (1971)	West, South, and East India	Farm-level data from Madhya Pradesh, Kerala, Andhra Pradesh, and Orissa (1,431 observations)	NSS	May not hold	Statistically weak basis for inverse relationship.
1954–68	G. R. Saini (1971)	All India	Disaggregated data from 9 states, 11 districts, and 25 cases	FMS	Holds	Statistically significant inverse relationship.
1955–57	N. Bhattacharya and G. R. Saini (1972)	North India	Disaggregated farm-level data from Uttar Pradesh and Punjab	FMS	May not hold	Intravillage differences; relationship holds for Muzaffarnagar, Uttar Pradesh, and not for Ferozepur, Punjab.
1954–57	K. Bharadwaj (1974a)	All India	Aggregate data from 6 states, 9 districts, 25 cases	FMS	Appears to hold	Not always statistically significant.
1956–71	G. K. Chaddha (1978)	North India	Twelve districts in Punjab	FMS/Agricultural census	Holds	In all districts.
1955–57 1968–73	A. K. Ghose (1979a)	North and East India	Farm-level data from Hooghly, West Bengal, and Ferozepur, Punjab	FMS	Holds	Relationship exists independent of production relationship.
1962–70	V. V. Rao and T. Chotigeat (1981)	South India	Pooled data from Kerala, Tamil Nadu, and Andhra Pradesh	FMS	Does not hold	Especially with higher capital and cropping intensities.

Note: AERC = Agro-Economic Research Center; FMS = Farm Management Surveys; NSS = National Sample Survey (India).

Table 4-2. Relationship between Farm Size and Efficiency: Evidence from South Asia

Study	Year of data	Region and data description	Remarks
		Pre-HYV Period	
T. W. Schultz (1964)	—	—	Traditional farming is efficient.
M. Paglin (1965)	—	—	Large farmers are less efficient.
W. D. Hopper (1965)	1954	Data for 43 farms in Uttar Pradesh	Traditional farming is efficient.
A. M. Khusro (1964)	1954–57	FMS data from Andhra Pradesh, Bombay, Madhya Pradesh, Madras, Punjab, Uttar Pradesh, West Bengal	Efficiency does not decrease by farm size.
G. S. Sahota (1968)	1955–57	FMS data from Madras, Uttar Pradesh, West Bengal	No significant differences in efficiency across farm sizes.
G. R. Saini (1969)	1955–57	FMS data from Punjab and Uttar Pradesh	Farmers are efficient but no efficiency differences across size of farms.
P. A. Yotopoulos, L. J. Lau, and K. Somel (1970)	1955–57	FMS data from Madhya Pradesh, Madras, Punjab, Uttar Pradesh, West Bengal	Small farmers are technically more efficient, but there are no differences in price efficiency by size.

		Post-HYV Period	
L. J. Lau and P. A. Yotopoulos (1971)	1955–57	FMS data from Madhya Pradesh, Madras, Punjab, Uttar Pradesh, West Bengal	Small farmers exhibit higher level of both price and technical efficiency.
P. A. Yotopoulos and L. J. Lau (1973)	1955–65	FMS data from Madhya Pradesh, Madras, Punjab, Uttar Pradesh, West Bengal	Small farmers are technically more efficient, but not different in their price efficiency.
S. S. Sidhu (1974b)	1967–71	FMS, old and new varieties of wheat, 150 farms, Punjab	No difference in economic, technical, and price efficiency by farm size.
P. N. Junankar (1978a)	1969–70	FMS data, local and HYV paddy, 150 farms, Tamil Nadu	Relatively equal economic, technical, and price efficiency of all farm sizes.
F. S. Bagi (1979a and b, 1981)	1969–70	Farm-level data for irrigated and unirrigated farms, Haryana	Small farmers are more efficient but not significantly different.
M. H. Khan and D. R. Maki (1979, 1980)	1974	Wheat and rice farms, Pakistan	No differences in efficiency by farm size.
K. Kalirajan (1981)	1977–78	Seventy farmers growing HYV rice in rabi season, Tamil Nadu	Small and large farmers exhibit equal price and technical efficiency.

— Not applicable.
Note: FMS = Farm Management Surveys.

Table 4-3. South Asia: Relationship between Farm Size and Productivity, the Post-HYV Period

Data years	Study	Region	Data notes	Inverse relationship	Remarks
1955–60/ 1966–70	C. H. H. Rao (1975)	North and South India	Andhra Pradesh, Punjab, Uttar Pradesh	Does not hold	Relationship breaks down under conditions of new technology.
1967–70	S. S. Johl (1971)	North India	Farm-size specific data, Ludhiana	Does not hold	Growing productivity and income disparities between large and small farmers.
1968–72	S. L. Bapna (1973)	West India	Kota District, Rajasthan	Does not hold	Growing productivity and income disparities between large and small farmers.
1969–70	W. Khan and R. N. Tripathy (1972)	South India	West Godavari, Andhra Pradesh	Does not hold	Growing productivity and income disparities between large and small farmers.
1969–70	F. S. Bagi (1981)	North India	Farm-level data, Haryana	Holds	Small farmers are at least as efficient as large farmers.
1954–70	G. R. Saini (1980)	All India and North India	Disaggregated data, 9 states, 11 districts, 25 cases along with business income data for Punjab and Uttar Pradesh	May not hold	Business incomes indicate that small farmers may be as productive as large farmers.

Period	Study	Region	Data	Relationship	Comments
1962–73	M. Chattopadhyay and A. Rudra (1977)	All India	Disaggregated data, 10 states, 12 districts, and 27 cases	May not hold	Generally holds for all crops, does not hold for individual crops, and does not hold in all cases and at all times.
1968–71	S. S. Bhalla in Berry and Cline (1979)	All India	Panel survey over three years for approximately 3,000 cultivating households	Holds	Holds but is weakening.
1970–71	A. Deolalikar (1981)	All India	Data for 272 districts	Does not hold	At low levels of technology (fertilizer use), inverse relationship holds; at higher levels the relationship is reversed and larger farms are more productive.
1970–73	B. Dasgupta (1977a)	All India	Village-level crop-specific studies	Does not hold	See consolidation of evidence in Dasgupta (1977a), table 3.15.
1974	M. H. Khan (1977)	Pakistan	Irrigated Indus Basin farms in Punjab (498)	May not hold	Holds for all crops, positive for wheat.
1974	M. H. Khan (1979b)	Pakistan	Irrigated Indus Basin farms in Punjab (498)	May not hold	Because of higher levels of non-traditional inputs in large farms.
1975–76	P. L. Roy (1981)	North India	Punjab farm households (821)	Does not hold	Districts with low levels of adoption show inverse relationship; in districts with high levels of adoption relationship is reversed.

and choices. Both the willingness and, indeed, the efficiency with which poor households respond to opportunities within their limited means need to be kept in mind when assessing ways to improve their situation.

There are two strategies for raising small-farm output, both of which are designed to draw on small farmers' main asset other than land—their labor resources. The first is intended to increase the output of a given crop per unit of area; the second is intended to increase the number of crops per unit of area in a given crop year. These strategies are discussed below, as well as the critical role of irrigation in increasing the output of food crops on small farms. The chapter concludes with a brief survey of small farmers' access to credit (which is essential if they are to buy the inputs needed for sustained growth in production) and markets (which provide the earnings needed to develop and expand South Asia's rural cash crop economies).

Better Cultivating Practices: The Training and Visit System

A noteworthy and successful approach to raising output of a given crop is the so-called training and visit (T&V) system of extension described by Benor, Harrison, and Baxter (1984). The system is designed to enable extension workers to convey information easily to farmers and persuade farmers to do simple things that will increase output immediately. The emphasis is on raising efficiency, especially that of costly inputs, by improving management practices and cropping sequences. In principle, these improvements are in land preparation, seedbed and nursery maintenance, the spacing and density of plant populations, use of seed (including appropriate improved varieties), seed treatment, the timing of tilling, weeding, and fertilizing, and the methods of using pesticides and fertilizers. In fact, T&V systems have also introduced line transplanting of paddy, faster growing varieties of paddy, and the production of wheat on residual moisture in Assam; seed selection and treatment in Madhya Pradesh; techniques to improve plant populations in Gujarat; faster growing HYV paddy and early jute varieties to allow the rotation of crops (paddy-wheat and rapeseed-jute) in West Bengal; new crops such as oilseeds, pulses, and HYV paddy in Orissa; lower-cost measures to protect cotton plants in Gujarat; and the ridge cultivation of maize in Rajasthan.

There are several reasons for this emphasis on cultivating and management practices. First, they are said to produce sure and immediate results, and adopting them exposes farmers to few risks. Second, although new practices may involve more work, they require little or no cash outlay. Third, the ability to derive the maximum benefit from new production technologies depends on first learning good crop management techniques. For example, if farmers apply fertilizers to a field that is not properly weeded or that has poor stands of plants, the net effect will be to fertilize weeds, which will successfully compete with crops for available soil, moisture, and light; the result can be a lower crop yield rather than a higher one.

Under the T&V approach, new cultivation and management practices are initially recommended for only a small part of a farmer's land, so that the methods do not appear unduly risky and so that the results can be compared with those of traditional practices on the farmer's own land. Since these practices are quite "well known and tested" (according to Benor, Harrison, and Baxter 1984), they can be incorporated into an extension service without elaborate and time-consuming screening and trials.[2]

The T&V method has been successfully used under a variety of rainfed and irrigated conditions. The achievements and impact of T&V are difficult to quantify, but evidence suggests that they are considerable. In Orissa, the area devoted to drought-resistant crops such as oilseeds and pulses has increased significantly since the inception of the T&V system in 1977. In Assam, the area sown to HYV increased fourfold and fertilizer use increased 144 percent in one year after the introduction of the system. In Rajasthan, farmers have raised paddy yield from 2.1 tons to more than 3 tons per hectare in two years, a 43 percent improvement. In Madhya Pradesh, unirrigated and irrigated wheat yields rose from 1.3 tons to nearly 2 tons per hectare after one season, an increase of nearly 54 percent. The area under high-yielding paddy and wheat varieties in the entire state of West Bengal is reported to have grown substantially in a single year, as have cropping intensities and the employment of family labor. These impacts were found to be greater on small holdings than on large (see Ray 1979).

These rapid gains in output were apparently not primarily because of better irrigation or weather, the discovery of a new crop variety, or greater use of fertilizer. In Rajasthan, for example, it was reported that yields rose while the use of purchased inputs fell. In irrigated areas where the T&V method was adopted, irrigation had been available for years but had been poorly managed and used. A survey of beneficiaries in one of the World Bank's projects in Uttar Pradesh found that although yields increased significantly with the installation of tubewells, they remained well below levels in irrigated areas in other states which had better extension organizations.[3] This suggests that better extension is critical for realizing the full potential of irrigation, fertilizer, and HYV investments.

Some of the gains were the result of *reduced* applications of costly fertilizers or protective chemicals, or the result of more timely and better applications. Such achievements are often missed in statistics that are geared to show increased input use as a sign of progress. These gains are especially important for small farmers. Available evidence strongly suggests that a professional agricultural extension service developed on the same principles in each of these diverse areas was a major force behind these changes (see Benor, Harrison, and Baxter 1984).

Evidence that following recommended practices has a significant impact on yields even on the smallest holdings is available from the Chambal canal project areas in Rajasthan and Madhya Pradesh (Cernea, Coulter, and Russell 1984, ch. 4). Yield increases of 50–60 percent are reported from the smallest holdings. Additional evidence on the effects of improved extension services comes from the monitoring and evaluation of two Bank projects in Rajasthan and Haryana (see tables A6–A14).

Although there are some minor differences, these and other data suggest the following generalizations:

- The adoption rates for recommended practices are slightly higher for contact farmers (those regularly visited by T&V agents) than for noncontact farmers.
- The adoption rates are higher in areas with T&V than in areas with traditional extension systems.
- There are substantial differences in yields between those who adopt recommended practices and those who do not, and these yield differences increase with the number of recommended practices adopted.
- Yields increase as the frequency of extension visits increases.
- There are no significant differences either in adoption rates or in yields between farms of different sizes.
- Small farmers are not being neglected by agents in favor of larger farmers.
- Extension agents are the main source of knowledge leading to higher yields.

Moreover, since the improved practices require more labor, rather than increased use of costly inputs, small farmers may in fact be able to adopt such recommendations more easily than larger ones (see Feder and Slade 1984 for detailed analysis of the Haryana data).

These findings come from areas with previously poor records of agricultural performance and large numbers of smallholders. They clearly suggest that small farmers have an enormous potential for raising yields through simple improvements in cropping practices implemented under extension systems. It is important, however, to distinguish carefully between yield increases that can be achieved merely with increased labor (associated with improved practices and of course knowledge) and those that require increases in other inputs, such as water, seeds, pesticides, nutrients, and credit. These inputs may not be available to small farmers—or they may not be profitable to use, a point that has often been ignored.

It is very difficult to separate the impact of extension alone from that of other inputs that often accompany the introduction of new practices via extension. To do this requires careful comparison of data from areas where T&V has been introduced against data from areas where traditional systems prevail. Feder and Slade (1984) analyzed the impact of the T&V system in districts in Haryana by comparing them with similar districts in Uttar Pradesh where T&V had not been introduced. Their results suggest that when compared with traditional extension services, the T&V system has significantly increased the diffusion of knowledge of recommended practices for HYV cereals; there was no evidence that visits to contact farmers by extension agents were biased by farm size; and significant yield increases occurred after the introduction of the T&V system.

Further, Feder, Slade, and Lau (1985) show that after accounting for the impact of other inputs, the impact on yield attributable to T&V *alone* was about 10 percent. The estimated rate of return of the T&V project, based on yield increases attributed to the new system alone, was approximately 40 percent in one district according to their calculations. Their findings refute the consistent criticism that T&V has few benefits to offer, that extension agents bypass smallholders, and that contact farmers fail to pass information to other farmers. Extension services are rapidly becoming major sources of knowledge, especially with respect to more complicated and costly practices, and their impact on yields and production is significant (Feder, Slade, and Sundaram 1986).

A growing body of research suggests that substantial increments in production and income are possible, even in semi-arid rain-fed areas, with improved cultivation practices and varieties, and with modest amounts of fertilizer properly applied. An example of the range of improvement possible is shown in table 4-4. These results suggest that technology already available can raise incomes substantially on the 70 percent of India's cropped land which is not irrigated.

Much of the work done by Benor and Harrison, and others who stress improved farming practices, is based on reducing the gaps between "average" yields and "best practice" yields in the same area. Although these gaps are smaller than those typically cited between

Table 4-4. Net Income Increases as a Percentage of Gross Farm Incomes

Country and crop	Mean yield (kilograms per hectare)[a]	Grain price (rupees or taka per kilogram)	Gross value of mean yield (rupees or taka)[b]	Net income increases as percentage of gross value			
				Current[c]		Improved[d]	
				HYV	Traditional	HYV	Traditional
Bangladesh							
Rice	1,043	198.0	2,065	29	7	93	63
India (irrigated)							
Rice	1,352	129.0	1,744	52	25	14	9
Wheat	1,572	136.2	2,141	33	9	9	28
Maize	1,749	86.0	1,504	—[e]	23	—[e]	6
Jowar	943	120.0	1,131	1	—[e]	-2	—[e]
India (unirrigated)							
Wheat	837	136.2	1,140	—[e]	7	—[e]	5
Maize	896	86.0	771	-2	46	0	34
Jowar	486	120.0	583	6	—[e]	0	—[e]

a. For India, 1973–74 average irrigated and unirrigated yields are used; for Bangladesh, 1972–73 yields are used.
b. For India, 1976 prices are used; for Bangladesh 1977, first quarter prices are used.
c. When moving from zero fertilizer use to current levels.
d. When moving from current levels of fertilizer use to optimum levels.
e. Less than 0.5 percent.
Source: World Bank data.

Table 4-5. *India: Examples of Yield Gaps in Cultivators' Fields, 1977*

	Present yields (kilograms per hectare)		Increase in yields possible (percent)
State and crop	Average	On best fields[a]	
West Bengal			
Rice			
Aman	1,100	2,500	127
Aus	1,000	2,000	100
Boro	2,500	5,000	100
Wheat	2,000	4,000	100
Pulses	600	1,200	100
Oilseeds	400	1,000	150
Madhya Pradesh			
Paddy	750	1,600	113
Wheat	730	2,000	174
Pulses	690	1,600	132
Other cereals[b]	720	1,800	150
Rajasthan			
Wheat	1,300	2,000	54
Pulses	500	1,600	220
Other cereals[b]	740	1,800	143

a. Average on best farmers' fields is lower than obtained under research conditions.
b. Sorghum, barley, maize, millets-barley.
Source: World Bank data.

farmers' yields and those obtained under research conditions, they can be very large—anywhere from 50 to 250 percent depending on the crop and region (table 4-5)—and they provide an easily observable measure of potential gains. The few data available suggest that, without any increase in inputs, output can be raised by 15–30 percent in rain-fed areas and by 25–50 percent in irrigated areas, depending on the crop (see tables 4-5 and A15). Further increases in yields require varietal changes or increased use of inputs, or both.

There are thus discrete stages in the adoption of improved practices, each providing an incremental yield. But not all stages are equally accessible to small farmers. Data from rain-fed areas in Assam (table A15) make this point. Stage 1 consists only of changes in cropping practices; stage 2a requires varietal changes, and 2b requires the use of additional nutrients; stages 3a and 3b involve not only new varieties and more nutrients, but also management-intensive practices such as the use of appropriate pesticides. Stage 2 requires the reorganization of research, extension, and marketing systems (for the delivery of inputs) to make sure that small farmers have access to them. Stage 3 requires management capabilities, which means farmers must be educated and given a proper understanding of soils, plants, and nutrients so they can make intelligent decisions.

All innovations do not come from experts or extension agencies. In Bangladesh small farmers themselves have pioneered a variety of techniques for multiple crops and intercropping. They include broadcast upland rice sown during pre-monsoon showers and followed by a second rice crop; on land that is susceptible to flooding, a quick-maturing upland rice and a longer-maturing deep-water rice sown together but harvested separately, followed by a crop of pulses, oilseeds, or wheat in the dry season using residual soil moisture (Brammer 1980). These practices demonstrate an amazing adjustment of the farmers' choice of crop and cropping patterns to the specific micro environment in their fields. One result is the multiplicity of rice varieties that have been adopted.[4] Double sowing of paddy and cultivation of wheat on soils unsuited for rice are other examples of innovations by the farmers themselves. Farmers as a community are not so dependent on research and government programs as governments and aid organizations widely presume. They readily adopt practices that maximize the use of their scarce land. These intercropping practices do not necessarily require mechanized cultivation, nor is irrigation essential where deep loamy soils have a high moisture content, as in parts of Bangladesh. Even fertilizers are not essential for continuous cropping on seasonally flooded soils (Brammer 1980).

To summarize, small farmers can easily increase their yields by 10–50 percent without any increase in inputs if they are taught better practices. Nevertheless, the data just presented and the apparent success they reveal should be treated with caution. The samples are small, the evidence is limited, and it is too early to evaluate the full impact of the changes over time. At best, these magnitudes should be treated as only indicative of the type of yield increases that can be brought about by changing simple cropping practices. Further increases (of 75–150 percent) will depend on the price and availability of inputs, access to these inputs, the availability of credit with which to purchase them (see below), and better-educated small farmers.

In India the reform of extension systems along the lines of the T&V approach involves the consolidation, reorganization, and strengthening of existing extension agencies rather than the creation of new organizations. This approach uses the experience and skills of the existing staff, avoids duplication of effort, and keeps costs low. Twelve states have already adopted the T&V extension system through World Bank-assisted projects. When fully developed these programs will cover some 70 percent of India's farm holdings and some 65 percent (45 million) of India's farm families. Bangladesh and Pakistan are in the process of adapting the T&V approach to their needs.

Scientific Multiple Cropping

In addition to better cultivation practices, multiple cropping—growing more than one crop on the same piece of land in a given year—can make the little land available to small farmers more productive. Multiple cropping increases both the area cropped per year and the total yield per unit of area.

Although an ancient practice on the subcontinent, multiple cropping has gained considerable attention lately. Until the early 1960s most multiple cropping was of vegetables grown near urban areas and irrigated with sewage. The recent concept of *scientific* multiple cropping is an outcome of the existence of reliable irrigation, awareness of the value of commercial fertilizers, and the development of quick-maturing, high-yielding varieties of cereals, grains, legumes, and other crops. The objective is to maximize production and economic returns per unit of area and per unit of time. (Rajat and Bhardwaj 1974.)

Table 4-6 gives figures for multiple cropping in selected countries in the 1960s. In South Asia 15–40 percent of the planted area was multiple cropped, in East Asia 30–80 percent. The multiple cropped area did not increase much from 1950 to 1969 in the subcontinent (see table 4-7), in spite of the increase in irrigation with which it is strongly linked. The index of multiple cropping remained fairly stable for India at between 112 and 115 during this period.[5] For Pakistan it has been even lower, but the range is about the same. In Bangladesh

Table 4-6. *Index of Multiple Cropping in Selected Economies*

Economy	Years	Index	Multiple cropped area (1,000 acres)
Burma	1965–66	111.1	2,162
Pakistan	1966–67	111.7	4,116
India	1962–63	115.0	48,456
Indonesia	1964	126.2	5,248
Philippines	1960	136.0	4,982
Bangladesh	1968–69	139.2	8,479
China	1968	147.4	127,388
Korea, Rep. of	1969	153.4	3,074
Egypt	1961–62	173.0	4,388
Taiwan	1969	184.3	1,905

Note: The index is derived by dividing the total land area planted during the year (including that planted as a result of double cropping) by the amount of cultivated land physically available and in use.

Source: Compiled from data presented in Dalrymple (1971).

Table 4-7. South Asia: Multiple Cropped Area and Index

Season	Bangladesh Multiple cropped area (1,000 acres)	Index	India Multiple cropped area (1,000 acres)	Index	West Pakistan Multiple cropped area (1,000 acres)	Index
1949–50	5,564	127.6	38,108	112.0	n.a.	n.a.
1950–51	5,708	127.8	32,486	111.1	3,131	111.1
1951–52	6,080	129.4	34,181	111.6	2,333	108.4
1952–53	6,574	131.4	35,169	111.5	2,066	107.4
1953–54	6,909	133.1	38,730	112.4	2,825	109.4
1954–55	6,572	131.4	40,119	112.7	3,503	112.0
1955–56	5,509	126.9	44,861	114.1	3,875	112.7
1956–57	5,468	126.7	45,916	114.2	3,774	112.1
1957–58	5,620	127.7	41,340	113.0	2,405	111.0
1958–59	5,366	127.0	48,928	115.0	4,520	114.3
1959–60	5,902	128.7	49,136	115.0	3,105	109.6
1960–61	6,732	132.3	48,330	114.7	2,421	107.5
1961–62	6,453	130.8	51,266	115.3	3,447	110.4
1962–63	6,796	132.5	50,465	115.0	3,187	109.4
1963–64	7,095	133.7	50,468	115.0	4,191	112.9
1964–65	7,434	135.2	51,931	115.2	5,140	114.7
1965–66	7,940	136.8	47,119	114.0	4,473	112.9
1966–67	7,926	137.6	48,456	114.4	4,116	111.7
1967–68	9,694	144.6	n.a.	n.a.	3,046	108.5
1968–69	8,479	139.2	n.a.	n.a.	n.a.	n.a.

n.a. Not available.
Note: The index is derived by dividing the total land area planted during the year (including that planted as a result of double cropping) by the amount of cultivated land physically available and in use.
Source: Dalrymple (1971).

a larger percentage of the area is multiple cropped (30–40 percent), and the trend has been positive.

Although aggregate data for South Asia suggest that multiple cropping could be increased substantially, they do not reflect the full picture for small farms. As one would expect, multiple cropping is inversely related to farm size. Small farmers farm their land more intensively, having the available family labor to do so; hence their yields per unit of area and per unit of time are much higher than those on large farms.

Although only 9 percent of the cultivated area is multiple cropped in India and 11 percent in Pakistan, figure 4-1 shows that the multiple cropped area on farms smaller than five acres ranges from 16 to 27 percent for India and from 30 to 52 percent for Pakistan. The figures for Bangladesh are even more dramatic. Whereas 53 percent of the cultivated area in Bangladesh is multiple cropped, 58–82 percent of the area of farms smaller than five acres is multiple cropped. Indeed, for farms of less than one acre the cropping intensity is almost as high as that in Taiwan, which is often cited as the prime example of effective multiple cropping systems. Raising the number of small farms in India and Pakistan that produce two crops a year ultimately depends

Figure 4-1. *South Asia: Multiple Cropped Area as a Percentage of Cultivated Area, by Farm Size*

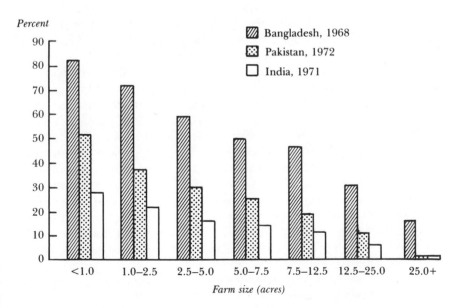

Sources: Bangladesh Bureau of Statistics (1972); India, Ministry of Agriculture and Irrigation (1975); and Pakistan, Ministry of Food and Agriculture (1975).

on the availability of water and its control through irrigation. In Bangladesh, where many farmers are already getting nearly two crops a year, the objective is to get three crops a year.

Tables 4-8, 4-9, 4-10, and A16 and A17 provide additional data on cropping intensities by farm size for Bangladesh, Pakistan, and India. They clearly highlight the inverse relationship between farm size and cropping intensities (see figure 4-2) as well as the importance of irrigation to higher intensities (see below). They show how small farms overcome the handicaps of their size by farming what they have far more intensively. This is a central reason why land area is not a good proxy for the income potential of small holdings.

The input requirements of multiple cropping can be substantial. Necessary (but not sufficient) conditions for its wider adoption include the use of improved varieties of seed, better water control, higher inputs of fertilizer, better insect and disease controls, and more efficient postharvest technologies. New varieties of crops are of central importance in promoting multiple cropping. Early maturing varieties are generally associated with a rise in multiple cropping; the shorter the growing season required by a given crop, the greater the possibility of raising an additional one within the available growing time (Dalrymple 1971, p. 23). Other desirable characteristics, especially for grains, are yield rather than vegetative responsiveness to fertilizers; short, strong stems that limit "logging"; as much insect and disease resistance as possible; and acceptability to consumers. In addition, varieties that are to be grown in rain-fed areas often need to be drought-resistant. The high-yielding varieties of wheat and rice developed in the late 1960s have many of these characteristics and have been extensively adopted in multiple cropping systems.

Since the rainfall in large areas of South Asia is both inadequate and unsuitably distributed for multiple cropping, increased irrigation is also essential. Irrigation is discussed separately in the next section; its role in raising cropping intensities is summarized here. A policy conflict can arise between increasing the supply of water during the single existing growing season or extending the growing season to cover other parts of the year. Although irrigation during appropriate periods helps make multiple cropping possible, the relationship works both ways: multiple cropping may be necessary to justify the expense of putting irrigation systems in place. Indeed, this is a necessary condition for many agricultural projects in South Asia. Many of the new irrigation projects pay particular attention to projected cropping intensities.

The extensive existing irrigation systems in South Asia were not designed to maximize output per acre, however, but rather to spread

Table 4-8. India: Cultivated Area, Cropping Intensity, and Irrigation by Size of Operational Holding, 1970–71

Size of holding (acres)	Total area of holdings (millions of acres)	Cultivated area		Gross cropped area (millions of acres)	Cropping intensity (percent)	Percentage of cultivated area	
		Millions of acres	As percentage of total			Irrigated	Unirrigated
< 1.0	13.46	12.52	93	15.93	127	34	66
1.0–2.5	22.48	21.14	94	25.89	122	31	69
2.5–5.0	47.62	44.21	93	51.40	116	28	72
5.0–7.5	40.38	37.52	93	42.66	114	27	74
7.5–25.0	152.85	138.76	91	150.15	108	23	77
25.0–50.0	70.44	62.47	89	63.60	102	16	84
50.0+	53.20	41.72	78	40.80	98	12	88
Total	400.43	358.34	89	390.43	109	23[a]	78[b]

Notes: Column may not add to total because of rounding.
a. 88.2 million acres.
b. 302.2 million acres.
Source: India, Ministry of Agriculture and Irrigation (1975).

Table 4-9. Pakistan: Cultivated Area, Cropping Intensity, and Irrigation by Size of Farm, 1960–61 and 1972

Farm size (acres)	Cultivated area			Gross cropped area			Cropping intensity[a]		Percentage of cultivated area			
	Percentage of total		Percentage increase in group	Percentage of total		Percentage increase in group			Irrigated		Unirrigated	
	1960–61	1972		1960–61	1972		1960–61	1972	1960–61	1972	1960–61	1972
< 1.0	1	—b	−73	1	—b	−67	138	152	54	65	46	35
1.0–2.5	3	1	−54	3.5	2	−46	130	137	63	72	37	28
2.5–5.0	7	4	−31	8	5	−22	128	131	66	75	34	25
5.0–7.5	8	8	2	9	9	12	127	125	70	78	30	22
7.5–12.5	17	20	28	18	22	37	124	119	73	81	27	19
12.5–25.0	29	29	10	30	29	15	119	111	74	78	26	22
25.0–50.0	20	19	5	19	18	10	115	103	68	70	32	30
50.0–150.0	10	13	35	9	11	53	109	97	47	60	53	40
150.0+	5	5	22	2.5	4	87	108	88	58	60	42	40
Total	100	100	9	100.0	100	17	120	111	68	74	32	26
Millions of acres	37.25	40.69		38.31	44.98				25.2	29.98		

a. Censuses provide cropping intensity based on net sown area (86 percent and 92 percent of total cultivated areas in 1960–61 and 1972 respectively).
b. Less than 0.5.
Sources: Pakistan, Ministry of Agriculture and Works (1960b), tables 13 and 17; Pakistan, Ministry of Food and Agriculture (1975), tables 24, 25, 26, and 27.

Table 4-10. Bangladesh: Cultivated Area, Cropping Intensity, and Irrigation by Size of Farm, 1960–61 and 1967–68

Farm size (acres)	Cultivated area[a] Percentage of total 1960–61	1967–68	Percentage increase in group	Gross cropped area Percentage of total 1960–61	1967–68	Percentage increase in group	Cropping intensity (percent) 1960–61	1967–68	Percentage of cultivated area,[b] 1960–61 Irrigated	Unirrigated
< 0.5	1	1	11	1	1	25	166	186	6	79
0.5–1.0	2	3	32	2	3	40	171	181	6	76
1.0–2.5	13	17	31	16	19	36	166	172	6	75
2.5–5.0	27	30	13	28	31	15	155	158	6	75
5.0–7.5	20	18	-8	20	17	-7	147	149	6	75
7.5–12.5	19	16	-19	18	15	-16	140	145	7	75
12.5–25.0	14	11	-20	12	9	-21	132	131	8	73
25.0–40.0	3	3	29	2	3	20	127	117	9	72
40.0+	1	1	-3	1	1	-7	117	113	13	73
Total	100	100	1	100	100	4	148	153	7	75
Millions of acres	18.85	19.03		27.88	29.08				1.32	14.3

Notes: Because of rounding, figures may not add to total. Increase in group is the absolute percentage increase.

a. Cultivated area is taken as net sown area, consistent with cropping intensity.

b. 1960–61 data show 18 percent of total cultivated area as flooded; this is not shown in this column.

Sources: Pakistan, Ministry of Agriculture and Works (1960a), tables 12, 13, and 18; Bangladesh Bureau of Statistics (1972), table 7.

Figure 4-2. *South Asia: Cropping Intensities by Farm Size*

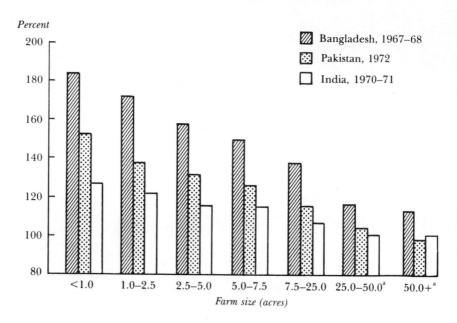

a. For Bangladesh, the largest size groups are 25.0–40.0 and 40.0+ acres respectively.
Sources: Tables 4-8, 4-9, and 4-10.

the available water as widely as possible in order to reduce the probability of crop failure (see Mellor and others 1968). Especially in the case of canal irrigation, which is widely used in the subcontinent, the quantity of water available depends largely on seasonal flows. The main drawback to canal irrigation in Pakistan is that the supply is unreliable (Mohammad 1965; Kaneda and Ghaffar 1970). When the water is most needed—in the dry season or for the second crop—it is likely to be most scarce (Dalrymple 1971, p. 25). This has led to the rationing of water in the winter in Pakistan, which has in turn limited opportunities for multiple cropping (Hussain 1970).

   Unless the seasonal distribution of water is improved, it is not possible to increase cropping intensities. In this connection, both well water and tubewell irrigation are preferable to canal-based systems, because they are less subject to seasonal variations in supply. There is clear evidence that the multiple cropping index is generally higher in regions where tubewell irrigation is practiced than in canal-irrigated regions. In the Indian Punjab the multiple cropping index in regions irrigated by wells in 1968–69 was 150 percent as opposed to 125 percent in canal-irrigated areas; it was expected to rise to between 180 and 200 percent by the 1980s (Billings and Singh 1970; I. Singh and Day 1975a). Similarly, in West Pakistan in 1963–64 the cropping index for tubewell farmers in three districts averaged about 138 percent, as opposed to 107 percent for those without tubewells.

Irrigation is only one aspect of the water control problem; the other is drainage. Adequate drainage is needed in the short run to ensure proper irrigation; in the longer run, it is essential in order to prevent chronic waterlogging or salinization of the soil (which is extensive in Pakistan). If drainage schemes are in the hands of local elites, small farmers may again be the last to receive adequate assistance.

One of the drawbacks of multiple cropping is that the soil is impoverished (unless replenished by annual flooding, as in Bangladesh). Thus, in addition to quick-growing crop varieties and reliable irrigation and drainage systems, the further expansion of multiple cropping on small farms requires the use of organic or chemical fertilizers to reinvigorate the soil.[6] Although extensive work has been done on the new high-yielding varieties, relatively little is known about the relationship between different crop rotations and fertilization needs. Ultimately, small farmers' use of fertilizer depends on whether they have access to supplies of it and whether they find its use profitable. Without the increased use of nutrients, however, extensive multiple cropping systems will be difficult to sustain (Swaminathan and Bains 1970).

Finally, multiple cropping requires a longer life span for plants, which in turn requires better controls for insects and diseases. Unfortunately, some of the new high-yielding crop varieties are much more susceptible to local diseases and insects than are the native varieties. Four possible solutions to this problem are: stepping up chemical control measures, breeding for natural plant resistance, attempting biological control, and arranging rotations so that no two crops sharing the same pests and diseases are grown in sequence (Dalrymple 1971, p. 28). The first three have major difficulties and limitations. Chemical control can be expensive and cause ecological problems; moreover, chemical pesticides are cash-intensive and may be out of small farmers' reach. Breeding for natural resistance and developing biological controls are time-consuming processes, and it is not certain whether all the necessary research has been done, especially in Bangladesh and Pakistan. The last method, the use of appropriate rotations, is the most logical starting point. What can be accomplished in practice depends, however, on adaptive research into the development of farming systems especially suited to the conditions and needs of small farmers on the subcontinent.

Thus, much needs to be done before the potential for multiple cropping in South Asia can be realized. Moreover, multiple cropping presents fewer opportunities for small farmers than for larger ones. Small farmers may have relatively limited access to the necessary new inputs, and raising the area under multiple cropping, especially with existing cropping intensities of over 150–160 percent, requires a huge advance in farmers' management capabilities. Small farmers are shrewd decisionmakers, but they generally lack the scientific information needed to handle complex cropping systems.

The most critical management problem has to do with timing. In South Asia, which has year-round sunshine and no climatic barriers to three or even four crops a year, the key obstacle to extensive multiple cropping is the length or timing of the growing season.[7] As more crops are planted and the growing period between them is shortened, less time is left between the harvesting of one crop and the planting of the next. Minimizing the number of days during which the land is left idle is a difficult job for the farm manager. A large number of operations need to be carried out in a relatively short period. The small farmer's advantage of having a relatively abundant supply of labor may well be offset by his disadvantages in obtaining other inputs. If seeds, nutrients, and irrigation water are not available on time, they might as well not be available at all; if small farmers have to wait for these inputs, their timing is likely to be upset and the probability of succeeding with multiple cropping practices is likely to be correspondingly reduced.

Even though adaptive research has provided appropriate cropping rotations for parts of India and Bangladesh, the problem of timing has prevented their general use. Most of these rotations leave little margin for delays caused by weather or the unavailability of inputs. Delays in crop maturity may reduce yields or create problems with harvesting one crop and planting the next.[8] Mechanization, which has been widely adopted in some parts of the subcontinent, can speed up the work, but it creates its own difficulties; in any event, this is not a viable solution for small farmers. Timing can therefore be expected to continue to be an obstacle to the development of extensive and stable multiple cropping systems.

If the various impediments to sustained increases in cropping intensities can be effectively reduced or removed, however, the benefits to small farmers and the agricultural sector as a whole could be considerable. Multiple cropping can virtually double the demand for labor and raise the net incomes of the poorest farmers by 30–60 percent.[9] An example of the possible net impact of multiple cropping systems on income is shown in table 4-11. Increases in incomes are low unless one moves beyond double cropping to triple and quadruple cropping, when increments of 50–100 percent are possible. I do not know how representative these data are, so it is difficult to predict the net increases in the incomes of small farmers. If a farmer has a very small holding and few off-farm employment opportunities, it may be necessary for him to move to higher cropping intensities simply to maintain a minimal income. Such a tendency is clearly evident from the data on cropping intensities on small farms in Bangladesh.[10]

It is reasonable to suppose that the total amount of labor used rises substantially with multiple cropping, but little empirical evidence is available on this point. Data from a sample of farmers in the Indian Punjab during the 1960s indicate that labor requirements rose faster than cropping intensities (Johl 1971). Evidence from northwestern India shows that when quadruple cropping increases production about threefold, the demand for labor rises about fivefold (Rajat and Bhardwaj 1974). Again, it is difficult to assess how representative these data are. But labor requirements also vary considerably with the type of water supply and with the kinds of crops, varieties, and cropping intensities. Canal irrigation requires twice the labor of tubewells, while water supply by persian wheels requires ten times more again (Singh, Day, and Johl 1968). When sugarcane is included in the rotation, labor requirements are far higher than with other crops. Improved crop varieties require more labor per unit of land (although not always per unit of output) than traditional varieties. Finally, the variation in incremental labor requirements widens as one moves from single to double and from double to triple cropping.

It is thus hard to assess how much additional employment could be generated if multiple cropping were adopted more widely. One such estimate for India suggests that about 17 million additional people could be employed directly, with an additional secondary and tertiary impact on employment in input services and transportation (Rajat and Bhardwaj 1974, p. 659).

It is not certain, however, how much the additional labor for multiple cropping would add to the number of jobs, and how much it would simply reduce the underemployment of existing farm labor. Experience in Pakistan shows that an increase in multiple cropping led to a less than comparable increase in the farm labor force, which suggests a substantial degree of previous underemployment (Cownie, Johnston, and Duff 1970). The same must certainly be true for India and Bangladesh. If labor requirements increase substantially, large operators (who have to hire labor) might find further increases in cropping intensity unattractive; on the other hand, small operators (who rely on their families' labor) might find them very profitable, especially where there are few off-farm jobs and consequently little or no loss of wage income if workers are needed on the family farm.

The extent of underemployment during much of the year, especially on small family farms, would be reduced. Farm management

Table 4-11. Northwestern India: Economics of Multiple Cropping Sequence

Cropping system	Crop	Rupees per hectare			Net profit index with base of single cropping	Benefit-cost ratio
		Gross income	Expenditure	Net profit		
Single cropping	Wheat	3,572	1,775	1,797	100	2.01
Double cropping	Wheat	3,420	1,775	1,645		
	Maize	2,200	1,813	387		
	Subtotal	5,620	3,588	2,032	113	1.57
Triple cropping	Green gram	1,000	636	364		
	Maize	2,200	1,813	387		
	Wheat	3,750	1,775	1,975		
	Subtotal	6,950	4,224	2,726	152	1.65

Maize	2,037	1,813	224		
Potato	4,954	3,055	1,899		
Onion	5,234	2,225	3,009		
Subtotal	12,225	7,093	5,132	286	1.72
Green gram	1,095	636	459		
Red gram	1,078	1,000	678		
Wheat	3,040	1,775	1,265		
Subtotal	5,813	3,411	2,402	134	1.70
Quadruple cropping					
Green gram	1,000	636	364		
Maize	2,200	1,813	387		
Potato	4,500	3,055	1,445		
Wheat	2,128	1,575	553		
Subtotal	9,828	7,079	2,749	153	1.39

Note: The table refers to the Northwest Plains zone comprising the states of Delhi, Haryana, Punjab, northeastern Rajasthan, and western Uttar Pradesh.

Source: Rajat and Bhardwaj (1974), p. 654.

studies in India have shown that as much as 25–30 percent of all family labor engaged in farming is not gainfully employed, because farm operations are not evenly spread over the year.[11] Multiple cropping clearly helps to shorten slack periods, but the problem of seasonal peaks in the demand for labor during planting and harvesting is likely to be exacerbated and may lead to mechanization (Billings and Singh 1970; Johl 1971; Day and Singh 1977). How much this will affect small farmers will depend on a host of factors. As noted earlier, mechanization is unlikely to be an option for this group in the short term. Eventually, however, some kind of labor-saving machinery for harvesting and planting operations will need to be developed for small farmers so that they can handle production bottlenecks.[12]

At any rate, multiple cropping promises to be more effective in creating employment and income for rural populations than either rural industries or rural work programs (discussed in chapters 6 and 7). Small farmers and the landless will be the most likely beneficiaries, if the delivery systems for fertilizers and water can meet their needs, and if appropriate solutions can be found for the other technological and management problems associated with multiple cropping.

Irrigation

Irrigation and controlled water management hold the key to increasing agricultural productivity in South Asia. Irrigation is essential for higher yields because it permits a shift to higher production functions; because the proper management of complex cropping systems calls for controlled water; because high-yielding varieties perform best under irrigated conditions; because irrigation reduces the risks associated with the variability of weather and monsoons; and because crops are more responsive to organic and inorganic fertilizers under irrigated conditions.

In India there is a clear inverse relationship between the size of holding and the area under irrigation. All farms in India taken together irrigated about 22 percent of their gross cropped area in 1970–71, but farms smaller than five acres irrigated significantly more—28 to 34 percent of their area (table 4-8). This relationship is much weaker in Pakistan. A far higher percentage of the total area was irrigated in 1972 (roughly 74 percent on all farms); for the smallest farms the irrigated percentage (65–75 percent) was not above the average (table 4-9). In Bangladesh a very small percentage of the area was irrigated (6–7 percent) and there were no substantial differences among farms of various sizes (table 4-10). By 1985, despite major investments in water development, irrigation covered no more than 22 percent of the cultivated area according to World Bank data.

Small farms may irrigate a higher proportion of their gross cropped area, but they account for only small proportions of the total irrigated areas of India and Pakistan. In India, farms of fewer than five acres accounted for 22 percent of the total irrigated area (and 19 percent of the cultivated area); in Pakistan for only 6 percent (5 percent of the cultivated area). In Bangladesh the figures are much higher, nearly 50 percent of the irrigated area (51 percent of the cultivated area).

The aggregate data show only that small farmers irrigate proportionately as much, if not more, than larger ones. They give no indication of the intensity of water use, the timing of the availability of water in farmers' fields, or the efficiency of water use once it gets to the fields. These issues are central to the problem of small farmers' access to irrigation.

We need to establish the extent of the unutilized potential for irrigation in the subcontinent and how much of this potential is likely to be made available to small farmers. There are two kinds of irrigation to be considered: surface irrigation, mainly through canals, and groundwater irrigation through wells and tubewells. Government studies indicate that there is considerable potential for increased irrigation from both these sources in South Asia (tables A18 and A19) subject to investment expenditures that may or may not be made. But despite this substantial potential for increased irrigation from both surface and groundwater, a number of factors may prevent small farmers from getting access to it.

With surface irrigation, the problems are:

- Lack of investment in farm-level tributary irrigation and proper field-level water courses and drainage systems. Old-style irrigation projects that left the development of secondary and tertiary systems to local authorities may have unwittingly biased the development of surface irrigation in favor of larger and better-off farmers.

- Lack of access to and control over water flows. Small farmers may be located fairly far downstream in the water distribution network and may not be able to get canal water released when they need it. Since timing is critical, especially in periods of drought or low rainfall, small farmers may suffer from being last in line to receive scarce water resources. Rationing during periods of scarcity is likely to benefit farmers who have good relations with the local authorities.

- Lack of credit for financing long-term on-farm investments such as water courses, drainage systems, and wells. This can be a special problem for sharecroppers and tenants who lack clear title

to the land they farm. Reliance on land and physical assets as collateral for long-term loans discriminates specifically against these
groups because they do not own such assets.

- Costs of water. Although not discriminatory, water rates can be
  prohibitive to the small farmer with little cash. Subsidizing water
  rates for small farmers is one solution but is not easy to administer.

With groundwater irrigation the problems are:

- Lack of investment funds or medium- and long-term credit to
  sink deep wells or put in tubewells.
- Economies of scale that militate against the use of private
  tubewells on small and fragmented holdings. Irrigation cooperatives can be established to overcome this problem, but organizations of this kind suffer from a problem endemic to cooperatives
  in general: the larger and better-off farmers end up controlling
  the system and getting most of the benefits.
- Lack of public wells and tubewells. A definite bias against
  smallholders and tenants who belong to lower castes restricts their
  use of existing public deep wells, and public tubewells that were
  installed to overcome the problems of lumpy investments have
  often turned out to benefit larger holders.
- Fragmentation of holdings prevents groundwater irrigation from
  being used to its best advantage.[13]

Where holdings are fragmented, cooperation between neighboring
farms is essential if wells are to be sunk and used productively. The
minimum economic area for well-water irrigation depends on how
the water is shared among farmers (see Dhawan 1977). Alternatively,
the operators of large fragments may install wells and sell water to
their neighbors, a solution that permits larger farmers to become monopoly suppliers of a scarce resource.

As I show in chapter 8, small farms are generally made up of fewer
parcels than larger farms. Nevertheless, fragmentation is a critical
problem, for a small farmer may be able to borrow only a little money
to install a well, and the investment cannot be spread effectively over
as many as six small parcels of land. Although other diseconomies
and inefficiencies are associated with the fragmentation of holdings,
the barriers to the effective use of groundwater are especially crip-
pling for the small farmer.

Smallholders are thus likely to get less than their share of increased
irrigation in the 1990s. Moreover, the further development of both
surface and groundwater irrigation systems faces real difficulties. In

India, for example, the actual use of irrigation systems lags far behind their completion. The government has introduced command area development (CAD) programs (see below) to improve the situation. The funding of such programs has not been easy, but the crucial constraint has been the time required to build the institutional framework to implement and administer the complex components of CAD schemes. An estimated 6.25 million acres was potentially irrigable from existing facilities by the end of the fifth plan (1974–79). In relation to the extent of the task, coverage by CAD projects has been modest—not more than 250,000 acres by 1985. Despite its ambitious plans, CAD cannot be expected to have a major impact on the gap between the potential created and its actual utilization for a long time.

In addition, the design and operating standards of existing and planned large and medium-size surface irrigation systems in India need to be upgraded if India's scarce water resources are to be used efficiently. Upgrading is of special concern since the introduction of high-yielding varieties, which require more water, and within more narrowly restricted periods, than do traditional varieties. Most of the irrigation systems built over the last 200 years were designed to deliver relatively small supplements to rainfall over a wide area to protect the crops. The systems generally lacked controlled structures to deliver water selectively when crops needed it. Furthermore, utilization efficiencies—that is, the proportion of the water entering the system that is beneficially used—are generally very low.

These difficulties have caused India to change its strategies for the development of surface irrigation. Initially, even when projects incorporated components to strengthen agricultural extension services or on-farm development, these features were largely ignored in practice. Experience with these earlier projects made it clear, however, that construction of irrigation infrastructure alone had little impact on agricultural output, and that the integration of irrigation and agriculture was essential to make better use of the water and to realize the anticipated benefits from projects more rapidly.

This conclusion led in the early 1970s to command area development, which constructs field channels and drains, and levels and shapes the land to ensure an effective and reliable water supply at the farm level. Some of the larger projects now involve 100,000 or more farmers, each of whom has to be dealt with individually. Before the actual work of land development can begin, the land records of every farmer must be updated, farm boundaries established, the land surveyed, and development plans prepared for loans from land development or commercial banks. As universal participation is essential, special arrangements must be made for providing finance from outside normal credit channels if a farmer's creditworthiness is in doubt. These arrangements are especially necessary for the small farmers included in the schemes.

The World Bank's experience with CAD has been mixed. The Rajasthan Canal project, which also included the reorganization of extension services, was very successful. This is an atypical example, however, since it was also a settlement project and hence involved no problems of land records and credit. In the Chambal project in Rajasthan and Madhya Pradesh, progress with CAD has been painfully slow, despite the special emphasis placed on organizational features associated with land tenure.

It is now generally agreed that if irrigation development is approached piecemeal, project by project, a significant program of on-farm works cannot be implemented, particularly in view of the estimated backlog of 25 million acres needing such works. To speed development, the problem is being approached on a statewide basis. It is believed that the solutions to organizational, administrative, financial, and legal problems associated with land development can be replicated across states.

Other breakthroughs have been to improve water use through better engineering design and to finance all works except land leveling from budgetary sources, thus bypassing credit institutions and ending the need for clear land titles. The main problems that remain have to do with cost recovery, either by raising water charges or by refinancing the budgetary portion of expenditures through credit institutions.

To what extent have small farmers benefited from surface irrigation, CAD or otherwise, in India? Areas have hitherto been earmarked for surface irrigation mainly on technical grounds, with preference being given to dry and drought-prone areas. These areas tend to have larger but very poor farms, which have considerable potential once they are irrigated. Traditionally, larger farmers (and particularly those at the head of a water course) have benefited most. Bringing the water supply to the farm level and financing irrigation schemes from budgetary sources rather than by credit should, however, greatly increase the participation of small farmers in the benefits of irrigation.[14]

To the extent that surface irrigation requires field channels, and to the extent that such investment requires valid and generally accepted land titles, both small farmers and tenants stand to gain little. The former lack the credit to invest in field channels, and the latter lack both credit and clear title to the land they cultivate. The inability of current organizational structures to deliver water from developed irrigation sources to small and tenant farmers is well known, but the reforms needed have not been defined satisfactorily.

Similarly, enormous problems exist in the development of ground-water potential. The major force in irrigation development in India has been private investment in open wells and tubewells. The number of open wells rose from about 3.6 million in 1956 to about 6.1 million in 1971 (India, Ministry of Agriculture and Irrigation 1976, pt. 5, p. 18); tubewells proliferated further in the wake of the new technologies. A private tubewell enables the cultivator to water his crops at the right time and with the required quantity—freedom of action of immense value.

In India at the end of the fourth plan (1969–73) there were some 6.8 million wells in use and about 4.1 million diesel and electric pumps. From the mid-1960s to the early 1970s this type of investment in irrigation added more to the irrigated area than all public programs combined. The government's role in this development has been mainly to provide rural electrification and medium-term credit.[15]

Private tubewell development has so far occurred mostly in Haryana, Punjab, Tamil Nadu, and western Uttar Pradesh—regions in which conditions are highly favorable for the adoption of seed-fertilizer-water technology in general and groundwater development in particular. If private tubewell development is to maintain its historical rate of growth, the impetus must now come from other areas.

One important geographical area that still has an untapped potential for large-scale groundwater development is India's eastern region, comprising Assam, Bihar, Orissa, eastern Uttar Pradesh, and West Bengal. But economic, climatic, and institutional conditions in the region provide relatively poor incentives for investment in tubewells. Agriculture is not highly productive and is based on traditional varieties of grain, mainly rice. Because existing rice varieties are neither as widely adaptable nor as broadly pest-resistant as the new wheat varieties, private investment in tubewells may be limited. Furthermore, because the area has fairly heavy rainfall, the need for irrigation is less obvious and the incremental benefits are few. The average size of holdings is small, so even the smallest private tubewell is a viable investment for relatively few farmers. In addition, the public infrastructure is not well developed in the eastern region. The area is not strong in cooperative or commercial credit institutions; consequently, credit for tubewell financing may be available, but there are few local institutions to channel funds to small farmers who might use them. Moreover, rural electrification is much less developed in the eastern region than elsewhere.[16]

A recent innovation in Bihar is a low-cost bamboo tubewell that irrigates five to ten acres. A large number of these were sunk in the districts of Purnea and Saharsa and were reported to perform well for more than four years. These low-cost tubewells hold great promise for rapid exploitation of groundwater where shallow aquifers exist, but how extensively they can be used is not known (India, Ministry of Agriculture and Irrigation 1976, pt. 5). Electric pumps for them are generally trouble-free, cheap, and easy to operate, but the low voltage in many areas of India means that they have not been used as effectively as they might have been. Moreover, a disproportionately small percentage of small farmers have access to electricity. Diesel pumps can be conveniently moved from one tubewell to another and can be rented; farmers thus save on capital costs, but the hourly operating costs are nearly double those of electric ones.

Pakistan has similar problems. Although irrigation systems have existed for centuries, recent developments have consisted mainly of large infrastructure projects designed to transfer water from western to eastern rivers. Some on-farm work has been undertaken to make water courses more efficient. As a result, farmers at the tail end of water courses (generally the smaller farmers) may now receive more reliable water supplies.

In Bangladesh, before independence in 1971, the emphasis was on large-scale flood control and gravity irrigation projects. These were costly and represented a poor allocation of scarce resources. Since independence the trend has been away from major infrastructure programs and toward simple, low-cost, quick-yielding minor irrigation projects. These newer projects have provided mainly low-lift pumps and tubewells.

Bangladesh has pioneered its own institutional arrangements for irrigation, and much of its groundwater has been reaching smaller farmers. Given the small size of most holdings in Bangladesh, it was essential to organize farmer groups to make the best use of minor irrigation facilities, which typically cover ten to fifty acres. Although there are few large farmers in Bangladesh, the relatively better-off farmers tend to dominate these groups. Evidence from the Northwest Tubewells project sponsored by the International Development Association (IDA), an affiliate of the World Bank, confirms this, although it also shows that small farmers have benefited significantly.

Recent World Bank projects have placed more emphasis on reaching small farmers. Under the Shallow Tubewells project, for example, if a farmer group is to be eligible for credit, "at least one-half of the proposed irrigated area must belong to farmers whose total holdings are less than three acres each." Even if programs with stipulations of this kind are fully successful, however, they cannot significantly reduce the inequalities between various segments of rural society or solve at a stroke the problems of improving small farmers' access to irrigation.

The relationship between access to groundwater and credit is well established in Bangladesh. Because of scale economies, smallholders must purchase tubewells as a group. The Thana Irrigation Program (TIP) is the only current example of this sort of arrangement in Bangladesh. The TIP begins with the formation of a pump group, which is encouraged to act as a cooperative and can expect to obtain credit to purchase tubewells. But according to Blair (1974), although a large proportion of the groups do become cooperatives, only a small proportion of the members obtain any loans. Possibly a few individuals take advantage of the program by padding their membership lists with nonexistent members. At least some of the groups are composed of farmers in a quasi-tenurial debt relationship to the group manager. Furthermore, because credit payments are made on the basis of irrigated area, farmers have no incentive to use water carefully. Though farmers are expected to assume all operating costs of the pumps for a five-year period, their operations were initially subsidized; moreover, the distribution of pumps has become "a distribution of favors."

The utilization of deep tubewells in Bangladesh was found to be positively related to the availability of cooperative credit and other inputs. The deep tubewells were rented to groups by the Bangladesh Agricultural Development Corporation. Although the groups included members with farms of all sizes, leadership rested mainly with medium and large cultivators. Because of the fragmentation of ownership holdings and lack of cohesiveness in the pump group, small farmers were not able to benefit. Myers (1973), quoting a study by A. H. Khan (1971) of a cooperative trying to take advantage of tubewell irrigation, reported that 24 percent of the cooperative's members received 62 percent of all loans. The larger landholders had greater indebtedness, and the larger the loan, the greater was the percentage of loan default. Khan found that the share of loans taken by management committee members (who were large farmers) was disproportionately large—managers made up 36 percent of all borrowers and received 65 percent of all loans.

To conclude, irrigation water is essential for raising small-farmer productivity, and the potential for expanding irrigation is substantial. Nevertheless, severe problems remain in ensuring that small farmers in the subcontinent will get a larger share of projected increases than in the past. Organizational arrangements designed to improve small farmers' access to both surface and groundwater irrigation are still in their infancy, and their success is far from assured.

Access to Credit, Markets, Research, and Extension

The sustained and substantial growth in small farmers' production of food grains depends critically on the increased use of purchased inputs—whether for multiple cropping or for the adoption of new high-yielding varieties (see the following section and chapter 5). Small farmers, however, typically have few if any financial resources for purchasing inputs. Hence they are in special need of agricultural credit. To what extent is credit in fact available to small farmers in South Asia, and does a lack of credit on reasonable terms seriously constrain their prospects for prosperity? The available data and some key policy issues relevant to the availability of credit are discussed below.

It might be possible to acquire cash to buy inputs by selling marketable surpluses. I have already shown that small farmers do in fact participate in the market economy. But is this participation currently limited by market distortions or other impediments, and can steps be taken to improve market access for small farmers? A brief overview of the evidence on small farmers' access to markets and related questions for policy is presented below.

Sources and Availability of Credit for Small Farmers

Credit can be obtained from both institutional sources (public agencies or banks) and noninstitutional sources (moneylenders, commission agents, friends, relations, and other private sources).[17] Institutional loans make up only a very small proportion of total agricultural credit (table 4-12), and they go to only 5–20 percent of all farmers. Noninstitutional sources provide 70–86 percent of the total volume of agricultural credit lending. In Bangladesh and Pakistan, all institutional loans come from public sources, while most noninstitutional credit is "noncommercial," that is, privately arranged through family or friends with interest rates and repayment terms that are hard to establish. In India, however, commercial credit predominates in the noninstitutional sector, and public institutions do not monopolize the institutional sector. Figure 4-3 shows the distribution of credit by country and by main source.

Small farmers rely particularly heavily on noninstitutional and noncommercial sources of credit, especially rural moneylenders and relatives (Reserve Bank of India 1976). Moreover, although small farmers account for a large proportion of the *number* of loans from all sources—51 percent in India, 73 percent in Bangladesh, and 40 percent in Pakistan—they account for a smaller proportion of the total *value* of lending—41 percent in India, 50 percent in Bangladesh, and only 23 percent in Pakistan (see figure 4-4).[18] And they pay much higher interest rates because they depend heavily on moneylenders, whose rates are two and a half to three times as high as those of institutional sources (table 4-13). There is little evidence on the interest rates charged by friends and relatives, the other major source of

Table 4-12. *South Asia: Estimated Distribution of Agricultural Loans by Type of Lender*

Item	Bangladesh	India	Pakistan
Institutional loans			
Percentage of farmers getting	15	20	5
Percentage of all agricultural credit	14	30	14
Percentage of all institutional loans			
Public	100	87	100
Private	0	13	0
Noninstitutional loans			
Percentage of all agricultural credit	86	70	86
Percentage of all noninstitutional loans			
Commercial	39	71	27
Noncommercial	61	29	73

Sources: Donald (1976); World Bank data.

credit for small farmers, but there is no reason to suppose that these rates are merely nominal.

Opinions differ on whether access to credit is a problem for small farmers. The traditional view is that it is indeed a considerable problem that hinders their adoption of new technologies. Abraham (1973) argues that special small-farmer credit agencies were set up in India largely to counter the bias of the institutional credit system against small farmers.[19]

Commercial banks have given small farmers better service since nationalization, but other institutional agencies remain strongly biased toward medium and large landholders. B. Sen (1974) points out that although credit from cooperative societies is supposedly available to large and small farmers alike, loans are granted in proportion to the share capital purchased. Consequently, even cooperatives set up to help small farmers end up discriminating against them. Small farmers' participation in the cooperatives' decisionmaking is limited; large farmers, with larger share purchases per acre, get more credit per acre from the cooperative movement. This problem is particularly serious because of the special role of cooperatives in fostering the spread of new technology for food-grain production. As Schluter (1973) pointed out, cooperative credit became important in the adoption of new technologies because traditional credit sources were unable or unwilling to meet the needs of small farmers and because farmers were unable or unwilling to use these sources owing to the high risks involved in taking up the new technologies. By contrast, cooperatives' more flexible arrangements for repayment made farmers more willing to take risks.

Figure 4-3. *South Asia: Sources of Agricultural Credit as a Percentage of Rural Borrowings*

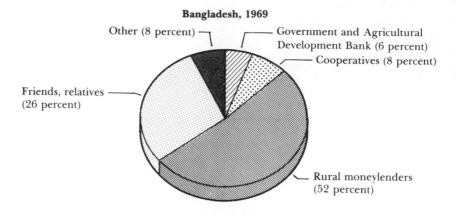

Bangladesh, 1969

Other (8 percent)

Government and Agricultural Development Bank (6 percent)

Cooperatives (8 percent)

Friends, relatives (26 percent)

Rural moneylenders (52 percent)

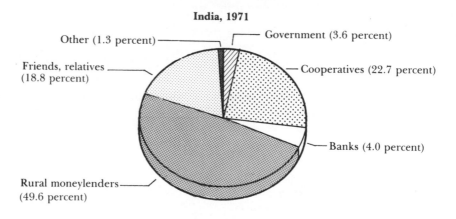

India, 1971

Other (1.3 percent)

Government (3.6 percent)

Friends, relatives (18.8 percent)

Cooperatives (22.7 percent)

Banks (4.0 percent)

Rural moneylenders (49.6 percent)

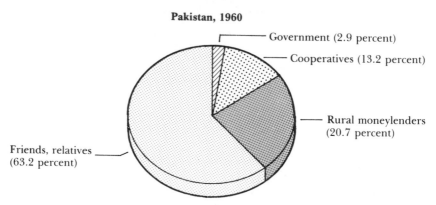

Pakistan, 1960

Government (2.9 percent)

Cooperatives (13.2 percent)

Rural moneylenders (20.7 percent)

Friends, relatives (63.2 percent)

Sources: Data for India are from the National Council of Applied Economic Research. Other data are from Tyers (1977); Surjit Bhalla in Berry and Cline (1979); the World Bank and the ILO; and Lowdermilk (1972).

Figure 4-4. *South Asia: Percentage Distribution of Loans by Farm Size, 1971–72*

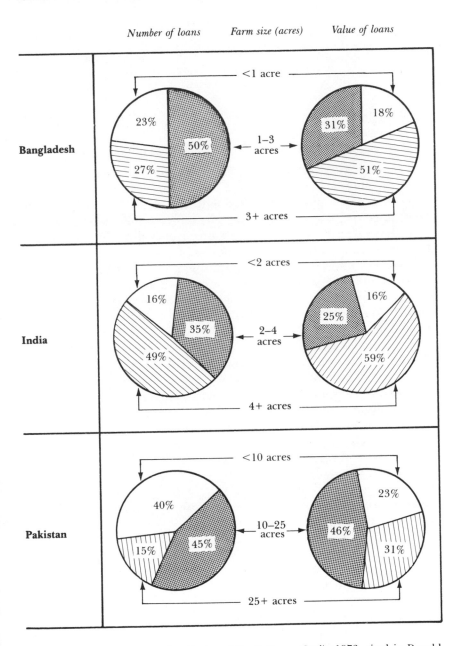

Source: Data from USAID *Spring Review of Small Farmer Credit*, 1973, cited in Donald (1976).

Table 4-13. *India: Average Rates of Interest by Farm Size and Sources*

Size of holding (acres)	Government	Cooperatives	Commercial banks	Money-lenders	Friends, relatives	All sources
0–5	8.9	8.9	7.2	22.5	n.a.	16.0
5–10	9.0	9.1	8.1	20.9	n.a.	14.3
10–15	8.3	9.0	9.4	23.3	n.a.	14.9
15+	8.4	9.0	9.2	16.3	n.a.	9.0
All holdings	8.8	9.0	8.4	21.8	n.a.	14.8

n.a. Not available.

Sources: Surjit Bhalla in Berry and Cline (1979); World Bank and ILO data.

C. H. H. Rao (1970) used evidence from the All-India Rural Credit Survey to show that small farmers had higher indebtedness than did large farmers, despite the fact that between 1962–63 and 1967–68 the percentage increase in credit taken by large farmers was far greater than that taken by small ones. Small farmers did get a better deal from large cooperative societies than from other sources, but the prevailing high interest rates in the free market gave large farmers an incentive to obtain credit from cooperatives and to re-lend these borrowings to smaller farmers. By taking up the lion's share of lending, large farmers actually shifted the burden of high interest rates to small ones.

Surjit Bhalla (in Berry and Cline 1979), looking at data from the All-India Debt and Investment Survey (1971–72), found that small farmers had relatively few assets to offer as collateral and relatively low discretionary income out of which to make repayments. He found data to support the assertion that as farm size rose, the cost of capital fell. Furthermore, institutional lenders were heavily biased toward HYV users, who were considered a better risk than farmers who used traditional crop varieties; thus loans for fertilizer for HYV were made available at low interest rates. Other evidence on problems of access to credit and their consequences for small-farmer productivity has been cited by Wills (1972) in Uttar Pradesh, Rajpurohit (1972) in Mysore, and Frankel (1971) in the Punjab.

Similar problems have been noted by Gotsch (1971) for Pakistan. He found that cooperatives in Pakistan had failed to provide adequate help to the small-scale sector. Contributory causes included the monopoly of institutions by large farmers, the diversion of funds to finance more lucrative ventures in towns, the failure to provide any kind of business management at the local level, and the cooperatives' inability to recover outstanding debts. In another study, Gotsch (1973) found that most programs aimed at making capital markets more responsive to small farmers' needs had been almost entirely ineffective. Creating local institutions to serve the weaker sections of the farming community had proved very difficult. Meanwhile, the direct distribution of government-subsidized credit encouraged the socially and politically powerful to try to secure the available funds for themselves. When credit was disbursed indirectly through organizations of farmer representatives, the disproportionate power of large cultivators undermined the objective of assisting small farmers.

M. H. Khan (1975), also citing evidence from Pakistan, showed that the percentages of farmers reporting debt and borrowing for production rose with farm incomes. He found that institutional loans made by the Agriculture Development Bank of Pakistan (ADBP) and cooperatives went mostly to farmers holding more than twenty-five acres, while most small farmers and the landless depended on friends and relatives for credit. He concluded that access to the gains from the new technologies was biased in favor of large commercial farmers at the expense of subsistence farmers, because the former were able to get the credit to purchase the appropriate inputs. Amjad (1972) pointed out that government credit was extended mainly to large farmers because small farmers could not provide security for loans. When he examined data from the ADBP for 1970–71 he found that the landless got 5.5 percent of all loans made, while farmers with between one and three acres got less than 0.5 percent; farmers with between three and twelve acres received 7.6 percent; and those with more than twelve acres received 86 percent. Further, he found that small farmers had trouble obtaining fertilizer and seeds because they had no way to pay premium prices for these inputs.[20]

Similar evidence can be found for Bangladesh. Bose (1974a), in a study of the Comilla cooperatives, found that large farmers got disproportionately large shares of credit, even though they defaulted more often than others. Better-off farmers sometimes used cooperative loans to buy and lease land rather than for production as the loans were intended. Even though the cooperative movement in Bangladesh had given small farmers some degree of economic and political power, the cooperatives had not yet become "trade unions of the small farmers" as initially envisaged. On the available evidence, Bose felt that a replication of the Comilla cooperative credit model could not ensure the diffusion of agricultural technology with a reasonably equal distribution of benefits.

Similarly, Rochin (1973) found both that credit was insufficient and that farmers in Bangladesh used credit for personal consumption rather than production purposes. Faidley and Esmay (in Stevens, Alavi, and Bertocci 1976) noted that the cooperatives' lending policies excluded those owning less than one acre. Cooperative members came mainly from farms larger than one acre, and since members controlled the operation of tubewells and pumps, they were able to irrigate a larger proportion of their farm land than nonmembers (who tended to have less than one acre or no land at all).

Credit and New Agricultural Technologies

How does one reconcile this litany of small-farmer credit woes with the extensive evidence on the adoption of new technologies by small farmers?[21] Obviously, small farmers must have been able to get cash or credit from somewhere to purchase the nonfarm inputs they have used. The answer is twofold: first, small farmers have turned to non-institutional sources (moneylenders, friends, or relatives) for credit; second, with the advent of new technologies, institutional sources have been more willing to provide credit to small farmers who adopt them. Thus, although new technologies have increased the demand for credit by small farmers, the supply has also increased considerably.

This point is well exemplified in the cultivation of HYV food crops— the new technology most frequently cited as increasing output and income. Data for India reviewed by Surjit Bhalla (in Berry and Cline 1979) suggest that small farmers who cultivate HYVs obtain a larger proportion of their credit from institutional sources than those who do not (table A20). The former account for 17 percent of all government loans, 9 percent of commercial bank loans, and 8 percent of moneylender loans. By contrast, non-HYV small farmers account for only 9 percent of government loans and 3 percent of bank loans, but 33 percent of moneylender loans. The proportions of small-farmer loans extended by cooperatives and noncommercial sources do not differ significantly by type of crop cultivated.

As table A21 shows, Surjit Bhalla found the differences in the cost of credit to HYV and non-HYV farmers to be most pronounced for small farmers: within this group, HYV growers paid an average of about 14 percent interest, non-HYV growers nearly 19 percent.

In Pakistan, Lowdermilk (1972) showed that although the majority of small farmers reported that the shortage of funds was a major constraint on nutrient use, this constraint seems to be felt less the higher the mean level of nutrient use.

Underlying the question of the absolute availability of credit are some more fundamental issues related to production systems and their profitability for small farmers. Both the farmer and his creditors must perceive that production with the new technologies will earn an appropriate return before he can obtain and make good use of credit. This in turn means that a number of conditions need to be fulfilled if credit programs are to be successful.

First, the inputs (such as seed and fertilizer) or improvements (for example, irrigation) financed by any credit arrangement must offer yield increases that are large enough to persuade risk-averse small farmers to depart from previous practices and to use credit to adopt new ones. Inputs and improvements that meet this condition are available in South Asia, and many small farmers are profiting from them. I have already discussed the yield improvements obtainable with multiple cropping and irrigation; data on the output and income gains from HYV adoption are given in chapter 5.

Second, the market has to offer the small farmer substantial returns on his borrowed capital. This means that he will be interested in questions of price—both the prices he must pay for inputs and the prices he can get for his marketed surplus. He will be concerned not only with relative price levels, but also with the risks and uncertainties of price changes in the market (this issue is discussed further below). Since substantial numbers of small farmers in South Asia have adopted new cropping practices and technologies, one can conclude that the relative prices of inputs and products, discounted for risks, have seemed to them to be favorable.[22]

Third, shortages of inputs at critical stages in the production process can ruin any credit program. In most cases, however, this problem is less important than the first two—yields and prices—because it is better understood and more easily controlled.

Fourth, delinquency and default can adversely affect credit programs. There is some controversy about whether small farmers typically have high rates of delinquency and default, but high rates seem generally to be associated with technologies that offer low yields and cash returns. There is not enough evidence, however, to determine with any real certainty whether changing farming practices and the advent of the new technologies have lowered default and delinquency rates among small farmers.[23] There is some evidence that households with larger families and higher dependency ratios are more prone to default, and these are more often than not households with larger holdings (Bhende 1986).

Fifth, for all but the poorest small farmers, credit may be unnecessary for the purchase of some inputs, such as seed and fertilizer packages (which require no single large outlay). The absence of medium- and long-term credit probably does, however, inhibit the widespread and rapid adoption of farm equipment and land improvements. Water pumps, for example, may be beyond a small farmer's self-financing capacity.

Sixth, the source of credit is an important consideration. Private credit systems, formal and informal, have largely met the modest demand for credit generated by small farmers, especially in the first phase of the adoption process. But these systems tend to have relatively inelastic supplies. Exclusive reliance on the informal sector will almost certainly slow the rate at which new technologies are adopted. Moreover, although private sources of credit will usually respond to profitable opportunities for investment, their interest rates may be so high that they discourage small farmers from borrowing. Public and institutional sources then become essential. Furthermore, it is important that institutional credit be available to compete against the monopoly of private lenders.

But let us not underrate the resilience or the utility of private moneylenders—the stereotypical villains of many discussions of credit problems. Whatever their putative vices of exploitation and extortion, moneylenders remain a key source of rural credit. Attempts to displace them by, for example, competing through lower interest rates have been relatively unsuccessful, which suggests that they perform useful services. Credit administrators tend too often to judge credit schemes exclusively in terms of rates of interest and to overlook other features such as simple procedures, flexibility, and timeliness. Although they charge higher interest rates, informal sources of credit may have better information about their communities and provide better services than institutional lenders.

Interest Rates and Interest Subsidies

Are the interest rates charged by some or all lenders too high for small farmers?[24] The evidence seems to suggest the opposite if small farmers can borrow at the rates they do without serious defaults.

Should agricultural credit be subsidized, especially by the institutional sector? The traditional view is that small farmers are especially in need of subsidized credit and low interest rates. It is argued that farmers are sensitive to changes in interest rates and that low rates are necessary to induce them to use credit for productive investments.[25] But small farmers are accustomed to and undeterred by high interest rates, and they appear willing to invest when profitable opportunities are available. Thus the case for low interest rates may be based on borrowers' welfare rather than on economic efficiency.[26]

Artificially low interest rates create problems for credit institutions. If they do not cover operating expenses or the cost of technical supervision, they may lead to portfolio losses and jeopardize the overall financial integrity of credit institutions. And they encourage institutions to maximize earnings by concentrating their lending on relatively reliable and prosperous farmers, particularly those with collateral. Thus the bulk of the small-farm sector is excluded, and one of the principal proclaimed purposes of low rates (giving small farmers access to credit) is defeated by the low-rate policy itself.

Adams (1973) has effectively argued that low interest rate policies defraud small farmers and do them more harm than good. He insists that more rational interest rates are essential in the field of small-farmer finance. He has also argued (and supporting evidence is available) that higher interest rates could stimulate a much greater growth of financial savings in the rural sector than is generally thought possible.[27]

Those who argue against raising interest rates point to the distortions in the input and output commodity markets in which small farmers operate and suggest that increasing interest rates is unlikely to improve the economic efficiency of these markets. They also argue that it is appropriate for institutions to charge much lower rates than moneylenders because the latter offer more or better services; that the hypothesized effect of high interest rates on the supply of commercial credit and rural savings is still untested except in a few countries; and that governments, politicians, farmers, and others support low interest rates, and their views are not likely to be easily overcome.

There are legitimate reasons for subsidizing small farmers: to redistribute income to them from other sectors; to maintain subsistence levels, especially among those with so few resources that greater access to (or even the free availability of) new technology would not make their farms viable; and to encourage production and the adoption of new technology on potentially viable farms. It is arguable, however, whether credit mechanisms should be used to promote these goals. If subsidies are deemed necessary on broad policy grounds, they should be incorporated in the price of services and supplies rather than in the price of credit. Subsidizing credit distorts credit markets, creates false opportunity costs that are artificially below their real economic levels, and leads to large farmers borrowing funds to invest in virtually useless enterprises.[28]

Credit and Uncertainty

Small farmers face many uncertainties that significantly affect the extent to which they will seek credit in order to adopt new technologies. In particular, those living at or near the margin of subsistence can be prevented from incurring debt by great uncertainty about crop yields and prices. The credit needed for even highly productive on-farm investments will therefore be sought only if these uncertainties are reduced (Naidu 1964).

Yield is probably the most serious area of uncertainty for small

farmers. The new technologies consistently show greater yield variations than do traditional methods of cultivation. If the weather is bad
and irrigation and water control systems are not available, HYVs sometimes yield even less than traditional varieties. Consequently, farmers
in areas with uncertain rainfall keep a relatively high percentage of
their crop area under drought-resistant crops or grow a mixture of
crops. Farmers must also consider the possible incidence of floods,
pests, disease, and even wars, all of which might adversely affect
yields. Crop insurance programs hold some promise for spreading
the weather risks faced by farmers, but these must be applied with
great care. The more successful credit programs normally provide
technical assistance to overcome local differences in yields.

Prices of inputs or products are also of concern to the farmer. They
fluctuate from year to year, yet the farmer must predict specific values
for each crop before the crop season. Kahlon and Johl (1964) found
that in the Indian Punjab farmers varied their cropped acreage according to price and yield fluctuations, and risks were anticipated by
a fund that grew larger with the use of new technologies. Government
price guarantees may help; price policies are also subject to change
even during the crop year, but they directly affect the profitability of
new technologies and are especially needed for small farmers who are
highly risk-averse. The most successful credit programs have been
supported by price policies which reduce the variability of input and
product prices to the farmer.

Organizational Aspects of Access to Credit

The way in which credit flows are organized can make access to it difficult for small farmers. As has been noted, the power structure in
rural societies is often heavily biased against the interests of small
farmers; consequently, the objectives of credit programs can all too
easily be frustrated unless the government is prepared to intervene.
Gotsch (1973) has made this point repeatedly and convincingly for
Pakistan.

Another much-debated question is whether it is better to organize
special new credit agencies for small farmers (such as the Small
Farmer Development Agency and the Marginal Farmer Agency in
India) or to reorient the existing organizational structure to serve
small farmers' needs. The evidence shows that the organizational
form in which credit is supplied seems to matter less than economic
questions related to technology and farm-level profitability (see Rice
1973; S. R. Bose 1974a; Schluter 1973; Stepanek 1973; Solaiman and
Huq 1973; Tinnermeir and Dowsell 1973).

A third organizational issue is the demonstrated need for programs to handle a large number of small-farmer clients and do it cheaply. High levels of administrative skills, low-cost credit delivery, efficient supervision and collection methods, and access to a large supply of funds are all needed. Decentralized agencies seem to perform best; in particular, private cooperatives have some outstanding features such as local participation, group sanctions against delinquency, and the ability to provide scarce technical training.

It is sometimes suggested that the problem of efficiently serving large numbers of small farmers could be solved simply by encouraging private moneylenders to continue. The advantages of the moneylender include low overhead and other administrative costs, and a personal familiarity with clients that can substantially reduce the rate of default. Reliance on moneylenders as conduits for credit would, however, perpetuate the status quo in two unsatisfactory respects: credit would continue to flow predominantly to the most solvent and progressive farmers and the current concentration of economic power would be reinforced rather than reduced.

That well-designed and well-managed credit programs targeted to the rural poor can be implemented is borne out by the experience of the Grameen Bank in Bangladesh. This bank originated as a private action-research project in one area near Chittagong University to supply capital to the poor without collateral. It was formally established in 1983 and has been an enormous success. By 1987 it had 298 branches and some 250,000 borrower-shareholders, and at the end of 1986 its loans outstanding were 301 million taka. The loans are given to even the most disadvantaged groups (women account for 69 percent of all loans) and are used mainly for noncrop activities such as livestock and poultry raising, trading, processing, and shopkeeping. The bank has succeeded in reaching its target group, the rural poor. Only some 4 percent of its members belong to households that own a half acre or more of cultivable land, while 60 percent belong to agricultural-labor households. The loan repayments have been excellent—only 0.5 percent of loans surveyed in 1985 were overdue—a record that destroys the myth that the rural poor default on their credit or are unable or unwilling to repay. The success is attributed to the ability of the bank to lend only to the really needy, to its strong management, and to the dedicated commitment of its staff; but it is also due to the fact that loans were only for income-generating activities and that repayments were scheduled in small amounts suited to the borrowers' ability to repay. The Grameen Bank shows how unorthodox banking, not based on collateral (the landless and the poor have none), can be made to work if there is a commitment to the program. A comprehensive review of the Grameen Bank's performance is provided by Hossain (1988).

Small Farmers' Access to Markets

Farm management studies in India have shown that 80–90 percent of total output on farms smaller than five acres is kept for home consumption.[29] Nevertheless, small farmers do participate in local product and labor markets. So-called subsistence farmers, who are isolated from local factor and product markets and supply their own minimal needs, simply do not exist in South Asia (see chapters 6 and 7, and Lele 1971).

The mere fact of market participation is not enough, however. If farmers (including small farmers) are to have the incentive and the funds to invest in raising their productivity, they need to be served by efficient marketing systems for the output they sell. Do rural markets in South Asia meet this need, or are they beset with distortions and other problems?

Some marketing problems may apply equally to small and large farmers. All farmers may suffer from being tied to particular market outlets because of credit or other service obligations. The efficiency of a market depends critically on infrastructure and information; if these are lacking, rural markets become costly for all farmers.

It has been suggested, however, that small farmers are especially prone to victimization by a so-called marketing connection made up of middlemen and petty traders, whom all governments in South Asia have castigated as exploiters and hoarders. The little verifiable evidence available on the working of marketing systems in South Asia does not support this image, at least in India.

The most extensive and detailed work in this area is by Lele (1972, 1974, 1976). She states that the "efficiency" of marketing systems depends on the availability and quality of their physical infrastructure, financial institutions, communication networks, and entrepreneurial and managerial manpower.[30] The extent to which individual contractual relationships between buyers and seller incorporate arrangements which substitute for these market features is a reflection of the pervasive inadequacy of many local markets. Traditional market systems in subsistence agriculture typically suffer from inadequate transport and storage facilities, lack of standardization in weights and measures, poor dissemination of information, a large number of intermediaries, and inadequate finance for trading. These problems affect all farmers, although small ones are especially hard hit by the costs they impose.

Nevertheless, Lele (1972) provides extensive evidence to refute the view that traditional rural markets encourage high and monopolistic profits for traders at the expense of small farmers. She found that although "strong bargaining positions" are enjoyed by some traders, monopolistic profits are usually ruled out by the large number of intermediaries. The high profits earned by a few traders are due to their large scale of operations or their command over scarce capital, not to a specific monopoly position. Furthermore, traders are well informed about prices and demand through local contacts even though they lack good information on overall stocks and supply conditions.

Regional and intraregional disparities in input and output prices are often cited as conclusive evidence of monopoly returns. Lele found, however, that prices of comparable varieties did not differ by more than the costs of shipment from one region or intraregional locality to another. The margins between primary and wholesale markets, which show marked seasonality, can be attributed mainly to the availability of transport during the pre- and postharvest periods. Price differences are then a consequence of general market imperfections and not of monopolistic advantages accruing to particular individuals or groups.

Seasonal price variations also reflect real changes in demand and in supply prices (which are strongly influenced by the costs of storage). The storage costs of food grains are often not covered by a rise in off-season prices; traders consequently turn their stocks over rapidly rather than capitalize on the full differences between the postharvest low purchase and the preharvest high sale price as is usually assumed.

Governments have nevertheless intervened extensively "to correct the imperfections" in marketing systems, in the belief that they are acting in the interest of farmers, especially small farmers. The results have been dismal. Black markets have often developed in essential inputs and outputs, thereby reducing the quantities traded on open markets, increasing marketing costs (especially in small markets), and adding illegitimate charges to regular costs, all to the special detriment of small farmers. Each of the various expedients tried has proved to have major flaws.

Lele (1976) has shown that government-controlled markets have not been more efficient than the private markets they were designed to replace. She found that the effective weighted average prices of the controlled and uncontrolled marketed surpluses were not significantly different and that, contrary to the popular view, the marketing margins of government and parastatal agencies were almost *higher* than those of traditional traders. Thus government regulations have typically led to illicit trade that has raised both marketing costs and the number of intermediaries involved.

Officially sponsored procurement systems have similarly been no boon to small farmers. Large commercial farmers have evaded the systems, while the politically less powerful small farmers have been their victims.[31] Lele notes that the lower effective weighted average prices earned by small farmers from sales of their marketed surplus to government agencies seem particularly paradoxical because these surpluses are usually distributed to urban consumers with relatively high incomes.

Price controls may not be very helpful to most farmers. If prices are set on the basis of new technologies, they discriminate against farmers who use less productive, traditional technologies. This problem becomes especially acute if new inputs are highly subsidized or if the majority of farmers do not have access to new technologies. More generally, however, the inelastic demand for food grains (and the consequent instability of prices) impinges much more heavily on large commercial farmers, who market a relatively large share of their output, than on small farmers. Therefore price stabilization programs, though they may be desirable on other grounds, may offer less to small farmers than is often assumed.

Marketing cooperatives have often been seen as a solution to the perceived exploitation of small farmers in the marketing of agricultural produce. But, as noted above, this exploitation may be more perceived than real. Lele (1977) found that differences in the prices received by small and large farmers in a given market are far less significant than those between markets with and without adequate transport connections. In addition, traders (like moneylenders) seem to provide important services to small producers—services that cannot be replaced by government programs and cooperatives except at substantially greater costs. Traders function in the least accessible areas and meet the small producers' credit needs (often including consumption credit). The timely availability and flexibility of badly needed credit explain why small farmers often turn to traders, even when cooperative marketing channels are available. Thus the marketing connection may have real benefits for small farmers, and there is little hard evidence of its exploitative elements, despite their wide notoriety.

Cooperatives may be effective in selling inputs when their market margins are fixed by government policy. But pushing cooperative development too rapidly may be counterproductive because it frequently becomes a haven for subsidies (Lele 1977). Furthermore, marketing cooperatives are likely to suffer from problems similar to those of credit cooperatives—poor management, financial instability, and subversion by powerful interests (usually of large farmers).

No soundly based empirical studies are available on the operation of rural marketing systems in Pakistan and Bangladesh. Anecdotal material suggests, however, that these systems have serious problems, including inefficient handling, marketing, and processing; inadequate storage; outmoded sales practices; and lack of marketing cooperatives. In Pakistan, large farmers are said to have an advantage in marketing because they sell through so-called nonfixed contracts which small farmers cannot utilize.

These suppositions notwithstanding, the evidence of bias against small farmers in markets is scanty and unverifiable. At least on the basis of available data from India, it is hard to support the contention that small farmers suffer from problems of market access that differ significantly from those facing all farmers.

Notes

1. For a fuller and more detailed examination of the points made in this chapter, see Singh (1988b).

2. This is not generally true everywhere, but in India extension systems can rely on an accumulation of agronomic research, especially for irrigated crops. The position is less clear-cut for Bangladesh and Pakistan, where adaptive agronomic research is not of such long standing.

3. The following yields (tons per hectare) were reported by Michael Baxter in 1981 (unpublished World Bank manuscript):

	Beneficiaries of recent irrigation	Other nearby farmers with irrigation for more than five years	Farmers in other irrigated areas with good extension
Paddy HYV	2.3	2.9	5.7
Wheat HYV	2.3	3.0	3.0
Sugarcane	37.5	41.2	60–80

4. The Bangladesh Rice Research Institute has identified some 4,500 varieties of rice and considers these to be only half the actual number in use by smallholders.

5. See table 4-7 for a definition of the multiple cropping index. A similar but slightly different measure is cropping intensity, which is the ratio of gross cropped area (net area sown plus areas sown more than once) to cultivated area. See Dalrymple (1971, pp. 1–8) for some definitional problems in measuring multiple cropping.

6. More than thirty years ago Indian scientists developed a simple method of fermenting cow dung to yield methane for use as fuel and nitrogen-enriched slurry for use as fertilizer and as a starter for compost heaps. Mixing the resulting manure with small quantities of urea and superphosphates produced a fertilizer with twice as much efficiency per gram of nutrient as urea alone. But in the 1960s the glamour of chemical fertilizers blinded users to the virtues of such simple and cheap methods of soil enrichment. They were remembered when price rises in 1974 put chemical fertilizers out of the reach of all but the richest Indian farmers. The untapped potential in the subcontinent for the use of cow dung to produce both fuel and soil-enriching organic fertilizers is enormous; it needs to be further developed, especially for small farms that lack the cash to buy either fuel or chemical fertilizers.

7. In northeastern India, for example, there is plentiful rain, but it has not been possible to sow wheat in addition to rice because the paddy takes

at least five and a half months to mature and harvesting is seldom completed before the middle of December. Similarly, in Bihar and eastern Uttar Pradesh, the nursery beds are planted in June and the seedlings are not ready to be transplanted until late July or early August. As a result, the crop does not ripen until late autumn, when the days are relatively short and the nights are cold, so that a second crop is not possible.

8. In the case of certain kharif crops in India, a delay of one week in sowing reportedly delays crop maturity by two weeks or more. See A. S. Kahlon (1970).

9. Returns from multiple cropping are highly variable; they depend partly on the frequency of cropping and partly on the crops included. Although the net returns per unit of land have decreased in a few cases, they are more likely to increase and then taper off as cropping intensities rise. Aside from the considerable evidence from the Philippines and Taiwan available in publications from the International Rice Research Institute (IRRI), a detailed study in India showed that when the index of returns was set at 100 for double cropping, triple cropping produced an index of 149 while quadruple cropping had an index of 191. (See Singh and Choubey 1969; Swaminathan 1972.) There is also some evidence that increased returns are in part a function of management skill (Dalrymple 1971, p. 52).

10. See Phukan (1972), S. L. Shah and R. Singh (1970), C. H. H. Rao (1975), and Pakistan, Ministry of Agriculture and Works (1968) for studies verifying the inverse relationship between farm size and cropping intensities.

11. Similarly, bullocks are not used during more than half of the year (see Dalrymple 1971).

12. The successful development of mechanized equipment at IRRI to suit the needs of rice farming systems is an example that will need to be duplicated in the subcontinent.

13. In India this problem has been frequently cited as a major barrier to the proper development of well irrigation. Legislation for the consolidation of holdings exists in most states, but only Haryana, Punjab, and Uttar Pradesh have begun consolidation, and only 89 million acres have been consolidated (20 percent of these states' cropped area). See chapter 8 for a general discussion of issues related to fragmentation of holdings.

14. For example, in the Orissa Irrigation project, 75 percent of the 30,000 farm families who were expected to benefit owned less than five acres.

15. Although not all investments in tubewell development have been financed by institutional credit, estimates of flows of funds through publicly controlled agricultural credit institutions tend to confirm that private tubewell development accelerated from the mid-1960s to the early 1970s. After that there was a decline, and only in the 1980s has the momentum been restored. The decline after 1970–71 did not reflect any shift in public policy. In fact it has been argued that agricultural credit institutions were further expanded and strengthened after the mid-1960s and that subsidies were eliminated before private tubewell development reached high rates of growth. The availability of credit for tubewell development has not been a problem; the slowdown appears instead to have been a function of decreased

demand for these funds on the part of farmers generally. Whether or not credit has been a particular problem for small farmers is not known, however.

16. At the end of the fourth plan (1969–73), 17 percent of the villages in the eastern region, including Uttar Pradesh, had electricity, compared with 37 percent in the rest of India and 27 percent in the northern region.

17. There is an extensive literature on issues related to credit for small farmers. See, for example, Donald (1976), which summarizes the *Spring Review of Small Farmer Credit* by the the U.S. Agency for International Development (USAID). See also Rice (1973); World Bank (1975); Tinnermeir and Dowsell (1973); and Braverman and Guasch (1986).

18. The size classes used for this comparison differ from those in the rest of this book: small farms in Pakistan are those up to ten acres in size (much larger than elsewhere in this book); small farms in Bangladesh are those up to three acres (much smaller than elsewhere in this book).

19. The special agencies are the Small Farmer Development Agency and the Marginal Farmer Agency. See Mavinkurve and Sundernathan (1975) for an extensive discussion of the role of these agencies.

20. An interesting feature of both the Pakistan and Indian data is that the lack of credit does not appear to be a binding constraint in the early phases of the adoption of new technologies. See Rochin (1971) and Lowdermilk (1972) on Pakistan. It appears to be after the new technologies have taken off that credit becomes a major problem.

21. See chapter 5 for an extensive discussion of the Green Revolution and HYV adoption. Here we deal only with the linkage between HYV cultivation and other new sources of higher output, such as multiple cropping and access to credit.

22. Since both prices and yields affect profits and therefore the success of credit programs, higher crop prices can compensate the farmer for lower yields. There is always a policy choice between raising administered prices and promoting new technology. Where new technologies are available, however, it is preferable in the long run to adopt a technology-based strategy for raising incomes rather than one based on pricing.

23. The evidence fails to distinguish between three different types of credit: a direct income transfer through debt write-offs or subsidized interest to increase small farmers' welfare, credit for consumption purposes, and production credit. Some credit programs are based on the assumption that no increase in production is to be expected from the provision of credit. They thus use credit as an income transfer; default rates are expected to be high, and are high. Credit for consumption poses more difficult problems because for farm households it cannot be easily separated from production credit. Equally, credit provided ostensibly for production can replace the farmer's own resources, which in turn can be used for consumption.

24. Simple comparisons of the gross rates charged by different sources may, however, tell us little. Bottomley (1963, 1964a, b, and c, 1973) has consistently argued that rural rates of interest have several component parts: the pure interest rate, the administrative premium, the risk premium, and the monopoly profit. From the point of view of the borrower, pure interest rates

differ little between institutional and noninstitutional sources. The administrative and risk premiums, however, are significant in credit to small farmers. Although some amount of monopoly profit remains, this element is far less than is often suggested. Bottomley has shown that blanket attempts by governments to finance the status quo at low rates of interest will not succeed. What is needed is a change in technology and a substantial reduction in risk premiums. He has further shown that it actually takes a technology-induced *increase* in the demand for productive loanable funds to bring about a lower rate of interest (Bottomley 1973).

25. Some research suggests an opposite view, on the hypothesis that if institutional interest rates were raised from, say, the average current rate of 5 percent to 20 percent, there would be few losses in terms of program goals and some major gains for small farmers. See especially the papers by Dale Adams, Claudio Gonzalez Vega, Millard Long, P. E. Church, and T. F. Carroll and I. J. Singh, all done for the *USAID Spring Review of Small Farmer Credit* (Washington, D.C., 1973).

26. A distinction is often drawn between the welfare or equity objectives of credit programs and their production objectives. No one can deny that credit programs are often set up for welfare objectives or that governments have a right to establish such objectives. No one can say that consumption credit is never justifiable or that credit programs are not a convenient way of transferring income. The real problem occurs when a conflict arises between welfare and production objectives within the same program. This conflict often creates problems both for the effectiveness of the program and for the evaluation of its success. Welfare or consumption credit at low interest rates must be seen as an income transfer.

27. For evidence from Taiwan, see Adams, Ong, and Singh (1975).

28. This argument does not invalidate the utility of subsidies to credit institutions (as opposed to beneficiaries), which may play a useful role in covering any initial deficits of young institutions.

29. See studies on the "Economics of Farm Management" carried out in various districts by the Directorate of Economics and Statistics, Ministry of Food and Agriculture, Delhi.

30. An "efficient" marketing system is one that provides a timely supply of inputs, distributes seasonally produced outputs to processors and consumers at a minimum cost, mobilizes market surpluses in the short run, and integrates local markets with national markets. See Lele (1974).

31. Large farmers in India have always succeeded in getting higher procurement prices than those recommended by the Agricultural Prices Commission and have evaded producer levies. See C. H. H. Rao (1975) for evidence.

5

The Rural Poor and the Green Revolution

The new technologies associated with the adoption of high-yielding varieties (HYVs) offer an unprecedented opportunity for raising small farmers' output and incomes. Nevertheless, the spread of these technologies—popularly known as the Green Revolution—has been accompanied by a growing chorus of criticism that focuses less on the real gains for the rural poor and more on the supposedly negative implications for income distribution and agrarian structures.

It is argued that small farmers have adopted HYV technologies to a relatively minor extent because they lack access to the necessary inputs, especially fertilizers, and that the gains from the introduction of HYVs have gone disproportionately or even exclusively to larger farmers (Griffin and Ghose 1979; Frankel 1971). Some critics even suggest that these technologies are not viable within the present agrarian structure in South Asia and that the rural poor stand to lose rather than gain from them (Dasgupta 1977a). Much of this criticism is misplaced and stems from an inadequate understanding of the technologies themselves and an improper interpretation of the evidence on their impact in the early years of their adoption. This chapter examines the available evidence on small farmers' adoption of HYVs and use of nutrients and the impact of these technologies on productivity, employment, and incomes among the rural poor.

It is useful to begin by dispelling some popular myths about HYVs. Most analysts now agree that the new technologies are "scale neutral"—that is, they present no systematic bias against those with few resources. Indeed, as Lipton (1979) points out, if researchers had been asked in the 1960s to develop a blueprint to help the rural poor, they would have specified a technology with precisely the attributes of cereal HYVs: one that increases the demand for labor, can be profitably adopted with little or no fixed capital, reduces the risks of not having the right complementary inputs (water, light, nutrients), concentrates on food (which looms large in the budgets of poor people), smooths the seasonal peaks in labor requirements and food availability, dramatically increases land productivity, and increases the links between farmers and researchers. Moreover, it is not true, as many argue, that HYVs require large amounts of costly and precisely balanced packages of inputs and cultivating practices, or that they actually reduce incomes unless planted under stringently controlled agronomic conditions of light, water, and nutrient use. In fact, "HYVs are increasingly available that produce more output, more profitably at all plausible levels of light, nutrient and water inputs, flooding excluded," and "with carefully selected HYVs farm incomes for all adopters can be increased under most circumstances, and dramatically increased under many" (Lipton 1979, p. 121).

Many critics still contend, however, that HYVs are more costly to cultivate than traditional varieties, require more working capital (credit) to purchase nonfarm (often imported) inputs such as fertilizers, are best cultivated under irrigated conditions, and increase the farmers' dependence on markets (both for the supply of inputs and for sales of increased surpluses). It is further asserted that the packages of inputs (seeds, fertilizers, pesticides) and the markets through which they are delivered, together with the necessary complementary factors (water, knowledge, credit) and the institutional mechanisms ("the system") through which they are disseminated, are far from scale neutral. Small farmers are said to lack information on HYVs, the managerial or educational abilities needed to cultivate them effectively and profitably, the capital and credit needed to buy the essential inputs, and the ability to take risks.[1] Since inputs, credit, water, and extension services all move through markets and institutions of one kind or another, and since these are often biased against small farmers, it is believed that the new varieties are not viable for small farmers.

On a more abstract level, it is said that "the system" determines the real impact of new technologies because it determines who gets what inputs and at what prices. Thus technologies that may initially be scale neutral become transformed by "the system" into cultivating techniques that favor the large and the rich and are denied to the small and the poor. Overall, however, the appropriate response to problems of access is not to damn the technologies and argue against their adoption, but rather to do everything possible to remove market and institutional barriers that retard HYV adoption.

Have institutional biases been a *major* obstacle to the adoption of HYVs by small farmers? The evidence suggests otherwise.

Patterns of HYV Adoption

There are so many studies relating to the Green Revolution and the farmer's response to it that a complete review is both impractical and undesirable.[2] Ruttan (1977) summarized the findings of a large body of literature:

- The new cereal HYVs were adopted exceptionally quickly in areas where they are technically and economically superior to local varieties.
- Neither farm size nor type of tenure has seriously constrained the adoption of new high-yielding grain varieties. Small farmers and tenants did tend to lag behind large farmers soon after the introduction of HYVs, but these lags typically disappeared within a few years.
- Neither farm size nor type of tenure has been an important determinant of growth in productivity; although small farmers do face relatively more severe constraints, these have not been serious enough to cause any significant differences in yields.
- The introduction of the new HYVs has increased the demand for labor.
- Landowners have gained more than tenants and laborers from the adoption of HYVs.
- Introduction of the new varieties has contributed to a widening of wage and income differentials between regions.
- Adoption of HYVs has reduced the rate of increase in food-grain prices to consumers.

The evidence from South Asia confirms these generalizations. The area under high-yielding cereal varieties has expanded rapidly since the late 1960s (figure 5-1), and HYV wheat has been almost universally adopted in areas suited to it. Almost two-thirds of the rice area in India and half the area in Pakistan was under HYV rice in the early 1980s. (The Pakistan figure is an underestimate, however; see note 6 at the end of the chapter.) The area under HYV rice in Bangladesh is still small because appropriate rice varieties have yet to be developed for medium to deep water, the prevalent conditions there. Thus despite early concerns about adoption, the new varieties have fairly well saturated the areas for which they are suited. It is unlikely that they will expand into deep-water or upland areas until varieties specifically designed for those conditions become available (Herdt 1980).

The evidence on adoption by farm size shows that small farmers lagged considerably in the early phases of adoption, but later caught

Figure 5-1. South Asia: Estimated Percentage of Wheat and Rice Areas Planted to High-Yielding Varieties, 1968–83

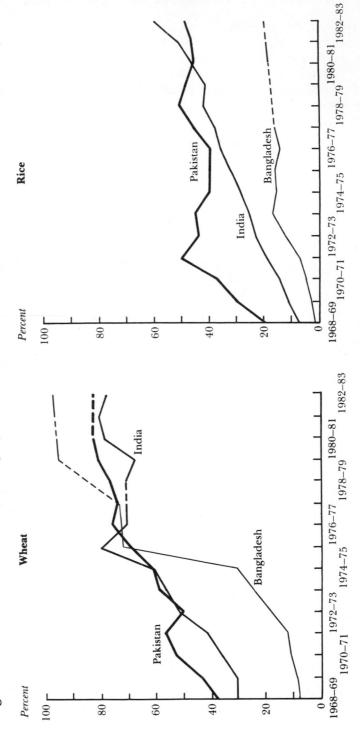

Note: Broken line indicates data were not available.
Sources: Dalrymple (1978); Herdt (1980); India, Ministry of Agriculture and Rural Development (1985a); Bangladesh Bureau of Statistics (1983); World Bank data; and IFDC (1983).

up rapidly. As a result, early studies of the spread of the new technologies tended to conclude that HYVs favored larger holdings and that small farmers were unlikely to benefit much.[3] Even in the early years of adoption, however, many studies found that although small farmers were lagging they were quickly catching up and often had a higher "intensity" of adoption—that is, they were planting a greater proportion of their areas to HYVs.[4]

Part of the difficulty in interpreting the evidence lies in what is meant by adoption. It can be measured either by the percentage of cultivators growing HYVs or by the area of a particular crop devoted to HYVs. The evidence suggests that a smaller percentage of small farmers may be growing HYVs but that once HYVs are adopted, small farmers tend to devote a higher percentage of their area to them. This supposition is confirmed by tables A27–A30, which present data from various regions in India on both the percentage of cultivators growing HYVs and the percentage of area planted to wheat and rice HYVs, by size of holding. The data show that the adoption of HYV wheat is almost universal in most states, in terms of both number of cultivators and area regardless of farm size.

In the early stages of the Green Revolution, evidence from the Indian Punjab showing almost 100 percent adoption of HYV wheats on even the smallest holdings (Kahlon and Singh 1973) was thought to be a special case. It was argued that abnormally favorable factors—a large average size of holding; a high percentage of irrigated land; greater availability of roads, markets, and electricity; good credit and extension facilities; and more motivated (Sikh) farmers—accounted for its success (Dasgupta 1977a). Other states were not expected to repeat this success.

In fact, however, data from the India Planning Commission, Programme Evaluation Organisation, show almost complete adoption of wheat HYVs by even the smallest holdings in such diverse states as Bihar, Haryana, Rajasthan, and Uttar Pradesh. The Punjab is no longer a special case. Thus either the infrastructural and institutional problems of access to inputs, knowledge, water, credit, and markets have been rapidly overcome in other states, or they were less of a constraint than originally assumed. The data also clearly show that small farmers did lag, but that the lags diminished rapidly—at least in the case of wheat. Data from Pakistan, though less extensive, confirm this (see table A31).

The data for rice are somewhat different. First, the overall adoption rates are lower for rice, with fewer states showing 100 percent adoption. Nevertheless, relatively high rates are found in such diverse regions as Andhra Pradesh, Orissa, Tamil Nadu, and Uttar Pradesh. Second, the total area devoted to HYVs is much smaller for rice than for wheat, which suggests that the adoption of rice varieties has been less successful overall. There are no significant differences by farm size, however. Evidence on this point from all states in India is shown in table 5-1. In states with large areas under HYV rice, small farmers have done as well as large ones; where such areas remain relatively small, small farmers have done no worse than their larger counterparts.

The proportion of farmers adopting HYVs and the proportion of area sown to them often differ by farm size but are two aspects of the same phenomenon. Combining the two is the *index of participation*, which is the product of the percentage of farmers using HYVs and the percentage of the area of a given crop sown to HYVs by adopting farmers. (An index of 100 implies that 100 percent of the farmers have adopted the HYVs and that 100 percent of the relevant crop area is sown to HYVs.)

Tables 5-2 and 5-3 present these indices for wheat and rice HYVs

Table 5-1. *India: Percentage of Rice Area in Modern Varieties (Irrigated and Unirrigated) by Farm Size, 1975–76*

	Farm size (hectares)				
State	*<1*	*1–2*	*2–4*	*4–10*	*10+*
Andhra Pradesh[a]	34.3	43.0	53.5	53.7	4.0
Assam[a]	6.9	2.7	6.3	2.9	11.2
Bihar[b]	34.0	36.4	39.5	25.0	29.2
Gujarat	12.1	2.5	19.8	6.0	2.1
Haryana	72.5	92.5	92.8	86.2	92.6
Himachal Pradesh	3.4	1.8	3.6	3.1	n.a.
Jammu and Kashmir	88.0	75.1	74.9	80.1	n.a.
Karnataka[a]	40.5	49.6	37.9	56.3	23.0
Kerala	48.7	39.8	50.7	100.0	n.a.
Madhya Pradesh	1.7	0.2	1.2	0.6	1.1
Maharashtra	9.8	21.0	8.3	17.9	n.a.
Orissa[a]	28.4	30.5	33.6	35.6	37.9
Punjab	98.9	99.9	100.0	100.0	100.0
Rajasthan	0	0	1.6	11.5	55.6
Tamil Nadu[a]	65.3	59.6	50.5	67.1	19.2
Uttar Pradesh	35.0	33.9	25.6	33.1	21.1
West Bengal[a]	21.3	14.8	19.8	20.9	50.0

n.a. Not available.
a. Average of summer, winter, and autumn paddy crops.
b. Average of autumn and winter paddy crops.
Source: NCAER (1978).

for different regions in India. By the middle of the 1970s the adoption of wheat was almost universal in terms of both the number of farmers adopting and area. The indices are far lower for rice for all farm sizes with only two states—Punjab and Tamil Nadu—coming even close to complete adoption. The index for small farmers may be lower than that for large farmers in a particular state and year, whereas the reverse may be true for other years and states. In the case of rice, however, one could at least hypothesize that overall participation has been somewhat lower for small farmers than for large ones.

The reasons for the slower adoption of HYV rice are well known, however, and are related more to incentives and to environmental and seasonal factors than to farm size. Lipton (1979), C. H. H. Rao (1975), IRRI (1975), and Subbarao (1980) provide extensive evidence to show that at least in India price incentives have been far poorer for rice production than for wheat production. Furthermore, appropriate rice varieties for upland, flooded, or deep-water areas have yet

Table 5-2. *India: Index of Participation for HYV Wheat by Size of Holding*

District and state	Year	Size of holding (hectares)				
		0–1	*1–2*	*2–4*	*4–8*	*8–20*
Gaya, Bihar	1967–68	24	31	26	26	30
	1969–70	21	68	47	14	49
	1972–73	64	80	69	100	100
	1974–75	65	99	100	100	100
Rohtak, Haryana	1967–68	n.a.	10	5	13	26
	1969–70	n.a.	30	80	80	93
	1972–73	n.a.	98	73	52	84
	1974–75	58	68	72	74	100
Ludhiana, Punjab	1967–68	n.a.	80	65	61	82
	1969–70	93	63	83	96	78
	1972–73	100	100	100	100	100
	1974–75	100	100	100	92	97
Muzaffarnagar, Uttar Pradesh	1969–70	30	34	37	24	17
	1972–73	100	100	100	100	100
	1974–75	100	100	100	100	100

n.a. Not available.

Note: The index of participation is the product of the percentage of cultivators using HYVs and the percentage of total wheat area sown to HYVs. Data are for selected villages.

Source: Compiled from data in India, Planning Commission (1976).

Table 5-3. *India: Index of Participation for HYV Rice by Size of Holding*

		Size of holding (hectares)				
District and state	Year	0–1	1–2	2–4	4–8	8–20
West Godavari, Andhra Pradesh	1972–73	65	63	63	64	34
	1974–75	55	57	64	66	78
Shahabad, Bihar	1972–73	6	10	20	16	14
	1974–75	n.a.	...	2	4	1
Palghat, Kerala	1972–73	44	52	57	59	88
	1974–75	16	18	25	26	50
Coimbatore, Tamil Nadu	1972–73	91	94	61	93	n.a.
	1974–75	79	82	86	92	n.a.
Thana, Maharashtra	1972–73	11	16	14	12	31
	1974–75	5	8	2	2	n.a.
Shimoga, Karnataka	1972–73	31	18	39	48	64
	1974–75	9	9	21	26	n.a.
Cuttack, Orissa	1972–73	32	18	13	10	n.a.
	1974–75	14	20	22	2	n.a.
Amritsar, Punjab	1972–73	n.a.	48	59	87	93
	1974–75	n.a.	71	85	80	72
Basti, Uttar Pradesh	1972–73	64	42	60	3	n.a.
	1974–75	29	25	36	19	n.a.
Midnapur, West Bengal	1972–73	23	11	7	2	29
	1974–75	16	13	8	6	n.a.

n.a. Not available.
... Negligible.
Note: The index of participation is the product of the percentage of cultivators using HYVs and the percentage of total rice area sown to HYVs. Data are for selected villages.
Source: India, Planning Commission (1976).

to be developed, and those already developed depend heavily on proper water control. In seasons and areas subject to drought, variable rainfall, or flooding or where other environmental factors such as photo periodicity are adverse, HYV rice has done poorly. Thus in Bangladesh in 1979–80, for example, 62 percent of the paddy area was sown to HYVs in the boro season, but only 21 percent in the aus season and 28 percent in the aman season (IFDC 1980, pp. 70–71; R. Ahmed 1979a). This is because aus and aman are the flood seasons, and the HYV rice varieties developed thus far are susceptible to moisture stress (Herdt 1980; IRRI 1978b).

Overall adoption rates for rice thus differ by size of holding because larger farmers have better access to credit and knowledge than do smaller farmers. The data from a sample survey in Bangladesh (table 5-4) clearly reflect differences by farm size. Relatively few small farmers had adopted HYVs by 1975 (though nearly two-thirds of those with holdings smaller than half an acre were planting HYVs, a proportion much higher than the overall data for Bangladesh show), but the gap is rapidly closing. Among adopters there are few differences by farm size in the percentage of HYV area devoted to rice; boro season areas planted to HYV are consistently higher. The overall index of participation is lowest for small holdings, at least in the boro season, but it increases with size of holding up to 2.5–5.0 acres and then decreases again. This suggests that adoption has been more common on medium-size holdings than on large ones; that it is not the smallest but often the largest farmers who are most conservative in taking up new technologies. (This tendency is not confined to HYV rice but is more generally true for many innovations.) Studies by Asaduzzaman and Islam (1976) in Bangladesh and by Gotsch (1973) in Pakistan confirm this view.[5] (See table A32 for the Bangladesh data.) Thus small farmers seem to have adopted HYV rice and continue to do so as extensively as large ones where the new varieties are available, suitable, and profitable.

To sum up the evidence in this section, small farmers' adoption rates for HYV wheat have initially lagged behind those of large farmers. Over time the size-adoption relationship begins to change and the evidence seems contradictory. This is not surprising: size of holding is a surrogate for a whole array of potentially important factors such as wealth, education, tenurial status, ability to bear risk, and access to credit, information, and scarce inputs (water, seeds, fertilizers). Since the importance of these factors varies in different areas and over time in the same area, so does the relationship between adoption and farm size. In some areas—notably Punjab—small farmers adopted HYVs as rapidly as large ones, even in the early years, and differences in the adoption rates of large and small farmers had disappeared by the mid-1970s, at least for wheat. By now, the adoption of HYV wheat is almost universal in areas where it is suitable and profitable.

The spread of rice HYVs has not been as rapid, extensive, or consistent as that of new wheat varieties. Rice HYVs were found to be more location-specific in their adaptation and yield response; they frequently competed with improved local varieties, which might yield as much and have other, more desirable characteristics (better taste, shorter growing time, lower water logging). Thus HYV rice adoption is far from universal;[6] in particular, small farmers have not adopted HYV rice as extensively as large farmers, although they have begun to catch up in all areas studied.

It is axiomatic that adoption ultimately depends on access to essential inputs, markets, credit, and information. If these are available

Table 5-4. Bangladesh: Percentage of Cultivators Growing HYV Paddy, HYV as a Percentage of Total Paddy Area, and Index of Participation by Farm Size, Selected Districts

Districts	Year	Farm size (acres)									
		0–0.5	0.5–1.0	1.0–1.5	1.5–2.0	2.0–2.5	2.5–3.0	3.0–3.5	3.5–5.5	5.5+	All
		Percentage of cultivators growing HYV									
Bogra, Sylhet, and Noakhali	1968	16.5	14.5	19.4	18.0	20.0	28.0	12.9	25.8	13.6	17.9
	1969	20.9	25.0	29.1	22.9	43.3	32.0	29.0	35.5	27.2	27.3
	1970	27.5	33.3	33.3	47.5	56.6	32.0	51.6	42.0	49.9	36.9
	1971	41.8	42.7	43.0	57.3	69.9	48.0	71.0	61.4	68.1	49.8
	1972	44.0	49.0	48.6	68.8	73.2	56.0	83.9	77.5	86.3	57.4
	1973	48.4	55.3	58.3	77.0	83.2	68.0	83.9	90.4	90.8	64.6
	1974	55.0	61.6	66.6	81.9	86.5	76.0	87.1	93.6	95.3	70.5
	1975	58.3	66.8	72.2	90.1	89.8	84.0	90.2	96.8	99.8	75.5
		Percentage of total paddy area planted to HYV									
Bogra, Sylhet, and Noakhali	1974–75[a]	44	52	44	58	49	71	49	57	56	51
	1975[b]	40	30	28	28	26	26	28	20	23	30
		Index of participation[c]									
Bogra, Sylhet, and Noakhali	1974–75[a]	22	32	25	41	36	62	38	50	51	34
	1975[b]	17	13	12	12	12	11	14	8	13	13

Notes: Data are from 459 rice holdings in three villages in 1974–75.
a. Boro.
b. Aman.
c. Product of the percentage of cultivators using HYV rice and the percentage of total rice area under HYV.
Source: Iftikhar Ahmed (1981).

small farmers catch up quickly after a short lag, but if these inputs and services continue to be difficult to obtain the lags will be prolonged. The available evidence suggests, however, that these constraints will eventually be overcome and that all small farmers will eventually adopt HYVs. Adoption will continue to be low in upland, deep-water, and flooded rice areas because suitable varieties have yet to be developed. The total area under HYV rice in Bangladesh continues to be low mainly because suitable technologies are not available, not because holdings are small or farmers lack access to inputs.

Nevertheless, the early lag in small farmers' response put them at a disadvantage. By being first to adopt, large farmers reduced the profitability of later adoption by small farmers—not only did they glut local crop markets but also, by securing a first lien, as it were, on credit and inputs, they made residual supplies more costly and difficult for latecomers to obtain, at least initially. Faiz (1986) makes exactly this point in analyzing the adoption of HYV technologies in Pakistan during the 1970s and concludes that large farmers gained the most from these technologies. In this he is supported generally by M. H. Khan (1975, 1981). But studies by M. G. Chaudhry (1982, 1983) reach just the opposite conclusion. The evidence is contradictory because of the difficulty of capturing the impact of an ongoing process. The early maldistribution of gains can be attributed largely to the lag in providing an adequate supply of essential inputs and services. But with input and credit supplies increasing in many parts of India, small farmers have continued to close the gaps. They may still have to compete for limited quantities of the essential inputs, but the lags are becoming shorter as access problems are resolved.

Yield Gains and Nutrient Use

Once HYVs are available and adopted, the impact on production is significant. Few countries publish production data separated by modern and local varieties, but Indian national data for rice suggest that the overall yields of modern varieties were 70–160 percent higher than those of local varieties between 1965 and 1975 (Evenson and Flores in IRRI 1978a). But this is an aggregate of all rice and irrigation conditions and overstates the case.

Farm management and field-level data are available, however, on yields of local and modern varieties under various conditions of soil, climate, and irrigation. The evidence suggests that when grown under *similar* conditions, modern varieties yield between 40 and 100 percent more than traditional varieties. Some of these data are shown in table 5-5. In nearly every case, the yields of the modern varieties are higher than those of the local varieties by an average of 40 percent or more in both wet and dry seasons. Data on rice yields from eastern India suggest even larger differences ranging from 40 to 160 percent, with smaller farmers reaping larger increases in yield (table A33).

A basic difficulty is that these yield data reflect not only varietal differences but also differences in the inputs used. If modern varieties need irrigated land and large amounts of fertilizer, then (it is argued) small farmers, who have less access to these inputs, will gain less than large farmers. Data on yield differences by farm size in the early 1970s seem to suggest that this was the case (see Dasgupta 1977a; C. H. H. Rao 1975); HYV yields are significantly correlated with the availability of irrigation and use of fertilizer. Since small farmers tend to have higher irrigation intensities, the real concern is with their ability to get fertilizer—which, because typically they have little cash, in turn entails the availability of credit.

The popular impression that HYVs require a lot of fertilizer to be profitable needs to be dispelled. The view that fertilizers are the sine qua non of the Green Revolution and that HYVs cannot yield more

Table 5-5. *South Asia: Comparison of Yields of Modern and Traditional Varieties from Farm-Level Surveys*

Location	Modern/traditional yield ratio		Study period
	Wet season	*Dry season*	
Bangladesh			
All regions (aman)	1.27	n.a.	1979
All regions (boro)	n.a.	1.85	1979–80
All regions (aus)	n.a.	1.89	1980
India			
Andhra Pradesh	1.40	1.93	1971–72
Tamil Nadu	1.56	1.61	1971–72
Uttar Pradesh	2.01	n.a.	1971–72
Karnataka	1.89	n.a.	1971–72
Orissa	n.a.	1.41	1971–72
West Bengal	1.47	n.a.	1972–73
Bihar	1.53	n.a.	1972–73
Orissa	1.45	n.a.	1972–73
Pakistan			
Punjab	1.60	n.a.	1971–72
Punjab	1.52	n.a.	1972–73
Sind	1.42	n.a.	1972–73

n.a. Not available.
Sources: For India and Pakistan, Herdt (1980); for Bangladesh, IFDC (1981).

than local varieties without high levels of nutrients is false and misleading. Lipton (1979) points out that it was the concentration of nutrient use on big farms and rich soils in the early phases of the Green Revolution that led to the fallacy that HYVs need lots of fertilizers to do well. Unfortunately, the "full package" idea promoted by many extension services in the first decade of the Green Revolution did much to discourage the early adoption of HYVs by small farmers. It spread the fallacy that any practice or input by itself was likely to yield only low returns, but that the right combination and levels of practices or inputs would yield high returns (Lipton 1979).

Lipton correctly notes that these packages and recommended doses of fertilizer have placed restrictions on scientists and extension workers too busy to read the fine print. Unrealistic packages that impose fixed and high doses of fertilizer regardless of farm-specific sunlight, soil, and water conditions and without reference to expected prices or returns deter farmers from adopting HYVs because the packages are thought to be an inflexible, all-or-nothing requirement. Policymakers too are deterred from disseminating HYVs to the poor if they believe that timely credit and many other inputs are indispensable. In fact, as Lipton points out, some HYVs are so robust that in most soils they will outperform local varieties even without extra fertilizers. (Some relevant evidence is shown in table 5-6.) Lipton concludes that small farmers are being discouraged not by the technological and economic requirements for massive doses of fertilizer, together with the loans and risks involved, but by the overselling of such inputs.

Even small amounts of fertilizer combined with the adoption of HYVs can prove profitable on small farms. But what evidence is there to support the idea that small farmers use less fertilizer, get lower yields, and earn lower incomes from modern varieties than do large farmers?

Herdt (1980) compiled data on rice yields and nutrient use by farm size from farm surveys in forty-three locations in Asia; thirty-one of these locations were in South Asia. Yields on large farms exceeded those on small farms by more than 0.1 ton per hectare in only a third of the cases. The average difference was less than 260 kilograms per hectare. Fertilizer use is also slightly higher on large farms with a few exceptions. Although no statistical tests were done on these figures, such tests on data from thirty-two Asian villages done by Barker and Herdt (1978) showed that in many cases—mostly in India and Indonesia—yields for HYV rice growers were significantly higher on large farms than on small ones. In Malaysia, Philippines, and Thailand, however, average yields on small farms were higher. This led them to conclude that in an environment of unequal distribution of landholdings, the disadvantage of small farmers in obtaining comple-

Table 5-6. *India: Average Yields without Fertilizers, 1967–71*
(kilograms per hectare)

Crop	Region	HYVs	Traditional	HYV/traditional yield ratio
Wheat	Northern (Delhi, Haryana, and Punjab	3,454	2,054	1.68
	Indo-Gangetic (Bihar, Uttar Pradesh, West Bengal)	1,809	1,574	1.15
	Western (Gujarat, Maharashtra, Rajasthan)	1,937	1,647	1.12
	Central (Madhya Pradesh)	1,514	1,312	1.15
	All regions	1,988	1,650	1.20
Rice	Southern (Andhra Pradesh, Mysore, Tamil Nadu)	3,704	3,018	1.23
	Northeastern (Bihar, West Bengal)	2,646	1,795	1.47
	Central (Madhya Pradesh)	2,552	2,966	0.86
	Northern (Haryana, Uttar Pradesh)	2,419	2,194	1.10
	All regions	2,913	2,493	1.17
Rice[a]	Southern (Andhra Pradesh, Mysore)	3,108	2,319	1.34
	Eastern (Orissa)	3,094	n.a.	n.a.
	All regions	3,101	2,319	1.34
Rice[b]	Southern (Kerala)	3,090	3,375	0.92

n.a. Not available.
a. Rabi, irrigated.
b. Rabi, unirrigated.
Source: Dasgupta (1977a).

mentary resources—irrigation, fertilizer, and credit to purchase inputs—may account for their lower yields.

A review of the available evidence from South Asia does not support the view that yields are smaller or input intensities lower on small farms. The evidence is mixed, but on balance it suggests that the proportion of those using *any* fertilizer is usually smaller among small farmers than among large farmers, and the proportion of total area fertilized is often also smaller among small farmers. When small farmers do use fertilizers, however, they tend to use them more intensively on the areas they fertilize.

Although some studies reported that small farmers tended to use fertilizers less intensively—for example C. H. H. Rao (1975), Ojha (1970), and Perrin and Winkelman (1976)—a majority of studies of India find either no significant relationship between farm size and intensity of fertilizer use or find small farmers using more fertilizers. For example, the extensive National Sample Survey 26th Round data for 1971–72 showed higher intensities of use for small rice holdings and no relationship between farm size and fertilizer use for wheat holdings (India, Ministry of Planning 1976b). The extensive data from the Programme Evaluation Organisation review of the HYV program in India in the late 1960s reveals some tendencies for fertilizer use to increase with farm size (India, Planning Commission 1971; see also tables A34 and A35). But this was in the early phases of adoption when the Integrated Agricultural Development Program was concentrating on large "progressive" farmers and recommending ridiculously expensive packages of inputs.

By the early 1970s, the pattern was already changing. According to an extensive survey of more than 4,000 farmers throughout India by the National Council of Applied Economic Research (NCAER), although small farmers fertilize a somewhat smaller proportion of their areas, they tend to use as much fertilizer per hectare as large farmers—or even more (NCAER 1978, and see table 5-7). The intensity of fertilizer use is higher and the area fertilized is larger for HYVs. Similar findings were reported by Parthasarathy and Prasad (in IRRI 1978b). A follow-up study of the HYV program in the mid-1970s found no significant relationship between farm size and fertilizer use (India, Planning Commission 1976).

Figures from the 1975–76 NCAER survey (NCAER 1978, and see tables A36 and A37) clearly show that although the percentage of total area fertilized continued to be positively related to farm size, there was no significant relationship between size and intensity of fertilizer use. Small farmers tend to conserve their scarce working capital by limiting the area they fertilize. A more appropriate measure is therefore the fertilizer use per fertilized area, information that is available in the NCAER survey.

Since rice is the main crop in the poorer eastern and southern regions of India, tables 5-8 and 5-9 show rice areas fertilized and nutrient use per fertilized area for each state in 1975–76 and for selected states in southern India (see also table A38). These data confirm that although a lower proportion of small farmers fertilize a smaller proportion of their areas, they tend to use more nutrients per fertilized area than large farmers. The data by variety and irrigation in table A38 show that even in some major rice-producing states where the percentage of *total* rice area fertilized remains small—Bihar and Uttar Pradesh—the percentage of the total area sown to HYVs that is fertilized is very high even among holdings smaller than 1 hectare, and the average nutrient use is much greater than on larger holdings.

The evidence from Pakistan is similar. Although Salam (1976),

Table 5-7. *India: Fertilizer Use on Irrigated Holdings by Size of Holding, 1970–71*

Size of holding (hectares)	Rice		Wheat		Maize	
	Area fertilized[a]	NPK[b]	Area fertilized[a]	NPK[b]	Area fertilized[a]	NPK[b]
HYV						
0–2.5	82.6	88.1	79.5	72.4	91.1	10.9
2.5–8.5	84.7	71.4	91.0	65.2	99.8	64.2
8.5+	93.9	83.8	95.2	58.7	89.6	53.8
All	85.8	81.8	88.5	63.4	95.0	77.6
Non-HYV						
0–2.5	49.0	49.2	34.2	39.8	28.0	65.2
2.5–8.5	60.6	39.4	49.6	47.7	56.1	56.2
8.5+	86.2	35.9	68.8	55.3	55.4	37.9
All	55.4	43.9	47.3	47.6	41.4	54.9
Total						
0–2.5	58.4	64.6	54.4	55.2	33.6	73.9
2.5–8.5	67.2	50.4	73.5	60.2	63.4	58.3
8.5+	91.1	67.6	82.1	57.3	58.1	39.8
All	64.8	59.5	68.7	58.2	47.3	59.9

a. As a percentage of total area planted to the crop.
b. Kilograms per hectare of nitrogen, phosphorus, and potash.
Source: NCAER (1978).

Kaneda (1972), and Naseem (1971) found nearly all farmers using fertilizers, Amjad (1972) and Rochin (in Stevens, Alavi, and Bertocci 1976) reported that small farmers used less than large farmers. Gotsch (in Stevens, Alavi, and Bertocci 1976), Moazam Mahmood (1977), and M. H. Khan (1975) report no significant differences in fertilizer use by size of farm, while Salam (1976) found higher fertilizer use among smaller farmers. M. H. Khan (1975) shows lower fertilizer use on smaller holdings in 1974 (table A39), but the differences are not large. A farm survey of the Indus basin by the Water and Power Development Authority (WAPDA) in Pakistan in 1976–77 suggests that there are no significant differences by farm size in fertilizer use per hectare (see table 5-10).

Until recently data on fertilizer use by farm size from Bangladesh have been sparse. Whereas a small sample survey by Quasem and Hossain (1979) showed small farmers using less fertilizer per hectare, another by Quasem (1978) found no significant differences by farm size, and Hossain (1977a and b) and I. Ahmed (1981) report that in-

Table 5-8. India: Percentage of Rice Area Fertilized and Fertilizer Consumption per Hectare, 1975–76

State	Percentage of rice area fertilized by farm size in hectares					Nutrients (kilograms per hectare) by farm size in hectares				
	<1	1–2	2–4	4–10	10+	<1	1–2	2–4	4–10	10+
Andhra Pradesh[a]	70.4	73.9	87.8	79.6	68.8	112.0	117.9	109.4	101.4	119.5
Assam[a]	1.6	8.6	5.6	3.6	67.0	108.6	43.9	58.7	48.4	8.4
Bihar[b]	27.9	47.0	61.1	46.0	48.2	54.6	51.6	37.0	36.4	31.0
Gujarat	49.1	56.0	64.9	55.8	95.3	72.1	49.1	62.3	63.4	43.9
Haryana	83.2	93.2	96.1	95.0	99.0	91.1	91.7	77.9	96.7	116.8
Himachal Pradesh	41.9	31.2	9.0	40.2	—	38.1	20.1	25.7	28.0	—
Jammu and Kashmir	77.7	72.0	72.2	61.3	—	46.1	46.7	47.8	34.6	—
Karnataka[a]	79.8	85.6	89.3	96.4	100.0	194.2	165.8	133.4	142.3	72.1
Kerala[a]	84.0	86.3	85.4	100.0	—	100.4	103.0	117.4	173.6	—
Madhya Pradesh	0.9	6.6	13.2	15.5	42.2	52.6	50.3	35.8	23.1	17.4
Maharashtra	43.1	53.2	55.9	52.8	63.1	83.5	76.5	53.5	64.3	62.6
Orissa[a]	33.2	38.4	42.6	46.0	60.9	81.2	82.2	85.1	105.9	106.5
Punjab	56.9	71.8	88.4	97.1	100.0	102.8	87.3	92.3	96.0	114.7
Rajasthan	2.1	7.6	32.4	48.2	100.0	143.3	63.1	32.0	44.4	50.5
Tamil Nadu[a]	82.2	89.0	91.3	92.2	100.0	134.7	137.4	121.1	122.6	108.2
Uttar Pradesh	21.6	30.8	44.0	55.2	28.5	47.9	46.1	39.3	38.8	71.4
West Bengal[a]	40.4	38.5	46.5	44.7	100.0	99.9	95.7	77.2	63.4	133.2
Average	46.8	52.3	58.0	60.6	76.6	91.9	78.1	70.9	75.4	75.4

— Not applicable.
a. Average of summer, winter, and autumn paddy crops.
b. Average of autumn and winter paddy crops.
Source: NCAER (1978).

171

Table 5-9. *South India: Households Fertilizing, Area Fertilized, and Fertilizer Use by Farm Size, Four States, 1976–77*

			Farm size in hectares			
Item	*<1*	*1–2*	*2–4*	*4–10*	*10+*	*All*
Andhra Pradesh						
Percentage of households fertilizing	44.9	66.5	75.2	76.0	90.0	62.2
Percentage of cropped area fertilized	43.8	46.1	47.8	41.1	51.2	45.4
Fertilizer use (kilograms per hectare)	124.3	113.8	124.5	115.4	48.3	104.8
Karnataka						
Percentage of households fertilizing	34.4	39.7	37.8	41.2	37.5	38.5
Percentage of cropped area fertilized	36.6	32.7	23.2	24.3	70.3	24.3
Fertilizer use (kilograms per hectare)	213.0	184.3	175.7	123.2	115.5	157.3
Kerala						
Percentage of households fertilizing	77.8	96.4	84.6	100.0	—	80.0
Percentage of cropped area fertilized	89.8	88.8	84.2	100.0	—	89.3
Fertilizer use (kilograms per hectare)	94.5	77.1	61.3	130.8	—	88.7
Tamil Nadu						
Percentage of households fertilizing	67.0	75.1	87.2	87.5	80.6	73.7
Percentage of cropped area fertilized	63.5	60.6	57.9	53.2	49.0	58.9
Fertilizer use (kilograms per hectare)	128.3	124.4	130.0	128.9	124.0	127.6

— Not applicable.
Source: NCAER (1979).

tensity of fertilizer use is negatively related to farm size. The evidence from Bangladesh is particularly significant because most farms are very small, income levels are very low, and rice is the predominant crop. A recent and extensive survey of fertilizer use on more than 1,800 farms throughout Bangladesh carried out jointly by the Bangladesh Agricultural Research Council (BARC) and the International Fertilizer Development Center (IFDC) provides extensive evidence on fertilizer use by farm size (see table 5-11). Although the data show no

Table 5-10. Pakistan: Nutrient Use by Farm Size, 1976–77
(kilograms of nitrogen and phosphorus per hectare planted)

Farm size (hectares)	Wheat					Rice				
	Average[a]	HYV	Traditional	Sellers[b]	Nonsellers	Average[a]	IRRI	Basmati	Sellers[b]	Nonsellers
<2	26.9	29.8	7.3	38.1	25.3	18.8	24.2	24.0	24.1	15.5
2–5	25.3	28.1	6.8	34.0	21.7	14.6	16.8	16.0	16.1	12.7
5–10	27.5	30.1	7.6	31.6	23.9	15.5	17.7	19.7	19.0	10.3
10–20	25.6	27.6	10.9	31.9	19.7	15.3	13.5	29.7	18.8	11.6
20+	20.2	21.4	n.a.	23.1	16.6	13.9	16.2	34.7	22.5	7.7
All	25.8	28.1	7.9	31.2	21.8	15.0	16.7	22.5	18.6	10.9

n.a. Not available.
Notes: The weight of nutrients used is weighted by the area planted.
a. The average for rice is not the average for IRRI and basmati, which cover approximately 50 percent of the area under rice.
b. Sellers are farmers who sell any portion of their crop output.
Source: Pakistan, Water and Power Development Authority (1977).

Table 5-11. Bangladesh: Percentage of Farmers Using Fertilizers and Fertilizer Use per Cropped Area by Farm Size, 1979–80

Size of holding (acres)	Boro season (1979–80)		Aus season (1980)		Aman season (1980)	
	Percentage fertilizing	Total nutrient use (maunds per acre)[a]	Percentage fertilizing	Total nutrient use (maunds per acre)[a]	Percentage fertilizing	Total nutrient use (maunds per acre)[a]
Landless[b]	50.0	2.20	100.0	0.21	0.0	
<0.5	68.9	1.55	60.6	0.87	53.3	0.88
0.5–1.0	65.1	1.30	59.0	0.83	55.2	0.79
1.0–1.5	64.6	1.24	56.0	0.72	55.5	0.73
1.5–2.0	65.4	1.11	65.1	0.80	62.1	0.89
2.0–2.5	71.0	1.27	59.6	0.63	55.3	0.62
2.5–3.0	67.2	1.02	61.9	0.60	67.4	0.83
3.0–3.5	64.0	0.90	62.2	0.65	66.3	0.83
3.5–4.0	79.2	1.24	60.7	0.88	73.2	0.94

4.0–4.5	67.2	0.76	57.8	0.58	61.3	0.82
4.5–5.0	62.5	0.79	72.9	0.83	72.1	0.88
5.0–6.0	79.5	1.08	63.0	0.68	70.1	0.69
6.0–7.0	84.6	1.24	74.5	0.82	72.6	1.01
7.0–7.5	58.3	0.88	53.8	0.54	73.3	0.95
7.5–8.0	78.6	0.93	71.4	1.19	64.3	0.38
8.0+	72.5	1.17	68.6	0.91	70.3	0.80
All	68.0	1.20	61.6	0.70	60.9	0.80
Number of farmers in sample[c]	1,097	—	1,039	—	1,142	—

— Not applicable.
a. Nutrients include urea, triple superphosphate, muriate of potash, and diamonium phosphate. 1 maund = 82.27 pounds = 37.3 kilograms.
b. Farmers who do not own any land, not even a homestead.
c. Only farmers with any cropped area in the season are included.
Source: IFDC (1981), appendix tables II.1.10, III.1.10, and IV.1.10.

significant relationship between the percentage of farmers fertilizing and farm size, small farmers tend to use more nutrients per hectare than large farmers, especially in the boro season when rainfall is assured and a large area is planted to HYVs.

To summarize, the extensive evidence on fertilizer use in South Asia confirms that a lower percentage of small farmers use fertilizers and that they probably fertilize a smaller proportion of their cultivated area than large farmers. But small farmers also tend to have a higher intensity of fertilizer use on the land that they do fertilize. The yields and productivity gains on the areas they fertilize or put under HYVs have been comparable to those on larger farms. The evidence does not suggest any severe problems of physical access to fertilizer supplies or difficulties with distribution. Why then do small farmers fertilize a smaller proportion of their area than large farmers? The various reasons could include risk aversion, lack of access to knowledge or credit, and higher real costs of acquiring inputs.

HYVs and the Landless

In areas where new technologies have had a significant impact, they have *directly* benefited even the smallest farmers. They have also *indirectly* benefited rural laborers by increasing the demand for labor. This is attested to by a significant increase in real wages in areas such as Haryana and the Indian and Pakistani Punjabs, in spite of the dampening effects of considerable in-migration and mechanization in these areas.

The landless and near landless have benefited in three ways:

- Irrigation, multiple cropping, and greater nutrient use with the adoption of HYVs have increased on-farm employment.

- Nonfarm employment in rural areas has increased, especially in ancillary and service activities.

- The increase in food-grain production has lowered food prices and made food more readily available.

The first two trends have attracted some attention, but little has been said about the last, although it may have had the most important real impact.

The new technologies have also had a *negative* impact on the landless and near landless. They have been accompanied by mechanization in some areas, so that the positive overall effect on employment has been reduced or neutralized. And the increased profitability of self-cultivation has led to the eviction of small tenants. These negative effects are not a necessary consequence of the Green Revolution, however. They arise more from the agrarian structure within which the new technologies have been introduced and from the economic policies that have been followed in South Asia.

Employment and Wage Effects

How have the land-intensive technologies of the Green Revolution affected employment, and what are the positive outcomes for the landless and near landless? The broad evidence from South Asia (and Southeast Asia as well) is summarized below.

The demand for labor increases significantly with the switch from local to high-yielding varieties. Additional demand, ranging from 10 to 100 percent depending on the crop, region, and other factors, generally takes the form of increased labor use in workdays per hectare. The increase is lower in terms of workdays per metric ton of yield, however, because yields increase faster than labor use per hectare with the switch from traditional to modern varieties. By now the evidence on this issue is fairly extensive.[7] Some of it is summarized in table 5-12 and figure 5-2.

The increase in labor demand varies by crop and region and is hard to generalize. The elasticity of employment with respect to overall increases in output also varies widely, partly because of the confounding effect of other variables (such as mechanization and input and output intensities) and partly because of the extreme diversity of crops and agronomic zones. Attempts to calculate overall employment elasticities are therefore not very successful, but micro data suggest that the elasticities are not very large and vary between 0.3 and 0.5 in most cases.

The increased demand for labor has been particularly pronounced for specific tasks—land preparation, transplanting, weeding, and harvesting, for example—so that the *seasonal* distribution of labor demand has changed significantly. Mechanization, however, has decreased the demand for some tasks, such as land preparation and threshing, more than others (see Day and Singh 1977; B. Agarwal 1980a and b, 1981). The Green Revolution has thus increased the overall demand for labor, but raised it by less than the increase in output and changed the seasonal nature of this demand.

Part of the higher demand for on-farm labor will be met by family workers. Especially on small farms there may be stocks of underutilized labor, and families may prefer extra employment on their own land to wage employment elsewhere. The near landless, too, might find increased work on their own land more remunerative than some types of wage employment. But it is the likely impact on

Table 5-12. South Asia; Hired Labor Used per Hectare by Farmers Growing Modern Varieties (MV) Compared with Farmers Growing Local Varieties (LV)

Crop and place	Labor unit	Labor per hectare		Ratio MV/LV	Study year	Source
		MV	LV			
Rice						
India						
Cuttack, Orissa	Rupees	260	110	2.4	1966–67	Desai (1971)
Varanasi, Uttar Pradesh	Rupees	230	225	1.0	1966–67	Desai (1971)
Saharanpur, Uttar Pradesh	Rupees	94	50	1.9	1966–67	Desai (1971)
Raipur, Madhya Pradesh	Rupees	99	115	0.9	1966–67	Desai (1971)
Kolaba, Maharashtra	Rupees	94	77	1.2	1966–67	Desai (1971)
Amritsar, Punjab	Rupees	199	178	1.1	1967–68	Desai (1971)
Krishna, Andhra Pradesh	Rupees	178	133	1.3	1966–67	Desai (1971)
East Godavari, Andhra Pradesh	Rupees	390	316	1.2	1968–69	Dasgupta (1977a)
West Godavari, Andhra Pradesh	Rupees	373	328	1.1	1967–68	Desai (1971)
West Godavari, Andhra Pradesh	Rupees	659	588	1.1	1968–69	Dasgupta (1977a)
Ernakulam, Kerala	Rupees	354	294	1.2	1966–67	Desai (1971)
Thanjavur, Tamil Nadu	Rupees	98	116	0.8	1966–67	Desai (1971)
Birbhum, West Bengal	Rupees	221	144	1.5	1968–69	Dasgupta (1977a)

Pakistan					
Gujranwala, Punjab	Rupees	106	86	1.2	1972–73	M. H. Khan (1975)
Sahiwal, Punjab	Rupees	37	27	1.4	1972–73	M. H. Khan (1975)
Jacobabad, Sind	Rupees	67	49	1.5	1972–73	M. H. Khan (1975)
Hyderabad, Sind	Rupees	67	45	1.5	1972–73	M. H. Khan (1975)
Punjab (overall)	Rupees	101	77	1.3	1972–73	M. H. Khan (1975)
Sind (overall)	Rupees	39	20	2.0	1972–73	M. H. Khan (1975)
Bangladesh					
Mymensingh	Days	114	71	1.6	1972–73	Muqtada (1974)
Bangladesh (aus)	Days	91	69	1.3	1975–76	R. I. Rahman (1981)
Bangladesh (aman)	Days	155	106	1.5	1975–76	R. I. Rahman (1981)
Bangladesh	Days	116	74	1.6	1972–73	Muqtada (1974)
Bangladesh (aus)	Days	198	143	1.4	1970–82	Hossain (1986)
Bangladesh (aman)	Days	163	125	1.3	1970–82	Hossain (1986)
Bangladesh (boro)	Days	242	207	1.2	1970–82	Hossain (1986)
Wheat (Pakistan)					
Jhelum	Rupees	2,950	410	7.2	1972–73	M. H. Khan (1975)
Gujranwala	Rupees	1,082	536	2.1	1972–73	M. H. Khan (1975)
Sahiwal	Rupees	282	146	1.9	1972–73	M. H. Khan (1975)
Punjab	Rupees	778	326	2.4	1972–73	M. H. Khan (1975)
Jacobabad	Rupees	267	112	2.4	1972–73	M. H. Khan (1975)
Sind	Rupees	892	111	8.0	1972–73	M. H. Khan (1975)

Sources: The evidence from Desai (1971) and Dasgupta (1977a) is compiled partly in Herdt (1980).

Figure 5-2. South Asia: Labor Use for Modern and Traditional Varieties, Selected Regions
(workdays per hectare)

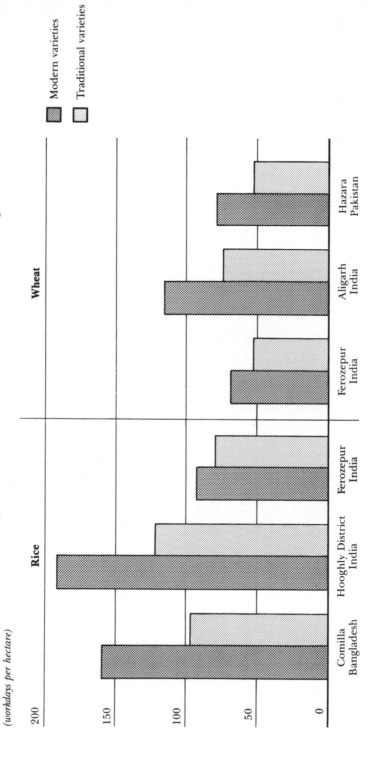

Source: Table 5-13.

hired labor that is of primary interest to the landless.

The demand for hired labor has also increased substantially. The increased volume of farm work has been too high to meet from family labor alone, at least on a seasonal basis. As a result, the proportion as well as the total amount of hired labor used in farm production has increased. Table 5-13 presents some of the relevant evidence from South Asia. Herdt (1980) gives supportive evidence from Bangladesh, India, and Pakistan as well as other Southeast Asian countries. He reports that in two-thirds of the studies reporting total labor the modern varieties used more than the local, and in 17 out of 22 studies reporting hired labor the same was true. When the findings of all studies were averaged, Herdt found that modern varieties absorbed 23 percent more labor and 21 percent more hired labor than traditional varieties.[8] Most of the increase in demand for hired labor takes the form of extra employment of casual laborers. Increases of this kind in India are reported by Dasgupta (1977a), in Pakistan by M. H. Khan (1975), and in Bangladesh by Clay (1975, 1979).

Additional outlays on hired labor have not been uniformly related to the adoption of HYVs. In some cases, the cost of hired labor may have actually declined as a percentage of total costs (which have increased significantly). Thus, although the total returns to labor have probably increased, the share going to labor in relation to other inputs may have declined, with negative consequences for the share of benefits accruing to labor (see Dasgupta 1977a, ch. 3). Because of the pronounced emphasis on hired labor in HYV cultivation, the percentage supplied by family labor has declined.

But it is not only family or local labor that is affected. Localities where HYVs have been adopted are normally more prosperous than others, and this has encouraged inflows of migrants from other areas to meet the increased demand, especially in peak periods. In the Indian Punjab, for example, in-migrants have come from very distant areas of Bihar, Rajasthan, and Uttar Pradesh. In-migration has also occurred in Andhra Pradesh, Haryana, Rajasthan, Tamil Nadu, and West Bengal, though to a lesser degree. Barker and Herdt (1978), in a study of rice-farming areas in thirty-six villages in South and Southeast Asia, found that an average of 39 percent of all farms in these villages reported using more labor; 56 percent hired more labor from within the village and 31 percent hired more from outside. Dramatic increases in off-farm employment are reported by Kaneda and Ghaffar (1970) and M. G. Chaudhry (1982) for the Pakistan Punjab and by Blyn (1983) and Sidhu and others (1979) in the Indian Punjab. Migration of labor out of states that have lagged and into areas that have led the Green Revolution is heaviest in the Indian Punjab. An estimated half a million migrant laborers from Bihar, Rajasthan,

Table 5-13. South Asia: Labor Use and Yields for Modern Varieties (MV) and Traditional Varieties (TV), Selected Regions

Region	Year	Labor input				Yield (metric ton per hectare)		MV/TV (percent)		Percentage of hired labor	
		Workdays per hectare		Workdays per metric ton				Workdays per hectare	Yield per hectare		
		MV	TV	MV	TV	MV	TV			MV	TV
		Rice									
Mymensingh, Bangladesh[a]	1969–70	194	137	57	62	3.4	2.2	142	155	59	52
Comilla, Bangladesh[b]	1967	160	97	42	48	3.8	2.0	165	190	—	—
Hooghly District, India[c]	1970–73	192	122	66	61	2.9	2.0	157	145	44	52
Thanjavur, India[c]	1967–70	116	134	55	61	2.1	2.2	87	95	80	77
Ferozepur, India[c]	1967–70	92	79	22	33	4.1	2.4	116	171	55	63
Sri Lanka[d]	1970–71	169	127	42	41	4.0	3.1	133	129	43	40
Gujranwala, Pakistan[e]	1972–74	45	45	16	24	2.8	1.9	100	147	68	61
Sahiwal, Pakistan[e]	1972–74	21	19	7	11	3.0	1.8	111	167	46	56
Lyallpur, Pakistan[e]	1972–74	n.a.	121	n.a.	67	n.a.	1.8	n.a.	n.a.	n.a.	73
Jacobabad, Pakistan[e]	1972–73	15	19	7	12	2.2	1.6	79	138	39	43

Wheat

Location	Year										
Ferozepur, India[a]	1967–70	68	52	27	33	2.5	1.6	131	156	56	54
Muzaffarnagar, India[a]	1966–69	63	58	20	32	3.1	1.8	109	172	n.a.	n.a.
Aligarh, India[f]	1967–68	115	73	31	38	3.7	1.9	158	195	n.a.	n.a.
Hazara, Pakistan[f]	1969–70	78	52	56	65	1.5	0.8	150	175	n.a.	n.a.
Gujranwala, Pakistan[e]	1972–74	31	45	17	35	1.8	1.3	69	138	65	66
Sahiwal, Pakistan[e]	1972–74	13	26	6	16	2.2	1.6	50	138	65	63
Lyallpur, Pakistan[e]	1972–74	25	n.a.	10	n.a.	2.4	n.a.	n.a.	n.a.	66	n.a.
Jacobabad, Pakistan[e]	1972–74	21	20	26	25	0.8	0.8	105	100	27	11

n.a. Not available.
a. IRRI (1978a).
b. Iftikhar Ahmed (1975).
c. Farm Management Surveys.
d. Hameed and others (1977).
e. M. H. Khan (1975).
f. Bartsch (1977).

and Uttar Pradesh have helped to relieve seasonal labor shortages there. Unfortunately, however, their settlements have led to social friction with communal overtones (G. Singh 1984; Gill 1976).

Thus the Green Revolution has increased the employment prospects not only for hired labor in the areas where it has been successful but also for in-migrants from more depressed areas. The consequences have not necessarily been positive. For example, the overall participation rates of village workers have declined; women, who specialize in harvesting and transplanting activities, are being displaced by migrant labor; although the overall volume of work has increased, a smaller number of the landless in a village may now find themselves being employed for longer hours; and labor mobility among jobs, villages, and regions has broken down traditional patron-client relationships between landowners and agricultural laborers. The Jajmani system in northern India, for example, has collapsed: cash payments are replacing payments in kind, and permanent or assured contracts are giving way to seasonal or casual day contracts (see Critchfield 1980). There are growing reports of rural conflicts over wages, conditions of work, and output-sharing arrangements as traditionally accepted contractual relationships dissolve.

Positive effects on wages are found in areas of heavy HYV *adoption, but they are often offset by downward aggregate pressures on real wages.* Changes in the demand for labor have had a complex, and not necessarily favorable, impact on real wages. Studies of changes in wages have been confounded not only by mechanization and other factors but also by a lack of analytical clarity. As Herdt (1980, p. 36) correctly points out:

> Some observers have confused the question of whether the new varieties absorb more labor than existing varieties with the question of whether the demand for labor has kept pace with its supply. An unfortunate lack of logic lies behind the idea that because labor absorption by agriculture using modern technology has failed to keep up with the growth in the supply of labor, the technology has caused the failure and should therefore be abandoned.

Since there has been little growth in per capita agricultural production in most regions of the subcontinent, it is hardly surprising to find that real wages have fallen. In areas of stagnation in output per capita, if the growth in employment were proportional to growth in output, and if the growth in the labor force were proportional to population growth, then one would expect real wages to fall in the absence of rapid growth in industrial employment (which has been characteristic of South Asia). Since employment elasticities with regard to output are generally less than unity and the rural labor force has grown faster than population in the subcontinent, labor supply has out-stripped demand. Declining real wages are thus a natural conse-quence of underlying demographic pressures; they do not signal the failure of the new technologies, which have added to aggregate de-mand. Without the technologies, real wages would have fallen even faster in most regions of South Asia. This judgment is supported by the clear evidence of rising real wages in areas where the Green Revo-lution has been most prominent—the Indian Punjab, Gujarat, Haryana, Tamil Nadu, Uttar Pradesh, and Pakistan (Mehra 1976). Strong correlations have been established between agricultural growth and increase in real wages by both M. S. Ahluwalia (1978) and Lal (1976) for India. Rising real wages in Pakistan are confirmed by Guisinger and Hicks (1978) and M. G. Chaudhry (1982).

Aggregate or even state-level data can be misleading because they often combine high-growth and low-growth districts. Subject to these limitations, two generalizations are possible: (a) *daily* real wages have definitely risen in states where HYVs or irrigation has been widely adopted, and (b) within a particular state or district real wages have been higher in localities with higher adoption rates.

In the Indian Punjab and Haryana the impact on real wages has differed for different activities (table 5-14). In general, real wages have risen most slowly for activities that have been extensively mechanized—especially plowing and harvesting—and far more rap-idly for those (such as weeding, sowing, and cotton picking) that have not. Real wages have also risen significantly in rural trades such as blacksmithing and carpentry.

Although real wages have increased in HYV areas, their rate of in-crease has usually fallen behind the rate of growth of production. As a consequence the share of wages in total labor income may in fact have declined, with a negative impact on income distribution.

There is a need to distinguish between *daily* and *yearly* real wages, for it is possible for daily wages to increase and yearly earnings to de-cline if the number of days worked declines. There is some evidence that this has not occurred, at least in the Punjab. Farm management data from the Punjab show that workdays per hectare of cultivated and cropped area increased by 40 percent and 25 percent respectively between 1955–56 and 1968–69, during a period when both cultivated and cropped areas were increasing (Mehra 1976). More credible data on wage shares and incomes of the landless before and after the Green Revolution are unavailable. But it is fair to conclude that where rates of agricultural growth have been high (in excess of 3–4 percent a year) real wages and incomes of the landless have gone up. Thus some benefits have "trickled down" to varying degrees, depending on institutional and technological conditions.

Table 5-14. India: Changes in Money and Real Wages in Punjab and Haryana for Agricultural Tasks

Year	Money wages								Real wages								CPIAL[a]
	(1)	(2)	(3)	(4)	(5)	(6)	(7)	(8)	(1)	(2)	(3)	(4)	(5)	(6)	(7)	(8)	
								Punjab									
1954	2.25	1.78	1.69	2.56	0.78	2.37	3.50	3.50	2.30	1.82	1.72	2.61	0.80	2.42	3.57	3.57	0.92
1955	2.19	1.76	1.69	2.69	0.81	2.50	3.62	3.50	2.23	1.80	1.72	2.74	0.83	2.55	3.69	3.57	0.98
1956	2.15	1.81	1.75	2.62	0.78	2.50	3.50	3.37	2.19	1.85	1.79	2.67	0.80	2.55	3.57	3.44	0.93
1957	2.29	2.02	2.02	3.13	1.80	2.37	3.76	3.77	2.29	2.02	2.02	3.13	1.80	2.37	3.76	3.77	1.00
1958	2.40	2.18	2.03	2.51	1.00	2.51	3.78	3.86	2.33	2.12	1.97	2.44	1.55	2.44	3.67	3.75	1.03
1959	2.46	2.23	2.12	2.30	2.25	2.36	3.76	4.00	2.24	2.03	1.93	2.09	2.05	2.15	3.42	3.63	1.10
1960	2.46	2.43	2.37	2.40	2.00	2.20	4.29	4.48	2.41	2.38	2.32	2.35	1.96	2.16	4.21	4.39	1.02
1961	2.46	2.53	2.39	2.48	2.00	2.28	4.18	4.37	2.37	2.43	2.30	2.38	1.92	2.19	4.02	4.20	1.04
1962	2.62	2.56	2.60	2.80	2.70	2.61	4.44	4.61	2.47	2.42	2.45	2.64	2.55	2.46	4.19	4.35	1.06
1963	2.79	2.85	2.59	2.88	2.31	2.52	4.70	4.74	2.63	2.69	2.44	2.72	2.18	2.38	4.43	4.47	1.06
1964	3.12	3.13	2.95	3.45	2.50	2.77	5.08	5.10	2.44	2.45	2.30	2.70	1.95	2.16	3.97	3.98	1.28
1965	3.45	3.40	3.31	4.01	2.69	3.02	5.46	5.46	2.48	2.45	2.30	2.70	1.95	2.16	3.97	3.98	1.28
1966	3.82	3.73	3.66	3.94	3.35	3.51	6.12	6.08	2.58	2.52	2.47	2.66	2.26	2.37	4.14	4.11	1.48
1967	4.27	4.18	3.94	4.93	4.00	4.14	7.02	7.11	2.20	2.15	2.03	2.54	2.06	2.13	3.62	3.66	1.94
1968	4.70	4.74	4.59	6.14	4.00	4.71	8.29	8.61	2.46	2.48	2.40	3.21	2.09	2.47	4.34	4.51	1.91
1969	6.15	6.12	5.83	7.43	3.97	5.57	10.29	10.20	3.19	3.17	3.02	3.85	2.06	2.89	5.28	5.28	1.93
1970	6.46	6.47	6.32	7.71	3.24	6.40	11.56	11.54	3.30	3.30	3.22	3.93	1.65	3.27	5.90	5.89	1.96
1971	6.62	6.62	6.55	7.94	3.48	6.46	12.31	12.31	3.25	3.25	3.21	3.89	1.71	3.17	6.03	6.03	2.04
1972	6.64	6.73	6.72	8.24	3.29	6.76	12.45	12.44	3.05	3.09	3.08	3.78	1.51	3.10	5.71	5.71	2.18
1973	7.14	7.24	7.12	8.98	3.93	7.62	13.04	13.03	2.94	2.98	2.93	3.70	1.62	3.14	5.37	5.36	2.43
1974	7.54	7.59	7.36	8.38	4.57	7.74	13.73	13.73	2.42	2.43	2.36	2.69	1.46	2.48	4.40	4.40	3.12
1975	8.43	8.58	8.48	10.34	5.44	8.60	14.68	14.68	2.56	2.61	2.58	3.14	1.65	2.61	4.46	4.46	3.29
1976	8.64	8.65	8.54	11.04	4.71	8.93	16.31	16.42	2.92	2.92	2.89	3.73	1.59	3.02	5.51	5.55	2.96

Year	Punjab (1)	(2)	(3)	(4)	(5)	(6)	(7)	(8)	Haryana (1)	(2)	(3)	(4)	(5)	(6)	(7)	(8)	CPI[a]
1977	9.21	9.21	9.01	9.96	5.53	9.18	18.44	18.65	2.83	2.83	2.77	3.06	1.70	2.82	5.67	5.74	3.25
1978	9.73	9.68	9.51	11.29	5.08	9.92	20.72	20.68	2.93	2.92	2.86	3.40	1.53	2.99	6.24	6.23	3.32
Percentage increase, 1954–78									27	61	66	30	91	24	75	74	238
1954	2.52	2.20	2.01	2.60	1.50	2.51	3.73	3.83	2.29	2.00	1.83	2.36	1.36	2.28	3.39	3.48	1.02
1955	2.78	2.48	2.64	2.51	1.75	2.43	3.52	4.09	2.73	2.43	2.59	2.46	1.72	2.38	3.45	4.01	1.02
1956	2.56	2.57	2.11	2.69	2.00	2.12	4.51	4.64	2.46	2.47	2.03	2.59	1.92	2.04	4.34	4.46	1.04
1957	2.99	2.78	2.52	2.97	2.75	2.63	4.74	4.98	2.82	2.62	2.38	2.80	2.59	2.48	4.47	4.70	1.06
1958	3.06	2.84	2.66	3.36	2.40	2.78	5.04	5.02	2.89	2.68	2.51	3.17	2.26	2.62	4.75	4.74	1.06
1959	3.23	3.03	2.73	3.29	2.25	2.96	4.85	5.00	2.52	2.37	2.13	2.57	1.76	2.31	3.79	3.91	1.28
1960	3.13	2.77	2.58	2.90	2.50	2.75	5.13	5.17	2.27	2.01	1.87	2.10	1.81	1.99	3.72	3.75	1.38
1961	3.47	3.21	2.98	3.33	3.16	3.20	5.66	5.54	2.34	2.17	2.01	2.25	2.14	2.16	3.82	3.74	1.48
1962	3.96	3.99	3.51	4.55	3.20	3.55	5.98	6.04	2.04	2.06	1.81	2.35	1.65	1.83	3.08	3.11	1.94
1963	4.66	4.33	3.75	4.80	3.42	4.18	7.44	7.49	2.44	2.27	1.96	2.51	1.79	2.19	3.90	3.92	1.91
1964	5.46	5.08	4.31	5.29	3.71	4.59	8.32	8.48	2.83	2.63	2.28	2.74	1.92	2.33	4.31	4.39	1.93
1965	6.07	5.75	4.84	6.01	3.82	5.17	9.00	9.10	3.10	2.93	2.47	3.07	1.95	2.64	4.59	4.64	1.96
1966	6.48	6.24	5.28	7.24	4.59	5.91	9.73	9.70	3.32	3.20	2.71	3.71	2.35	3.03	4.99	4.97	1.95
1967	6.76	6.34	5.46	5.97	4.50	5.71	10.13	10.09	3.07	2.88	2.48	2.71	2.18	2.60	4.60	4.59	2.20
1968	7.04	6.45	5.69	6.02	4.23	5.85	10.02	10.05	2.90	2.65	2.34	2.48	1.74	2.41	4.12	4.14	2.43
1969	7.11	6.57	5.45	6.61	5.03	5.81	10.25	10.60	2.28	2.11	1.75	2.12	1.61	1.86	3.29	3.40	3.12
1970	7.99	7.53	6.60	7.68	6.58	6.77	12.24	11.94	2.43	2.29	2.01	2.33	2.00	2.06	3.72	3.63	3.29
1971	8.37	8.15	6.88	8.45	8.25	7.42	10.99	12.56	2.83	2.75	2.32	2.85	2.79	2.51	3.71	4.24	2.76
1972	8.92	8.53	7.64	8.87	7.14	7.38	12.79	13.55	2.74	2.62	2.35	2.73	2.20	2.27	3.94	4.17	3.25
Percentage increase, 1954–73									20	31	28	16	61	-1	16	20	218

Notes: The tasks are as follows: (1) plowing, (2) weeding, (3) sowing, (4) harvesting, (5) cotton picking, (6) other agricultural labor, (7) blacksmithing, and (8) carpentry.

a. Consumer price index for agricultural laborers.

Sources: Statistical Abstract of the Punjab and *Statistical Abstract of Haryana* (Chandigarh, various years); Sheila Bhalla (1979).

Effects of Mechanization

Meanwhile, two other factors, mechanization and the displacement of tenants, have had a consistently negative impact on the prospects of the landless. They are related in the sense that the former has in some cases encouraged the latter. A series of linked developments is briefly outlined here.

Labor use and hence the employment prospects of the landless have been reduced by mechanization. Mechanization is generally inconsistent with the factor endowments and social organization of labor prevailing in most regions of South Asia. There is a distinction, however, between land-intensifying mechanization (motors, low-lift pumps, tubewells, and small power tillers) and labor-displacing mechanization (tractors; various types of harvesting equipment such as threshers, combines, cotton pickers, and vegetable harvesters; and chemical weed control). Land-intensifying mechanization generally raises cropping intensities as a result of better irrigation or higher plant densities, or both. Although it displaces some task-specific labor, it raises the demand for labor in other activities—and can therefore have a net positive effect on labor use. The second type of mechanism only lowers labor demand.

Analysts are still debating whether tractors are labor displacing, with some arguing that tractors raise both yields and intensity. A large number of studies specifically directed at tractor use have been carried out in South Asia, and an informative analytical and empirical review has been compiled by Binswanger (1979). He found that tractors have not significantly raised cropping intensities and that double and even triple cropping can be achieved without them. They have few yield-increasing effects, and the differences in yields between farms with tractors and those without owe more to the higher intensity of fertilizer use on the former. Tractors produce a few gains associated with timeliness, mainly in arid and semi-arid areas, and are responsible for only a few changes in cropping patterns (such as the reduction in fodder areas as animals are displaced).

The type of on-farm labor likely to be affected by mechanization will depend on the activities being mechanized and the size of farm (as noted earlier, the proportion of hired labor generally rises with farm size). Because mechanization is often task-specific, its impact on family and hired labor can vary considerably. Tractors, harvesters, threshers, and chemical weed control considerably reduce the amount of hired (often casual) labor required for plowing, sowing, weeding, and harvesting. Tubewells, however, tend to offset the labor-displacing effects of this mechanization, as has been shown in a large number of detailed studies for South Asia.[9] The net effect on employment of mechanization, more intense use of land and irrigation, and HYV adoption can be either positive or negative. Most studies show an overall decline in farm employment over time (Day and Singh 1977; D. Singh, Singh, and Singh 1981; Joshi, Bahl, and Jha 1981; Mehra 1976; and McInerney and Donaldson 1975).

Nevertheless, many cross-sectional farm surveys show tractors to be associated with neither an increase nor a decrease in labor use per hectare.[10] This anomaly partly reflects variations in the level of adoption of HYVs and in the intensity of fertilizer use and irrigation—all of which, being capital-intensive, are associated with size of holding, at least in the initial phase of adoption.

The confounding effects of these variations are illustrated by the conflicting evidence from West Pakistan. Although there is general agreement that tubewells have increased the demand for labor considerably (Kaneda 1969; Nulty 1972), there is little agreement on the impact of tractorization on employment. Bose and Clark (1969) and McInerney and Donaldson (1975) show a negative impact on employment, whereas Gotsch (1973) and Naseem (1971) argue that the effects have been positive. There is general agreement, however, that mechanical cultivation was both cost reducing and output augmenting in Pakistan. M. G. Chaudhry (1986) even argues that the impact on income distribution has been favorable for both small farmers and landless laborers, who have been major beneficiaries of the tubewell-tractor technology associated with technical change in Pakistan.

B. Agarwal (1981) provides evidence from India not only on the negative impact of tractor use but also on the positive impact of tubewells on labor use per hectare in HYV wheat cultivation in farms of all sizes in the Punjab. She estimated that the net impact was negative, especially on smaller farms. A survey of other recent findings from India is provided in Basant (1987).

On balance, it seems that the potential positive impact of HYVs on employment has been seriously eroded by mechanization in many parts of South Asia. A full picture of the adverse effect of mechanization needs to go beyond the observed decline in employment per hectare and estimate the *potential employment forgone*—that is, the employment that would have been possible if more labor-intensive techniques had been combined with HYV adoption. Two studies give some idea of the direct impact of mechanization on total labor use in farm production. The first, by Joshi, Bahl, and Jha (1981), attributes the changes in total labor use to various technologies on farms in Uttar Pradesh between 1966–67 and 1977–78. The results (see table 5-15) clearly indicate that irrigation and the use of HYVs greatly increased labor use—by 55.4 hours per hectare in wheat production and 6.4 hours per hectare in rice production. But these gains were offset by

Table 5-15. India: Changes in Total Labor Input, 1966–67 to 1977–78, Uttar Pradesh and Punjab
(work hours per hectare)

Technology	Wheat			Rice			Wheat, Punjab
	East Uttar Pradesh	West Uttar Pradesh	Uttar Pradesh	East Uttar Pradesh	West Uttar Pradesh	Uttar Pradesh	
Irrigation of additional area	16.9	22.0	25.7	1.5	4.9	3.3	16.4
Irrigation technology (switch to tubewells)	−11.7	−4.0	−6.4	−0.7	−1.8	−1.3	−34.6
Seed variety (HYV)	35.5	19.9	22.1	1.7	6.7	2.6	17.4
Tractor plowing	−12.4	−44.4	−19.1	−15.7	−65.2	−37.3	−5.3
Mechanical threshing	−13.2	−50.7	−0.1	−0.7	−0.7	−0.4	−70.6
Chemical weed control	−6.2	−15.4	−6.7	−0.4	−1.4	−6.9	n.a.
Irrigation-varietal interaction	7.4	6.5	7.6	0.5	1.2	0.5	} −14.8
Other interactions	−6.0	−14.4	−0.3	−0.2	0.3	−0.3	
Change in total labor use	10.3	−89.5	−21.4	−13.4	−55.3	−39.8	n.a.
Linear annual growth rate of employment (percent)	−0.2	−1.7	−0.2	−0.2	−1.1	−0.7	n.a.

n.a. Not available.
Source: Basant (1987), p. 1348.

the irrigation technology used (tubewells have a positive impact on intensity but use less labor than traditional persian wheels) and by tractor plowing, mechanical threshing, and chemical weed control. The net effect was a decline in labor use per hectare in Uttar Pradesh.

A second, similar result is from the Punjab. I have used a dynamic model developed in Day and Singh (1977), which traced the impact of the Green Revolution and labor use in the central districts over twenty-five years, to project what would have happened to labor use if tractors, threshers, power cane crushers, and tubewells had not come on the scene—that is, if mechanization had not occurred (see table 5-16). Three scenarios are explored: case A, with the mechanization that occurred during the period; case B, without mechanization and without allowing for increases in the supply of animal draft power or for the in-migration of labor to offset the absence of mechanization; and case C, without mechanization but allowing for an increased supply of draft animals and the in-migration of labor as needed to substitute for mechanization. Going from A to B increases labor use per hectare, but reduces the cropped area because of lack of farm power and additional labor; private profits per hectare also fall.

The interesting comparison is between scenarios A and C. When machines are taken away but fully replaced by animal and human labor, so that the same area is cropped and cropping intensities remain unchanged, the impact on labor use is dramatic (figure 5-3). Without mechanization (case C) total labor use would have been higher than case A by 12, 59, 134, and 477 percent in 1955, 1965, 1970, and 1980 respectively! Furthermore, of the total net increase of 144 million and 493 million days of labor use in 1970 and 1980 (when certain tasks were almost totally mechanized), more than 48 percent in 1970 and more than 80 percent in 1980 would have been met by hired or migrant labor. These results vividly illustrate the massive negative impact of mechanization on farm employment in crop production and on opportunities for the landless. This negative impact has also been documented by Basant (1987) with data from Uttar Pradesh and Punjab (table 5-15).

Some mechanization has also been associated with displacement of tenants. Two types of displacement have occurred. In the first, tenants on medium or large holdings have been displaced because mechanization makes it possible for owners to farm a larger holding with their own household labor. Less permanent and casual labor is hired, tenant farmers are evicted, and larger operated holdings appear. This pattern is especially common in Pakistan. Tractor use there has been associated with a decrease in the number of medium-size holdings (5–10 acres) and an increase in the average size of holding.

Table 5-16. India: Impact of Mechanization on Labor Use in Central Punjab, 1955–80

Item	1955			1965			1970			1980		
	A	B	C	A	B	C	A	B	C	A	B	C
Area cropped (millions of hectares)	1.41	1.24	1.41	1.77	1.49	1.77	2.03	1.47	2.03	2.64	1.13	2.44
Total labor use (millions of workdays)	108	113	121	108	165	172	107	186	251	102	149	595
Labor use per hectare (workdays)	76.6	91.1	85.8	61.0	100.7	97.2	52.7	126.5	123.6	39.0	131.8	225.4
Tractor use (millions of hours)	2.3	0.0	0.0	5.5	0.0	0.0	12.1	0.0	0.0	29.2	0.0	0.0
Tractor use per hectare (days)	1.63	—	—	3.1	—	—	6.0	—	—	11.1	—	—
Private profits per hectare (constant 1970 rupees)	546	488	583	1,027	909	1,161	1,885	1,269	1,701	2,513	1,270	2,175

— Not applicable.
A: With mechanization—that is, tractors, threshers, harvesters, and tubewells.
B: Without mechanization and without increases in animal draft power or migrant labor.
C: Without mechanization but with increases in animal draft power and migrant labor.
Source: Model results; see Day and Singh (1977) for a description of model.

Figure 5-3. *Central Punjab, India: Labor Use*
under Scenarios A and C

(workdays per hectare)

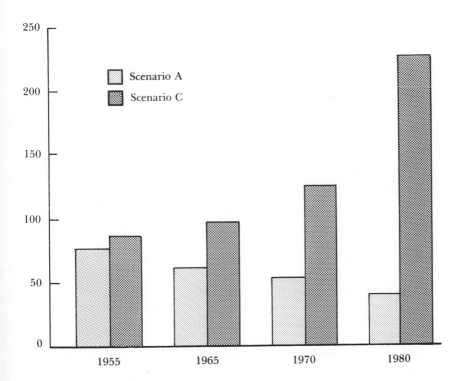

Note: See Table 5-16 for scenario details.
Source: Table 5-16.

McInerney and Donaldson (1975) calculated that 4.5 tenants had been displaced per tractor in Pakistan and that the average size of operated holdings had increased from 18 to 44 hectares. Similar evictions were reported by M. H. Khan (1981) and B. Ahmad (1972); those affected are by no means the poorest rural households.

A second type of displacement, which is much more common in India and Bangladesh, occurs when small tenants are evicted because the owners (who have previously leased out their land) realize that they can now profitably farm the land themselves with Green Revolution technology. Such evictions are reported by Dasgupta (1977a) and A. R. Khan (in ILO 1977a). The high productivity of land under HYVs has thus given the landowners an additional incentive to evict tenants and do their own cultivation, thereby swelling the ranks of landless agricultural laborers. This kind of eviction has been more severe where farms are large enough to make mechanization privately profitable.

Mechanization and HYV technologies are by no means the chief causes of tenant displacement, however. Ironically, most evictions happened in earlier years, in response to announced "reforms" that set ceilings for landholdings but were never carried out. Tenancy promptly went underground instead. In the Indian Punjab, for example, the percentage of total cultivated area leased to tenants declined from 77 percent in 1955–56 to 35.4 percent by 1960–61, *before* the Green Revolution; it fell by much less, to 28 percent, by 1970–71. Similar evidence is available for Pakistan (M. H. Khan 1979b). Thus well-meaning land reforms that were not implemented evicted more tenants than technological change did (see chapter 8 for a more detailed discussion of land reform).

Mechanization is not a necessary concomitant of the Green Revolution, and the new technologies have been adopted without it. It has been claimed that the HYV technologies form an indivisible package, in which the labor-enhancing components (seeds, nutrients, and irrigation) cannot be separated from the labor-displacing effects of mechanization. Consequently, the net effect on labor use is said to be slight or negative. For example, Griffin and Ghose (1979) have stated that tractors and modern varieties are politically linked, and therefore the undesirable aspects of modernization (tractorization) cannot be eliminated and only the desirable aspects (modern varieties) retained.

Contrary to this view, there is ample evidence that modern varieties are being widely adopted without tractors in many areas. Auden-Laerina and Barker (1978) and Barker and Herdt (1978), for example, present data from thirty villages in Southeast Asia (India, Indonesia, Malaysia, Pakistan, and Thailand) which show that modern varieties have been widely adopted without mechanization. In twelve villages studied in India 96 percent of all farmers reported using modern varieties, whereas only 27 percent reported using tractors. In Pakistan the association is higher—all farmers reported using modern varieties, and 73 percent reported using tractors.[11] Barker and Herdt (1978) found that 50–60 percent of the tractor users in India used more hired labor *after* they began using new varieties, while 60–70 percent of those without tractors also used more hired labor. Extensive evidence has already been provided in this book on the adoption of HYVs by small farmers throughout South Asia with little or no mechanization.

The adoption of tractors is an example of how government policies have induced the rapid spread of capital-intensive technologies generally unsuited to South Asia, where labor is abundant. The quantifiable gains from the use of tractors seem mainly to be the reduced costs of animal and human labor. Less tangible benefits (such as leisure, conspicuous consumption, status seeking, and reduced reliance on human labor that is deemed "unreliable" or "undesirable") have also been associated with tractorization. Substitution of mechanical for human or animal power can sometimes be justified by circumstances—for example, very hard soils, acute seasonal labor shortages, or the need for timely operations to permit multiple cropping —but by and large it has been encouraged by inappropriately cheap credit and low capital costs.

In general, the private benefits of mechanization far exceed the social costs.[12] The latter can be substantial, however. To subsidize tractors either directly or through exchange rate or credit policies is to subsidize unemployment, not only because tractors reduce the demand for labor but also because the foreign exchange (or domestic resources) used to buy tractors and fuels could have been used for job-creating purchases of fertilizer. The landless are the main losers because they have been replaced by machines for the heavy tillage, weeding, and harvesting operations. The main beneficiaries are a few large landholders who, because they have access to land and capital, can reap the economies of scale inherent in farm machinery. The already skewed distribution of income and assets in rural areas thus becomes worse.

The rate of mechanization can be slowed considerably if credit and capital policies are corrected to bring the very high private rates of return in line with the lower social ones. Ultimately, however, mechanization reflects the enormous inequality in the distribution of owned and operated holdings, a phenomenon that can be corrected only by the redistribution of rural assets.

Food Prices

Perhaps the greatest positive effect of the Green Revolution is that food prices have been lower than they would have been. The benefits to the landless (who gain both as consumers and producers) exceed all other distributional benefits or costs associated with the Green Revolution. As I have already noted, the poor spend a disproportionately large share of their incomes on food grains; by raising food-grain output dramatically (and faster than total output in the agricultural sector), the Green Revolution has also ensured that the poor as consumers and producers have been the major gainers. Astonishingly, this point is almost totally ignored by the critics of the new technologies. Bad as the conditions of the rural poor are, what do the critics imagine their prospects would have been had there been no Green Revolution?

Food-grain prices do not have to fall either nominally or in real terms for this point to be valid; they need only to be lower than they otherwise would have been. Prices are determined by both demand and supply; since demand is partly demographically determined, if the Green Revolution had failed to increase food supplies it would have doomed the landless poor to higher prices and less employment and income. Mass starvation for the growing population in South Asia—an outcome predicted often enough as recently as the 1970s—would have been the most likely outcome.

Analysts have long emphasized that the poor as consumers are the chief beneficiaries of measures to increase food output (see, for example, Mellor and Lele 1973; Mellor 1976; and Lipton 1977, 1978). Hayami and Herdt (1977) have shown that producers who consume a large proportion of the rice they produce recoup much of the benefits of technical change. They further show that the degree to which the benefits are internalized by producers is inversely related to the proportion of output sold, implying that smaller farmers gain more than larger ones. I have calculated the effect of an increase in cereal prices on the demand for food grains among different rural groups, using Indian data and taking account of differences in expenditure elasticities and proportions of output marketed. I found that for every 1 percent increase in cereal prices, the landless would be forced to reduce their demand by 0.9 percent, marginal farmers by 0.7 percent, small farmers by 0.4 percent, and medium-size farmers by 0.03 percent, while large farmers would actually increase their consumption by 0.13 percent because their incomes would increase enough to offset the price effects. Thus it is the landless and the near landless (and urban consumers) who stand to gain the most when increased production causes food prices to fall.

Food prices did not actually fall in India, because higher production was used to replace food imports rather than to increase the domestic availability of food.[13] Rationing prevented prices from rising further than they did, but the major beneficiaries of rationing were urban consumers (the rural poor had little or no access to ration shops). In Bangladesh, too, the major benefits of rationing are confined to urban groups (World Bank 1979).

To sum up, it is totally wrong to state that the landless or near landless did not benefit from the Green Revolution. On the contrary, they have benefited considerably from increases in food-grain production and employment. Mechanization has dampened these gains, but real wages have risen rapidly in the areas where mechanization has been most rapid. This is because the Green Revolution has increased incomes in general and has therefore indirectly increased nonfarm employment opportunities where it has been most successful.

Distribution of Gains from the Green Revolution

It is now widely accepted that HYV technologies have distributed their benefits unevenly, with the largest gains going to large farmers, smaller gains going to smaller farmers, and the smallest gains going to the landless. But although there is extensive evidence to support the view that *all* rural households have gained to one degree or another from the Green Revolution, many continue to assert that the new technologies have benefited only the rich and that they have positively damaged the prospects of the poor.

Such a belief was understandable in view of the experience in the 1960s, when small farmers lagged considerably in HYV adoption and the benefits for the landless were little known. Some observers based their pessimistic conclusions on the distribution of gains from even earlier programs, such as the Integrated Agricultural Development Program in India, which were specifically directed toward large and progressive farmers.[14] Many then agreed with Gotsch (1971) that the rapid growth of the 1960s had made most of the small farmers relatively worse off, or with Bardhan (1973b) that despite great progress in agricultural development the extent of poverty of agricultural labor households had not declined. The repetition of this early evidence led many to doubt that increases in agricultural production or rapid agricultural growth associated with HYVs would do much to improve conditions of the rural poor. Indeed, Griffin and Ghose (1979) concluded that it had no effect whatsoever on the underlying dimensions of rural poverty. Others argued as did Saith (1981) that, although the nominal incomes of the rural poor had certainly increased, higher agricultural prices had offset all these gains—leaving the poor little better off.

With the second decade of the Green Revolution—and it must be recalled that the process is still far from complete in most of South Asia—the evidence now supports a different view. Small farmers may have gained relatively less and the landless have probably gained the least from the HYV technologies, but *all* rural households have gained absolutely and in real terms. According to this view, the benefits to the rural poor have been seriously eroded, however, by mechanization and by institutional biases in the agrarian structure that have reduced access to essential inputs. As a consequence, income distributions have worsened in rural areas.

Whether one attributes the worsening of income distribution and the unequal distribution of gains to the HYVs alone, or to the systemic unequal distribution of landholdings, depends on whether net returns per hectare are positively related to farm size. A number of studies seem to confirm that they are. Where per hectare gains on large farms outstrip the gains on small farms, income distribution among farming households would have worsened even if the size distribution of land assets had been even.[15] But other studies cite no significant differences in net returns per hectare between small and large farms as a result of the introduction of HYVs.[16] In these cases, the relative gains of small farmers would have been the same as for larger farms, but the skewed size of holdings meant that large farmers would have gained absolutely more. Rural income distribution could have become even more skewed because of the smaller gains by the landless.

A third group of studies has shown that the net returns per hectare on small farms have actually exceeded those on large farms or that farm income distributions have improved with the introduction of HYVs.[17] Of course, overall rural income distribution could still worsen, according to this view, unless the incomes of the landless keep up with those of the landed. Although a number of studies report considerable gains for the landless, few cite evidence that the landless have gained relatively more than those who have land to operate.[18] Thus most of the evidence would support the view that rural income distribution has worsened.

Part of the problem of assessing the gains from HYVs or other technologies has been that the process of technological change is still in progress and its consequences have yet to work themselves out fully. The areas of South Asia in which the Green Revolution is now complete—the Indian and Pakistani Punjabs—offer a preview of the likely consequences of widespread adoption of HYVs in South Asia. Recent evidence from these areas suggests that the gains for all classes of the rural poor have indeed been dramatic and mostly positive.

In the Indian Punjab a detailed and careful study by Bhalla and Chadha (1982) in the mid-1970s found that farmers with marginal (fewer than 2.5 acres) and small (between 2.5 and 5 acres) holdings were able to raise output and farm income per acre along with large farmers. The gains were distributed more or less in proportion to the initial landholdings, and because landholdings were skewed, so were the gains. But because of more opportunities for nonfarm earnings, total incomes were less skewed.

Mundle (1982), reviewing changes in the Indian Punjab from the early 1960s through the 1970s, found a sharp decline in the proportion of those who did not own land and a significant tendency for the number of people below the poverty line to decrease over the period as a result of increased production (see table A40). Although he found no real trend (increase or decrease) in the real wages of agricultural laborers, when all sources of income were included the per capita real income of rural agricultural labor households (those without land) was 50 percent higher in 1974–75 than a decade earlier (table A41). This is significant because rural labor households have been the fastest growing segment of the rural population, and before the large-scale adoption of the HYV technologies their real incomes were actually falling.

Although substantial segments of the rural population remain below the poverty line, a broader study (Mundle 1983) finds a significant negative correlation between agricultural production and rural poverty in almost every state—thus confirming Ahluwalia's (1978) contentions and refuting those of Griffin and Ghose (1979). Mundle also shows a significant trend toward a decline in poverty in Haryana, Punjab, and Tamil Nadu—three Indian states in which the Green Revolution has progressed the furthest. Field visits by other social scientists a decade after their first visits in the 1960s confirmed that all segments of the rural population had gained and that agricultural growth in the Punjab had more than offset the increases in population and large-scale in-migration. Leaf (1983) found the relative position of small farmers and the poor to have improved; he concluded that the gains had gone as much to the poorer villagers as to the wealthier and that social stability had increased. Blyn (1979, p. 707) found that although all farmers had gained from the Green Revolution, the gain was more apparent for the smaller cultivators. He concluded that

> though the universality of gain was apparent to my eye, I was amazed to find that urban, educated people generally took for granted that only rich, large landlords had gained, that by corruption they had cornered the input markets, monopolized the credit, oppressed the laborers—a kind of cant catechism. The most charitable view I can take of such talk is that it may represent the lag of public knowledge behind actual circumstances and that it may accurately reflect the early years of the Green Revolution.

These findings should lay to rest once and for all the view of some scholars that the Green Revolution in the Indian Punjab not only intensified inequalities, but also perpetuated poverty and destitution (see Bardhan 1973b; Byres 1972; and ILO 1977a).

Similar evidence is now available from Pakistan. Chaudhry (1982) has shown that the per acre incomes of small farmers nearly doubled between 1965–66 and 1970–71, while those of larger farmers increased by only 50–60 percent;[19] that relative income disparities have decreased; and that the indirect effects on employment were large (often exceeding the direct effects), with the result that real wages for rural labor increased fourfold and the share of income going to the rural landless greatly improved. He concluded that in Pakistan the Green Revolution has actually been responsible for a decline in income disparity between small and large farmers, between farm and nonfarm rural classes, and between well-to-do and poorer agricultural regions. This is in sharp contrast to the earlier assessment by Gotsch (1971). There will always be those who argue that the Punjabs are a special case, but the evidence suggests that they may simply be harbingers of what is likely to happen all over the subcontinent.

Conclusions

I have provided considerable evidence to show that, contrary to popular perceptions about the Green Revolution and HYV technologies, small farmers have adopted and continue to adopt HYVs when they are suitable and profitable. Although small farmers lagged behind larger farmers in initial adoption, they quickly caught up and matched their gains in productivity. Because small farmers lack resources, they cannot fertilize as large a proportion of their areas as can large farmers, but they compensate by applying higher input intensities. Meanwhile the landless and near landless have also benefited considerably—directly through increased on-farm employment opportunities and indirectly via increases in nonfarm employment and lower food prices. Mechanization has seriously eroded these benefits, but it is not a necessary concomitant of the HYV technologies and stems from faulty policies. The urban poor have also gained through lower food prices, as have all classes of rural households. Benefits have been unevenly distributed, but this is a consequence of the initial skewed distributions of landholdings and not of the new technologies. Indeed, *without* the HYVs and their widespread adoption, the lot of the urban and rural poor in South Asia would have been far worse than it is today. As Lipton (1978, p. 330) points out, "common sense suggests that without the extra food and work provided by the HYVs the poor would have been even worse off and in many cases dead."

Many other negative consequences have been attributed to the HYVs, including increasing landlessness, growing proletarianization of the peasantry, and growing concentration of land assets (Dasgupta 1977a). As I have argued in chapter 3, these are more the consequences of demographic pressures in an environment of unequal distribution of land assets than of new agricultural technologies. HYVs do have problems, but rural poverty or the worsening of agrarian conditions cannot be blamed on them; without HYVs, the difficulties facing the poor would have been far worse. There is little hope of redressing poverty without an even more widespread and rapid adoption of HYVs. They cannot alleviate poverty by themselves, however, and have failed to do so even where they are most successful; they are absolutely necessary but by no means sufficient for the reduction of poverty.

The gains of the worse-off would have been even more widespread if they had been preceded or accompanied by a really effective program to redistribute rural assets. Without new technologies, such a program would merely have redistributed poverty; without reforms the widespread adoption of new technologies has greatly helped but cannot solve the problems of poverty. They may have bought policy-makers some time, but demographic pressures over the years make it less and less likely that reforms plus new technologies will be able to give the rural poor a decent and reasonably secure livelihood. The time gained may also have been time lost, as I shall show in chapter 8, which examines how reforms failed in the past and why they may be even less feasible today.

Notes

1. See Bergmann and Eitel (1976); Farmer (1977); Frankel (1971); C. H. H. Rao (1975); and Dasgupta (1977a).

2. Several good reviews are available, including Herdt (1980); Dasgupta (1977a); Palmer (1972, 1975, 1976); Hameed and others (1977); Vyas (1975) Lockwood, Mukherjee, and Shand (1971); and India Planning Commission (1976).

3. See early evidence from India by Ladejinsky (1977); Harriss (1972); Frankel (1971); Michie (1973); Ojha (1970); Bell (1974b); R. Singh (1973); Parthasarathy (1973); C. H. H. Rao (1972, 1975); Wills (1972); Rajpurohit (1972). Similar findings for Pakistan are in Gotsch (1971, and in Stevens, Alavi, and Bertocci 1976); Naseem (1971); Amjad (1972); Lowdermilk (1972); and Eckert (1970) and for Bangladesh in Asaduzzaman and Islam (1976).

4. This was confirmed for India in studies by Muthiah (1971); Schluter (1971); Sharma (1973); Mencher (1974); Schluter and Mellor (1972); Subbarao (1980); Bhattacharya and Majid (1976); Sen (1970); and Vyas (1975) and in the extensive reviews of the HYVs and of farm-level data from agroeconomic research centers by Dasgupta (1977a). In particular, the inverse relationship between intensity of adoption and farm size has been clearly documented in the extensive review of India's HYV program by Lockwood, Mukherjee, and Shand (1971) and the follow-up study by the India Planning Commission (1976), as well as in the analysis by Bhalla (in Berry and Cline 1979) of the extensive data collected by the NCAER. (Some of the relevant evidence is shown in tables A22–A26 in the statistical appendix.)

Similar evidence from Bangladesh is provided by Faidley and Esmay (in Stevens, Alavi, and Bertocci 1976); I. Ahmed (1975); and Bose (1974a), who found farmers adopting HYVs at about the same rate regardless of size. Studies by I. Ahmed (1975); Rochin (1972); and Muqtada (1974) in Pakistan also found no farm size differences in adoption rates. Some studies continued, however, to find some differences. I. Ahmed (1981) found not only seasonal differences in adoption rates in Bangladesh, but also a positive relationship between farm size and adoption. M. H. Khan (1975) provides similar evidence for Pakistan.

5. The general thesis that it is middle-class, not upper-class farmers who are the first and fastest innovators was advanced by Cancian (1977). He looked at data on the adoption of new agricultural technologies in India, Kenya, Mexico, Pakistan, Philippines, and Taiwan and confirmed the hypothesis that it is not the lowest but the upper-middle classes who are most conservative.

6. By 1982–83 only 60 percent of the rice area in India and 20 percent of the rice area in Bangladesh was under HYVs. In Pakistan only 47 percent of the area was under HYVs, but another 42 percent was sown to basmati rice, which is more profitable and preferred for domestic consumption and exports. Local rice varieties account for only 10 percent of the rice area.

7. A review is available in Bartsch (1977). Billings and Singh (1970), C. H. H. Rao (1975), Dasgupta (1977a), Mehra (1976), Bapna (1973), Lakshminarayan (1973b), Acharya (1973), Joshi, Bahl, and Jha (1981), and Kumar, Mathur, and Singh (1981) among others confirm the above pattern for Indian data. Also see the series of studies reported in the *Indian Journal of Agricultural Economics* 36 (4), October–December 1981, and their review by Kartar Singh in the same issue.

Work by Johnston and Cownie (1969), Falcon (1970), Rochin (1972), M. H. Khan (1975), B. Ahmad (1972), and Haider (1977a) provides evidence of higher labor demand for Pakistan, while relevant information for Bangladesh is available in I. Ahmed (1975, 1981), Clay (1978), Clay and Khan (1977) Muqtada (1974), and Rahman (1981).

8. Further evidence for India is available from Dasgupta (1977a), while Haider (1977a) and I. Ahmed (1981) provide evidence for Pakistan and Bangladesh, and Herdt (1980) for rice-growing regions in Asia.

9. See I. Singh and Day (1975a and b); Acharya (1973); Mehra (1976); Kumar, Mathur, and Singh (1981); D. Singh, Singh, and Singh (1981); I. Ahmed (1981); B. Agarwal (1980a and b, 1981); and Blyn (1983).

10. See Binswanger (1979) for evidence. In some cases farms with tractors show higher labor use while those without show a lower labor use per hectare (see Mehra 1976, for example).

11. There is evidence that tractors may be used for specific tasks without the farms being fully mechanized. The use of tractors for one or two primary tillage operations displaces family labor from those tasks but leaves hired labor unchanged on other farms. See Day and Singh (1977); Herdt (in IRRI 1978a).

12. See Gotsch (1973); Kaneda (1972); Bose and Clark (1969); and Lockwood (1981).

13. I am indebted to Michael Lipton for making this point to me.

14. The most widely quoted study is Frankel (1971), which is based on data far predating the actual widespread introduction of HYVs in India. Its conclusion that small farmers were systematically excluded from gains was quickly generalized and widely accepted, even though it turned out to be wrong.

15. See C. H. H. Rao (1975), Lipton (1979), Bardhan (in Srinivasan and Bardhan 1974), Saini (1976), Parthasarathy and Prasad (in IRRI 1978b), and Clay (1975) for studies in India, and Stepanek (1979) and Clay (1978) for studies in Bangladesh.

16. These include Kahlon and Singh (1973) in the Punjab; Shanmugasundram (1973) in Tamil Nadu; R. Singh (1973), Bapna (1973), and Srinath Singh (1977) in Uttar Pradesh; Bhattacharya and Majid (1976) and Vyas (1975) in various regions of India; and M. H. Khan (1975) for Pakistan.

17. These include the studies by Sidhu and others (1979), Swenson (1976), A. J. Singh, Miglani, and Singh (1979), Leaf (1983), Gill (1976), Blyn (1979) in India and M. G. Chaudhry (1982) in Pakistan.

18. Clay (1975), Chaudhry (1982), Blyn (1979), and Mundle (1982) report gains for the landless; Ranade and Herdt (1978) in the Philippines show gains of hired labor exceeding those of operators.

19. M. H. Khan (1981) has taken M. G. Chaudhry to task for using too small a sample to reach this conclusion, but Chaudhry (1983) defends this by saying that the data he used are the only ones available for intertemporal comparisons.

6
Noncrop Employment for the Rural Poor

Too much attention has been focused on land as the source of rural income and employment and on access to land as a means of alleviating rural poverty. By contrast, too little attention has been given to noncrop and nonfarm employment as sources of income for the small farmers and the landless. Inasmuch as crop production will be unable to generate enough growth in the demand for labor to match the growth in the rural labor force, more reliance will have to be placed on other activities.

Noncrop activities are those which complement agriculture—livestock and dairying, small stock raising, poultry, fisheries, forestry—and are often carried out in farming and rural areas. Nonfarm activities are far more diverse and difficult to define; they include a variety of jobs in services, commerce, construction, transport repair and maintenance, and processing. Apart from being primary sources of income, they are also very important sources of secondary income for small farmers and the landless. Noncrop and nonfarm activities together account for between 20 and 25 percent of the labor force and income in India and 30 percent in Bangladesh. Data are less adequate for Pakistan, but over 20 percent of the total rural income is generated by nonfarm activities. In areas where there has been relative stagnation in agriculture, the lack of growth in employment opportunities has forced the poor into very marginal low-income activities as a secondary source of employment to supplement their income. In areas of rapid agricultural growth, totally new employment opportunities have been generated in the nonfarm sector with generally higher wages, and this has been a primary source of employment and income for the rural poor.

This chapter briefly discusses some of the noncrop activities, and chapter 7 examines the links between agricultural growth and the growth of nonfarm employment in rural industries.

Livestock and Dairying

Next to crop production, livestock rearing and dairying are the most important economic activities in rural South Asia. Livestock farming accounts for about 15 percent of the gross value of agricultural production in India and for about 25 percent of this aggregate in Pakistan; in Bangladesh it contributes about 7 percent of agricultural value added (Anderson and Leiserson 1978, 1980). The subcontinent's livestock herds consist predominantly of cattle, but also include buffaloes, sheep, goats, and pigs. Although animals are generally of poor quality, they nevertheless provide draft power for farming and transport, animal protein to supplement meager diets, and cash income (from hiring out cattle or buffaloes for draft services or from the sale of live animals or their products—milk, meat, hides, skins, and wool). Even animal waste products have their uses as fertilizer and as fuel for cooking and heating. Livestock farming contributes to the agricultural economy of the subcontinent not only by diversifying the resources of the rural poor, but also by providing a degree of income stability since, unlike crops, animal products such as milk can yield income throughout the year.

Key Features of the Livestock Economy

Despite the fact that South Asia has one-fourth of the world's population of cattle, analysts of the region's rural economy have paid much less attention to livestock and dairying activities than to crop production. Nevertheless, any serious attempt to understand or influence rural change and the prospects of the rural poor in the subcontinent must take account of cattle as an integral part of its farming systems. Over 40 percent of Indian cattle are working oxen, and the need for draft power dominates the pattern of cattle ownership in the subcontinent. All farmers who can afford to do so keep a pair of bullocks (or male buffaloes in wetter regions). Those who cannot afford bullocks cannot farm the land they own; those without land can rarely rent it in unless they own bullocks. Cows are kept primarily to breed replacement bullocks; milk and female calves are by-products. The strong complementarity between cattle farming and food-grain production, however, is particularly important on small holdings. Cattle provide manure for crops, crop residues are used to feed cattle, and the price of the straw fed to cattle affects the production of the main crop.[1] Meanwhile, cash incomes from the sale of milk can be used to purchase fertilizers and better seeds.

The distribution of livestock ownership suggests that livestock represents an important resource for poor and landless households (see tables 6-1, 6-2, and 6-3 for data from the 1970s). Livestock owner-ship is distributed far more evenly among households than land. In India landless households (27 percent of all households) owned roughly 2–10 percent of the cattle and buffaloes; however, there were wide variations between states. In Pakistan 3.3 million households (8 percent of the total) were classified as "livestock households"—that is, they were primarily engaged in livestock activities—and owned 20 percent of the country's milk cattle and buffaloes. In Bangladesh about half a million livestock households with holdings smaller than 1.5 acres (20 percent of the total) owned 12 percent of all cattle. Dependence on livestock as the main source of income is more usual in arid areas where the land is too poor for cultivation and is instead used for communal grazing.

Small farmers and those operating no land own a relatively insig-nificant proportion of draft animals, and as a result shortages of draft power can occur at peak periods.[2] Oxen are scarce and expensive be-cause the poor have difficulty making the investment needed to rear healthy calves and waiting to get a return on this investment over the eighteen years or so of an ox's life. This leads to the "apparent para-dox of 5 million weaned male calves annually being allowed to perish while smallholder cultivation is frequently limited by the non-availability of oxen at peak work periods" (Crotty 1980, p. 171).

Smallholders and households operating no land own a relatively large proportion of heifers and supply a large share of total milk pro-duction and of marketed calves. In India these households owned 8–10 percent of the heifers and young cattle and buffaloes. In 1972 about 40 percent of Pakistan's beef and milk was produced by land-less households and those with holdings smaller than 5 acres. In Ban-gladesh 28 percent of the milk cows and 6 percent of the milk buffa-loes were owned by households with fewer than 2.5 acres (table 6–3).

It is clear that the rural poor own a disproportionate share of live-stock assets (except for draft animals). These assets represent a valu-able potential source of income, especially since 90 percent of the cost of their rearing is accounted for by feed and labor—inputs that can be provided largely by small family farms from their own resources. But so far this potential has not been fully realized owing to a number of unsatisfactory characteristics of South Asia's livestock economy.

First, unless the quality of animals is improved, the incomes to be made from them will remain low. With few exceptions, mainly in northwestern India, the cattle owned by the majority of smallholders and the landless are underfed, overworked, infested with parasites, weak, and of poor quality both as working animals and as milk and meat producers. Mortality rates are high—about 25 to 30 percent during the first year and as high as 50 percent during the first two years. The average liveweights of cattle are 25 to 30 percent below their potential.[3]

Second, there is a general shortage of feed for cattle. Crop residues make up over 50 percent of all feeds; natural herbage foraged or gathered by hand, 35 percent; cultivated fodder, 9 percent; and concentrates, 5 percent, measured in terms of energy content (Halse 1980, p. 266). The landless often have to rely on communal grazing, but most production is farm-based and relies on agricultural by-products. Communal lands are overgrazed, and there has been a growing reliance on supplementary feeds and fodders, which are increasingly in short supply. Between 15 and 20 percent of India's gross cropped area is devoted to fodder crops. Feed costs are high. In some areas, notably in Bangladesh, the shortage of fodder has become so critical that the average liveweight of cattle has been decreasing.

The poor quality of herds and fodder shortages result in very low yields of milk and meat—no more than 2.5 to 3 kilograms of milk per cow per day, or about 525 to 720 kilograms over a 210- to 240-day lactation period.[4] The yields are higher for buffaloes, but not by much. With better feeding and proper health care, indigenous cows can yield up to 800 to 1,000 kilograms of milk a year in excess of their calves' requirements. Crossbreeds of indigenous and European cattle yield between 1,000 and 2,000 kilograms per cow. Indigenous cattle slaughtered for meat yield an average dressed weight per animal of 50 to 60 kilograms—only two-fifths of the averages recorded in Europe.[5]

These yield gaps are analogous to those often calculated for crops and reflect similar productivity problems. As in the case of food grains, the feed, management skills, and quality of breeding stock—let alone changes in attitudes and institutions—needed to raise yields to the levels implied by the gaps are probably unattainable. Nonetheless the figures suggest that even at realistic levels of inputs, significant improvements are possible.[6]

Third, because cows will generally produce milk only when their calves are alive and nearby, and because milk is highly prized, more calves are produced than can be supported after weaning. Surplus calves commonly starve to death (Crotty 1980). Meanwhile, the cost of cows (as opposed to bullocks) is low, but the price of milk is high. Crotty (1980, p. 174) calculated that in 1970 the variable costs per gallon of milk were 23 pence in East Punjab compared with 4 pence in Ireland. Relative milk prices have been rising steadily as demand continues to outpace supplies and as marginal costs rise from the introduction of crossbreeds and more expensive concentrate feeds.[7] The high price of milk allows those who produce milk for sale—particularly the landless, who do not produce their own crop

Table 6-1. India: Percentage Distribution of Livestock and Cattle by Size of Operated Holdings, 1971–72

Item	Landless	Size group of operated holdings (acres)						All sizes
		0–1.0	1.0–2.5	2.5–5.0	5.0–10.0	10.0–20.0	20.0+	
Households								
Millions	21.5	11.7	14.1	12.9	10.1	5.4	2.7	78.4
Percent	27	15	18	16	13	7	3	100
Percentage not owning draft livestock	96.8	76.4	41.1	22.7	15.7	12.8	13.4	52.4
Operated area								
Average size (acres)	0.00	0.45	1.67	3.59	6.92	13.56	33.94	3.96
Percent	0	2	8	15	23	24	28	100
Livestock ownership								
Male cattle								
Millions	1.3	3.9	13.6	18.6	19.1	12.8	8.8	78.0
Percent	2	5	17	24	24	16	11	100
Female cattle								
Millions	4.2	3.8	7.6	10.4	11.4	7.0	6.3	52.2
Percent	8	8	15	21	22	13	12	100
Young stock								
Millions	3.0	2.8	5.7	7.9	9.0	5.9	4.6	39.0
Percent	8	7	15	20	23	15	12	100
Male buffaloes								
Millions	0.2	0.6	1.8	2.6	2.3	1.3	0.8	9.65
Percent	2	6	18	27	24	14	8	100

Female buffaloes								
Millions	2.5	1.2	3.2	3.9	5.5	4.6	3.3	25.2
Percent	10	5	13	16	22	18	13	100
Young buffaloes								
Millions	1.5	0.6	1.5	2.6	3.0	2.7	2.0	13.8
Percent	10	4	11	19	22	19	15	100
Sheep								
Millions	2.9	1.0	3.7	4.5	7.1	5.5	4.9	29.6
Percent	10	3	13	15	24	19	16	100
Goats								
Millions	6.7	4.7	8.2	8.6	9.2	6.7	3.3	47.7
Percent	14	10	17	18	19	14	7	100
Pigs								
Millions	1.1	0.4	0.5	0.8	0.4	0.2	···	3.4
Percent	33	11	14	22	13	6	1	100
Value of livestock								
Cattle								
Millions of rupees	9.8	14.3	43.6	67.9	82.2	66.5	52.2	336.5
Percent	3	4	13	20	24	20	16	100
Buffaloes								
Millions of rupees	14.1	5.9	18.5	31.4	35.8	30.3	20.4	156.4
Percent	9	4	12	20	23	19	13	100
Other								
Millions of rupees	6.5	2.9	6.3	7.3	8.2	7.5	8.3	47.0
Percent	14	6	13	16	17	16	18	100

··· Negligible.

Note: "Percent" refers to the percentage distribution within all size groups.

Source: National Sample Survey, 26th Round (1971–72), Report 215, tables 5, 7, 9, 10,

Table 6-2. *Pakistan: Percentage Distribution of Livestock among Livestock and Farming Households, 1972*

Size group (acres)	House- holds	Bullocks	Cows	Buffaloes Male	Buffaloes Female	Sheep	Goats
Landless livestock							
households	7.4	3.6	6.2	8.4	14.1	22.3	29.6
<1.0	1.0	0.4	2.2	0.8	1.4	1.3	1.6
1.0–2.5	4.2	2.8	6.2	3.9	5.0	4.3	5.2
2.5–5.0	10.8	8.9	12.1	10.1	12.8	6.6	7.3
5.0–7.5	14.4	13.1	13.2	14.6	14.8	8.4	8.6
7.5–12.5	25.3	25.5	22.2	23.6	21.7	16.4	15.2
12.5–25.0	23.6	27.0	23.7	22.4	19.6	20.6	17.1
25.0+	13.3	18.7	14.2	16.2	10.6	20.1	15.4
All sizes	100.0	100.0	100.0	100.0	100.0	100.0	100.0
Number (millions)	3.3	11.8	0.8	3.6	5.8	7.9	10.1

Note: Although the distributions are for work animals only, the totals include milk cattle and buffaloes. Data giving the distribution of all livestock by size of holding are not available.

Source: Pakistan, Ministry of Food and Agriculture (1975).

residues—to use supplementary concentrates as feed, even though they are costly. This in turn keeps the price of milk high, since yields per cow are low.

By and large the traditional cattle economy is both stable and efficient, given the low incomes of most milk producers, the Hindu taboo against slaughtering cattle, the available technologies, and the poor quality of the stock. The number of cows tends to be held to the point at which milk production is maximized. In view of the limited grazing land and shortage of fodder, an increase in the stock of cows would reduce milk output per cow and fodder costs would rise. Draft oxen essential for crop production are costly, reflecting the costs of rearing calves to maturity as work animals. The supply of draft power and of animal protein is stable, even though all those who need oxen cannot get the right kind and quality at the going price, and those who need animal protein cannot afford it at the going price (see Crotty 1980, ch. 11, for a full exposition).

Like the low-level equilibrium of traditional farming, this bovine equilibrium can be destabilized by the introduction of new technologies. Evidence from all parts of India confirms that dairying on a scientific basis can significantly raise employment and incomes, especially for smallholders and the landless (R. K. Patel 1980; D. S. Sidhu 1975). Interventions are needed to (a) improve the quality of the stock, (b) tackle the problem of feed shortages, (c) improve yields in

Table 6-3. Bangladesh: Percentage Distribution of Livestock and Poultry by Farm Size, 1977

Operational holding (acres)	All cattle		Cows		Buffaloes				Goats		Sheep		Poultry	
			All	Milk	All		Female	Milk						
	N	A	A	A	N	A	A	A	N	A	N	A	N	A
<0.5	2.4	1.3	1.4	1.3	0.4	0.3	0.2	0.4	3.6	2.6	1.5	1.0	4.0	3.0
0.5–1.0	6.7	4.0	4.5	4.0	1.0	1.0	0.3	0.2	7.6	5.7	3.9	2.4	9.1	6.9
1.0–1.5	10.4	7.1	8.0	7.1	2.3	1.8	0.9	1.0	10.0	8.1	7.8	5.1	11.4	9.5
1.5–2.5	19.6	15.5	17.1	15.6	5.3	4.0	3.6	3.9	18.0	15.7	14.8	10.3	19.3	17.4
2.5–5.0	29.5	29.7	29.5	29.1	17.8	13.3	12.1	10.6	28.3	28.1	27.4	22.9	27.4	27.9
5.0–7.5	12.0	16.1	14.6	15.2	19.0	15.1	15.2	13.6	12.2	14.3	15.2	15.8	11.0	13.2
7.5–10.0	4.5	7.4	6.5	6.9	13.5	11.2	11.6	10.6	4.8	6.3	7.2	8.7	4.2	5.5
10.0–12.5	2.3	4.6	3.9	4.2	11.8	11.7	12.2	11.6	2.6	3.5	5.2	7.3	2.2	3.1
12.5–15.0	1.0	2.2	1.9	2.1	6.3	5.9	6.3	6.5	1.2	1.7	2.1	3.1	1.0	2.5
15.0–25.0	1.6	4.1	3.4	3.7	14.8	18.3	18.9	14.8	1.7	2.8	3.7	5.4	1.5	2.5
25.0+	0.4	1.4	1.1	1.3	5.7	14.9	16.4	18.0	0.4	0.9	1.7	8.0	0.4	0.8
All holdings	100.0	100.0	100.0	100.0	100.0	100.0	100.0	100.0	100.0	100.0	100.0	100.0	100.0	100.0
Millions	5.83	20.51	6.71	3.55	0.15	0.47	0.14	0.06	2.77	8.44	0.14	0.51	4.85	41.46

N = Number of holdings reporting category of livestock.
A = Number of animal heads associated.
Source: Bangladesh Bureau of Statistics (1977).

211

a manner consistent with rural people's social values and their need for draft animals, and (d) provide a marketing link for small producers. To reach small farmers and the landless, improvements must be sought that do not require costly feeds or unaffordable capital and that bypass the marketing middlemen. Much of the evidence that dairy development among the poor can be successful comes from cooperatives that operate in accordance with the so-called Anand model. Before reviewing the potential for further dairy development, therefore, it is worth briefly describing this model.

The Anand Dairy Cooperative and Operation Flood

The Anand Dairy Cooperative in Gujarat, India, has been highly successful in designing a program to benefit small farmers and the landless. This approach is now being extended to fourteen Indian states under the National Dairy Development Board's Operation Flood and is also being replicated in Pakistan. The Anand model organizes small producers into dairy cooperatives, provides them with the necessary inputs and services, and markets their output. Under the Anand scheme, the poorest households with one or two milk animals have benefited particularly; employment has been provided especially to women, whose social status has consequently improved; incomes from crop production have risen as a result of inputs purchased with cash from dairying; and caste and sex barriers are being reduced.

Operation Flood, an enterprise run by the National Dairy Development Board (NDDB), began in 1975 and is estimated to cost Rs4.75 billion (US$600 million). Described as the world's biggest dairy development project, its goal is to improve the availability of dairy products, with emphasis on small producers. By 1985, it had planned to set up a national grid, covering 155 producer districts and 10 million small producers, to supply milk to 15 million consumers in 148 cities. The project's main functional objectives are (a) to supply better quality cattle to small farmers and landless laborers, because only high-producing milk animals will give small producers in dairying the economic foundation they need; (b) to provide loans and subsidies to small producers, especially for crossbred heifers; and (c) to organize small producers into dairy cooperatives and dairy unions to facilitate marketing and to provide services which they could not otherwise afford.

Since much of the success with dairying so far has been based on the Anand model, its special features should be noted (Korten 1980; Kurien 1977; Alderman, Mergos, and Slade 1987):

- Its benefits are accessible to even the poorest groups in the community.
- It uses technologies that have been proven under local conditions.
- The village cooperative system is backed by a highly disciplined support system that provides an array of services through the union of cooperatives.
- There is a strong externally audited management system, which leaves little room for dishonesty in daily payments to members or in public transactions.
- The cooperatives make minimal demands on their members either for communal labor or complex decisions.
- The overall approach is based on learning-by-doing through cooperative action and on experimenting with new ideas.
- An independent national organization, the NDDB, has been given control and oversight of the program as a whole.
- The system has benefited from the strong and sustained leadership of one man (V. Kurien, the chairman of the NDDB, based in Anand), supported by a large number of dedicated young professionals with relevant skills.
- Both the Indian government and overseas agencies (including the World Bank) have given the system strong administrative and political support.
- Market orientation and concern for profitability are emphasized.

Perhaps the most important of these features are the mix of technology used and the participation of the poor on an equal basis; in these respects, the Anand model is unique. Capital-intensive technology to process and market a large volume of milk products is combined with a relatively simple labor-intensive production technology used by a large number of small producers (Brumby 1980). This pattern departs from the principle of "small is beautiful," which stresses the need to use simple, low-cost processing methods and sell in local markets (Schumacher 1973). Capital costs in Anand are large (US\$30 per liter of capacity) and so are operating costs (around US\$3.5 per liter). The Anand experience shows that producers who lack capital and skills can benefit from capital- and skill-intensive public or cooperative services—not just marketing and processing but also extension, credit, and research. As such, it should stimulate new thinking on how advanced, intermediate, and simple technologies can be blended to serve the rural poor.

With regard to the participation of the poor, the Anand model belies the conventional wisdom in South Asia that cooperatives end up serving rural elites. In other experiments, such an outcome has indeed occurred, as is documented by Nyholm, Schaumburg-Muller, and Westergaard (1974) in a review of the Bangalore Milkshed Area in Karnataka in the 1960s. Though many smallholders belonged to this organization of cooperatives, and though overall milk production increased in the area, neither the technology it introduced (crossbred cows and artificial insemination) nor its form of organization (cooperative, but dominated by large farmers) benefited the small farmer because of the local social and political situation. These cooperatives have now been reorganized on the Anand model, and Mishra (1980) suggests that most of the earlier problems are being overcome.

One of the most intensive empirical investigations of dairy development in India—Alderman (1987) on the benefits of a similar dairy scheme in Karnataka—finds not only that local production increased, but also that the benefits of the project appeared to be spread among members of all farm-size classes, including the landless, many of whom own livestock. The incomes of larger landholders increased more than those of smaller landholders, but relative as opposed to absolute income differences did not increase. No group lost absolutely. In addition, consumer prices of milk increased in the cooperative villages, and there was a reduction in fluid milk consumed. Nutritionally, however, consumption was not affected significantly because calories from other sources were substituted. The evidence at present is limited and calls for caution. But many more dairy schemes based on the Anand model are now being implemented in India, although they have yet to be tried in Bangladesh and Pakistan. Excellent reviews of some of the issues relating to cooperative dairy development and the commercialization of milk production are provided in Alderman (1987), Alderman, Mergos, and Slade (1987), Terhal and Doornbus (1983), and George (1985).

Economic Impact of Dairying

Dairy cooperatives are enabling an increasing number of India's poor to raise their incomes; moreover, there is evidence that a larger share of the benefits go to the poor than is usually the case with other rural development programs.

How much of an impact can dairying have on the incomes of the poor? The assessment of the Anand scheme by a U.N. evaluation team (reported by Jul 1979) found that by joining milk cooperatives, rural people could earn twice as much from dairying and other activities as their counterparts who were not members. Farmers with fewer than five acres achieved the largest increases in total net income. In the Kaira district, 97 percent of the landless and 75 percent of the farmers with fewer than 2.5 acres had at least one milk animal.[8] An indigenous animal yielded a net income of Rs700 annually if given improved feed—a significant amount for participants. As income elasticities of demand for food energy intake are high (about 0.3) for the landless and small farmers, the study concluded that this doubling of incomes resulted in a 30 percent increase in food energy intake among the poor.

Patel and Pandey (1976) undertook a comprehensive study sponsored by the National Dairy Development Board of milk producers in Kaira district, where the Anand model had its genesis. Data from three milk unions, and from control villages not covered by the unions, showed that incomes increased for all groups of households, particularly for the poorest, on joining the cooperative. The landless and small farmers with holdings of fewer than five acres made up nearly 75 percent of the producers in villages with a dairy cooperative, compared with only 48 percent in the control villages. A typical cooperative member owned two buffaloes and tilled 2.5 acres of land, and thus seasonal agricultural work was a main source of income.

Several studies have examined the returns to dairying. Returns vary among income groups and depend to a large extent on the technologies used. Mishra (1980) found that daily returns from dairying ranged from Rs10 (local cows) to Rs135 (exotic cows), net of the imputed cost of family labor. Households with small and marginal holdings gained higher returns from dairying than larger farmers.

The study by Appa Rao and Krishna (1978) notes that landless laborers have either to collect fodder or purchase it, while those with even very small holdings have crop residues or can grow green fodder. Thus the maintenance costs per animal for the landless were nearly 30 percent higher than for those in farming households. But the landless also used better feed, provided more care, and consequently had better yields and net incomes from dairying—25 to 40 percent higher than those of small and marginal farmers.

The returns from crossbred cattle are higher than from indigenous animals, since the former convert feed into milk more efficiently.[9] In a district in Kerala where 97 percent of the holdings were small or marginal, Gangadharan (1980) found that although feed requirements and costs for crossbred cows were often 1.5 to 2.0 times those for indigenous cows, feed costs per kilogram of milk produced were 20–30 percent lower because crossbreeds had higher conversion efficiencies.[10] This study also found that relatively costly compound cattle feeds (including groundnuts, oilcakes, and green fodders) were nevertheless the most economical feeds for crossbred dairy cattle on small farms. Dairy activities can therefore offer important benefits for poverty alleviation.

Dairying and Nutrition

There is concern that as market-oriented dairying evolves, the nutritional status of the rural poor will suffer. The evidence does not support this contention.

Patel and Pandey (1976) note that milk production has been transformed from a subsistence to a commercial activity for cooperative members in Kaira. Because milk is a perishable commodity, the ability to sell it daily is a considerable advantage to the small producer. In the absence of storage, processing, or transport facilities, farmers previously had to sell their milk to private traders, who offered relatively low prices. Milk producers in villages covered by the Anand scheme were found to obtain prices that were nearly 20 percent higher than those received by their counterparts in control villages. In control villages nearly 15 percent of the milk produced by landless households and 24 percent of that produced on small farms was consumed at home, mainly as ghee, because fluid milk could not be marketed easily. In dairy villages 80 to 85 percent of the fluid milk production was marketed and none was processed into ghee. Furthermore, the smaller a household's farm, the higher was the proportion of its milk that was marketed—a trend opposite to that observed in food grains.

Small cultivators and the landless thus apparently prefer to sell a relatively large share of their milk in order to earn extra cash income. Thakur's (1975) findings on this point, also for Kaira, are more equivocal: though the landless in cooperative villages sell more of their milk than do their counterparts in other villages, there is no systematic relationship between the size of holding and the proportion of milk sold.

Some commentators have expressed concern that the commercialization of dairying may reduce the amount of milk consumed by poor producers and reduce their intake of necessary nutrients. Available evidence is mixed but does not seem, on balance, to support this anxiety (Patel and Pandey 1976; Alderman, Mergos, and Slade 1987). Thakur (1975) notes, however, that landless cooperative households both sold more of the milk they produced and consumed appreciably less than their counterparts in other villages (0.8 liters compared with 1.13 liters per household daily).

Even if producing households' consumption of milk per person were in fact to fall after dairy projects had been established, this would not necessarily imply a decline in nutritional standards as long as per capita income was increasing. Milk is a relatively expensive source of protein and calories. Jul (1979) has shown that in India, given the relative prices of food in the open market, buffalo milk supplies only one-sixth as much energy per rupee as rice and one-tenth as much as wheat. Landless families who can sell milk and buy food grains are doing infinitely better than those who have no market for milk and no cash income to purchase food grains, so that they end up being forced to consume their own milk output.

Thus there seems little reason to fear that commercial milk production schemes would have a negative impact on nutrition levels in general. A more rational cause for concern is the possible reduction in milk consumption by children in producing households (Huria and Acharya 1980; Acharya and Huria 1986). Including education components on maternal and child health and nutrition in dairy projects may be the most effective way of ensuring that this does not happen.

Combining Dairying with Crop Production

Although dairying helps the landless directly, it can help those with small holdings even more. Several microeconomic studies from India attest that incomes per unit of area can be much higher from mixed dairy and crop production than from crop production alone (A. S. Saini 1975; Radhakrishnan and Sivanandham 1975; Pandey and Bhogal 1980).

Returns to mixed farming in drought-prone areas unsuitable for intensive cultivation are also generally greater than for crop farming alone. In the dry farming areas of Andhra Pradesh and Karnataka, the net returns from mixed farming with fodder crops and milk animals were twice those from dryland grain production (Huria and Acharya 1980; Acharya and Huria 1986).

Incomes from dairying also help crop production. Both Patel and Pandey (1976) and Thakur (1975) observe the use of cash income from dairying in Kaira district to purchase modern inputs for crops. Thakur notes that the percentage of farmers using modern inputs for crops and dairying was significantly higher in dairy villages, and the value of such inputs per acre operated was 33 percent higher than in the control villages. In addition, crop incomes were 10 percent higher, dairy incomes 65 percent higher.

Criticizing conclusions about the success of dairying in Kaira, Crotty (1980) states that dairy villages were located in areas of higher yields and better infrastructure than control villages and that dairy programs have worsened income distribution. But historically crop yields in Kaira district have not differed significantly from those in other Gujarat districts, and although the district's present infrastructure is better, there is no evidence that it was better than elsewhere to begin with. Although income gaps are large in the dairy villages (the ratio of total incomes on large farms to the incomes of the landless is 9.3 in dairy villages compared with 2.6 in control villages), these gaps would be even larger without dairy enterprises as a source of income. (The same income ratio *excluding* earnings from dairying is 23 in dairy villages compared with 3.9 in control villages). The major source of inequality is not dairying, but the crop incomes that large farmers obtain in dairy villages.

World Bank staff have repeatedly noted that villages where dairy farming is well established have also experienced marked increases in food crop production (Anderson and Leiserson 1978). Dairying substantially raises cash incomes—especially for small farmers, who market only about 10–15 percent of their food-grain output. A large part of this incremental cash income—by Bank estimates, about 50 percent—is spent on fertilizer, improved seeds, and irrigation water. More manure from better-fed cows is also available, though this may be used mainly for fuel.

Milk production and the income and employment it creates do not detract from food-grain production. Food crops and dairy cattle do not compete for land if the cattle are fed on crop residues. If crossbred high-yield cattle are introduced, however, low-energy, roughage-based diets will have to be replaced, and the availability of fodder may become a cause for concern.

Employment in Dairying

Microeconomic studies of various Indian regions have sought to estimate the labor needed to maintain dairy cattle on small holdings and have examined how introducing dairying to supplement crop production on these holdings can raise the demand for labor (see Grewal and Rangi 1980; Amrik Singh and R. V. Singh 1977; Sirohi and others 1980; Verma and Pant 1978; and Pandey and Bhogal 1980). Although their assumptions vary, these studies show that dairying can increase the demand for labor per unit of area by between 30 and 100 percent on small and marginal farms, depending on the type and number of milk animals kept and the crops grown (see table 6-4 and figure 6-1).

Most smallholders and landless rural families have surplus labor that can easily be used for dairying. Women usually have the main responsibility for this activity. Milk output is generally highest in December and January, when it is two or three times its April-August levels, so that the demands of dairying on smallholder labor do not

Table 6-4. India: Impact of Dairying and Poultry on Incomes and Employment in Various Farm Sizes, Union Territory of Delhi, 1979

Item	Marginal farms (average 0.81 hectare)		Small farms (average 1.62 hectares)		Medium farms (average 3.85 hectares)	
	Existing plan	Optimal plan[a]	Existing plan	Optimal plan[a]	Existing plan	Optimal plan
Total cropped area (hectares)	1.62	1.72	3.34	3.44	7.69	8.01
Intensity (percent)	200	212	200	212	200	208
Cows (number)	0	1	0	1	0	2
Buffaloes (number)	1	0	1	0	1	1
Poultry (number)	0	489	0	269	0	0
Family labor (days)	251	1,446	405	1,072	947	993
Total labor (days)	251	1,525	405	1,144	1,046	1,253
Own capital (rupees)	3,731	3,731	4,917	4,917	7,684	7,684
Borrowed capital (rupees)	—	23,925	—	14,355	—	11,784
Total net returns (rupees)	4,769	12,661	5,793	14,353	20,796	25,133
Percentage increase over existing plans						
Net returns	—	265	—	248	—	121
Total employment	—	608	—	282	—	120

— Not applicable.
a. With improved cows and poultry farming.
Source: Sirohi and others (1980).

Figure 6-1. *Labor Demand and Total Net Return with and without Dairying and Poultry Farming for Marginal, Small, and Medium-Size Farms, Union Territory of Delhi, India, 1979*

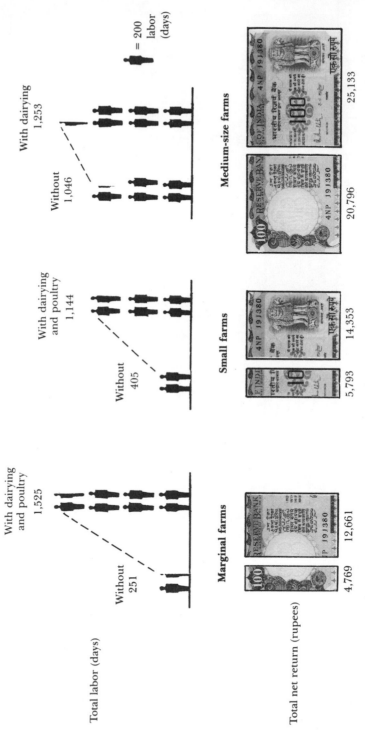

Source: Table 6-4.

conflict with those for crop production, which peak in the March-June harvest period.

Dairying offers impressive possibilities for increasing employment. It has been estimated that producing each additional 6–10 liters of milk requires an additional workday of labor in cattle feeding and care (Brumby 1978, 1980). Consequently, a dairy project that produces 100,000 liters of milk per day from some 50,000 smallholders or landless households creates an annual demand for their labor equivalent to that created by an additional 12,000–14,000 hectares of irrigated rice or 30,000–40,000 hectares of irrigated wheat.[11] This would imply an equivalent of between 12,000 and 30,000 additional farm jobs in the area. The processing capacity of cooperative dairying in India in 1980 was around 5 million liters a day and was expected· to expand at around 10 percent a year. This implies an employment equivalent of around 150,000 hectares of wheat annually. Since projects of this size cost around US$5 million equivalent to put in place, the investment cost per job created is US$200–500.[12] The expansion of dairying also indirectly creates employment by increasing the demand for services, although these benefits are unlikely to accrue primarily to the rural poor.

Income from Dairying and Crop Production

The significance of dairying as a source of income for smallholders and the landless is highlighted by comparing the net returns from an irrigated acre of land with those from a cow (see table 6-5). The net return from one crossbred cow, for example, is equal to the net income from approximately five acres of irrigated land sown to HYV or two to fifteen acres of land sown to traditional varieties of wheat or rice.

For the landless household, at an assumed average wage of 3 rupees a day, the net income from one local cow can be viewed as equivalent to the wages from 70 days of employment, and the income from one crossbred cow as equivalent to 282 days' worth. In most cases this represents *additional* income for the household, not a substitute for other wage income forgone. Further, it represents cash that can be earned by women and children, who would otherwise be unlikely to work for wages.

In summary:

- On holdings smaller than two acres, income from even one local cow can potentially be higher than that from crops. Income from one crossbred cow can equal that from five acres of irrigated land

Table 6-5. India: Comparison of Net Incomes from an Irrigated Acre of Land and from Dairying, 1976–77

Item	Traditional crops					HYV crops				
	Wheat		Rice		Local cows	Wheat		Rice		Crossbred cows
	North	West	South	East		North	West	South	East	
Crop estimates[a]										
Average yield (quarts per acre)	5.2	3.0	4.8	4.5		13.2	8.1	10.0	10.1	
Price (rupees per quart)	110	110	80	75		110	110	80	75	
Gross return (rupees per acre)	572	330	384	338		1,452	891	800	758	
Costs (percentage of gross return)[b]	25	37	33	33		45	57	53	53	
Net income (rupees per acre)[c]	430	208	253	127		799	383	376	356	
Dairy estimates[d]										
Milk yield (liters per year)					500					2,300
Milk price (rupees per liter)					1.30					1.30
Milk income (rupees per cow)					650					2,990
Manure income (rupees per cow)					200					400
Gross return (rupees per cow)					850					3,390

	Local cows	Crossbred cows
Costs for landless (percentage of gross income)[e]	75	75
Costs for farmers (percentage of gross income)	45	45
Net income for landless (rupees per cow)	213	848
Net income for farmers (rupees per cow)	468	1,865

Acre equivalent of one cow	Local cows				Crossbred cows			
Landless, irrigated HYV	0.5	1.0	0.8		1.1	2.2	2.3	2.4
Landless, traditional					2.0	4.1	3.4	6.7
Farmers, irrigated HYV	1.1	2.3	1.9	3.7	2.3	4.9	5.0	5.2
Farmers, traditional					4.3	9.0	7.4	14.7

a. Average yields are taken from World Bank project experiences; prices are from the procurement price of grain for 1976–77.

b. It is assumed that, as a percentage of gross returns, costs of inputs (excluding family labor) are 20 percent higher for HYV than for traditional crops.

c. Excluding the cost of family labor.

d. The economics of milk production with local and crossbred cows are taken from recent World Bank dairy projects.

e. Since the landless have to buy their feed while small farmers can use crop residue, their costs differ; sometimes net returns to dairying also differ.

Sources: Acharya and Huria (1986), Bowonder and others (1987); World Bank project data.

planted with HYVs; this is equivalent to more than the income being realized on nearly half of all holdings of fewer than four acres in South Asia.

- One crossbred cow may do more to raise the standard of living of landless households than giving each of them two to four acres of irrigated land in most parts of India. Providing such a cow is also equivalent to providing a year of employment.
- The potential earnings from dairying are even greater for smallholders who are able to combine dairying with crop farming. On holdings of two to four acres in most parts of India, the income from an additional crossbred cow can be equivalent to doubling the size of holding or doubling the cropping intensity. For smallholders using local crop varieties, introducing dairying with crossbreeds is equivalent to quadrupling the size of holding or cropping intensity.

The Constraints

Dairy programs need to address many constraints if the schemes are to be effective. These include (a) fodder shortages, especially the acute shortages of concentrates, and the need to bring fodder within the reach of the small farmers—and the landless in particular (S. Singh 1979; Shah, Tripathi, and Desai 1980); (b) credit shortages, especially the need to finance the purchase of milk animals and feed by the landless (Amrik Singh and R. V. Singh 1977; Nyholm, Schaumburg-Muller, and Westergaard 1974); and (c) the lack of transport, extension, and management services that are necessary for successful marketing. It is also important to ensure that the dairy program does not simply enrich commercial dairies and that the market for milk does not become so saturated that returns are reduced. If possible, projects of this nature should not be limited to better-off areas, but should be distributed so as to decrease interregional inequalities (Baviskar and George 1987).

Dairying as a Means of Alleviating Rural Poverty

The shortage of land is the greatest limitation on raising the incomes of the rural poor. The scope for redistributing land into viable holdings is limited, however, and as the past thirty years have shown, land reform is difficult and seldom confers good land on the poor (see chapter 8). A program to give small farmers or the landless quality cows, or to upgrade the cattle they already own through artificial insemination, would present fewer physical and economic difficulties than giving them good irrigated land. Moreover, experience suggests that dairy cooperatives—at least if modeled on Anand—can remain relatively free from the undue influence that wealthy farmers have tended to exert in food-crop development programs.

The credit requirement for such dairy programs would be feasible and would provide high rates of return. In 1975 the average price of a crossbred cow was around Rs2,000, but it yielded a minimum net cash flow of around Rs500 a year. If a landless family got a loan to buy, say, two crossbred cows, the principal and interest (at the then current rate of 5.5 percent) could be paid back in six years, while still yielding a net annual cash flow of around Rs600 (US$80) to the family (George and Srivastava 1975). By comparison, to purchase two acres of irrigated wheat or paddy land would have cost between Rs20,000 and Rs40,000 in the same year, depending on quality, location, and other factors, and would have yielded a net income of between Rs1,000 and Rs2,000 an acre each year if planted to HYVs. Assuming the higher of these two income flows, and a retained amount of Rs600 per year for the family (as in the two-cow dairying model), a loan of Rs20,000 at 5.5 percent interest would take more than twenty-eight years to pay back. The differences in the relative payback periods have not changed much in the intervening years.

Even if dairying is expanded on a large scale, demand for milk is likely to remain robust. Crossbreeding can increase milk output dramatically, but the population of low-grade dairy cows in India is extremely large and their milk production potential is very poor. Furthermore, demand for milk and milk products is highly responsive to increases in income. In the near future, milk sales are thus likely to increase most rapidly in urban areas, but subsequently demand in rural areas can also be expected to rise as average rural incomes grow. There is reason to believe that imports of donated milk, which at present fill the gap between India's demand and supply, will decline; any future disincentives from this source are therefore unlikely to be large.

Raising milk output entails increasing feed intakes and in the longer run replacing weak or low-yielding animals, which tend to be owned by the poorest households. Animal feeds are already in very short supply, and even more acute scarcities are forecast. The size of feedstuff deficits may well determine whether dairy programs can help the rural poor; most of the landless depend on purchased feeds and cannot afford high prices. Given the pressure on arable land in the subcontinent, the large-scale expansion of dairying should initially be based on indigenous cattle, which can be fed partly on crop residues and thus compete less with food crops than do crossbreeds.

(This strategy is being followed by Operation Flood II and III.)

Setting up adequate support services and institutions is not a quick or easy task, and it will be particularly difficult where agricultural growth has been slow. In addition to good transport, marketing, and communication facilities, sustained dairy development and increases in milk yields require a network of veterinary and artificial insemination services. Even where the necessary skills and trained personnel exist—and they are inadequate in Bangladesh, Pakistan, and many parts of India—the organization of such services on a scientific basis is still a distant prospect. Even when they are organized, it will be necessary to take special care to ensure that the poor have adequate access to them.

For dairying as for food crops, continued research and development efforts are necessary to develop new technologies and to adapt them to small producers' resources. More work is needed on cross-breeding of cattle and in particular on the development of new varieties of forage crops suitable for different locations. Such research is in its infancy in India and has yet to begin in Bangladesh and Pakistan.

Small Stock Development

Small stock—goats, sheep, and pigs—are the poor man's cattle and are widely owned by small farmers and those not cultivating land. Data show that in India 41 percent of the sheep, 59 percent of all goats, and 80 percent of all pigs were owned by the landless or households with fewer than five acres; in Pakistan about one-fourth of all small stock were owned by nonfarming households; in Bangladesh 32 percent of the goats and 19 percent of the sheep were owned by those with fewer than 2.5 acres of operated area (tables 6-1 to 6-3).

Small stock thus represent a considerable income potential for these households, but very little is known about the small stock economy.

Although extensive research efforts are under way for increasing the quality and productivity of draft and milk cattle—which tend to be owned by the richer strata in rural areas—virtually no research in the animal sciences or economics has been done on how to increase milk and meat production from goats and sheep indigenous to developing countries. Therefore little can be said about how to raise the productivity of these assets owned by the poor or about their possible contribution to incomes. Nevertheless, the potential must be significant, simply because of the sheer numbers of these stock available in South Asia—some 66 million goats and some 39.5 million sheep. Clearly, there is an urgent need for research; the absence of such work is another example of the inherent bias against the rural poor (see Winrock International Livestock Research and Training Center 1983).

Poultry

Small-scale poultry farming might seem a practical way for the rural poor to supplement their incomes, and a large number of them do so. In India small farmers and the landless already own a considerable share of the poultry stock—15–20 percent in some Indian states; in Pakistan small farmers (those with fewer than five acres) account for a third of poultry production. Like dairying, however, poultry farming needs to be placed on a new technological and commercial footing if it is to have any major impact on the incomes of the poor. The requirements include: (a) a new, tested technology that uses improved poultry strains to raise yields of meat and eggs; (b) a system to deliver credit, feed supplies, and veterinary services; (c) a marketing and transport system to handle processing, cleaning, grading, and delivery of output; and (d) a cooperative organization to make these services available to small producers.

Unlike dairying, there is very little experience, cooperative or otherwise, against which to evaluate the potential for small poultry producers. Several researchers have speculated about the impact of introducing poultry production on crop and mixed farms (Rudra and Sen 1980, p. 394). The very few available empirical studies suggest, mainly on the basis of large-scale commercial operations, that poultry farming might have the potential to increase farmers' incomes significantly, especially if it is ancillary to crop production (Mathur and Gupta 1978). To date most of the gains in poultry production have been confined to a few states in the northwest and south of India.

The investment costs of commercial poultry activities have hitherto been too high for the rural poor to afford. Economies of scale also seem significant: on the basis of a study in Jabalpur, Rajasthan, in 1978–79, Karanjkar and Soni (1980) report that the optimum scale of business seems to be around 1,000 birds. To set up an operation of this size would require an investment of around Rs20,000—an unthinkable sum for most small farmers. Obviously, the rural poor could neither undertake such enterprises themselves nor easily compete with those already in operation.

If small producers are to realize the potential income gains of this kind from poultry, however, several initiatives need to be taken:

- More plants are needed to produce feed, perhaps operated as cooperatives on the Anand dairy model.

- Farmers need credit for operating capital, and the government needs to ensure that smallholders have adequate access to these funds.
- Marketing arrangements, both for buying chicks of desirable strains and for selling eggs and meat, need to be improved.
- Veterinary services and research must be organized on a cooperative basis (again perhaps using the Anand model) if small producers are to benefit from them.

Some landless households may lack space to keep poultry efficiently, but the requirements are modest. Based on Mathur and Gupta's (1978) estimates, a unit of 200 birds in cages would need 1,000–1,500 square feet of space. This is less than one-fifth of an acre, and the land does not have to be suitable for cultivation. Opponents of land reform often suggest that redistribution would result in holdings too small to be viable for crop production; even a holding that was not viable for food crops, however, could permit a peasant farmer to earn some additional income from poultry farming or dairying.

Fisheries

Fishing is a major activity for many people in rural areas.[13] It accounts for 1–4 percent of GDP in South Asian countries and is undertaken mostly on a small scale. Table 6-6 provides some preliminary data. Fishing is undertaken largely by small-scale rural enterprises (often based on family and caste) and is often a seasonal activity. In Bangladesh, for example, it peaks in the dry season when the water level falls and fish are trapped in depressions flooded by the monsoons.

Efforts to develop fisheries need to take account of three factors. First, many fishing resources are publicly owned, so that the way fishing rights are organized will determine who reaps their benefits. Sec-

Table 6-6. *Importance of Fishing in South Asia, 1973*

Country	Total value of fishing (millions of U.S. dollars)	Percentage of GDP	Value per capita (U.S. dollars)	Production from small-scale fisheries (percentage of total)
Bangladesh	155.7	3.6	2.2	95.0
India	443.3	0.8	0.8	80.0
Pakistan	68.7	1.3	1.0	n.a.

n.a. Not available.
Source: World Bank (1982).

ond, although fisheries are a renewable resource, uncontrolled large-scale commercial fishing can make rapid inroads into the livelihoods of small-scale fishermen. Third, because fish are perishable, the organization of markets is of crucial importance.

Catching fish in the sea, rivers, or lakes should be distinguished from aquaculture—raising fish under human control. The World Bank estimated in 1981 that half a million households in Bangladesh were engaged in fish farming; typically each managed a small pond no larger than a hectare. New and highly profitable technologies exist in aquaculture. Indian or exotic carp, stocked at the rate of 5,000 to 8,000 per hectare in a freshwater pond and fed on aquatic weeds or oil cakes and rice bran, can yield from 4,000 to 10,000 kilograms of fish per hectare per year. If fish are valued at around $250 per ton, a one-hectare pond could in principle produce a gross income of US$1,250–2,500 a year—equivalent at present levels to the incomes of five to ten landless households. Much more preparatory work needs to be undertaken, however, before hypothetical estimates of this kind can be translated into real-life earnings opportunities.[14]

Forestry

The scarcity of fuelwood has been called the energy crisis of the rural poor (see Eckholm 1975). With the rapid erosion of forests in South Asia, most rural families use animal dung for cooking. Dung that is burned cannot be used as fertilizer. In India, for example, the equivalent of 6 million tons of nitrogenous fertilizer is burned every year—more than India's total annual fertilizer consumption (World Bank 1978). Meanwhile, those who still rely on firewood for fuel have to spend considerable amounts of time and energy in gathering it. Soaring wood prices drain meager incomes. Deforestation has led to massive erosion of the soil and desertification. Increasing the availability of fuelwood would thus not only improve the well-being of poorer households but also release supplies of dung for use as manure.[15]

In response to this need, a series of state social forestry programs was started in India in the early 1980s. The programs are centrally sponsored by organizations such as the Rural Fuelwood Programs, National Rural Employment Progam, and more recently the US$500 million fuelwood agroforestry effort of the National Wasteland Development Board and the World Bank. Many have criticized the programs for failing to increase the fuelwood supply for domestic consumption. Chandrashekhar, Murti, and Ramaswamy (1987) have attacked Karnataka's forestry programs because they have replaced natural forests with eucalyptus plantations, favored large private holdings, and failed to meet the fodder and fuelwood requirements of rural society. Blair (1986), in a study of Maharashtra's forestry program, finds that trees are grown as cash crops either for the pulp and rayon industries or for sale to urban consumers. Although this does not meet the original goal of supplying fuelwood, trees are nevertheless an important and growing source of income for the poor landed households whose soils are unsuited for agricultural crops.

Very little is known about how to organize wood production to benefit the rural poor. The major problem is that forestry projects take years to mature. Gupta and Mohan (1979) compared the net returns per hectare to wood and annual food crops on marginal agricultural land in Rajasthan. They found that net returns from wood crops were anywhere from ten to seventy times higher than from good crop production on this land, once the benefits were discounted over the life cycles of the various types of tree (table 6-7). On better agricultural land, the returns to annual crops would be two to three times higher, and this gap would be reduced accordingly. The trees take from six to twenty-five years to mature, however. The rural poor can hardly be expected to commit land, labor, and other resources to wood production with an uncertain and distant outcome. Nor would they be likely to risk forgoing other low but certain income even if some kind of subsistence fund were set up to support them in the interim.

Nevertheless, it seems essential to try to promote village-based forestry projects in view of their enormous indirect benefits to ecology as well as the direct gains from the production of a cash crop. Over the long term, the most appropriate approach would seem to be social forestry projects—the creation of cooperative societies in which all households in a project area participate. To avoid being dominated by large landowners, such projects would need to use publicly ac-

Table 6-7. *India: Expected Annual Net Returns to Annual and Tree Crops in the Hot Arid Zone of Rajasthan, 1978*

	Net returns (rupees)		Years to maturity
Crop	Per hectare	Per household	
Annual crops	30	550	1
Tree plantations			
Acacia tortilis	360	4,990	8
Albizzia lebbek	550	7,560	15
Prosopis juliflora	950	13,160	6
Prosopsis cineraria	1,610	22,200	20
Zizyphus species	2,910	40,110	15
Lucaena lencocephala	20,080	28,630	8

Source: Gupta and Mohan (1979), p. 86

quired land, and shares in the cooperative would need to be distributed evenly among all the members. But getting cooperative efforts with long payback periods under way and seeing them to completion is a tall order indeed. Recent experience with the funding of social forestry projects in South Asia offers some hope. (See Cernea 1985, chs. 8 and 9; Anderson 1987.)

Conclusions

The evidence suggests that noncrop activities can become a major source of income and employment opportunities for the rural poor. As yet, however, the necessary research and implementation efforts are missing. The main benefits seem to be from dairying, which is complementary to crop production for small farmers and has been shown to benefit the landless. Opportunities for small stock, poultry, fishing, and forestry also exist but remain underutilized. A concentrated effort is needed to exploit these activities to benefit the poor, as has been done in the case of dairying. The focus of research as well as of poverty alleviation programs needs to be shifted away from land-based crop production systems and toward a variety of ancillary activities that the poor can undertake with or without land, given some help from credit and marketing institutions and the knowledge to undertake new productive endeavors.

Notes

1. Halse (1980) estimates that nearly 38 percent of the fertilizer applied in India in 1975 came from manure. It is also estimated that less than 40 percent of India's crop output can be eaten by people; the balance is used for animals.

2. As an internal World Bank staff report on livestock in Bangladesh (1981) observes, "Field surveys . . . show that farmers plow their fields only 3–6 times instead of the required 4–8 times. At the same time, the incidence of humans pulling plows and of field cultivation exclusively by hand now is increasing rapidly."

3. In East Punjab and Sind bullocks weigh around 350 kilograms; those in Bangladesh weigh around 200 kilograms.

4. Yields vary widely in the subcontinent, but are generally low by international standards. The average is estimated to be 250 kilograms per cow per year in Bangladesh, compared with 700 kilograms for all Asia, 500 kilograms in India, 684 kilograms in China, and 800 kilograms in Pakistan. Yields in Europe average 3,358 kilograms, and in Norway, Sweden, and the United States they exceed 5,000 kilograms per cow annually.

5. Among the Hindus in India beef is taboo, and many states forbid the

slaughter of cows. Although more than 120 million Indian Muslims eat beef, as do outcasts and people in tribal areas, the incentives for rearing cattle for beef do not exist in most parts of India.

6. The yield gaps are much more dramatic in livestock than in grain production. The "best" yields of grain in developed countries exceed those in South Asia (and developing countries in general) by a factor of 4 or 5; the "best" yields of milk in developed countries exceed those in South Asia by a factor of 50 or 60.

7. Data from Kaira Dairy Union cited in Brumby (1980) show that in 1970–71 the official procurement price of milk was Rs0.86 per kilogram; in 1978–79 it was Rs1.15 per liter.

8. The corresponding figures were 39 and 36 percent in Punjab, and 34 and 43 percent in Madura, Tamil Nadu.

9. See studies summarized in *Indian Journal of Agricultural Economics* 35 (4), October-December 1980.

10. Measured by the ratio of milk yields to feed inputs, excluding capital, labor, and management costs.

11. To produce 100,000 liters per day requires 10,000 workdays over a lactation period of 240 days; this provides 2.4 million days of additional employment. On average, the direct labor requirements of one hectare planted with HYV rice amount to about 200 workdays (for local rice about 175 workdays), while a hectare of HYV wheat requires about 80 workdays (for local wheat, about 60 days).

12. Compare this with the US$200 "equipment cost per workplace" that Schumacher (1973, p. 169) assigned to intermediate technologies "that would be immensely more productive than the indigenous technology, but would also be immensely cheaper than the sophisticated highly capital-intensive technology of modern industry."

13. Clay (in Bangladesh, Ministry of Agriculture and Forests 1978) estimates that fishing provided 5 percent of total employment in Bangladesh in 1975–76.

14. For a "state of the art" paper with a large number of references on the problems involved in exploiting fishing resources in the Asian context, see Emmerson (1980). For a discussion of problems relating to small-scale fishing and fishing communities, see also Lawson (1977); de Silva (1977); and Pollnac (1981 and in Cernea 1985).

15. Dung could produce biogas for fuel and still be available as a nutrient. Some 300 million to 400 million tons of wet dung are used for fuel in India annually (Eckholm 1975).

7
Rural Industrialization and Employment

The growth of nonfarm employment in rural areas depends on linkages between agriculture and related rural activities, and between agricultural activities in general and those in other sectors, notably industry. The importance of these linkages for the creation of rural jobs has been repeatedly emphasized.[1] Little empirical work has been done, however, to establish in concrete terms either the specific nature of the linkages or their effects on employment.

Rural enterprises for small-scale food processing, manufacturing, and services are widely dispersed, use much labor, require little capital, and are ideally suited to provide jobs for the rural poor. They also meet locally generated demand. Here I discuss the experience of other countries in including these activities in a broad framework of rural industrialization to increase employment opportunities. I draw lessons for South Asia and argue that in the medium term, and in the absence of rapid agricultural growth, the growing problems of rural unemployment require more direct measures than those previously employed. In this context I examine rural public works and other specialized programs that complement direct efforts to raise farm and nonfarm employment and incomes, and review their role in an overall strategy for alleviating rural poverty.

The available evidence seems to suggest that employment generation in rural areas is strongly correlated with the rate of agricultural growth, but this evidence comes mainly from areas that have experienced high agricultural growth rates over long periods, such as the Indian and Pakistan Punjabs, the Republic of Korea, Malaysia, and Taiwan.

Employment Linkages

Farm and nonfarm activities are linked in at least five ways:

- *Production linkages* are based on the inputs and services needed to meet final demand for agricultural output. Growth in farm output generates demand (and employment) through forward linkages as the output is marketed, processed, and transported to final consumers in rural or urban areas. It also generates demand through backward linkages by increasing the need for farm and nonfarm inputs such as fertilizers, fuels, machinery, and pesticides, together with the systems to produce, transport, market, service, and repair these items. Jobs are also created by the growth of credit and extension services and of power and transport infrastructure.

- *Consumption linkages* are based on changes in the size and distribution of rural incomes, which in turn have a multiplier effect on both the level and composition of final demand and expenditure in rural areas. Mellor (1976) and others have contended that there is a strong positive relation between rural incomes and the demand for rural nonfarm goods.[2] Household expenditure studies in many developing countries have found that the share of nonfood and off-farm goods and services in rural household budgets rises with income and that income (expenditure) elasticities of demand for these items are strongly positive (see Lluch, Powell, and Williams 1977, pp. 52 and 54). Some recent studies of rural areas that have experienced rapid economic growth show that expenditure elasticities for nonfarm goods are on the order of 2 to 3. In this case a 5 percent increase in rural (farm plus wage) incomes—a rate experienced in some Indian states and Pakistan—could imply a rise in demand for nonfarm goods of as much as 10–15 percent a year. This extra demand would have a multiplier effect on the growth in nonfarm rural employment.

- *Savings-investment linkages* are produced by new demand for quasi-fixed and fixed capital goods—including private investment in tractors, tubewells, farm machinery, and land improvements and public investment in rural infrastructure. The size and composition of private investment depend mainly on how rural incomes and savings are distributed, while public investment depends more on policy choices.

- *Employment linkages* are the consequence of changes in the proportions of the labor force in different sectors and of income transfers from one sector to another. Rapid out-migration of labor from rural areas creates labor shortages that encourage farmers to adopt labor-saving production technologies, while slow out-migration (or immigration from other areas) may have the opposite effect. Meanwhile, income transfers in the form of remittances of earnings from other sectors create demand for both consumer and investment goods.

• *Foreign sector linkages* have effects determined by the extent to which the pattern of exports and imports modifies the other linkages described above. For example, if agricultural output is exported unprocessed, production linkages based on intermediate demand will be relatively weak. Similarly, if some of the direct consumption needs of the rural population are satisfied by imports, consumption-based links to other sectors of the domestic economy are weakened.

These rural linkages have important implications for rural growth and employment. Such empirical work as has been done in estimating their quantitative impact has focused on the first two categories listed above. Some key findings from this work are described in the subsections that follow.

Forward and Backward Production Linkages

As Johnston and Kilby (1975) have pointed out, production linkages depend on the composition as well as the size of demand. The composition of demand will be affected by the distribution of income among rural households, and this will in turn be strongly influenced by the distribution of land. Where incomes (and land) are more or less evenly distributed among broad sections of the population, there will probably be a large local market for comparatively simple goods and services that can be produced locally with the use of little capital or technical skill.

Evidence from India, Pakistan, and Taiwan suggests that goods such as bicycles, wooden furniture, bricks, metal utensils, improved farm implements, irrigation pumps, and electric motors are likely to be made by small-scale workshops in rural centers. These establishments use favorable factor proportions (low ratios of capital and skills to unskilled labor) and are locally competitive. Their output is relatively unstandardized, uses local raw materials, and is sold to low-income groups. In such an environment the small-scale sector would expand naturally. If these producers can obtain access to the technology and credit they need, they can expand in pace with the growth of farm-based demand.

In other areas, incomes (and landholdings) may be more skewed, and growth in farm output may be confined to a small group of medium-size or large farmers. The resulting composition of demand will tend to support a relatively narrow market for relatively expensive goods that are likely to be produced in urban centers and to need more capital and skills. This type of demand structure limits the number of new jobs based on rural linkages and may lead to capital-intensive industrial development and inefficient import substitution policies. In Pakistan, for example, the industrial structure is based on capital-intensive urban industries promoted by policies that have undervalued capital. In contrast, Taiwan, where factor prices reflect resource endowments relatively accurately, has very labor-intensive industries that are characterized by vigorous rural activity and labor-intensive exporting. Rurally based industries have supplemented their core supplies of labor with part-time agricultural workers, women, and teenagers; their output is geared mainly to lower-income labor households (Ho 1979).

Taiwan and the Indian subcontinent can also be contrasted in the way in which backward linkages have been established for farm equipment. In Taiwan, and to some extent in the Indian Punjab, farm tools and equipment such as irrigation pumps and motors, threshers, harrows, and tillers are largely fabricated by small-scale enterprises in small rural centers (Cartillier 1975; Child and Kaneda 1975). By contrast, the manufacture of farm implements by rural artisans has been of relatively little importance in India and has involved few nonfarm linkages.

Although several studies have noted the changing structure of occupations in South Asia and the importance of the effects of production linkages in rural areas, few have empirically documented these phenomena. Vyas and Mathai (1978) examined the prospects for nonfarm employment in rural India and noted that nonfarm activities represented a declining source of jobs, especially for agricultural labor households.[3]

The only study that has actually tried to quantify the extent of intersectoral production linkages was done by the Asian Development Bank (ADB 1977). Using input-output studies from various countries, it found that (a) the agricultural sector depends more heavily on its own output than does the nonagricultural sector, (b) forward as well as backward linkages with the agricultural sector were weak, particularly in India, and (c) export and import linkages were weaker in India than in other countries. It also found that the overall linkage between increased food-crop production and growth in the rest of the economy was weak in most of the countries studied, including India. It attributed this fact to an insufficiently broad diffusion of new technologies, the heavy dependence of the high-growth sectors on imports, and a considerable degree of import leakage.

Linkages and the Composition of Final Demand

Increases in rural incomes are spent mainly on consumer goods. The distribution of income among different income classes determines the composition of final demand, which in turn depends on the type and extent of consumption linkages. Table 7-1 gives figures for the proportion of marginal income spent on different categories of consumption goods by various expenditure classes in rural India, grouped by approximate size of holdings.

The data show that the cereals category accounts for more than half of the marginal outlays of the landless but falls increasingly rapidly as incomes rise, to less than 10 percent for large farmers. Overall, however, a relatively large share of any increase in food output, especially if achieved by labor-intensive small farms with the use of wage labor, will be directly absorbed back into the rural sector: production will provide its own demand. If most of a production increase is accounted for by larger farmers or by labor-saving methods, however, most of the higher output will have to seek its demand on open mar-

Table 7-1. *India: Marginal Budget Shares among Commodity Groups by Rural Expenditure Group*
(percent)

		Size of landholding corresponding to the expenditure group[a]			
Commodity	Landless	*0–1* acre	*1–5* acres	*5–10* acres	*10+* acres
Agricultural	85.59	79.59	68.80	54.28	29.39
Cereals	57.74	46.53	29.22	17.92	8.02
Milk and milk products	3.61	7.75	13.68	15.60	7.26
Edible oil	4.05	3.95	3.09	2.30	2.79
Meat, fish, and eggs	2.71	3.69	4.02	2.96	1.28
Sugar and gur	2.47	3.79	4.40	4.53	2.82
Other food items	14.95	13.88	14.39	10.98	7.22
Clothing	1.52	2.08	8.12	13.70	12.16
Fuel and light	5.37	7.27	5.48	3.43	2.13
Other nonfood items	7.58	11.06	17.60	28.59	56.33

Notes: Data from Rounds 3–25 of the National Sample Survey, consumer expenditure surveys, have been used for all expenditure groups to estimate the linear expenditure system.

a. Expenditure classes of the 17th Round, at 1961–62 prices, have been grouped to form corresponding landholding groups: the landless (Rs0–8); 0–1 acres (Rs8–11, 11–13); 1–5 acres (Rs13–15, 15–18, 18–21); 5–10 acres (Rs21–24, 24–28, 28–34); 10+ acres (Rs34–43, 43–55, 55–75, 75+).

Source: Radhakrishna and Murty (1978), table 3.2.

kets and will likely be bought by labor households outside the food-
grain sector. The cash incomes accruing to larger farmers will then
be allocated to other goods and services in accordance with their budget shares.

Agricultural commodities other than food grains constitute 30–40
percent of the budget shares of nearly all expenditure groups. The
strong apparent linkage between increased rural incomes and the
propensity to consume these commodities suggests that demand for
them is powerful enough to support a variety of ancillary and
processing activities. Small-scale, labor-intensive production of
these commodities in rural areas could have significant second-
order income and employment effects. Until recently, however,
governments in South Asia have been preoccupied with the food-
grain sector, with the result that credit, marketing, extension, and
price support policies for other agricultural commodities have been
neglected.

As table 7-1 shows, milk and milk products have a 13–15 percent
share in the marginal budgets of small and medium-size farm households, a larger proportion than even fuel or clothing. Poultry and
meat products, though a relatively small share of their budgets, can
considerably improve the diet of rural households as incomes rise
above poverty levels. India has given considerable attention to dairy
and livestock development in recent years, but Pakistan and Bangladesh have not as yet.

Other goods—including clothing, fuel and light, education, consumer services, and durable and semidurable items—account for
15–20 percent of the incremental expenditures of marginal farmers
and the landless and for increasingly large shares in the case of
higher-income groups. The paucity of data prevents a breakdown of
the wide variety of goods and services involved, making it difficult to
identify linkages. These linkages, however, depend critically on how
fast incomes grow for the majority of the rural population. If the incomes of the poor stagnate at low levels, the total final demand multi-
pliers for these goods will be low because their marginal budget
shares are small.

Data on expenditure elasticities for the same set of commodities
and expenditure classes reinforce the findings based on marginal
budget shares (see table 7-2). Since the expenditure elasticities of cereals for the two poorest expenditure groups are close to unity, these
groups' demand for cereals is dominated by changes in incomes and
food prices; for higher income groups, demand is likely to be determined mainly by changes in household population. In the short run,
if prices are stable, the main determinant of demand for food grains
will be the rate of growth in the incomes of the poor. If prosperity

is widespread and incomes of the lower income groups increase via a Green Revolution in food grains, their expanding demand will absorb most of the higher output and confine a large part of the linkages to rural areas.

The real level of demand and the distributive effects of any growth also depend on what happens to cereal prices. An increase in cereal prices has two opposing effects. It will in principle lower consumption by raising costs, but may also increase incomes. If a substantial proportion of the cultivated area of households is devoted to food grains, and if marketed surpluses are large enough, the negative cost effect may be offset by a positive expenditure effect as higher prices raise farm profits and incomes (Barnum and Squire 1979; Ahn and Singh 1981).

Cross-price and own-price elasticities with respect to cereal prices for the same nine commodity groups by expenditure class are consistently negative; any increase in grain prices will reduce the demand for *all* items consumed by the lowest and even middle income groups. The landless are hardest hit by a rise in cereal prices; those who possess land and have net marketed surpluses may register gains, however, because of the offsetting effects on their incomes of the higher prices for the commodities they can sell. Thus, as noted in the previous paragraph, price increases may actually increase food-grain consumption for some income groups.

Increases in food-grain prices, which dominate the consumer price

Table 7-2. *India: Rural Expenditure Elasticities for Nine Commodity Groups by Expenditure Group*

		Size of landholding corresponding to the expenditure group			
Commodity	Landless	0–1 acre	1–5 acres	5–10 acres	10+ acres
Cereals	0.954	0.827	0.583	0.460	0.343
Milk and milk products	1.962	2.245	2.222	1.701	0.728
Edible oil	1.527	1.247	0.968	0.783	0.985
Meat, fish, and eggs	1.546	1.693	1.569	1.149	0.606
Sugar and gur	1.363	1.655	1.537	1.379	0.803
Other food items	1.115	1.008	1.121	0.871	0.674
Clothing	0.823	0.644	1.468	1.541	1.044
Fuel and light	0.589	0.963	0.814	0.587	0.508
Other nonfood items	1.072	1.370	1.763	1.816	1.781

Note: Expenditure elasticities are computed at mean expenditure levels in each class. See table 7-1 for definitions of expenditure groups.
Source: Radhakrishna and Murty (1978), table 3.3A.

indexes, and especially for lower income groups in rural areas, result in lower demand for *all* commodities, except among the highest income groups, whose expenditure elasticities offset the cross-price effects. Small and marginal farmers and the landless reduce their consumption of food grains and all other goods. The linkage effects are considerably weakened if food-grain prices rise significantly in real terms. Thus, unless increases in food-grain output are accompanied by a decline in real food-grain prices, these demand linkages will be weakened. In South Asia real food-grain prices have been rising. The total effect on each commodity group depends on how incremental expenditures are distributed.

The expenditure elasticities for milk products, edible oils, meat, fish, eggs, and sugar are in the 1.5 to 2.0 range for the lowest and middle income groups that make up the bulk of the rural population. This suggests that high rates of growth in output (incomes) among these groups—say, 3–4 percent a year—would be accompanied by an increase in demand and employment (if increased output retains the same labor intensity) of 4.5–8 percent a year. If most of the output and income growth is confined to large farmers, however, the growth in demand for these products would be considerably reduced because this group's expenditure elasticities for these goods are relatively low. The successful development of agriculture other than food grains thus depends significantly on income growth being widely distributed across rural expenditure classes.

The expenditure elasticities for nonfarm goods and services (other than clothing and fuel and light) exceed unity for all expenditure classes. A 3–4 percent increase in rural incomes would therefore have high secondary effects on this subsector by raising demand between 5 and 8 percent a year.

The strength of consumption linkages depends on the distribution of incremental earnings among different income groups in rural areas. Mellor and Lele (1973) have pointed out that raising the employment and income levels of the poor depends on increasing the food supply via the marketed surpluses of the rural rich. But the link between larger surpluses and higher levels of employment and earnings is weak, because the new HYVs, for example, generate relatively small increases in labor demand and incomes, while sharply raising crop yields and the net incomes of cultivators.

The share of the poorest expenditure classes in increased production payments seems very small; most of the incremental benefits and incomes accrue to cultivating households. As has been explained in previous chapters, however, marginal and small farmers account for a significant proportion of these households and of cultivated area and output. If they continue to adopt HYVs, the benefits would spread widely to these groups. The extent of this diffusion cannot be determined without more extensive data.

The use of more labor-intensive methods, more rapid growth of output among small and marginal farmers and in backward regions, redistribution of land assets, and rural works programs are, in principle, all ways to redistribute incremental income in favor of the rural poor. Joint employment and production strategies for the food-grain sector and other rural activities is the surest way of promoting strong linkages within the rural economy. But will the supply of products other than food grains be forthcoming? Inelasticity of supply in the relevant industries would definitely weaken the linkages. Where it occurs, this inelasticity is not likely to be caused by a lack of capital: such objects of incremental expenditures as livestock, fruits, vegetables, and small consumer goods can be produced by relatively labor-intensive methods.[4]

Rather, supply inelasticities are likely to be caused by institutional constraints, including (a) neglect by policymakers of the relevant industries' concerns and failure to appreciate their role in development policy; (b) more specifically, the absence of institutions for providing inputs, credit, and marketing and extension services in support of these industries; and (c) a dearth of project investments in these sectors, especially in rural areas. A more decentralized and labor-intensive pattern of industrialization than that currently apparent in the subcontinent, combined with a supporting network of appropriate institutions, could go a long way toward correcting these problems.

The extent of the intersectoral linkages is also affected by the intersectoral terms of trade. When the terms of trade are moving in favor of agriculture, those who buy agricultural commodities will be adversely affected, but those who sell agricultural output will benefit. Thus in periods of favorable terms of trade the demand of the agricultural sector for nonagricultural commodities is likely to increase. Tyagi (1987) has shown that the terms of trade for agriculture in India were adverse from 1952–53 to 1963–64, were favorable from 1964–65 to 1974–75, but again turned against agriculture from 1975–76 to 1983–84. The terms of trade have had a cyclical effect on the demand linkages between sectors, which suggests that pricing policies are a major determinant of the strengths of these linkages.

Employment Implications

What are the likely employment implications of a labor-intensive rural development strategy? Unfortunately, very few empirical studies have examined the direct and indirect employment effects of labor-intensive growth. Some estimates are available for India, however, based on a simulation model incorporating a conceptual framework of the sort discussed above (Mellor and Mudahar 1974a and b). The model attempts to determine the *potential* level of employment that could be generated in the nonagricultural sector in response to an expansion in the food-grain sector and the consequent changes in intermediate and final demand. The main findings are that, if food-grain production rises at about 4 percent a year and the rural labor force grows at about 2.5 percent a year, then:

- Demand in sectors other than food grains will grow at about 6 percent a year.
- Demand for nonfarm goods and services (through forward and backward linkages) will also grow at about 6 percent a year.
- Employment in the food-grain sector (direct on-farm employment) will grow at about 3 percent a year.
- Employment in other sectors (mainly noncrop) will grow at about 6 percent a year.
- Employment in the nonfarm sectors (rural and urban because location is unspecified) will grow at about 4 percent a year and will account for over half of the incremental employment in rural areas.
- As a consequence of these different rates of growth, nonfarm employment will increase its share of total rural employment from about 45 to 55 percent in little over a decade.
- Employment in the economy as a whole will grow at about 4 percent a year.
- An initial rate of rural "unemployment" of about 30 percent will be reduced to about 3 percent in twelve years.

The model thus suggests that growth of 4 percent a year in agricultural (mainly food-grain) production will generate a parallel 4 percent increase in employment (economywide, not just in the rural sector). Even a slightly more rapid adoption of high-yielding varieties does not substantially change the results. A slower rate of output growth will dampen the consumption linkages and will reduce the elasticity of employment with respect to output to below unity.

Lower rates of growth in food-grain production impose substantial penalties over time because of their cumulative employment effects. Rates of growth in food-grain production of 2.75 percent, 3.0 percent, or 3.9 percent are associated with 2.7, 3.0, or 4.0 percent rates of growth in employment respectively. These different rates in turn mean that it would take 39, 27, or 12 years respectively to bring about "full employment"—that is, to absorb the assumed 30 percent unemployed and 2.5 percent annual growth in the labor force. Similarly, a population growth rate of, say, 3 percent instead of 2 percent means that the "full employment" nirvana recedes, on the best assumption about output growth, another one to two decades. In the nonfarm sector Mellor (1976) conjectures that it would be reasonable to expect output to rise twice as fast as employment—that is, by 8 percent a year if employment were growing at 4 percent—provided that policies to increase the rate of investment in this sector were in place. The basic point made by these studies is the strong interaction between agricultural and nonfarm growth in rural areas. Without a high rate of agricultural growth, reducing rural unemployment will be impossible.

Other studies that measure direct and indirect employment effects of agricultural growth are more pessimistic; they predict unemployment increasing despite high growth (Krishna 1974). The evidence clearly points out that the extent of the increase in indirect employment induced by linkages depends crucially on the choice of technology in all sectors. The use of capital-intensive technologies in any sector considerably dampens the induced employment effects—to such an extent, indeed, that additional entrants into the labor force can find only marginal, low-productivity employment in the informal sectors of rural and urban labor markets.

In summary, the findings of the studies discussed in this section suggest the following broad generalizations:

- The indirect or secondary effects of agricultural growth on employment and income can be very important factors in regional development.
- To generate a viable, dynamic nonfarm sector, however, a sustained rate of growth in agricultural output of 3.5–4 percent for about a decade may be needed.
- A 1 percent change in agricultural output is likely to increase *total* employment by no more than 1 percent. (In technical language, the economywide induced employment elasticity with respect to agricultural output is likely to be no more than unity.) For *rural* employment, the indirect effects are likely to be less, unless they are wholly localized.
- These indirect effects can be dampened considerably by the use of relatively capital-intensive technologies, which raise prices (particularly for wage goods), or by the location of producing units in urban areas.
- These effects can considerably improve the employment and income prospects of the landless poor, particularly in nonfarm activities, but income distribution may actually worsen if the lion's

share goes to those in nonfarm activities who are already relatively well-off.

- Supportive investments in infrastructure and institutions are essential: without them, these effects could be considerably reduced (Lele and Mellor 1972b, 1981).

Rural and Small-Scale Industrialization

Linkages of the kind I have been discussing have not been effectively exploited in South Asia, other than in a few isolated areas. This becomes apparent from an examination of such few data as are available on rural and small-scale industrialization in the subcontinent.

India's Experience

A study by Mazumdar (1980) found that in 1971 more than half of *all* employment in manufacturing, processing, and repair establishments combined was in rural areas. Of this subtotal, nearly half was provided by household units, which were by definition small (90 percent of them employed fewer than ten persons, none employed more than twenty). The other half of all rural employment was provided by nonhousehold units, nearly half of which employed fewer than twenty workers. Thus nearly 75 percent of all rural manufacturing employment was carried out in small-scale units (fewer than twenty workers). Rural household units (all definitionally small in scale) accounted for a significant proportion of total employment in several industries—wool and synthetic textiles (26 percent), cotton textiles (38 percent), textile products (26 percent), wood and furniture (39 percent), leather and fur (30 percent), nonmetallic mined products (25 percent), and food (21 percent).

Among nonhousehold units, Mazumdar found that rural areas again accounted for a significant proportion of total employment—close to half in Bihar, Haryana, and Uttar Pradesh, for example. But data on enterprises in six northern states by firm size (table 7-3 and figure 7-1) reveal two peculiar features of the nonhousehold manufacturing sector: the distribution is strongly bimodal, with large percentages in very small units (up to 4 workers) and very large ones (more than 500 workers); and large enterprises appear to be very important in rural areas. Medium-size enterprises (50–500 workers) that could effectively exploit linkages and raise labor productivity are missing in both rural and urban areas, despite policies designed to favor their growth.

The differences between West Bengal and the Indian Punjab are

Table 7-3. India: Percentage of Employees in Each Size Group of Firms in Rural Areas, 1971

State	Firm size (number of employees)							Percentage of all nonhousehold enterprise employment
	1–4	5–9	10–49	50–99	100–299	300–499	500+	
Bihar	45.6	8.2	19.2	6.3	7.4	2.0	11.4	43.1
Haryana	17.5	3.9	15.5	12.0	16.3	9.4	25.5	42.0
Madhya Pradesh	20.2	7.2	38.0	34.7[a]	—	—	—	24.1
Punjab	47.2	4.7	12.3	12.2	12.7	1.8	9.2	26.8
Uttar Pradesh	30.2	9.2	21.4	11.7	8.3	1.1	18.2	49.8
West Bengal	26.5	8.8	20.0	9.4	15.7	3.0	16.7	23.5

Notes: Of the total employment of 12.7 million in manufacturing, processing, or service establishments, 46.6 percent is rural (5.92 million), of which nearly half (3.0 million) is in nonhousehold enterprises in rural areas. Of this 3.0 million, nearly half (1.4) are in establishments with fewer than twenty workers. The Economic Census of Establishments in 1977 reports nearly 20 million employees spread over 1.7 million establishments in all rural areas of India.

a. Percentage in all firms with fifty or more employees.
Sources: Mazumdar (1980); Census of India, Establishment Tables, 1971.

Figure 7-1. *India: Distribution of Manufacturing Employment in Rural Areas by Firm Size, 1971*

(percent)

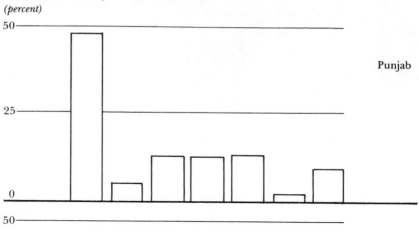

Punjab

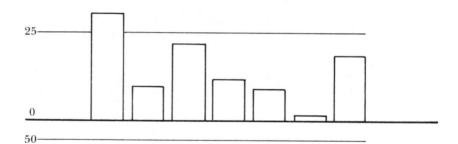

Uttar Pradesh

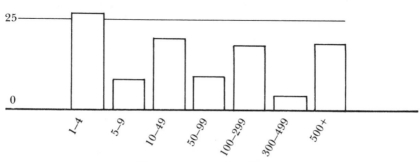

West Bengal

Firm size (number of employees)

Source: Table 7-3.

Table 7-4. *India: Employment in Selected Industries in Punjab and Haryana Combined*

	Number of workers		Annual percentage increase
Industry	*1969–70*	*1976–77*	*(1970–77)*
Khadi and village industries[a]	25,642	43,290	7.8
Cycle and cycle parts	18,642	40,337	11.7
Agricultural implements and machine and hand tools	32,857	35,376	1.1
Rice shelling, cotton ginning and pressing	11,673	18,777	7.0
Sewing machines and parts	6,984	8,418	2.7
Hosiery	24,521	46,509	9.6

a. Includes processed food and vegetable oil, soap, gur-khandsari, pottery, handmade paper and textiles, and leather and leather goods.

Sources: *Statistical Abstract of the Punjab 1978*, pp. 334–40; *Statistical Abstract of Haryana 1977–78*, pp. 170–73, 182–83.

also striking. In urban areas in West Bengal the percentage of employment in large units with more than 500 workers is very much higher than in the other states covered by the table. By contrast, the Punjab has a much smaller percentage of employment in very large units and a moderate amount in medium-size ones, while small units (fewer than 50 workers) provide 30 percent of total employment. Punjab alone among the states for which data are given has developed a strong segment of medium-size and small industrial firms producing a variety of goods. West Bengal's industry, however, is concentrated around Calcutta and in a few subsectors such as jute textiles and steel. These differences are repeated in rural areas, except that West Bengal's bias toward large units is not repeated in the rural economy. Bihar, Haryana, and Punjab also have heavy concentrations of employment in very small units.

Industries have grown at very different rates. The nonmetallic mineral products subsector, which is dominated by relatively large units, has generally shown the most rapid rate of growth in rural areas, and its growth has been at the expense of food processing industries that generally operate with smaller units (Mazumdar 1980, p. 38).

This is not true everywhere. Table 7-4 shows the growth rates of selected industries in Punjab and Haryana. In these states it appears that traditional village industries, which are dominated by smaller units, have not stagnated as in the rest of India. Meanwhile, some newer industries specializing in consumer goods and agricultural processing (often dominated by small and medium-size units) have also shown vigorous growth. These industries tend to have higher ratios of value added to employment and lower ratios of fixed capital to employment than most of the heavy industries—chemicals, steel, and power—that dominate the industrial sector in other states.[5]

The industrial experience of Punjab and Haryana is particularly relevant because these areas were considered industrially far behind West Bengal at the time of independence.[6] Partition dealt a further blow to the region's industry, and a totally new start had to be made. Yet twenty-five years later the region was recording high rates of growth and its industrial output had increased more than fiftyfold. Between 1947 and 1974 the number of registered factories rose from 547 to 7,400; by 1973 registered small-scale industrial units had grown from some 18,000 to 49,000, and there was an equal number of unregistered units in these states. The region has emerged as an important producer of many industrial goods in the country, despite the fact that it lacks both major raw materials and the large markets that generally form the basis for industrial expansion.

Table 7-5 shows the share of the Indian Punjab and Haryana in national output and employment in thirteen industries, for both large- and small-scale units. It demonstrates the dominant position of the region in the country's modernized small-scale sector of many industries—the two states' share of total employment and output in India exceeds 40 percent in more than half the industries listed. Even their share in the industrial output of the large-scale sector is high, given that Punjab and Haryana together account for only about 4.5 percent of India's population.

Few other states that were industrially backward before independence have achieved anything approaching this record of industrial growth. Moreover, most of the region's industrial success is based on newly emerging industries in which it has no comparative advantage in the supply of raw materials. Markets, too, are mainly in other states or abroad.[7] Pandit (1978) argues that the key features of this remarkable industrialization process have been the availability of a cadre of industrial entrepreneurs (mainly persons displaced by partition) with previous experience in trade, business, or industry and the rapid emergence of a large and disciplined skilled labor force. The state government played its part by allotting materials and factory sites, providing loans for construction and machinery, training and organizing industrial institutes, and giving special allotment quotas to help displaced persons. Displaced agricultural classes also spearheaded the Green Revolution, which suggests the importance of migrants—or remigrants, in the case of the Punjab, because their ancestors had gone to settle the new canal colonies in West Pakistan only two generations before partition—in pioneering entrepreneurial activity.

Table 7-5. India: Share of Punjab and Haryana in All Output and Employment for Selected Industries and Sectors

| | Percentage of all India | | | |
| | Small-scale sector (1972)[b] | | Large-scale sector (1969)[c] | |
Industry[a]	Output	Employment	Output	Employment
Woolen hosiery and other knitted wear	88.9	92.7[d]	28.8[d]	13.1[d]
Rubber footwear	68.3	56.1	13.9	8.8
Small hand and cutting tools	50.2	43.0	15.5	18.5
Plumbing fixtures and metal fittings	18.9	18.5	63.2[d]	62.4[d]
Nuts, bolts, and other minor hardware	36.2	36.8	3.8	5.4
Agricultural implements and hand tools	36.6	29.6	18.2	15.6
Utensils and light metal products	13.2	9.2	4.3[e]	4.3[e]
Machine tools	42.5	44.4	9.6	11.0
Sewing and knitting machines	68.5	73.0	17.5	15.3[d]
Automobile parts and machinery	17.0	18.8	14.4	16.8
Bicycles, motorcycles, and parts	59.3	55.8	30.6	28.7
Laboratory and scientific instruments	26.9	27.5	13.7[e]	21.3[e]
Sports goods	48.3	47.6	78.7	57.2[e]
All industries	13.2	10.4	4.4	3.9

a. Industries are grouped according to definitions standardized in the Annual Survey of Industries.
b. The small-scale sector is defined by "Census of Small-Scale Industrial Units" of the Indian Ministry of Industry.
c. The large-scale sector is composed of units employing 50 or more workers and using power or 100 or more workers without power.
d. Refers to Punjab only.
e. Refers to Haryana only.
Source: Pandit (1978), p. 1936.

Skilled workers make up more than two-thirds of the total number employed in most of the industries which the region dominates; this is true even in the small-scale sector. This labor force is drawn mainly from urban centers in which skilled refugees from Pakistan had settled. Because they and other migrants from rural areas have stressed the importance of education for their children and have acquired skills through learning-by-doing, the efficiency of this labor force has increased in the postindependence decades.

Skilled labor with an entrepreneurial spirit and experience of adversity together with enlightened state policies have transformed this region through small-scale industrialization in a way unparalleled in the subcontinent. The region has been able to absorb the growth of its own labor force and in-migration from other regions attracted by rising real wages in agricultural and other occupations. The early development of industry, initially rural, small-scale, and modest, has promoted the formation of both skills and finance capital that should ensure rapid future growth.

The region's lesson for other areas seems to be that a rapid expansion of small-scale industries, both as direct producers of consumer goods and as ancillaries to larger firms, is a highly effective way to expand employment. In general, however, evidence on the industrial structure in India and on the linkages discussed earlier suggests that rurally based strategies for growth have been exploited on only a very limited scale in South Asia. This has been a major failure of rural development efforts generally in the subcontinent.

Lessons from Taiwan

That a strategy based on rural small-scale industries can be made to work is evident not only from experience in the Indian Punjab but also from developments in several Southeast Asian economies, including China, the Republic of Korea, Malaysia, and Taiwan. The experience in China and Taiwan is especially instructive.

Ho (1979) has shown how in Taiwan nonfarm sources of income increased from 25 percent of total farm household income in 1962 to 43 percent in 1975. Although total rural employment grew at a slower rate than urban employment, employment in many rural industries grew more rapidly (manufacturing employment in rural Taiwan grew at 7.2 percent between 1956 and 1966) and led to a large shift toward nonagricultural rural jobs. In 1956 agriculture employed 73 percent of the rural labor force. By 1966 this share had fallen to 54 percent, with the rest employed in manufacturing, commerce, and services. Further industrialization has not been accompanied by a concentration of nonagricultural employment in major metropolitan areas.

In rural areas, small-scale units with low capital intensity predominate. Establishments with fewer than ten workers employed 41 percent of the manufacturing workers in rural Taiwan. Fixed assets per person employed in rural areas were half those in urban areas,[8] the output-capital ratios were higher in some industries, and the ratio of net value added to fixed assets did not differ much from those in urban Taiwan. These facts suggest that rural-based industries used capital as efficiently as, if not better than, urban-based industries.

The impact on rural employment was particularly significant. With the labor force growing by over 2.5 percent and the size of holdings averaging about one hectare (Fei, Ranis, and Kuo 1979), increasing nonfarm employment enabled farm households to combine farming with part-time or full-time (for some members of the household) employment, which eased the pressure on land and on rural-urban migration. In 1960, 45 percent of all farm households relied exclusively on farms while 23 percent earned more income from nonfarm activities. By 1970 these ratios stood at 30 percent and 29 percent respectively. The share of small farmers was even higher, and this contributed to the greater equality of total incomes in rural areas. Nonfarm activities grew by 12 percent a year between 1960 and 1970. The real income of farm households doubled between 1952 and 1972, mainly as a result of this growth, although rising agricultural productivity also contributed. This was accompanied by an upgrading of skills of the rural population via almost universal education and the development of rural infrastructure.

The geographical size of Taiwan has certainly contributed to the decentralization of its industries in rural areas. But it is clear that rapid and equitable agricultural development (based initially on a very successful land reform) has also contributed by providing an important market for nonfarm goods and services. Practically all of the services and many nonfarm consumer goods demanded by farm households are produced in rural areas. Many of these have relatively high income elasticities, and their production in small-scale, capital-efficient units with low technology and skill requirements has created rural nonfarm employment.

Rural Industry in China

The experience in China is of special relevance because of characteristics it shares with the countries of South Asia—notably size of land area and population. Rural linkages and nonfarm activities are strongly emphasized in China. Although noncrop agricultural activities have always been important—especially pig production—they have been accelerated and integrated since the 1970s at both the private and the communal level.[9] Nonagricultural rural employment, for example, rose from about 15 percent of the labor force in 1957 to over 24 percent by 1975.

More than 100 million people worked in China's nonfarm rural sector in 1975, reflecting a growth rate of over 7 percent a year between 1957 and 1975. The expansion was most marked in collective-communal industries in rural areas. Trade, food processing, personal and financial services, health, education, transport, and communications all showed above average rates of growth (Rawski 1979). Social services—health, education, and population control—have been actively encouraged and have grown rapidly.

One unique feature of rural development in China has been the promotion of rural small-scale industries designed to meet local production (intermediate) and consumption (final) demand locally. A second unique feature has been the integration of these activities with agricultural seasons; in the slack period much of the labor force is employed in noncrop and nonagricultural rural activities. Communes and "brigades" ran small-scale enterprises organized on this basis. In the 1980s these have been largely decollectivized through the use of the personal responsibility system (PRS). These enterprises almost doubled in number and in the value of their output between 1975 and 1978. These activities were expected to contribute about half the total value of communes' output by 1985 (Perkins and Yusuf 1984).

Small-scale rural industries in China include iron and steel, cement, and chemical fertilizers (over half the total output of these industries was produced in small plants in 1973),[10] together with local enterprises that manufacture and repair farm machinery, process agricultural output, and produce consumer goods. Most of the durable consumer goods available in rural areas, including bicycles, radios, furniture, and textiles, are also produced in small-scale units linked to communes—the result of a conscious policy "to use local materials, produce locally and distribute locally" (Sigurdson 1972, p. 324).

The Chinese have also gone to unusual lengths to promote indigenous intermediate technologies in support of the official strategy. Locally developed methods, equipment, and adaptive innovations are encouraged (Riskin 1978). As a direct consequence, in addition to the considerable intensification of agriculture, the vast rural economy not only absorbed nearly 100 million new entrants into the rural work force between 1957 and 1975, but also raised the average number of days of employment for the entire farm labor force of more than 300 million men and women (Rawski 1979, p. 126 and ch. 4).

The development of China's rural industry before the late 1970s has since been dwarfed by a burst of growth.[11] With the breakdown of the communes and the onset of rural reforms in 1978, the farm sector was transformed by the personal responsibility system, which was introduced in 1978 but fully implemented in 1980–83. Under the PRS land can be leased for private farming by rural households for up to fifteen years (up to fifty years in mountainous regions), and leases can be transferred to heirs. The result has been a tremendous surge in agricultural and rural economic activity. Further changes in government policies have progressively liberalized the growth of private enterprises and permitted the establishment of a variety of new enterprises in rural areas. The labor surplus, which was extensive but hidden under the old commune system, suddenly became open and visible with the growth of private family farming. This in turn has generated pressure in rural areas to use the large labor surplus effectively.

Between 1978 and 1987 the value of gross agricultural output grew at 6.8 percent a year in real terms, the gross value of industrial output in rural areas grew at more than 23 percent a year in real terms, while rural employment in industry, commerce, transport, and construction increased by 124 percent. This tremendous growth of rural industrial and other activities has been accompanied by a large increase in personal incomes and in the demand for rural housing and consumer goods. As a result, millions of new township and village enterprises (TVEs) have emerged to meet this demand. Large increases in rural credit have been provided to the TVEs by the expanding banking system, and internal accumulation of funds has been generated in part by concessional tax treatment. Rapid growth in incomes in the rest of the economy (at rates of more than 10 percent a year) together with high investment demand (gross investment to GDP ratios in China in the 1980s have exceeded 30 percent a year) have helped support this expansion.

The growth in the TVE sector has also brought about massive shifts in the rural labor force. In 1978 about 11 percent of the total rural labor force of around 306 million was in nonfarm activities. By 1986 this share had grown to about 20 percent of a total rural labor force of 380 million. The nature of rural industry has also changed. Previously many of the TVEs were geared to processing and sideline activities that supplemented incomes in the communes in the off-seasons. With few links to the larger economy, they were inward oriented and static, offering no competition to the state-owned urban-industrial sector. Now TVEs are characterized by dynamism, rapid growth, and an ability to adjust quickly to changing market conditions; they compete effectively in many product areas with state-owned enterprises and reach out to local and even provincial product markets.

A continuing characteristic of Chinese rural industry is its strong ties to the local community. The institutional structure of China's TVE sector is linked very closely to a three-tier system of rural community governance—township, village, and production team—that has been in place since the 1950s. Community governments at the township and village levels resemble mini-states in that they have fixed membership, often share incomes within the community, and exhibit a large degree of financial self-reliance. Many of them continue to be communally owned, but at the same time seem to operate as profit-oriented business entities.

Agroindustries in other countries, especially in South Asia, often suffer from an inability to develop strong farm linkages with private peasant suppliers of raw materials, but this problem does not seem to be evident in China. Although forms of individual ownership and proprietorship are emerging, it is still the strong ties to local government and communities that link the Chinese TVEs with the farm sector and underlie their success. These strong community links are a cultural trait that is shared with Japan, Korea, and Taiwan, where rural industrial activities have also been flourishing. Whether these cultural norms can be transferred to the South Asian context is debatable.

TVEs in China are not without their problems. They suffer from limited factor mobility in a socialist setting where labor has never been mobile, face increasingly severe competition and market saturation in many industries, are hindered by lack of scale economies and by excessive spatial dispersion, lack support services (credit and marketing networks, transport, and communication), and are denied many essential materials distributed by the state-controlled system. But above all they are still in a sort of legal limbo: their rapid growth has caught the government off guard, and it is not exactly sure how to deal with the expansion of this "private" sector in a socialist setting.

The recent mushrooming of TVEs in China is further evidence, if more were needed, of the impetus that the growth of agricultural output provides for growth of the rural nonfarm sector. South Asian countries generally lack this impetus and have not been able to benefit to the same extent from rapid growth in rural industry. This is particularly disturbing because, given the population densities in South Asia and China, growth in industrial employment cannot be expected to keep up with the growth in the labor force, even with high rates of growth in the industrial sector. In this regard too, China has outpaced India. Whereas industry in China grew at around 10 percent a year all through the 1950s and 1960s, India's industrial growth stagnated around 5 percent a year. Between 1973 and 1984 the industrial sector grew 8.7 percent a year in China but only 4.4 percent in

India. Even with such high rates of industrial growth, most of the employment growth in China is expected to be in the TVE sector. The same will have to be the case in South Asia. But rapid employment growth has been possible only where agricultural growth has been robust (Northwest India and Punjab). For further growth, it will be necessary to have rapid industrial growth in the urban sector as well. Better links between rural and urban industrialization will have to be developed. China and Taiwan both point the way in this context.

Another important element of Chinese strategy has been their conscious reliance on the growth of the TVE sector to prevent rapid urban growth and to meet most of the growing employment needs in rural areas. Earlier this was done mainly by restricting any labor movement whatsoever. Now the reliance is on rapid growth of rural industrial employment. In South Asia the absence of any rational strategy to provide employment in rural industries has led to rapid urbanization with all the associated costs of heavy social overhead and urban blight. Disguised rural unemployment and poverty have too often been converted into open urban unemployment and despair through lack of growing opportunities in rural areas. To its credit, China has so far avoided this. It is a lesson well worth learning in South Asia.

Comparison of India and China

The different approaches to rural industrialization taken in India and China have been examined by Sigurdson (1978). He points out that both countries recognize the need to develop nonfarming activities through rural industrialization and both have some 20 million people engaged in rural industrial activities. Nevertheless, as he shows, the organization and structure of rural industries in the two countries exhibit major differences—differences that offer some helpful insights into what can be learned from the Chinese experience.

Industrial activity in India's rural sector is dominated by traditional, household-based artisanal handicrafts, together with a modest but growing nonhousehold sector; China's rural industries are run mostly by collectively owned units. This denotes not only a difference in ownership—private or collective—but also differences in size, technology, skill levels, productivity, and the consequent ability to generate investable capital. Some of the results of these contrasting approaches are briefly outlined in the next few paragraphs.

First, India has tried to preserve village and artisanal activities based on Gandhian traditions. To this end, it has imposed quotas, differential pricing, preferential treatment for credit and raw materials, and a "reserved" listing of goods that can be produced only by this sector. As a result, primitive (and not necessarily appropriate) technologies involving limited use of machinery and power have been preserved at the cost of more efficient alternatives. It has also meant that new skills have not been learned, new occupations have been discouraged, and low labor productivity has been institutionalized. The integration of these household units with other industrial processes is minimal; they have consequently not been exposed to any modernizing influence. Attempts to promote more modern, technology-based rural industries in semirural towns via the Rural Industries Projects (RIP) have had few results.

In China, by contrast, under the communes, the collectivization of household and village industrial and artisanal activities meant that the 20 million people in the rural industrial sector in 1973 were employed in modern or semimodern industrial activities as part of an overall program for rural modernization. The total number of nonagricultural TVE employees, including part-time and seasonal workers, rose from 22 million in 1978 to 77 million in 1986, an increase of 55 million. Levels of technical development and skills were consciously upgraded, and access to modern tools, machinery, and power were encouraged. The long-term benefits of skill formation have outweighed the costs of production equipment. This systematic organization of rural industrial activities continues under the personal responsibility system.

The basic approaches underlying rural industrial programs are thus quite different in the two countries. China emphasizes upgrading village crafts by transforming their technologies, while India preserves outmoded and stagnant production methods for their own sake, regardless of their high opportunity costs when compared with more appropriate systems. As a result, China operates with larger units and higher capital intensity, but also with higher labor productivity and greater diversification of output.

Second, Indian programs stress the labor-absorbing aspects of rural industrialization—in effect, treating it as a residual source of jobs that agriculture has failed to provide. China, however, has paid only marginal attention to using industrial employment in rural areas as a means of righting the overall imbalance between labor supply and demand in these areas. It has instead concentrated on dovetailing industrial activities with seasonal labor needs in farm production and has used massive rural works to mop up rural labor. The Chinese have thus not been the victims of the obsession to use labor at any cost that has prevented Indian rural industries from choosing more productive and efficient techniques. Rural industrialization has rightly been seen not as providing employment opportunities for certain rural groups—often precisely those who are least able to take advantage of them—but rather as an integrated function of a modernization program designed to upgrade the rural economy as a whole.

Third, rural industries in India are considered in isolation both from urban industries and from programs for regional rural development. Rural industrialization is organized in an economic vacuum. Vertical integration and linkages with urban industries through subcontracting is missing; there is no overall plan for meeting local needs through local production. Farm machinery and fertilizers come from distant urban centers or from abroad. Only primary food processing is located anywhere near rural areas. Neither intermediate nor final local demand is systematically met by local production using local materials.

In China rural industries are part of both an overall industrial strategy and an integrated rural strategy based on the TVE system. Not only is considerable attention paid to producing for local needs by local units using local raw materials and skills, but also the interdependence of units is planned for and promoted through links within counties, between counties, and with higher-level enterprises. Large numbers of people are mobilized to participate in overall rural development through regional planning that is dovetailed with local participation down to the brigade level. Rural industrialization is thus seen as only one element of China's strategy for rural development. A number of integrated components form a "package," and it may be difficult or impossible to hive off individual parts (see Aziz 1978).

In both China and India, population pressures on land are intense, the rural labor force is growing rapidly, and the economic welfare of farm and landless households depends critically on whether they have access to rapidly expanding sources of nonfarm employment. The Chinese model suggests that this access can be provided by creating and developing a process of spatially decentralized industrialization, based on small-scale rural production units that are linked to the intermediate and final demand generated by a rapidly growing agricultural sector. All these activities need not be planned by the state, as in China, but a system of incentives must be devised to achieve similar results. Rural industrialization can thus serve as a base for economywide industrialization.

Conclusions

The experience of other countries suggests that the broad elements of a rural development strategy for South Asia include:

- An accelerated expansion of food-grain production, based as much as possible on labor-intensive methods and small and marginal farms

- Massive public investment in irrigation, transportation, communications, electrification, feeder roads, and other infrastructure in rural areas
- A change in the structure of industrial production toward consumer goods whose quality, price, and product mix are specifically designed to reflect the demand structure of the rural population
- A rapid growth in ancillary industries—both those ancillary to agriculture (dairying, poultry, fishing, forestry, and food processing) and those ancillary to urban medium- and large-scale industries (through subcontracting for and vertical integration with those industries)—together with the expansion of institutions to provide the inputs, credit, and marketing and extension services needed to support these industries' growth
- A conscious policy of encouraging, in rural areas and provincial towns, productive small-scale enterprises that use local materials and develop local skills whenever this is cost-effective
- A shift of emphasis away from household-based, low-productivity village handicraft and artisan units, and toward the rapid development of units that, although still small in scale, use machinery, power, and new skills to raise labor productivity
- As in the case of ancillary industries, the development of supporting institutions to deliver inputs, credit, and marketing and extension services to these small-scale "modern" enterprises
- The development of appropriate price, tax, and credit incentives and assured access to needed raw materials
- The delivery of basic social services such as health and education, not only to improve the quality of rural life but also more specifically to upgrade skills and labor productivity in rural areas
- The promotion of a new attitude toward rural industries that defines them as a dynamic part of an integrated strategy to transform rural areas, rather than as a "make-work" means of absorbing labor and providing residual employment for the rural poor who cannot find agricultural work.

Such a strategy would raise the incomes of peasant cultivators and small-scale rural entrepreneurs and would thus initially worsen income distribution. At the same time, however, the living standards of the rural poor would improve as a result of lower food-grain prices and greater employment opportunities.

The organizational arrangements (communal or private) and the means (central planning or a system of market incentives) of implementing the strategy are probably less important than the establishment of an environment in which the poor have increasing access to resources and opportunities. Experience from other countries in Asia suggests that redistribution of land may be a necessary (but by no means sufficient) condition for such an environment.

Both equity and growth can be served if rising incomes and their induced effects can be widely and equitably distributed. The demand structures associated with rising rural incomes can then support a decentralized and labor-using pattern of industrialization. Growth and equity conflict when the distribution of rural incomes is highly skewed and incremental incomes are inequitably distributed. Such a situation produces a narrowly based, urbanized process of industrialization that caters to the needs of the few who are relatively rich and neglects the needs of the many who are poor.

It needs to be understood that the long-run answer to the problems of rural unemployment and underemployment must be sought not in the rapid growth of agriculture alone, but in rapid and appropriate industrialization, in both rural and urban areas, that proceeds hand in hand with rising agricultural output. Whatever the long-term prospects for the expansion of rural employment and incomes in South Asia, however, given past and reasonably predictable future rates and types of growth in the rural economy, the problem of rural unemployment will not be solved quickly. Indeed, rural unemployment can be expected to increase further in the near and medium term, under even the most optimistic scenarios for accelerated agricultural growth, at least in Bangladesh and most of India. Therefore a case for medium-term relief to the unemployed becomes unassailable.

Policymakers have been forced to rely on large-scale public works programs, both to create additional employment in rural areas and to construct some of the physical assets needed for the dynamic expansion of the rural economy in the long term. Experience with programs of this kind in the subcontinent is discussed in the next section.

Rural Public Works Programs

Examples of public works programs in South Asia include three programs in Bangladesh (the Works Program, the Thana Irrigation Program, and the Integrated Rural Development Program), two in Pakistan (the Rural Works Program and the People's Works Program), and three in India (the Scarcity Relief Program, the Crash Scheme for Rural Employment, and the Drought Prone Areas Program). A great deal of controversy exists about the usefulness of such programs in alleviating rural poverty and unemployment. This section summarizes the findings of a detailed World Bank study of experience with these programs in the 1960s and 1970s (Burki and others 1976) and also examines the Maharashtra Employment Guarantee Scheme (EGS), which has adopted a novel, comprehensive, and apparently successful approach to public works (Thomas and Hook 1977).

Main Characteristics

Table 7-6 summarizes some of the characteristics of selected public works programs in South Asia. The programs have generally been geared to provide employment to specific target groups such as the rural poor, the "most needy," or "poor surplus agricultural labor," but in practice their targeting has been neither very specific nor very effective.

Although all the programs have promoted long-term employment and the development of infrastructure, they have been designed primarily to provide relatively short-term disaster relief or income supplements. Moreover, they have tended to be planned and implemented in isolation rather than as part of any broad strategy to create new rural assets in an efficient way or to attack the fundamentals of the unemployment problem. The physical, budgetary, and political constraints inherent in these programs have made it impossible for them to make an appreciable difference. They cannot employ all those without jobs or provide supplemental sources of income to all those who need them.

In Bangladesh a number of important and innovative programs provide employment opportunities for the poor in construction, while creating economically justified infrastructure in rural areas. By far the largest of these is the Food for Work Program (FWP), which started in 1974–75. The allocation of food to the FWP increased almost twelvefold in the following decade to reach 500,000 tons in 1986, equivalent to about US$114 million (IFPRI 1985). The FWP now generates annually nearly 100 million days of employment for workers who would otherwise be unemployed and at least 17 days of additional employment for every landless worker in Bangladesh in construction alone. Recent evaluation studies suggest that if FWP projects are well selected, designed, implemented, and maintained, the employment effects will be enormous. A recent review by the World Food Program, however, has criticized the program's lack of integration with local development schemes such as those financed by the Upazila Development Grant. It also identifies technical and managerial problems, the underpayment of beneficiaries, and the overestimation of work done. Nevertheless, those who found jobs with public works projects considerably improved their short-term income and consumption.

The percentage of GDP represented by the programs' expenditures

Table 7-6. South Asia: Characteristics of Selected Public Works Programs to Augment Income

Item	Bangladesh, Works Program	India		Pakistan, Rural Works Program
		Crash Scheme for Rural Employment	Drought Prone Areas Program	
Duration	1962 to present	1971–74	1970 to present	1962–72
Nature of unemployment	Seasonal; estimated at 30 percent of available workdays	Seasonal; estimated at 40 percent of rural labor force	None	Underemployment estimated at 27 percent
Target group	Rural poor	Most needy		Poor surplus agricultural labor
Population per square kilometer, 1965	456	153		51
Workdays of employment generated (millions)	28.8	178.0	37.9	4.4
Average annual program expenditure of GDP	0.57	0.15	0.05	0.19
Wages as a percentage of total program expenditure	63 (1962–67); 16 (1971–78)	76	50	30

Note: The main objective of income-augmenting programs is to supplement the normal earning activities of those they employ, usually in rural areas. They generally take account of seasonal variation in employment. This objective distinguishes them from disaster relief works designed to replace earning opportunities destroyed or reduced by natural calamity and from long-term employment programs designed to absorb structural unemployment.

Source: Burki and others (1976).

has varied, but has generally been low (Burki and others 1976). Since their overall inflationary impact has consequently been negligible, little can be concluded about how the price of wage goods might be affected by an expanded program designed to reduce rural unemployment rates significantly. Inflationary pressures on food prices have occurred, however, especially where crisis relief programs have concentrated on a small geographical area. This was so in Maharashtra in 1973–74, for example, when the Scarcity Relief Program generated an estimated 290 million days of labor at a time when successive crop failures had already produced strong upward pressures on cereal prices.

The need for income-augmenting rural works programs varies inversely with the demand for agricultural labor. If they are to reach those who need additional employment, the programs must be based on a detailed knowledge of local on-farm and off-farm seasonal employment patterns. In this regard, most of the programs effectively coordinated public works activities with seasonal needs and concluded, deferred, or interrupted projects to avoid conflicts. Programs which offer year-round jobs can present serious problems, however, especially if they pay high wages; they may outbid the agricultural sector for peak-season labor and create a shortage of workers in agriculture.

The detailed evidence on alternative employment patterns and wage rates that would make it possible to calculate the real opportunity cost of the programs was not available. But the wage rates obtainable under, for example, the Pakistan Rural Works Program seem high enough to run the risk of diverting rural labor from other activities. The extent to which this could occur in practice depends partly on how much emphasis a particular program places on employment generation to the exclusion of other outcomes. One measure of the strength of this emphasis is the percentage of total expenditures going to wages (see the last column in table 7-6). Both programs in Pakistan were classified in the low employment-creating category, while portions of the Bangladesh Work Program (1962–67) were judged to have generated large amounts of employment. Both the Crash Scheme for Rural Employment and the Drought Prone Areas Program in India are considered medium-to-high employment-creating programs (see Thomas and Hook 1977).

Most of the programs in South Asia have concentrated on directly productive projects and the provision of physical (as opposed to social) infrastructure. This bias effectively counters fears that public works programs do not create useful rural assets. According to Burki and others (1976), however, only India's Drought Prone Areas Program spent substantial sums on creating assets that could be expected to have a direct impact on agricultural growth. In many cases, expenditure is thought to have emphasized road construction in rural areas, an activity that has traditionally been well organized under existing administrative structures in South Asia. Efforts of this kind often concentrate on the so-called construction phase of a project to the exclusion of its long-term impact on unemployment or poverty. Wages paid purely for this kind of work are unlikely to have any lasting effect on poverty or to cause any long-term changes in the position of those employed or in the distribution of income in rural areas.

In the construction phase, the programs transfer resources to those believed to be in deepest poverty through the wages paid, but their secondary and tertiary benefits depend on the type of works being constructed. Projects for the development of irrigation, drainage, or soil conservation, for example, have the greatest impact on future production and thus the highest potential for creating additional demand for labor. By and large, however, they help those who already own land or assets, and this help is directly proportionate to the amount of land or assets owned. Thus, where land distribution is bimodal, as in Pakistan, secondary benefits are regressive—that is, they accrue mainly to the better-off and accentuate inequities in the ownership of rural assets. Where land distribution is more even, as in Bangladesh, the benefits may be more evenly shared but are still distributed among landowners only; the landless remain excluded from all but the primary wage benefits. An illustrative case analyzed for Bangladesh shows that the returns to land (and hence to landowners) claimed by public works projects are five times higher than the returns to labor (Burki and others 1976, p. 50). It is of course possible that the programs provide work for some very small owner-cultivators. Nevertheless, rural income distribution is unlikely to improve much if some short-term increase in employment is the only benefit this group receives.

Projects that emphasize economic infrastructure (roads, reforestation, markets) tend to have the largest short-run redistributive effects because they are usually located on public land. But again longer-term benefits will accrue to landowners in proportion to the size of their holdings and, more important, the size of their marketable surpluses. Traders and intermediaries providing farmers with inputs or buying their output will also gain. The only nonwage benefits of infrastructure programs (notably roads) for the landless may lie in providing greater labor mobility and opening up remote areas—developments which may lead to better employment opportunities.

Social infrastructure projects (such as schools, clinics, and low-cost housing) can provide broad benefits, although they may not reach the poorest groups if access to these facilities is limited. The rural power structure can often restrict the effects of such programs.

Thus gains from public works programs (other than short-term employment) may percolate through to smallholders and the landless only if land is reasonably evenly distributed or if small holdings are geographically segregated from larger ones. In South Asia, where small and large holdings are intermixed, it is almost impossible to direct the longer-term benefits of public works programs to small farmers or the landless. The existing distribution of scarce resources, especially of land, is the single most important determinant of the flows of nonwage benefits from works programs.

Both the design and the implementation of most public works programs in South Asia have been subject to political influence. The two most important factors in bringing about what Burki and others (1976) call "program mutations" are (a) political commitments and objectives that are rarely articulated explicitly, and (b) local elites that bend public works programs to serve their own interests. Pressures can be applied at key decisionmaking stages, including the choice of subprojects and of the location of the program as a whole; the choice of technology, especially its labor intensity; the choice of agents for project implementation; the establishment of wage rates; and the selection of employees. Depending on the choices made, benefits can be diverted to suit the interests of (usually) higher-income groups.

Program mutation has been especially evident in Pakistan, with its sharply skewed distribution of land assets and political power. In both the People's Works Program and the Rural Works Program, political loyalty rather than project performance became the basis for public works allocations. "Large land owners, rural contractors and small town tradesmen quickly shaped the program to serve their own interests" (Thomas, in Falcon and Papanek 1971, p. 306) by shifting decisionmaking from the lowest tier of government, the union councils, to the much larger district councils, which were controlled by these interests. Work was given to contractors, which led to a rapid decline in labor intensity and employment creation.

In Bangladesh a more egalitarian rural structure appears to have slowed the process of mutation, the consequent emergence of power brokers, and the dilution of broad participation in project decisions and benefits. In addition, the Works Program in Bangladesh has benefited from giving local bodies the authority to make decisions and to implement programs within a framework structured by the central government.

To summarize, overall experience with rural works programs in the

1960s and early 1970s was unimpressive, and much of the skepticism about their effectiveness was justified.

Maharashtra's Employment Guarantee Scheme

The Employment Guarantee Scheme (EGS), begun by the Maharashtra state government in 1972, seems to provide an alternative to the earlier rural works programs.[12] The EGS offers guaranteed employment to the rural poor, including small and marginal farmers, landless agricultural workers, and rural artisans. In ways that are productive to the economy, it aims to provide gainful employment to all unskilled persons in rural areas who are willing to do manual labor but cannot find work. In a country as large as India with widespread rural unemployment and underemployment, such a program clearly has enormous appeal.

The main features of the scheme are:

- Beneficiaries cannot choose the work for which they will be employed.
- Guarantees are given that work will be available within a radius of five kilometers of the village where potential beneficiaries have registered. If employment is more than five kilometers away, arrangements for camping (including water, sanitation, and medical and shopping facilities) have to be made.
- Work has be be provided within fifteen days of a request for it.
- Work has to be provided for a continuous period of not less than fifteen to thirty days. It is not clear whether workers can repeatedly reregister after having worked thirty days, but presumably this is so.
- Works are undertaken under government auspices, not through contractors, and at least 60 percent of total expenditures must be for wages to laborers. (This provision is designed to meet the criticism that public works programs have often spent their money through contractors and have provided only limited employment and wage benefits to participants.)
- Wages are determined by piece rates calculated to ensure that, as far as possible, a laborer working seven hours a day gets the minimum agricultural wage, or at least Rs3 a day. Wages are paid weekly, on the basis of output or work done.
- Works are chosen according to a particular set of priorities, such as the completion of earlier works or the continuation of labor-intensive activities that directly or indirectly stimulate agricultural

production. Works may include minor irrigation infrastructure, water and soil conservation, command area development, land development, or flood control. Road construction is undertaken where no other productive activities are available.

- As far as possible, on-farm and related labor needs are to be met before the EGS becomes active in any area.

The scheme has some unique administrative features. First, since priority is given to existing or incomplete projects, only if no such projects are available can new ones be started. Second, to the extent possible, each project is intended to be completed within one or two work seasons, and any requiring more than 4,000 workdays to complete need prior authorization from the state government. Third, each project must have a blueprint that shows how work is to be allocated over each two-week work period, and a manpower budget showing labor demand and supply must be prepared at the block level. Fourth, a register of work seekers is used to forward requests for work to the block level where the program is coordinated by the district collector who is in overall charge of the EGS. Fifth, half of the budget allocation for the EGS comes from the state's regular budget and the other half is raised by special taxation. Sixth, local administrative units enjoy wide discretionary powers; each district has its own quarterly budget for managing the scheme.

Table 7-7 shows the expenditures of the EGS and workdays of employment generated. Its employment impact has been massive, even when compared with the nationwide Crash Scheme for Rural Employment (which generated only 178 million workdays over a five-year period). The World Bank estimated in 1978 that rural unemployment and underemployment in Maharashtra amounted to roughly 620 million workdays a year. The scheme was intended to provide about 140 million workdays per year, a figure estimated to have been surpassed by 1977–78. At its planned level the EGS was thus expected to generate work for nearly a quarter of the rural unemployed and underemployed; if the projections in table 7-7 were fully realized, this proportion would have risen to nearly 35 percent.[13] The wage component of expenditures has typically been much higher than the levels previously experienced in public works programs in South Asia, attesting to the labor intensity and employment emphasis of the scheme. Wage rates actually paid have been at or above planned levels.

The EGS was supposed to supplement existing projects already incorporated in state plans, but all evidence indicates that it has in fact been an initiator of new projects. More than 5,000 individual projects

Table 7-7. *India: Expenditure and Employment in Maharashtra's Employment Guarantee Scheme*

Year	Annual expenditure (millions of rupees)	Days of employment generated (millions)	Wage component (percent)	Average daily wage[a] (rupees)
1972–73	18.8	4.5	n.a.	4.18
1973–74	18.9	5.1	n.a.	3.71
1974–75	137.2	48.1	99	2.85
1975–76	344.5	109.5	86	3.14
1976–77	485.4	133.0	77	3.64
1977–78 (est.)	560.0	160.0	75	3.50
1978–79[b]	738.6	188.0	70	3.93
1979–80[b]	867.8	220.9	70	3.93
1980–81[b]	1,100.0	260.0	65	4.23
1981–82[b]	1,292.5	305.5	65	4.23
1982–83[b]	1,518.7	359.0	65	4.23

n.a. Not available.

a. Annual wage expenditure divided by days of employment.

b. Projected.

Source: World Bank data.

have been undertaken each year, but the rate of completion was expected to fall.

Some tentative estimates of the preliminary benefits from the first three years are given in table 7-8. Few conclusions can be drawn from the data, other than that the impact on agricultural production in the state was only slight in these years.

Despite problems of project planning and selection, a majority of EGS expenditures can be classified in the "directly productive" category. Between 80 and 90 percent of all expenditures have been for irrigation of one kind or another or for soil conservation and land development projects. This emphasis is one of the distinctive features of the EGS.

The costs of financing the EGS have been growing fast (table 7-7), but half of its expenditures are funded by special taxes, nearly 70 percent of which are in turn generated by a tax on professional incomes, mainly in urban areas. The inflationary impact of EGS spending should therefore be minimal provided that deficit financing is avoided; to do so, other state expenditures will need to fall as EGS outlays increase. Although the primary inflationary potential of the scheme as currently constituted thus appears to be small, its secondary impact on food-grain prices could be high because most of its outlays are on wages and wage recipients are likely to have high marginal

Table 7-8. *Maharashtra's Employment Guarantee Scheme: Area Benefited and Estimated Cumulative Impact on Production and Employment, October 1977*

Program	Area benefited (hectares)	Additional production (tons)	Additional annual employment (thousands of workdays)
Minor irrigation	150,000	150,000	6,000
Completed	14,500	14,500	580
Incomplete	135,500	135,500	5,420
Percolated tanks	45,000	45,000	1,800
Completed	10,000	10,000	400
Incomplete	35,000	35,000	1,400
Contour bunding	560,000	28,000	n.a.
Irrigation channel bunding	2,000	2,000	80
Completed	900	900	36
Incomplete	1,100	1,100	44
All programs	n.a.	225,000	7,880
Completed	n.a.	53,000	1,016
Incomplete	n.a.	172,000	6,864

n.a. Not available.

Note: Total food-grain production in Maharashtra in 1974–75 was 7.8 million tons. The 225,000 tons expected additional production (assumed to be food grains) from completed and *incomplete* projects over nearly three years of operation amounts to 75,000 tons annually, or less than 1 percent of total annual production.

Source: World Bank data.

propensities to consume and high income elasticities for food-grain consumption.

The EGS has had its share of problems. These include:

- *Low completion rates of projects.* Although detailed data are unavailable, surveys indicated to the World Bank that in 1978, 35 percent of the works on the master list had been completed, but they accounted for less than 7 percent of the total value of works scheduled. Thus there appeared to be a predictably strong correlation between the size of the work and the speed of completion.

- *Inequitable distribution of benefits.* The scheme has focused mainly on intermediate outputs—workdays of employment and asset creation—rather than final benefits. Although it was intended mainly to help landless laborers and the lowest decile of landowners, preliminary evidence shows that only about 46 percent of the beneficiaries have come from these groups. The remaining 54 percent own larger holdings—but this may be more an indication of the poverty of landowners in rural areas of Maharashtra than a sign of the failure of the EGS to reach its target groups. Large landowners have also gained from the creation of assets on their holdings. To the extent that these investments have increased the demand for labor, however, indirect distributional benefits are still progressive.[14]

- *Planning and selection of projects.* The greatest weakness in the management of the EGS may be the limited ability of local authorities to undertake the physical surveys needed to prepare suitable new works or to develop integrated projects. So far the state has not been prepared to pay for preliminary design work. Moreover, there is little scope in many areas for EGS projects on publicly owned land. Projects on private land usually involve a 50 percent loan and a 50 percent state subsidy.

The EGS, however, offers several important lessons for the successful use of public works programs to reduce widespread rural unemployment. These are:

- Rural public works programs can be designed and administered on a large scale. In addition, they can have a significant impact on long-term employment prospects in rural areas.
- If properly financed, such programs need not be inflationary and can even serve as a means for urban-rural transfers.
- Political commitment to employment creation is needed at the highest level. The EGS represents such a commitment. Sometimes viewed as a social contract between the state and the citizen, it incorporates concepts such as the dignity of labor, the right to employment and group participation, and the state's responsibility for the timely execution of public works. It can also be seen as an opportunity for mobilizing and organizing rural labor throughout the state or as a first step toward the unionization of rural labor.
- Perhaps the most important contribution of the EGS is its adoption of the watershed as the appropriate unit for the planning and management of rural development. This approach is based on the belief that a watershed is a stronger economic community than a village. It raises the possibility of using the systems approach advocated by Minhas (in Srinivasan and Bardhan 1974) to undertake jointly three components usually thought of as separate and distinct—land consolidation, development, and rural public works for employment. Although the EGS does not include a land consolidation program, its choice of the watershed as the planning basis for rural public works and its emphasis on irriga-

tion and soil conservation projects certainly contain the other two elements.

The Indian National Rural Employment Program

The experience with Maharashtra's EGS and the earlier Food for Work Program encouraged the government of India to institute the nation-wide National Rural Employment Program (NREP) in 1980. This program, whose purposes and modes of operation are similar to those of the EGS, uses unemployed and underemployed labor in rural areas to create productive community assets. The program focuses not only on productive assets such as irrigation infrastructure, drainage systems, and soil conservation schemes, but also on support for basic social services such as wells, village schools, health subcenters, and rural housing and roads, which are being developed under the Minimum Needs Program (see below). In 1980 an estimated 1.5 million person years of employment were provided under NREP. This was less than 8 percent of the total rural unemployment of some 19 million estimated by the World Bank in that year.

These programs, however, are not meant to provide full-time year-round employment; they merely attempt to supplement the income of a broad segment of the rural population—especially during the agricultural slack seasons. As such they can significantly raise employment opportunities in rural areas and narrow the gap between labor supply and demand. The creation of productive assets is expected to generate permanent jobs, while increases in social assets will improve the quality and productivity of rural life. Although it is too early to assess the overall impact of the NREP, it represents a major commitment on the part of the government of India to address the problems of rural unemployment. No such nationwide programs exist yet in Pakistan or Bangladesh.

Conclusions

Although the extension of Maharashtra's EGS experience on a nation-wide basis through the NREP offers a glimmer of hope for new jobs in rural South Asia, rural public works programs cannot solve the problem of rural unemployment. It is a structural problem caused by unduly rapid growth in the labor force coupled with unduly slow growth in the demand for rural labor. Rural-urban migration merely displaces the problem from the countryside to the cities. Extensive and ongoing labor mobilization in rural areas may well be part of the answer. But in the long run, rural works programs, no matter how comprehensive and well executed, cannot be more than a palliative.

Substantial long-run reductions in rural unemployment will be achieved only by structural change that raises the demand for labor through vigorous agricultural growth and associated rural industrialization.

Rural works programs will therefore be inadequate; growth in farm and nonfarm incomes remains the only viable solution to poverty in the long run. In the interim there seems to be a need for special programs to assist the rural poor and to alleviate the burden of poverty.

Specialized Poverty Programs

In addition to rural work programs like the NREP, an extensive effort is now being made to develop programs specially designed to assist the rural poor. The commitment to such programs, at least on a nationwide basis, is currently confined to India.

The main nationwide poverty programs now operating in India are the Minimum Needs Programs (MNP) and the Integrated Rural Development Program (IRDP). Whereas the purpose of the NREP is to provide more employment opportunities in rural areas, the MNP is geared to improving the human capital and quality of life for the rural poor and the IRDP to helping poor rural households acquire productive assets.

Minimum Needs Program

Over the years, the government of India has sponsored a wide variety of programs to make certain minimum social services available to all. A core group of these programs—elementary education, adult education, rural health, rural water supply, rural electrification, rural roads, housing for the rural and urban poor, and nutrition—are now being implemented through the Minimum Needs Program, which started in 1980. Some of these programs (education, health, water supply, nutrition) explicitly invest in human capital, while others (such as electrification and roads) develop a minimum level of infrastructure in less advanced rural areas.

Some Rs58 billion were allocated to MNP during the sixth plan period (1980–85) (see tables 7-9 and 7-10). Although performance under such umbrella programs is always difficult to assess, data available to date suggest that overall results have been fairly good. Rural electrification, roads, and water supply improve living conditions for all rural households, whereas health, nutrition, education, and housing programs have a more than proportional benefit for the rural poor.

The rural poor, especially the poorest, suffer disproportionately from inadequate nutrition and lack of access to health care and education, and they typically have relatively large families and high child-to-adult ratios (see chapter 2). Therefore, improving their access to family planning, nutrition, health care, better water supplies, and housing will not only improve their quality of life but substantially improve their ability to work.

But in the long run providing minimum or basic needs solely as consumed services, without increasing the productive capabilities of the rural poor, would only burden already poor societies. It is precisely because improvements in health, nutrition, and education actually increase the productive capacity of the poor that such programs make economic sense. Better health and nutrition, along with educa-

Table 7-9. *India: Planned Outlays on Selected Poverty Programs*
(billions of rupees in 1979–80 prices)

Item	1980–81 to 1983–84[a] (1)	Original planned allocation, 1980–85 (2)	Percent (1) / (2) (3)
Selected poverty programs			
Minimum needs	34.6	58.1	59.6
Rural development[b]	26.0	34.9	74.0
Memo items			
Crop production	16.1	29.6	54.4
Irrigation	62.6	121.0	51.7
Total plant	596.6	975.0	61.2

a. Actuals for 1980–81 and 1981–82, except for rural development expenditures which are revised estimates; revised estimates for 1982–83 and budget estimates for 1983–84.

b. Excludes community development and cooperation; includes Integrated Rural Development Program and National Rural Employment Program.

Source: World Bank data.

Table 7-10. *India: Government Expenditure on Antipoverty Programs*
(millions of rupees)

Program	1980–85, sixth plan	1985–86, revised	1986–87 budget	1987–88, revised	1988–89 budget
Integrated Rural Development Program	15,000	2,786	4,274	2,970	3,462
National Rural Employment Program	18,000	3,372	4,427	6,820	7,300
Rural Landless Employment Guarantee Program	4,000	6,063	6,337	6,529	5,294
Total	37,000	12,221	15,037	16,310	16,050

Sources: Dandekar (1986); Rath (1988).

tion and the promotion of family planning, will also decrease population growth rates. This itself can have enormous economic benefits, particularly for the rural poor (see Quizón and Binswanger 1986).

The Integrated Rural Development Program

The IRDP was initiated in India on a nationwide basis in the early 1980s to increase the income-generating assets of the poor directly through a mixture of subsidies and credits. The IRDP was allocated nearly Rs15 billion under the sixth plan (see table 7-10). It integrates a number of earlier programs (notably the Small Farmers Development Agency and the Marginal Farmers and Landless Labor Agency) which had offered credit subsidies to the poor. The purpose of the IRDP is to provide a group of selected beneficiaries (identified as those below the poverty line) with a mixture of credits and subsidies (the ratio specified is Rs2 credit to Rs1 subsidy) in sufficient amounts to purchase assets such as draft and milk animals, small stock, and farm equipment. The intention is to generate additional income to raise the recipients above the poverty line.

The program grew very rapidly in the early 1980s, from Rs4 billion in 1980–81 to Rs10 billion in 1982–83, the number of recipients increased from 2.8 million to 3.3 million families a year, and the investment per family more than doubled in current prices. The IRDP and related programs now account for 5.13 percent of the total outlay for the agricultural sector in the seventh plan (Rath 1988).

Any program of this size and scope and with this rapid a growth in commitments and beneficiaries is bound to have implementation problems. Funds are inadequate for the scope of the job. In addition, they are allocated in a fixed amount per block without any reference to the number of poor, which leads to anomalies in allocations. The beneficiaries are supposed to be the "poorest of the poor," but identification of the targeted group is a pervasive problem. Other concerns are with the overconcentration on livestock, the question of whether the effects will be lasting, and the strain placed on the administration of other services.

The problem of identifying target groups also plagued the earlier programs. Part of the problem is administrative: first, the program has grown fast; and second, because progress is measured by the number raised above the poverty line, there may be an incentive to concentrate on those at or near that line. But a more fundamental difficulty is that, since substantial subsidies are involved, relatively better-off farmers use their influence to participate in the program. In Tamil Nadu and Maharashtra the average per capita income of the beneficiaries in each district was higher than that of the control group of nonbeneficiaries before the program started. Moreover, a significant proportion of the beneficiaries (15–60 percent) were better-off farmers (India, Planning Commission 1982, pp. 41–49). Only in cases where local villages were involved in selecting the beneficiaries was the selection concentrated toward the very poor. Community participation should therefore be made mandatory in selecting beneficiaries. Only in this way can the powerful and the rich be prevented from milking such programs for their own benefit, often in collusion with the bureaucratic apparatus set up to administer such programs.

The budgetary commitments do seem inadequate to make a dent in the problem. With an average annual investment of about Rs2,000 per beneficiary in 1979–80 prices, and even with an optimistic investment-output ratio of 2.0, the most that can be generated is a gross monthly income stream of about Rs80 per household (or Rs15 per capita, assuming an average household size of 5.6). Since the *average* monthly per capita expenditure for those *below* the poverty line was about Rs50 and the poverty line was about Rs75 in 1979–80, an increase of Rs80 would offer a major breakthrough in living standards, especially for those in the lowest decile with per capita expenditures of around Rs30. But this is before deducting loan repayments (at 10.25 percent interest these are an estimated Rs9.5 per capita), working expenses (fodder for animals, for example), and legal and illegal administrative costs and fees associated with participating in the program.

Evidence suggests that few IRDP beneficiaries have been able to raise their incomes significantly more than the control group of nonbeneficiaries. Also, given the extreme poverty of recipients and the risks attendant on being poor, there are strong incentives to sell the assets acquired by these loans to meet contingencies or consumption needs, rather than to wait for gains from the investment. At any rate, much higher sums will have to be made available if net consumption is to be raised. If those at the lowest levels get these loans and use them appropriately, the income-generating benefits could be substantial.

The largest component of IRDP assistance is for the purchase of livestock. Because of the potentially high returns associated with dairying and the use of draft animals, however, the problems are not with this concentration as such. Rather, the difficulties are that beneficiaries often lack experience, veterinary services are lacking, funds remain inadequate to purchase more productive and higher grade animals, and working funds (for fodder or grazing payments) are unavailable. Still, poor beneficiaries who acquire dairy or small stock can make a viable return when complementary marketing and other services are provided. The National Dairy Development Program is one source of assistance, but more attention needs to be given to expanding such services.

With nearly 3 million families a year joining the IRDP, government agencies in rural areas are strained, and other development services, such as extension, may suffer as a result. Some rural credit agencies are already under serious financial pressure, with high and rising amounts overdue on loans of increasing maturity (see chapter 2 and Tendulkar 1983), and there is skepticism about whether these loans will be paid back.

Conclusions

It is too early to assess whether these special programs will make a major contribution to alleviating rural poverty. Nevertheless, they tackle the problem via *direct* efforts to help the rural poor, and both their scope and their expenditures are extensive. Whatever their current shortcomings, they demonstrate the government's commitment to a substantial effort to help those with the greatest needs—the rural poor. Given the pervasive poverty in South Asia, the need for such a commitment and for the practical means to make it effective is obvious. Whether the programs will succeed in doing what they are intended to do is not yet clear. What can be said, however, is that only in India (perhaps reflecting the pressures exerted within its democratic polity) is there yet even a commitment in principle to exploring ways of direct alleviation of rural poverty.

Notes

1. See Hirschman (1958); Lele and Mellor (1972a and b); Johnston and Kilby (1975); and Mellor (1976).

2. See also Liedholm and Chuta (1976) for an example based on Sierra Leone, and ILO (1972, 1974) for studies of Kenya and the Philippines.

3. For Bangladesh see N. Islam (1978) and Stepanek (1979), and for Pakistan see D. A. Khan (1978).

4. Analysis of data on consumer goods industries by Lele and Mellor (1972a and b) suggested that capital-labor ratios were relatively low and that such high ratios as were found applied primarily to industries catering to the demands of urban consumers.

5. Fixed capital requirements range between Rs10,000 and Rs20,000 per unit of employment in most food processing industries (rice milling is low with Rs5,400), around Rs30,000 in chemicals, and Rs10,000–55,000 in bicycles, sewing machines, light engineering, tanning, and the aluminum, brass, and copper industries (data for 1954–56). Generally, value added per worker increases significantly with the size of establishment. Labor productivity is

four to six times higher in large firms than in small ones. The value added per unit of employment ranges from Rs3,000–15,000 in food processing, to Rs13,000 in bicycles and sewing machines, and to Rs20,000–35,000 in chemical-related industries.

6. Much of this section is based on an excellent article by Pandit (1978); see also D. Gupta (1980).

7. In 1971–72 the shares of Punjab alone in India's exports of various commodities were as follows: woolen hosiery, 100 percent; sports goods, 68 percent; bicycle parts, 67 percent; completed bicycles, 29 percent; domestic sewing machines, 14 percent; and pipe fittings, 12 percent. In 1969–70 Haryana accounted for 80 percent of the country's exports of hand tools and small tools and 73 percent of exports of plumbing fixtures (Pandit 1978).

8. This estimate is biased upward because data on very small, informal, less capital-intensive units are not available below the two-digit classification used.

9. See Burki (1969); Perkins and Yusuf (1984); Rawski (1979); and for the Chinese experiences, Keesing (1975).

10. See Sigurdson (1972, 1977, and 1978); Riskin (1978); and report of the American Rural Small-Scale Industries Delegation to China, *Rural Small-Scale-Industries in the People's Republic of China* (Berkeley, Calif., 1972).

11. The discussion of China's rural industry that follows is based on World Bank material and data. For a more extensive treatment, see Byrd and Lin (1990).

12. The major sources for this section are Reynolds and Sunder (1977); Dandekar and Sathe (1980); Abraham (1980); World Bank data; a newspaper article, "Miles To Go in Maharashtra," *Financial Express*, January 29, 1977; and India and Maharashtra (1980). On the Integrated Rural Development Program, Dandekar (1986); Kurian (1987); and Saxena (1987).

13. This record may be more impressive than that of other public works programs, but it compares unfavorably with the 496 million workdays generated under scarcity relief in 1973–74 in Maharashtra.

14. Minimum wage legislation may also be a factor. Some farmers have reported that workers prefer EGS work to farm labor, even when higher wages are offered. But workers may prefer EGS less for its wage benefits than for the opportunity to escape irksome and even degrading relations with farm employers.

8
Land Reform:
The Missed Opportunity

Several times in this book I have referred to the contention that rural poverty in South Asia has its roots in the structure of landholding. It is reasonable then to maintain, as many do, that the only remedy lies in the radical alteration of this structure, mainly through fundamental measures of tenancy reform and land redistribution. This view may be too simplistic, however, and is often inconsistent with observed reality. This chapter briefly summarizes the institution of tenancy, examines land reform in general, including measures to reform tenancy and to alleviate the concentration and fragmentation of operated holdings, and assesses the feasibility and desirability of land reform as a means of reducing rural poverty in the subcontinent.

How important is tenancy? Accurate data on the number of tenants, area under tenancy, and the type of tenurial relations are hard to find and vary from source to source. Unrecorded tenancy relationships are widespread, so it is safest to assume that the available figures are underestimates. The extent, type, efficiency, and changes in the patterns of tenancy in South Asia are examined in some detail by Singh (1988c). Here I summarize the main findings from that study.

The best available data are for India in the early 1970s, and they show that only a quarter of all holdings were under tenancy. The vast majority of these were *partial* tenancies (operators own part of their area and lease-in part of it), with *pure* tenancies (wholly leased-in area) an insignificant 4 percent of all holdings. There had been a slow decline in the number of mixed tenant holdings, but a rapid decline in the number of pure tenancies. The total area under tenancies (leased-in area) of all types was small (around 11 percent) and had declined significantly countrywide (Sanyal 1977b). There was considerable variation among states, but nowhere was the percentage overwhelmingly large and everywhere it had been declining. The highest rates of tenancy (25–30 percent of the leased-in area) remained in areas where the Green Revolution was the most successful—Punjab and Haryana. But tenancy had always been highest there, and even there tenancy had dramatically declined (Sanyal 1977b).

Tenancy was not exclusively associated with small holdings—those smaller than 5 acres accounted for 72 percent of all holdings but for only 37 percent of the area leased-in. It is true that in many states, mainly in eastern India, most of the area under tenancy was in small holdings, but most of the holdings were small. Of the households leasing-in land, nearly a third were landless. The practice of leasing-out land was very common among smallholders (those with fewer than 5 acres), who accounted for nearly a third of all area leased out. So the simple association between "small" and "tenant" and "large" and "landlord" cannot be made—many smallholders are landlords, and others are both landlords and tenants at the same time (tables 8-1, 8-2, and 8-3). The dichotomy between landlords on the one hand and tenants on the other is therefore invalid.

Sharecropping (mainly though not exclusively 50:50 shares) is the most predominant form of tenancy in most states. Fixed-kind tenancies predominate in some southern states where plantation crops are important, and fixed-cash tenancies are becoming prevalent in areas most affected by the Green Revolution, such as Punjab and Haryana. The high incidence of small holdings, of tenancy among small holdings, and of sharecropping poses a triple threat to areas in some eastern Indian states where tenancy was formerly characterized by rent collectors known as *zamindars*. There the relationship between small share tenancies and technological change and the distribution of its benefits is of special concern.

The data on tenancy in Bangladesh (table 8-4) are of somewhat dubious quality, but they suggest that in the 1970s over a third of the holdings and a quarter of the cultivated area were under mainly mixed tenancies; pure tenancy accounted for only about 8 percent of both holdings and area. Tenancy seemed to be increasing in terms of both holdings and area (Jabbar 1977). Most mixed tenancies are not small but were dominated by medium and large holdings of between 2.5 and 12.5 acres. Sharecropping (almost exclusively 50:50 shares) was the absolutely dominant form of tenancy, and there was little evidence of a transition to fixed-cash or other forms of tenancies (Sanyal 1977b). Most sharecropping arrangements are of short duration—a third are for a year or less—which indicates the extreme lack of security of these tenures.

In Pakistan the available data show that in 1972 tenancy was a predominant fact of agrarian conditions with owner-tenant and pure-tenant farms accounting for two-thirds of all holdings and area (table 8-5). Pure tenancy was significant and accounted for two-thirds of

Table 8-1. India: Tenancy in Small Farms by Size of Operated Holdings, 1971–72
(percent)

Size (acres)	Maharashtra		Gujarat		Kerala		Punjab		All India	
	Number	Area	Number	Area	Number	Area	Number	Area	Number	Area
0–1.0	11.4	0.2	9.3	1.0	63.0	22.4	0.6	...	19.7	3.3
1.0–2.5	13.0	0.7	17.8	3.3	19.5	20.7	2.9	0.7	28.4	13.2
2.5–5.0	24.6	10.7	14.2	6.9	10.6	26.0	19.3	9.0	24.2	20.4
5.0+	51.0	88.4	58.7	88.8	6.9	30.9	77.8	90.3	27.7	63.1
All sizes	100.0	100.0	100.0	100.0	100.0	100.0	100.0	100.0	100.0	100.0
Number (hundreds)	558	—	218	—	389	—	355	—	14,655	—
Area (thousands of acres)	—	2,729	—	827	—	242	—	1,880	—	32,814
All operated area (millions of acres)		44.4		8.6		2.8		6.7		310.4
All operated holdings (millions)	4.7	—	2.3	—	2.3	—	0.7	—	57.1	—

— Not applicable.
... Negligible.
Note: The table shows the percentage distribution of the number of holdings leasing-in and the area leased-in by the size group of operated holdings.
Source: National Sample Survey (NSS), Report 215, 26th Round (1971–72), "Tables on Landholdings," State Reports, table 19.

Table 8-2. India: Operating Households by Tenancy Status

Operational holdings	1953–54	1961–62	1971–72
Number (millions)	55.5	50.8	57.1
Percent			
Entirely owned	60.2	72.6	74.4
Partly owned, partly tenanted	22.9	21.8	21.7
Entirely tenanted[a]	16.9	5.5	3.9

a. These are not necessarily operated by landless households.

Sources: NSS, Reports 30, 36, 74, 8th Round (1953–54); Report 144, 17th Round (1961–62); Report 215, 26th Round (1971–72).

Table 8-3. India: Changes in Leased-in Area as a Percentage of Total Area Cultivated

State	1953–54	1960–61	1970–71
Andhra Pradesh	19.07[a]	9.15	9.01
Assam	43.54	15.36	19.69
Bihar	12.39	10.25	14.50
Gujarat	n.a.	5.83	3.91
Haryana	—	—	23.26
Punjab	76.89[b]	35.39[c]	28.01
Jammu and Kashmir	22.17	14.13	8.06
Karnataka	16.37	18.16	15.90
Kerala	23.63	15.30	8.59
Madhya Pradesh	18.61	6.40	7.46
Maharashtra	n.a.	8.74	6.15
Orissa	12.58	10.75	13.46
Rajasthan	12.92	4.87	5.26
Tamil Nadu	27.53	16.55	13.07
Uttar Pradesh	11.38	8.06	13.01
West Bengal	25.43	17.65	18.73

— Not applicable.

n.a. Not available.

a. Figure is for Andhra region. The figure for Hyderabad State, which is included in present-day Andhra Pradesh, was 18.04.

b. Punjab includes present-day Haryana plus Delhi and Himachal Pradesh.

c. Punjab includes present-day Haryana and parts of Himachal Pradesh.

Source: Bardhan (1976).

all tenancies and 30 percent of the total operated area. There were notable regional differences with mainly mixed tenancies concentrated in medium-size (5–25 acre) holdings in the Punjab and smaller pure tenant holdings that were sharecropped in Sind (M. H. Khan 1981). The "pure-tenants at will" (the *haris*) were at a special disad-

Table 8-4. *Bangladesh: Changes in Tenant Holdings and Area, 1960–78*

	Cultivating households		Operational holdings		
Item	1960	1967–68	1973–74	1977	1978
Operational holdings or cultivating households					
Number (millions)	6.1	6.9	7.0	8.2	9.3
Percent					
Owner-operators	61.0	66.0	67.0	61.2	64.5
Owner-tenants	37.0	30.0	27.0	32.0	28.1
Pure tenants	2.0	4.0	6.0	6.8	7.4
Area cultivated					
Millions of acres	21.7	21.6	n.a.	18.8	24.3
Percent					
Owner-operated	54.0	57.8	n.a.	54.0	58.5
Owned and leased in	45.0	38.9	n.a.	41.7	37.7
Purely leased in	1.0	3.4	n.a.	4.3	3.8
Under all forms of leasing in	18.0	17.0	25.0	22.9	23.7

n.a. Not available.

Sources: Bangladesh Agriculture Census, 1960; Bangladesh Bureau of Statistics (1972, 1977); Bangladesh, Ministry of Agriculture and Forests (1978); and Jannuzi and Peach (1980).

vantage in relation to their landlords who were large owners, and the dichotomy between landlords on the one hand and tenants on the other was certainly valid.

There were significant differences between East and West Punjab. Tenancy in the East Punjab was less important in holdings and area, pure tenancy was insignificant, sharecropping was giving way to fixed-cash tenancies, and most tenancies were concentrated in the 5–10 acre range. In the West Punjab, the proportion of total area under tenancy was almost twice as large, pure tenancy was significant, sharecropping was the dominant form, and the average size of the tenant holdings was more than two times larger. Whether medium and large mixed tenancies are a barrier to technological innovation is the pertinent question to ask in the case of the Punjabs (Singh 1988c).

Tenancy as an Institutional Constraint

Much of the traditional debate on agrarian conditions has been colored by an altogether negative view of tenancy as an institution. In particular, it is argued that tenancy, share tenancy especially, is an economically inefficient way to organize production; impedes the adoption of new, particularly yield-increasing, technologies; allows

Table 8-5. Pakistan: Regional Changes in Tenancy, 1960–72

Item	1960		1972		Percentage change between 1960 and 1972	
	Number of farms	Total area in operational holdings	Number of farms	Total area in operational holdings	Number of farms	Total area in operational holdings
Pakistan						
All farms (millions)	4.9	48.9	3.8	49.1	−23	...
Percent						
Owner operated	41	38	42	40	−21	4
Owner-tenant operated	17	23	24	31	8	38
Tenant operated	42	39	34	30	−36	−24
Punjab						
All farms (millions)	3.3	29.2	2.4	31.0	−29	6
Percent						
Owner operated	43	38	42	39	−29	7
Owner-tenant operated	19	25	29	36	10	54
Tenant operated	39	37	29	26	−47	−26
Sind						
All farms (millions)	0.7	9.7	0.7	9.5	10	−2
Percent						
Owner operated	20	29	24	31	30	3
Owner-tenant operated	9	15	13	19	62	25
Tenant operated	71	56	63	51	−2	−12

... Negligible.
Source: M. H. Khan (1981), pp. 108–11.

landlords a disproportionate share of the income from cultivation and the incremental gains from new technologies and leaves few gains to the tenants; and serves few, if any, functions in the agrarian economy, except the exploitation of tenants by landlords (Ladejinsky 1977).

As a consequence, tenancy is seen as a major barrier to the redress of poverty. The remedy sought is to abolish tenancy and "give the land to the tiller" or, where this is not feasible, to restrict tenancy by a variety of tenurial reforms. Legislation has been proposed to limit the rental shares going to landlords, give security of tenure to tenants, and force landlords to bear a larger share of cultivation costs.

The Role of Tenancy

Those who want to abolish tenancy fail to understand that it is a robust and dynamic institution with many important functions in the existing agrarian structure. It has long been known (since Adam Smith) and widely recognized (by Marx and Marshall among others) that share tenancy is a mechanism for adjustments between land and other resources, an incentive system that brings forth more effort at less cost for supervision than does farming with wage labor, and a credit system that allows those without assets to acquire capital and credit (Braverman and Srinivasan 1980).

More recent literature has added the views that share tenancy serves to spread production risks among differently risk-averse agents (Cheung 1968; Reid 1974; Stiglitz 1974), to overcome the indivisibility of inputs where lease markets are imperfect, to reduce transaction costs where information is incomplete and supervision costly (Jaynes 1979a and b), to allow agents to share their managerial and entrepreneurial skills, and to allow labor contracts where labor markets are risky and imperfect and nonstandard labor is involved. Share contracts are seen as only a second-best solution—an imperfect response to incomplete and imperfect markets for land, credit, labor, management, information, and insurance. Indeed, much of the recent rigorous work suggests that with high transaction costs, incomplete markets, and uncertainty, first-best Pareto-efficient solutions are just not possible.

But it is because these markets *are* imperfect and incomplete that share tenancy serves important functions. If it is abolished, these functions will have to be served by other institutions—markets or government agencies. As markets develop, the reasons for sharecropping become more tenuous, and other forms of tenancy with a fixed rent become more common. There is considerable evidence of this transition in the agriculturally more advanced regions of South Asia.

Efficiency

Many economists have agreed with Marshall (1961) that share tenancy is inefficient; others, along with Cheung (1969) and Newbery and Stiglitz (in Roumasset, Boussard, and Singh 1979) to mention only a few, have argued that it can be efficient. Since the theoretical arguments are logically correct, the conflicting results must follow from different assumptions about the nature of share contracts. The central differences revolve around the degree of control that landlords can exercise. Thus if landlords can control and supervise the combination of inputs to some extent, share in the costs of cultivation, and evict tenants at will by using only short-term leases, it is recognized that share tenancy would be as efficient as fixed-rent or owner-cultivated systems (Vyas 1970; C. H. H. Rao 1971; Bliss and Stern 1980). The question of efficiency rests on how share tenancy operates in practice, not on any theoretical grounds. Since the issue can be resolved only empirically, what is the evidence from South Asia?

Testing for differences in efficiency is not a straightforward matter. At a minimum, there is a need to control for farm size when comparing, say, owner-operated with tenant farms (Chakravarty and Rudra 1973). But other confounding influences such as quality of land, access to irrigation and credit, different attitudes toward risk, and different skill and factor endowments make it difficult to interpret the results. There are very few empirical studies that are completely satisfactory.

To compare sharecropped with owner-operated farms, I first examine input intensities and output per hectare after controlling for farm size and then look at cost-sharing, duration of leases, and ability on the part of landlords to control inputs.

In India evidence from many geographically diverse regions suggests that there are no marked differences in input-output patterns of owner- and tenant-operated farms *of the same size* and hence no significant tenancy-related inefficiencies. There are perhaps two exceptions: on very small tenant farms (fewer than 5 acres) input intensities are lower in Bihar, and Bell (1977) shows input intensities and outputs to be lower on leased-in land than on owned land operated by the *same farmer* (this is one way to control for other sources of variation). But Bardhan and Rudra (1980a and c, 1981) find no differences in West Bengal.

There is only one study from Pakistan (West Punjab), and it found no significant differences between tenant and nontenant farms. A few studies done in Bangladesh also found no differences, when size is controlled for, between tenant- and owner-operated farms. Where owned and sharecropped land under the *same* cultivators was observed, mixed tenants were found to cultivate leased-in land less intensely (Hossain 1977b).

Even given the difficulty of controlling for confounding effects and the great diversity of agrarian conditions, the weight of the evidence suggests no significant inefficiencies associated with sharecropping systems, at least where tenanted farms are of medium or large size.

Some inefficiencies have been noted on very small share tenancies (including owned and leased land cultivated by the same operator). This finding is of some significance because in many states in India—Bihar, Kerala, Orissa, Tamil Nadu, Uttar Pradesh, and West Bengal—and in Bangladesh such tenancies account for more than 50 percent of the tenanted area. But in these cases, sharecropping per se may not be the source of all the inefficiencies. They may be caused by lack of resources or poorly developed or imperfect factor and product markets that place small farmers at a disadvantage. The true source of the inefficiency is hard to identify, and removing tenancy or changing its terms may not be the best way to deal with the problem.

Evidence on cost-sharing reveals that in India it is a new but not unusual part of a tenancy contract, and its importance is increasing, especially where HYVs and irrigation have increased productivity. In some areas affected significantly by the Green Revolution, where costs are equally shared, efficiency is restored. But in most areas, only partial cost-sharing systems are prevalent. Cost-sharing is more common in the *ryotwari* areas—western, southern, and northwestern states in which landholders pay land taxes or rents directly to the state—than in the former *zamindari* areas in eastern India where intermediaries (*zamindars*) collected taxes for the state (Bell 1977; Newbery 1974; Jodha 1979).

In Pakistan there is some evidence that costs are equally shared in the Punjab (Naseem 1971). Elsewhere costs are not shared or are shared unequally. In Bangladesh cost-sharing does not yet seem to be widely reported (Zaman 1973; Jannuzi and Peach 1980).

Lease contracts are for a short time—predominantly one year but sometimes from two to four years—and getting shorter. Some are now given on a seasonal basis. The shorter leases are correlated with greater intensity of cropping and changing technology, but they may also be the result of uncertainty created by legislation. Although designed to give tenants "secure rights in land," this legislation may paradoxically have increased the insecurity of tenants. There is also evidence that landlords are deeply involved in their tenants' decisions and in Bangladesh closely supervise the work. Both short-duration leases and close supervision and participation are means by which landlords attempt to control inputs and hence reduce inefficiencies.

The weight of the overall evidence suggests that share tenancies are likely to show some inefficiency where the tenancies are small (fewer than 2 hectares), cost-sharing is minimal, technical change and productivity increases are slow, tenants are not under threat of eviction or have long leases, markets of all kinds are imperfectly developed, and semifeudal patron-client systems are prevalent. Such areas are found predominantly in eastern India, Bangladesh, and to some extent Northwest Frontier Province in Pakistan. Elsewhere there are not likely to be any significant inefficiencies associated with share tenancy as such.

Barrier to Innovation

What of the argument that tenancy impedes the spread of innovations—in particular, that small tenants will not adopt HYVs or use fertilizers because they cannot or because usurious, "semifeudal" landlords are more interested in making consumption loans than productive investments (Bhaduri 1973)?

The "semifeudal" paradigm used as a basis for these arguments is, however, counterfactual. Evidence from West Bengal, the very region from which the paradigm is often drawn, shows that although landlords do give consumption loans to their tenants, most of them are interest free. Furthermore, landlords do give production loans for new inputs, are interested in productive investments, do not have moneylending as a principal occupation, and do not bond labor at lower than market rates via consumption loans. Even small tenants themselves hire labor. Thus empirically many of the features of "semifeudalism" do not hold (Bardhan and Rudra 1980a and c, 1981).

On the adoption of new technologies, extensive evidence shows no systematic relationship between tenancy status and either adoption of HYVs or nutrient use per hectare in most of the subcontinent. Where some evidence of such a relationship existed it was confined to eastern Indian states and Bangladesh. But much of it could probably be explained by sharecroppers' far more limited access to credit and other inputs in these areas. Certainly where tenancies are mainly mixed or for larger plots, and where credit and new inputs have been readily available, tenants have done just as well as owner-cultivators. Thus it is safe to conclude that tenancy as such is unlikely to hinder the adoption and widespread diffusion of technologies, especially where tenants have adequate and timely access to modern inputs.

Tenancy probably inhibits longer-term investment by tenants because of the insecurity of small sharecropped holdings and lack of credit. But there is little direct evidence available. Where mixed tenancies exist and tenant holdings are larger—as in the Punjabs—

tenants have been investing in tubewells and farm machinery, contrary to conventional expectations of observers.

The distribution of gains from share tenancy go disproportionately to landlords where the rental share is 50 percent of the harvest. Full cost-sharing (where landlords contribute 50 percent of the cost of inputs) is the exception rather than the rule, and tenants often bear all the costs, not only for inputs but also for transactions in credit, labor, or product markets. The gains particularly from new technologies have been generally lower on tenant- than on owner-operated holdings.

Direct evidence reveals, however, that new technologies *have* benefited all classes of farmers, including tenants. Landlords seem to take a larger share of the gains, especially from smaller tenants and in areas where small share tenancies are predominant, but the absolute size of the gains is related more to the size of the holding than to tenancy status.

The impact of new technologies on tenurial systems has been varied. In general, where HYVs, irrigation, multiple cropping, and other technologies are prominent the area under tenancy may even increase, but fixed-tenancy systems begin to replace sharecropping and pure tenancies. Poor landless sharecroppers may then have to rely on wage employment. Mixed fixed tenants with larger holdings become predominant. Reverse tenancies—with smallholders leasing out their land to larger owners—increase (Bell 1977). In the long run technological progress displaces the poorer sharecroppers, reduces sharecropping in favor of fixed-rental systems and partial cost-sharing systems, and may or may not reduce the area under tenancy. Although technological progress should not be slowed, policymakers must find ways of ameliorating its impact on the poorer segments of the sharecropping population who will be rendered landless.

In the end, sharecropping will be replaced, and it can be viewed as a transitional (though long-lasting) phase in the development of land-lease markets. It will continue to be prevalent as long as farms are small and farmers are poor, markets are underdeveloped, and infrastructure is weak in rural areas. It is poverty that leads to sharecropping, and not sharecropping that causes poverty.

Conclusions

There is no clear or direct relationship between the unequal distribution of holdings and the incidence of poverty. Nor does the incidence of tenancy or the proportion of landless rural labor households in a region have a direct bearing on the extent to which the poor have benefited from various programs. The evidence in hand does not support the view that existing agrarian systems, or modes of production, have prevented small farmers and tenants from expanding output and taking advantage of new opportunities. Nor is it possible to ascribe backwardness and poverty to a semifeudal agrarian relationship in which exploitative landlords and moneylenders oppose technological change; as has been noted in earlier chapters, the balance of available evidence supports just the opposite tendencies. Tenancy does not in fact seem to be a major barrier to efficiency, innovation, and productivity gains since few differences can be found between tenant- and owner-operated farms once size is accounted for.

It does indeed appear that the gains from innovation have been unevenly distributed between those with access to land, water, and inputs and those without and that the "have-nots" in this context frequently (but by no means always) tend to be small tenant farmers. But this has been because of the imperfect nature of the markets in these goods and because institutions serving agriculture have been biased against small landowners, tenants, and the landless alike, rather than solely because of the nature of landholding arrangements as such. Where there has been technological progress, smallholders, including tenants, have gained directly while the landless have benefited less and indirectly, irrespective of the agrarian structure. The evidence does not support the view that such growth as has taken place has further impoverished the rural poor or ineluctably "proletarianized" them even where agricultural growth rates have been relatively high.

Rather, the evidence seems to suggest that the main causes of agrarian backwardness and poverty lie in generally low or nonexistent rates of growth in agriculture and in the low productivities inherent in the traditional ways of deriving income from both land and labor. Relentless demographic pressures and the consequent exhaustion of land resources have reduced opportunities in the countryside, especially where agricultural output has failed to grow significantly. In areas of stagnation the result has been increasing poverty, a rural economy in which holdings have become smaller (though not more unevenly distributed), and a rise in the proportion of the rural population that has had to depend on wage labor for its livelihood. Thus the need is to accelerate growth—in both the farm and nonfarm sectors—and to increase the productivity of both land and labor inputs. Where this has been done and the growth of agricultural output has outpaced that of population, poverty has been reduced, though slowly.

Nevertheless, the central tenet of the "structuralist" viewpoint is that the only long-run remedy to the problems of rural poverty is to change the present agrarian structure by radical land reforms. This proposition deserves serious consideration, if only because when stated in these simple terms it is correct and remains an influential idea. The case for reforms can be appreciated when one considers the sheer magnitude of the problem and the numerous remedies already proposed: agricultural growth via new technologies in irrigated and semiarid areas; reforms of credit, irrigation, marketing, research, and other institutions serving agriculture to make this growth more accessible to small farmers (owners and tenants); growth in ancillary activities for the rural poor; supplementary growth in employment opportunities for rural labor both on farms and in rural industries, marketing, transportation, construction, and other rural services as well as in special programs for rural public works; and poverty programs to provide the poor with assets or human capital. Yet all these measures may not be enough to alleviate the problems of absolute rural poverty in South Asia, at least in the short run.

Stagnation only compounds the problem. But continued and sustained growth in agriculture, accompanied by rapid growth in industrial output and employment—conditions still not met in most of South Asia—could over a longer period solve at least the problems of absolute poverty. Problems of relative poverty will always remain. Extensive evidence provided here makes the case that rapid growth can in the long run solve the problem of poverty, but not that of unequal development.

If, like the structuralists, one is unwilling to wait for the uncertain prospects of the longer run, then one accepts the argument that only a radical transformation of the rural patterns of landholding will suffice. The nonstructuralists, however, argue that although radical reforms may seem desirable in the abstract, the experience to date with reforms has not been salutary. The structuralists counter by saying that the reforms undertaken so far actually amount to "nonreforms," and what is needed is not only a strict implementation of current reforms but even more radical measures. The nonstructuralist response is that, given the present balance of political forces in South Asia (or any reasonably credible alternative), the prospects for more radical reforms are extremely poor—even those already on the statute books have not been implemented. Furthermore, in the absence of radical reforms, there are many other good measures that can help and that need to be undertaken—measures such as those that have been outlined in other chapters. There the argument rests.

All those who have worked on problems of rural poverty in South Asia—structuralists and nonstructuralists alike—agree that growth is better than stagnation, that growth has not been rapid enough in either agriculture or industry, and that the benefits of growth will continue to be unevenly distributed as long as the patterns of landholding remain unequal. The case for redistributive land reforms is further strengthened by the evidence provided here that smaller holdings could enhance employment and farming intensities and encourage wider use of new technologies. A more equitable distribution of holdings would also create more equitable demand patterns, which in turn should enhance nonfarm growth and remove some of the institutional biases in credit, marketing, and research that arise from the unequal distribution of assets and associated power. Many argue that the best solution to rural poverty would be a radical redistribution of assets accompanied by rapid growth in agriculture and industry.

Why then has this "best solution" been neglected? It is beyond the scope of this work to provide a complete answer, but one simple response might be that any fundamental change in the structure of agrarian relations in a predominantly agricultural economy is by its very nature revolutionary and can be undertaken only under a revolutionary and coercive policy, not an evolutionary and democratic one. For a variety of historical, cultural, and political reasons the political regimes in South Asia were and remain nonreformist and noncoercive in nature. And their present polity is not likely to change dramatically; on the contrary, the evidence suggests that evolutionary, nonreformist tendencies may have been strengthened. Radical reforms which seemed at least feasible at independence seem to have become a remote possibility. In this sense such reforms represent a missed opportunity.

This is not the place to argue about the socioeconomic aspects of wholesale and fully egalitarian land redistribution in South Asia. Suffice it to say that such an initiative could not be carried out under existing social, political, or constitutional arrangements, that it would probably be only an interim stage on the road to collectivization, and that, as a revolutionary act, it could only be carried out as part of a broad, radical transformation of political, social, and economic relations. South Asia seems far from developing the preconditions for genuinely revolutionary change—and experience in other countries suggests that its consummation does not always lead to better conditions.

In the following section I examine the relevant facts and try to show that land reforms, though well intended, have not amounted to much. In particular, quite apart from the political and administrative problems associated with legislation and implementation, the reforms to date have not necessarily been helpful to the poor. Even successful and radical changes in landholding arrangements are not, under present conditions, a sufficient condition for rural prosperity, and there are no quick fixes for what is essentially a long-term problem. Because these reforms have been delayed, the task of alleviating poverty has become far more difficult as populations have continued to increase and available alternatives have continued to shrink. What was possible three decades ago seems less possible and even less desirable today.

A great deal has been written on the subject of land reform, especially in South Asia.[1] At least three broad sets of measures are meant when land reform is discussed: tenancy reforms, the establishment of ceilings on holdings and the redistribution of land, and the consolidation of fragmented holdings. To the extent that data permit, I will discuss the desirability and feasibility of each of these approaches and assess the experience with them in South Asia.

Tenancy Reform

The term "tenancy reform" covers a bewildering variety of proposals that reflect very different perceptions of the so-called tenancy problem. At one end of the spectrum are modest proposals to record the terms of leases for each crop season so as to give tenants access to crop loans. (Because land is used as collateral, recording of leases is supposed to encourage loans against crop shares.) At the other extreme are measures to grant tenants security of tenure in perpetuity and the right to pass on leases to their heirs, with no right of resumption for self-cultivation by owners. Between these extremes there are proposals for fixing rental payments, forcing landlords to share cultivating costs, or limiting landlords' rights to resumption for self-cultivation. Bangladesh, India, and Pakistan have extensive tenancy reform legislation.[2] A review of the vast experience in this area suggests that efforts have all too often been ill-conceived, poorly implemented, and ineffective or counterproductive. In fact, tenancy reforms seem generally to have done more harm than good to those they were meant to help.

Tenancy as a Constraint: Some Myths and Realities

The previous discussion of the nature of tenancy in South Asia presents at least five findings, all of which run counter to the generally accepted wisdom that has influenced existing or proposed legislation.

First, tenancy is not as important as it is sometimes made out to be. It does not account for an extensive area or for a large percentage of cultivated holdings—even if official figures are underestimates—except in Pakistan, where pure tenancy is mainly confined to relatively large holdings. Moreover, tenancy is declining in overall importance, although it remains significant in some regions of India and mixed tenancies have increased somewhat in Bangladesh in recent years. This suggests that the amount of legislation and effort devoted to combating it may be excessive and that it is unlikely to be an over-whelming constraint on aggregate agricultural growth. The problems of small tenants remain critical in some states, but few of the measures designed to help them are likely to be effective, as I will show.

Second, tenancy performs some very important functions in rural markets and may often represent an appropriate second-best response to a host of problems confronting the parties to contracts in land. This response is made necessary in part because land and factor endowments are unequally distributed and in part because complete and perfect markets are nonexistent. The solution, however, is not to restrict tenancy contracts or to abolish tenancy. If this is done, the functions it now performs will have to be undertaken by other institutions, such as inefficient markets or government agencies. There is no guarantee that these alternatives will represent an improvement on the present system.

Third, tenancy in itself is neither necessarily inefficient nor a barrier to technological innovations. In particular, tenants have adopted new HYV technologies where they have been available, profitable, and agronomically suitable. Further improvements in productivity through better farming practices, multiple cropping, and new inputs are and will continue to be possible on tenant holdings. Tenants have by and large performed as well as owner-cultivators and reaped similar benefits. They have had to share these benefits with landlords—unevenly in some areas but less so in regions where relatively equal cost-sharing or fixed-rental systems have evolved. That landlords have had the lion's share of the gains from technological change is attributable not to tenancy per se, but rather to the imperfections of local markets and the fact that land is scarce, unevenly distributed, and becoming more productive.

Fourth, in South Asia there is often no neat dichotomy between landlords and tenants. The poor may often rent out their land (becoming landlords) while the better-off may often augment their existing holdings by renting in land (becoming tenants). Thus legislation simplistically designed to help tenants against landlords may militate against many of the poor and benefit others who are far better-off. It is at best a blunt instrument that may end up doing the poor more harm than good.

Fifth, a tenancy contract is more often than not a part of a series of linked, interdependent, and simultaneous contracts in a number of product and factor markets for land, labor, credit, and other inputs. These linkages are organic and not some "deviation" from "normal" agrarian relations. Nor are they necessarily exploitative; many have been shown decidedly to benefit tenants. In the case of those that are exploitative, attempts to redress the linkages in one market may be thwarted because the monopolistic or monopsonistic power involved can often be maintained by shifting the terms of the interlinked contracts to other markets.[3] Yet tenancy legislation is all too often designed as if existing conditions in other markets are immutable.

In view of these considerations, what can be said about the desirability of the various kinds of tenancy reform that have been implemented or proposed? I review the three most widely discussed measures below.

Abolition of Intermediary Interests

In the often confused debate on agrarian reform in South Asia it is sometimes forgotten that one of the most critical phases of tenancy reform has in fact been carried out. The *zamindari* system of rent-collecting intermediaries, which dated back to the Permanent Settlement of Bengal in 1793, was abolished in India between 1951 and 1956, despite administrative problems and widespread opposition (Ladejinsky 1977). In Bangladesh, too, intermediate rent-receiving interests were eliminated by 1956.[4] As a result of these generally successful and forgotten reforms, millions of tenants were made secure on their land and freed from a host of illegal exactions; many of them acquired ownership of their land at moderate cost. The greatest shortcoming of the abolition measures was that they left unchanged the inequalities of land holdings and the position of sharecroppers and laborers. Their overall achievements were significant, however: the system of illegal exactions was abolished; permanent, heritable, and transferable rights were conferred on occupants; and the top layer of absentee landlords (those with the largest holdings) was skimmed off.

But these reforms had their costs. Many *zamindars* acquired ownership rights over land from which they had previously only collected revenue, many tenants were evicted, and the large amounts of compensation paid to some *zamindars* turned them into rich agro-industrialists.[5]

The *zamindari* system has remained essentially intact in Pakistan despite moves to abolish it, largely because of the ability of the landed elite to sabotage reform. Landlords have traditionally held the balance of power in rural areas, and by and large their position has not been changed.[6] Tenancy remains a significant factor in Pakistan, and much of the current maldistribution of land holdings there may owe much to this initial failure.

There is nothing in the existing features of tenancy to prevent the abolition of intermediary interests. Both this type of reform and the direct granting of occupancy rights to subtenants are highly desirable. But such reforms need to be carried out at a single stroke and with no delay; where they have not been undertaken, as in Pakistan, the chance has probably been missed.

Security of Tenure

Many measures have been proposed for enhancing security of tenure. They include prohibitions on the eviction of tenants, granting of permanent and transferable occupancy rights to tenants, prohibitions on the resumption of land by landlords for self-cultivation, and restrictions on the subletting of land. Most existing legislation in South Asia has, however, been subject to the landlord's right of resumption, and this has been its Achilles' heel.

The usual argument advanced in favor of these measures is that without security of tenure tenants will have no incentive to make permanent improvements in the land, especially if there is no way to compensate them if they are later evicted. The obvious question to ask is, what would prevent landlords from making these improvements? They could presumably recover their costs and earn sufficient rates of return on their investments by charging higher rents. One answer lies in the supposed paradigm of the antigrowth landlord. But the paradigm is internally inconsistent and does not fit the observed facts. It is difficult to think of a situation in which those who own the land, have overwhelming economic power over their tenants, and retain the lion's share of the benefits of cultivation would not have an interest in making that land as productive as possible. Yet this is what is being argued by those who maintain that landlords will neither encourage their tenants to increase productivity nor undertake productive investments themselves. As I showed in the previous section, however, landlords do in fact encourage yield-increasing technologies, provide production loans, and take a great deal of interest in productive investments. Investment has been considerable, especially in areas in which new technologies have promised dramatic gains in productivity.

Measures to provide greater security to tenants would be desirable if good intentions could be turned into reality. In fact, however, most measures of this kind have had the reverse effect of making tenants *less* secure. Legislative loopholes that allow resumption of land for self-cultivation have been mercilessly exploited by landlords, while the impossibility of policing every contract has flawed the legislation from its conception. The good intentions of lawmakers have been frustrated by their failure to generate political commitment throughout the system, to ensure that law enforcers have access to local sources of information about contracts, or to act quickly enough to prevent the counteractions of landlords.

Speedy and wholehearted enforcement are crucial for the success of legislation to grant security of tenure. Any hesitation between announcement of a measure and its implementation gives landlords time to develop a counterstrategy—as they have in fact done in India when the time lag has been significant. Evictions in response to half-hearted legislation started in many areas long before mechanization began to affect the eviction rate. At least evictions done to take advantage of mechanization have put land into the hands of cultivators with more economic assets, but evictions and shorter leases in response to poorly implemented tenancy legislation have created insecurity without necessarily improving productivity. Tenancy has been driven underground (hence my skepticism about official statistics), and the duration of leases has been reduced to as little as a single crop season.[7] These effects of tenancy reform are, of course, the opposite of those intended by the sponsors of the relevant legislation.

There is evidence, however, that with political will and commitment, together with access to grass-roots rural power, state governments can in fact enforce measures to increase tenants' security of tenure. In Kerala land legislation was effectively implemented because it was backed by a mass movement of potential beneficiaries, which was organized when the Communist party came to power (see Oomen 1971b, 1975). For two decades Kerala was unique, but in 1979 Operation Barga was initiated by West Bengal's Left Front government with the Land Reform Amendment Act.[8] This act tried to plug at least four loopholes in the previous legislation by preventing *benami* (illegal or fictitious) transfers of holdings, defining personal exemptions from land ceilings in terms of family rather than personal ownership, shifting the onus of proof in disputes about tenancy rights from the tenant to the landlord, and attempting to record all bona fide *bargardars* (sharecroppers) so as to give them previously legislated occupancy rights.[9]

This last feature is critical, because a program to grant rights to tenants can work only if there are records of who the tenants are. Since contracts have traditionally been oral, landlords have avoided giving security of tenure by disavowing or changing tenants, placing land in *benami* holdings, or resuming tenanted lands for self-cultivation. The West Bengal government's response has been described as follows:

One of the important achievements of the Left Front government has been to record the rights of bargardars through group action. Group meetings are held with bargardars and they are encouraged to speak out their de facto status. This is followed by public verification of bargardar claims in the presence of both landowners and the claimant sharecroppers. Landowners are given opportunity to express their objections which are also heard and verified in the field in public. Thereafter certificates of bargardari rights are distributed among sharecroppers whose claims have been vindicated by the public. This group action is far more helpful to the bargardars than the traditional approach where bargardars would themselves have to seek the protection of the law. (Dutt 1981, p. A5a).

Three ingredients seem essential for success: group action, the public nature of the proceedings, and state power exercised on behalf of the tenants.[10] Even with these ingredients, speed remains crucial; as these measures were being contemplated, a large number of bargardars were evicted and land was "reformed" for so-called self-cultivation under "personal exemption" by landlords in West Bengal.

It is too early to tell how Operation Barga will turn out. In its initial stages it was very successful; three-quarters of a million bargardars were identified and recorded in the first year alone. Two years later, however, only 1 million out of an estimated 2 million bargardar claims had been recorded; the remaining 50 percent were still unregistered (Khasnabis 1981, p. A45).

Nevertheless, Operation Barga is an important achievement in view of earlier failures. It calls into question the idea that nothing can be done about tenancy reform in South Asia or that any new efforts are now too late. Above all, it shows that if measures to bring real security to tenants are to succeed, they must be backed by the power of the state at the local level.[11] Without such backing, no amount of well-intentioned legislation will succeed in making tenants secure, for as soon as the government's intentions are known, tenants will be evicted unless the state has the local political power to enforce the measures. Thus, providing security to tenants depends on grass-roots enforcement and speedy action before landlords respond with evictions. A better approach would be to give tenants their land outright.

Regulation of Rents and Cost-Sharing

In the absence of the outright transfer of ownership rights in leased land to tenants—which has never been successfully undertaken in South Asia—the accepted route of reform has been to regulate the relations between landlords and tenants by fixing either landlords' rental share or their share of input costs. I have noted that 50:50 rental shares are common in traditional sharecropping arrangements.

Input cost shares have varied widely, but landlords generally seem to appropriate between 45 and 55 percent of any value added (Bell 1977).

Extensive legislation was enacted in India in the 1950s, and in later years in Pakistan and Bangladesh, to fix the maximum rental share for landlords and to specify their input share. Legislated rents varied from one-fifth of the gross product of tenanted land in some states to one-half in others. (Tables A42 and A43 summarize legislation on rent control and security of tenure.) Although it was seldom specified just how much tenants would benefit from such measures, it was widely felt that enforcing maximum rental shares would significantly raise tenant incomes, perhaps even double them.[12] Their effect in practice was never tested, however, because the legislation was never enforced, and landlords generally continued to take their traditional share of rents. (See M. H. Khan 1981, p. 169, for a review of the Pakistan reforms and Parthasarathy 1977 on the Indian reforms.)

It is now generally agreed that legislation to fix rental ceilings did more harm than good: it prompted evictions or voluntary surrenders and, where tenancy continued, led to informal agreements with much greater insecurity for tenants.[13] These measures displaced more tenants in the 1950s than the much criticized displacements in the name of mechanization or the Green Revolution in the 1960s and 1970s. The pace of evictions actually slowed in the early 1960s, once it was recognized that this type of legislation could not be enforced and was in fact a paper tiger. But the shift toward informal tenancy agreements brought about by these measures became permanent; tenancy effectively went underground and many tenants became landless laborers.[14] Consequently, few of the official figures of the extent and nature of tenancy in South Asia can now be deemed reliable.

Parthasarathy (1979, p. 342) sums the position up as follows:

> Powerful and enterprising landowners succeeded in evicting the tenants and in engaging them as labourers. The dramatic effect of tenancy legislation in the fifties was the gradual demise of the tenant and his exit into the ranks of the landless, more insecure conditions of tenancy and the shift of land from the urban middle class to the resident big landlord.

It is not difficult to see why these measures failed. In the first place, to legislate is not the same as to enforce. And enforcement is not merely a matter of political will: given the sheer scale of the task, even the strongest political will may not be up to it. To stipulate the landlord's rental share and share of input costs under varying agronomic conditions and in different regions would require recording, monitoring, supervising, and policing millions of field-level contracts, many of which may have been orally made. The administrative machinery needed for enforcement is almost unimaginable.

Second, because rural markets for labor, credit, products, and land are interdependent and interlinked, with landlords acting as agents, any measure to help tenants in land markets at the expense of landlords can be offset by rearranging contracts in other markets. Where these interlinked contracts are prevalent—and they are particularly so in areas where share tenancy is extensive and markets are least developed—legislation to control one element in a set of linked contractual arrangements is an exercise in futility. Policies other than direct redistribution of land will leave the welfare of tenants generally unaltered.[15] It is now realized that under these circumstances legislation will fail unless the entire set of contracts is monitored and supervised. Monitoring all contracts of all kinds seems even more impractical than monitoring all tenancy contracts.

Much of course depends on the extent of interlinking and the degree of monopoly or monopsony power that landlords exercise in various markets. Empirical research in this area is lacking. But what is surprising is that the most strenuous advocates of legislated ceilings on landlords' rental shares tend also to be those who adamantly maintain that landlords have broad "exploitative powers" which would nullify the effects of the ceilings.

Third, as noted earlier, most of these measures assume a neat but false dichotomy between rich, big, "exploitative" landlords and poor, small "exploited" tenants. In reality, millions of smallholders are both tenants and landlords, and in many parts of South Asia relatively rich operators may hold part of their land as tenants (often of poor and small landlords). Any legislation to provide relief to poor tenants would first have to identify those who are both tenants *and* poor, and then discriminate in their favor. By contrast, blanket ceilings on rents are meaningless if not counterproductive. For example, as was shown in chapter 3, all leased-in operational holdings of fewer than 5 acres in India in 1971–72 accounted for only 36 percent of the total leased-in area. If income gains accruing to tenants are roughly proportional to the area under tenancy, then nearly two-thirds of the benefits of such reforms, if effectively implemented, would accrue to tenants outside the target group of the poor. Similarly, since only 20 percent of the area under tenancy in Bangladesh is in this size group, 80 percent of the benefits would accrue outside the target group. In Pakistan less than 3 percent of the tenanted area is in holdings of fewer than 5 acres, so over 97 percent of benefits would have accrued to the nonpoor!

Basically, then, tenancy reforms do not represent a well-targeted instrument for redressing rural poverty, and as often as not they are unworkable or perverse in their effects. Experience suggests that tenancy reforms per se have been a failure in South Asia and that no amount of tinkering with existing laws—to plug loopholes and improve implementation—is likely to work (Appu 1975). Unless the overall balance of economic and political power shifts in favor of the weaker sections of the rural community, further tenancy reform is useless. The greatest shifts are likely to occur where technological change breaks down old class structures and brings about a new alignment of interests. Measures designed to "give the land to the tiller"— that is, to grant ownership rights in land to persons who work on it as tenants or hired laborers—are unlikely to succeed. The alternatives to interventionist or regulatory reforms are either a laissez-faire policy with no attempt to intervene on tenants' behalf or a genuinely radical decision to make the actual cultivator the owner of the land.

Meanwhile, part of the tenancy problem seems to be solving itself as some areas switch from pure sharecropping to partial cost-sharing leases and fixed-rent systems. Technological innovation, especially where the Green Revolution has spread, is helping to transform contractual arrangements in the desirable direction of both efficiency and equity. Technological changes have also helped to break down traditional rural class structures, polarizing those who have gained significantly—the well-off and the moderately rich peasantry—and those who have gained less—the small peasantry made up of tenants and landless laborers. The likely outcome of this polarization is not yet clear. In some areas in northwestern India and Pakistan, for example, a powerful class of middle-income peasants has emerged and the poor remain weak. Elsewhere, as in Tamil Nadu, the organized power and militancy of agricultural laborers have led to action to promote more effective reform (see Byres 1972, 1974, 1977, and 1981 on these issues). It will be through power shifts of these kinds, not through legislation in the name of simplistic abstractions, that the institution of tenancy will evolve.

Ceilings on Landholdings and Redistribution of Land

Tenancy reform is only one element in the structuralists' agenda for land reform. A second set of proposals addresses the inequitable distribution of landownership—which is less skewed than is often thought, but inequitable nonetheless—and the plight of the landless and those with very little land. Schemes for placing a ceiling on the ownership of land and redistributing holdings above these ceilings are designed to benefit these groups (see especially Dandekar and Rath 1971 on the case for ceilings).

It is clear that land ceilings and redistribution would promote greater equity. A more equal size structure of holdings would also have beneficial effects on employment and income distribution, although the impact on output and productivity may be less desirable.[16] It would lead to better labor use, the creation of rural assets for the poor, and more appropriate patterns of output and choices of technology; both private and social ends would be well served.

Arguments for the benefits of a more equal distribution of land are not new, and measures designed to limit the size of holdings and redistribute so-called surplus land have had a long history in the region.[17] Despite the enormous volume of legislation on the subject, however, little has in fact been achieved.

The Record since Independence

Table 8-6 shows the impact of various redistributive measures in the three decades since independence. In Pakistan less than 4 percent of the operated area—only 0.77 million hectares—was acquired by the government under the 1959 Martial Law Regulation 64. Over half of this total was uncultivated wasteland or forest, so only about a quarter million hectares were actually available for distribution.[18] Under the 1972 decrees, the surplus land acquired amounted to only a quarter million hectares (about 1 percent of the operated area); by mid-1974 only half of this had been redistributed.[19]

Similarly in Bangladesh (then East Pakistan), only about 200,000 hectares were transferred to tenants and tenants-at-will during the 1960s, although the operated area was around 8.9 million hectares. The land ceiling legislation of 1972 applied to only about 3.3 percent of the operated area; only 0.8 percent was actually acquired, although the availability of additional land as a result of silting meant that some 134,000 hectares, about 1.5 percent of the operated area, were eventually distributed (see Abdullah 1976 and Jannuzi and Peach 1980 for details).

In the case of India, estimates of surplus land available for redistribution vary according to the source and year.[20] Moreover, figures for the different states are hard to obtain or to reconcile. In the sixteen Indian states that implemented land ceiling legislation between 1958 and 1971, however, only 0.99 million hectares had been declared surplus by 1971, representing only 0.7 percent of the operated area. Of this total, less than 0.49 million hectares or 0.9 percent of the operated area had been redistributed to poor farm households and landless laborers (ADB 1977, pp. 100–01). Later figures do not significantly change the picture: by 1977 only some 0.7 percent of the total oper-

Table 8-6. *South Asia: Impact of Land Redistribution before 1977*

(area in thousands of hectares)

Total area	Operated area (1)	Estimated as surplus (2)	Acquired through legislation (3)	Percent (3) / (1) (4)	Redistributed under reforms (5)	Percent (5) / (1) (6)
Bangladesh						
1977	8,890	295	69	0.8	134[a]	1.5
India						
1957–77	125,684	2,154[b]	n.a.	—	850	0.7
1971[c]	139,368	988	n.a.	—	493	0.4
Pakistan						
1959	20,206	2,217	771	3.9	252[d]	1.2
1972	19,854	432	239	1.2	125[d]	0.6

— Not applicable.

n.a. Not available.

a. Most of this land was settled with *ryots* (owner-cultivators) and was acquired as a result of siltation or by means other than legislation. See Abdullah (1976), p. 95.

b. Estimates of the surplus land available for redistribution range from 1.7 million to 11.0 million hectares. See India, "Draft Five-Year Plan 1978–83," vol. 1, p. 29.

c. Estimates for 1971 by the ADB (1977), p. 100.

d. Sold to landless tenants or to tenants who were small owners. An additional 74,700 hectares were sold to others in 1959. In 1972 the area was allotted without cost. Data for Pakistan have been converted from acres in the original source.

Sources: M. H. Khan (1981), pp. 165–78; NSS Report 215, 26th Round, p. 87; India, "Draft Five-Year Plan 1978–83," vol. 1, pp. 29–30, vol. 3, pp. 6–8; Abdullah (1976), pp. 94–96; ADB (1977), p. 100.

ated area had been redistributed under land reforms (Dandekar and Rath 1971).

These figures illustrate the abject failure of land reform to match intentions. Meanwhile, population increases and landlords' concealment of holdings are eroding the available surplus. Redistribution has been bedeviled by a whole series of difficulties (many of them imposed by the relevant legislation). These include absurdly high ceilings for permissible holdings, long lists of exemptions, fictitious transfers by landholders to avoid the ceilings, and delays as reforms became bogged down in legal maneuvers designed to make them ineffective.

The most egregious flaw in the legislation was that the ceilings above which land was to be declared surplus were far too high in relation to the inequities of existing patterns of landownership (see table A44)—although lower ceilings would not have solved all the problems, as shown below. In addition, exemptions to even these high ceilings provided loopholes. As a result, the amount of surplus land available for redistribution was too small to secure a meaningful livelihood per capita for the landless.

In Pakistan, for example, the 1959 land reform set ceilings of 500 acres of irrigated and 100 acres of unirrigated land per person. Although these figures were lowered to 150 acres of irrigated and 300 acres of unirrigated land in 1972, this change had little impact because the so-called Bhutto Reforms remained unimplemented. Furthermore, exemptions designed to reflect the "productivity of land" in effect permitted an individual to retain far more than the ceiling. In Sind, for example, an owner could keep at least 1,800 acres of irrigated land of average productivity—a holding nearly four times the theoretical limit of 500 acres. Another 150 acres could be retained for orchards, livestock, and stud farms; land was allowed for house lots, and an individual could transfer large amounts of land to heirs and female dependents. The 1972 legislation lowered the ceilings, but actually gave a bonus of extra land to owners of tractors and tubewells. The new regulations did abolish the exemptions on orchards and also limited intrafamily transfers but, as noted above, their impact has been minimal (M. H. Khan 1981).[21]

In Bangladesh the 1950 reform legislation set the ceiling at 100 bighas (33.3 acres) per family or 10 bighas per family member, whichever was larger. In 1961 the family ceiling was actually raised to 375 bighas (125 acres), although it was brought back down to the 1950 level in 1972. These figures are manifestly absurd in a country where an average household's operated holding is only about 2.5 acres. As in Pakistan, exemptions were also permitted (for plantation crops and mechanized and dairy units).

Indian legislation followed the same flawed pattern. Ceilings were set too high in relation to the average operated area per rural household, and various exemptions and loopholes were adopted by individual states. Generally, however, ceilings were lower than in Pakistan and loopholes were fewer. A comparison of ceilings in Pakistan and in the Indian Punjab and Haryana show that those on the Indian side of the border were one-tenth to one-twentieth of those on the Pakistani side. This fact, together with better implementation in India, has contributed to the substantial differences in landholding structures in the two Punjabs noted in chapter 3. The Indian legislation, however, does seem to have been somewhat of a deterrent; in Pakistan very large units continue to operate with impunity, but in India the threat of legislated ceilings seems to have prevented the further expansion of larger holdings.

The failure of land redistribution efforts is not simply a matter of faulty legislation. Even the existing legislation has not been effectively implemented. This is due partly to a lack of political will, but there are other difficulties. Accurate land records are lacking, and local *patwaris* (record keepers) are open to bribery; land is illegally transferred (with the connivance of the *patwaris*) into the names of relatives or fictitious (*benami*) owners to evade the law; legal delays and lawsuits often drag on for decades; compensation for acquired land is inappropriate (it tends to be set too high for states to afford the land but too low in relation to market values for landowners to find it attractive); and those holding the levers of local power actively oppose the law.[22]

Further problems arise even after land has been acquired. Much of it is either very poor or even uncultivatable, and landless families have all too often been the least likely recipients of any distributed land—which is not necessarily given away free.[23] Sale, rather than free distribution, was required by many of the reform acts that tried to make redistributive measures self-financing (India, Ministry of Agriculture and Irrigation 1976). To sum up the position, "the ceiling legislation of the late fifties and early sixties was a great hoax perpetrated on the land hungry of India" (Parthasarathy 1979, p. 344).

Political and constitutional traditions in the region also place severe limitations on radical reform. Private property is protected by the law and cannot be alienated from owners without "just compensation." The processes of alienation and compensation are subject to endless legal delays—and even if procedures are rationalized, their implementation is far from assured.

Alternative Redistribution Schemes

Even if redistributive measures were to be fully implemented, how effective would they be in offering the smallest cultivators and the landless the chance to earn a tolerable livelihood from agriculture? Table 8-7 shows the effects of alternative approaches to redistribution, scheme A giving priority to the landless, scheme B giving it to marginal cultivators to bring them up to subsistence levels. (The data sources, assumptions, and implications are discussed in detail in appendix B). The results of the calculations indicate that redistribution would be of little value, even if existing ceilings were reduced. Scheme A, "land to the landless first," appears to be workable only in areas where it is least needed (Pakistan and northwestern India); in areas of real need (Bangladesh and southern and eastern India) there is simply too little surplus land to provide the landless with holdings large enough for basic subsistence. Another disadvantage of this scenario is that it would set the poorest against the poor by discriminating against the latter. A major drawback is that possession of land alone is not enough to ensure a livelihood from agriculture; complementary inputs (water, seeds, draft power) are also needed. Moreover, labor previously hired out by landless households would now

Table 8-7. South Asia: Alternative Land Redistribution Scenarios

	Scheme A				Scheme B			
	Landless labor		Below subsistence farmers		Landless labor		Below subsistence farmers	
Country and region	Thousands	Percent	Thousands	Percent	Thousands	Percent	Thousands	Percent
Bangladesh								
Case 1	71	2	0	0	173	7	0	0
Case 2	2,763	84	0	0	2,451	100	751	53
India	6,377	44	4,612	12	9,937	84	2,963	21
Jammu and Kashmir	13	100	301	100	310	100	13	100
Punjab	414	100	54	100	54	100	414	100
Haryana	174	100	72	100	72	100	174	100
Uttar Pradesh	108	8	0	0	159	2	0	0
North India	709	36	427	5	586	7	601	30
Rajasthan	111	100	857	100	851	100	111	100
Gujarat	468	55	0	0	664	31	0	0
Madhya Pradesh	781	100	1,846	100	1,846	100	781	100
Maharashtra	394	57	0	0	863	25	0	0
West India	1,954	70	2,697	33	4,224	51	892	32

Karnataka	438	49	0	0	569	19	0	0
Kerala	21	8	0	0	25	1	0	0
Tamil Nadu	788	38	0	0	1,584	100	155	7
Andhra Pradesh	1,944	100	1,488	68	2,187	100	1,315	68
South India	3,191	62	1,488	16	4,365	47	1,470	28
Orissa	280	67	0	0	441	23	0	0
West Bengal	151	7	0	0	198	5	0	0
Bihar	90	6	0	0	120	2	0	0
Assam	2	1	0	0	2	...	0	0
East India	523	12	0	0	761	6	0	0
Pakistan	2,000	100	720	100	720	100	2,000	100

... Negligible.

Notes: This table presents the results of alternative redistribution schemes.

Scheme A: The surplus land available for redistribution is allocated first to landless labor households in amounts large enough to produce subsistence requirements, and then if any land remains it is allocated to households cultivating below-subsistence holdings so as to bring them up to subsistence requirements.

Scheme B: The available surplus is first allocated to cultivating households with holdings below subsistence levels so as to bring them up to subsistence requirements; any land that remains is then allocated to landless labor households.

The number and percentage of households in each group likely to benefit under both schemes are given.

Sources: The data, assumptions, and sources are discussed in appendix B.

need to be devoted to farming the household plot, so incomes would be depleted by the wage earnings forgone.

Scheme B, "land to marginal cultivators first," should face fewer difficulties with the need for complementary inputs because this group is likely already to have access to at least some inputs. But there is still the drawback that household members who formerly hired out their labor would have to divert some of their effort into work on the newly acquired land. Furthermore, this scheme is open to the objection that its primary target group is not the very poorest (the landless) but a group that already has some land; this priority may make economic sense but would be politically controversial. The critical objection, as with the first alternative, is that the available land would be insufficient to satisfy the objective of the scheme—in this case, raising all marginal cultivating households to subsistence levels.

In principle, if the ceilings on holdings were lowered, more surplus land ought to be made available for redistribution. Can ceilings in fact be lowered further? Realistically, it is hard to avoid the conclusion that, if the present ceiling levels have not been enforced, there are even slimmer chances of lower ones coming into effect.[24] Lower ceilings are possible in Pakistan and some states in northern and western India; where they are being lowered, however, the results are not quite what might be expected by advocates of land reform as a solution to rural poverty.

In 1972 the Indian state of Maharashtra enacted legislation under which new surplus lands were acquired in 1975 and distributed to the landless poor in 1976. But as Pardeshi and Kazar (1981) have shown, the effect on the prospects of the poor was marginal. Although their average net sown area was around 2.5 acres (and acquired land raised the value of their assets threefold), crop incomes remained insignificant. The contribution of newly allotted land to total income was marginal (around 5 percent) because this land was of very poor quality; meanwhile, lacking essential inputs for cultivation, beneficiaries continued to rely mainly on wage income for their livelihood. Animal husbandry showed real improvement: livestock incomes increased by 130 percent. But by and large the landless poor who were now given access to land remained what they had been before—poor and mainly dependent on wage income.

Two specific lessons seem to emerge: (a) even if enough surplus land were available, redistribution (especially if the land is poor) is not helpful unless other inputs—draft animals, irrigation, credit, fertilizers—are provided; and (b) the distribution of small parcels of poor land could, however, open up prospects for livestock and other ancillary activities that might make better use of the land than crop cultivation.

More generally, the record of how little has actually been achieved by land ceilings and redistribution, together with the discussion in appendix B of the two hypothetical examples shown in table 8-7, suggests that radical measures for the redistribution of land are not the panacea for poverty they are often believed to be. What Dandekar and Rath (1971, p. 106) correctly concluded a decade ago is even more true today: "A major means of production in the Indian economy is land. Therefore a suggested remedy to the problem of poverty is to redistribute available land among all those who depend on it. But there is not enough land to redistribute so that everyone may employ himself on his land and earn a minimum desirable living." So, however simple it may appear, it is futile to attempt to resolve the problem of rural poverty in an overpopulated land by redistributing land that is in short supply.

Moreover, as the hypothetical examples show, land surpluses and the potential beneficiaries of redistribution are not themselves distributed evenly over the subcontinent; available data suggest that redistribution seems to be feasible where it may not be necessary, and less feasible where it seems more urgently needed. It can no longer be argued that the redistribution of land into smaller holdings would increase productivity. Evidence cited in chapter 4 suggests productivity may actually fall if holdings are made smaller unless other market and institutional biases are also corrected.

Does this mean that all thoughts of land redistribution should be set aside, at least in states and regions where there is not enough land to distribute into viable holdings for everyone? Not necessarily: some redistribution, even of land parcels too small to form viable units for crop farming, could still be valuable. In particular, a relatively modest redistribution program could usefully give the landless plots for simple homesteads and space for small-scale vegetable or livestock farming.

Giving the millions who do not have a roof over their heads some land on which to build shelter seems to be a worthwhile and achievable goal. In Bangladesh in 1978 nearly 3.5 million rural households (out of a total of 12 million) owned either no land or only enough for their houses. Nearly half did not have any land at all, not even house lots. I have no comparable figures for India and Pakistan, but if the same ratio is used, landless families without homesteads would be estimated at 7.5 million in India and 1 million in Pakistan in 1980.

Serious consideration should be given to formulating and implementing homestead legislation that would provide enough land for the landless at least to build themselves shelter and have a small vegetable garden or space to rear small stock and poultry. Of course land alone will not be enough; money and effort will be needed to help those who are given land to build low-cost housing and learn to grow vegetables and rear small stock. However flimsy or poorly constructed the houses, they would be better than what most of the landless have now. Moreover, even the simplest homestead arrangement would provide an asset base whose value would rise over the long term.

The amount of land needed for a homestead is very small. Even small amounts of land can be effectively used for activities such as vegetable gardening, dairying, poultry, and fisheries—all of which could greatly increase the incomes of the landless over their present levels. For dairying, as little as a quarter or a half acre can provide fodder for a cow; one-eighth of an acre is enough to set up a poultry unit of economic size; in fisheries, a quarter-acre pond represents a large unit if farmed intensively. A vegetable plot of a quarter acre can yield a large income.

Realistically, redistribution of the surpluses available cannot provide holdings large enough to support even subsistence food-grain farming for the landless and marginal cultivators. Once the focus shifts to ancillary activities, however, the redistribution of land parcels as small as one-eighth to one-quarter acre in size begins to make sense. In some cases—poultry and fisheries for example—even poor land can be effectively used; locational factors (distance from markets, roads, electricity supplies, extension services) are probably a more important consideration. In the case of dairying and vegetable farming, although land quality remains important, other factors such as credit, marketing, and extension are probably critical.

Thus a land redistribution scheme that provides a minimum amount of land—say, a quarter to a half acre per household—is both desirable and feasible everywhere. Such a scheme will not make the landless into self-sufficient farmers, as past reforms have misleadingly promised and fruitlessly attempted to do, but it will give them access to sources of income other than casual wage labor and the opportunity to build shelter for their families. Unlike the grandiose abstractions of the radical structuralists, this seems an achievable goal that would give all poor rural families some modest but tangible gains.

Consolidation of Fragmented Holdings

The concentration of holdings in the hands of relatively large operators is not the only troublesome feature of landholding arrangements in South Asia. The fragmentation of even the smallest holdings severely constrains the evolution of productive peasant agriculture. A fragmented holding consists of physically scattered parcels of land operated by one household; if they are widely scattered, the individual parcels define the scale of farming operations regardless of the size of the total holding. As has rightly been pointed out, "For a country's agricultural economy, whether owner- or tenant-operated, fragmentation is an unmitigated evil for which no advantages can be claimed" (Ladejinsky 1977, p. 374).

Fragmentation has occurred primarily through subdivision. Under the traditional system of inheritance, landholdings have been subdivided among heirs. Inheritances may include pieces of land from different parts of the original holding, so as to even out any inequities in land quality and productivity.

In 1928 the Royal Commission on Agriculture had this to say: "In extreme cases the result is ludicrous . . . the size of individual plots is sometimes as small as 1/160th of an acre . . . fields have been formed a mile long and but a few yards wide, while areas have been brought to notice where fragmentation has been carried so far as to prevent all attempts at cultivation."[25]

The severity of the problem of fragmentation in the three countries can be seen in tables 8-8 to 8-10 and figure 8-1. In 1960–61 the average operational holding in India consisted of six parcels of land. In Bangladesh more than half the farms reported six or more fragments in 1960, and by 1977 the average number of fragments had risen to ten, with over 70 percent of the farms reporting more than seven fragments on average. Data from Pakistan for 1960 and 1972 suggest that fragmentation may be becoming more acute as a smaller percentage of farms report unfragmented areas.

Fragmentation usually increases with the size of operational holdings, but even the very smallest holdings are highly fragmented. In India holdings smaller than 5 acres contain an average of two to five parcels of land, each with an average area of 0.1 to 0.4 acres. In Bangladesh more than half of all holdings smaller than 0.5 acres reported two to three fragments or more, as did 90 percent of holdings of 0.5–1.0 acres. A somewhat similar picture emerges for Pakistan, especially for small and marginal farms (see M. H. Khan 1979b).

Regional data for India show that fragmentation is higher than the Indian average in the eastern states of Bihar, Orissa, Uttar Pradesh, and West Bengal, with holdings of 2.5–4.9 and 5–7.5 acres recording as many as eight to ten parcels each (see table A45). In these states the countryside is a patchwork of tiny parcels of 0.1 to 0.2 acre on which millions of small cultivators—by no means all of them owners—eke out a living.

Fragmentation leads to economic inefficiency and depresses productivity. Apart from the time lost in moving human and animal labor from one parcel to another, scarce land is wasted in the construction of boundaries and irrigation channels between fields. Hired labor and land-labor contracts become hard to supervise. Above all, however,

Table 8-8. India: Average Number and Size of Fragments in Operational Holdings, by Size of Holding, 1960–61

Size of operational holding (acres)	Estimated number of holdings (millions)	Estimated area operated		Fragments per holding	
		Percentage of total	Acres per holding	Average number	Average acres per fragment
<0.5	4.3	0.3	0.2	1.8	0.1
0.5–1.0	4.3	0.9	0.7	3.1	0.2
1.0–2.5	11.1	5.6	1.6	4.4	0.4
2.5–5.0	11.4	12.3	3.5	6.0	0.6
5.0–7.5	6.5	11.7	5.9	6.8	0.9
7.5–10.0	3.5	9.0	8.4	7.6	1.1
10.0–12.5	2.6	8.2	10.6	7.6	1.4
12.5–15.0	1.5	5.9	13.3	8.0	1.7
15.0–20.0	1.9	9.6	16.6	7.9	2.1
20.0–25.0	1.2	7.4	21.0	8.8	2.4
25.0–30.0	0.7	5.3	26.3	8.0	3.3
30.0–50.0	1.1	12.0	35.8	8.1	4.4
50.0+	0.5	11.6	73.4	9.4	7.8
Total	50.7	100.0[a]	6.5	5.7	1.1

Notes: Columns may not add to total because of rounding.
a. Estimated total area operated is 329.6 million acres.
Source: NSS data.

fragmentation makes it extremely difficult to use irrigation water effectively or to implement measures for water conservation. Even small tubewells or mechanized tillers are uneconomic on many small holdings, and mobile units become harder to manage. In a broader context it becomes very difficult to carry out any rational plan for efficient exploitation of land and water resources within a watershed.

Consolidation of fragmented holdings is thus essential for improving the efficiency and productivity of small-farm agriculture. The small farmer needs a compact area equal in value as well as in size to his former patchwork of scattered plots. Consolidation is not just a matter of physical regrouping of plots, however; it is a complex and difficult process, requiring villagers to make voluntary agreements (at best difficult) to undertake consolidation on an equitable basis. This in turn entails

a conviction on the part of the farmer that in the process of consolidation (correction of land records, land measurements, land classification, land valuation, and reassignment of the consolidated land) his interest will be protected. The touchiest of questions is land val-

Table 8-9. Bangladesh: Agricultural Land Holdings and Fragmentation per Holding by Farm Size, 1977

Size (acres)	Holdings		Acreage				Fragments per holding	
	Number	Percent	Number	Percent	Average		Average number	Average acres per fragment
0.0–0.5	342,040	5.5	109,009	0.5	0.319		2.9	0.109
0.5–1.0	648,302	10.4	472,029	2.1	0.730		4.4	0.167
1.0–1.5	799,282	12.8	961,580	4.4	1.203		5.7	0.209
1.5–2.5	1,322,258	21.1	2,574,475	11.7	1.947		7.5	0.260
2.5–5.0	1,829,458	29.2	6,402,140	29.2	3.499		10.5	0.334
5.0–7.5	726,272	11.6	4,335,620	19.7	5.970		14.2	0.420
7.5–10.0	269,296	4.3	2,279,487	10.4	8.465		17.4	0.488
10.0–12.5	140,796	2.3	1,540,086	7.0	10.938		20.1	0.545
12.5–15.0	62,901	1.0	849,186	3.9	13.500		21.8	0.620
15.0–25.0	93,357	1.5	1,691,215	7.7	18.116		25.9	0.699
25.0+	23,211	0.4	744,664	3.4	32.082		32.8	0.977
Total or average	6,257,173	100.0	21,959,476	100.0	3.509		9.6	0.367

Source: Bangladesh Bureau of Statistics (1977).

311

Table 8-10. *Pakistan: Fragmentation of Farms by Size of Operational Holding, 1960 and 1972*

Size of operational holding (acres)	Total area (millions of acres)	Unfrag-mented area (percent)	Total number of farms (millions)	Percentage of unfrag-mented farms	Percentage of farms reporting		
					2–3 fragments	4–5 fragments	6+ fragments
1960							
<1.0	0.334	70	0.742	77	21	2	—[a]
1.0–2.5	1.345	51	0.856	55	34	8	3
2.5–5.0	2.911	37	0.806	37	37	14	12
5.0–7.5	3.546	32	0.581	32	35	15	18
7.5–12.5	7.357	25	0.759	26	36	15	23
12.5–25.0	12.533	20	0.729	21	35	17	27
25.0–50.0	9.468	13	0.286	14	29	21	36
50.0–150.0	6.539	8	0.088	9	19	19	53
150.0+	4.896	5	0.014	6	17	15	62
All	48.929	19	4.860	39	33	12	16
1972							
<1.0	0.076	66	0.154	73	24	3	1
1.0–2.5	0.563	55	0.351	56	33	8	3
2.5–5.0	1.859	45	0.527	45	35	12	8
5.0–7.5	3.349	40	0.566	41	39	10	10
7.5–12.5	8.732	33	0.903	34	45	11	10
12.5–25.0	12.778	27	0.778	29	41	15	11
25.0–50.0	8.832	19	0.277	21	41	19	19
50.0–150.0	6.848	12	0.095	13	37	22	29
150.0+	3.594	9	0.014	10	27	20	41
All	46.672	25	3.664	38	40	12	11

a. Less than 0.5 percent.

Sources: 1960 Pakistan Census of Agriculture: A Summary of West Pakistani Data (Karachi: Agricultural Census Organization), p. 63; *1972 Pakistan Census of Agriculture: All Pakistan Report* (Lahore: Agricultural Census Organization, 1975), p. 4.

uation. While it is a truism to say that plots of land vary greatly in quality of soil, facilities of irrigation, productivity, and distance from the village, it is a Herculean task to evolve methods of valuation by which different classes of land can be reduced to a comparable basis. Unless valuation of land satisfies the community, consolidation cannot succeed. (Ladejinsky 1977, p. 374)

Even the correction of land records—another prerequisite for successful consolidation—is likely to be enormously difficult, since rec-

Figure 8-1. *India and Bangladesh: Average Number of Fragments per Holding by Size of Holding*

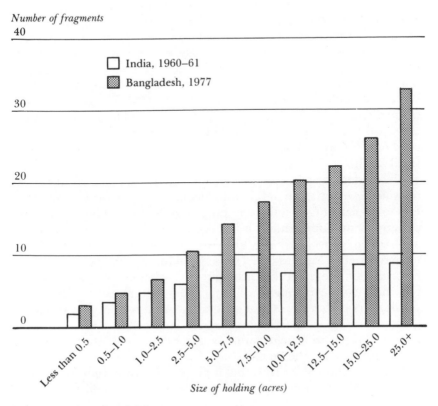

Number of fragments

□ India, 1960–61

▨ Bangladesh, 1977

Size of holding (acres)

Sources: Tables 8-8 and 8-9.

ords tend to be nonexistent, incomplete, or subject to corruption.

Despite these difficulties, some progress has been made. Land consolidation was begun a century ago in South Asia, first on a voluntary basis and later compulsorily once a certain percentage of landlords agreed to it. With the exception of the Indian states of Kerala and Tamil Nadu, legislation exists almost everywhere in the subcontinent for the prevention of further fragmentation and for consolidation where it is deemed to be necessary.[26]

Precise and up-to-date information on how far consolidation has progressed is scarce. In Pakistan some 13.6 million acres had been consolidated by 1968 out of about 40 million acres of arable cropland (Elkinton 1970), but later data are unavailable. Very little consolidation has occurred in Bangladesh. Available data for the Indian states (table 8-11) show a great deal of progress in some states, but very little overall. Consolidation has made virtually no headway in eastern and southern India where rural poverty is most critical. Punjab and Haryana have achieved complete consolidation, while Uttar Pradesh and Maharashtra report considerable progress. In the south and east, only Karnataka and Orissa had even planned significant consolidation efforts as of 1979. The areas in which new agricultural technologies have had the greatest impact are also the ones that have implemented successful land consolidation programs, a fact that suggests the two phenomena may be linked. One might be tempted to wonder whether the consolidation of fragmented holdings represents a necessary precondition for spreading the gains from the new technologies to very small holdings.

The evident benefits of consolidation make it a structural reform on which everyone can agree in principle. The practical problems of how to implement consolidation programs, however, have led to some disagreement. For example, it has been suggested that the traditional approach to consolidation is likely to take too long and to yield only limited benefits. Minhas (1974) has called for an alternative approach involving an integrated (and compulsory) scheme for land consolidation, national development of land and water resources, and rural public works. He argues that such a program would give farmers a greater incentive to participate because land consolidation would be part of a larger package of public works. Such an integrated program would also involve the landless.

There are difficulties with this approach. It would require substantial economic and administrative resources, and it could be achieved only if legislation on land ceilings were effectively implemented--a development that, as I have noted, seems unlikely. But consolidation of fragmented holdings does not in fact require a systems approach of this kind. The eastern and southern states could follow the example of Haryana, Maharashtra, Punjab, and Uttar Pradesh under existing legislation. Such a goal seems both administratively reasonable and economically desirable.

Conclusions

This brief overview of the unfinished business of land reform suggests a number of general conclusions. Most important, it seems hard to believe that legislation or even the enforcement of structural change in landholding systems in South Asia will solve the problem of rural poverty. At best, efforts in this direction represent only one element in a much broader strategy. Moreover, different kinds of

Table 8-11. *India: Area Covered under Land Consolidation by State and Region*
(area in millions of acres)

| Region and state | Geographical area | Operated area | Cultivable area | Area consolidated | | | |
| | | | | By 1974 | | 1974–79 targets | |
				Area	Percent	Area	Percent
North							
Haryana	4.4	3.4	—	—	—	—	—
Himachal Pradesh	5.6	0.9	0.8	0.2	25.0	—[a]	25.0
Jammu and Kashmir	22.2	0.9	1.0	—[a]	—[a]	...	—[a]
Punjab	5.0	4.0	8.0	9.1[b]	100.0	...	100.0
Uttar Pradesh	29.4	18.2	20.1	11.8	58.7	3.0	73.6
Subtotal	66.7	27.4	29.9	21.2	70.9	3.1	81.3
West							
Gujarat	19.6	10.0	11.1	1.2	10.8	0.4	14.4
Madhya Pradesh	44.3	21.1	22.1	3.6	16.3	1.2	21.7
Maharashtra	30.8	21.2	20.8	9.8	47.1	6.1	76.4
Rajasthan	34.2	20.3	25.0	1.7	6.8	...	6.8
Subtotal	128.9	72.7	79.0	16.3	20.6	7.7	30.4
South							
Andhra Pradesh	27.7	13.6	15.5	0.4	2.6	...	2.6
Karnataka	19.2	11.4	12.4	1.0	8.1	0.8	21.0
Kerala	3.9	1.6	2.3	...	0.0	...	0.0
Tamil Nadu	13.0	7.7	8.2	...	0.0	...	0.0
Subtotal	63.7	34.3	38.5	1.4	3.6	0.8	5.7
East							
Assam	10.0	2.9	27.0	...	0.0	...	0.0
Bihar	17.4	11.5	11.5	0.3	2.6	0.5	7.8
Orissa	15.6	6.4	7.6	...	0.0	1.7	22.4
West Bengal	8.8	5.1	5.9	...	0.0	...	0.0
Subtotal	51.7	25.9	52.0	0.3	0.6	2.3	5.0
All India	311.0	160.2[c]	199.4	39.2	19.7	13.9	26.6

— Not applicable.
... Negligible.
a. Fewer than 25,000 hectares.
b. Includes parts of Himachal Pradesh also.
c. The operated area calculated by the census differs significantly from the operated area estimated by the NSS for 1970–71.
Sources: India, Ministry of Agriculture and Irrigation (1975), p. 42; (1976), pp. 2, 33–34.

structural change seem to have very different degrees of promise. I assess each briefly below.

Consolidation of Fragmented Holdings

The most desirable and feasible of the items on the structuralist agenda, consolidation is a prerequisite for other measures to increase small-farm productivity, and real benefits accrue from implementing it. Although consolidation is not easy to carry out, the fact that it has been implemented effectively in some areas suggests that it is feasible. Where it has yet to be carried out, consolidation remains a priority.

Tenancy Reform

Most efforts to reform tenancy have not succeeded, and they are unlikely to do so, given the complex nature of tenancy arrangements and the interlinked nature of land and other markets. The major exception to this generalization is the relative success of measures to abolish intermediary interests. This has been a helpful change; further progress remains possible where state power is used on behalf of tenants—although it may be that the opportunity has now passed for areas in which nothing has yet been done.

By contrast, measures to provide security of tenure have largely failed. Existing legislation to prohibit evictions and restrict subletting or resumption of land by landlords is difficult to implement and enforce, and its net effect has often been to reduce security of tenure. Without good records and firm state backing at the grass-roots level, additional legislation combined with halfhearted enforcement will only make life more difficult for tenants and place further restrictions on land-lease markets. These measures are not worth pursuing unless governments are prepared to make a much more uncompromising commitment to them—and to back that commitment with the full force of state power.

Legislation to fix rental shares and cost-sharing has been a total failure. The complex nature of contracts and intractable problems of enforcement make it unlikely that regulation could ever work; moreover, it appears in practice to have done more harm than good to tenants. These measures should be abandoned.

Apart from all the problems of implementation, tenancy reform faces another major difficulty in attempting to redress poverty. Reform efforts cannot be targeted specifically at the poor, because poor and small farmers appear on both sides of land-lease contracts. Such efforts are therefore crude and potentially counterproductive. Poor tenants would benefit most from being given ownership rights to some land—but any program of this kind would have to be implemented in a discriminatory way so as not to benefit the rich as well. The political chances of such an initiative seem slim. In general, tenancy reform seems likely to remain ineffective and ought now to be abandoned.

Land Ceilings and Redistribution

Realistic land ceilings should be legislated and implemented because they have the beneficial effect of limiting the size of operational units. They cannot be expected to solve the problem of poverty, however, and they face formidable enforcement problems. Efforts to give the landless viable subsistence holdings are impractical in the areas where they would be likely to do the most good, because there is not enough land to go round; where they are feasible, they make little economic sense because they would raise the number of subsistence holdings at the expense of more productive ones.

Redistribution is, however, practical and sensible if it is more narrowly conceived—not as a way of making all marginal and landless rural households into viable farmers, but as a transfer mechanism for more modest parcels of land (enough for a home, a small vegetable plot, and activities such as livestock or poultry farming).

In some areas—Pakistan, for example—enough land is available for redistribution to provide the landless with viable holdings. But in these areas, land redistribution may be beside the point. Agricultural output is growing, real wages are rising, and the landless are already seeking new and better sources of income and employment.

Whether large-scale or modest, redistribution programs alone cannot produce solid or lasting improvements in the livelihood of the poor. Other inputs and services, such as credit, marketing, and extension, must also be made available if beneficiaries are to use their newly allotted land productively. Thus, although redistribution may be a necessary condition for relieving the problems of poverty in some areas, it can never be the only condition.

As I have shown, redistribution is least possible in the areas where it seems most desirable, because there is too little available land. Even a totally egalitarian redistribution in these areas would make no economic sense; the problem of rural poverty cannot be resolved simply by redistributing land in overpopulated areas where land is in short supply, even supposing such a policy were administratively or politically feasible. But more limited measures to distribute some land assets to the landless and the rural poor would be both feasible and desirable elements in a broader program to diversify sources of rural earnings. The greater the delay in enacting such a program, the less useful it will ultimately be. Without such a program, extreme poverty and the severe penalty it imposes on the lives of millions in South Asia will continue at least into the next century.

Notes

1. For a comprehensive review and bibliography on the Indian literature, see Joshi (1975); for Bangladesh, see Zaman (1976) and Jannuzi and Peach (1980); and for Pakistan, see M. H. Khan (1979b). For a fuller treatment of the problems of agrarian reform in the Asian context, see Ladejinsky (1977). In addition, see Minhas (in Srinivasan and Bardhan 1974), Dandekar and Rath (1971), and Parthasarathy (1977) on the Indian experience, and Abdullah (1976) and Herring and Chaudhry (1974) on the recent experience in Bangladesh and Pakistan.

2. In India this legislation is a state matter, so provisions vary from state to state. There have also been variations over time in the legislation of all three countries. For details on India, see the discussion in Wunderlich (1970), the state-by-state legislation described in Wadhwa (1973), and the bibliography in Joshi (1975). Two large volumes are required simply to list the various acts legislated in India since 1793 (Joshi 1975). Those interested in Pakistan will find Akram (1973), Herring and Chaudhry (1974), M. H. Khan (1981), and Hirashima (1978) useful. For Bangladesh, see Abdullah (1976) and Zaman (1976). For a summary of the main provisions of various agrarian reforms, see tables A43 and A44.

3. For a review of the literature on interlinked product and factor markets in rural areas and their implications, see Binswanger and Rosenzweig (1981) and Bardhan (1980). For the literature on interlinked contracts and their implications in South Asia, see, for example, Braverman and Srinivasan (1980), Braverman and Stiglitz (1980), P. Mitra (1979), Bardhan (1981), Bardhan and Rudra (1978, 1980a, b, c, 1981), Sheila Bhalla (1976), and Rosensweig (1978).

4. See Abdullah (1976). A class of subtenants has now emerged, however; see M. H. Khan (1981) and Jannuzi and Peach (1980).

5. By 1968 an estimated total of Rs6.1 billion had been paid to *zamindars* in India (see Dantwala 1972). For information on the eviction of tenants that accompanied these measures, see Khusro (1965) and Jannuzi (1974).

6. How land reform measures have been negated in Pakistan is too complex a subject to pursue here; see Stevens, Alavi, and Bertocci (1976) and M. H. Khan (1981) for a critical evaluation.

7. "After the initial spurt of evictions in the late fifties the subsequent period was marked not so much by a decline in tenancy, but changes in its character from kind to share, from written to oral and from stable to unstable relationships," Parthasarathy (1979), p. 348.

8. See Bandhopadhyaya (1981), Sengupta (1981), Rudra (1981), and Khasnabis (1981) for a flurry of articles on Operation Barga. Of course the provisions of the act were already in existence; it is the nature of their implementation that is claimed to be different.

9. West Bengal had already made considerable progress toward land reform, and most of these provisions were not new. By 1981 more than a mil-

lion acres had been acquired, of which 0.67 million acres had been distributed to some 1.2 million people, which amounts to about 0.6 acre per beneficiary. See Bandhopadhyaya (1981) and Dutt (1981).

10. Note the similarities between this process and what happened in China in the 1950s, when land was redistributed and local landed elites were confronted in public by the poor. See Hinton (1966) for a description of the process in China, as well as Selden (1971) on the importance of public confrontations.

11. Even in West Bengal, it is argued, reform measures of this kind in a class society will do no more than slightly rearrange property relations, because the notion of "bourgeois property rights" imposes severe limitations. See Khasnabis (1981).

12. Bell (1977) suggested that moving from a 50 percent rental share to a maximum of 25 percent would increase tenants' direct income by more than half since they bore most of the costs of intermediate inputs. Further, on the assumptions used by Bell, "the indirect increases in the incomes of the tenant through a rental share reduction to 25 percent would be at least as large as the direct increase" (p. 26). The assumptions used are not far from observed conditions, so his conclusions seem valid, at least as a first approximation.

13. "Evictions and voluntary surrenders, and where there were neither of these two, informal tenancy agreements with much greater insecurity for tenant become common. By the middle fifties there were large-scale evictions . . . . There was a shift to more informal agreements in tenancy" (Parthasarathy 1979, p. 339). "As for the security of tenure, there have been more evictions and changes of tenants during the years following the tenancy legislation than in the previous period in recent history" (Dantwala 1958).

14. For an early review of Indian experience, see Dantwala (1958) and Parthasarathy (1977); for Bangladesh, see Abdullah (1976) and Jannuzi and Peach (1980); for Pakistan, see M. H. Khan (1981).

15. Braverman and Srinivasan (1980) give a clear exposition of some of the implications of interlinking—especially the interlinking of credit and tenancy arrangements—for land reform and tenant welfare.

16. As shown in chapter 4, productivity is not necessarily inversely related to farm size, especially since the advent of new technologies. This undermines the argument, based on this supposed inverse relationship, that redistribution would improve not only equity but also productivity and growth.

17. See Joshi (1975) and Wadhwa (1973). For the case in favor of redistributive land reform, see also Eckholm (1979), Lehman (1977), and Raup (1963). There is an extensive literature on the problem of land ceilings, especially in India. See in particular Joshi (1961), Parthasarathy and Raju (1972), C. H. H. Rao (1972), India, Ministry of Agriculture and Irrigation (1972), and Ladejinsky (1977).

18. Sometimes these figures are reported as a percentage of net cropped areas. I have used operated area because it gives more consistent results for comparative purposes.

19. For further details by district and various periods, see M. H. Khan (1981, ch. 4) and Herring and Chaudhry (1974). Qayyum (1977) gives the following statistics for Pakistan as of April 1977: of some 3.4 million acres acquired, 1.5 million were distributed to tenants at no cost; some 0.15 million

families benefited. There were about 19,000 complaints of illegal ejection of tenants, and some 14,000 tenants were restored to their tenancies.

20. In the late 1950s, for example, before the abolition of *zamindari* systems, there were an estimated 25 million hectares of surplus land in India. For the 1960s Dandekar and Rath (1971) estimated the surplus at 16.9 million hectares on the basis of 1960–61 data. In the mid-1970s the Planning Commission estimated a surplus of 8.6 million hectares, but recent estimates by the same authority give only 1.7 million hectares as surplus. See B. M., "Land Reforms: Concealing the Surplus," *Economic and Political Weekly* 13 (26), July 1, 1978, pp. 1051–52. Estimates of operated areas in the National Sample Survey and the Agricultural Census differ by more than 15 million hectares.

21. The so-called productivity index units on which the exemption regulations were based were determined in accordance with 1949 revenue figures; the subsequent fourfold or fivefold increases in productivity were not taken into account in the calculations (M. H. Khan 1981, pp. 158–60). Khan estimates (p. 177) that even with these "tightened" regulations 400 acres of irrigated land in the Punjab and 480 acres in Sind could be retained per person. For owners of tractors or tubewells the ceiling was raised by 66 and 80 acres respectively.

22. By the 1950s political power at the state level had shifted to the rural landowning classes, and big landlords became effective brokers of rural votes and power. See Bell (1974b), Alavi (1973), and Byres (1981) among others on the role of the so-called bourgeoisie-kulak alliance in thwarting the implementation of reform.

23. About half of the resumed land in the Pakistan Punjab after the 1950 act was uncultivated area, about two-thirds of which was uncultivatable waste, "which was producing nothing and most of it would require improvements after it was sold to new owners" (M. H. Khan 1981, p. 164). In Bangladesh "most of the khas lands were uncultivatable [because] the proprietors had the choice of which land they would retain. The result has been that of even the paltry total of land acquired, a large portion would be unfit for settlement" (Abdullah 1976, p. 83). The fee to acquire land was set at five to ten times the annual rent; this was later raised to 50 percent of market value and still later to full market value. See also Ladejinsky (1977).

24. The ceilings in appendix B that are used for the calculations are much lower than the maximum permitted by existing legislation, and the illustrative figures show at best only partial coverage of target groups. Dandekar and Rath (1971) did a similar exercise and proposed lower ceilings. Their ceilings are in many cases higher than those used here, and their floor (the minimum amount of land required for subsistence per household) is in many cases higher. See table B-1 in appendix B for floor and ceiling figures.

25. Quoted by Ladejinsky (1977, p. 373). Fifty years later the Indian National Commission on Agriculture stated: "One of the major causes of low agricultural productivity in India is the fragmentation of holdings."

26. See Herring and Chaudhry (1974), Abdullah (1976), Hirashima (1978), and ADB (1977) for a summary of the land reform legislation in Bangladesh, India, and Pakistan.

APPENDIX A
Caveats in Using Data on Poverty in South Asia

Both the imperfect nature of the data used to calculate the incidence of poverty and the problems associated with the methodology used for the calculations suggest that extreme care needs to be exercised in drawing inferences from the numbers obtained. Some of the main methodological pitfalls are discussed below.

1. *The use of a minimum calorie "norm" to define a poverty line is arbitrary and potentially misleading.* Although there are difficulties in translating the notion of a minimum nutritional level (on which there is disagreement) into a poverty line defined in terms of consumption expenditures, all studies have started from a base of this kind. The nutritional levels generally used (between 2,100 and 2,300 calories per capita per day) are not minimum requirements at all; rather, they are average requirements for so-called reference men and women, based on the Sukhatme-FAO recommended diets.[1] There are such enormous variations in these requirements between one individual and another—the standard deviation is around 15 percent—that, even by FAO standards, 10 percent of the population would require up to 1,800 additional calories. Moreover, these diets are obviously expensive, and few of the rural poor can afford them. Attempts to adjust the minimum requirements only lead to defining other arbitrary poverty lines giving differing results. Thus, for example, Naseem (in ILO 1977a), using 2,100 calories per person, found that over 85 percent of rural households (or 80 percent of the population) in Pakistan fell below his norm; his definition of new poverty lines based on 95, 92, and 90 percent of this arbitrary norm does not remove the essentially arbitrary nature of the exercise.

2. *The concept of the incidence of poverty is extremely sensitive to the choice of poverty line.* It is now well established that the relation between per capita expenditures (the basis for calculating the percentage of the population in poverty) and calorie consumption (based on the food

bundle purchased at each expenditure level) is nonlinear, but highly sensitive precisely around the so-called norm often used in these studies. The elasticity of calorie intake with respect to income (expenditures) is very low around a consumption level of about 2,200 calories but changes dramatically as the level of calories is reduced. Its inverse, the elasticity of the incidence of poverty with respect to the poverty line or calorie norm specified in the studies, is consequently very high. The results of Naseem's study for Pakistan and A. R. Khan's study for Bangladesh (both in ILO 1977a) can be used to illustrate the point.

Naseem's results for 1971–72 show that, as the poverty line changes from 95 percent of the "norm" of 2,100 calories (1,975 calories) to 92 percent (1,932 calories) and to 90 percent (1,890 calories), the percentage of the population in poverty declines from 74 percent to 55 percent and 43 percent respectively. The implied elasticities (percentage change in the incidence of poverty for a unit percentage change in the calorie norm) are 8.1 and 10.0 respectively. This means that for a 1 percent change in the calorie norm that defines the poverty line (a mere 19–20 calories per person per day) the study shifts nearly 8–10 percent of the rural population—4 to 5 million people in Pakistan—from one category of poverty to another.

In Khan's study of Bangladesh, the data for 1973–74 imply that for a 1 percent change in per capita monthly expenditures (a mere 0.24 taka per person per month), 1.7 percent of the rural population— nearly 1.1 million persons—could be included in or excluded from the ranks of the "extremely poor." How many calories per day did 0.24 taka per person per month buy in 1963–64? Khan's study does not give the calorie equivalent, but if the "absolutely poor" consumed 1,935 calories per person per day and his "extremely poor" consumed 1,720 calories (see R. Ahmed 1979a), then the implied elasticity is 4.2. A change in consumption of 20 calories per person per day would therefore move 4.2 percent of the rural population into or out of the category of the "poor."

Data from a large variety of expenditure surveys in developing countries show that income and consumption expenditures may be underestimated by as much as 20–30 percent (see Surjit Bhalla 1980). The difference may be particularly large among the poor because of underestimation of the consumption of home-produced as opposed to purchased food. Thus, for example, an analysis of Indonesian food expenditure data reveals that 10 percent of the population consumed fewer than 1,000 calories, more than three standard deviations below the norm of 2,100 calories.

Given the enormous disagreement on calorie norms as well as the possibility of data errors, especially in measuring expenditure levels, how seriously should one take the estimates of the incidence of rural poverty in these studies and the numbers of the rural poor they imply?

3. *Samples from which the calorie-expenditure (income) relationships are calculated (and on which estimates of the incidence of poverty are based) are small and sometimes of questionable composition.* Naseem's study, for example, used fifty-six observations from grouped data in six different surveys, while Khan's study used eleven observations based on grouped data. Other studies have used even fewer observations. In addition, grouped data require extrapolation from the outer limits of the range of expenditures that define the poverty line (to avoid a typically wide range of estimates of the number of poor).

4. *The use of price deflators raises special problems when estimating trends in real expenditures over time.* To reflect the way changing relative prices affect the commodity composition of consumption over time, current prices must be deflated to some "real price" level. Getting reliable price data to construct appropriate deflators can be very difficult, however. And the incidence of poverty is particularly sensitive to the choice of deflator. At a norm of around 2,200 calories per capita per day, the elasticity of calories consumed is low with respect to income but is high with respect to prices, whereas at a norm of around 1,800 calories one would expect the opposite to be true. The results can therefore vary enormously depending on the reliability of the price data and the choice of norm and deflator.

5. *The choice of end points in calculating trends can be arbitrary when adequate, consistent, and comparable time series on consumer expenditures are not available.* Each of these problems can significantly change estimates of the incidence of poverty, even if the underlying data are reliable. In reality, many data (especially in Bangladesh and Pakistan) are unreliable and skimpy. Even the state-level data for India are aggregated so much that high-growth and low-growth districts are lumped together. The use of average nutritional requirements to measure poverty has been vigorously challenged, and other more comprehensive measures have been recommended (see A. K. Sen 1980 for a review of these issues). Although poverty may be all too apparent, it remains a daunting task to measure it.

Note

1. Even Sukhatme (1965) and FAO (1973) recommended that their figures not be used. Moreover, they are based on outdated nutrition theory. We now know that the body can convert proteins into calories at low levels of nutrition so that their separation is not very useful. For an extensive discussion of the problems associated with measuring malnutrition, see Srinivasan (1979c).

APPENDIX B
Hypothetical Redistribution Schemes: Data Sources and Policy Issues

A full-scale land redistribution program must start by estimating the number of beneficiaries to be served. Table B-1 shows estimates for 1980 based on the agrarian structure in the 1970s (cols. *a* and *d*) and the estimates of rural labor households in chapter 2. State-specific land requirements for subsistence agriculture (col. *f*; calculated in chapter 2) are used to determine the number of households cultivating land at below subsistence levels (col. *h*). Then for different size groups of holdings too small to provide subsistence, I calculate the average amount of land required to bring holdings in each group up to the subsistence level in different states.[1] Using data on operated areas in the 1970s (col. *b*) and median levels of legislated land ceilings (col. *j*), I determine the area that would become "surplus" if all land above this ceiling were available for redistribution (col. *l*).[2]

This surplus land has been generously overestimated for two reasons. Not only are the ceilings shown far lower than would actually be imposed, but also it is likely that there have been major changes in the operated area since the 1970s when these data were collected. For example, as population has increased many holdings must have been subdivided. This means that in the 1980s the amount of surplus land above indicated ceilings will be smaller than the estimates shown, while the area needed to give every household the indicated minimum subsistence holding will be greater. Without more up-to-date information, however, I can give no better picture than that shown in the table.

On the basis of these data I then evaluate two redistribution schemes: *scheme A*, in which surplus land is first redistributed to all landless labor households and then, if further land is available, to cultivating households with too little land for subsistence; and *scheme B*, in which the available surplus is first redistributed to marginal cultivating households so as to bring them up to subsistence and then, if further land is available, to landless households. The outcome is shown in table 8-7 in chapter 8.

Land to the Landless First

The results for scheme A, in which land is first given to the landless, show the limitations of large-scale redistribution schemes. Only in Pakistan and in some states in northern and western India—Andhra Pradesh, Haryana, Jammu and Kashmir, Madhya Pradesh, Punjab, and Rajasthan—is there enough land to meet the needs of all landless labor households.[3] But these are not areas in which landlessness is most severe. Indeed, the landless labor households in these six Indian states account for less than a quarter of all rural households in India (3.43 million out of an estimated total of 14.34 million in 1980). Moreover, rapid agricultural growth in some of these states has already led to higher real wages for landless laborers and growing employment and income opportunities in the nonfarm sector. This is especially true in Haryana, Punjab, and Rajasthan in India and, of course, in Pakistan. Land redistribution nevertheless remains a worthwhile option because it is feasible and the landless represent a significant proportion of all rural households in many of the Indian states listed. Similarly in Pakistan, the great inequalities in existing landholdings and the high proportion of rural labor households without land make the implementation of redistributive land reforms highly desirable. Furthermore, except for Andhra Pradesh, there is enough land in all these areas to bring marginal farmers up to subsistence level as well as to give land to all the landless.

Elsewhere, however, an altogether different picture emerges. In southern and eastern India and in the large states of Gujarat, Maharashtra, and Uttar Pradesh there is too little surplus land available to provide the landless with subsistence holdings, even given our low ceilings. These states account for more than two-thirds of all landless labor households in India. In Bangladesh, even though we have used a very low ceiling of 1.2 hectares per family as the median, the shortage of land is also a constraint.[4] The exercise clearly shows that in Bangladesh and the Indian states just listed, most of the landless and all very small holders would simply be ignored by redistribution. But these are also the areas where landlessness is high, lack of agricultural growth has limited nonfarm employment opportunities, real wages have stagnated or declined, and poverty and rural employment are most severe. It thus appears that where redistributive land reforms seem likely to do the most good they are the least feasible.

Any redistributive reforms would of necessity be inequitable (because many landless households would have to be excluded) and

Table B-1. South Asia: Alternative Land Redistribution Scenarios

Country and state	All rural households, 1980 (millions) (a)	Total operated area, 1971-71 (millions of hectares) (b)	Average area per rural household, 1980 (hectares) (c)	Landless labor households, 1980		Estimated hectares required per household		Households below subsistence level, 1980		Ceiling (hectares)		Surplus land available (thousands of hectares)	
				Thousands (d)	Percentage of (a) (e)	Assumption I[a] (f)	Assumption II[b] (g)	Thousands (h)	Percentage of (a) (i)	I[a] (j)	II[b] (k)	I[a] (l)	II[b] (m)
Bangladesh													
Case 1	14.3	8.9[c]	0.6	3,300	23.1	0.8	—	5,751	40	8.7	—	57	—
Case 2										1.3	—	2,210	—
India	88.5	128.4	1.5	14,344	16.2	—	—	52,129	59	—	—	15,826	16,913
Jammu and Kashmir	0.7	0.7	1.0	13	18.6	1.3	1.0	314	45	5.1	6.2	275	17
Punjab	1.8	2.8	1.6	414	23.0	0.3	2.0	468	26	14.4	10.3	294	502
Haryana	1.2	2.3	1.9	174	14.5	0.4	2.0	246	21	14.5	10.3	186	
Uttar Pradesh	15.4	16.5	1.1	1,388	9.1	1.5	1.0	9,396	61	12.8	6.2	162	1,572
North India	19.1	22.3	1.2	1,988	10.1	—	—	10,424	55	—	—	917	2,091

Rajasthan	3.7	15.2	4.1	111	3.0	0.9	4.0	962	26	12.6 20.1	2,550	1,779
Gujarat	4.5	10.2	2.3	855	19.0	2.1	3.0	2,970	66	13.0 10.3	983	1,394
Madhya Pradesh	7.1	16.2	2.3	781	11.0	1.5	3.0	2,627	37	5.7 12.4	3,966	1,738
Maharashtra	7.0	17.9	2.6	1,050	15.0	2.6	3.0	4,480	64	13.4 12.4	1,545	2,292
West India	22.3	59.6	2.7	2,797	12.5	—	—	11,039	50	— —	9,044	7,203
Karnataka	4.5	10.3	2.3	900	10.0	6.4	3.0	3,960	88	6.2 10.3	2,804	1,347
Kerala	3.5	1.0	0.3	256	7.3	0.9	0.4	2,671	76	5.3 3.1	19	205
Tamil Nadu	7.2	4.7	0.7	2,088	29.0	0.4	1.0	3,672	51	9.1 4.1	315	206
Andhra Pradesh	8.1	12.0	1.5	1,944	24.0	0.6	2.0	4,131	51	13.0 6.2	1,970	3,133
South India	23.3	28.0	1.2	5,188	22.3	—	—	14,434	62	— —	5,180	5,291
Orissa	4.3	4.8	1.1	419	9.7	1.4	1.0	2,354	55	4.1 6.2	393	582
West Bengal	7.2	4.3	0.6	2,232	31.0	1.2	1.0	6,264	87	6.0 4.1	182	417
Bihar	9.8	8.0	0.8	1,470	15.0	1.2	1.0	6,664	68	12.1 5.2	108	1,189
Assam	2.5	1.5	8.6	250	10.0	1.1	1.0	950	38	7.8 3.1	2	140
East India	23.8	18.6	0.8	4,371	18.4	—	—	16,232	68	— —	685	2,328
Pakistan	10.1	19.9	2.0	2,000	19.8	1.1	—	2,720	27	61.0 —	3,000	—

— Not applicable.
a. Assumption I uses subsistence land requirements based on state-specific yield data for 1971–72.
b. Assumption II uses subsistence land requirements suggested in Dandekar and Rath (1971a and b) and based on 1960s data.
c. For 1977.

would substantially raise the number of noneconomic holdings in the countryside. In India almost 52 million rural households are estimated to be below state-specific subsistence levels (col. *h*). If "land to the landless" redistributive schemes were actually implemented, they would add another 15.8 million holdings to this category (col. *l*). In Bangladesh the number of rural households to be given land would more than double under such a redistribution.

But "land to the landless" is in any case not enough. How are beneficiaries to farm their land without complementary inputs—bullocks, water, credit—and above all without training in farming skills? Either inputs will also have to be redistributed (and skills will have to be learned) or the new cultivators will not be able to farm their plots. And the allotted holdings will not necessarily provide beneficiaries with an income that is adequate or even higher than the one previously earned from wage employment. (The average income in wage labor households is higher than in households with marginal holdings.) The new owners of the allotted holdings may well be worse off than other farmers with holdings of the same size because the surplus land that is surrendered and redistributed will (if past experience is any guide) be of the poorest quality. Meanwhile allottees' wage incomes will be reduced, as able-bodied family labor will have to be withdrawn from wage employment to work the farm. Given all these difficulties, the viable class of small peasant proprietors that redistribution is supposed to promote may in fact fail to emerge.

Rath (1979) has argued against any reforms that redistribute only land without changing the conditions of production. The consequences were cogently summarized by Dandekar and Rath (1971, p. 87) earlier:

> It will be worth nobody's while to cultivate such land in the small pieces into which it will be distributed. It will also be beyond the means of the new holders to develop these lands. No amount of credit, long term or short term, from the cooperatives or the nationalized banks can make the uneconomic holdings economically viable. Most probably the small uneconomic holders, old and new, will sell their land and turn landless. The entire operation of redistribution will be nullified. If this is prevented by law, the small uneconomic holders will lease out their land to bigger cultivators and tenancy will emerge in a new and reverse form. If it has not been easy to enforce tenancy legislation on the bigger owners, it will be impossible to do so in respect of the innumerable small owners. If this is attempted the small uneconomic holders will mortgage their lands but they will not cultivate them because it will not be worthwhile. . . . A patently uneconomic proposition cannot be sus-

tained by law. It is not entirely for doctrine that communist countries after redistribution of land have immediately proceeded to collectivize them in large cooperatives.

Land to Marginal Cultivators First

The alternative scheme B is based on the idea that since there is not enough land available to make all households self-sufficient, it would be better to focus on small cultivators currently living below the margin of subsistence whose holdings could be made viable with a little additional land.[5] Unlike the landless, this group is at least likely to have some of the complementary inputs and farming skills necessary to make the exercise a success. The results of pursuing this alternative are also shown in table 8-7. The scheme seems viable in a number of Indian states and in Pakistan, but the bulk of marginal farmers would be left out of the redistribution in many states. Such an alternative would make some sense from the point of view of organizing agricultural production rationally, but again Dandekar and Rath (1971, p. 86) point out why it is impractical:

> It does not solve the problem of rural poverty or rather admits that the problem of poverty cannot be solved by redistribution of land to anyone who needs it. Yet for that reason the proposition will not be politically acceptable. In any programme of redistribution of land it will be impossible to set aside politically the claims of the landless and very small cultivators who are hardly different from the landless. With these priorities the consequences of even very low ceilings can only be a vast increase in the number of uneconomic non-viable holdings.

Notes and Sources for Table B-1

Col. a: The number of rural households is estimated by dividing 1980 estimates for rural population (obtained by projecting 1970–71 population on the basis of growth rates between 1971 and 1981) by estimates of rural household size for Indian states and Pakistan. For Bangladesh the 1977 household size is used along with a 1980 World Bank projection of rural population. *Sources*: Afzal (1974), p. 47, for a rural household size of 5.8; Reserve Bank of India (1975), table 2, gives rural household counts for all states; Government of India, *Report of the Expert Committee on Population Projections*, 1971 Census, Series I, paper 1, provides five-year growth rates of rural areas (Part II-A, ii, Union Primary Census Abstract, 1971, pp. xxviii–xxix, was used to project 1971 figures to 1980); preliminary results of the Bangladesh

1977 Agriculture Census, tables 02 and 39, provide number of households and population by size group of operated holdings; and World Bank data were used for 1971 and 1979 state population figures for India.

Col. b: Data on operated holdings differ considerably between the National Sample Survey (NSS) and the Indian Agricultural Census; the latter shows approximately 162 million hectares compared with 130 million hectares for the NSS in 1971–72! State-specific data on rural operated area for 1971–72 are unavailable. The state-specific data for 1961–62 (NSS 17th Round) on operated area are used and state-specific percentage changes between 1961–62 and 1971–72 (computed by Sirohi, Ram, and Singh 1976) are applied to estimate the operated area for 1971–72. For Pakistan the 1972 Agricultural Census figure is used (tables 1 and 2 give the distribution of operated holdings by farm size). For Bangladesh the 1977 Agricultural Census data are used. *Sources*: M. H. Khan (1981); India, Ministry of Agriculture and Irrigation (1975) provides the mean value of the largest size group of holdings, which enables the number of holdings in the last size group of operated holdings to be calculated when the application of a ceiling requires it (table 8.2 in this source indicates 162 million hectares of operated area in all of India); India, Ministry of Planning (1976b) gives data from the NSS 26th Round on changes in the size distribution of holdings (table 5 estimates 130 million hectares of operated area in all of India); Dandekar and Rath (1971), table 5.1, give state distributions of operational holdings by size group; Sirohi, Ram, and Singh (1976) present percentage changes in the distribution of operational holdings based on the NSS 17th Round, which are reconciled with data from the 26th Round cited above to provide estimates of the 1971–72 distributions.

Col. c = col. *b*/col. *a*.

Col. d = col. *e* x col. *a*.

Col. e: There are no data for Pakistan on the percentage of rural landless labor households. These were estimated for 1972 at 19.8 percent. There are no reliable data on landlessness for Bangladesh. The 1977 Land Occupancy Survey states that 29 percent of all rural households do not own any land other than house lots. We have assumed that 80 percent of these—that is, 23 percent of the total—are rural labor households. *Source*: India, Ministry of Labour (1978) gives the number of rural labor households with and without land in 1964–65 and 1974–75.

Col. f: Calculated earlier on the basis of state-specific data on yields, family size, and cropping intensity.

Col. g: For India, Dandekar and Rath (1971) have used a "floor area" to connote a "viable size of holding" in each state. These are presented here for purposes of comparison.

Col. h: The state-specific distributions of operated holdings for 1961–62 from the NSS 17th Round have been updated on the basis of size-specific percentage changes in area and number of holdings between 1961 and 1971 as reported by Sirohi, Ram, and Singh (1976) to obtain the 1971–72 distributions. Then, assuming a linear intra-size group variation, data for the proportion of households cultivating land below the subsistence level are interpolated for 1971–72. These are then multiplied by col. *a* to get the number of cultivating households below subsistence in 1980.

Col. i: For Pakistan and Bangladesh, 1972 and 1977 data on the size distribution of holdings are used directly to obtain the percentage of rural households that have less than enough land to support subsistence. Data on both percentages and numbers are presented. *Sources*: Same as for col. *b*.

Col. j: Table A44 gives the different legislated ceilings in each state. These ceilings differ widely because they are designed to account for differences in productivity. Setting aside the very large ceilings for orchards and forest and desert land, I have taken the midvalues of the remaining range. They are usually far below the maximum ceilings allowed. In Bangladesh there are two ceilings because there are two legislated criteria. The first allows 1.3 hectares per person (Case 1); the second allows 1.3 hectares per household (Case 2). I have used the first assumption. *Sources*: India, Ministry of Agriculture and Irrigation (1976) gives details of legislated ceilings applicable to holdings of various types in each state; ADB (1977), app. I.5.1, gives ceilings in Bangladesh and Pakistan.

Col. k: For India, Dandekar and Rath (1971, table 4.2) have selected what they call "reduced ceiling levels" to calculate the impact on the available surplus. I have presented these here for comparative purposes, so as to indicate that the ceiling levels I have used are similarly "low" (and far below the permitted ceilings for each state).

Col. l: The surplus areas are computed by taking the total operated area in holdings above ceiling levels and subtracting the amount of the ceiling area.

Col. m: These are surplus areas calculated by Dandekar and Rath (1971) on the basis of their "floor" and "reduced ceiling" levels and 1961–62 data on size distribution of holdings for India. They are given for comparison.

Notes

1. I use the median for each group because the data are given in that form—for example, 0.25 hectare for the 0.0–0.5 hectare category and 0.75 hectare for the 0.5–1.0 hectare category—and subtract this from the subsistence level.

2. Because of differences in productivity, most land ceilings are expressed as a range, and I therefore use the median of legislated areas.

3. The National Sample Survey data on operated area in three of these states (Andhra Pradesh, Madhya Pradesh, and Rajasthan) are far from reliable.

4. This problem has been noted by all who have looked at the efficacy of land redistribution. For India, see Dandekar and Rath (1971); for Bangladesh, see Jannuzi and Peach (1979).

5. This idea was first suggested by Dandekar and Rath (1971), who carried out a similar exercise with data on operational holdings from the 1960s. Their data and results are shown in table B-1 for comparison.

STATISTICAL APPENDIX
Tables A1 through A45

Table A1. India: Percentage of Rural Population in Poverty by State and Region

Region and state	1957–58	1959–60	1960–61	1961–62	1963–64	1964–65	1965–66	1966–67	1967–68	1968–69	1970–71	1973–74
North												
Punjab and Haryana	28.0	24.2	18.8	22.3	29.4	26.5	26.5	29.5	33.9	24.0	23.6	23.0
Uttar Pradesh	52.3	36.7	37.9	35.4	56.6	53.7	47.1	55.2	60.2	46.4	40.6	47.3
West												
Gujarat	n.a.	41.5	31.6	39.7	45.7	49.8	50.7	54.1	50.8	42.8	43.8	35.6
Madhya Pradesh	57.7	46.4	43.8	40.0	43.6	42.1	47.2	58.3	62.3	56.0	52.9	52.3
Maharashtra	n.a.	54.5	48.4	43.6	48.2	59.1	57.8	63.2	57.2	54.8	46.6	49.8
Rajasthan	33.4	n.a.	32.3	33.0	32.6	31.8	30.8	37.1	35.9	41.4	41.8	29.8
South												
Andhra Pradesh	53.4	48.8	50.1	47.2	45.6	41.5	45.4	47.9	46.0	47.3	41.0	39.8
Karnataka	41.3	48.9	39.1	35.4	50.5	55.1	63.9	59.5	56.9	58.8	47.2	46.9
Kerala	59.6	62.3	57.8	50.3	52.8	60.7	70.7	67.1	63.4	64.6	62.0	49.3
Tamil Nadu	67.8	64.4	53.9	51.0	52.0	57.4	59.5	62.7	58.1	60.6	57.3	48.3
East												
Assam	28.0	31.4	25.6	29.4	24.4	24.2	31.3	46.8	38.4	47.3	35.3	39.3
Bihar	59.7	55.7	41.5	49.9	52.3	54.3	59.4	74.4	70.9	59.4	59.0	58.4
Orissa	66.6	63.4	62.4	49.3	60.0	61.9	62.1	64.2	64.7	71.2	65.0	58.0
West Bengal	62.3	61.4	40.4	58.3	63.3	64.0	56.5	64.3	80.3	74.9	70.1	66.0
All India	53.4	48.7	42.0	42.3	49.1	50.4	51.1	57.4	57.9	53.5	49.1	47.6

n.a. Not available separately.
Source: Montek S. Ahluwalia (1978), table 3(a).

Table A2. India: Different Indices of Incidence of Absolute Poverty in Rural India by NSS Round

NSS Round	Survey period	Head count (percent)			Sen's poverty index	
		Ahluwalia's estimates		Indian Statistical Institute estimates	Ahluwalia's estimates	Indian Statistical Institute estimates
		Estimate I	Estimate II			
12	March–August 1957	54.1	n.a.	n.a.	0.230	n.a.
13	September 1957–May 1958	50.2	53.4	n.a.	0.220	n.a.
14	July 1958–June 1959	46.5	n.a.	n.a.	0.190	n.a.
15	July 1959–June 1960	44.4	48.7	n.a.	0.170	n.a.
16	July 1960–June 1961	38.9	42.0	n.a.	0.140	n.a.
17	September 1961–July 1962	39.4	42.3	n.a.	0.140	n.a.
18	February 1963–January 1964	44.3	49.1	n.a.	0.160	n.a.
19	July 1964–June 1965	46.8	50.4	45.7	0.170	0.170
20	July 1965–June 1966	53.9	51.1	48.7	0.210	0.189
21	July 1966–June 1967	56.6	57.4	56.0	0.240	0.237
22	July 1967–June 1968	51.0	57.9	55.7	0.240	0.232
23	July 1968–June 1969	n.a.	53.5	50.5	0.200	0.199
24	July 1969–June 1970	47.5	n.a.	49.0	n.a.	0.186
25	July 1970–June 1971	n.a.	49.1	45.2	0.180	0.168
27	October 1972–September 1973	46.1	n.a.	46.4	n.a.	0.176
28	October 1973–June 1974	n.a.	47.6	46.1	0.170	0.164
32	October 1977–June 1978	n.a.	n.a.	40.2	n.a.	0.143
38	January 1983–December 1983	n.a.	n.a.	32.8	n.a.	0.108

n.a. Not available.
Sources: Montek S. Ahluwalia (1978) and personal communication from Robin M. Mukherjee, Economic Research Unit, Indian Statistical Institute, Calcutta.

Table A3. India: Percentage of Rural Population in Poverty for Selected States by NSS Round

NSS Round	Survey period	Head count (percent)					
		Bihar	Haryana	Kerala	Punjab	Tamil Nadu	West Bengal
13	September 1957–May 1958	59.7	—[a]	59.6	28.0	67.8	62.3
15	July 1959–June 1960	55.7	—[a]	62.3	24.2	64.4	61.4
16	July 1960–June 1961	41.5	—[a]	57.8	18.8	53.9	40.4
17	September 1961–July 1962	49.9	—[a]	50.3	22.3	51.0	58.3
18	February 1963–January 1964	52.3	—[a]	52.0	29.4	52.0	63.3
19	July 1964–June 1965	54.3	—[a]	60.7	26.5	57.4	64.0
20	July 1965–June 1966	57.7	21.9	72.8	31.0	59.6	72.1
21	July 1966–June 1967	74.1	21.6	68.1	28.4	62.8	76.4
22	July 1967–June 1968	70.7	30.6	63.1	32.2	58.3	80.7
23	July 1968–June 1969	59.8	26.7	64.8	17.3	60.9	75.9
24	July 1969–June 1970	57.2	26.4	69.1	24.1	62.2	67.7
25	July 1970–June 1971	58.7	27.9	61.9	16.5	58.0	69.4
27	October 1972–September 1973	59.9	16.2	55.0	15.8	49.5	66.1
28	October 1973–June 1974	60.2	26.2	49.8	18.3	50.2	69.4
32	October 1977–June 1978	54.9	19.8	41.6	10.7	48.7	62.0
38	January 1983–December 1983	56.2	12.0	27.7	8.6	44.4	54.5

a. Punjab and Haryana data are combined prior to the 20th Round.
Sources: Montek S. Ahluwalia (1978) for data prior to the 26th Round, rest from personal communication from Robin M. Mukherjee, Economic Research Unit, Indian Statistical Institute, Calcutta.

Table A4. India: Relative Inequality of Consumption: Gini Coefficients

Region and state	1957–58	1959–60	1960–61	1961–62	1963–64	1964–65	1965–66	1966–67	1967–68	1968–69	1970–71	1973–74
North												
Punjab and Haryana	0.32	0.30	0.37	0.35	0.30	0.32	0.33	0.31	0.31	0.28	0.30	0.29
Uttar Pradesh	0.30	0.30	0.30	0.32	0.30	0.30	0.29	0.28	0.28	0.31	0.29	0.25
West												
Gujarat	n.a.	0.33	0.26	0.27	0.30	0.30	0.29	0.30	0.29	0.29	0.28	0.24
Madhya Pradesh	0.41	0.34	0.30	0.34	0.35	0.31	0.32	0.29	0.32	0.33	0.32	0.29
Maharashtra	n.a.	0.29	0.29	0.28	0.29	0.28	0.29	0.29	0.26	0.29	0.26	0.28
Rajasthan	0.41	0.36	0.32	0.37	0.31	0.32	0.32	0.35	0.34	0.40	0.33	0.29
South												
Andhra Pradesh	0.33	0.30	0.33	0.32	0.31	0.31	0.31	0.28	0.28	0.29	0.28	0.30
Karnataka	0.38	0.32	0.29	0.37	0.29	0.28	0.31	0.31	0.30	0.32	0.29	0.28
Kerala	0.35	0.34	0.33	0.33	0.30	0.34	0.30	0.30	0.32	0.42	0.33	0.32
Tamil Nadu	0.32	0.33	0.31	0.31	0.31	0.30	0.29	0.28	0.28	0.19	0.27	0.28
East												
Assam	0.26	0.29	0.24	0.23	0.22	0.20	0.21	0.25	0.19	0.20	0.19	0.22
Bihar	0.32	0.29	0.40	0.28	0.29	0.29	0.31	0.32	0.31	0.28	0.27	0.29
Orissa	0.32	0.31	0.33	0.30	0.28	0.27	0.28	0.25	0.30	0.29	0.29	0.30
West Bengal	0.27	0.27	0.26	0.28	0.27	0.24	0.27	0.26	0.25	0.23	0.27	0.30
All India	0.34	0.32	0.33	0.32	0.30	0.30	0.30	0.30	0.29	0.31	0.29	n.a.

n.a. Not available separately.
Source: Montek S. Ahluwalia (1978), table 8.

Table A5. Bangladesh and West Bengal (India): Recent Changes in Landownership

West Bengal

Size group (acres)	Number of households (cumulative percent)			Acres owned (cumulative percent)			Average size of holding (acres)		
	1961	1971	Percentage change	1961	1971	Percentage change	1961	1971	Percentage change
0	12.6	9.8	-3.7	—	—	—	—	—	—
0-1	51.1	56.5	50.2	4.1	6.8	39.3	0.25	0.23	-8.0
1-5	86.1	90.3	19.6	17.5	52.9	189.0	2.61	2.14	-18.0
5-10	95.9	97.6	-7.8	72.3	80.7	-57.4	6.80	5.99	-11.9
10-15	98.5	99.3	-19.0	85.7	92.2	-28.9	11.92	10.64	-10.7
15+	100.0	100.0	-42.2	100.0	100.0	-54.2	21.64	17.52	-19.0
All groups	4.91[a]	6.08[a]	23.8	11.38[a]	9.56[a]	-16.0	2.31	1.57	-32.0

Bangladesh

Size group (acres)	Number of households (cumulative percent)			Acres owned (cumulative percent)			Average size of holding (acres)		
	1977	1978[b]	Percentage change	1977	1978	Percentage change	1977	1978	Percentage change
0	11.1	14.7	34.8	—	—	—	—	—	—
0-1	58.5	59.6	-4.4	9.3	8.3	-4.0	0.32	0.32	0.0
1-5	92.4	91.9	-3.9	57.0	51.6	-2.5	2.30	2.33	1.3
5-10	98.1	97.7	3.3	80.4	74.5	5.7	6.70	6.85	2.2
10-15	99.2	99.2	34.8	88.7	84.9	33.8	12.32	12.03	-2.4
15+	100.0	100.0	0.0	100.0	100.0	43.6	23.06	32.76	42.1
All groups	11.85[a]	11.99[a]	1.2	19.35[a]	20.81[a]	7.5	1.63	1.76	8.0

— Not applicable. a. Millions. b. Percentages are adjusted from the original as necessary.

Sources: Sanyal (1977b); Reserve Bank of India (1976); Jannuzi and Peach (1980), appendix tables D.1 and E.1.

Table A6. *Yields among Adopters and Nonadopters: Chambal Agricultural Extension Program, Rajasthan, 1976–77*

	Kilograms per hectare		Yield increases over nonadopters (percent)
Season and crop	Adopters[a] (contact farmers)	Nonadopters[b] (other farmers)	
Kharif (1976–77)			
Paddy (288 observations)	4,169	2,877	45
Sorghum (250 observations)	854	555	54
Rabi (1976–77)[c]			
Wheat (266 observations)	2,215	1,947	14
Gram (530 observations)	985	895	10

a. Farmers adopting 50 percent or more of the recommended practices.
b. Farmers adopting less than 50 percent (including none) of the recommended practices.
c. In 1976–77, drought reduced yields in this season.
Source: Rajasthan (1977).

Table A7. *Extent of Adoption of Recommended Practices: Chambal Agricultural Extension Program, Rajasthan, 1976–77*
(percentage of total)

	Farmers adopting recommended practices			Area on which practices were adopted		
Crop	A	B	C	A	B	C
Paddy	57	36	6	56	38	6
Sorghum	38	39	23	36	37	27
Wheat	49	51	0	n.a.	n.a.	n.a.
Gram	43	50	3	n.a.	n.a.	n.a.

n.a. Not available.
A: Farmers adopting more than 50 percent of the practices recommended.
B: Farmers adopting less than 50 percent of the practices recommended.
C: Farmers adopting none of the recommended practices.
Source: Rajasthan (1977).

Table A8. *Adoption Rates for Different Practices: Chambal Agricultural Extension Program, Rajasthan, 1974–77*
(percentage of farmers adopting recommended practices)

Wheat	1974–75 (first year)	1975–76 (second year)	1976–77 (third year)
Seed treatment	59	49	60
Maintenance of optimum plant population	31	62	70
Interculture operations	67	69	70
Use of HYV	89	93	92

Source: Rajasthan (1977).

Table A9. *Impact of Number of Practices Adopted on Sorghum Yields: Chambal Agricultural Extension Program, Rajasthan, 1976–77*

Item	Practices adopted for sorghum[a]					
	None	1	1–2	1–3	1–4	All 5
Yield (kilograms per hectare)	505	578	616	855	872	919
Percentage increase over none	—	14	22	69	72	82

a. Practices: (1) clean cultivation, row planting; (2) treatment of seeds before sowing; (3) maintenance of optimum plant populations; (4) application of nitrogenous fertilizer immediately after hoeing; (5) use of plant protection measures.
Source: Rajasthan (1977).

Table A10. *Adoption Rates for Selected Practices by Farm Size: Chambal Agricultural Extension Program, Rajasthan, 1976*
(percentage of farmers adopting recommended practices)

	Farm size (hectares)					
Crop and practice	*0–1*	*1–2*	*2–4*	*4–8*	*8+*	*Overall*
Wheat						
Use of HYV	100	86	100	89	89	90
Seed treatment	45	54	43	40	53	44
Timely sowing[a]	43	42	53	42	42	51
Optimum plant population	53	58	55	65	62	61
Interculture operations	83	56	58	47	41	52
Use of fertilizer[b]	52	65	55	60	51	58
Gram						
Timely sowing[a]	44	13	7	11	16	16
Plant population	100	81	74	82	79	89
Control of pests	29	27	13	32	38	28

a. Sowing was delayed by rains in November 1976.
b. Nitrogen and phosphorus.
Source: Rajasthan (1977).

Table A11. *Adoption of Nitrogen Fertilizers among Hybrid Bajra Growers, Haryana, 1976*

Farm size (acres)	Contact farmers		Noncontact farmers	
	Sample size	*Percentage adopting*	*Sample size*	*Percentage adopting*
Irrigated				
0–4.9	17	88	36	67
5.0–9.9	20	70	55	60
10.0–20.0	59	75	59	81
20+	37	78	33	70
All irrigated	133	77	183	70
Rain-fed				
0–4.9	26	12	43	30
5.0–9.9	35	31	67	28
10.0–20.0	51	35	54	43
20+	34	29	28	29
All rain-fed	146	30	192	33

Source: World Bank data.

Table A12. Adoption of Fertilizers by Growers of Dwarf Wheat, 1976

Group	Jind district				Karnal district			
	Sample size	Adoption rate (percent)			Sample size	Adoption rate (percent)		
		Nitrogen	Phos- phorus	Potash		Nitrogen	Phos- phorus	Potash
Contact farmers								
Small[a]	102	95	42	15	68	97	78	51
Large	155	98	65	21	109	99	81	54
All	257	97	56	18	177	98	80	53
Noncontact farmers								
Small	165	95	33	13	103	95	62	49
Large	140	96	44	14	79	100	84	66
All	305	96	38	13	182	97	72	58

a. Farmers owning less than ten acres are defined as small farmers.
Source: World Bank data.

Table A13. Visits to Farmers by Extension Worker More Than Four Weeks before the Interview, 1976

Farm size (owned acres)	Jind district, Haryana					Karnal district, Haryana					Muzaffarnagar district Uttar Pradesh[b]	
	Contact farmers		Noncontact farmers		All farmers (weighted average)[a]	Contact farmers		Noncontact farmers		All farmers (weighted average)[a]		
	Sample size	Percent visited	Sample size	Percent visited	Percent visited	Sample size	Percent visited	Sample size	Percent visited	Percent visited	Sample size	Percent visited
0–4.9	52	77 (81)	58	17 (34)	23.0 (36.4)	18	83 (81)	44	32 (7)	37.1 (14.4)	46	6
5.0–9.9	51	71 (85)	91	22 (37)	26.9 (41.8)	48	88 (84)	44	30 (15)	35.8 (21.9)		
10.0–19.9	89	82 (90)	97	20 (32)	26.2 (37.8)	63	90 (85)	49	41 (35)	45.9 (40.0)	46	15
20+	58	83 (89)	57	25 (38)	30.8 (43.1)	48	98 (88)	22	59 (41)	62.9 (45.7)		
All	250	79 (87)	303	21 (35)	26.8 (40.2)	177	91 (85)	159	38 (22)	43.3 (28.3)	92	11

Notes: Figures in parentheses refer to rabi 1981–82.
a. The weighted averages are calculated assuming that the percentage of contact farmers in the population is 10 percent and that of noncontact farmers is 90 percent.
b. Control district.
Source: World Bank data.

Table A14. *Average Levels of Fertilizer Use, 1976*

	Jind district				Karnal district				Recommended dose
	Contact farmers		Noncontact farmers		Contact farmers		Noncontact farmers		
Fertilizer	Small	Large	Small	Large	Small	Large	Small	Large	
Nitrogen									
Average use (kilograms per acre)	26.9	30.3	26.0	26.2	37.5	38.8	34.7	41.3	48
Standard deviation	12.7	15.3	12.0	12.4	12.9	15.4	13.6	15.4	
Sample size	93	147	154	132	64	108	9	75	
Phosphate									
Average use (kilograms per acre)	13.7	14.4	13.4	13.7	17.6	16.5	16.3	15.9	24
Standard deviation	5.4	7.2	6.3	6.0	7.4	6.4	4.6	5.0	
Sample size	42	98	53	57	52	87	61	62	
Potash									
Average use (kilograms per acre)	5.4	7.02	5.8	6.3	8.0	8.4	8.1	7.7	24
Standard deviation	2.6	1.8	2.4	2.2	1.7	2.4	1.9	1.6	
Sample size	14	27	18	18	35	59	47	48	

Source: World Bank data.

Table A15. Expected Increases in Yield from Recommended Practices, Assam, India, 1977

				Package of practices						
Practice	0	1		2a		2b		3a		3b
Improved practices	No	Yes		Yes		Yes		Yes		Yes
Improved and HYVs	No	No		Yes		Yes		Yes		Yes
Fertilizer[a]	0	0		0		25		50		100
Seed treatment	No	Optional		Optional		Yes		Yes		Yes
Other pesticides	No	Emergencies		Emergencies		Emergencies		Routine		Routine

	0	1		2a		2b		3a		3b	
Crop	Yield (tons per hectare)	Yield (tons per hectare)	Percentage gain	Yield (tons per hectare)	Percentage gain	Yield (tons per hectare)	Percentage gain	Yield (tons per hectare)	Percentage gain	Yield (tons per hectare)	Percentage gain
Rain-fed crops											
Aus rice	0.6	0.8[b]	35	1.0	25	1.1	13	1.5	27	n.a.	n.a.
Sali and boro rice	1.0	1.3	25	1.5	20	1.6	9	2.0	23	n.a.	n.a.
Wheat	1.1	1.4	25	n.a.	n.a.[c]	1.5	9	1.9	24	n.a.	n.a.
Pulses	0.4	0.5	25	0.6	20	0.7	21	n.a.	n.a.	n.a.	n.a.
Coarse grains	0.5	0.6	25	0.8	19	0.9	17	1.2	31	n.a.	n.a.
Oilseeds	0.4	0.5	25	0.6	20	0.7	22	n.a.	n.a.	n.a.	n.a.
Jute	1.2	1.4	25	1.7	20	1.9	7	2.3	23	n.a.	n.a.
Sugarcane[d]	30.0	38.0	25	45.0	18	54.0	20	60.0	11	65.0	8

(Table continues on the following page.)

Table A15 (*continued*)

	0	1		2a		2b		3a		3b	
Crop	Yield (tons per hectare)	Yield (tons per hectare)	Percentage gain	Yield (tons per hectare)	Percentage gain	Yield (tons per hectare)	Percentage gain	Yield (tons per hectare)	Percentage gain	Yield (tons per hectare)	Percentage gain
Irrigated crops											
Aus rice	0.8	1.1[b]	35	1.4	25	1.6	18	2.1	29	2.4	15
Sali and boro rice	1.2	1.5	25	1.8	20	2.1	16	2.6	24	2.9	11
Wheat	1.5	1.9	25	n.a.	n.a.[c]	2.1	13	2.7	25	3.0	11
Pulses	0.5	0.6	25	0.8	19	1.0	33	1.4	38	n.a.	n.a.
Coarse grains	0.8	1.0	25	1.2	20	1.5	20	1.9	31	2.2	16
Oilseeds	0.5	0.6	25	0.8	19	1.0	33	1.4	38	n.a.	n.a.
Jute	1.3	1.6	25	2.0	20	2.2	13	2.8	25	n.a.	n.a.
Sugarcane	45.0	56.0	25	68.0	21	80.0	18	88.0	10	94.0	6

n.a. Not available.

a. Nitrogen, phosphorus, and potash; kilograms per hectare.

b. Includes change from broadcast to transplanting.

c. All wheat is HYV already.

d. Fertilizer doses of 50, 100, and 150 kilograms per hectare for packages 2b, 3a, and 3b, respectively.

Source: World Bank data.

Table A16. *Pakistan: Cropping Intensity by Irrigation Status and Farm Size, 1972*

Farm size (acres)	Average cropping intensity		
	Irrigated farms[a]	Unirrigated farms	All farms
0.0–1.0	159	141	152
1.0–2.5	144	121	137
2.5–5.0	138	110	131
5.0–7.5	133	101	125
7.5–12.5	125	96	119
12.5–25.0	118	92	111
25.0–50.0	113	87	103
50.0–150.0	112	86	97
150+	105	70	88
All	120	92	110

a. Cropping intensities of farms with over 76 percent of their cultivated area irrigated.

Source: Pakistan, Ministry of Food and Agriculture (1975), table 24.

Table A17. *India: Statewide Cropping Intensities by Farm Size, 1970–71*

Farm size (hectares)	Maharashtra	Punjab	Tamil Nadu	West Bengal
<0.5	110.1	164.1	127.9	129.0
0.5–1.0	109.6	161.6	123.1	127.8
1.0–2.0	107.9	159.6	120.0	127.0
2.0–3.0	106.9	158.2	118.2	126.6
3.0–4.0	106.4	157.0	117.3	124.6
4.0–5.0	105.8	155.5	116.4	124.7
5.0–10.0	105.2	151.2	115.5	122.1
10.0–20.0	104.5	143.4	113.7	119.6
20.0–30.0	104.1	135.7	111.8	116.4
30.0–40.0	103.8	132.2	111.0	123.6
40.0–50.0	103.3	131.7	110.3	n.a.
50.0+	103.1	142.3	109.0	101.3

n.a. Not available.

Source: Nairain and Roy (1980), table 12.

Table A18. *South Asia: Irrigated Area and Estimates of Additional Potential*
(millions of hectares)

Country and year	Surface irrigation	Tubewell irrigation	Other	Total
Bangladesh				
1985 irrigated area	0	5.1[a]	—	5.1[b]
1987 estimates of				
additional potential	11.6[c]	—	7.0	18.6
India				
1970–71 irrigated area	30.2	12.2	29.5	71.9
1980 estimates of				
additional potential	46.4	7.7[a]	—	54.1
Pakistan				
1972 irrigated area	24.0	5.1	3.8	32.9
Estimates of additional				
potential by 1990	1.2	7.9[a]	—	9.1

a. Includes "Other" also.

b. Estimated from World Bank (1987b), p. 55.

c. Includes tubewells also.

Sources: Pakistan, Ministry of Food, Agriculture, and Rural Development (1978); India, Ministry of Agriculture and Irrigation (1975) and (1976), pt. 5, table 15.6; FAO (1977); and World Bank data.

Table A19. *India: Irrigation Summary*

(millions of hectares)

Item	Surface irrigation		Minor surface	Total area utilized	Ground-water	Total irrigated area utilized
	Major and medium					
	Potential	Utilization				
Ultimate potential	58	58	15	73	40	113
Position at the end of:						
1950–51	9.7	9.7	6.4	16.1	6.5	22.6
1st plan	12.2	11.0	6.4	17.4	7.6	25.0
2nd plan	14.3	13.0	6.5	19.5	8.3	27.8
3rd plan	16.6	15.2	6.5	21.7	10.5	32.2
Annual plans, 1966–69	18.1	16.8	6.5	23.3	12.5	35.8
4th plan	20.7	18.7	7.0	25.7	16.5	42.2
5th plan	24.8	21.2	7.5	28.7	19.8	48.5
Annual plans						
1978–80	26.6	22.3	8.0	30.6	22.0	52.6
1980–81	27.5	23.0	8.2	31.2	23.2	54.4
1981–82	28.5	24.4	8.4	32.8	24.5	57.3
1982–83 (estimate)	29.4	25.3	8.6	33.9	25.7	59.6
1984–85 (target)	32.3	27.9	9.0	36.9	29.0	65.9
Average annual increase						
1st plan	0.5	0.3	n.a.	0.3	0.2	0.5
2nd plan	0.4	0.4	0.0	0.4	0.1	0.5
3rd plan	0.5	0.4	n.a.	0.4	0.4	0.8
Annual plans, 1966–69	0.5	0.5	n.a.	0.5	0.7	1.2
4th plan	0.5	0.4	0.1	0.5	0.8	1.3
5th plan	1.0	0.6	0.1	0.7	0.8	1.5
Annual plans						
1978–80	0.9	0.7	0.2	0.9	1.1	2.0
1980–81	0.9	0.7	0.2	0.9	1.2	2.1
1981–82	1.0	1.4	0.2	1.6	1.3	2.9
1982–83 (estimate)	0.9	0.9	0.2	1.1	1.2	2.3
1984–85 (target)	1.1	1.1	0.2	1.3	1.4	2.1

n.a. Not available.

Source: World Bank data.

Table A20. India: Distribution of Loans by Farm Size and Source for HYV and Non-HYV Farmers
(percent)

Source	HYV (farm size in acres)					Non-HYV (farm size in acres)				
	0–5	5–10	10–15	15+	All holdings	0–5	5–10	10–15	15+	All holdings
Government	17.0	34.0	15.1	15.3	81.4	9.4	2.5	0.7	6.0	18.6
Cooperatives	10.9	15.7	9.3	26.1	62.0	11.8	11.2	5.6	9.4	38.0
Commercial banks	9.0	18.4	0.2	7.1	34.7	2.9	5.9	28.6	27.9	65.3
Moneylenders	7.6	8.5	8.5	4.7	29.3	33.3	21.1	6.7	9.6	70.7
Friends, relatives	9.6	3.4	1.3	70.8	85.1	9.4	3.0	0.4	2.1	14.9
All	9.0	10.4	7.1	22.8	49.3	21.7	13.9	6.5	8.6	50.7

Sources: Surjit Bhalla in Berry and Cline (1979); ILO and World Bank data.

Table A21. *India: Average Rates of Interest by Farm Size and HYV Classification*
(percent a year)

Farm size (acres)	HYV growers	Non-HYV growers	All
0–5	13.9	18.6	17.3
5–15	12.3	14.8	13.8
15–25	11.6	12.7	12.2
25+	9.7	13.0	11.8
All	12.4	15.8	14.5

Sources: Surjit Bhalla in Berry and Cline (1979); ILO and World Bank data.

Table A22. *India: Adoption of High-Yielding Wheat Varieties, 1968–71*

Farm size (hectares)	1968–69	1969–70	1970–71	Percentage gain, 1968–69 to 1970–71
Percentage of farmers using HYVs				
<2	26	27	37	42
2–6	30	35	38	26
6–10	31	43	47	51
10+	34	36	40	17
All	29	34	39	34
Percentage of sown area under HYVs				
<2	15.8	11.7	18.5	17
2–6	13.1	11.4	15.8	20
6–10	13.5	12.9	17.7	31
10+	10.5	9.4	17.0	62
All	13.7	11.5	17.1	25

Source: NCAER cited in Roy and Sanderson (1972).

Table A23. *India: Rate of Adoption of HYV Wheat by Farm Size, Muzaffarnagar, Uttar Pradesh, 1967 and 1972*

Farm size (hectares)	Percentage of adopters		Percentage of cultivated land under HYVs	
	1967	*1972*	*1967*	*1972*
<2.88	26.7	95.1	18.6	48.3
2.88–4.71	45.7	99.0	12.7	40.7
4.72–6.96	59.4	100.0	13.8	39.5
6.97–10.65	66.7	98.2	11.8	37.5
10.65+	66.7	100.0	9.8	40.0
All	44.0	97.5	15.4	41.3

Source: Roshan Singh (1973).

Table A24. *India: Adoption of HYV Wheat by Farm Size, Ferozepur, Punjab, 1967–72*

Farm size (hectares)	1967–68	1968–69	1969–70	1971–72
		Percentage of adopters		
Small (<6)	14.3	42.9	88.9	100.0
Medium (6–14)	7.4	78.6	81.8	100.0
Large (14+)	11.1	77.8	80.0	100.0
		Percentage of land under HYV		
Small (<6)	55.0	86.9	94.6	100.0
Medium (6–14)	42.1	92.7	100.0	100.0
Large (14+)	44.1	93.8	98.2	100.0

Source: Kahlon and Singh (1973).

Table A25. *India: Percentage of Land under HYV Wheat by Farm Size, Kota, Uttar Pradesh, 1968–69 and 1971–72*

Farm size (acres)	1968–69	1971–72
<5	29.6	91.3
5–10	22.1	83.9
10–15	20.6	79.7
15–20	17.7	75.8
20–30	28.7	75.7
30–40	38.7	98.3
40–60	12.7	65.6
60+	23.4	61.0

Source: Bapna (1973).

Table A26. *India: Percentage of Nonadopters of HYV Rice by Farm Size, West Godavari, Andhra Pradesh, 1972*

Farm size (hectares)	Percentage
<1	65.5
1–2	47.6
2–3	35.1
3–4	9.1
4–6	15.0
6+	4.4

Source: Parthasarathy (1973).

Table A27. *India: Percentage of Cultivators Growing HYV Wheat by Size of Holding, Selected Districts*

District, state, and year	Size of holding (hectares)					
	0–1	*1–2*	*2–4*	*4–8*	*8–20*	*20+*
Ludhiana, Punjab						
1967–68	50	100	96	100	100	100
1969–70	93	93	96	97	98	100
1972–73	100	100	100	100	100	100
1974–75	100	100	100	100	100	100
Rohtak, Haryana						
1967–68	0	10	11	22	56	56
1969–70	25	30	82	85	97	100
1972–73	10	98	100	100	100	100
1974–75	73	84	94	99	100	100
Muzaffarnagar, Uttar Pradesh						
1968–69	53	80	82	83	94	100
1969–70	37	72	78	95	94	100
1972–73	100	100	100	100	100	100
1974–75	100	100	100	100	100	100
Gaya, Bihar						
1967–68	43	68	63	89	100	100
1969–70	45	88	94	94	75	50
1972–73	82	91	99	100	100	100
1974–75	95	99	100	100	100	100

Source: Compiled from data in India, Planning Commission (1976).

Table A28. *India: Percentage of Irrigated Wheat Area Sown to HYV Wheat by Size of Holding, Selected Districts*

District, state, and year	Size of holding (hectares)					
	0–1	*1–2*	*2–4*	*4–8*	*8–20*	*20+*
Ludhiana, Punjab						
1967–68	n.a.	89	68	61	82	100
1969–70	100	100	85	99	100	100
1972–73	100	100	100	100	100	100
1973–74	100	100	100	100	97	100
Rohtak, Haryana						
1967–68	n.a.	100	49	53	47	100
1969–70	n.a.	100	97	94	96	n.a.
1972–73	n.a.	100	73	52	89	100
1974–75	80	81	86	75	100	n.a.
Muzaffarnagar, Uttar Pradesh						
1969–70	82	47	47	25	18	100
1972–73	100	100	100	100	100	100
1974–75	100	100	100	100	100	100
Gaya, Bihar						
1967–68	55	46	41	27	30	100
1969–70	47	77	50	15	65	100
1972–73	92	88	70	100	100	n.a.
1974–75	100	100	100	100	n.a.	100

	Size of holding (acres)							
	0–5	*5–10*	*10–15*	*15–20*	*20–30*	*30–40*	*40–60*	*60+*
Kota, Rajasthan								
1968–69	30	22	21	18	29	39	13	23
1971–72	91	84	80	76	76	98	66	61

n.a. Not available.

Sources: Compiled from data in India, Planning Commission (1976) and Bapna (1973).

Table A29. *India: Percentage of Cultivators Growing HYV Paddy by Size of Holding, Selected Districts*

District, state, and year	Size of holding (hectares)					
	0–1	*1–2*	*2–4*	*4–8*	*8–20*	*20+*
West Godavari, Andhra Pradesh						
1967–68[a]	4	3	4	10	25	43
1969–70[a]	62	78	75	58	86	100
1972–73	88	85	93	89	100	67
1974–75	100	100	100	100	100	100
Shahabad, Bihar						
1967–68	40	65	71	63	75	100
1969–70	57	88	94	88	93	100
1972–73	14	27	67	70	91	100
1974–75	20	23	52	52	57	n.a.
Palghat, Kerala						
1967–68	0	3	9	8	67	100
1969–70	9	53	56	71	67	100
1972–73	60	80	79	93	100	100
1974–75	65	84	93	100	100	100
Coimbatore, Tamil Nadu						
1967–68[a]	36	48	50	64	83	100
1969–70[a]	55	51	46	71	83	100
1972–73	100	100	100	100	100	100
1974–75	81	85	86	92	100	100
Thana, Maharashtra						
1967–68[b]	21	32	34	32	25	n.a.
1969–70[b]	23	43	45	36	25	50
1972–73	25	47	55	78	92	n.a.
1974–75	39	39	35	53	50	n.a.
Shimoga, Karnataka						
1967–68[a]	36	25	46	44	67	n.a.
1969–70[a]	65	61	75	89	89	n.a.
1972–73	33	32	55	79	100	n.a.
1974–75	46	45	51	70	100	n.a.

(Table continues on the following page.)

Table A29 *(continued)*

District, state, and year	Size of holding (hectares)					
	0–1	*1–2*	*2–4*	*4–8*	*8–20*	*20+*
Cuttack, Orissa						
1967–68[b]	n.a.	n.a.	14	n.a.	n.a.	n.a.
1969–70[b]	27	26	57	50	n.a.	n.a.
1972–73	98	100	100	100	n.a.	n.a.
1974–75	54	98	100	100	100	n.a.
Basti, Uttar Pradesh						
1967–68[b]	1	26	62	29	75	100
1969–70[b]	49	83	79	71	75	100
1972–73	100	100	100	100	100	n.a.
1974–75	68	91	93	90	100	n.a.
Midnapur, West Bengal						
1967–68[b]	5	8	40	25	100	n.a.
1969–70[b]	15	33	67	40	100	n.a.
1972–73	58	48	65	67	100	n.a.
1974–75	55	60	60	75	100	n.a.

	Size of holding (acres)			
	0–1.99	*2–4.99*	*5–9.99*	*10+*
Surat, Gujarat				
1968–69	0	4	21	20
1969–70	0	46	43	36
1970–71	50	74	61	82
1971–72	65	65	61	82
1972–73	55	74	71	82

n.a. Not available.
a. Rabi season only.
b. Kharif season only.
Sources: Compiled from India, Planning Commission (1976) and Schluter (1973).

Table A30. *India: Percentage of Total Paddy Area Sown to HYV Rice by Size of Holding, Selected Districts*

District, state, and year	Size of holding (hectares)				
	0–1	*1–2*	*2–4*	*4–8*	*8–20*
West Godavari, Andhra Pradesh					
1972–73	74	74	68	64	51
1974–75	55	57	64	66	78
Shahabad, Bihar					
1972–73	40	37	30	23	15
1974–75	n.a.	1	3	8	1
Palghat, Kerala					
1972–73	74	65	72	63	88
1974–75	25	21	27	26	50
Coimbatore, Tamil Nadu					
1972–73	91	94	61	93	n.a.
1974–75	97	96	100	100	n.a.
Thana, Maharashtra					
1972–73	42	33	26	15	34
1974–75	13	20	7	4	n.a.
Shimoga, Karnataka					
1972–73	95	56	70	61	64
1974–75	19	19	42	37	n.a.
Cuttack, Orissa					
1972–73	33	18	13	10	n.a.
1974–75	25	20	22	2	n.a.
Amritsar, Punjab					
1972–73	n.a.	93	83	89	93
1974–75	n.a.	89	96	90	92
Basti, Uttar Pradesh					
1972–73	64	42	60	3	n.a.
1974–75	43	28	39	21	n.a.
Midnapur, West Bengal					
1972–73	39	23	10	3	29
1974–75	29	21	13	8	n.a.

n.a. Not available.

Source: Compiled from data in India, Planning Commission (1976).

Table A31. *Pakistan: Percentage of Crop Area Sown with HYVs by Farm Size, 1972–73*

District and farm size (acres)	Mexi-Pak wheat	IRRI rice	Improved cotton	Improved maize
Jhelum	21.1	—	—	—
<12.50	—	—	—	—
12.50–25.00	—	—	—	—
25.00–50.00	—	—	—	—
>50.00	66.7	—	—	—
Gujranwala	97.2	50.3	—	—
<12.50	98.8	48.7	—	—
12.50–25.00	94.9	36.5	—	—
25.00–50.00	98.0	46.3	—	—
>50.00	95.1	63.2	—	—
Sahiwal	89.1	8.7	92.6	100.0
<12.50	83.3	1.3	91.6	100.0
12.50–25.00	82.0	5.8	87.6	100.0
25.00–50.00	84.1	16.0	93.5	100.0
>50.00	94.8	7.2	98.0	100.0
Lyallpur	100.0	—	100.0	97.8
<12.50	100.0	—	100.0	87.0
12.50–25.00	100.0	—	100.0	94.8
25.00–50.00	100.0	—	100.0	100.0
>50.00	100.0	—	100.0	100.0
Rahimyar Khan	79.5	1.9	83.7	—
<12.50	65.8	—	74.8	—
12.50–25.00	70.7	33.3	82.1	—
25.00–50.00	67.4	—	89.8	—
>50.00	96.1	—	82.6	—
Punjab	91.7	31.0	93.7	98.8
Jacobabad	64.5	15.8	100.0	—
<12.50	—	2.0	—	—
12.50–25.00	44.4	—	—	—
25.00–50.00	72.3	18.2	—	—
>50.00	70.4	21.0	100.0	—
Larkana	—	98.1	—	—
<12.50	—	100.0	—	—
12.50–25.00	—	100.0	—	—
25.00–50.00	—	97.7	—	—
>50.00	—	97.6	—	—

Table A31 *(continued)*

District and farm size (acres)	Mexi-Pak wheat	IRRI rice	Improved cotton	Improved maize
Nawabshah	46.1	—	91.8	—
<12.50	29.6	—	73.4	—
12.50–25.00	64.8	—	79.9	—
25.00–50.00	48.5	—	100.0	—
>50.00	42.2	—	93.5	—
Hyderabad	100.0	95.9	88.2	—
<12.50	100.0	93.1	90.7	—
12.50–25.00	100.0	98.7	87.8	—
25.00–50.00	100.0	92.8	82.9	—
>50.00	100.0	94.8	89.2	—
Sind	89.6	61.4	90.8	—

— Not applicable.

Source: M. H. Khan (1975), p. 20. Reprinted with permission.

Table A32. *Bangladesh: HYV Paddy Adoption by Farm Size, Four Villages*

Size of holding (acres)	Number of holdings	Adopters[a] (1)	HYV area[a] (2)	Index of participation (1) × (2)
Very small (< 1)	127	25.2	31.3	7.8
Small (1–3)	267	53.9	22.6	11.9
Lower medium (3–5)	168	63.4	18.4	11.7
Upper medium (5–7.5)	46	73.9	14.3	10.6
Large (7.5+)	20	50.0	14.3	7.2
All	628	52.0	18.5	9.6

a. As a percentage of all paddy cultivators or total paddy area.

Source: Asaduzzaman and Islam (1976).

Table A33. Eastern India: Rice Yields by Farm Size in Three Districts, 1971–72
(kilograms per hectare)

Farm size (hectares)	Burdwan			Shahabad			Farm size (hectares)	Sambalpur		
	Local	HYV	Percentage increase	Local	HYV	Percentage increase		Local	HYV	Percentage increase
0.01–1.0	2,152	3,543	64.6	1,977	3,163	60.0	0.1–2.50	1,483	3,875	161.3
1.01–2.0	2,686	4,117	53.3	1,636	—	—	2.51–5.00	1,483	3,800	156.2
2.01–3.0	2,392	4,186	75.0	1,648	2,735	66.0	5.01–7.50	—	3,753	—
3.01–4.0	2,471	3,370	36.4	1,480	2,511	70.0	7.51–10.0	2,224	3,845	72.9
4.01–6.0	2,236	4,193	87.5	1,510	2,382	57.8	10.01–15.00	1,977	2,849	44.1
6.01–8.0	2,511	3,188	27.0	1,761	2,261	28.4	15.01–21.00	—	3,489	—
8.01–10.0	—	—	—	1,441	2,459	70.6	21.01–25.00	—	3,123	—
10.01–12.0	—	—	—	1,574	2,337	48.5	25+	2,471	4,359	76.4
All	2,414	3,926	62.6	1,587	2,434	53.4	All	2,152	3,558	65.3

— Not applicable.
Source: Mandal and Ghosh (1976).

Table A34. *India: Application of Chemical Fertilizer on HYV Wheat Crops by Size Group, 1967–69*
(kilograms per acre)

State and district	Size group			
	I	*II*	*III*	*IV*
Punjab				
Amritsar	260	213	243	232
Ferozepur	155	135	133	131
Ludhiana	250	278	301	254
Patiala	187	172	227	183
Haryana				
Hissar	204	167	197	159
Rohtak	105	134	99	154
Uttar Pradesh				
Aligarh	93	123	147	148
Allahabad	253	277	279	284
Basti	98	154	229	346
Muzaffarnagar	123	237	240	292
Saharanpur	207	269	272	275
Sitapur	145	139	163	269
Rajasthan				
Sriganganagar	116	156	176	252
Bihar				
Gaya	122	126	140	144

Note: The chemical fertilizer consists of nitrogen, phosphorus, and potash. The size groups are as follows: I, the smallest 30 percent (deciles 1–3); II, the next 30 percent (deciles 4–6); III, the next 30 percent (deciles 7–9); IV, the largest 10 percent.

Source: India, Planning Commission (1971).

Table A35. *India: Application of Chemical Fertilizer on HYV Paddy Crops by Size Group, 1967–69*
(kilograms per acre)

	Size group			
State and district	*I*	*II*	*III*	*IV*
Tamil Nadu				
Coimbatore	286	182	163	225
North Arcot	48	156	100	90
Thanjavur	30	51	85	66
Karnataka				
Shimoga	189	129	185	135
Orissa				
Cuttack	0	123	11	116
Sambalpur	159	168	377	207
West Bengal				
Burdwan	100	139	84	129
Hooghly	94	162	148	191
Midnapur	105	169	182	307
Kerala				
Palghat	50	158	156	80
Trichur	34	111	65	297
Andhra Pradesh				
Krishna	224	270	208	442
Nellore	0	0	173	128
Nizamabad	344	210	266	238
West Godavari	251	149	181	159
Uttar Pradesh				
Basti	164	247	300	259
Varanasi	8	161	221	27
Punjab				
Amritsar	0	279	284	116
Bihar				
Gaya	92	48	76	167
Shahabad	169	232	220	173
Maharashtra				
Bhandara	11	52	71	107
Thana	72	109	87	103

Note: The chemical fertilizer consists of nitrogen, phosphorus, and potash. Size groups are defined in table A34.

Source: India, Planning Commission (1971).

Table A36. *India: Percentage of Fertilizer to Total Cropped Area,*
1975–76

Zone and state	\<1	1–2	2–4	4–10	10+	All
			Size of farm (hectares)			
Northern						
Haryana	45.0	46.7	38.6	47.8	64.2	48.7
Himachal Pradesh	21.1	32.6	28.9	31.2	70.0	27.6
Jammu and Kashmir	38.9	27.1	24.8	19.7	—	28.5
Punjab	63.4	69.0	74.9	78.8	76.8	76.3
Western						
Gujarat	45.9	39.9	46.7	41.9	43.4	43.1
Maharashtra	28.0	32.8	25.1	27.8	26.5	27.3
Central						
Madhya Pradesh	2.9	5.1	8.9	11.6	15.6	10.8
Rajasthan	11.8	19.4	24.0	25.3	16.2	20.1
Uttar Pradesh	22.7	28.6	37.8	52.0	54.5	52.1
Eastern						
Assam[a]	5.4	3.8	3.5	3.4	57.5	4.9
Bihar	24.1	34.2	40.3	37.8	36.7	35.3
Orissa	8.3	15.7	19.0	23.6	47.1	20.7
West Bengal	47.8	47.6	53.9	49.5	15.7	49.8
Southern						
Andhra Pradesh	47.5	46.7	49.2	38.8	32.7	41.7
Karnataka	46.0	43.0	40.4	26.6	26.5	33.4
Kerala	69.4	78.9	69.6	100.0	—	72.6
Tamil Nadu	60.6	53.9	56.5	51.4	37.8	55.4

— Not applicable.

a. Includes Manipur, Meghalaya, and Tripura.

Source: NCAER (1978).

Table A37. *India: Fertilizer Use by Size of Holding in Various States,*
1975–76
(kilograms per hectare)

Zone and state	Size of farm (hectares)					
	<1	*1–2*	*2–4*	*4–10*	*10+*	*All*
Northern						
Haryana	54.6	64.2	57.0	74.5	98.2	76.6
Himachal Pradesh	41.7	26.0	20.9	22.3	17.3	28.5
Jammu and Kashmir	45.6	50.8	47.0	34.4	—	47.0
Punjab	88.1	80.3	90.9	90.8	93.6	90.8
Western						
Gujarat	78.7	64.7	59.7	43.1	34.7	45.8
Maharashtra	90.5	95.8	85.4	75.3	63.3	77.3
Central						
Madhya Pradesh	72.1	66.9	55.4	41.3	41.9	46.5
Rajasthan	59.2	55.6	57.9	59.0	48.1	55.5
Uttar Pradesh	73.5	66.0	65.4	65.6	47.7	64.6
Eastern						
Assam[a]	69.1	51.2	56.2	50.1	15.4	49.4
Bihar	64.7	50.8	45.7	45.4	49.3	49.7
Orissa	86.9	71.5	77.6	97.3	111.5	90.8
West Bengal	100.0	103.6	77.3	65.9	177.5	89.5
Southern						
Andhra Pradesh	109.0	118.5	115.9	117.4	85.6	111.7
Karnataka	169.1	131.7	106.3	97.4	39.3	104.6
Kerala	93.4	88.6	73.4	171.4	—	92.0
Tamil Nadu	133.5	133.0	122.5	120.5	127.3	128.1

— Not applicable.
a. Includes Manipur, Meghalaya, and Tripura.
Source: NCAER (1978).

Table A38. India: Percentage of Area Fertilized and Fertilizer Use per Hectare for Irrigated Paddy by Size of Holding in Selected States

| | | | Size of holding (hectares) | | | | | |
| | | | < 1 | | 1–2 | | 10+ | |
Crop	Season[a]	State	Use[b]	Percent[c]	Use[b]	Percent[c]	Use[b]	Percent[c]
Irrigated HYV paddy	K	Haryana	100.0	88	94.4	98.0	119.8	99.0
	K	Punjab	103.1	57	87.3	72.0	114.6	100.0
	K	Gujarat	62.6	81	n.a.	n.a.	203.4	100.0
	K	Uttar Pradesh	47.5	27	44.8	44.0	85.1	99.0
	K(A)	Bihar	60.8	58	71.0	93.0	35.9	100.0
	K(A)	West Bengal	121.7	100	117.4	96.0	133.2	100.0
	K(A)	Andhra Pradesh	114.8	62	121.3	80.0	159.5	100.0
	K(A)	Tamil Nadu	124.3	86	130.7	96.0	297.3	100.0
	K(W)	Bihar	65.2	87	49.7	93.0	33.9	100.0
	K(W)	Andhra Pradesh	131.2	61	114.8	86.0	159.5	67.0
	K(W)	Tamil Nadu	163.4	96	148.6	99.0	75.8	100.0
	R(S)	Andhra Pradesh	136.2	65	187.8	77.0	135.6	100.0
	R(S)	Tamil Nadu	114.7	99	146.3	100.0	18.3	100.0
	R(S)	Orissa	181.3	98	174.1	100.0	243.2	100.0
Irrigated non-HYV paddy	K	Haryana	63.6	83	39.9	86.0	79.0	100.0
	K	Gujarat	60.1	71	68.6	61.0	50.1	100.0
	K	Maharashtra	105.3	64	71.2	62.0	49.5	22.0
	K	Andhra Pradesh	34.6	1	78.8	23.0	29.7	72.0
	K	Rajasthan	143.3	6	63.1	32.0	56.8	100.0
	K	Uttar Pradesh	53.7	22	47.7	32.0	30.7	5.0

(Table continues on the following page.)

Table A38 (continued)

| Crop | Season[a] | State | Size of holding (hectares) | | | | | |
| | | | < 1 | | 1–2 | | 10+ | |
			Use[b]	Percent[c]	Use[b]	Percent[c]	Use[b]	Percent[c]
Irrigated non-HYV paddy	K(A)	Andhra Pradesh	109.9	85	73.3	63.0	80.8	100.0
	K(A)	Karnataka	194.8	86	170.7	88.0	95.9	100.0
	K(W)	Bihar	64.0	37	44.2	54.0	67.5	70.0
	K(W)	Orissa	42.3	17	42.3	14.0	28.7	94.0
	K(W)	Andhra Pradesh	90.0	68	102.6	82.0	93.7	60.0
	K(W)	Tamil Nadu	162.0	67	142.5	78.0	140.8	100.0
	R(S)	Andhra Pradesh	117.5	85	108.5	78.0	26.7	100.0
	R(S)	Tamil Nadu	147.5	82	130.2	97.0	156.1	100.0
Unirrigated non-HYV paddy	K	Gujarat	98.6	33	38.4	55.0	18.7	86.0
	K	Maharashtra	80.3	33	48.6	36.0	63.2	68.0
	K	Madhya Pradesh	54.4	1	22.5	4.0	23.8	33.0
	K	Uttar Pradesh	21.8	12	30.2	2.0	34.3	15.0
	K(A)	Orissa	24.4	8	27.5	11.0	6.9	17.0
	K(A)	Karnataka	90.7	21	76.7	21.0	114.9	100.0
	K(A)	Tamil Nadu	77.0	32	47.1	15.0	25.2	100.0
	K(W)	Bihar	33.6	13	25.0	30.0	9.2	27.0
	K(W)	Orissa	29.8	2	34.1	12.0	65.5	21.0
	K(W)	Karnataka	79.7	98	51.9	100.0	21.1	100.0

n.a. Not available.

a. K, kharif; A, autumn; W, winter; S, summer; R, rabi.
b. Fertilizer use in kilograms per hectare.
c. Percentage of area fertilized.
Source: NCAER (1978).

Table A39. Pakistan: Use of Fertilizers, 1974
(bags per acre)

Size of holding (acres)	Mexi-Pak wheat crop						
	Jhelum	Gujranwala	Sahiwal	Lyallpur	Rahimyar Khan	Nawabshah	Hyderabad
<12.5	—	0.7	1.7	0.9	2.5	1.7	1.3
12.5–25.0	—	1.0	1.6	1.5	1.9	1.6	2.3
25.0–50.0	—	1.4	1.6	2.1	2.4	1.6	1.7
50.0+	0.1	1.0	1.7	2.0	3.6	1.6	2.6

	IRRI rice crop					
	Gujranwala	Sahiwal	Rahimyar Khan	Jacobabad	Larkana	Hyderabad
<12.5	0.5	1.0	n.a.	0.5	1.4	0.7
12.5–25.0	1.2	2.2	2.0	0.8	1.5	0.8
25.0–50.0	1.0	1.6	n.a.	0.8	1.4	1.4
50.0+	1.0	2.2	n.a.	0.4	1.4	1.4

— Not applicable.
n.a. Not available.
Source: M. H. Khan (1975), pp. 160–77. Reprinted with permission.

Table 40. *India: Poverty, Production, and Prices in Rural Punjab, including Haryana*

| Year | Percentage of population below the poverty line | | | Per capita food-grain production (kilograms)[a] | CPIAL[b] (1960–61 = 100) |
	Below	Well below	Far below		
1963–64	39.49	31.42	20.63	346	114
1964–65	41.12	30.35	18.57	422	139
1965–66	40.89	32.93	19.06	313	138
1966–67	38.52	30.53	18.78	386	174
1967–68	44.58	36.18	24.02	527	193
1968–69	34.03	26.22	15.13	512	193
1969–70	37.86	30.25	16.19	627	196
1970–71	35.44	27.42	13.80	648	194
1971–72	31.31	24.60	15.26	662	205
1972–73	25.18	18.64	9.52	616	228
1973–74	34.00	25.26	13.79	597	273

a. Per capita food-grain production has been calculated by dividing total estimated food-grain production of Punjab (including Haryana) by its total rural population.

b. Consumer price index for agricultural laborers.

Source: Mundle (1982).

Table A41. *India: Annual Income of Agricultural Labor Households in Punjab, including Haryana*

Agricultural labor households	1956–57	1964–65	1974–75
Money income (current rupees)			
With land	626	987	4,773
Without land	656	917	3,388
All households	731	928	3,508
Real income (rupees at 1956–57 prices)			
With land	626	705	1,404
Without land	656	655	996
All households	731	663	1,032
Average size of household			
With land	n.a.	5.9	6.6
Without land	n.a.	5.4	5.6
All households	5.2	5.5	5.7
Per capita real income (rupees at 1956–57 prices)			
With land	n.a.	119	213
Without land	n.a.	121	178
All households	141	121	181

n.a. Not available.

Note: The annual income of all households in 1956–57 is larger than for households with and without land because the latter pertain to casual labor households only. The real incomes have been calculated using the consumer price index for agricultural laborers as deflator and 1956–57 as base. For 1974–75 Punjab and Haryana data have been combined using the number of households in the relevant category as weights.

Source: Mundle (1982).

Table A42. South Asia: Summary of Land Reform Legislation

Region	Major legislation and period	Summary enactment and salient features
North India		
Uttar Pradesh	Land Reform Act (1977) Zamindari Abolition Acts (1950–58)	Ceiling (100–200 acres); compensation for resumption of land *Zamindars* compensated up to eight times net assets with rehabilitation grant
Punjab and Haryana	Four acts (1952–54)	Approximately 650,000 occupancy tenants acquired 2 million acres with the abolition of rent-receiving intermediaries and compensation of landowners
Himachal Pradesh	Punjab and East Punjab States Union Acts (1952–54) and another in 1971	Government compensated *zamindars* according to land revenue, conferring proprietary rights on tenants
West India		
Rajasthan	Land Reform and Resumption of Jagirs Act (1952) with subsequent amendments	Problematic implementation in princely and religious estate holdings; staged resumption of all *jagirs*; erstwhile tenants elevated through registration
Maharashtra	Series of seventeen acts (1949–58)	Abolition of *ryots* and various kinds of land grants; compensation dependent upon intermediary interests forgone
Madhya Pradesh	Abolition of proprietary rights (1950)	*Zamindari* and *jagirdari* abolished; staged compensation with minimal or no rehabilitation grant
Gujarat	Numerous acts for Saurashtra and Bombay states (1949–62)	Abolition of intermediaries, upgrading of tenant cultivators to occupancy status with no payments for occupancy rights

South India

Tamil Nadu	Series of twelve acts (1948–72)	Abolition of intermediaries with multiple compensations based on returns from estates
Pakistan	Muslim League Agrarian Committee (1949) and Punjab and Sind Tenancy Acts (1950)	Abolition of *jagirs*; ownership to tenants; security of tenure; fixation of rent; land over ceilings (150–450 acres) resumed by state with compensation; redistribution to tillers and smallholders (<12.5 acres)
	Land Reform Regulation no. 64 (1959)	Ceiling (500–1,000 acres) based on land productivity; resumption and redistribution of excess land; abolition of *jagirs*; tenant security; consolidation of holdings
	Land Reform Regulation no. 115 (1972)	Ceiling (150–300 acres) based on productivity; no eviction without cause, no compensation for resumed land; tenants have first choice on sale

Note: A *ryot* is a landowner who pays land taxes or rent directly to the state. A *jagir* is a land grant awarded by states for services rendered.
Sources: M. H. Khan (1981); Abdullah (1976); India, Ministry of Agriculture and Irrigation (1976).

Table A43. South Asia: Summary of Provisions on Rent Control and Security of Tenure

State	Fixation of rent	Security of tenure
Bangladesh	Yes	Government acquires rent-receiving interests for tenants-at-will.
North India		
Jammu and Kashmir	1/4 of produce on wetland, 1/3 of produce on dryland if landlord holds under 12.5 acres	Tenants have secure tenure subject to landlord's right of resumption. Tenants in possession have right of purchase.
Himachal Pradesh	1/4 of produce	Tenants whose landlords pay more than Rs125 a year in revenue have security. Landlord resumption privilege has expired. Non-occupancy tenants of small landowners have little security.
Punjab	1/3 of gross produce	Security of tenure subject to landlord right of resumption (expired) leaving tenant 5 standard acres. Tenants have purchase option in some areas.
Uttar Pradesh	No; no official leasing although *batai*[a] is practiced, and payment is 1/2 of output	Tenancy abolished except for those with *batai*, who have no security of tenure.
West India		
Gujarat	Lesser of 1/6 of gross produce or 2 to 5 times assessment	Tillers deemed to be owners. Many unable or unwilling to purchase at 20 to 200 times assessment. Resumption for personal cultivation by landlord restricted to half the holdings except for surrendered land.
Rajasthan	1/6 of gross produce	Some tenants have fixity of tenure. Security of tenants of *khudkasht* (personal land of landlords) and subtenants subject to resumption (expired), which left tenant 15.6 to 125 acres.
Madhya Pradesh	2 to 4 times assessment	All tenants are occupancy tenants. Tenure is secure but subject to landlord resumption (expired). Tenant to be left with at least 25 acres depending on length of lease and class of land.
Maharashtra	Lesser of 1/6 of produce or 2 to 5 times assessment	Compulsory transfer except in Vidharba area. Many purchases by tenants are "ineffective." Efforts to confer ownership may have decreased security.

372

	Rent	Tenure and security
South India		
Karnataka	1/5 to 1/4 of produce depending on land class	Tenure is fixed subject to landlord resumption of up to half the leased area.
Kerala	Paddy land 1/8 to 1/4 of produce; garden 1/10 to 1/3; dry land 1/8 for cultivated; Rs4.00 per acre for other land	Tenure for all tenants permanently fixed subject to landlord resumption (expired). Tenants purchase ownership for 16 times fair rent.
Madras	40% of *normal* gross produce for wetland; 33.3% of normal gross produce for dry-land (for less than 3/4 of normal yields, rent may be reduced)	Interim act (1955) forbidding eviction expired in 1965. Tenants have right to reclaim up to 6.6 acres if evicted.
Andhra Pradesh	In Andhra area 1/2 of gross produce on land irrigated by baling; in Hyderabad area lesser of 1/5 of produce or 3 to 5 times assessment; 1/2 of output on irrigated lands	In Andhra area eviction of tenants prohibited; in Hydera-bad tenants in possession 6 years protected from eviction; landlord resumption limited to 3 family holdings (expired).
East India		
Bihar	1/2 of gross produce	Tenant obtains occupancy right after 12 years of possession; under-*ryots* have little security.
Orissa	1/4 of gross produce	Fixity of tenure subject to landlord's resumption (expired) of up to half area.
West Bengal	No regulation except for *bargadars* (sharecroppers); 1/2 of produce if landlord supplies plow, manure, and seed; 40% if cropper supplies	Tenancy abolished. *Bargadars* do not have tenancy status but have security subject to owner's right to resume 2/3 of the area leased. If area is less than half an acre, owner may resume all.
Assam	1/2 of produce if landlord supplies bullocks; 1/5 of produce if tenant (*adhiar*) supplies bullocks	Rights of resumption expired 1963. Occupancy *ryots* have permanent transferable interest. Nonoccupancy *ryots* and under-*ryots* have no security.
Pakistan	Yes; rents to be paid in kind according to established tradition	Ejectment only for just cause; occupancy tenants to be made owners.

a. A *batai* is an arrangement under which tenants exchange their labor and a share of the output for use of the land.
Source: Wunderlich (1970), pp. 40–42.

Table A44. *South Asia: Statewide Legislation on Ceiling on Holdings,*
1969–74

(hectares)

Region and state	Range of ceilings per household	Operated area per rural household	Median ceiling levels[a]
Bangladesh	1.3–13.7[b]	0.6	8.7[c]
North India			
Jammu and Kashmir	n.a.	1.0	5.1
Himachal Pradesh	4.1–12.2	n.a.	8.1
Punjab	7.0–21.8	1.6	14.4
Haryana	7.3–21.8	1.9	14.5
Uttar Pradesh	7.3–18.3	1.1	12.8
West India			
Rajasthan	7.3–21.9[d]	4.1	12.6
Gujarat	4.1–21.9	2.3	13.0
Madhya Pradesh	4.1–7.3[e]	2.3	5.7
Maharashtra	7.3–19.4	2.6	13.4
South India			
Karnataka	4.1–8.2[e]	2.3	6.2
Kerala	2.4–8.1	0.3	5.3
Tamil Nadu	6.2–12.2	0.7	9.1
Andhra Pradesh	4.1–21.9	1.5	13.0
East India			
Orissa	0.8–7.3[e]	1.1	4.1
West Bengal	5.0–7.0	0.6	6.0
Bihar	6.1–18.2	0.8	12.1
Assam	6.7–8.7	0.6	7.8
Pakistan			
1959 (per person)	207–414	2.0	61.0
1972 (per person)	62 or 124		

n.a. Not available.

a. These median ceiling levels are used for the exercise on land redistribution schemes in appendix B, table B-1.

b. Originally set at 100 bighas (33.3 acres) per household in 1950, raised to 375 bighas in 1961, and reset at 100 bighas in 1972.

c. The median size of 8.7 hectares is too large, so a minimum value of 1.3 hectares was used to construct alternative scenarios for Bangladesh in appendix B, table B-1.

d. Desert land is excluded.

e. Based on the standard acre (approximately 1 acre of wetland).

Sources: India, Ministry of Agriculture and Irrigation (1976), pp. 135–44; M. H. Khan (1981); Abdullah (1976).

Table A45. *India: Fragmentation of Operational Holdings by State,*
1960–61

	Number of fragments per operational holding		
State	*All size classes*	*2.5–4.9 acres*	*5.0–7.5 acres*
Andhra Pradesh	4.32	4.32	5.03
Assam	2.75	2.96	3.50
Bihar	7.18	8.04	10.97
Gujarat	4.40	3.49	4.17
Jammu and Kashmir	5.09	5.83	6.63
Kerala	2.01	3.40	3.73
Madhya Pradesh	5.30	4.31	4.95
Madras	4.96	5.40	6.58
Maharashtra	3.78	3.50	3.51
Mysore	3.79	3.18	3.85
Orissa	6.39	6.08	8.32
Punjab (including Haryana)	4.76	4.32	4.65
Rajasthan	4.27	3.66	3.89
Uttar Pradesh	7.78	8.33	9.27
West Bengal	7.12	7.48	10.02
All India	5.66	6.05	6.79

Source: Minhas (in Srinivasan and Bardhan 1974), tables 3 and 4.

Bibliography

Abdullah, Abu. 1976. "Land Reform and Agrarian Change in Bangladesh." *Bangladesh Development Studies* 4 (1) January: 67–112.

Abdullah, Abu, M. Hossain, and R. Nations. 1976. "Agrarian Structure and the IRDP: Preliminary Considerations." *Bangladesh Development Studies* 4 (2) April.

Abraham, A. 1980. "Maharashtra's Employment Guarantee Scheme." *Economic and Political Weekly* 15 (32) August 9.

Abraham, S. 1973. "Cooperative Credit for Small Farmers in India." *Small Farmer Credit in South Asia.* USAID Spring Review of Small Farmer Credit. Washington, D.C.: U.S. Agency for International Development.

Acharya, K. T., and V. K. Huria. 1986. "Rural Poverty and Operation Flood." *Economic and Political Weekly* 21 (37) September 13: 1651–56.

Acharya, S. S. 1973. "Green Revolution and Farm Employment." *Indian Journal of Agricultural Economics* 28 (3).

Adams, D. W. 1973. "The Case for Voluntary Savings Mobilization: Why Rural Capital Markets Flounder." *Analytical Papers* 19. USAID Spring Review of Small Farmer Credit. Washington, D.C.: U.S. Agency for International Development.

Adams, D. W., M. L. Ong, and I. J. Singh. 1975. *Voluntary Rural Savings Capacities in Taiwan, 1960 to 1970.* Economics and Sociology Paper 175. Columbus, Ohio: Department of Agricultural Economics and Rural Sociology, Ohio State University.

ADB (Asian Development Bank). 1977. *Asian Agricultural Survey 1976: Rural Asia.* Manila.

Adnan, S. 1977. *Differentiation and Class Structure in Village Shamraj.* Village Studies Project Paper 8. Dhaka: Bangladesh Institute for Development Studies.

Adnan, S., and others. 1978. "A Review of Landlessness in Rural Bangladesh, 1877–1977." Rural Economics Program, Department of Economics, University of Chittagong, Bangladesh. August.

AERC (Agro-Economic Research Center). 1969. "A Study of High-Yielding Varieties Programme in the District of Cuttack, Orissa, with Special Reference to Credit, 1967." Vishwa-Bharati, Shantiniketan.

————. 1970a. "Evaluation of the High-Yielding Varieties Programme, Khariff, 1968: A Study of IR8 Paddy in Karnal District, Haryana." Delhi.

————. 1970b. "Report on High-Yielding Variety Programme in Paddy in Sibsagar District, 1968–69." Jorhat.

————. 1970c. "Report on the High-Yielding Varieties Programme in Varanasi District, 1968." University of Allahabad.

————. 1970d. "Report on the Study of the High-Yielding Varieties Programme (Rabi 1968–69)." Waltair: Andhra University.

————. 1972. "Study on the Problems of Marginal Farmers and Landless Agricultural Labourers in the District of Hooghly, West Bengal." Vishwa-Bharati, Shantiniketan.

————. 1974. "Study of the Small Farmers Development Agency, Nalgonda District, Andhra Pradesh (Rabi 1972–73)." Waltair: Andhra University. October.

————. 1975a. "Study on Marginal Farmers and Agricultural Labourers in Bankura, West Bengal." Vishwa-Bharati, Shantiniketan. July.

————. 1975b. "Study of the Marginal Farmers and Agricultural Labourers Development Agency, Vishakapatnam District, Andhra Pradesh (1972–73 and 1973–74)." Waltair: Andhra University. August.

————. 1975c. "Study of the Small Farmers Development Agency, Nalgonda District, Andhra Pradesh (1973–74)." Waltair: Andhra University. December.

————. 1976a. "Marginal Farmers and Agricultural Labourers in Pondicherry." University of Madras.

————. 1976b. "Report on the Evaluation Study of Small Farmers Development Agency in South Arcot District, Tamil Nadu (1972–73)." Department of Economics, University of Madras.

————. 1976c. "Study of Incomes, Savings and Investments of Selected Cultivator and Labour Households in East Godavari, Andhra Pradesh." Waltair: Andhra University.

————. 1976d. "A Study of Rural Poverty and Inequality in a Developed District (East Godavari)." Waltair: Andhra University.

————. 1976e. "Study of Small Farmers Development Agency, Ganjami, Orissa." Vishwa-Bharati, Shantiniketan.

————. 1978. *Annual Report on: (1) Farm Structure Study: 1976–77 and (2) Economic Analysis of New Farming Practices: Kharif 1976.* Jodhpur, Rajasthan: Central Arid Zone Research Institute.

Afzal, M. 1974. *The Population of Pakistan.* CICRED series. Islamabad: Pakistan Institute of Development Economics.

Agarwal, Bina. 1980a. "Effect of Agricultural Mechanization on Crop Output: A Study of Operation-wise Effects for HYV Wheat in the Punjab." *Indian Economic Review* 15 (7) January-March: 29–51.

———. 1980b. "Tractorisation, Productivity and Employment: A Reassessment." *Journal of Development Studies* 16 (3) April: 375–86.

———. 1981. "Agricultural Mechanization and Labor Use: A Disaggregated Approach." *International Labour Review* 120 (1) January-February: 115–27.

Agarwal, N. L., and R. K. Kumawat. 1974. "Green Revolution and Capital and Credit Requirements of the Farmers in the Semi-Arid Regions of Rajasthan." *Indian Journal of Agricultural Economics* 29 (1): 67–75.

Agarwal, S. 1968a. "Impact of Consolidation of Land Holdings." *Agricultural Situation in India* 23 (12) March.

———. 1968b. "Impact of Consolidation of Land Holdings: A Field Study." *Artha Vijnana* 10 (1) March.

———. 1971. *Economics of Land Consolidation in India.* New Delhi: S. Chand and Co.

Agarwala, R. 1964a. "Size of Holdings and Productivity: A Comment." *Economic and Political Weekly*, April 11.

———. 1964b. "Size of Holdings and Productivity: Further Comments." *Economic and Political Weekly*, November 21.

Ahluwalia, I. J. 1985. *Industrial Growth in India.* Oxford: Oxford University Press.

Ahluwalia, Montek S. 1978. "Rural Poverty and Agricultural Performance in India." *Journal of Development Studies* 14 (April): 298–323.

Ahmad, Bashir. 1972. "Farm Mechanization and Agricultural Development: A Case Study of the Pakistan Punjab." Ph.D. diss., Michigan State University, East Lansing.

Ahmad, Ehtisham, and Stephen Ludlow. 1989. "Poverty, Inequality and Growth in Pakistan." Paper presented at the World Bank–International Food Policy Research Institute Policy Research Conference, Airlee, Va., October.

Ahmad, M. 1974. "Farm Efficiency under Owner Cultivation and Share Tenancy." *Pakistan Economic and Social Review* 12 (2) Summer: 131–43.

Ahmed, Iftikhar. 1975. *The Green Revolution, Mechanization, and Employment.* ILO Working Paper. Geneva: International Labour Office.

———. 1978. "Unemployment and Underemployment in Bangladesh Agriculture." *World Development* 6: 1281–96.

———. 1981. *Technological Change and Agrarian Structure: A Study of Bangladesh.* Geneva: International Labour Office.

Ahmed, R. 1979a. *Foodgrain Supply, Distribution and Consumption Policies within a Dual Pricing Mechanism: A Case Study of Bangladesh.* Research Report 8. Washington, D.C.: International Food Policy Research Institute.

———. 1979b. "Production and Consumption Linkages among Rural Enterprises: A Case Study of Bangladesh: A Project Proposal." International Food Policy Research Institute, Washington, D.C. Draft.

―――. 1987. *A Structural Perspective of Farm and Non-Farm Households in Bangladesh*. Washington, D.C.: International Food Policy Research Institute.

Ahn, Choong Yong, and Inderjit Singh. 1981. "A Model of an Agricultural Household in a Multi-Crop Economy: The Case of Korea." *Review of Economics and Statistics* 63 (4) November: 520–25.

Aiyaswamy, U., and H. G. Bhole. 1981. "Market Access as Constraint on Marginal and Small Farms." *Economic and Political Weekly* 16 (13) March 28.

Akbar, Ali. 1975. "1974 Famine in Bangladesh." Rajshahi University. November.

Akram, C. M., ed. 1973. *Manual of Land Reforms*. Lahore: Government of Pakistan.

Alagh, Y. K., G. S. Bhalla, and A. Bhaduri. 1978. "Agricultural Growth and Manpower Absorption in Indian Agriculture." In P. K. Bardhan, A. Vaidyanathan, and Y. K. Alagh, eds., *Labor Absorption in Indian Agriculture*. Bangkok: International Labour Organisation and Asian Regional Programme for Employment Promotion.

Alagh, Y. K., and P. S. Sharma. 1980. "Growth of Crop Production: 1960–61 to 1978–79: Is It Declining?" *Indian Journal of Agricultural Economics* 35 (2) April-June.

Alam, M. S. 1974. "The Economics of Landed Interests: A Case Study of Pakistan. *Pakistan Economic and Social Review* 12 (Spring): 12–24.

Alamgir, M. 1975. "Poverty, Inequality and Social Welfare: Measurements, Evidence and Policies. *Bangladesh Development Studies*, April.

―――. 1978. *Bangladesh: A Case of Below Poverty Level Equilibrium Trap*. Dhaka: Bangladesh Institute of Development Studies.

―――. 1980. *Famine in South Asia: Poltical Economy of Mass Starvation*. Cambridge, Mass: Oelgeschlager, Gunn and Hain.

Alauddin, T. 1975. "Mass Poverty in Pakistan: A Further Study." *Pakistan Development Review*, Winter.

Alavi, Hamza. 1973. "Elite Farmer Strategy and Regional Disparities in the Agricultural Development of Pakistan." *Economic and Political Weekly*, Review of Agriculture 8 (12) March 24: A31–A39.

Albrecht, Herbert. 1976. *Living Conditions of Rural Families in Pakistan*. Frithjof Kuhnen, ed.; V. June Hager, trans. Socioeconomic Studies on Rural Development. Saarbrücken: ssɪᴘ-Schriften Breitenbach.

―――. 1981. "New Technologies and Income Distribution in Agriculture: The Case of the Pakistan Punjab." Institute for Rural Development, University of Göttingen. Draft.

Alderman, H. 1987. *Co-operative Dairy Development in Karnataka, India: An Assessment*. Research Report 64. Washington, D.C.: International Food Policy Research Institute.

Alderman, H., G. Mergos, and R. Slade. 1987. *Co-operatives and the Commer-*

cialization of Milk Production in India: A Literature Review. Working Paper on Agriculture 2. Washington, D.C.: International Food Policy Research Institute.

Ali, A. 1980. "Part-Time Farming in Bangladesh." *Labour, Capital and Society* 13 (2) November.

Allen, R. 1978. "Employment of the HYV Strategy." U.S. Agency for International Development, Dhaka. Draft.

Allison, Christine. 1989. "Poverty, Inequality and Public Policy in Pakistan." Paper presented at the World Bank–International Food Policy Research Institute Poverty Research Conference, Airlee, Va., October.

Allison, S. 1974. "Progress Towards Development of a More Appropriate Technology for Land and Water Development in Bangladesh." World Bank, Dhaka. March.

Amjad, Rashid. 1972. "A Critique of the Green Revolution in West Pakistan." *Pakistan Economic and Social Review* 10 (1) June.

Anderson, Dennis. 1987. *The Economics of Afforestation: A Case Study in Africa.* Baltimore, Md.: Johns Hopkins University Press.

Anderson, Dennis, and Mark Leiserson. 1978. *Rural Enterprise and Nonfarm Employment.* Washington, D.C.: World Bank.

———. 1980. "Rural Non-Farm Employment in Developing Countries." *Economic Development and Cultural Change* 28 (2) January: 227–48.

Appa Rao, V., and R. R. Krishna. 1978. "Impact of Dairying on Small and Marginal Farmers and Agricultural Labourers: A Case Study of Two Villages in Arakapalli." Waltair: Technical Cell, Andhra University. Draft.

Appu, P. S. 1975. "Tenancy Reform in India." *Economic and Political Weekly* 10 (33–35) August.

Asaduzzaman, M., and M. Hossain. 1974. *Some Aspects of Agricultural Credit in Two Irrigated Areas in Bangladesh.* Research Report 18. Dhaka: Bangladesh Institute of Development Studies.

Asaduzzaman, M., and Faridul Islam. 1976. *Adoption of HYVs in Bangladesh: Some Preliminary Hypotheses and Tests.* Research Report, n.s. 23. Dhaka: Bangladesh Institute of Development Studies.

Asian and Pacific Center for Women and Development. 1979. *Women's Employment: Possibilities of Relevant Research.* Section 5, *Impact on Women: The Anand Pattern of Dairy Development.* Anand: National Dairy Development Board.

Athreya, V. B, G. Boklin, G. Djurfeldt, and S. Lindberg. 1986. "Economies of Scale or Advantage of Class." *Economic and Political Weekly* 21 (13) March 29: A2–A26.

Attwood, D. W. 1979. "Why Some of the Poor Get Richer: Economic Change and Mobility in Rural Western India." *Current Anthropology* 20 (3) September: 495–515.

Auden-Laerina, T., and R. Barker. 1978. "The Adoption of Modern Varieties." In *Interpretive Analysis of Selected Papers from "Changes in Rice Farming in Selected Areas of Asia."* Los Baños: International Rice Research Institute.

Azad, M. P., R. N. Yadar, and H. K. Nigan. 1980. "Economics of Poultry Farming in Kanpur: Case Study, 1979–80." *Indian Journal of Agricultural Economics* 35 (4) October-December: 170.

Aziz, S. 1978. *Rural Development: Learning from China*. London: Macmillan.

Bagchee, S. 1987a. "Rural Development Strategies." *Economic and Political Weekly* 22 (30) July 18: 1189–90.

———. 1987b. "Poverty Alleviation Programmes in the Seventh Plan: An Appraisal." *Economic and Political Weekly* 22 (4) January 24: 139–48.

Bagi, F. S. 1979a. "Irrigation, Farm Size and Economic Efficiency: An Analysis of Farm-Level Data in Haryana (India) Agriculture." Tennessee State University, Nashville. June.

———. 1979b. "Relationship between Farm Size, Tenancy, Productivity and Returns to Scale in Haryana (India) Agriculture." Tennessee State University, Nashville. October.

———. 1979c. "Technical and Allocative Efficiencies of Share-Cropping in Haryana (India) Agriculture." Tennessee State University, Nashville. May.

———. 1980. "The Stochastic Frontier Production Function and Sources of Measured Technical Efficiency." Tennessee State University, Nashville. April.

———. 1981. "The Stochastic Frontier Production Function and the Effect of Irrigation on the Average Technical Efficiency." Department of Rural Development, Tennessee State University, Nashville. July.

Ballabh, V., and B. Sharma. 1987. "Adoption of HYV Paddy and Wheat in Flood-Prone and Flood-Free Districts of Uttar Pradesh: Implications for Research Strategy." *Indian Journal of Agricultural Economics* 42 (1) January-March: 76–90.

Bandhopadhyaya, N. 1981. "Operation Barga and Land Reform Perspectives in West Bengal: A Discursive Review." *Economic and Political Weekly* 16 (25–26) June 20–27: A38–A42.

Bangladesh Bank. 1978. "Problems and Issues of Agricultural Credit and Rural Finance." Deliberations of the International Workshop on Providing Financial Services to the Rural Poor, Dhaka, October 23–25.

Bangladesh Bureau of Statistics. 1972. *Master Survey of Agriculture in Bangladesh, 1967–68*. 7th Round, 2nd phase. Dhaka.

———. 1977. *Agriculture Census, 1977*. Dhaka: Government Press.

———. 1983. *Report on Bangladesh Pilot Agricultural Census 1982*. Dhaka: Government Press.

———. 1985. *Statistical Pocket Book of Bangladesh, 1985*. Dhaka: Government Press.

———. 1986a. *The Bangladesh Census of Agriculture and Livestock: 1983–84*. Dhaka: Government Press.

———. 1986b. *Final Report: Labor Force Survey 1981–82*. Dhaka: Ministry of Planning.

———. 1986c. *Household Expenditure Survey for Bangladesh, 1981–82*. Dhaka.

————. 1986d. *Report of the Bangladesh Household Expenditure Survey, 1981–82.* Dhaka: Ministry of Planning.

Bangladesh, Ministry of Agriculture and Forests. 1978. *Agrarian Structure and Change: Rural Development Experience and Policies in Bangladesh.* Background Papers to the Bangladesh Country Report for the World Conference on Agrarian Reform and Rural Development, Dhaka, May.

Bansie, P. 1977. *Agricultural Problems in India.* New Delhi: Sterling.

Bapna, S. L. 1973. "Economic and Social Implications of the Green Revolution: A Case Study of Kota District." Vallabh, Vidyanagar: Agro-Economic Research Center, Sardar Patel University.

BARC (Bangladesh Agricultural Research Council). 1978. *Incidence of Landlessness and Major Landholding and Cultivation Groups in Rural Bangladesh.* Agricultural Economics and Rural Social Science Paper 5. Dhaka.

Bardhan, Pranab K. 1970. "The Green Revolution and Agricultural Labourers." *Economic and Political Weekly* 5 (29–31) January: 1239–46.

————. 1971. "Trends in Land Relations in India: A Note." *Economic and Political Weekly*, Annual Number.

————. 1973a. "Size, Productivity and Returns to Scale: An Analysis of Farm-Level Data in Indian Agriculture." *Journal of Political Economy* 81: 1370–86.

————. 1973b. "Variations in Agricultural Wages: A Note." *Economic and Political Weekly* 8 (21) May 26: 947–51.

————. 1976. "Variations in Extent and Forms of Agricultural Tenancy." *Economic and Political Weekly* 11 (37–38) September 11–18.

————. 1977a. "Rural Employment and Wages with Agricultural Growth in India: Some Intertemporal and Cross-Sectional Analyses." Studies in Employment and Rural Development 38. World Bank, Development Economics Department, Washington, D.C. March.

————. 1977b. "Rural Employment, Wages and Labor Markets in India: A Survey of Research." *Economic and Political Weekly* 12 (26–28) June 28, July 2–9.

————. 1977c. "Variations in Forms of Tenancy in a Peasant Economy." *Journal of Development Studies* 4 (June): 105–18.

————. 1978. "On Measuring Rural Unemployment." University of California, Berkeley. Unpublished.

————. 1979. "Agricultural Development and Land Tenancy in a Peasant Economy: A Theoretical and Empirical Analysis." *American Journal of Agricultural Economics* 61 (1) February.

————. 1980. "Interlocking Factor Markets and Agrarian Development: A Review of Issues." *Oxford Economic Papers*, March.

————. 1981. "Labor Tying in a Poor Agrarian Economy: A Theoretical and Empirical Analysis." University of California, Berkeley. May. Unpublished.

————. 1984. *Land, Labour and Rural Poverty.* Essays in Development Economics. Oxford: Oxford University Press.

————. 1986. *The Political Economy of Development in India.* Oxford: Oxford University Press.

Bardhan, P. K., and A. Rudra. 1978. "Interlinkage of Land, Labor and Credit Relations." *Economic and Political Weekly* 13 (6–7) February.

————. 1980a. "Labour, Employment and Wages in Agriculture: Results of a Survey in West Bengal, 1979." *Economic and Political Weekly* 15 (45–46) November 8–15.

————. 1980b. "Terms and Conditions of Sharecropping Contracts: An Analysis of Village Survey Data in India." *Journal of Development Studies* 16 (April): 287–302.

————. 1980c. "Types of Labor Attachment in Agriculture: Results of a Survey in West Bengal, 1979." *Economic and Political Weekly* 15 (35) August 30.

————. 1981. "Terms and Conditions of Labour Contracts in Agriculture." *Oxford Bulletin of Economics and Statistics* 43: 89–111.

Bardhan, P. K., and T. N. Srinivasan. 1971. "Crop Sharing Tenancy in Agriculture: A Theoretical and Empirical Analysis." *American Economic Review* 61 (1) March: 48–64.

Barker, K., and R. Herdt. 1978. "Equity Implications of Technology Changes." In *Interpretive Analysis of Selected Papers from "Changes in Rice Farming in Selected Areas of Asia."* Los Baños: International Rice Research Institute.

Barker, R., and V. Cordova. 1978. "Labor Utilization in Rice Production." In *Economic Consequences of the New Rice Technology.* Los Baños: International Rice Research Institute.

Barnum, Howard N., and Lyn Squire. 1978. "Technology and Relative Economic Efficiency." *Oxford Economic Papers* 30 (2) July: 181–98.

————. 1979. *A Model of an Agricultural Household: Theory and Evidence.* Baltimore, Md.: Johns Hopkins University Press.

Bartsch, W. H. 1977. *Employment and Technology Choice in Asian Agriculture.* New York: Praeger.

Basant, R. 1987. "Agricultural Technology and Employment in India: A Survey of Recent Research." *Economic and Political Weekly* 22 (31) August 1: 1297 and (32) August 8: 1348.

Basu, K. 1981. "Food for Work Programmes: Beyond Roads That Get Washed Away." *Economic and Political Weekly* 16 (1–2) January 3–10: 37–40.

Basu, S. 1979. *Commercial Banks and Agricultural Credit: A Study of Regional Disparity in India.* Bombay: Allied Publishers.

Baviskar, B. 1988. "Development and Controversy." *Economic and Political Weekly* 23 (13) March 26: A35–A43.

Baviskar, B., and S. George. 1987. "Operation Flood: A Different View." *Economic and Political Weekly* 21 (44–45) November 1–8: 1961–62.

Bell, Clive. 1972. "The Acquisition of Agricultural Technology: Its Determinants and Effects." *Journal of Development Studies* 9 (1) October: 123–59.

———. 1974a. "Crop Sharing Tenancy in Agriculture: A Rejoinder." *American Economic Review* 64 (6) December: 1007–09.

———. 1974b. "Ideology and Economic Interests in Indian Land Reform." In David Lehmann, ed., *Peasants, Landlords and Governments: Agrarian Reform in the Third World*. New York: Holmes and Meier.

———. 1976. "Production Conditions, Innovation and the Choice of Lease in Agriculture." *Sankhya: The Indian Journal of Statistics* 38 (ser. C, pt. 4) December.

———. 1977. "Alternative Theories of Sharecropping: Some Tests Using Evidence from Northeast India." *Journal of Development Studies* 13 (July).

———. 1978. "Some Reflections on Tenancy in South Asia." Development Research Center, World Bank, Washington, D.C. January. Draft.

Bell, Clive, and Peter Hazell. 1980. "Measuring the Indirect Effects of an Agricultural Investment Project on Its Surrounding Region." *American Journal of Agricultural Economics* 62 (1) February.

Bell, Clive, Peter Hazell, and Roger Slade. 1982. *Project Evaluation in Regional Perspective: A Study of an Irrigation Project in Northwest Malaysia*. Baltimore, Md.: Johns Hopkins University Press.

Bell, Clive, and P. Zusman. 1976. "A Bargaining Theoretic Approach to Cropsharing Contracts." *American Economic Review* 66 (September): 578–87.

Benor, Daniel, James Q. Harrison, and Michael Baxter. 1984. *Agricultural Extension: The Training and Visit System*. Washington, D.C.: World Bank.

Bergmann, T., and D. Eitel. 1976. *Promotion of the Poorer Sections of the Indian Rural Population*. Socioeconomic Studies on Rural Development. Saarbrücken: SSIP-Schriften Breitenbach.

Berry, R. Albert, and William L. Cline. 1979. *Agrarian Structure and Productivity in Developing Countries*. Baltimore, Md.: Johns Hopkins University Press.

Berry, R. Albert, and R. Sabot. 1978. "Labour Market Performance in Developing Countries: A Survey." *World Development* 6 (11–12): 1199–1246.

———. 1984. "Unemployment and Economic Development." *Economic Development and Cultural Change* 33 (October): 99–116.

Bertocci, P. 1972. "Community Structure and Social Relations in Two Villages in Bangladesh." *Contributions to Indian Sociology* (6): 28–35.

Beteille, A. 1965. *Caste, Class and Power: Changing Patterns of Stratification in a Tanjore Village*. Berkeley: University of California Press.

———. 1974. *Studies in Agrarian Social Structure*. Delhi: Oxford University Press.

———. 1975. "Agrarian Relations in Tanjore District, South India." University of New Delhi.

Bhaduri, A. 1973. "Agricultural Backwardness under Semi-Feudalism." *Economic Journal* 329 (83) March.

———. 1977. "On the Formation of Usurious Interest Rates in Backward Agriculture." *Cambridge Journal of Economics* 1 (4): 341–52.

Bhagwati, J. 1988. "Poverty and Public Policy." *World Development* 16 (5): 539–55.

Bhagwati, J., and Sukhamoy Chakravarty. 1969. "Contributions to Indian Economic Analysis: A Survey." *American Economic Review* 59 (4, pt. 2) September.

Bhalla, G. S., and Y. K. Alagh. 1979. *Performance of Indian Agriculture: A Districtwise Study.* New Delhi: Sterling.

Bhalla, G. S., and G. K. Chadha. 1982. "Green Revolution and the Small Peasant: A Study of Income Distribution in Punjab Agriculture." *Economic and Political Weekly* 17 (2) May 15–22: 826–33, 870–77.

———. 1983. *Green Revolution and the Small Peasant: A Study of Income Distribution among Punjab Cultivators.* New Delhi: Concept Publishers.

Bhalla, Sheila. 1976. "New Relations of Production in Haryana Agriculture." *Economic and Political Weekly*, Review of Agriculture 9 (13) March 27: A23–A30.

———. 1977. "Changes in Acreage and Tenure Structure of Land Holdings in Haryana, 1962–1972." *Economic and Political Weekly* 12 (13) March 26: A2–A15.

———. 1979. "Real Wage Rates of Agricultural Labourers in Punjab, 1961–1977: A Preliminary Analysis." *Economic and Political Weekly*, Review of Agriculture 14 (26) June 30: A57–A68.

Bhalla, Surjit. 1980. "Measurement of Poverty: Issues and Methods." Development Economics Department, World Bank, Washington, D.C. January. Draft.

———. 1983. "Does Land Quality Matter: Theory and Measurement." Development Economics Department, World Bank, Washington, D.C. December. Processed.

Bhalla, Surjit, and P. L. Roy. 1983. "Mis-Specification in Farm Productivity Analysis." Development Economics Department, World Bank, Washington, D.C. November. Processed.

Bharadwaj, Krishna. 1974a. "Notes on Farm Size and Productivity." *Economic and Political Weekly* 9 (13) March 30.

———. 1974b. *Production Conditions in Indian Agriculture: A Study Based on Farm Management Surveys.* Department of Applied Economics, Occasional Paper 33. Cambridge: Cambridge University Press.

Bharadwaj, Krishna, and P. K. Das. 1975a. "Tenurial Conditions and the Mode of Exploitation: A Study of Some Villages in Orissa." *Economic and Political Weekly* 10 (5–7) February: 221–39.

———. 1975b. "Tenurial Conditions and the Mode of Exploitation: A Study of Some Villages in Orissa—Further Notes." *Economic and Political Weekly* 10 (25–26) June 21–28.

Bhatt, V. 1988. "Growth and Income Distribution in India: A Review." *World Development* 15 (5): 641–47.

Bhattacharya, G., and M. Chattopadhyay. 1986. "Growth of Indian Agriculture: A Reappraisal." *Indian Journal of Agricultural Economics* 42 (1) January–March: 67–76.

Bhattacharya, N., M. Chattopadhyay, and A. Rudra. 1987. "Changes in Level of Living in Rural West Bengal: Social Consumption." *Economic and Political Weekly* 22 (28) July 11 and (33) August 15: 1410–13.

Bhattacharya, N., and G. R. Saini. 1972. "Farm Size and Productivity: A Fresh Look." *Economic and Political Weekly*, June 24.

Bhattacharya, P., and A. Majid. 1976. "Impact of the Green Revolution on Output, Cost and Income of Small and Big Farmers." *Economic and Political Weekly* 11 (52) December 25: A147–A150.

Bhende, M. 1986. "Credit Markets in Rural South Asia." *Economic and Political Weekly* 21 (38–39) September 20–27: A119–A125.

Billings, Martin H., and Arjan Singh. 1970. "Farm Mechanization and the Green Revolution, 1964–1984: The Punjab Case." U.S. Agency for International Development, New Delhi. April. Processed.

Binswanger, Hans P. 1979. *The Economics of Tractors in South Asia: An Analytical Review*. New York: Agricultural Development Council.

Binswanger, Hans P., and J. McIntire. 1987. "Behavioral and Material Determinants of Production Relations in Land-Abundant Tropical Agriculture." *Economic Development and Cultural Change* 36 (1) October: 73–99.

Binswanger, Hans P., and M. R. Rosenzweig. 1981. *Contractual Arrangements, Employment and Wages in Rural Labour Markets: A Critical Review*. New York: Agricultural Development Council; and Hyderabad: International Crops Research Institute for the Semi-Arid Tropics.

Blair, H. 1974. *The Elusiveness of Equity: Institutional Approaches to Rural Development in Bangladesh*. Dhaka and Ithaca, N.Y.: Cornell Center for International Studies.

———. 1986. "Social Forestry: Time to Modify Goals?" *Economic and Political Weekly* 21 (30) July 26: 1317–22.

Bliss, C. J., and N. H. Stern. 1980. *Palampur: Studies in the Economy of a North Indian Village*. New Delhi: Oxford University Press.

Blyn, George. 1979. "The Green Revolution and Rural Social Structure in India." *Rural Development: Contributions to Asian Studies* 13, ed. Mohinder Chaudhry. Leiden: E. J. Brill.

———. 1983. "The Green Revolution Revisited." *Economic Development and Cultural Change* 31 (4) July: 705–25.

Bose, Ajit N. 1978. *Calcutta and Rural Bengal: Small Sector Symbiosis*. Calcutta: Minerva Associates.

Bose, Swadesh R. 1968. "Trend of Real Income of the Rural Poor in East Pakistan, 1949–66." *Pakistan Development Review* 5 (3) Autumn.

———. 1974a. "The Comilla Co-operative Approach and the Prospects for Broad-Based Green Revolution in Bangladesh." *World Development* 2 (8) August: 21–28.

————. 1974b. "Movement of Agricultural Wage Rates in Bangladesh." In A. Mitra, ed., *Economic Theory and Planning: Essays in Honour of A. K. Dasgupta.* Oxford: Oxford University Press.

Bose, S. R., and E. M. Clark. 1969. "Some Basic Considerations on Agricultural Mechanization in West Pakistan. *Pakistan Development Review* 9 (Autumn): 273–308.

Bottomley, Anthony. 1963. "The Premium for Risk as a Determinant of Interest Rates in Underdeveloped Areas." *Quarterly Journal of Economics* 76: 637–47.

————. 1964a. "The Determination of Pure Rates of Interest in Underdeveloped Rural Areas." *Review of Economics and Statistics* 46: 301–04.

————. 1964b. "Monopoly Profit as a Determinant of Interest in Underdeveloped Rural Areas." *Oxford Economic Papers* 16: 431–37.

————. 1964c. "The Structure of Interest Rates in Underdeveloped Rural Areas." *Journal of Farm Economics* 46 (May): 313–22.

————. 1973. "A Tide in the Affairs of Men." *Small Farmer Credit Summary Papers* 20. Washington, D.C.: U.S. Agency for International Development. June.

Bottrall, A. 1974. *Serving the Small Farmer: Policy Choices in Indian Agriculture.* London: Overseas Development Institute.

Bowonder, B., and others. 1987. "Further Evidence on the Impact of Dairy Development Programmes." *Economic and Political Weekly* 22 (13) March 28: A6–A15.

Brammer, Hugh. 1980. "Some Innovations Don't Wait for Experts: A Report on Applied Research by Bangladeshi Peasants." *Ceres: FAO Review on Agriculture and Development*, March-April.

Brannon, R., and D. Jessee. 1977. *Unemployment and Underemployment in the Rural Sectors of the Less Developed Countries.* Occasional Paper 4. Washington, D.C.: Economics and Sector Planning Division, Technical Assistance Bureau, U.S. Agency for International Development.

Braverman, Avishay, and J. L. Guasch. 1986. "Rural Credit Markets and Institutions in Developing Countries: Lessons for Policy Analysis from Practice and Modern Theory." *World Development* 14 (October-November): 1253–69.

Braverman, Avishay, and T. N. Srinivasan. 1980. *Agrarian Reforms in Developing Rural Economies Characterized by Interlinked Credit and Tenancy Markets.* World Bank Staff Working Paper 433. Washington, D.C.

Braverman, Avishay, and J. E. Stiglitz. 1980. "Sharecropping and Interlinking of Agrarian Markets." Development Research Center, World Bank, Washington, D.C. October. Draft.

————. 1981a. "Cost Sharing Arrangements under Sharecropping: A Multidimensional Incentive Program." Development Research Center, World Bank, Washington, D.C. April. Draft.

————. 1981b. "Landlords, Tenants and Technological Innovations." Development Research Center, World Bank, Washington, D.C. April. Draft.

Brown, D. 1971. *Agricultural Development in India's Districts*. Cambridge, Mass.: Harvard University Press.

Brown, L. 1970. *Seeds of Change: The Green Revolution and Development in the 1970s*. New York: Praeger.

Bruce, R., Jr. 1982. "Agrarian Organization and Resource Distribution in South India: Bellany District, 1800–1979." Ph.D. diss., University of Wisconsin, Madison.

Brumby, P. 1978. "Complementarity between Milk and Foodgrain Production: A Linear Programming Exercise." South Asia Projects Department, World Bank, Washington, D.C. March. Draft.

———. 1980. "The Dairy Situation in India." In *Proceedings of the Agricultural Sector Symposia*. Washington, D.C.: World Bank.

Burki, S. J. 1969. *A Study of Chinese Communes*. Cambridge, Mass.: East Asian Research Center, Harvard University.

Burki, S. J., and others. 1976. *Public Works Programs in Developing Countries: A Comparative Analysis*. World Bank Staff Working Paper 224. Washington, D.C.

Bussink, W., and K. Subbarao. 1986. "Living Standards Improvement in India: An Agenda for Studies." World Bank, New Delhi. July. Processed.

Byerlee, D. 1973. *Indirect Employment and Income Distribution Effects of Agricultural Development Strategies: A Simulation Approach Applied to Nigeria*. African Rural Employment Paper 9. East Lansing: Department of Agricultural Economics, Michigan State University.

Byrd, William A., and Lin Qingsong, eds. 1990. *China's Rural Industry: Structure, Development, and Reform*. New York: Oxford University Press.

Byres, T. 1972. "The Dialectic of India's Green Revolution." *South Asian Review* 5 (2) November-January.

———. 1974. "Land Reform, Industrialization and the Market Surplus in India: An Essay on Rural Bias." In David Lehman, ed., *Agrarian Reform and Agrarian Reformism*. London: Faber and Faber.

———. 1977. "Agrarian Transition and the Agrarian Question." *Journal of Peasant Studies* 4 (3) April.

———. 1981. "The New Technology, Class Formation and Class Action in the Indian Countryside." *Journal of Political Studies* 8 (4) July.

Cain, M. 1981. *Landlessness in India and Bangladesh: A Critical Review of Data Sources*. Working Paper 71. New York: Population Council.

Cancian, Frank. 1977. "The Innovators' Situation: Upper-Middle Class Conservatism in Agricultural Communities." Social Science Working Paper 132. School of Social Sciences, University of California, Irvine. November.

Cartillier, M. 1975. "Role of Small-Scale Industries in Economic Development: Irrigation Pumpsets Industry in Coimbatore." *Economic and Political Weekly* 10 (44–45) November 1.

Castillo, G. 1973. "All in a Grain of Rice: A Review of Philippine Studies on the Social and Economic Implications of the New Rice Technology." University of the Philippines, Los Baños. December.

Center for Management of Indian Economics. 1986. *Basic Statistics Relating to Indian Economy.* Bombay.

Cernea, Michael M., ed. 1985. *Putting People First: Sociological Variables in Rural Development.* New York: Oxford University Press.

Cernea, Michael M., John K. Coulter, and John F. A. Russell, eds. 1984. *Agricultural Extension by Training and Visit: The Asian Experience.* Washington, D.C.: World Bank.

Chaddha, G. K. 1978. "Farm Size and Productivity Revisited: Some Notes from Recent Experience of Punjab." *Economic and Political Weekly* 13 (39) September 30: A87–A96.

Chadha, V. 1984. "The Landless and the Poor in Green Revolution Regions in India." *Agricultural Situation in India* 39 (5) August: 295–303.

Chakravarty, Aparijita. 1981. "Tenancy and Mode of Production." *Economic and Political Weekly* 16 (13) March 28.

Chakravarty, Aparijita, and A. Rudra. 1973. "Economic Effects of Tenancy: Some Negative Results." *Economic and Political Weekly* 13 (28) July 14: 1239–46.

Chakravarty, Sukhamoy. 1987. *Development Planning: The Indian Experience.* Oxford: Clarendon Press.

Chambers, Robert. 1979. *Health, Agriculture and Rural Poverty: Why Seasons Matter.* Discussion Paper 148. Brighton: Institute of Development Studies, University of Sussex.

———. 1981. "A Lesson for Rural Developers: The Small Farmer Is a Professional." *Development Digest* 19 (3) July: 3–12.

Chandrashekhar, D., K. Murti, and S. Ramaswamy. 1987. "Social Forestry in Karnataka." *Economic and Political Weekly* 22 (24) June 13: 935–41.

Chattopadhyay, M. 1979. "Relative Efficiency of Owner and Tenant Cultivation: A Case Study." *Economic and Political Weekly* 14 (39) September 29: A93–A96.

Chattopadhyay, M., and A. Rudra. 1976. "Size-Productivity Revisited." *Economic and Political Weekly* 11 (39) September 25: A100–16.

———. 1977. "Size-Productivity Revisited—Addendum." *Economic and Political Weekly* 12 (11) March 12: 476–89.

Chaudhri, D., and A. Dasgupta. 1985. *Agriculture and the Development Process.* Kent: Croom Helm.

Chaudhry, M. G. 1982. "The Green Revolution and the Redistribution of Rural Incomes: Pakistan's Experience." *Pakistan Development Review* 21 (3) Autumn: 173–205.

———. 1983. "The Green Revolution and the Redistribution of Rural Incomes: Pakistan's Experience—A Reply." *Pakistan Development Review* 22 (2) Summer: 117–23.

———. 1986. "Mechanization and Agricultural Development in Pakistan." *Pakistan Development Review* 25 (4) Winter: 431–46.

Chaudhry, M. G., and M. Anwar Chaudhry. 1974. "Cost of Living Indexes for Rural Labourers in Pakistan." *Pakistan Development Review*, Spring.

Chaudhry, P. K. 1960. "Ceilings on Land Holdings: August Measures to Hoodwink People." *Economic and Political Weekly* 12 (12) March 19.

Chaudhry, Rafique Huda. 1978. "Some Aspects of Seasonal Dimensions to Rural Poverty in Bangladesh." Paper presented at the Conference on Seasonal Dimensions to Rural Poverty, Institute of Development Studies, University of Sussex, Brighton, July 3–6.

Chaudry, N. K. 1976. "Farm Efficiency under Semi-Feudalism: A Critique of Marginalist Theories and Some Marxist Formulations." *Economic and Political Weekly* 11 (39) September.

Chauhan, K., S. Mundle, N. Mohanan, and D. Jadhav. 1973. *Small Farmers: Problems and Possibilities of Development: A Study in Sangli District of Maharashtra.* Ahmedabad: Center for Management in Agriculture, Indian Institute of Management.

Chawdhari, T. P. S., and others. 1969. *Resource Use and Productivity on Farms: A Comparative Study of Intensive and Non-Intensive Agriculture Areas.* Hyderabad: National Institute of Community Development.

Chayanov, A. N. 1976 [1929]. *The Theory of the Peasant Economy.* B. Kerblay, D. Thorner, and R. Smith, eds. Homewood, Ill.: Irwin.

Chen, Lincoln. 1975. "An Analysis of Per Capita Foodgrain Availability, Consumption and Requirements in Bangladesh: A Systematic Approach to Food Planning." *Bangladesh Development Studies* 3 (2) April: 93–126.

———, ed. 1973. *Disaster in Bangladesh: Health Crisis in a Developing Nation.* New York: Oxford University Press.

Cheung, S. N. S. 1968. "Private Property Rights and Sharecropping." *Journal of Political Economy* (76): 1107–22.

———. 1969. *The Theory of Share Tenancy.* Chicago, Ill.: University of Chicago Press.

Child, F. C., and H. Kaneda. 1975. "Links to the Green Revolution: A Study of Small-Scale Agriculturally Related Industry in Pakistan Punjab." *Economic Development and Cultural Change* 23 (January): 249–75.

Chothani, A. n.d. "Identifying the Critical Components in a Successful Cooperative." National Dairy Development Board, Anand. Processed.

Choudhry, K. M. 1965. "Factors Affecting Acceptance of Improved Agricultural Practices: A Study of an I.A.D.P. District in Rajasthan." Agro-Economic Research Center, Vallav, Vidyanagar.

Chowdhury, A. 1978. *A Bangladesh Village: A Study of Social Stratification.* Dhaka: Center for Social Studies.

Chowdhury, A., T. Alauddin, and L. C. Chen. 1977. "The Interaction of Nutrition, Infection and Mortality during Recent Food Crises in Bangladesh." *Food Research Institute Studies* 16 (2): 47–61.

Chowdhury, A., and M. Haque. 1976. "Agrarian Hierarchy in a Kushtia Village." Indian Rural Development Project Paper. Dhaka: University of Dhaka.

Chuta, Enyinna, and Carl Liedholm. 1979. *Rural Non-Farm Employment: A Review of the State of the Art.* MSU Rural Development Paper 4. East Lansing: Department of Agricultural Economics, Michigan State University.

Clay, Edward J. 1975. "Equity and Productivity Effects of a Package of Technical Innovations and Changes in Social Institutions: Tubewells, Tractors and High-Yielding Varieties." *Indian Journal of Agricultural Economics* 30 (4) October-December.

————. 1976. "Institutional Change and Agricultural Wages in Bangladesh." *Bangladesh Development Studies* 4 (4) October.

————. 1978. "Environment, Technology and the Seasonal Patterns of Agricultural Employment in Bangladesh." Paper presented at the Conference on Seasonal Dimensions to Rural Poverty, Institute of Development Studies, University of Sussex, Brighton, July 3–6.

————. 1979. "The Rice Harvester Revisited: A Micro Study of Forms of Payment to Agricultural Labor in Bangladesh." Agricultural Development Council and International Crop Research Institute for Semi-Arid Tropics, Hyderabad. August.

Clay, Edward J., and M. S. Khan. 1977. *Agricultural Employment and Underemployment in Bangladesh: The Next Decade.* Agricultural Economics and Rural Social Science Paper 4. Dhaka: Bangladesh Agricultural Research Council.

Colmenares, J. 1975. *Adoption of Hybrid Seeds and Fertilizers among Colombian Corn Growers.* Mexico City: Centro Internacional de Mejoramiento de Maíz y Trigo (CIMMYT).

Connell, J., and others. 1976. *Migration from Rural Areas: The Evidence from Village Studies.* Delhi: Oxford University Press.

Cownie, J., B. F. Johnston, and B. Duff. 1970. "The Quantitative Impact of the Seed-Fertilizer Revolution in West Pakistan: An Exploratory Study." *Food Research Institute Studies* 1 (January).

Critchfield, R. 1978. "India Ready to Reap a Farming Revolution." *Agricultural World*, May.

————. 1979. *The Changing Peasant: Part III, The Modern Farmer.* American University Field Staff Report 46. Hanover, N.H.

————. 1980. "The Greening of Ghungrali." *Asia*, May-June.

Crotty, R. 1980. *Cattle, Economics and Development.* Commonwealth Agricultural Bureau. Old Woking, Surrey: Gresham Press.

Dalrymple, Dana G. 1971. *Survey of Multiple Cropping in Less Developed Nations.* FEDR-12. Washington, D.C.: Foreign Economic Development Service, U.S. Department of Agriculture.

————. 1975. *Measuring the Green Revolution: The Impact of Research on Wheat and Rice Production.* Foreign Agricultural Economic Report 106. Washington, D.C.: U.S. Department of Agriculture.

———. 1976; 6th ed. 1978. *Development and Spread of High-Yielding Varieties of Wheat and Rice in Less Developed Nations.* Foreign Agricultural Economic Report 95. Washington, D.C.: Economic Research Service, U.S. Department of Agriculture and U.S. Agency for International Development.

Damodaran, A. 1987. "Structural Dimensions of the Fodder Crisis." *Economic and Political Weekly* 22 (13) March 28: A16.

Dandekar, V. M. 1962. "Economic Theory and Agrarian Reform." *Oxford Economic Papers* 12 (February): 69–80.

———. 1964. "Prices, Production and Marketed Supply of Foodgrain." *Indian Journal of Agricultural Economics* 19 (July-December): 186–95.

———. 1976. "Crop Insurance in India." *Economic and Political Weekly* 11 (26) June: A61–A80.

———. 1986. "Agriculture, Employment and Poverty." *Economic and Political Weekly* 21 (38-39) September 20–27: A90–A101.

Dandekar, V. M., and N. Rath. 1971. "Poverty in India." *Economic and Political Weekly* 6 (1–2) January 2–9.

Dandekar, V. M., and M. Sathe. 1980. "Employment Guarantee Scheme and Food for Work Programme." *Economic and Political Weekly* 15 (5) April 12: 707–13.

Dantwala, M. L. 1958. "Prospects and Problems of Land Reforms in India." *Economic Development and Cultural Change* 6 (1) October.

———. 1962. "Failure in Land Reform." *Janta* 17 (1) January 26.

———. 1972. "Financial Implications of Land Reforms: Zamindari Abolition." *Indian Journal of Agricultural Economics* 17 (4) October-December.

———. 1973. "Poverty and Unemployment in Rural India." Report of the Study Conducted with the Assistance of the International Development Research Center, Ottawa, Canada, September.

———. 1985. "Garibi Hatao: Strategy Options." *Economic and Political Weekly* 20 (11) March 16.

———. 1986. "Agrarian Structure and Agrarian Relations in India." In Indian Society of Agricultural Economics, *Indian Agricultural Development since Independence.* Bombay: Oxford University Press and IBH Publishing Co.

———. 1987a. "Growth and Equity in Agriculture." *Indian Journal of Agricultural Economics* 42 (2) April-June: 149–60.

———. 1987b. "Rural Assets: Distribution and Composition of the Labour Force." *Indian Journal of Agricultural Economics* 42 (3) July-September: 294–301.

Dantwala, M., and C. Shah. 1971. "Evaluation of Land Reforms." University of Bombay.

Dantwala Committee. 1970. *Report of the Committee of Experts on Unemployment Estimates.* New Delhi: Government of India, Planning Commission.

Darling, M. 1977 [1925]. *The Punjab Peasant in Prosperity and Debt.* Reprinted with a new introduction. New Delhi: Oxford University Press.

Dasgupta, Biplab. 1977a. *Agrarian Change and the New Technology in India.* Geneva: United Nations Research Institute for Social Development.

———. 1977b. *Village Society and Labor Use.* Delhi: Oxford University Press.

Dasgupta, B., and R. Laishley. 1975. "Migration from Villages." *Economic and Political Weekly* October 18.

Datta, S. 1980a. "Choice of Agricultural Tenancy in the Presence of Uncertainty and Transaction Costs." Ph.D. diss., University of Rochester, Rochester, New York.

———. 1980b. *Sharecropping as a "Second-Best" Form of Tenancy in Traditional Agriculture.* Modelling Research Group Working Paper 8011. Los Angeles: Department of Economics, University of Southern California.

Datta, S., and D. O'Hara. 1980. *Choice of Agricultural Tenancy in the Presence of Transaction Costs.* Modelling Research Group Working Paper 8010. Los Angeles: Department of Economics, University of Southern California.

Day, R. H. 1967. "The Economics of Technological Change and the Demise of the Share-Cropper." *American Economic Review* 57 (June): 427–49.

Day, R. H., and Inderjit Singh. 1977. *Economic Development as an Adaptive Process: The Green Revolution in the Indian Punjab.* New York: Cambridge University Press.

de Haan, H. 1980. *Rural Industrialization in India.* Discussion Paper 54. Rotterdam: Center for Development Planning, Erasmus University.

de Janvry, A., and K. Subbarao. 1986. *Agricultural Price Policy and Income Distribution in India.* New Delhi: Oxford University Press.

de Kruijk, H. 1986a. *When Poverty Declines and Inequality Increases: The Case of Pakistan during the 1970s.* Discussion Paper 37. Rotterdam: Center for Development Planning, Erasmus University.

———. 1986b. "Income Inequality in the Four Provinces of Pakistan." *Pakistan Development Review* 25 (4) Winter: 685–705.

Deolalikar, A. 1981. "The Inverse Relationship between Productivity and Farm Size: A Test Using Regional Data from India." *American Journal of Agricultural Economics* 63 (2) May.

Desai, B. M., ed. 1979. *Intervention for Rural Development: Experiences of the Small Farmer Development Agency.* Ahmedabad: Institute of Management.

Desai, Gunvant M. 1971. "Some Observations on the Economics of Cultivating High-Yielding Varieties of Rice in India." In *Viewpoints on Rice Policy.* Los Baños: International Rice Research Institute.

de Silva, M. W. A. 1977. "Structural Change in a Coastal Fishing Community in Southern Sri Lanka." *Marga* 4 (2): 67–88.

Dhanagare, D. 1987. "Green Revolution and Social Inequalities in Rural India." *Economic and Political Weekly* 22 (19) May 21: 137–45.

Dhar, P., and H. Lydall. 1961. *The Role of Small Enterprises in Indian Economic Development.* Bombay: Allied Publishers.

Dhawan, B. D. 1977. "Tubewell Irrigation in the Gangetic Plains." *Economic and Political Weekly* 12 (39) September 24.

———. 1987. "How Stable Is Indian Irrigated Agriculture?" *Economic and Political Weekly* 22 (39) September 26: A93–A97.

Divatia, V. V. 1976. "Inequalities in Asset Distribution of Rural Households." *Indian Reserve Bank Staff Occasional Papers* 1 (1) June: 1–45.

Dobbs, T., and P. Foster. 1972. "Incentives to Invest in New Agricultural Inputs in Northern India." *Economic Development and Cultural Change* 21 (1) October.

Dogra, B. 1986. "Can Seventh Plan Targets Be Achieved?" *Economic and Political Weekly* 21 (16) April 19: 689.

Donald, Gordon. 1976. *Credit for Small Farmers in Developing Countries.* Boulder, Colo.: Westview.

Dorner, P., and D. Kanel. 1971. "The Economic Case for Land Reform: Employment, Income Distribution and Productivity." In *Land Reform, Land Settlements, and Cooperatives.* Rome: Food and Agriculture Organization.

Dutt, Kalyan. 1970. "A Critique of Land Redistribution." *Mainstream* 9 (5) October 3.

———. 1981. "Operation Barga: Gains and Constraints." *Economic and Political Weekly* 16 (25–26) June 20–27: A58–A60.

Dwivedi, H., and A. Rudra. 1973. "Economic Effects of Tenancy: Some Further Negative Results." *Economic and Political Weekly* July 21: 1291–94.

Eckert, J. B. 1970. "The Beginnings of Change in West Pakistan's Agriculture." Ford Foundation, Lahore. June.

———. 1972. "Rural Labor in Punjab: A Survey Report." Punjab Planning and Development Department, Lahore. July.

Eckert, J. B., and D. A. Khan. 1977. "Rural-Urban Labor Migration: The Evidence from Pakistan." Economic Research Institute, Lahore. Processed.

Eckert, J. B., and others. 1973. "An Employment Strategy for Rural Areas of Pakistan." Paper by Ad Hoc Working Group, Economic Research Institute, Lahore.

Eckholm, E. 1975. *The Other Energy Crises: Firewood.* Worldwatch Paper 1. Washington, D.C.: Worldwatch Institute.

———. 1979. *The Dispossessed of the Earth: Land Reform and Sustainable Development.* Worldwatch Paper 30. Washington, D.C.: Worldwatch Institute.

Elkinton, C. 1970. "Land Reform in Pakistan." In *Land Reform in Turkey, Pakistan and Indonesia.* USAID Spring Review Country Paper. Washington, D.C.: U.S. Agency for International Development.

Emmerson, Donald K. 1980. *Rethinking Artisanal Fisheries Development: Western Concepts, Asian Experiences.* World Bank Staff Working Paper 423. Washington, D.C.

Epstein, T. 1973. *South India: Yesterday, Today and Tomorrow.* London: Macmillan.

Ercelawn, A. 1984. "Income Inequality in Rural Pakistan: A Study of Sample Villages." *Pakistan Journal of Applied Economics* 3 (1) Summer: 1–29.

Esman, M. J. 1978. "Landlessness and Near-Landlessness in Developing Countries." Rural Development Committee, Cornell University, Ithaca, N.Y. September.

Faiz, Mohammed. 1986. "Wealth Effects of the Green Revolution." *Pakistan Development Review* 25 (4) Winter: 489–511.

Falcon, Walter P. 1970. "The Green Revolution: Generation of Problems." *American Journal of Agricultural Economics* 52 (December).

Falcon, Walter P., and Gustav F. Papanek, eds. 1971. *Development Policy II: The Pakistan Experience*. Cambridge, Mass.: Harvard University Press.

FAO (Food and Agriculture Organization). 1973. *Monthly Bulletin of Agricultural Economics and Statistics,* January.

————. 1977. *Report of the Seminar on Agricultural Perspective Planning, Islamabad*. Rome.

FAO and UNDP (United Nations Development Programme). 1975. *Pakistan: Report of FAO Sector Programming Mission*. FAO Sector Programming Mission Series 6, PAK/75/010. Rome: Food and Agriculture Organization.

Farmer, B., ed. 1977. *Green Revolution?* Boulder, Colo.: Westview Press.

Farouk, A., and others. 1976. *The Vagrants of Dacca City*. Dhaka: Bureau of Economic Research, University of Dhaka.

Feder, Gershon. 1979. "Adoption of Interrelated Agricultural Innovations: Credit, Risk and Scale Effects." Development Research Center, World Bank, Washington, D.C. December. Processed.

————. 1980. "Farm Size, Risk Aversion, and the Adoption of New Technology under Uncertainty." *Oxford Economic Papers* 32 (2) July: 263–82.

Feder, Gershon, Richard Just, and David Zilberman. 1981. *Adoption of Agricultural Innovations in Developing Countries: A Survey*. World Bank Staff Working Paper 444. Washington, D.C. Rev. ed. 1982, World Bank Staff Working Paper 542.

Feder, Gershon, and Gerald O'Mara. 1981. "On Information and Innovation Diffusion: A Bayesian Approach." Development Research Center, World Bank, Washington, D.C. January. Processed.

Feder, Gershon, and Roger Slade. 1984. *Aspects of the Training and Visit System of Agricultural Extension in India: A Comparative Analysis*. World Bank Staff Working Paper 656. Washington, D.C.

Feder, Gershon, Roger Slade, and Lawrence Lau. 1985. *The Impact of Agricultural Extension: A Case Study of the Training and Visit Systems in Haryana, India*. World Bank Staff Working Paper 756. Washington, D.C.

Feder, Gershon, Roger Slade, and A. Sundaram. 1986. "The T and V Extension System: An Analysis of Operations and Effects." *Agricultural Administration* 21: 33–59.

Fei, John C. H., Gustav Ranis, and Shirley W. Y. Kuo. 1979. *Growth with Equity: The Taiwan Case*. New York: Oxford University Press.

Franda, M. 1979. *Small Is Politics: Organizational Alternatives in India's Rural*

Development. American University Field Staff. New Delhi: Wiley Eastern Limited.

Frankel, F. 1971. *India's Green Revolution: Economic Gains and Political Costs.* Princeton, N.J.: Princeton University Press.

Gadre, N., and B. Sapte. 1980. "Impact of Dairy Projects on Rural Economy: A Case Study." *Indian Journal of Agricultural Economics* 35 (4) October-December: 173.

Gafsi, S. 1976. *Green Revolution: The Tunisian Experience.* Mexico City: Centro Internacional de Mejoramiento de Maíz y Trigo (CIMMYT).

Galgalikar, V., N. Gadre, and C. Joshi. 1976. "Changes in the Structural Distribution of Land Holdings: A Case Study." *Indian Journal of Agricultural Economics* 3 (July-September): 32–40.

Gangadharan, T. P. 1980. "Feed Economy in Milk Production: A Probe under New Dairy Farm Technology in Kerala." *Indian Journal of Agricultural Economics*, October-December.

Garg, J., and M. Azad. 1975. "Economics of Cross-Bred Cows: A Case Study." *Indian Journal of Agricultural Economics* 30 (3): 149–50.

Garg, J., and V. Prasad. 1975. "An Economic Investigation into the Problems of the Cooperative Milk Board, Kanpur." *Indian Journal of Agricultural Economics* 30 (3) July-September: 143.

George, M. V., and P. T. Joseph. 1976. "Changes in the Structure of Land Ownership and Use in Kerala and Their Economic Implications." *Indian Journal of Agricultural Economics* 31 (3) July-September: 27–31.

George, P. S. 1985. *Some Aspects of Procurement and Distribution of Foodgrains in India.* Working Paper on Food Subsidies. Washington, D.C.: International Food Policy Research Institute.

———. 1986. "Emerging Trends in Size Distribution of Operational Holdings in Kerala." *Economic and Political Weekly* 21 (5) February 1.

George, P. S., and V. V. Choukidar. 1972. *Production and Marketing Pattern of Paddy.* CMA Monograph 27. Ahmedabad: Center for Management in Agriculture, Indian Institute of Management.

———. 1973. *Dynamics of the Paddy-Rice System in India.* CMA Monograph 42. Ahmedabad: Center for Management in Agriculture, Indian Institute of Management.

George, P. S., and V. K. Srivastava. 1975. "Institutional Finance for Dairy Development." *Indian Journal of Agricultural Economics* 30 (3) July-September: 90–96.

George, Shanti. 1985. *Operation Flood: An Appraisal of Current Indian Dairy Policy.* New Delhi: Oxford University Press.

———. 1987. "Stemming Operation Flood: Towards an Alternative Dairy Policy for India." *Economic and Political Weekly* 22 (39) September 26: 1654–64.

Ghafar, M., M. Amir, and E. Clark. 1968. *Statistical Series on Private Tubewell Development in West Pakistan: Size of Holding of Private Tubewell Owners.* Research Report 69. Karachi: Pakistan Institute of Development Economics.

Ghose, A. K. 1979a. "Farm Size and Land Productivity in Indian Agriculture: A Reappraisal." *Journal of Development Studies* 16 (1) October.

————. 1979b. "Institutional Structure, Technological Change and Growth in a Poor Agrarian Economy: An Analysis with Reference to Bengal and Punjab." *World Development* 7 (April-May): 385–96.

————. 1980. "Wages and Employment in Indian Agriculture." *World Development* 8 (5–6) May-June.

————. 1987. "Agricultural Research and Rural Development." *Economic and Political Weekly* 22 (14–15) April 4.

————. 1988. "The 1988–89 Budget: Does It Tackle Any of India's Problems?" *Economic and Political Weekly* 23 (14–15) April 2–9: 711–19.

Ghose, A. K., and A. Saith. 1976. "Indebtedness, Tenancy and the Adoption of New Technology in Semi-Feudal Agriculture." *World Development* 4 (4) April.

Ghosh, Arabinda. 1973. "Size-Structure, Productivity and Growth: A Case Study of West Bengal Agriculture." *Bangladesh Economic Review* 1 (1) January: 59–70.

Ghosh, M. G. 1970. "A Study of High-Yielding Varieties Programme in the District Birbhum, West Bengal, with Reference to Kharif Paddy, 1968–69." Agro-Economic Research Center, Vishwa-Bharati, Shantiniketan.

————. 1986. "Farm-Size Productivity Nexus under Alternative Technology." *Indian Journal of Agricultural Economics* 41 (1) January-March: 17–29.

Ghosh, Ratan. 1976. "Effect of Agricultural Legislation on Land Distribution in West Bengal." *Indian Journal of Agricultural Economics* 31 (3) July-September: 40–46.

Gill, M. S. 1976. "The Green Revolution: Success in the Indian Punjab." *Progressive Farming* December: 7–15.

Gotsch, Carl H. 1971. "The Distributive Impact of Agricultural Growth: Low Income Farmers and the System." Paper presented to the Seminar on Small-Farmer Development, Agricultural Development Council and Ohio State University, Columbus, September.

————. 1972. "Technical Change and the Distribution of Incomes in Rural Areas." *American Journal of Agricultural Economics* 54 (2) May.

————. 1973. "Tractor Mechanization and Rural Development in Pakistan." *International Labour Review* 107 (2) February.

————. 1977. "Agricultural Mechanization in the Punjab: Some Comparative Observations from India and Pakistan." Food Research Institute, Stanford, Calif. Draft.

Gotsch, Carl H., and others. 1975. "Linear Programming and Agricultural Policy: Micro Studies of the Pakistan Punjab." *Food Research Institute Studies* 14 (1).

Grawe, R., J. Krishnamurti, and J. Baah-Dwomoh. 1979. "India: Employment and Employment Policy: A Background Paper." South Asia Projects Department, World Bank, Washington, D.C. October.

Grewal, S. S., and P. S. Rangi. 1980. "Economics and Employment of Dairying in the Punjab." *Indian Journal of Agricultural Economics,* October-December.

Griffin, Keith. 1974. *The Political Economy of Agrarian Change: An Essay on the Green Revolution.* Cambridge, Mass.: Harvard University Press.

Griffin, Keith, and A. K. Ghose. 1979. "Growth and Impoverishment in the Rural Areas of Asia." *World Development* 7 (4–5) April-May.

Guha, H. 1980. "Operation Flood II: Some Constraints and Implications: A Comment." *Economic and Political Weekly* 15 (17) April 26.

Guisinger, S., and N. Hicks. 1978. "Long-Term Trends in Income Distribution in Pakistan." *World Development* 6: 1271–80.

Gupta, D. 1980. "A Critical Evaluation of Government Policies and Programs of Rural Industrialization with Special Reference to the Punjab Region in Northern India." Institute of Economic Growth, Delhi. Draft.

Gupta, T., and D. Mohan. 1979. *Economics of Trees vs. Annual Crops on Marginal Agricultural Lands.* CMA Monograph 81. Ahmedabad: Center for Management in Agriculture, Indian Institute of Management.

Gupta, V. K., and D. P. Mathur. 1976. *Wheat Production, Marketing and Procurement.* CMA Monograph 58. Ahmedabad: Center for Management in Agriculture, Indian Institute of Management.

Gupta, V. K., and R. K. Pandey. 1975. "Consumption and Availability of Milk in India." *Indian Journal of Agricultural Economics* 30 (3) July-September: 142.

Guttman, J. 1980. "Villages as Interest Groups: The Demand for Agricultural Extension Services in India." *Kyklos* 33 (1): 121–41.

Haggblade, S., P. Hazell, and J. Brown. 1987. "Farm/Nonfarm Linkages in Rural Sub-Saharan Africa: Empirical Evidence and Policy Implications." Development Economics Department, World Bank, Washington, D.C. December.

Haider, A. S. 1977a. *An Economic Survey and Analysis of Factors Affecting Farm Production and Income in Selected Areas of Punjab.* Faisalabad: Department of Agricultural Economics, University of Agriculture.

―――. 1977b. *Emerging Occupations in a Rural Setting: Selective Evidence from Punjab, Pakistan.* Faisalabad: University of Agriculture.

Halse, M. 1980. "Increasing the Incomes of Landless Labourers and Small-Holders: Part I, The Experience of India's Dairy Cooperatives." *Agricultural Administration* 7: 259–72.

Hameed, N. D. Abdul, and others. 1977. *Rice Revolution in Sri Lanka.* Geneva: United Nations Research Institute for Social Development.

Harriss, B. 1972. "Innovation Adoption in Indian Agriculture: The High-Yielding Variety Program." *Modern Asian Studies* 6 (1) November.

―――. 1987. "Regional Growth Linkages from Agriculture and Resource Flows in Nonfarm Economy." *Economic and Political Weekly* 22 (1–2) January 3–10.

Havens, A. E., and W. Flinn. 1975. "Green Revolution Technology and Community Development: The Limits of Action Programs." *Economic Development and Cultural Change* 23 (3) April.

Hayami, Y., and R. Herdt. 1977. "Market Price Effects of Technological Change in Income Distribution in Semi-Subsistence Agriculture." *American Journal of Agricultural Economics* 59 (2): 245–56.

Hazell, P. 1984. "Sources of Increased Instability in Indian and U.S. Cereal Production." *American Journal of Agricultural Economics* 60 (3) August: 302–11.

Herdt, R., and C. Capule. 1983. *Adoption, Spread, and Impact of Modern Rice Varieties*. Manila: International Rice Research Institute.

Herdt, R. W. 1980. "Changing Asian Rice Technology: Impact, Benefits and Constraints." Paper prepared for the World Bank Seminar on the Introduction and Sustenance of High-Yielding Varieties, Washington, D.C., January 8.

Herdt, R. W., and E. A. Baker. 1972. "Agricultural Wages, Production and the High-Yielding Varieties." *Economic and Political Weekly* 7 (13) March 25: A23–A30.

Herdt, R. W., and A. Mandac. 1981. "Modern Technology and Economic Efficiency of Philippine Rice Farmers." *Economic Development and Cultural Change* 29 (2) January.

Herring, R., and M. G. Chaudhry. 1974. "The 1972 Land Reforms in Pakistan and Their Economic Implications: A Preliminary Analysis." *Pakistan Development Review* 13 (3) Autumn: 245–79.

Herring, Ronald. 1983. *Land to the Tiller*. New Haven, Conn.: Yale University Press.

Hinton, William. 1966. *Fanshen: A Documentary of Revolution in a Chinese Village*. New York: Monthly Review Press.

Hirashima, S. 1978. *The Structure of Disparity in Developing Agriculture*. Tokyo: Institute of Development Economics.

Hirschman, Albert O. 1958. *The Strategy of Economic Development*. New Haven, Conn.: Yale University Press.

Hirway, I. 1985. "Garibi Hatao: Can IRDP Do It?" *Economic and Political Weekly* 20 (13) March 30.

Ho, Samuel P. S. 1979. "Decentralized Industrialization and Rural Development: Evidence from Taiwan." *Economic Development and Cultural Change* 28 (1) October: 79–96.

Hodgdon, L. 1966. *Adoption of Agricultural Practices in Madhya Pradesh: Factors Associated with the Adoption of Recommended Agricultural Practices in Two Villages*. Hyderabad: Hyderabad National Institute of Community Development.

Honavar, R., and others. 1984. *An Economic Assessment of Poverty Eradication and Rural Unemployment Alleviation Programs and Their Prospects*. Madras: Institute for Financial Management and Research.

Hopper, W. D. 1965. "Allocative Efficiency in a Traditional Indian Agriculture." *Journal of Farm Economics* 47 (August): 611–29.

———. 1977. "Distortions to Agricultural Development Resulting from Government Prohibitions." Paper presented to workshop on Constraints in

World Agricultural Production with Special Reference to Distortion of Incentives, University of Chicago, Illinois, September.

Hossain, Mahabub. 1977a. "Agrarian Structure and Land Productivity in Bangladesh." Ph.D. diss., Cambridge University.

———. 1977b. "Farm Size, Tenancy and Land Productivity: An Analysis of Farm Level Data in Bangladesh Agriculture." *Bangladesh Development Studies* 5 (3) July: 285–348.

———. 1986. "A Note on the Trend of Landlessness in Bangladesh." *Bangladesh Development Studies* 14 (2) June: 95–100.

———. 1988. *Credit for Alleviation of Rural Poverty: The Grameen Bank in Bangladesh*. Research Report 65. Washington, D.C: International Food Policy Research Institute.

Huang, C. J., and F. S. Bagi. 1980. "Stochastic Frontier Production Functions and Average Efficiency in Indian Agriculture." Department of Rural Development, Tennessee State University, Nashville. October.

Huffman, W. E. 1977. "Allocative Efficiency: The Role of Human Capital." *Quarterly Journal of Economics* 91 (February): 59–79.

———. 1981. "Black-White Human Capital Differences: Impact on Agricultural Productivity in the U.S. South." *American Economic Review* 71 (1) March: 94–117.

Huq, A., ed. 1976. *Exploitation and the Rural Poor*. Comilla: Bangladesh Academy for Rural Development.

Huria, V. K., and K. T. Acharya. 1980. "Dairy Development in India: Some Critical Issues." *Economic and Political Weekly* 15 (45–46) November 8–15.

Hussain, A., and M. Muazzami. 1973. "Co-operative Farming in Bangladesh." Report of the Workshop. Bangladesh Agricultural University, Mymensingh. April.

Hussain, S. M. 1970. "Price Incentives for the Production of High-Yielding Mexican Varieties of Wheat." *Pakistan Development Review*, Winter.

IFDC (International Fertilizer Development Center). 1980. "Bangladesh: Equity Effects of Fertilizer Use." Joint Report of the Bangladesh Agricultural Research Council and the IFDC, Muscle Shoals, Alabama. Draft.

———. 1981. *Agricultural Production, Fertilizer Use, and Equity Considerations: Results and Analysis of Farm Survey Data, 1979–80*. Muscle Shoals, Alabama.

———. 1983. *Bangladesh: Policy Options for the Development of the Fertilizer Sector*. Muscle Shoals, Alabama.

IFPRI (International Food Policy Research Institute). 1985. *Development Impact of the Food for Work Program in Bangladesh*. Technical Papers. Washington D.C.

ILO (International Labour Organisation). 1971. *Problems of Employment Promotion in Pakistan*. Geneva.

———. 1972. *Employment, Income and Equality: A Strategy for Discovering Employment in Kenya*. Geneva.

————. 1974. *Sharing in Development: A Programme of Employment, Equity and Growth in the Philippines.* Geneva.

————. 1977a. *Poverty and Landlessness in Rural Asia.* Keith Griffin and A. R. Khan, eds. Geneva.

————. 1977b. *Report on the National Seminar on Landless Labour and Job Opportunities in Rural Areas.* Dhaka.

————. 1978. *Labor Absorption in Indian Agriculture.* Bangkok.

————. 1980. *Problems of Rural Workers in Asia and the Pacific.* Asian Regional Conference in Manila, Report 3. Geneva.

ILO and ARTEP (Asian Regional Team for Employment Promotion). 1980. *Employment Expansion in Asian Agriculture: A Comparative Analysis of South Asian Countries.* Bangkok: International Labour Office.

India, Government of, and Government of Maharashtra. 1980. *Joint Evaluation Report on Employment Guarantee Scheme for Maharashtra.* New Delhi.

India, Ministry of Agriculture and Irrigation. 1972. *Interim Report on Ceiling on Land Holdings.* Working Group, National Commission on Agriculture. New Delhi.

————. 1975. *All India Report on Agricultural Census, 1970–71.* New Delhi.

————. 1976. *Report of the National Commission on Agriculture.* New Delhi: Government Press.

India, Ministry of Agriculture and Rural Development. 1985a. *Indian Agriculture in Brief.* 20th ed. New Delhi: Directorate of Economics and Statistics, Department of Agriculture and Cooperation.

————. 1985b. *Instructions for the Implementation of the Rural Landless Employment Guarantee Programme.* New Delhi.

————. 1986. *Concurrent Evalution of* IRDP: *The Main Findings of the Survey for October 1985–March 1986.* New Delhi.

India, Ministry of Labour. 1978. *Rural Labour Enquiry, 1974–75: Summary Report.* New Delhi: Labour Bureau.

India, Ministry of Planning. 1961. "Tables with Notes on Some Aspects of Landholdings in Rural India, 16th Round (July 1960–June 1961)." National Sample Survey Organization, Department of Statistics.

————. 1976a. "Tables with Notes on Earnings, Indebtedness, Cultivated Holdings and Assets of the Weaker Section Households in Rural India, 25th Round: July 1970–June 1971." National Sample Survey Organization, Report 233.

————. 1976b. "Tables on Landholdings, 26th Round: July 1971–September 1972." All India and Statewide Reports for Punjab, Kerala, Gujarat, and Maharashtra. National Sample Survey Organization, Department of Statistics, February.

————. 1976c. "Some Summary Information on the Survey on Employment-Unemployment, 27th Round, October 1972–September 1973." National Sample Survey Organization, Report 255. Draft.

————. 1978. "Employment, Unemployment Situation at a Glance." *Sarvekshana* 2 (2) October.

————. 1982. "Tables on the Pattern of Land Ownership, 37th Round." National Sample Survey Organization, Department of Statistics.

————. 1983. "Tables on Unemployment, 38th Round." National Sample Survey Organization, Department of Statistics.

————. 1985. "Results of Indebtedness of Rural Labour Households, 32nd Round." *Sarvekshana* 7 (3–4) January-April.

————. 1986a. "Results of the Third Quinquennial Survey on Consumer Expenditure, 38th Round." *Sarvekshana* 9 (4) April: S1–S103.

————. 1986b. "Results on Assets and Liabilities of Rural and Urban Households: 37th Round, 1982." *Sarvekshana* 10 (1) July.

————. 1987. "Results on Indebtedness of Rural and Urban Households: 37th Round (January–December 1982)." *Sarvekshana* 11 (1) July.

————. 1988. *Economic Survey, 1987–88.* New Delhi.

India, Planning Commission. 1968. *Report on Evaluation of High-Yielding Varieties Programme, Kharif, 1968.* Delhi: Programme Evaluation Organisation.

————. 1971. *Evaluation Study of the High-Yielding Varieties Programme: Report for the Rabi 1968–69: Wheat, Paddy, and Jowar.* Delhi: Programme Evaluation Organisation.

————. 1976. *The High-Yielding Varieties Programme in India, 1970–75.* Part II. New Delhi: Programme Evaluation Organisation and Australian National University.

————. 1982. *Integrated Rural Development Programme: A Quick Preliminary Evaluation.* New Delhi: Programme Evaluation Organisation.

————. 1985a. *Evaluation Report on Integrated Rural Development Programme.* New Delhi.

————. 1985b. *The Seventh Five-Year Plan, 1985–90.* New Delhi.

Indian Society of Agricultural Economics. 1972. *Problems of Farm Mechanization.* Seminar Series 9. Bombay.

————. 1974. *Rural Development for Weaker Sections.* Seminar Series 12. Bombay.

Institute of Food and Nutrition Sciences. 1978. *Economic and National Effects of Food for Relief Work Projects.* Dhaka: University of Dhaka.

————. 1981. *Nutrition Survey of Rural Bangladesh.* Dhaka: University of Dhaka.

IRRI (International Rice Research Institute). 1972. *Rice, Science and Man.* Los Baños.

————. 1975. *Major Research in Upland Rice.* Los Baños.

————. 1978a. *Economic Consequences of the New Rice Technology.* Los Baños.

————. 1978b. *Changes in Rice Farming in Selected Areas of Asia.* Los Baños.

Isenman, P. I., and H. W. Singer. 1977. "Food Aid Disincentive Effects and Their Policy Implications." *Economic Development and Cultural Change* 25 (2) January: 205–37.

Islam, M. M. 1978. *Bengal Agriculture 1920–1946: A Quantitative Study.* Cambridge: Cambridge University Press.

Islam, Nurul. 1978. *Development Strategy of Bangladesh.* Oxford: Pergamon Press.

————. 1980. *Poultry Raising in a Comilla Village: A Survey of Existing Facilities and Problems.* Comilla: Bangladesh Academy for Rural Development.

Islam, Rizwanul. 1979. "What Has Been Happening to Rural Income Distribution in Bangladesh?" *Development and Change* 10 (3) July.

Jabbar, M. A. 1977. "Relative Productive Efficiency of Different Tenure Classes in Selected Areas of Bangladesh." *Bangladesh Development Studies* 5 (1) January.

Jain, Shail. 1975. *Size Distribution of Income: A Compilation of Data.* Baltimore, Md.: Johns Hopkins University Press.

Jannuzi, F. Tomasson. 1974. *Agrarian Crisis in India: The Case of Bihar.* Austin: University of Texas Press.

————. 1976. *Preliminary Report Concerning the Need for Further Research on the Hierarchy of Interests in Land in Bangladesh.* Dhaka: U.S. Agency for International Development.

Jannuzi, F. Tomasson, and James T. Peach. 1977a. *Report on the Hierarchy of Interests in Land in Bangladesh.* Washington, D.C.: U.S. Agency for International Development.

————. 1977b. *Summary Report of the 1977 Land Occupancy Survey of Rural Bangladesh.* Dhaka: Bureau of Statistics.

————. 1979. "A Note on Land Reforms in Bangladesh: The Efficacy of Ceilings." *Journal of Peasant Studies* 6 (3) April: 342–47; comment by K. Siddiqui, pp. 348–50.

————. 1980. *The Agrarian Structure of Bangladesh: Impediments to Development.* Boulder, Colo.: Westview Press.

Jayaraman, T. 1984. "A Review of the Special Credit Programme in an Irrigation Project in India." *Agricultural Administration* 16: 1–16.

Jayasuriya, J., and R. Chand. 1986. "Technical Change and Labor Absorption in Asian Agriculture: Some Emerging Trends." *World Development* 14 (3): 415–18.

Jaynes, G. D. 1979a. "The Economics of Land Tenure." Paper presented at the Conference on Adjustment Mechanisms of Rural Labor Markets in Developing Areas, Agricultural Development Council and International Crop Research Institute for Semi-Arid Tropics, Hyderabad, August 22–24.

————. 1979b. *Production and Distribution in Agrarian Economics.* Discussion Paper 309. New Haven, Conn.: Economic Growth Center, Yale University.

Jha, L., and others. 1984. *Report of the Evaluation Committee on Operation Flood II.* New Delhi: Ministry of Agriculture.

Jodha, N. S. 1972. "A Strategy for Dry Land Agriculture." *Economic and Political Weekly* 7 (13) March.

―――. 1973. "Special Programmes for the Rural Poor: The Constraining Framework." *Economic and Political Weekly* 8 (13) March.

―――. 1979. "Agricultural Tenancy in Semi-Arid Tropical Parts of India." International Crops Research Institute for the Semi-Arid Tropics, Hyderabad. Draft.

―――. 1986. "Common Property Resources and Rural Poverty in Dry Regions of India." *Economic and Political Weekly* 21 (27): 1169–81.

Johl, S. S. 1971. *Mechanization, Labor Use, and Productivity in Indian Agriculture.* Occasional Paper 23. Columbus: Department of Agricultural Economics and Rural Sociology, Ohio State University.

―――. 1975. "Gains of the Green Revolution: How They Have Been Shared in Punjab." *Journal of Development Studies* 2 (3) April.

Johnson, D. 1950. "Resource Allocation under Share Contracts." *Journal of Political Economy* 58: 111–23.

Johnston, B., and J. Cownie. 1969. "The Seed Fertilizer Revolution and Labor Force Absorption." *American Economic Review* 59 (4) September.

Johnston, B., and P. Kilby. 1975. *Agriculture and Structural Transformation.* New York: Oxford University Press.

Jose, A. V. 1974. "Trends in the Real Wage Rates of Agricultural Workers." *Economic and Political Weekly* 30 (3).

―――. 1978. "Real Wages, Employment and Income of Agricultural Labourers." *Economic and Political Weekly*, Review of Agriculture 12 (42) March.

Joshi, P. C. 1961. "Problems and Prospects of Ceilings on Land Holdings in India." *Agricultural Situation in India* 15 (5) August.

―――. 1974. "Agrarian Structure and the Rural Poor: Review of Perspectives." *Social Change* 4 (September-December).

―――. 1975. *Land Reforms in India.* Bombay: Allied Publishers.

―――. 1979a. "Perspectives on Poverty and Social Change: The Emergence of the Poor as a Class." *Economic and Political Weekly* 14 (7–8) February: 355–66.

―――. 1979b. "Technological Potentialities of Peasant Agriculture." *Economic and Political Weekly* 14 (June): A47–A57.

Joshi P., D. Bahl, and D. Jha. 1981. "Direct Employment Effect of Technical Change in Uttar Pradesh Agriculture." *Indian Journal of Agricultural Economics* 36 (4) October-December.

Juergensmeyer, M. 1979. "Cultures of Deprivation: Three Case Studies in Punjab." *Economic and Political Weekly* 14 (7–8) February: 255–62.

Jul, M. 1979. "Unexpected Benefit from a Dairy Project." *Food and Nutrition Bulletin* 1 (3) May.

Junankar, P. N. 1977. *Tests of the Profit Maximisation Hypothesis: A Study of Indian Agriculture.* Discussion Paper 96. Colchester: Department of Economics, University of Essex.

————. 1978a. "Do Indian Farmers Maximise Profits?" Department of Economics, University of Essex, Colchester. May. Draft.

————. 1978b. *Profit Maximization: Translog Functions Applied to Indian Agriculture*. Discussion Paper 313. Kingston, Ontario: Institute of Economic Research, Queens University.

Kahlon, A. S. 1970. "Farm Technology: Its Implications in Agricultural Economics." Presidential Address, Indian Society of Agricultural Economics, October 23.

Kahlon A. S., K. Dhawan, and G. Gill. 1975. "Relative Profitability of Dairy Enterprise vis-à-vis Crop Cultivation in the Punjab." *Indian Journal of Agricultural Economics* 30 (3) July-September: 120–28.

Kahlon, A. S., and S. S. Johl. 1964. "Nature and Role of Risk and Uncertainty in Agriculture." *Indian Journal of Agricultural Economics* 19 (January-March).

Kahlon, A. S., and G. Singh. 1973. "Social and Economic Implications of Large-Scale Introduction of High-Yielding Varieties of Wheat in Punjab with Special Reference to the Gurdaspur District." United Nations Development Programme Global Project. Department of Economics and Sociology, Punjab Agricultural University, Ludhiana.

Kalirajan, K. 1981. "The Economic Efficiency of Farmers Growing High-Yielding Irrigated Rice in India." *American Journal of Agricultural Economics* 63 (3) August: 566–607.

Kaneda, Hiromitsu. 1969. "Economic Implications of the Green Revolution and the Strategy of Agricultural Development in West Pakistan." *Pakistan Development Review* 10 (2) Summer.

————. 1972. "Economic Implications of the Green Revolution and the Strategy of Agricultural Development in West Pakistan." In Keith Griffin and A. R. Khan, eds., *Growth and Inequality in Pakistan*. New York: St. Martin's.

Kaneda, Hiromitsu, and M. Ghaffar. 1970. "Output Effects of Tubewells on the Agriculture of the Punjab: Some Empirical Results." *Pakistan Development Review* 10 (1) Spring: 71–72.

Kansal, S. 1981. "Data on Income Distribution in Bangladesh." Working Paper 1981-8. EPD Income Distribution Project, World Bank, Washington, D.C. July.

Kapteyn A., T. Wansbeek, and J. Buyze. 1979. "Maximizing or Satisficing?" *Review of Economics and Statistics* 61 (November): 549–63.

Karanjkar, S. V., and S. N. Soni. 1980. "Economics of Poultry Enterprise in Jabalpur." *Indian Journal of Agricultural Economics* 35 (4) October-December: 170.

Katyal, R., and V. Sood. 1976. "Real Growth in Agriculture at State Level." Indian Association for Research in National Income and Wealth, Tenth General Conference. January.

Kaul, J., and S. Kahlon. 1971. "Problems of Marginal Farmers and Agricultural Laborers in Hoshiarpur District of Punjab." Department of Economics and Sociology, Punjab Agricultural University, Ludhiana.

Keesing, D. 1975. "Economic Lessons from China." *Journal of Development Economics* 2: 1–32.

Kelkar, G. A., and S. Subramanian. 1977. "Pattern of Assets of Rural Households, 1961–71." *Indian Reserve Bank Staff Occasional Papers* 2 (1) June: 1–57.

Khan, Akhtar Hameed. 1971. *Tour of 20 Thanas*. Comilla: Bangladesh Academy for Rural Development.

Khan, A. R. 1972. *The Economics of Bangladesh*. London: Macmillan.

Khan, A. R., and others. 1981. *Employment, Income and the Mobilisation of Local Resources: A Study of Two Bangladesh Villages*. Asian Employment Programme. Bangkok: International Labour Organisation.

Khan, Ahmed Syed, A. M. Chaudhry, and M. Aslam. 1969. "Economics of Modern Poultry Production in West Pakistan." Faculty of Agricultural Economics and Rural Sociology, West Pakistan Agricultural University. October.

Khan, D. A. 1978. *Employment and Occupational Change in the Rural Punjab: Consequences of the Green Revolution*. Lahore: Economic Research Institute.

Khan, M. H. 1975. *The Economics of the Green Revolution in Pakistan.* New York: Praeger.

———. 1977. "Land Productivity, Farm Size and Returns to Scale in Pakistan Agriculture." *World Development* 5 (4) April: 317–23.

———. 1979a. "Agrarian Institutions and Change in Pakistan." Department of Economics, Simon Fraser University, Vancouver. Draft.

———. 1979b. "Farm Size and Land Productivity Relationships in Pakistan." *Pakistan Development Review* 18 (1) Spring: 9–76.

———. 1981. *Underdevelopment and Agrarian Structure in Pakistan*. Boulder, Colo.: Westview Press.

Khan, M. H., and D. R. Maki. 1979. "Effects of Farm Size on Economic Efficiency: The Case of Pakistan." *American Journal of Agricultural Economics* February: 64–69.

———. 1980. "Relative Efficiency by Farm Size and the Green Revolution in Pakistan." *Pakistan Development Review* 19 (1) Spring: 51–64.

Khan, S., and others. 1977. *Agricultural Employment and Underdevelopment in Bangladesh: The Next Decade*. UNDP/FAO Working Paper. New York: United Nations Development Programme and Food and Agriculture Organization.

Khan, T. M., and S. Bose. 1968. "Report on Income of Agricultural Workers in Pakistan." Pakistan Institute of Development Economics, Islamabad. November. Processed.

Khan, Waheeduddin, and V. B. R. S. Somasekhara Rao. 1974. "On Tenancy, Rent Systems and Improved Technology: An Investigation in West Godavari District." *Community Development and Panchayati Raj Digest*, April.

Khan, Waheeduddin, and R. N. Tripathy. 1972. "Intensive Agriculture and

Modern Inputs: Prospects of Small Farmers–A Study in West Godavari District." National Institute of Community Development, Hyderabad.

Khandker, R. H. 1973. "Distribution of Income and Wealth in Pakistan." *Pakistan Economic and Social Review* 11 (1) Spring.

Khasnabis, Ratan. 1981. "Operation Barga: Limits to Democratic Reformism." *Economic and Political Weekly*, Review of Agriculture 16 (25–26) June 20–27: A43–A48.

Khilji, N. 1986. "Optimum Resource Utilization in Pakistan's Agriculture." *Pakistan Development Review* 25 (4) Winter: 469–86.

Khusro, A. M. 1964. "Returns to Scale in Indian Agriculture." *Indian Journal of Agricultural Economics* 19 (3–4) July-December. Also in Khusro (1973).

———. 1965. "Land Reforms since Independence." In V. B. Singh, ed., *Economic History of India, 1857–1956*. Bombay: Allied Publishers.

———. 1973. *Economics of Land Reform and Farm Size in India*. Institute of Economic Growth. Delhi: Macmillan.

Kishore, D. 1986. "An Alternate Strategy for the Transfer of Technology with Special Reference to India." *Agricultural Administration* 21: 197–204.

Korten, David C. 1980. "Community Organization and Rural Development: A Leasing Process Approach." *Public Administration Review* September-October: 480–511.

Krishna, P. V., and S. C. Bandhopadhyay. 1975. "A Case Study of a Successful Dairy." *Indian Journal of Agricultural Economics* 30 (3) July-September: 145.

Krishna, Raj. 1959. "Agrarian Reform in India: The Debate on Ceilings." *Economic Development and Cultural Change* 7 (April).

———. 1967. "Government Operations in Foodgrains. *Economic and Political Weekly* 3 (37) September 16.

———. 1973a. "Unemployment in India." *Economic and Political Weekly* 8 (9) March 3.

———. 1973b. "Unemployment in India: Presidential Address." *Indian Journal of Agricultural Economics* 28 (1) January-March.

———. 1974. "Unemployment in India." *Teaching Forum* 38 (March). Agricultural Development Council, New York.

———. 1975. "Measurement of the Direct and Indirect Effects of Agricultural Growth with Technical Change." In Lloyd G. Reynolds, ed., *Agriculture in Development Theory*. New Haven, Conn.: Yale University Press.

———. 1976. *Rural Unemployment: A Survey of Concepts and Estimates for India*. World Bank Staff Working Paper 234. Washington, D.C..

Krishna, Raj, and A. Chhibber. 1983. *Policy Modelling of a Dual Grain Market: The Case of Wheat in India*. Research Report 38. Washington, D.C.: International Food Policy Research Institute.

Krishnaji, N. 1971. "Wages of Agricultural Labour." *Economic and Political Weekly*, Review of Agriculture 6 (39) September 25: A35–A41.

——. 1987. "Agricultural Growth, Prices and Rural Poverty." *Economic and Political Weekly* 22 (26) June 27.

Krishnamurty, N. S., and S. Subramanian. 1977. "Financial Assets of Rural Households." *Indian Reserve Bank Staff Occasional Papers* 2 (1) June: 84–135.

Kumar, P., V. C. Mathur, and R. P. Singh. 1981. "Estimating Labor Demand Functions and Labor Absorption in Agriculture: A Case Study of Delhi Wheat Farms." *Indian Journal of Agricultural Economics* 36 (4) October-December: 7–13.

Kurian, N. 1987. "IRDP: How Relevant Is It?" *Economic and Political Weekly* 22 (52) December 26: A161–A176.

Kurien, C. T. 1977. "Putting the Instruments of Rural Development into the Hands of Producers." Paper presented at the Ramon Magsaysay Award Workshop, National Dairy Development Board, Anand, February 7–9.

——. 1986. "Reconciling Growth and Social Justice Strategies and Structures." In M. L. Dantwala and others, *Rural Development: The Asian Experience*. New Delhi: Oxford University Press and IBH Publishing Co.

Ladejinsky, Wolf. 1977. *Agrarian Reform as Unfinished Business: The Selected Papers of Wolf Ladejinsky*. Louis J. Walinsky, ed. New York: Oxford University Press.

Lakshminarayan, H. 1973a. "Small Farmers' Development Program: A Note." *Economic and Political Weekly* 8 (17) April 28.

——. 1973b. "The Social and Economic Implication of Large-Scale Introduction of High-Yielding Varieties of Wheat in Haryana." UNDP Global Project. Agricultural Economic Research Center, University of Delhi, New Delhi.

——. 1979. "Inter-Size Group and Inter-State Variations in Distribution of Agricultural Assets." *Economic and Political Weekly* 14 (26) June 30: A69–A74.

Lakshminarayan, H., and S. Tyagi. 1976. "Some Aspects of Size Distribution of Agricultural Holdings." *Economic and Political Weekly* 11 (44) October 9: 1637–40.

——. 1977. "Inter-State Variations in Types of Tenancy." *Economic and Political Weekly* 12 (39) September 24.

Lal, D. 1975. "The Agrarian Question." *South Asian Review* 8 (4) July-October.

——. 1976. "Agricultural Growth, Real Wages and the Rural Poor in India." *Economic and Political Weekly*, Review of Agriculture 11 (26) June 26.

——. 1977. "Agricultural Growth and Rural Real Wages: A Reply." *Economic and Political Weekly* 12 (20) May 14.

Lau, L., and P. Yotopoulos. 1971. "A Test for Relative Efficiency and Application to Indian Agriculture." *American Economic Review* 61 (March): 94–107.

Lawson, R. 1977. "New Directions in Developing Small-Scale Fisheries." *Marine Policy* 1 (1) January: 45–51.

Leaf, M. 1983. "The Green Revolution and Cultural Change in a Punjab Village, 1965–1978." *Economic Development and Cultural Change* 31 (2) January: 227–70.

Lehman, D. 1977. "The Death of Land Reform." Paper presented at the World Bank Workshop on the Analysis of Distributional Issues in Development Planning, Bellagio, Italy, April.

Lele, Uma. 1968. "The Traders of Sholapur." In John W. Mellor, T. L. Weaver, Uma Lele, and S. Simons, eds., *Developing Rural India*. Ithaca, N.Y.: Cornell University Press.

———. 1971. *Food Grain Marketing in India: Private Performance and Public Policy*. Ithaca, N.Y.: Cornell University Press.

———. 1972. "Distributional Efficiency and Agricultural Price Policy: Food Grain Marketing in India." Teaching Forum Paper, Marketing Price Analysis and Trade no. 21. Agricultural Development Council, New York. October.

———. 1974. "The Roles of Credit and Marketing in Agricultural Development." In Nurul Islam, ed., *Agricultural Policy in Developing Countries*. Proceedings of a Conference of the International Economics Association, Bad Godesberg, Federal Republic of Germany. New York: Wiley.

———. 1976. "Considerations Related to Optimum Pricing and Marketing Strategies in Rural Development." Paper presented at the 16th International Conference of Agricultural Economics, Nairobi, July–August.

———. 1977. "Cooperatives and the Poor: A Comparative Perspective." Paper presented at the Experts' Consultation on Cooperatives and the Poor, International Cooperative Alliance, Loughborough, U.K., July.

Lele, Uma, and John W. Mellor. 1972a. "Jobs, Poverty and the Green Revolution." *International Affairs* 47 (1): 20–32.

———. 1972b. *Technological Change and Distributive Bias in a Dual Economy*. Occasional Paper 43. Ithaca, N.Y.: Department of Agricultural Economics, Cornell University.

———. 1981. "Technological Change, Distributive Bias and Labor Transfer in a Two-Sector Economy." *Oxford Economic Papers* 33 (November): 426–41.

Liedholm, Carl, and Enyinna Chuta. 1976. *The Economics of Rural and Urban Small-Scale Industries in Sierra Leone*. African Rural Economy Paper 14. East Lansing: Department of Agricultural Economics, Michigan State University.

Lipton, Michael. 1968. "The Theory of the Optimizing Peasant." *Journal of Development Studies* 4: 327–51.

———. 1974. "Towards a Theory of Land Reforms." In D. Lehman, ed., *Peasants, Landlords and Governments: Agrarian Reform in the Third World*. New York: Holmes and Meier.

———. 1976. "Agricultural Finance and Rural Credit in Poor Countries." *World Development* 4 (2) July.

———. 1977. *Why Poor People Stay Poor: Urban Bias in World Development*. Cambridge, Mass.: Harvard University Press.

———. 1978. "Inter-Farm, Inter-Regional and Farm/Non-Farm Income Distribution: The Impact of the New Cereal Varieties." *World Development* 6 (3): 319–37.

———. 1979. "The Technology, the System and the Poor: The Case of the New Cereal Varieties." In Institute of Social Studies, *Development of Societies: The Next Twenty-Five Years.* Dordrecht, Netherlands: M. Nijhoff.

———. 1983a. *Demography and Poverty.* World Bank Staff Working Paper 623. Washington, D.C.

———. 1983b. *Labor and Poverty.* World Bank Staff Working Paper 616. Washington, D.C.

———. 1983c. *Poverty, Undernutrition, and Hunger.* World Bank Staff Working Paper 597. Washington, D.C.

———. 1984. "Conditions of Poverty Groups and Impact on Indian Economic Development and Cultural Change: The Role of Labour." *Development and Change* 15: 473–93.

———. 1985. *Land Assets and Rural Poverty.* World Bank Staff Working Paper 744. Washington, D.C.

———. 1988. *Poor and the Poorest: Some Interim Findings.* World Bank Discussion Paper 25. Washington, D.C.

Lluch, Constantino, Alan A. Powell, and Ross A. Williams. 1977. *Patterns in Household Demand and Saving.* New York: Oxford University Press.

Lockheed, Marlaine E., Dean T. Jamison, and Lawrence T. Lau. 1980. "Farmer Education and Farm Efficiency: A Survey." *Economic Development and Cultural Change* 29 (1) October: 37–76.

Lockwood, Brian. 1981. "Farm Mechanization in Pakistan: Policy and Practice." Working Paper 17. The Consequences of Small Rice Farm Mechanization Project, Agricultural Development Council, Lahore.

Lockwood, Brian, P. K. Mukherjee, and R. T. Shand. 1971. *The High-Yielding Varieties Programme in India.* Part I. Delhi: Planning Commission of India and Australian National University.

Longhurst, R., and Michael Lipton. 1989. *New Seeds and Poor People.* Baltimore, Md.: Johns Hopkins University Press.

Longhurst, R., and P. Payne. 1979. *Seasonal Aspects of Nutrition: Review of Evidence and Policy Implications.* Discussion Paper 5. Brighton: Institute of Development Studies, University of Sussex. September.

Lowdermilk, Max K. 1972. "Diffusion of Dwarf Wheat Production Technology in Pakistan's Punjab." Ph.D. diss., Cornell University, Ithaca, N.Y.

Lowdermilk, Max K., Alan C. Early, and David M. Freeman. 1978. *Farm Irrigation Constraints and Farmers' Responses: Comprehensive Field Survey in Pakistan.* Water Management Research Project, Technical Report 48A-F. Fort Collins: Colorado State University, September.

Lowdermilk, Max K., and David M. Freeman. 1977. "Organising Farmers to Improve Irrigation Water Delivery: The Problem and Prospects for Solutions in Pakistan." *Pakistan Economic and Social Review* 15 (Autumn-Winter): 152–73.

Lowdermilk, Max K., R. Frey Scott, and David M. Freeman. 1979. "Cancian's 'Upper Middle Class Conservatism' Thesis: A Replication from Pakistan." *Rural Sociology* 44 (2): 420–30.

Lucas, R. 1977. *Sharing, Monitoring and Incentives: Marshallian Misallocation Reassessed.* Discussion Paper 10. Boston, Mass.: Department of Economics, Boston University.

Ludden, D. 1978. "Patronage and Irrigation in Tamil Nadu: A Long-Term View." *Social History Review* 16 (3).

———. 1979a. "Dimensions of Agrarian Political Economy: Focus on Tamil Nadu, India." *Peasant Studies* 8 (4) Fall.

———. 1979b. "Ecological Zones and the Cultural Economy of Irrigation in Southern Tamil Nadu." *South Asia: Journal of South Asian Studies* 9.

Mahendradev, S. 1986. "Growth of Labour Productivity in Agriculture." *Economic and Political Weekly* 21 (25–26) June 21–28.

———. 1987. "Growth and Instability in Foodgrains Production: An Interstate Analysis." *Economic and Political Weekly* 22 (39) September 26: A82–A93.

Mahmood, Moazam. 1977. "The Pattern of Adoption of Green Revolution Technology and Its Effects on Land Holdings in the Punjab." *Pakistan Economic and Social Review* 15 (1–2) Spring-Summer.

Mahmud, W. 1979. "Foodgrain Demand Elasticities of Rural Households in Bangladesh: An Analysis of Pooled Cross-Section Data." *Bangladesh Development Studies* 7 (1) Winter.

Mallum, D., and V. Gupta. 1977. *Changing Pattern of Wheat Production and Marketing.* CMA Monograph 67. Ahmedabad: Center for Management in Agriculture, Indian Institute of Management.

Mandal, G. P., and M. G. Ghosh. 1976. *Economics of the Green Revolution: A Study in East India.* Muzaffarnagar: Asian Publishers.

Marbro, R. 1971. "Employment and Wages in a Dual Agriculture." *Oxford Economic Papers* 23: 401–17.

Marshall, A. 1961. *Principles of Economics.* 9th ed. Cambridge: Cambridge University Press.

Masum, M. 1976. "Unemployment and Underemployment in Agriculture: A Case Study of Bangladesh." Ph.D. diss., School of Economics, Delhi University.

———. 1979. "Unemployment and Underemployment in Bangladesh: A Micro Study." *Bangladesh Development Studies* 7 (2) Summer: 47–69.

Mathai, P. 1972. "Rural Industrialization and the Maximization of Employment Opportunities in India." *Small Industry Bulletin for Asia and the Far East* 9.

Mathur, D. P., and V. K. Gupta. 1978. *Management of Small Poultry Farms.* CMA Monograph 73. Ahmedabad: Center for Management in Agriculture, Indian Institute of Management.

Mavalankar, N. 1971. "Economics of Consolidation in India: A Case Study Revised." *Artha Vijnana* 13 (4) December.

Mavinkurve, B. S., and P. K. Sundernathan. 1975. *The Small Farmers Develop-ment Agencies (1972–73): A Field Study.* Bombay: Reserve Bank of India.

Mazumdar, Dipak. 1963. "On the Economics of Relative Efficiency of Small Farms." *Economic Weekly*, Special Number (July): 1259–63.

———. 1965. "Size of Farm and Productivity: A Problem of Indian Peasant Agriculture." *Economica* 32 (126) May: 161–73.

———. 1975a. "The Theory of Sharecropping with Labor Market Dualism." *Economica* 42 (167) August: 261–71.

———. 1975b. *The Theory of Urban Underemployment in Less Developed Countries.* World Bank Staff Working Paper 198. Washington, D.C.

———. 1975c. *The Urban Informal Sector.* World Bank Staff Working Paper 211. Washington, D.C.

———. 1980. "A Descriptive Analysis of the Role of Small-Scale Enterprises in the Indian Economy." Development Economics Department, World Bank, Washington, D.C. Draft.

McInerney, John, and Graham Donaldson. 1975. *The Consequences of Farm Tractors in Pakistan.* World Bank Staff Working Paper 210. Washington, D.C.

Mead, C. 1981. *Landless in India and Bangladesh: A Critical Review of Data Sources.* Working Paper 71. New York: Population Council.

Mehra, Shakuntala. 1976. *Some Aspects of Labor Use in Indian Agriculture.* Tech-nological Change in Agriculture Project. Occasional Paper 88. Ithaca, N.Y.: Department of Agricultural Economics, Cornell University, June. Also *Indian Journal of Agricultural Economics* 31 (4).

Mellor, John W. 1976. *The New Economics of Growth.* Ithaca, N.Y.: Cornell Uni-versity Press.

Mellor, John W., and Gunvant M. Desai, eds. 1985. *Agricultural Change and Rural Poverty: Variations on a Theme by Dharm Narain.* Baltimore, Md.: Johns Hopkins University Press.

Mellor, John W., and Uma Lele. 1973. "Growth Linkages of the New Foodgrain Technologies." *Indian Journal of Agricultural Economics* 28 (1) Jan-uary-March: 35–55.

Mellor, John W., and M. Mudahar. 1974a. *Modernizing Agriculture, Employment and Economic Growth: A Simulation Model.* Occasional Paper 75. Ithaca, N.Y.: Department of Agricultural Economics, Cornell University.

———. 1974b. *Simulating a Developing Economy with Modernizing Agriculture Sector: Implications for Employment and Economic Growth.* Occasional Paper 76. Ithaca, N.Y.: Department of Agricultural Economics, Cornell Uni-versity.

Mellor, John W., and others. 1968. *Developing Rural India: Plan and Practice.* Ithaca, N.Y.: Cornell University Press.

Mencher, J. 1974. "Conflicts and Contradictions in the Green Revolution: The Case of Tamil Nadu." *Economic and Political Weekly* 9 (February).

———. 1978. "Agrarian Relations in Two Rice Regions of Kerala." *Economic and Political Weekly*, Annual Number (February).

Michie, Barry H. 1973. "Variations in Economic Behaviour and the Green Revolution: An Anthropological Perspective." *Economic and Political Weekly* 3 (26) June 30.

Minhas, B. S. 1974. "Rural Development for the Weaker Sections: Experience and Lessons." In *Rural Development for Weaker Sections*. Seminar Series 12. Bombay: Indian Society of Agricultural Economics and Indian Institute of Management.

Mishra, G. 1980. "Impact of Dairy Development in Rural Areas of Karnataka." Institute for Social and Economic Change, Bangalore. Processed.

Mishra, V. N., and D. S. Tyagi. 1972. "An Economic Analysis of the HYV of Wheat: A Study of Kota District." *Artha Vikas* January 1.

Mitra, Ashok. 1979. *The Status of Women: Literacy and Employment*. New Delhi: Indian Council of Social Science Research.

Mitra, P. K. 1979. "A Theory of Interlinked Rural Transactions." Development Research Center, World Bank, Washington, D.C. August. Draft.

Mohammad, Ghulam. 1965. "Private Tubewell Development and the Cropping Patterns in West Pakistan." *Pakistan Development Review* Spring: 25–26.

Mohan, Rakesh. 1974. "Contribution of Research and Extension to Productivity Change in Indian Agriculture." *Economic and Political Weekly*, Review of Agriculture 9 (39) September 18.

Moore, J. R., S. S. Johl, and A. M. Khusro. 1973. *Indian Foodgrain Marketing*. New Delhi: Prentice Hall of India.

Moorti, T. 1971. "A Comparative Study of Well Irrigation in Aligaoli District, India." *Cornell International Agricultural Development Bulletin*, May 19.

Moreland, W. 1929. *The Agrarian Structure of Muslim India*. Allahabad: Central Book Report.

Moscardi, E. 1976. "A Behavioral Model for Decision under Risk among Small-Holding Farmers." Ph.D. diss., University of California, Berkeley.

———. 1979. "Methodology to Study Attitudes Towards Risk: The Puebla Project." In A. Valdes, G. S. Scobie, and J. Dillon, eds., *Economics and the Design of Small-Farmer Technology*. Ames: Iowa State University Press.

Mudahar, M. S. 1973. *Dynamic Models of Agricultural Development with Demand Linkages*. Occasional Paper 59. Ithaca, N.Y.: Department of Agricultural Economics, Cornell University.

———. 1974. *Dynamic Analysis of Direct and Indirect Implications of Technological Change in Agriculture: The Case of Punjab, India*. Occasional Paper 79. Ithaca, N.Y.: Department of Agricultural Economics, Cornell University.

Mukherjee, M. 1980. "Some Aspects of Agrarian Structure of Punjab 1925–47." *Economic and Political Weekly* 15 (26) June 28.

Mukherjee, P. K. 1970. "The HYVP: Variables That Matter." *Economic and Political Weekly* 5 (13) March 28: A15–A22.

Mukherjee, Ramakrishna. 1961. "Rural Class Structure in West Bengal." In

A. R. Desai, ed., *Rural Sociology in India.* Bombay: IBH Publishing Co.

Mukherjee, Robin M. 1986. "Statistical Information on Final Consumption in India and the National Sample Survey." *Economic and Political Weekly* 21 (5) February 1: 206–09.

Mukund, K. 1986. "Bank Credit and IRDP: Madhya Pradesh Experience." *Economic and Political Weekly* 21 (41) October 11.

Muller, J. 1974. "On Sources of Measured Technical Efficiency: The Impact of Information." *American Journal of Agricultural Economics* 56 (4) November: 730–38.

Mundle, S. 1981. "Land, Labor and the Level of Living in Rural Bihar." Asian Regional Team for Employment Promotion, International Labour Organisation, Geneva. Processed.

———. 1982. "Land, Labor and the Level of Living in Rural Punjab." Asian Regional Team for Employment Promotion, International Labour Organisation, Geneva. June. Processed.

———. 1983. "Effect of Agricultural Production and Prices on the Incidence of Rural Poverty: A Tentative Analysis of Interstate Variations." *Economic and Political Weekly*, Review of Agriculture (June): A48–A53.

Muqtada, M. 1974. "The Seed-Fertilizer Technology and Surplus Labor in Bangladesh Agriculture." *Bangladesh Development Studies* 3 (4): 403–28.

Murty, C. 1987. "Influence of Socio-Economic Status on Contractual Terms of Tenancy: A Study in Two Delta Villages of Andhra Pradesh." *Economic and Political Weekly* 22 (39) September 26: A111–A121.

Muthiah, C. 1971. "The Green Revolution: Participation by Small vs. Large Farmers." *Indian Journal of Agricultural Economics* 26 (1) January-March.

Myers, Desaix. 1973. "Comilla: Reassessment and Replication—The Cooperative under Stress." *Small Farmer Credit in South Asia.* USAID Spring Review of Small Farmer Credit. Washington, D.C.: U.S. Agency for International Development.

Myrdal, Gunnar. 1968. *The Asian Drama: An Inquiry into the Poverty of Nations.* New York: Pantheon.

Naidu, V. T. 1964. "Risk and Uncertainty in Agriculture in Relation to Credit." *Indian Journal of Agricultural Economics* 19 (January-March).

Nair, K. 1979. *In Defense of the Irrational Peasant.* Chicago, Ill.: University of Chicago Press.

Nakajima, C. 1970. "Subsistence and Commercial Family Farms: Some Theoretical Models of Subjective Equilibrium." In C. R. Wharton, Jr., ed., *Subsistence Agriculture and Economic Development.* Chicago, Ill.: Aldine.

Narain, Dharm, and P. Joshi. 1969. "Magnitude of Agricultural Tenancy." *Economic and Political Weekly*, Review of Agriculture, September 27.

Narain, Dharm, and Shyamal Roy. 1980. *Impact of Irrigation and Labor Availability on Multiple Cropping: A Case Study of India.* IFPRI Research Report 20. Washington, D.C.: International Food Policy Research Institute.

Naseem, S. M. 1971. "Small Farmers and Agricultural Transformation in Pakistan Punjab." Ph.D. diss., University of California, Davis.

―――. 1973. "Mass Poverty in Pakistan: Some Preliminary Findings." *Pakistan Development Review* 12 (4) Winter.

―――. 1979. "A National Profile of Poverty in Pakistan." Joint ESCAP-Quaid e Azam University project, Bangkok. Draft.

Nayyar, R. 1976. "Wages for Agricultural Labourers in Uttar Pradesh." *Economic and Political Weekly* 6 (11).

NCAER (National Council of Applied Economic Research). 1974. *Credit Requirements for Agriculture*. New Delhi.

―――. 1975. *Changes in Rural Income in India, 1968–71*. New Delhi.

―――. 1977. *Resource Use, Productivity and Land Reforms in Uttar Pradesh*. New Delhi.

―――. 1978. *Fertilizer Demand Study: Interim Report, 1975–76*. New Delhi.

―――. 1979. *Survey Data on Patterns of Fertilizer Use on Selected Crops: 1975–76 and 1976–77*. Fertilizer Demand Study, Final Report, vol. 10. New Delhi.

NDDB (National Dairy Development Board, India). 1977. *Operation Flood II: A Proposal by the National Dairy Development Board*. Anand, June.

Netherlands, Ministry of Foreign Affairs. 1978. *Bangladesh: Rural Development in Four Tharas in Kushtia District: Study on the Problems of the Rural Poor*. The Hague: International Technical Assistance Department.

Newbery, David. 1974. "Cropsharing Tenancy in Agriculture: A Comment." *American Economic Review* 64: 1060–66.

―――. 1975a. "The Choice of Rental Contract in Peasant Agriculture." In Lloyd G. Reynolds, ed., *Agriculture in Development Theory*. New Haven, Conn.: Yale University Press.

―――. 1975b. "Tenurial Obstacles to Innovation." *Journal of Development Studies* 11 (3) July: 263–77.

―――. 1977. "Risk Sharing, Sharecropping and Uncertain Labor Markets." *Review of Economic Studies* 44: 585–94.

Noronha, Raymond. 1985. "A Review of the Literature on Land Tenure Systems in Sub-Saharan Africa." Agriculture and Rural Development Department, World Bank, Washington, D.C.

Nulty, L. 1972. *The Green Revolution in West Pakistan: Implications of Technological Change*. New York: Praeger.

Nyholm, Klaus, Henrik Schaumburg-Muller, and Kirsten Westergaard. 1974. "Socio-Economic Aspects of Dairy Development: Report from the Bangalore Milkshed Area." *Economic and Political Weekly*, Review of Agriculture (December 17): A127–A136.

Oberoi, A., and I. Ahmed. 1981. "Labour Use in Dynamic Agriculture: Evidence from Punjab." *Economic and Political Weekly* 16 (13) March 28.

Oberoi, A., and S. Manmohan. 1980. "Migration, Remittances and Rural Development: Findings of a Case Study in the Indian Punjab." *International Labor Review*, March.

Ojha, Gyaneshwar. 1970. "Small Farmers and HYV Programmes." *Economic and Political Weekly* 5 (14) April 4.

Oomen, M. 1971a. "Green Revolution and Agrarian Conflict." *Economic and Political Weekly*, Review of Agriculture 6 (26) June 26.

———. 1971b. *Land Reforms and Socioeconomic Change in Kerala*. Madras: Christian Literature Society.

———. 1975. "Agrarian Legislations and Movements as Sources of Change: The Case of Kerala." *Economic and Political Weekly* 10 (40) October.

Pacey, C., R. Longhurst, and R. Chambers. 1981. *Why Seasons Matter: Seasonal Dimensions of Rural Poverty*. London: Croom Helm.

Padki, M. 1965. "Consolidation of Holdings." *Agricultural Situation in India* 19 (5) August.

Paglin, M. 1965. "Surplus Agricultural Labor and Development: Facts and Theories." *American Economic Review* 55 (September).

Paine, Suzanne. 1977. "Agricultural Development in Less Developed Countries (Particularly South Asia): An Introduction to Bhaduri." *Cambridge Journal of Economics* 1 (4) December: 335–39.

Pakistan, Government of. 1951. *Census of Pakistan*. Islamabad: Government Press.

Pakistan, Ministry of Agriculture and Works. 1960a. *Agricultural Census of Pakistan: A Summary of East Pakistan Data*. Lahore: P. C. and M. G. Press.

———. 1960b. *Agricultural Census of Pakistan: A Summary of West Pakistan Data*. Karachi.

———. 1968. *Farm Management Research in Pakistan*. Planning Unit. Islamabad: Government Press.

Pakistan, Ministry of Food and Agriculture. 1975. *Census of Agriculture, 1972: All Pakistan Report*. Lahore: Agricultural Census Organization.

Pakistan, Ministry of Food, Agriculture, and Rural Development. 1978. *Yearbook of Agricultural Statistics*. Islamabad.

Pakistan, Water and Power Development Authority (WAPDA). 1977. *Extended Agroeconomic Survey of the Indus Basin*. Lahore.

Palmer, Ingrid. 1972. *Food and the New Agricultural Technology*. Geneva: United Nations Research Institute for Social Development.

———. 1975. *The New Rice in the Philippines*. Geneva: United Nations Research Institute for Social Development.

———. 1976. *The New Rice in Asia: Conclusions from Four Country Studies*. Geneva: United Nations Research Institute for Social Development.

Pandey, R. K., and T. S. Bhogal. 1980. "Prospects of Increasing Income and Employment on Mixed Farms." *Indian Journal of Agricultural Economics* 35 (4) October-December: 144–51.

Pandey, R. K., H. P. Singh, and B. C. Saxena. 1981. "Economic Impact of Dairy Development Programmes in the Milk Collection Areas of Madhararam Milk Supply Scheme, Chinglepur (Tamil Nadu)." *Indian Journal of Agricultural Economics* 35 (4) October-December: 172.

Pandey, S. M., ed. 1976. *Rural Labor in India: Problems and Policy Perspectives.* New Delhi: Sri Rami Center for Industrial Relations and Human Resources.

Pandit, M. L. 1978. "Some Less Known Factors Behind Recent Industrial Changes in Punjab and Haryana." *Economic and Political Weekly* November 25: 1935–40.

Pant, Chandrasekhar. 1980. "Tenancy and Cropping Patterns in India." Ph.D. diss., Indian Statistical Institute, New Delhi.

———. 1981. *Tenancy in Semi-Arid Tropical Villages of South India: Determinants and Effects on Cropping Patterns and Input Use.* Economic Program Report 29. Andhra: International Crops Research Institute for the Semi-Arid Tropics.

Pant, S. P., and S. V. Karanjkar. 1965. "Economics of Dairy Enterprises in Jabalpur with Special Reference to the Scale of Enterprise." *Indian Journal of Agricultural Economics* 20 (1).

Papanek, Gustav. 1977. *Economic Growth, Income Distribution and the Political Process in Less Developed Countries.* Discussion Paper 9. Boston, Mass.: Department of Economics, Boston University.

———. 1979a. *Methodological and Statistical Appendix.* Discussion Paper 30. Boston, Mass.: Department of Economics, Boston University.

———. 1979b. *Real Wages, Growth, Inflation, Income Distribution and Policies in Pakistan, India, Bangladesh, Indonesia.* Discussion Paper 29. Boston, Mass.: Department of Economics, Boston University.

Pardeshi, J. M., and D. V. Kazar. 1981. "An Economic Evaluation of Land Allotment to the Landless Poor in Ahmednagar District of Western Maharashtra: A Case Study." *Indian Journal of Agricultural Economics* 36 (1) January-March: 109–18.

Pardhy, M. K. 1968. "Rural Projects: Assessment of Achievements and Failures." *Yojana*, February 18.

Parthasarathy, Gogula. 1973. "Changes in Rice Farming and Their Economic and Social Impact: Case Study of a Delta Village." Department of Cooperation and Applied Economics, Andhra University, Waltair, Andhra Pradesh.

———. 1977. "Land Reform, Rural Dynamics, and Rural Poverty: Review of Indian Experience." Paper presented at the International Seminar on Agrarian Reform, Institutional Innovation, and Rural Development: Major Issues in Perspective, Land Tenure Center, University of Wisconsin, Madison. July.

———. 1979. "Land Reform and the Changing Agrarian Structure." In C. H. Shah and C. N. Vakil, eds., *Agricultural Development of India.* New Delhi: Orient Longmans.

———. 1985. "Reorientation of Rural Development Programmes: A Note on Some Basic Issues." *Economic and Political Weekly* 20 (48) November 30: 2125–29.

———. 1987. "Changes in the Incidence of Rural Poverty and Recent Trends in Some Aspects of the Agrarian Economy." *Indian Journal of Agricultural Economics* 42 (1) January-March: 1–22.

Parthasarathy, Gogula, and D. H. Babu. 1970. "HYVP, Variables That Matter: A Comment." *Economic and Political Weekly* 5 (25) June 20: 980.

Parthasarathy, Gogula, and D. S. Prasad. 1974. "Responses to and Impact of HYV Rice according to Land Size and Tenure in a Delta Village, Andhra Pradesh, India." *Developing Economies* 12 (2) June.

Parthasarathy, Gogula, and K. S. Raju. 1972. "Is There an Alternative to Radical Land Ceilings?" *Economic and Political Weekly* 7 (27) July 1.

Patel, R. K. 1980. "Rapporteur's Report on Economics of Livestock Enterprises with Special Reference to Its Employment Potential." *Indian Journal of Agricultural Economics* 35 (4) October-December: 174–90.

Patel, S. M., and M. K. Pandey. 1976. *Economic Impacts of Kaira District Cooperative Milk Producers' Union (Anand Dairy) in Rural Areas of Kaira District (Gujarat State)*. Ahmedabad: Institute of Cooperative Management.

Patel, V. 1987. "Social Forestry: A Farmer's Viewpoint." *Economic and Political Weekly* 22 (32) August 8: 1365–66.

Patnaik, U. 1987. *Peasant Class Differentiation*. Oxford: Oxford University Press.

Perkins, Dwight H., and Shahid Yusuf. 1984. *Rural Development in China*. Baltimore, Md.: Johns Hopkins University Press.

Perrin, R., and D. Winkelman. 1976. "Impediment to Technical Progress on Small vs. Large Farms." *American Journal of Agricultural Economics* 58 (5) December.

Phukan, Umananda. 1972. *A Study of Double Cropping in Sibsagar District, Assam (1968-69) India*. Jorhat: Agro-Economic Research Center for Northeast India, Assam Agricultural University.

Pinckney, Thomas C. 1986. "Stabilizing Pakistan's Supply of Wheat: Issues in the Optimization of Storage and Trade Policies." *Pakistan Development Review* 25 (Winter): 451–67.

Pingali, Prabhu, Yves Bigot, and Hans P. Binswanger. 1987. *Agricultural Mechanization and the Evolution of Farming Systems in Sub-Saharan Africa*. Baltimore, Md.: Johns Hopkins University Press.

Planning, Research and Action Institute. 1961. "Impact of Consolidation of Holdings: An Evaluation Study." Lucknow.

Pollnac, Richard B. 1981. *Sociocultural Aspects of Developing Small-Scale Fisheries: Delivering Services to the Poor*. World Bank Staff Working Paper 490. Washington, D.C.

Prasad, P. 1976. "Poverty and Bondage." *Economic and Political Weekly* 11 (31–33) August.

———. 1979. "Caste and Class in Bihar." *Economic and Political Weekly* 14 (7–8) February: 481–83.

———. 1987. "Toward a Theory of Transformation of Semi-Feudal Agriculture." *Economic and Political Weekly* 22 (31) August 1: 1287–91.

Pray, Carl E., and Jock R. Anderson. 1986. *Bangladesh and the CGIAR Centers: A Study of Their Collaboration in Agricultural Research*. CGIAR Study Paper 8. Washington, D.C.: World Bank.

Punjab, Economic and Statistical Office. 1971. *The Evaluation of the Rural Industrialization Programme in the Punjab.* Report 109. Chandigarh.

Qayyum, A. 1977. "Land Reforms (Pakistan): Review of Implementation." Land Tenure Center, University of Wisconsin, Madison. July.

Quasem, M. A. 1978. "Factors Affecting the Use of Fertilizers in Bangladesh." *Bangladesh Development Studies* 6 (3) Monsoon.

Quasem, M. A., and Mahabub Hossain. 1979. "Fertilizer Use in Two Selected Areas of Bangladesh." *Bangladesh Development Studies* 7 (4) Autumn.

Quibria, M. 1976. "A Note on Farm Size, Efficiency and the Socioeconomics of Land Distribution." *Bangladesh Development Studies* 4 (January).

Quizón, Jaime, and Hans P. Binswanger. 1986. "Modeling the Impact of Agricultural Growth and Government Policy on Income Distribution in India." *World Bank Economic Review* 1 (1) September: 103–48.

Rabbani, G. 1966. "Surplus Labour in Padi Cultivation in East Pakistan in 1964–65." Bureau of Statistics, Government of East Pakistan.

Radhakrishna, R., G. V. S. N. Murthy, and N. C. Shah. 1979. *Models of Consumer Behaviour for the Indian Economy.* Ahmedabad: Sardar Patel Institute of Economic and Social Research.

Radhakrishna, R., and K. N. Murty. 1978. *Food Demand Model for India.* Ahmedabad: Sardar Patel Institute of Economic and Social Research.

Radhakrishna, R., and A. Sharma. 1979. "Analysis of Sectoral Price Movements in a Developing Economy: Effects of Movement in Agricultural Prices and Production on Industrial Prices, Demand Pattern and Income Distribution." Paper presented at the Seventh International Conference on Input/Output Techniques, Innsbruck, April.

Radhakrishnan, S. A., and M. Sivanandham. 1975. "Dairying as a Subsidiary Enterprise for Farmers: A Micro Level Analysis." *Indian Journal of Agricultural Economics* 30 (3): 159.

Rahman, M. A. 1975. "Farm Size, Efficiency and the Socioeconomics of Land Distribution." *Bangladesh Development Studies* 3 (3).

Rahman, R. I. 1978. "Measurement of Rural Unemployment: A Disaggregative Approach." *Bangladesh Development Studies,* Winter.

———. 1981. "New Technology in Bangladesh Agriculture: Adoption and Its Impact on Rural Labor Markets." Asian Employment Programme Working Paper. International Labour Organisation, Geneva.

Raj, K. N. 1970. "Ownership and Distribution of Land." *Indian Economic Review* 1 (5 n.s.) April: 1–42.

———. 1976. "Trends in Rural Unemployment in India: An Analysis with Reference to Conceptual and Measurement Problems." *Economic and Political Weekly* 11 (31–33) August.

Rajaraman, I. 1975. "Poverty, Inequality, and Economic Growth: Rural Punjab, 1960–61 to 1970–71." *Journal of Development Studies,* July.

Rajasthan, Government of. 1977. *Crop Estimation Study under Agricultural Extension Program in Chambal Command Area.* Vols. 1 and 2. Kota.

Rajat, D., and R. B. L. Bhardwaj. 1974. *Systems of Multiple Cropping to Maximize Economic Returns and Employment.* Proceedings of the First FAO/SIDA Seminar on Improvement and Production of Field Crops for Plant Scientists from Africa and the Near East, Cairo, September 1–20, 1973. Rome: Food and Agriculture Organization.

Rajpurohit, A. R. 1972. "Study of HYV Programme in Mysore (1967–68): Mexican Wheat in Bijapur District." Gokhale Institute Series 17. Poona. Processed.

———. 1975. "Bovine Feed Availability and Requirements in Karnataka with Reference to Dairy Development Programmes." *Indian Journal of Agricultural Economics* 30 (3) July-September: 111–20.

Ranade, C., and R. Herdt. 1978. *Shares of Farm Incomes from Rice Production.* Los Baños: International Rice Research Institute.

Ranadive, B. T. 1979. "Caste, Class and Property Relations." *Economic and Political Weekly* 14 (7–8) February: 337–48.

Randhawa, M. S. 1974. *Green Revolution.* Delhi: Vikas.

Rani, Usha. 1971. "Size of Farm and Productivity." *Economic and Political Weekly* 6 (26) June 26: A85–A89.

Rao, A. P. 1967. "Size of Holdings and Productivity." *Economic and Political Weekly,* November 11.

Rao, B. P. 1973. *The Economics of Agricultural Credit Use in Southern Brazil.* Andhra: Andhra Pradesh University Press.

Rao, C. H. H. 1966. "Alternative Explanations of the Inverse Relationship between Farm Size and Output per Acre in India." *Indian Economic Review* 1 (2) October.

———. 1970. "Farm Size and Credit Policy." *Economic and Political Weekly* 5 (52) December 26.

———. 1971. "Uncertainty, Entrepreneurship and Sharecropping in India." *Journal of Political Economy* 79: 580.

———. 1972. "Ceiling on Agricultural Land Holdings: Its Economic Rationale." *Economic and Political Weekly,* Review of Agriculture 7 (26) June 24.

———. 1975. *Technological Change and the Distribution of Gains in Indian Agriculture.* Delhi: Macmillan.

———. 1976. "Rapporteur's Report on Changes in the Structural Distribution of Land Ownership and Use (since Independence)." *Indian Journal of Agricultural Economics* 31 (3) July-September: 56–62.

———. 1977a. "Agricultural Growth and Rural Poverty: Some Lessons from Past Experience." *Economic and Political Weekly* 12 (33–34).

———. 1977b. *Caste and Poverty: A Case Study of Scheduled Castes in a Delta Village.* Malikipuram: Savithri Publications.

———. 1986. "Changes in Rural Poverty in India: Implications for Agricultural Growth." *Mainstream* January 11.

Rao, K., and A. Sirohi. 1986. "Risk of Fertilizer Application to Paddy in West

Godavari District: Use of Contingency Matrix Approach." *Indian Journal of Agricultural Economics* 41 (1) January-March: 42–51.

Rao, M. 1981. "Commercialisation and Agricultural Growth in Asia: A Comparative Study of South Korea and Coastal Andhra." Paper presented at the International Workshop on Rural Transformation in Asia, New Delhi, October 2–4.

Rao, P. V. G. K. 1969. *Economic Aspects of High-Yielding Wheat and Punjab (Special Reference to Amritsar District Rabi 1968–69.* Delhi: Agro-Economic Research Center.

Rao, V. M., and R. S. Deshpande. 1986. "Agricultural Growth in India: A Review of Experiences and Prospects." *Economic and Political Weekly* 21 (38–39) September 20–27: A101–A113.

Rao, V. V. Bhanoji. 1982. "Data on Income Distribution in India." Working Paper 1980-2. EPD Income Distribution Project, World Bank, Washington, D.C. June.

———. 1987. "Changing Village Structure: Impact of Rural Development Programmes." *Economic and Political Weekly* 22 (13) March 28: A2.

Rao, V. V. Bhanoji, and T. Chotigeat. 1981. "The Inverse Relationship between Size of Land Holdings and Agricultural Productivity." *American Journal of Agricultural Economics* 63 (3) August: 571–74.

Rath, N. 1988. "The 1988–89 Budget: Does It Tackle Any of India's Problems?" *Economic and Political Weekly* 23 (15) April 9: 739–45.

Rath, R. K. 1979. "Towards a Functional Land Redistribution Programme." *Economic and Political Weekly* 14 (2) June 13.

Raup, P. 1963. "The Contribution of Land Reforms to Agricultural Development: An Analytical Framework." *Economic Development and Cultural Change* 12 (1) October.

Rawski, Thomas G. 1979. *Economic Growth and Employment in China.* New York: Oxford University Press.

Ray, A. K., B. R. Atteri, A. C. Sen, and P. N. Mathur. 1979. "Quantitative and Qualitative Impact of Training and Visit Systems on Different Groups of Farmers: A Case Study of Hooghly District, W. Bengal." *Indian Journal of Agricultural Economics* 34 (4) October-December.

Ray, Amal. 1979. "Organizational Problems of Small Farmers Development Administration." *Economic and Political Weekly* December: A161–A165.

Reddy, Y., and others. 1987. "Dryland Farming: Constraints to Improved Technologies." *Margin* 19 (3) April-June.

Reid, J. 1974. "Sharecropping as an Understandable Response: The Post-Bellum South." *Journal of Economic History* 33: 106–30.

Reserve Bank of India. 1975. *Small Farmers Development Agencies: A Field Study, 1972–73.* Bombay.

———. 1976. *Assets of Rural Households, as on June 30, 1971 (All-India Debt and Investment Survey, 1971–72).* Bombay.

Reynolds, N., and P. Sunder. 1977. "Maharashtra's Employment Guarantee

Scheme: A Program to Emulate?" *Economic and Political Weekly* 12 (29) July 16: 1149–58.

Rice, E. B., ed. 1973. "Summary of the Spring Review of Small Farmer Credit." *Small Farmer Credit Summary Papers*. Washington, D.C.: U.S. Agency for International Development.

Ridker, R. G., and H. Lubell, eds. 1971. *Employment and Underemployment Problems of the Near East and South Asia*. New Delhi: Vikas.

Riskin, C. 1978. "Intermediate Technology in China's Rural Industries." *World Development* 6 (11–12): 1297–1311.

Robinson, W. C. 1969. "Disguised Unemployment Once Again, 1951–1961." *American Journal of Agricultural Economics*, August.

Robinson, W. C., and N. Abbasi. 1979. "Underemployment in Pakistan." *Pakistan Development Review* 18 (4) Winter.

Rochin, Refugio I. 1971. "A Micro-Economic Analysis of Small Holder Response to High-Yielding Varieties of Wheat in West Pakistan." Ph.D. diss., Department of Agricultural Economics, Michigan State University, East Lansing.

————. 1972. "Responsiveness of Subsistence Farmers to New Ideas: Dwarf Wheat on Unirrigated Small Holdings in Pakistan." Reprint 88. Land Tenure Center, University of Wisconsin, Madison. May.

————. 1973. "A Study of Bangladesh Farmers' Experiences with IR-20 Rice Variety and Complimentary Production Inputs." *Bangladesh Economic Review* 1 (1) January.

Rosenstein-Rodan, Paul N. 1981. "The New International Economic Order or Relations between the Haves and Have Nots (North-South)." University Lecture 16. Boston University, Boston, Mass. March.

Rosensweig, Mark M. 1978. "Rural Wages, Labor Supply and Land Reform: A Theoretical and Empirical Analysis." *American Economic Review* 68: 874–961.

Roumasset, J. A. 1976. *Rice and Risk: Decision Making among Low-Income Farmers*. Amsterdam: North-Holland.

————. 1978. "The Case against Crop Insurance in Developing Countries." *Philippine Review of Business and Economics*, March.

————. 1979. "Sharecropping, Production Externalities and the Theory of Contracts." *American Journal of Agricultural Economics* 61 (4) November: 640–47.

Roumasset, J. A., J. M. Boussard, and I. J. Singh, eds. 1979. *Risk and Uncertainty in Agricultural Development*. New York: Agricultural Development Council.

Roy, Prannoy. 1981. "Transition in Agriculture: Empirical Indicators and Results (Evidence from Punjab, India)." *Journal of Peasant Studies* 8 (2) January.

Roy, Shyama. 1987. "The Tilona Model: A Successful Indian Grass-Roots Development Strategy?" *Canadian Journal of Development Studies* 8 (2): 355.

Roy, Shyama, and Fred Sanderson. 1972. *The Green Revolution in India: An Appraisal.* Brookings Institution Discussion Paper. Washington, D.C.

Rudra, A. 1968. "Farm Size and Yield per Acre." *Economic and Political Weekly* (Special Number) July.

———. 1969. "Big Farmers of Punjab: Second Installment of Results." *Economic and Political Weekly*, Review of Agriculture (December): A213–A219.

———. 1975a. "Loans as a Part of Agrarian Relations: Some Results of a Preliminary Survey in West Bengal." *Economic and Political Weekly* 10 (28) July 12.

———. 1975b. "Sharecropping Arrangements in West Bengal." *Economic and Political Weekly* 10 (39) September 27.

———. 1976. "Hiring of Labour by Poor Peasants." *Economic and Political Weekly* 11 (1–2) January 10: 33–36.

———. 1978a. "Class Relations in Indian Agriculture." Parts I, II, and III. *Economic and Political Weekly* 13 (24) June 3: 916–23; 13 (25) June 10: 963–68; and 13 (26) June 17: 998–1004.

———. 1978b. "Organization of Agriculture for Rural Development: The Indian Case." *Cambridge Journal of Economics* 2: 381–406.

———. 1981. "One Step Forward, Two Steps Backward." *Economic and Political Weekly* 16 (25–26) June 20–27: A61–A68.

———. 1987. "Share of Agriculture in the Labor Force." *Economic and Political Weekly* 22 (50) December 12: 2157.

Rudra A., A. Majid, and B. Talib. 1969. "Big Farmers of Punjab." *Economic and Political Weekly* 4 (39) September 27.

Rudra, A., and A. Sen. 1980. "Farm Size and Labor Use: Analysis and Policy." *Economic and Political Weekly* 15 (5–7): 391–94.

Ruttan, Vernon W. 1971. "Tenure and Productivity of Philippine Rice Producing Farms." *Philippine Economic Journal* 79: 587–95.

———. 1973. *Induced Technical and Institutional Change and the Future of Agriculture.* New York: Agricultural Development Council.

———. 1977. "The Green Revolution: Seven Generalizations." *International Development Review* 19 (4) December.

Rutten, M. 1986. "Social Profile of Agricultural Entrepreneurs: Economic Behaviour and Life-Style of Middle-Large Farmers in Central Gujarat." *Economic and Political Weekly* 21 (13) March 29: A15.

Sagar, S., and others. 1987. "Poverty among Identified Weaker Sections in Rajasthan." *Economic and Political Weekly* 22 (26) June 27.

Sahota, G. S. 1968. "The Efficiency of Resource Allocation in Indian Agriculture." *American Journal of Agricultural Economics* 50 (August): 584–605.

Sain, K. 1977. "Changes in Ownership and Operational Holdings in West Bengal: An Analytical Study." *Bangladesh Development Studies* 5 (2) April: 201–10.

Saini, A. S. 1975. "Impact of Dairy Enterprises on Farm Incomes in Punjab." *Indian Journal of Agricultural Economics* 30 (3) July-September: 159.

Saini, G. R. 1969. "Resource-Use Efficiency in Agriculture." *Indian Journal of Agricultural Economics* 24 (April-June): 1–18.

––––––. 1971. "Holding Size, Productivity, and Some Related Aspects of India's Agriculture." *Economic and Political Weekly* 6 (26) June: A79–A85.

––––––. 1976. "Green Revolution and the Distribution of Farm Incomes." *Economic and Political Weekly* 11 (13) March 27.

––––––. 1979. *Farm Size, Resource Use Efficiency and Income Distribution.* New Delhi: Allied Publishers.

––––––. 1980. "Farm Size, Productivity and Some Related Issues in India's Agriculture: A Review." *Agricultural Situation in India* February: 777–83.

Saith, A. 1981. "Production, Prices and Poverty in Rural India." *Journal of Development Studies* 17 (2) January.

Saith, A., and A. Tankha. 1972. "Agrarian Transition and the Differentiation of the Peasantry: A Study of a West U.P. Village." *Economic and Political Weekly* 7 (13) April 1.

Salam, Abdul. 1976. "Resource Productivity in the Punjab's Agriculture." *Pakistan Development Review* 15 (2) Summer.

Salimullah, S., and Shamsul Islam. 1976. "A Note on the Conditions of the Rural Poor in Bangladesh." *Bangladesh Development Studies* 4 (2) April.

Sanghvi, P. 1969. *Surplus Manpower in Agriculture and Economic Development.* Bombay: Asia Publishing House.

Sankhayan, P. L., and others. 1978. "An Analysis of Income and Expenditure Patterns of Punjab Farmers." Department of Economics and Sociology, Punjab Agricultural University, Ludhiana.

Sanyal, S. K. 1969. "Size of Holding and Some Factors Related to Production." *Economic and Political Weekly* August 16: 1345–47.

––––––. 1972. "Has There Been a Decline in Agriculture Tenancy?" *Economic and Political Weekly* 7 (19) May 6.

––––––. 1976. "A Review of the Conceptual Framework of Land Holding Surveys." *Indian Journal of Agricultural Economics* 31 (3) July-September: 2–10.

––––––. 1977a. "Long Haul to Agrarian Reform." *Economic and Political Weekly* 8 (5) December.

––––––. 1977b. "Trends in Some Characteristics of Land Holdings: An Analysis for a Few States." Parts I and II. *Sarvekshna* 1 (1) July:1–13 and 1 (2) October: 65–76.

––––––. 1979. "Changes in the Structural Distribution of Land Ownership and Use: A Few Comments." *Indian Journal of Agricultural Economics* 34 (1) January-March: 101–07.

Sanyal, S., and S. Sinha. 1976. "Methodological Problems in Large-Scale Sample Surveys: Experiences from the National Sample Survey." Paper presented at the Symposium on Recent Developments in Survey Methodology, Indian Statistical Institute, Calcutta, March 22–27.

Sau, R. 1971. "Agricultural Revolution by Production Function." *Economic and Political Weekly* 6 (26) June 26.

————. 1973. "Political Economy of Indian Agriculture: What Is It All About?" *Economic and Political Weekly* 7 (20).

————. 1988. "The Green Revolution and Industrial Growth in India." *Economic and Political Weekly* 23 (16) April: 789–96.

Sawant, S. 1983. "Investigation of the Hypothesis of Deceleration in Indian Agriculture." *Indian Journal of Agricultural Economics* 38 (4) October-December.

Saxena, A. 1987. "Concurrent Evaluation of IRDP: Selected Aspects for Administrative Follow-up." *Economic and Political Weekly* 22 (39) September 26: A121–A124.

Scandizzo, Pasquale L. 1979. "Implications of Sharecropping for Technology Design in Northeast Brazil." In A. Valdes, G. Scobie, and J. Dillon, eds., *Economics and the Design of Small-Farmer Technology*. Ames: Iowa State University Press.

Schaefer, R. 1978. "What Are We Talking about When We Talk about Risk? A Critical Survey of Risk and Risk Preference Theories." Research Memorandum 78-69. International Institute for Applied Systems Analysis, Laxenberg, Austria. December.

Schluter, M. 1971. *Differential Rates of Adoption of the New Seed Varieties in India: The Problem of Small Farms*. Occasional Paper 47. USAID Employment and Income Distribution Project. Ithaca, N.Y.: Department of Agricultural Economics, Cornell University.

————. 1973. *The Role of Cooperative Credit in Small Farmer Adoption of the New Cereal Varieties in India*. Occasional Paper 64. USAID Employment and Income Distribution Project. Ithaca, N.Y.: Department of Agricultural Economics, Cornell University.

————. 1974. *The Interaction of Credit and Uncertainty in Determining Resource Allocation and Income on Small Farms: Surat District, India*. Occasional Paper 68. USAID Employment and Income Distribution Project. Ithaca, N.Y.: Department of Agricultural Economics, Cornell University.

Schluter, M., and R. Longhurst. 1972. *Some Aspects of the Suitability of High-Yielding Rice and Bajra Varieties for the Small Farm: Thanjavur and Mehsana Districts, India*. Occasional Paper 57. Ithaca, N.Y.: Department of Agricultural Economics, Cornell University.

Schluter, M., and J. Mellor. 1972. "New Seed Varieties and the Small Farm." *Economic and Political Weekly*, Review of Agriculture 7 (13) March 25.

Schultz, Theodore W. 1964. *Transforming Traditional Agriculture*. New Haven, Conn.: Yale University Press.

————. 1977. "Farm Entrepreneurs, Incentives, and Economic Policy." Agricultural Economic Research Paper 77-20. University of Chicago, August. Draft.

————. 1979. "The Economics of Being Poor." Nobel Lecture, Stockholm, December 8.

Schumacher, E. F. 1973. *Small Is Beautiful*. New York: Harper & Row.

Schutjer, W., and M. Van der Veen. 1977. *Economic Constraints on Agricultural*

Technology Adoption. Occasional Paper 5. Washington, D.C.: Economic and Sector Planning Division, U.S. Agency for International Development.

Selden, M. 1971. *The Yenan Way in Revolutionary China*. Cambridge, Mass.: Harvard University Press.

Sen, Amartya K. 1962. "An Aspect of Indian Agriculture." *Economic and Political Weekly*, Annual Number, February.

―――. 1964. "Size of Holdings and Productivity." *Economic and Political Weekly*, Annual Number, February.

―――. 1966. "Peasants and Dualism with or without Surplus Labor." *Journal of Political Economy* 74: 425–50.

―――. 1973. "Poverty, Inequality, Unemployment: Some Conceptual Issues in Measurement." *Economic and Political Weekly* 8: 31–33.

―――. 1975. *Employment, Technology and Development*. London: Oxford University Press.

―――. 1980. *Levels of Poverty: Policy and Change*. World Bank Staff Working Paper 401. Washington, D.C.

―――. 1981. *Poverty and Famines: An Essay on Entitlement and Deprivation*. Oxford: Clarendon Press.

Sen, Bandhudas. 1970. "Opportunities in the Green Revolution." *Economic and Political Weekly* 5 (13) March 28.

―――. 1974. *Green Revolution in India: A Perspective*. New York: John Wiley.

Sen, S. 1974. *A Richer Harvest*. Bombay: Tata McGraw-Hill.

Sengupta, S. 1981. "West Bengal Land Reforms and the Agrarian Scene." *Economic and Political Weekly*, Review of Agriculture 16 (25–26) June 20–27: 169–75.

Shah, C. H. 1972. "Impact of Tenancy Reform on Level of Technology (Gujarat and Maharashtra)." *Artha Vikas*, July.

Shah, S. L., and R. Singh. 1970. "The Impact of New Agricultural Technology on Rural Employment in North-West U.P." *Indian Journal of Agricultural Economics*, July-September.

Shah, T., A. K. Tripathi, and M. Desai. 1980. "Impact of Increased Dairy Productivity on Farmers' Use of Feedstuffs." *Economic and Political Weekly* 15 (33) August: 1407–12.

Shanmugasundram, V. 1973. "Economic and Social Implications of High-Yielding (Paddy) Varieties Programme." Department of Economics, University of Madras.

Sharma, A. C. 1973. "Influence of Certain Economic and Technological Factors on the Distribution of Cropped Area under Various Crops in the Ludhiana District." *Journal of Research of the Punjab Agricultural University*, June.

Sharma, R. K. 1974. "Green Revolution and Farm Employment: An Analysis of the Experience in Punjab." *Indian Journal of Industrial Relations*, January.

Shavell, S. 1979. "Risk Sharing and Incentives in the Principal and Agent Relationship." *Bell Journal of Economics* Spring: 55–73.

Shigemochi, H. 1978. *The Structure of Disparity in Developing Agriculture: A Case*

Study of the Pakistan Punjab. Occasional Papers Series 16. Tokyo: Institute of Development Economics.

Shivakumar, S. S. 1978. "Aspects of Agrarian Economy in Tamil Nadu: A Study of Two Villages. Part I, Class Structure." *Economic and Political Weekly* 13 (18) May 6: 762–70.

Shukla, V. P., and S. V. Karanjkar. 1975. "Economic Analysis of Government Milk Supply Scheme in Jabalpur." *Indian Journal of Agricultural Economics* 30 (July-September): 144.

Shyam, R., and D. P. Gupta. 1975. "Study of Marginal Farmers and Agricultural Labourers in Ballia (1973–74)." Agro-Economic Research Center, Motilal Institute of Research, University of Allahabad.

Sidhu, D. S. 1975. "Rapporteur's Report on Dairy Development and the Bovine Economy." *Indian Journal of Agricultural Economics* 30 (3) July-September: 161–71.

———. 1977. *Wheat Production, Marketable Surplus and Price Policy in India.* CIMMYT Monograph 13. Mexico City: Centro Internacional de Mejoramiento de Maíz y Trigo.

Sidhu, D. S., and S. S. Grewal. 1981. *Agricultural Growth and Employment Shifts in Punjab: Findings of a Field Survey.* New Delhi: Birla Institute of Scientific Research.

———. 1987. "The Changing Land Holdings Structure in Punjab." *Indian Journal of Agricultural Economics* 42 (3) July-September: 294–301.

Sidhu, D. S., and others. 1979. "An Analysis of Income and Expenditure Patterns of Punjab Farmers (Report for the Year 1977–78)." Department of Economics and Sociology, Punjab Agricultural University, Ludhiana.

Sidhu, S. S. 1974a. "Economics of Technical Change in Wheat Production in the Indian Punjab." *American Journal of Agricultural Economics* 56 (May).

———. 1974b. "Relative Efficiency in Wheat Production in the Indian Punjab." *American Economic Review* 64 (September): 742–51.

Sidhu, S. S., and C. A. Baavante. 1979. "Farm Level Fertilizer Demand for Mexican Wheat Varieties in the Indian Punjab." *American Journal of Agricultural Economics* 61 (3) August: 455–62.

———. 1980. *The Environmental Factors and Farm Level Input Demand and Wheat Supply in the Indian Punjab: An Application of the Translog Profit Function.* Muscle Shoals, Ala.: International Fertilizer Development Center.

Sigurdson, Jon. 1972. "Rural Industry: A Traveller's View." *China Quarterly,* April-June.

———. 1977. *Rural Industrialization in China.* Cambridge, Mass.: Harvard University Press.

———. 1978. "Rural Industrialization: A Comparison of Development Planning in China and India." *World Development* 6: 667–80.

Singh, A. J., S. S. Miglani, and Tirath Singh. 1979. "Changes in the Pattern of Cost, Productivity and Farm Income Distribution in Punjab: A Case Study of Ferozepur District." *Economic Affairs* October-December: 287–92.

Singh, Amarjit, and A. S. Kahlon. 1976. "The Impact of New Technology on Farm Size, Tenurial Relations, and Land Rents in the Punjab." *Indian Journal of Agricultural Economics* 31 (3) July-September.

Singh, Amrik, and R. V. Singh. 1977. "Impact of Dairy Enterprises on Productivity and Employment." *Agricultural Situation in India* 32 (3) June: 139–42.

Singh, Daulat, V. K. Singh, and R. K. Singh. 1981. "Changing Patterns of Labor Absorption on Agricultural Farms in Eastern U.P.: A Case Study." *Indian Journal of Agricultural Economics* 36 (4) October-December: 39–44.

Singh, Gopal. 1984. "Socio-Economic Bases of the Punjab Crisis." *Economic and Political Weekly* 19 (1) January 7.

Singh, Harpal. 1976. "Structural Changes in the Size Distribution of Holdings: A Macro View." *Indian Journal of Agricultural Economics* 31 (3) July-September.

Singh, Inderjit. 1982. *Small Farmers and the Landless in South Asia*. World Bank Staff Working Paper 320. Washington, D.C.

———. 1988a. *Land and Labor in South Asia*. World Bank Discussion Paper 33. Washington, D.C.

———. 1988b. *Small Farmers in South Asia: Their Characteristics, Productivity, and Efficiency*. World Bank Discussion Paper 31. Washington, D.C.

———. 1988c. *Tenancy in South Asia*. World Bank Discussion Paper 32. Washington, D.C.

Singh, Inderjit, and R. Day. 1975a. "Factor Utilization and Substitution in Economic Development: A Green Revolution Case Study." *Journal of Development Studies* 2 (3) April.

———. 1975b. "A Microeconomic Chronicle of the Green Revolution." *Economic Development and Cultural Change* 23 (4) Spring: 661–86.

Singh, Inderjit, R. H. Day, and S. S. Johl. 1968. *Field Crop Technology in the Punjab, India*. Madison: Social Systems Research Institute, University of Wisconsin.

Singh, Inderjit, Lyn Squire, and John Strauss. 1986. "A Survey of Agricultural Household Models: Recent Findings and Policy Implications." *World Bank Economic Review* 1 (1): 149–79.

Singh, J. 1986. *The Role of Institutional Finance in Agriculture*. New Delhi: Ashish.

Singh, Kartar. 1973. "The Impact of New Technology on Farm Income Distribution in the Aligarh District of U.P." *Indian Journal of Agricultural Economics*, April-June.

———. 1981. "Rapporteur's Report on Labor Absorption in Agricultural and Rural Development." *Indian Journal of Agricultural Economics* 36 (4) October-December: 57–65.

Singh, Prem, and S. D. Choubey. 1969. "For Jabalpur an Intensive Cropping Schedule." *Indian Farming*, November.

Singh, R. P., and H. G. Goswani. 1975. "Study of Small Farmers Development

Agency, Purnea, North Bihar, 1973–74." Ad Hoc Study A-19, Publication 57. Agro-Economic Research Center, University of Allahabad.

Singh, Roshan. 1973. *The Social and Economic Implications of the Large-Scale Introduction of High-Yielding Varieties in Foodgrains (Wheat) in Muzaffarnagar (U. P.).* Agra: Raja Balwant Singh College.

Singh, Srinath. 1977. "Agricultural Development and the Small Farmer." Land Tenure Center, University of Wisconsin, Madison. July.

Singh, Surinder. 1979. "Operation Flood II: Some Constraints and Implications." *Economic and Political Weekly* 14 (41) October 27: 1765–74.

Singh, Surinder, and R. K. Sharma. 1981. "Some Implications of Area Choice in the Operation Flood II Programme." *Economic and Political Weekly* 16 (13) March 28.

Sinha, J. N. 1978. "Rural Development Planning: Dimensions and Constraints." *Economic and Political Weekly*, Annual Number.

Sinha, S. K. 1976. "Land Reforms and the Emerging Agrarian Structure in Bihar." *Indian Journal of Agricultural Economics* 31 (3) July-September: 23–27.

Sirohi, A. S., G. S. Ram, and C. B. Singh. 1976. "Interstate Disparities in the Structural Distribution of Land Holdings in Rural India." *Indian Journal of Agricultural Economics* 31 (3) July-September: 14–23.

Sirohi, A. S., and others. 1980. "Role of Dairy-Poultry Enterprises for Increasing Income and Employment in Farms in the Union Territory of Delhi." *Indian Journal of Agricultural Economics*, October-December.

Sivanandan, P. 1979. "Caste, Class and Economic Opportunity in Kerala: An Empirical Analysis." *Economic and Political Weekly* 14 (7) February: 475–79.

Smith, Adam. 1976. *The Wealth of Nations.* Edwin Cannan, ed. Chicago, Ill.: University of Chicago Press.

Solaiman, M., and A. Huq. 1973. "Small Farmer Credit in Bangladesh." *Small Farmer Credit in South Asia.* USAID Spring Review of Small Farmer Credit. Washington, D.C.: U.S. Agency for International Development, June.

Somjee, A., and G. Somjee. 1978. "Cooperative Dairying and Profiles of Social Change in India." *Economic Development and Cultural Change* 26 (3) April: 577–90.

Squire, Lyn. 1979. *Labor Force, Employment and Labor Markets in the Course of Economic Development.* World Bank Staff Working Paper 336. Washington, D.C.

Srinivasan, T. N. 1972. "Farm Size and Productivity: Implications of Choice under Uncertainty." *Sankhya: The Indian Journal of Statistics*, ser. B, 34 (4): 409–18.

———. 1974. "Income Distribution: A Survey of Policy Aspects." *Sankhya: The Indian Journal of Statistics*, ser. C, 36 (2–4) June-December: 369–96.

———. 1976. *The Remembered Village.* Delhi: Oxford University Press.

———. 1977. "Poverty: Some Measurement Problems." Conference Proceedings of the 41st Session of the International Statistical Institute, New Delhi, December.

————. 1979a. "Agricultural Backwardness under Semi-Feudalism: A Comment." *Economic Journal,* June.

————. 1979b. "Bonded Labor Contracts and Incentives to Adopt Yield-Raising Innovations in Semi-Feudal Agriculture." Development Research Center, World Bank, Washington, D.C. March. Draft.

————. 1979c. "Malnutrition: Some Measurement and Policy Issues." Development Research Center, World Bank, Washington, D.C. Draft.

Srinivasan, T. N., and P. K. Bardhan. 1974. *Poverty and Income Distribution in India.* Calcutta: Statistical Publishing Society.

Srinivasan, T. N., and A. Bhaduri. 1979. "Agricultural Backwardness under Semi-Feudalism: An Interchange." *Economic Journal* 35 (4) June: 89.

Srivastava, U. K., and E. O. Heady. 1973. "Technological Change and Relative Factor Shares in Indian Agriculture: An Empirical Analysis." *American Journal of Agricultural Economics,* August.

Staub, W. J., and Melvin Blase. 1974. "Induced Technological Change in Developing Agriculture: Implications for Income Distribution and Agricultural Development." *Journal of Developing Areas* 8 (4) July.

Steele, David B. 1975. "Rural Industrialization and Employment." Rural and Urban Employment Policies Branch, International Labour Organisation, Geneva. November.

Stepanek, J. F. 1973. "Comilla Cooperative Production Loans: A Note on the Cost of Capital." *Small Farmer Credit in South Asia.* USAID Spring Review of Small Farmer Credit. Washington, D.C.: U.S. Agency for International Development.

————. 1979. *Bangladesh: Equitable Growth?* New York: Pergamon.

Stevens, R. D., H. Alavi, and P. J. Bertocci, eds. 1976. *Rural Development in Bangladesh and Pakistan.* Honolulu: University of Hawaii Press.

Stiglitz, J. 1974. "Incentives and Risk Sharing in Sharecropping." *Review of Economic Studies* 61 (April): 219–56.

Stokes, Eric. 1978. *The Peasant and the Raj.* Cambridge: Cambridge University Press.

Stone, B., ed. 1987. *Fertilizer Pricing Policy.* Washington, D.C.: International Food Policy Research Institute.

Streifkerk, H. 1981. "Too Little to Live on—Too Much to Die on: Employment in Small-Scale Industries in Rural South Gujerat." *Economic and Political Weekly* 16 (15) April 11.

Subbarao, K. 1980. "Institutional Credit Uncertainty and Adoption of HYV Technology: A Comparison of East U.P. with West U.P." *Indian Journal of Agricultural Economics* 35 (1) January-March.

————. 1985a. "Regional Variations in the Impact of Anti-Poverty Programmes: A Review of Evidence." *Economic and Political Weekly* 20 (43) October 26.

————. 1985b. "State Policies and Regional Disparity in Indian Agriculture." *Development and Change* 16: 523.

Sukhatme, P. V. 1965. *Feeding India's Growing Millions*. London: Asia Publishing House.

Sundrum, R. 1986. *Growth and Income Distribution in India*. London: Sage.

Swaminathan, M. S. 1972. "Recent Research on Multiple Cropping." Research Bulletin. New Delhi: Indian Agricultural Research Institute.

Swaminathan, M. S., and S. S. Bains. 1970. "Latest Technology for Multiple Cropping: Principles, Practices, and Problems." Report of the National Seminar on Multiple Cropping, Ministry of Agriculture, New Delhi, May.

Swenson, G. 1976. "The Distribution of Benefits from Increased Rice Production in Thanjavur District, S. India." *Indian Journal of Agricultural Economics* 31 (January-March).

Tendulkar, S. 1983. "Rural Institutional Credit and Rural Development: A Review Article." *Indian Economic Review* 18 (1) January-June.

Terhal, Piet, and Martin Doornbus. 1983. "Operation Flood: Development and Commercialization." *Food Policy* 8 (August): 235–39.

Thakur, D. S. 1975. "Impact of Dairy Development through Milk Cooperatives: A Case Study of Gujarat." *Indian Journal of Agricultural Economics* 30 (3) July-September.

Thiesenbusen, W. 1974. "What Changing Technology Implies for Agrarian Reform." *Land Economics* 50 (1) February.

Thomas, John W., and R. M. Hook. 1977. *Creating Rural Employment: A Manual for Organizing Rural Works Programs*. Washington, D.C.: U.S. Agency for International Development.

Thorner, D. 1956. *The Agrarian Prospect in India*. Delhi: Delhi University Press.

Timmer, C. Peter. 1971. *Some Comments on the Mellor-Lele Labor Supply Theory of Economic Development and Its Applications*. Discussion Paper 71-76. Stanford, Calif.: Stanford Food Research Institute, Stanford University.

Tinnermeir, R., and C. Dowsell. 1973. "Small Farmer Credit." Workshop Report. Agricultural Development Council, Research and Training Network, New York. March.

Tyagi, D. 1982. "How Valid Are the Estimates of Trends in Rural Poverty?" *Economic and Political Weekly* 17 (26) June 26: A54–A61.

———. 1987. "Domestic Terms of Trade and Their Effects on Supply and Demand in the Agricultural Sector." *Economic and Political Weekly* 22 (13) March 28: A30–A37.

Tyers, R. 1977. *Small Farmers in Bangladesh: A Study of Their Prospects*. Cambridge, Mass.: Center for Population Studies, Harvard University.

Vaidyanathan, A. 1986a. *Agricultural Development and Rural Poverty*. Madras: Institute of Development Studies.

———. 1986b. "Labour Use in Rural India: Spatial and Temporal Variations." *Economic and Political Weekly* 21 (52) December: A130.

———. 1986c. "On the Validity of NSS Consumption Data." *Economic and Political Weekly* 21 (3) January 18.

Verma, R. C., and D. C. Pant. 1978. "Potentialities of Increasing Farm Income and Employment through Dairying." *Indian Journal of Agricultural Economics* 33 (3) July-September.

Visaria, Pravin. 1970a. "Farmers' Preference for Work on Family Farms." In *Report of the Committee of Experts on Unemployment.* New Delhi: Planning Commission, Government of India.

——. 1970b. "Unemployment in India in Perspective." *Economic and Political Weekly* 5 (29–31).

——. 1972. "Rapporteur's Report on Rural Unemployment." *Indian Journal of Agricultural Economics* 27 (4) October-December: 179–89.

——. 1975. "A Survey of Research on Employment in India." In *Survey of Research on Agriculture.* Delhi: Indian Council of Social Science Research.

——. 1977a. "Living Standards, Employment and Education in Western India, 1972-73." Development Research Center, World Bank, Washington, D.C. Draft.

——. 1977b. "Trends in Rural Unemployment in India." *Economic and Political Weekly* 12 (5) January 29: 139–45.

——. 1978. "Size of Holding, Living Standards and Employment in Rural Western India, 1972–73." Development Research Center, World Bank, Washington, D.C. October. Draft.

——. 1979. "Demographic Factors and the Distribution of Income: Some Issues." *Economic and Demographic Change: Issues for the 1980s. Proceedings of the Conference.* Liège: International Union for Scientific Study of Population. Vol. 1. Also in World Bank Reprint Series 129. Washington, D.C.

——. 1980. *Poverty and Unemployment in India: An Analysis of Recent Evidence.* World Bank Staff Working Paper 417. Washington, D.C.

——. 1981. "Poverty and Unemployment in India: An Analysis of Recent Evidence." *World Development* 9 (23): 277–300.

Visaria, Pravin, and L. Visaria. 1973. "Employment Planning for the Weaker Sections in Rural India." *Economic and Political Weekly* 8 (4–6).

Von Blackenburg, K. 1972. "Who Leads Agricultural Modernization? A Study of Some Progressive Farmers in Mysore and Punjab." *Economic and Political Weekly* 40 (7).

Vyas, V. S. 1970. "Tenancy in a Dynamic Setting." *Economic and Political Weekly* 5 (26) June: A73–A80.

——. 1971. "Mainsprings of Agricultural Growth in India." Pause Memorial Lecture, New Delhi, August 9.

——. 1975. *India's High-Yielding Varieties Programme in Wheat, 1966/1967–1971/1972.* Mexico City: Centro Internacional de Mejoramiento de Maíz y Trigo (CIMMYT).

——. 1976. "Structural Change in Agriculture and the Small Farm Sector." *Economic and Political Weekly* 11 (1–2) January 10.

——. 1979. "Some Aspects of Structural Change in Indian Agriculture: Presidential Address." *Indian Journal of Agricultural Economics* 34 (1) January-March.

————. 1987. "India's Rural Development Strategies: Lessons in Agricultural Growth and Poverty Alleviation." Paper presented at the International Association of Agricultural Economists Symposium, Beijing, October.

Vyas, V. S., Anil Bhatt, and S. M. Shah. 1985. *Decentralised Planning in India*. Bombay: Oxford University Press and ɪʙʜ Publishing Co.

Vyas, V. S., and N. Jagannathan. 1985. "Cooperation in Farm Production: Conditions of Viability." In T. Bergmann and T. Ogura, eds., *Cooperation in World Agriculture*. Tokyo: Food and Agriculture Policy Research Centre.

Vyas, V. S., and G. Mathai. 1978. "Farm and Non-Farm Employment in Rural Areas: A Perspective for Planning." *Economic and Political Weekly* 13 (6–7) February.

Vyas, V. S., and H. V. Shivamaggi. 1983. "Agricultural Labour in India." Indian Institute of Management, Ahmedabad. Processed.

Wade, Robert. 1975. *Irrigation and Income Distribution: Three Papers*. Paper 85. Brighton: Institute of Development Studies, University of Sussex. November.

————. 1980a. "Water to the Fields: India's Changing Strategy." *South Asian Review* 8 (4) July-October.

————. 1980b. "On Substituting Management for Water in Canal Irrigation: A South Indian Case." *Economic and Political Weekly*, Review of Agriculture, 15 (52) December 27: A147–A160.

————. 1982. "The System of Administrative and Political Corruption: Canal Irrigation in South India." *Journal of Development Studies* 18 (April): 287–328.

————. 1984. "Irrigation Reform in Conditions of Populist Anarchy: An Indian Case." *Journal of Development Economics* 14 (April): 285–303.

————. 1987a. "Management of Common Property Resources: Collective Action as an Alternative to Privatisation or State Regulation." *Cambridge Journal of Economics* 11 (June): 95–106.

————. 1987b. "Management of Common Property Resources: Finding a Co-operative Solution." *World Bank Research Observer* 2 (July): 219–34.

Wade, Robert, and Robert Chambers. 1980. "Managing the Main System: Canal Irrigation's Blind Spot." *Economic and Political Weekly* 15 (39) September 27.

Wadhwa, D. C. 1973. *Agrarian Legislation in India, 1793–1966*. Vols. 1 and 2. Poona: Gokhale Institute of Politics and Economics.

Warriner, Doreen. 1973. "Results of Land Reforms in Asian and Latin American Countries." *Food Research Institute Studies* 12 (2): 115–33.

Westley, J. 1986. *Agriculture and Equitable Growth: The Case of Punjab and Haryana*. Boulder, Colo.: Westview Press.

Wharton, C. R., Jr. 1963. "The Economic Meaning of Subsistence." *Malayan Economic Review* 8: 46–58.

Whitcombe, E. 1973. "The New Agricultural Strategy in Uttar Pradesh, India, 1968–70: Technical Problems." In R. T. Shand, ed., *Technical Change in Asian Agriculture*. Canberra: Australian National University Press.

Williamson, Cheryl R. 1980. "The Nutritional Impact of Operation Flood: A Framework for Analysis." Institute for International Development, Harvard University, Cambridge, Mass. May. Draft.

Wills, I. R. 1972. "Projection of Effects of Modern Inputs on Agricultural Income and Employment in a C.D. Block, U.P., India." *American Journal of Agricultural Economics* 54 (3).

Winrock International Livestock Research and Training Center. 1983. *Sheep and Goats in Developing Countries: Their Present and Potential Role.* World Bank Technical Paper 15. Washington, D.C.

Wood, D. G. 1973. "From Raiyat to Rich Peasant." *South Asian Review* 7 (1) October.

World Bank. 1975. *Agricultural Credit.* Sector Policy Paper. Washington, D.C.

————. 1978. *Forestry.* Sector Policy Paper. Washington, D.C.

————. 1979. *Bangladesh: Current Trends and Development Issues.* Washington, D.C.

————. 1980. *World Development Report 1980.* New York: Oxford University Press.

————. 1982. *Fishery.* Sector Policy Paper. Washington, D.C.

————. 1984. *Pakistan: Review of the Sixth Five-Year Plan.* World Bank Country Study. Washington, D.C.

————. 1986. *Poverty and Hunger: Issues and Options for Food Security in Developing Countries.* World Bank Policy Study. Washington, D.C.

————. 1987a. *Agricultural Mechanization: Issues and Options.* World Bank Policy Study. Washington, D.C.

————. 1987b. *Bangladesh: Promoting Higher Growth and Human Development.* World Bank Country Study. Washington, D.C.

————. 1988a. *World Development Report 1988.* New York: Oxford University Press.

————. 1988b. *World Tables 1987.* Washington, D.C.

Wunderlich, G. 1970. *Land Reforms in India.* USAID Spring Review Country Paper. Washington, D.C.: U.S. Agency for International Development.

Yap, Lorene Y. L. 1975. *Internal Migration in Less Developed Countries: A Survey of the Literature.* World Bank Staff Working Paper 215. Washington, D.C.

Yelamanchili, Satyanarayana. 1981. "Wage Trends in India, 1830 to 1976: An Analysis, Discussion and Compilation of Data." Studies in Employment and Rural Development 74. Employment and Rural Development Division, World Bank, Washington, D.C. October.

Yotopoulos, P. A. 1972. "Economic Rationality and Efficiency through the Production Function, Darkly." Paper presented at the Purdue Conference on Small Farm Agriculture, Purdue University, West Lafayette, Indiana. November.

Yotopoulos, P. A., and L. J. Lau. 1973. "A Test for Relative Economic Efficiency: Some Further Results." *American Economic Review* 63 (1) March: 214–23.

Yotopoulos, P. A., L. J. Lau , and K. Somel. 1970. "Labour Intensity and Relative Efficiency in Indian Agriculture." *Food Research Institute Studies in Agricultural Economics, Trade, and Development* 9 (1): 43–55.

Zaman, M. A. 1976. "Land Reform in Bangladesh to 1970." Research Paper 66. Land Tenure Center, University of Wisconsin, Madison. February.

Zaman, M. Raquibuz. 1973. "Share-cropping and Economic Efficiency in Bangladesh." *Bangladesh Economic Review* 1 (2) April: 149–72.

Index